MEDIA and MEANING
an introduction

colin stewart
marc lavelle
adam kowaltzke

 Publishing

First published in 2001 by the
British Film Institute
21 Stephen Street, London WIT ILN

Reprinted 2003

The British Film Institute promotes greater understanding of,
and access to, film and moving image culture in the UK.

Cover design: Mark Swan
Layout and design by Siobhan O'Connor/Design Consultants
Original page design: Gary Gravatt Design
Printed in Great Britain by St Edmundsbury Press, Suffolk

British Library Cataloguing-in-Publication Data
A catalogue record for this book is available from the British Library
ISBN 0–85170–843–9 pbk
ISBN 0–85170–844–7 hbk

contents

Introduction for teachers v

Notes to students vii

Preface ix

Acknowledgements x

CHAPTER 1: KEY CONCEPTS IN MEDIA EDUCATION

▶ The mass media in the new millennium 2

▶ Media: new ways and meanings 6

▶ Institutions and industries 8

▶ Audiences 25

▶ The violence debate 32

▶ Representation 35

▶ Genre 41

▶ Language 45

▶ Media products: contexts, texts
and meanings 51

CHAPTER 2: COMPUTER-BASED MEDIA

▶ The language of computer-based media 60

▶ New technology: issues 64

▶ The Internet: the medium 69

▶ Structure of Internet communication 72

▶ Audiences 77

▶ Representation issues 79

▶ Internet institutions and industries 84

▶ Legal issues 87

▶ Censorship 94

▶ Web page design .98

▶ Internet advertising 104

▶ Multimedia 109

▶ Multimedia narrative 114

▶ Representation and industry isssues 117

▶ Computer games 119

▶ Types of computer games 121

▶ The narrative structure of
computer games 124

▶ Representation issues 132

▶ Audience and institution issues 136

CHAPTER 3: FILM (Revised by Vivienne Clarke)

▶ The language of film and television 148

▶ Editing: shot-to-shot relationships 154

▶ Pre-production: scripts and storyboards . . .162

▶ Film: the medium 166

▶ Film audiences 176

▶ Film institutions .186

▶ Film products 191

▶ Docudrama feature films 207

▶ Docudrama representation issues 213

▶ Film adaptations of literary texts 217

▶ Films about school 225

▶ Representation and audience issues
in school films 229

CHAPTER 4: TELEVISION

▶ Television: the medium 234

▶ Measuring audiences 238

▶ Institutions and policy 241

▶ Television news: purposes and functions 250

▶ The structure of television news 256

▶ Television news grammar 259

▶ Writing a television news script 262

▶ Writing a lead 263

▶ Writing the rest of the story 264

▶ Planning the news bulletin 266

▶ Representation issues in news,
current affairs and documentaries 270

▶ Television documentaries and
current affairs 270

▶ Developing the documentary or
current affairs concept 279

▶ Scripting and structuring the documentary . .281

▶ Soap operas 285

▶ Soap opera plots 287

▶ Soap opera characters 290

▶ Soap opera settings 293

▶ Representation on soap operas 295

▶ The soap opera audience 297

▶ Television comedy 299

▶ Situation comedy 304

▶ Sitcom plots 306

▶ The crime drama genre 307

▶ Crime drama plots 312

▶ Crime drama characters 314

▶ Crime drama: issues 316
▶ Crime drama settings 319
▶ The television advertisement 321
▶ Types of television advertisement 323
▶ Writing the television advertisement 326
▶ Television advertisements pictures:
    scripts and storyboards 329
▶ Representation issues in television
    advertisements 332
▶ Television advertisements: audience issues . .336
▶ Talk shows 341

CHAPTER 5: RADIO

▶ The language of radio 352
▶ The medium of radio 355
▶ Radio audiences .357
▶ Radio institutions 360
▶ Radio music formats 365
▶ Radio news 369
▶ Radio documentaries 372
▶ Radio comedies .374
▶ Radio dramas 378
▶ Radio advertisements 384

CHAPTER 6: NEWSPAPERS AND MAGAZINES

▶ The language of the print media 390
▶ The medium of newspapers 399
▶ Print media readership 405
▶ The editorial 413
▶ The news story 417
▶ The structure of the news story 421
▶ Newspaper representation issues 424
▶ The feature story 428
▶ Magazines: the medium 431
▶ Magazine representation and
    audience issues 434
▶ Magazine front covers 437
▶ The magazine article 440
▶ Magazine display advertisements 443

Glossary of key terms 449
List of contacts 453
Bibliography 455
List of figures 458
Index 459

introduction

Introduction for Teachers

Media studies is a demanding subject for teacher and student alike, both in terms of the depth of study and breadth of reference to several media forms required. *Media and Meaning: An Introduction* presents a comprehensive account of the forms and production processes of the main media industries, together with consolidation of the many conceptual and theoretical perspectives that have arisen from media study over the past century.

It is aimed *principally* at students and teachers of **AS/A Level Media Studies** who are following the specifications offered by **OCR**, **AQA** and **WJEC** awarding bodies and **undergraduates** commencing their studies in media for the first time. The new specifications, offered from September 2000, have seen yet a further increase in the uptake of the subject at this level, as students now have a greater choice of subjects at **AS** Level and **Media Studies** has continued to be a popular and successful option.

The new assessments represent a challenge for teachers, however, first in requiring them to teach new topics and, secondly, in ensuring that their students are able to develop depth of knowledge as well as breadth. Furthermore, the new structure of January and June assessments in the first year of the A-Level course means that students need to engage in detailed study of media texts and their contexts right from the start. In these respects, this book has been designed especially to meet the challenges of the new Media Studies specifications.

It is also suitable to support the study of a number of subjects with a media-related focus or aspect, for example:

► **AVCEs** and **GNVQs (Internediate)** in Media Communicaton and Production, and **GSUQs** in Communication and Media

► **BTEC** and City and Guild courses in Film, Media and Television
► **AS/A** Level **Communication Studies**
► **AS/A** Level **General Studies**
► **AS/A** Level **English**
► Key skills assessment
► **SQA** Higher National Diploma in **Communication/SQA** National Certificate in **Media Studies**

The book is also an invaluable resource for anyone seeking an introduction to media studies.

Media and Meaning: An Introduction is organised around the main media forms of the twenty-first century, in order to help readers to locate topics easily. However, the increasing convergence of production and exchange of all media forms via digital processes and platforms is acknowledged in the main text that follows.

The book may be used in a variety of contexts. It has been designed to complement the common content covered in media studies at AS/A Level by all awarding bodies. Teachers should use the detailed requirements of their chosen specification, together with guidance from in-service training programmes and specification support materials offered by their preferred awarding body, in order to construct their schemes of work.

Specimen and past examination papers, past mark schemes and examiners'/moderators' reports on previous examination sessions are also available from awarding bodies for additional guidance and use with staff and students alike. Through the use of such materials directly with students, the teacher can encourage them to function in the role of an examiner themselves, by assessing their own work against mark schemes, as well as to pass on to them the useful advice contained in such documents. This has been found to be an effective strategy for raising student attainment.

The book may be used, in any order, to support schools' and colleges' schemes of work, as key concepts and terms are featured throughout every chapter and highlighted for ease in the index. Students may use it to support their own independent study and it can be used in class for selected assignments or sections set by the teacher as background reading. Non-media studies students and teachers can locate specific topics as appropriate to their particular course of study via the **index** and **glossary**.

There are references to examples from media texts/products and to further reading and research sources, which may be found at the end of the book. It will also be clear that there are frequent opportunities for overlap and reinforcement between chapters and topics. For example, a topic appearing in the **newspapers and magazines** chapter may also be appropriate to the study of **computer-based media**.

Each major chapter contains an introductory section on the **language** specific to each main **media form**, for example, film and television. This is then followed by **topics of study** (e.g. film docudrama), together with analysis of **key features** (e.g. the structure of television news) and presentation of issues relating to the **core concepts**: namely, **institutions and industries**, **audiences**, **representation** and **genre**. Major features of the book are the **activities** found throughout and the inclusion of three types of assignment – **oral**, **written** and **practical** – at regular intervals. These are intended to give a very wide menu of classroom and homework options that reflect the variety of ways in which the media communicate.

The role of practical media production in AS/A Level Media Studies is resolutely not a vocational one, just as creative writing assignments in AS/A Level English could not possibly be considered as a vocational training for writers. In the course of its evolution, the engagement of students in practical activities has been an integral part of media education.

The purposes of practical work at AS/A Level were, and remain, for students to develop knowledge and understanding of media production processes and techniques in order to facilitate a critical understanding of their practices, output and reception. In addition, it gives students opportunities to develop their own creativity and competencies. In many cases, students discover skills and aptitudes that they wish to develop further, by following dedicated vocational training courses, work experience or degree level study.

Vocational qualifications such as AVCES, BTEC and City & Guilds have been designed to develop a range of media production skills. However, these courses also contain elements of theory and contextual study, and this book has been constructed with these courses in mind as well.

Teachers seeking further information on professional development opportunities, events for teachers and students, guidance on resources and useful contacts should consult visit the BFI website: '**www.bfi.org.uk/education/**'. A further list of useful addresses (including awarding bodies) and places to find additional resources is listed in the **Contacts** appendix at the back of the book.

The following 'Notes to Students' explains what is required of students studying the media and how to use this book to support their studies.

Notes to Students

Studying media products is very different from consuming them. Accordingly, the level of responses required from you in the course assessments are also very different from first impressions and casual responses, although these are a good place to start your analysis of the media and how they make meaning.

Media products, like plays, novels and poems, were created to be consumed and enjoyed, not to be studied. During the course of your study of the media, you must keep their original purposes in mind. However, media study is dynamic and complex. Media products can tell us a great deal about other things; anything from global politics to personal relationships. Moreover, new products emerge daily.

The media exist in the midst of many other different sorts of environments (political, personal, historical) which influence the way the media are and the stories they can tell.

Media studies developed as a discrete academic subject at GCSE and A Level throughout the 1980s and 1990s, with its origins in many different disciplines, from sociology, economics, history, film, communication studies and English/English literature. It also shares some objects of study, concepts and skills with additional subjects, such as art and design, graphics, information technology, design and technology, drama, politics, psychology and business studies.

The world of work is not compartmentalised like a school or college curriculum and, in the twenty-first century, the media are common to all subjects on the curriculum, as they are now our primary sources of information and entertainment. The centrality of the media is just one of many justifications for its academic study and this book will engage you in consideration of many others.

After the age of sixteen, what you study is largely your choice. You have decided to pursue further study rather than the world of work, for the time being. Non-compulsory study means that greater self-reliance and independent learning is required of you. Whatever the reason for your choice of this media-related course of study, you need to invest in your own success in an increasingly competitive education and career market.

Managing your time carefully – whether studying in formal time-slots or independently, at home, school or college – and undertaking more than the minimum required of you, will be your keys to success at this level. Deadlines need to be managed very carefully, too, so that you will be able to cope with the demands of studying several subjects.

You may be facing examinations after one term of starting this subject and, whether you previously studied GCSE Media Studies or not, you need to prepare for a variety of different assessment methods and learn new skills, concepts and topics quickly. This book was designed to help you to do this and can support your study whether you are following a one- or two-year course.

Media studies is a challenging subject, as there are several media forms to acquire knowledge of and many texts and topics to learn. But the study of any media product and its context can be approached through a conceptual framework that is built on a number of key, or core, concepts and skills that you will see integrated throughout this book. If you grasp the key concepts listed below and outlined in the first chapter, you will understand the main aims and objectives of media study in relation to any media product:

- **institutions/industries**
- **audiences**
- **representation**
- **genre**

You will also need to relate this to the specific language with which each media form communicates.

Any media product may be studied from all of the above areas; however, this would be an enormous undertaking and, more typically, teachers will choose a selective focus of study, e.g. the topic of representation of consumerism in lifestyle magazines.

You obviously do not have to read this book from start to finish. Each major chapter contains an introductory section on the **language** specific to each main media form (e.g. film or television), followed by **topics of study** (e.g. docudrama), together with analysis of **key features** (e.g. the structure of television news) and presentation of issues relating to the core concepts listed immediately above. Three types of assignment appear in the text: oral, written and practical.

There are two main methods used to assess what you have learnt: examination under timed conditions (either of prereleased, unseen material or topics that have been preprepared) and coursework (such as written assignments and practical media production work completed over time). Each require their own preparation and organisation on your part and this book contains useful sections to support your preparation.

Your teachers will be following a specification, what used to be termed a 'syllabus', produced by one of the national awarding bodies, whose contact details are given in the appendix. It may also be possible for you to borrow a copy of the full specification from your teacher or to visit the relevant awarding body's website to access details of the specification yourself. Your teacher will also be using specimen and past examination papers, mark schemes and examiners'/moderators' reports which will help you to see how marks are awarded.

You will find that the activities and assignments in the book also contain suitable material for your key skills portfolio.

A list of useful addresses (including awarding bodies) and places to find additional resources is listed in the appendix entitled **Contacts** at the back of the book.

Research is a very important part of the study of any subject and the success of your studies at this level depends on it. This book contains many references to media texts and further reading for you to follow up. Your own learning institution will hopefully have a well-stocked library – but it is worth remembering that you can order any book, free of charge, from the inter-loan library service from your local library.

The Internet is a rich source of research and the 'Facts on Film' section of the BFI website (www.bfi.org.uk/facts) contains a range of information and suggested sources to help you find the answers to your film and television queries. Also on the BFI site is 'The Film Links Gateway', which contains annotated links to other websites about film. Within that, a section headed 'Education' has some useful links of specific interest to students and teachers of media studies.

Studying anything to do with the media is a dynamic activity as new media products appear daily and successful students are those who keep up to date with new developments from the sources listed in the Contacts appendix.

Media studies is also an enjoyable and rewarding subject and you may develop specific areas of interest that you could choose to develop at a higher level, by choosing a media-related degree, embarking on vocational training or a work placement. BFI Publishing produces an annual publication entitled *Media Studies UK*, edited by Lavinia Orton, which is the most useful directory of media courses available.

If your interest in the media is more than a passing one, securing a work experience placement early on is important for a number of reasons. As competition for places on media-related courses is considerable, some higher education institutions look more favourably on candidates who have relevant work experience in addition to requisite grades.

Relevant work experience may also help to you decide whether a job in the media is really what you are suited to and may support a job application. Once on a course, try to develop a portfolio or showreel of your work (indeed, why not start now!) and make good use of any contacts you make along the way.

You will find that various people may try to deter you from seeking a job in the media and many myths surround how to get into various sectors of the media. But if you develop the necessary skills and determination, there are various routes into a wide range of jobs. You need to start planning your next stage now. Someone has to fill a space in the work place – so why not you?

Learning does not stop with school or college; it is a lifelong process and need not necessarily be linked to a career. Develop an enthusiasm or a skill, join a regional film theatre or make use of the many opportunities to participate in extra-mural and short courses and film festivals.

Good luck and enjoy your studies.

Vivienne Clark
Chief Examiner GCSE Media Studies;
BFI Associate Tutor and Head of Media Studies
at Ravens Wood School, Kent

preface

We are at the dawn of a wholly-new era in terms of what we define *as* the mass media.

Study of the media naturally concentrates on the traditional mass forms of television, radio, cinema, and the press. This book differs from most, however, in two major respects. Firstly, in that it adopts an essentially '*generic*' approach to these subjects. Close analysis of the actual products of the media industries forms the basis of our scrutiny: types of film and TV programmes and their defining features, as well as newspaper, magazine and radio products.

Secondly, a major new addition to the 'media family' is with us now in the form of the Internet. Although most people are very familiar with this term, it is likely that the scale of its impact *on all of our lives* has yet to be realised. Many of the distinctive products, as well as the social and political implications of this 'new arrival' will be examined in a dedicated section of this book.

The recent history of Media Studies has seen a surge in publishing of textbooks. Only ten years ago, there was something of a shortage of materials to assist the ever-mushrooming numbers of teachers and students wishing to embrace the subject – particularly at advanced levels. Today, the market is more abundantly supplied, and continues to grow. Does this mean there is no need for yet another?

The present authors would argue that of course it does not. Not only does the subject itself continue to evolve (witness the recent revisions to the A-level syllabuses), but the insights and expertise of those engaged in delivering the courses evolve too. Agreement on what exactly makes up the subject grows and develops with the passage of time; so too does our understanding of what it takes to teach it. In a world that changes rapidly – especially a part of it that does so more than most – this understanding will need to keep pace also.

One of the distinctive features of this particular textbook is that places heavy emphasis on the exploration of key areas of knowledge through practical activity. A wide variety of both creative and analytical activities have been attached to the end of each section, within every chapter. Most of these have been based on actual classroom experience, over a considerable period of time. They offer scope for a breadth of interests and ability levels, and aim to cover both practical and theoretical considerations.

The genesis of this book enables it to claim *itself* to be a product of modern Internet technology: the genuine product of international co-operation. Extensive collaboration between the authors has led to this current edition. It can be truly stated that this publication would not have been possible (certainly not by its actual publication date!) without the facility and speed of up-to-date computer communication systems.

The knowledge, skills and resources of a very wide range of people have been drawn on to compile this book. In the best traditions of all mass media production, consultation, co-operation and cross-fertilisations have combined to create a comprehensive and up-to-date survey of the contemporary media.

Acknowledgments

Many people have made valuable contributions to the writing of this book. Foremost, I would like to thank my family for their patient support and understanding over my long absences and occasional frustrations. Extra thanks to my children for their help with the more esoteric aspects of contemporary television culture.

To my co-authors, I offer thanks not only for their original contributions, but also for their considered feedback on my own.

Next, and scarcely less, my special thanks to Ann Simmonds for her unflagging support and exhaustive patience with a host of technical and administrative tasks. She has brought an irreplaceable professionalism to the whole project.

Warm thanks, too, to all the following colleagues for their diverse responses and many useful suggestions: Peter Darling, Janey Gordon, Dave Green, Ian McCormack, Alexis Weedon, and Richard Wise.

Finally, my sincere and grateful appreciation to staff at the BFI for myriad contributions, especially Andrew Lockett.

Marc Lavelle,
7 September 2001

chapter one
Key Concepts in Media Education

1 ▶

The Mass Media in the New Millennium

What is meant by the mass media?

Quite simply, the mass media are modes of communication that are able to address large numbers of people.

Print was the first of these, although for many years its audience was severely limited by the fact that not many people could actually read. Books were the main products, initially. By the mid-eighteenth century, however, large circulations existed for a range of newssheets and pamphlets. Even though illiteracy was still widespread, people could always listen to others reading them aloud.

By the beginning of the twentieth century, a rush of other media began to arrive: first cinema, then radio, then television. With each new medium, the scale of the audiences grew; so, it might reasonably be said, did the *immediacy* of what was being presented. For instance, during the Boer War at the end of the nineteenth century, it took several weeks for news from the front line to reach home; during the Gulf War, a century later, we were able to watch *live* as missiles landed on Baghdad.

Problems of control

Many benefits have undoubtedly issued from the development of mass media forms. People are now much more able to keep up with significant social and political events. In the United States, one judge even ruled that television was an essential service, like water and electricity. In a modern democracy, he asserted, access to infor-mation was a fundamental human right. Without the broad social knowledge brought by the news, and even the moral and ethical debates aired by other programmes, no citizen could feel equipped to deal with the complexities of modern society.

Nevertheless, some shortcomings have also been identified, principally in the one-way nature of the flow of information. The *few-to-the-many* model of mass media communications points up how a relatively tiny number of people decide on the material that is supplied to the general public. This, of course, begs the vital questions of exactly who those 'few' are and what it is that they choose to transmit, as well as how they present these topics.

The right of access to the media has been a keenly debated topic for some time. Minority groups, in particular, feel that they have been denied a voice or adequate representation in traditional mainstream media outlets. The much-trumpeted multi-channel age which is now being unleashed *could* result in greater inclusiveness and better viewing opportunities for diverse audiences.

Just as this may be about to happen, however, the arrival of the Internet could also make the need for it rather less pressing. There is ample evidence of people making constructive use of their home computers for *interactive two-way* communication. Dependence on *passive* reception of traditional media products may well see a steep decline, as awareness of the possibilities here becomes more universal.

The Internet: how much 'hype' in hypertext?

A great deal of hype surrounds the Internet – some commentators maintain that this new tool of communication offers more capability than all the other mass media forms put together. On the face of it, that sounds like a massive claim: suspi-ciously like a manufacturer's 'puff', when somebody has a particular product they wish to promote.

However, when you begin to examine the full range of features already available, it is hard to disagree.

First, it appears to *replicate* those forms, in terms of audio and visual, as well as the print-based products that can be accessed. Next, it goes further, by *extending* those facilities (by way of websites, both personal and official, e-mail, chat rooms – in other words, *interactive modes of communication*).

It is already possible to get live pictures – and sound – and printed news from the Internet. DVD allows us to play films on our home computers – and it surely cannot be long before we can download, store and then watch them at our convenience. Radio is already available on the Internet and television will not be long in following. These features alone suggest that the *convergence* of media products via the Internet means it will certainly dominate the early part of the new millennium. The mergers of various large broadcast and Internet companies, such as Time-Warner and AOL, confirm this.

Over and above all of these things, however, there is yet another feature of the Internet that is perhaps even more exciting still: the scope for interaction between individuals on a global basis. For the first time in the history of humankind, the means now exists for people to communicate with each other, on topics of mutual interest, *instantaneously*. The implications of this, for culture, for economies, for systems of government, as well as for personal perception of and responses to the world, have scarcely begun to be recognised.

Taken all round, the Internet marks a sea change in the nature of what is meant by the term *mass medium*.

One of the most startling features it offers is the capacity for individual citizens, *anywhere in the world*, effectively to transmit information live, on any topic. Not only this, but also to include with that the option of visual images and even the possibility of *two-way* correspondence. In other words, individuals now have the ability to report on events taking place in their locale to a global audience, bypassing official, highly mediated sources of information, such as government agencies, the military and even the media institutions themselves. We are perhaps still a long way from turning to our computers rather than

Figure 1.1
The Internet brings a dramatic new challenge to traditional media reporting. Today, individuals can offer live, on-the-spot coverage of events anywhere in the world. However, although their reports are not subject to the filtering processes of mainstream media organisa-tions, this provides no guarantee against bias.

to our televisions for the latest news on particular events. It was a defining moment, however, when television cameras were directed at a screen displaying a website for the first, 'leaked' version of the Starr Report (the investigation into former US President Bill Clinton's sexual misconduct). Television news itself seemed at that moment to be acknowledging its own rejection as the *first* source of up-to-the-minute information.

In another example, the number of 'hits' to individual websites set up during the conflict in the Balkan states in the late 1990s suggest that this is a trend which is already firmly established.

Other devices have allowed for two-way communication, uncensored and over great distances: such as the telephone and citizen-band radio. Both have enabled free, live exchange between individuals. However, the nature of the communication has remained essentially private, with severe limitations on the numbers who could communicate at once.

New medium: new cautions

There are, of course, a number of checks on the euphoria with which this area should be greeted. Perhaps foremost is the realistic appraisal of just who has access to this exciting new facility. Great concern has been voiced about the division of the world into *information-rich* and *information-poor* populations. The West already has a considerable lead, in terms of development – this is likely to be greatly increased in the new world which is unfolding. Moreover, within Western society itself, access to this technology is very unequally distributed across the social spectrum. Without some kind of intervention to redress the imbalance, internal divisions can only grow.

Moreover, with regard to the nature of the *materials* on offer through the Internet, the validity of information on any website – official or unofficial – has always to be treated with a degree of caution. The greatest challenge that the Internet is going to present to us all will probably be how to discriminate between the multiple views, opinions and 'factual' accounts with which it presents us. In 1999, during the bombardment of Serbia, NATO and the British Government established websites to provide information about the conflict. These were declared to be a great success, with thousands of visits recorded – particularly from Serbia itself. However, when the propaganda value of these sites was recognised, viruses were devised to attack and corrupt the information stored there. This was billed by one commentator, writing in *The Independent*, 1 April 1999, as the first 'battle in cyberspace'. It may also serve as a useful reminder that the very birth of the Internet actually came about in response to military requirements.

Larger issues of censorship have equally dominated discussions about the impact and development of the Internet. Many governments around the world are deeply unhappy at the prospect of their citizens having access to news and information which has not been 'processed'. Some go to great lengths to block free access to the World Wide Web, often by allowing only one (state-controlled) service provider.

It is relatively easy to impose these types of restrictions, but there are consequences for all sorts of uses that governments may at the same time wish to promote – chiefly trade. Adam Powell, Vice President of the Freedom Forum, noted in a conference on guerrilla journalism that authoritarian regimes face a tension between censorship and development: 'More and more it is development which is winning.'

The past twenty years have seen phenomenal growth in the market for home-computer purchase. With its combination of educational, recreational and communications facilities, the home computer seems likely to oust even the television as the dominant item of domestic technology. Indeed, *convergence* of the two technologies is very much the target of the major media companies: the race is on to produce a single unit combining all the features of both. OnDigital and Sky Digital were the first to offer combined facilities: many others are sure to

MEDIA PASTIMES

Figure 1.2
Media pastimes per capita in the US. The table shows the average time and money spent on each media category by one person during 1994. To determine the average, the estimated total in each category is divided by the number of people surveyed. (Source: Veronis, Suhler & Associates)

(Per capita) MEDIUM	HOURS	$ SPENT
Television	1560	110
Radio	1102	0
Recorded music	294	56
Daily newspaper	169	49
Consumer books	102	79
Consumer magazines	84	36
Home video	52	73
Video games	22	17
Cinema movies	12	25
Consumer online and Internet services	3	7

CHARACTERISTICS OF THE MEDIA

Modern media may possess all or some of the following characteristics.

■ **Large numbers of people are reached**

The audience may truly be a mass audience, or it may be a much smaller *narrowcast* audience. With the exception of films in cinemas, media products are usually consumed privately, but produced centrally.

■ **Media products are often multi-modal**

Language has a variety of *modes of delivery*. These include speaking, writing, audio, non-verbal and visual modes of communication. Media products commonly combine several modes and computer-based media, in particular, can combine all of them.

■ **Some form of technology is employed**

Although the technology may possibly be simple, most media in fact use advanced technological processes.

■ **Industrial corporations are involved in production**

Especially in the case of the more traditional one-to-many media, large-scale government or commercial organisations control the production processes.

■ **There is often multiple authorship**

As media production is an industrial process, workers often have specialised roles as though on an assembly line. The list of credits at the end of a film, for example, reveals how many people were involved in making it. Other media products also have a variety of roles in their production: the journalist may write the story, but others have input into editing the copy, adding headlines and captions, the layout and design of the page, and so on.

■ **Governments regulate the media**

The media are usually regarded as a 'special case' and are subject to some degree of government regulation, even in societies favouring deregulated economies (where lack of interference in the operation of markets is fiercely promoted). Despite the notions we have of freedom of expression and liberty in the West, there are in fact many restrictions both on *what* can be produced (see p. 19) and *who* can produce them (see regulations on ownership, p. 20).

---

follow. Television will, in the very near future, seek to incorporate Internet capacity, in order to absorb its potential ... or should that perhaps the other way around?

How people use the media differently now

Until recently, for most people, the prospect of participation in the media was non-existent. Broadcast and print media were one-to-many providers with centralised production control. Video saturation of the consumer market in the late 1980s and early 1990s, however, allowed a further evolution in broadcast media participation. Home video cameras have allowed people to make television images of their own lives.

Homemade tapes are now being seen by a sizeable audience on mainstream television in shows such *You've Been Framed*. On a more serious level, video has allowed dissident groups to communicate their view of reality and break the power of central media, at least to a limited extent. There have been examples of this from within dictatorial countries. In East Timor, victims of brutal oppression carried out by the Indonesian army and government collaborated with Western journalists to send out reports of atrocities there. Evidence of brutality has also been gathered from within countries such as the United States.

When police in Los Angeles beat up an African-American man in a racially motivated attack, an eyewitness on the balcony of a nearby apartment block grabbed his home video camera and began filming the incident. Within hours of it taking place, the Rodney King beating was replayed to an audience of millions around the world. Within a day, airing of the thirty-second video clip had sparked full-scale urban rioting. In other instances, individual citizens have provided live eyewitness accounts – and even video footage, in some cases – of violent civil conflicts taking place around them.

Computer-based media have increased the possibility of mass participation in the creation of media products. On the Internet, it is possible for people to be both the producers and distributors of their own media products.

Media: New Ways and Meanings

To come to an understanding of the media, whether traditional or new, more than just the medium itself needs to be considered. The media are a whole set of social practices and relationships, as well as being buildings, steel transmission towers and printing presses. Study of the media consists of the following elements.

MEDIA PRODUCTS The television programme and the newspaper story both have their own ways of looking at the world. Each uses a specialised language, both visual and written. Media products have distinctive ways of telling stories and they have particular narratives and recognisable genres. The term 'text' tends to be used to refer to them, regardless of whether they are printed, still or moving images.

MEDIA INDUSTRIES AND INSTITUTIONS Media products are always influenced by the organisations that produce them. Ownership patterns, government regulation and how the products are assembled all have an effect.

MEDIA AUDIENCES While the members of an audience may not immediately think of themselves as part of the whole equation, without them the media would have no meaning.

MEDIA REPRESENTATIONS The way in which the media construct a view of the world provides an insight into their relationship with society.

MEDIA TECHNOLOGY The technologies of *production*, *distribution* and *exhibition* (sometimes also referred to as *exchange*) are an integral part of the media themselves. Advances in a technical area can have significant effects on what gets made and how popular it is. Audiences for film were in steep decline during the 1980s. Dolby stereo and heavy investment in sophisticated sound systems certainly contributed substantially to their dramatic revival during the 1990s.

GENRE In the study of the media, a *genre* is a category, type or style of media product. Films, for example, cover a range of genres that includes the horror film, the Western, action/adventure, romance and romantic comedy. Television has a similar range of genres, including soap operas, sitcoms, chat shows, game shows, docudramas, etc.

In the television and radio industries, these genres are often called *programme formats*. They are sometimes simply referred to as *formats*. A radio comedy and a television quiz show could both be considered particular types of programme format.

Figure 1.3
Codes of dress, of location, of appearance and facial expression combine to provide meanings in screen narratives. In the television play **Goodnight Mr Tom**, *set during World War II, John Thaw plays a grumpy old bachelor whose heart is gradually opened by the younger generation.*

MEDIA LANGUAGE The ways in which media products are constructed constitute methods of communication that we all recognise and readily decipher. This applies as much to verbal as to visual, and indeed to aural codes.

MEDIATION *Mediation* is the term used to describe the processes by which something is altered when it is passed on via a media outlet. A football match, for example, is a real event that has distinctive qualities when viewed live. Although the same original event, it is experienced quite differently when viewed at home. Multiple cameras, zoom lenses, action replays and so on *transform* the original experience. Arguments may rage about the relative merits of both, but the key point is that the two are very *different*.

Mostly, this process of mediation seeks simply to enhance the original event and make it more enjoyable. Some, however, have pointed to more sinister manipulations – of the press especially – and the ways in which they seek to control reception of raw events. Propaganda is a prime example of this.

In the rest of this chapter, we explore each of these areas in close detail.

▼ ▼ ▼ ▼ ▼ ▼ ▼

activities

1. Examine the ways in which other media products may have transformed the original events that they are representing. Find examples of photographs in newspapers and magazines, for example, and consider how framing, angle of shot and perspective may influence our view of a subject (see 'The Language of Film and Television', pp. 148).

2. Survey the media pastimes of the members of your class. To do this, interview class members on the hours and financial expenditure they allocate to different media. Add the totals and divide by the number of people in the survey to gain the average media consumption for the group.

Institutions and Industries

> Though a highly consumer-oriented good, [the media] is very different from most other such goods, like cars, toasters, washing machines. Whereas the latter provide the means, the former trades in the meanings of life.
>
> J. Blumler, *Television and the Public Interest*, 1992

▼ ▼ ▼

The media have been called the 'consciousness industries'. Over and above the products they sell, via advertising, they also promote ways of thinking and ways of seeing, or understanding, the world. The media are engaged in the production and distribution of states of mind.

According to some critics, there can be no disinterested position on the media; their social function is so profound, so central. Everybody, or every organisation, has an 'agenda' or point of view that they wish to promote.

The media institutions are also different from other knowledge institutions such as schools, churches or art galleries in several ways:

■ **They carry all types of knowledge**

Some of this knowledge is transmitted directly, in the form of educational programmes; some of it indirectly, through various kinds of entertainment, and advertisements.

■ **They are open to all members of society**

Ability to purchase is the only entry requirement.

■ **The relationship between sender and receiver is possibly more complex**

Passive reception is no longer assumed: diverse forms of participation are encouraged. From live audiences, to reader/viewer responses – not forgetting the imperative to go out and buy! – active engagement is the name of the game today.

■ **The media reach more people, for longer over a lifetime than any other institution**

The NHS may wobble in its delivery of services, but the media can truly be counted on to look out for us 'from cradle to grave'. With the exception of that other great institution of public service, the BBC, the media are of course all privately owned businesses.

Ownership

Lord Thompson of Fleet, one of the grand 'press barons' of a former age, once said owning a television station was 'a licence to print money'. A later and more notorious successor, Robert Maxwell, declared on purchasing *The Daily Mirror* (as it then was): 'I have bought a megaphone – and I intend to use it!' Between them, these two comments reveal the twin attractions of media ownership: money and power.

It is not always the case, however, that both are automatically attained; in recent years, newspapers particularly have been significant loss-makers, requiring massive subsidies from their owners to remain in business. Readership levels have been declining steadily for most, year after year. However, the simple fact that newspaper proprietors are prepared to go on pouring millions into these publications confirms their importance in terms of the status and influence which it is felt come with ownership of a major national newspaper.

The opportunity to influence public opinion, or even government policy, is a very powerful incentive to maintain involvement in newspaper production – particularly in view of the fact that most are now owned by conglomerates, as part of a portfolio of other businesses.

If prestige is one part of the attraction, manipulation of the environment for business activity is most certainly another. Many of their other corporate interests may benefit from this.

MEDIA AS BUSINESS

The essential fact is that the majority of media organisations are private businesses. They are companies with shareholders. Their prime concern is to make a profit for those shareholders. Huge investments of money are made. Taking the film industry as perhaps the most visible example, *Titanic* (USA, 1997) cost more than $200 million to produce and needed to take more than $350 million just to break even. In fact, it went on to gross more than $1 billion!

Film-making remains, however, a hugely risky business. *Last Action Hero* (USA, 1993) cost around $100 million, but failed to recoup anything like this at the box office, despite the bankable presence of Arnold Schwarzenegger. Even worse, the losses incurred by *Heaven's Gate* (USA, 1980) famously led to the collapse of United Artists, the studio that had made the film.

In the United Kingdom, the film industry is nowhere near as lucrative. It does have its own occasional spectacular successes: *The Full Monty* (UK/USA, 1997), for example, grossed £140 million worldwide (although most of the money returned to US investors).

The pattern is very varied. Many newspapers are actually losing money; however, this does not always seem to matter unduly, as proprietors may have reasons other than profit for being involved in the industry.

If newspapers are not always profitable, many television companies are decidedly the opposite. In 1998, Carlton declared profits of £166 million for the first half-year alone. Its total worth at that point was estimated to be in the region of £3.5 billion.

The BBC, of course, is both a substantial and a very different kind of organisation (see Chapter 4, p. 245). Funded by the licence fee and run traditionally on a non-commercial basis, it has no shareholders and does not seek to make profits – at least, not for private use. Although it did, in fact, begin life as a private company, the granting of a Royal Charter, in 1926, reconstituted the BBC as a public corporation, with the very distinctive status that that identity brings.

Before the privatisation drive of the 1980s, there were quite a number of national organisations which operated under this mantle: today, very few remain and even those that do – such as the Post Office – may yet be required to yield at least some of their traditional character. The jury is still out on whether this will apply to the BBC, too!

The BBC has always been a very influential organisation in terms of setting standards in broadcasting and in developing programme material and formats. In the past few decades, however, it has been increasingly squeezed both by cuts to its core funding and by the growing number and size of commercial competitors. One result of this is that it has come to resemble those channels more in terms not only of output, but also of operational practice. Its management structure has been ruthlessly shaken up and its programme-making subjected to rigorous 'internal

market' principles, which seek to imitate the systems used by industry on a much wider basis. The actual achievements of all this change are less than clear.

THE INFLUENCE OF THE OWNERS

Press baron Lord Beaverbrook once told the Royal Commission on the Press that he ran his newspapers 'purely for propaganda and no other purpose'. As for the worth of Beaverbrook's opinion on world affairs, Hugh Cudlipp (editor of *The Daily Mirror* in its heyday during the 1950s and 1960s) commented that Beaverbrook merited no more attention than a bearded nutcase in Trafalgar Square carrying a placard claiming that 'Judgement is nigh'. But he owned newspapers!

The Canadian media magnate Conrad Black owns media outlets in the United Kingdom (*The Telegraph*) and Australia. Black once told a Canadian Senate Committee that he believed journalists were 'opinionated and inadequately supervised'. His comments led analysts to accuse him of bullying journalists.

More notoriously, Rupert Murdoch, head of News International, has been responsible for numerous interventions, both direct and indirect, in the activities of his various media outlets. Most famously, in 1998, he ordered the publishing house HarperCollins to drop a book by former Hong Kong governor Chris Patten because it contained sharp criticism of China. This followed the dropping of the BBC World Service from Murdoch's Asian satellite, Star TV, when the government of that country objected to coverage from this source – usually noted for its impartiality – of some of its activities. Murdoch was very keen to get into the Chinese market: its enormous and commercially untapped population was an advertisers' dream. Moreover, the rightward thrust of the political outlook of *The Times* and *Sun* newspapers (up until the Labour victory in the 1997 UK general election, in the latter's case) under his control has been pointed out by many commentators.

SUPPORT OF THE POWERFUL

Media organisations are felt to have considerable influence over their audiences, especially in the realm of newspapers and most especially in the run-up to general elections. Prior to the landslide victory of the Labour party in 1997, Tony Blair paid a very well-documented visit to Rupert Murdoch's private island on the Great Barrier Reef, Australia. Many people felt that the strong anti-Labour front page of the *Sun* at the time of the previous election had been influential in turning that party's slim lead into a significant defeat.

The reason for Blair's visit was to address the Labour Party's attitude towards Murdoch's company, Newscorp, the media interests of which include the *Sun* and Sky television: its purpose was clearly to reassure that individual that a Labour Government would not be injurious to his business interests. The text of his speech on that day was not made public. However, what is certain is that shortly after this encounter, Murdoch was to speak very favourably of Blair; historically, on the day of the election, Murdoch's newspaper swung its weight fully behind Blair.

Whether this was a case of the *Sun* following a decisive shift in public opinion or helping to create it has remained a source debate ever since.

THE OWNERS

Karl Marx, the German political economist and philosopher, and founder of communism, proposed that the owners of big businesses are the 'ruling class'. They make up around 5 per cent of the population, but control roughly three-quarters of the national wealth. The remaining people work for them, exchanging labour for wages. In a Marxist view, the media owners, as members of the ruling class, represent reality from the viewpoint of 'the bosses'. Studies of television news have found a tendency to favour authority

figures, and the greater powers that they represent, in coverage of political and industrial events of various kinds. The views of 'ordinary' members of the public are very rarely featured, except as a bit of local colour to round off more weighty contributions from officials.

For the most part, the degree to which the media are manipulated to serve the interests of this powerful group is largely concealed. Occasionally, however, the sophistication of the system is bypassed – when the stakes are high enough. In Italy, businessman Silvio Berlusconi successfully used his television and radio outlets to support a political campaign to become prime minister in 1994. Prior to the election, he owned all three of the national commercial television stations: after it, he added the remaining public sector station to his list. For a while, he had complete control of what was broadcast throughout Italy. Berlusconi was also the head of the largest retail-industrial corporation in Italy after Fiat cars.

The process of acquiring this degree of control should not be seen as simplistic, however. Media producers have developed highly sophisticated methods of attracting consumers to their products, with an apparently wide range of fare on offer. If the material on offer has sufficient appeal, the majority of the public will not worry too much about the ins-and-outs of ownership. In Berlusconi's case, a good deal of his programming success depended on abundant use of scantily clad women, a resource long since established as effective by tabloid newspapers in the United Kingdom.

Nevertheless, schedulers have also learnt to

Figure 1.4
With multiple media outlets snared in the embrace of a giant octopus-like organisation, what chance is there of objective reporting? In the West, a handful of businessmen control the flow of all news.

diversify their material, in order to attract a wide range of audiences. Aside from the obviously populist variety and entertainment shows, some 'anti-Establishment' programmes have achieved enormous success – satirical and irreverent shows such as *Not the Nine O'clock News* (BBC/UK, 1980s), for instance. To make profits, they often present material that does not directly support the interests of the owners of big business. Occasionally, through television programmes such as *Roseanne*, a less well-heeled view of the world is presented (although the programme has now made Roseanne Barr herself extremely wealthy). Analysis of news programmes, however, has shown much more clear support for the capitalist establishment.

The Glasgow University Media Group has done many in-depth studies of news coverage (see *Bad News, More Bad News*) and has clearly established a preference for lending weight to 'official' comments from authority figures, rather than to representatives from among ordinary people, for instance. Coverage of the struggles between miners and police during the strike of 1984, in a classic instance, was more often than not conducted from behind police lines, rather than among the strikers themselves. Distortions in the representation of this conflict were inevitable: the police were perceived as victims of violence, rather than as perpetrators, and the miners as instigators. However, subsequent court cases threw out countless charges against the miners, firmly contradicting the picture of lawlessness created around them in the media at that time.

HEGEMONY

Political theorist Antonio Gramsci developed the concept of *hegemony* to chart how governments require the *consent* of their peoples to be governed. In a democracy, this is essential as, without consent, law and order can easily break down. Large-scale, popular dissent (such as that seen during protests in 1990 over the introduction of the notorious poll tax in the United Kingdom) can result in the people becoming literally ungovernable. French lorry drivers and farmers are good examples of this, with their readiness to take direct action and block major roadways and city centres, in order to force their government to listen to their demands.

The consent of the people to abide by the law and be ruled, therefore, is crucial.

This consent, however, has to be won: and the media play a considerable part in this process. The entertainment, excitement and other diversions they proffer are key to maintaining the complacency of the general populace. More recent theorists such as Noam Chomsky suggest a much more manipulative 'propaganda role' for the media. They actively conspire, he suggests, to promote particular values and foster interest in certain kinds of activity (such as sport) – and, of course, to focus consumer desires on certain kinds of products. These, Chomsky maintains, are largely distractions from more important concerns about things that actually matter in people's lives, such as how their society is being organised and governed, for instance.

TENDING TOWARDS MONOPOLY

Imagine a primeval swamp with a few bloated dinosaurs confronting each other. They exist in uneasy truce, but, if one beast turns its head momentarily, another will deliver a death blow. If one is smaller and grows more slowly, it will be hunted by the others. Eventually, only one or two of the largest, most ungainly dinosaurs survive. These are the media conglomerates!

IN A MEDIA MONOPOLY a single firm dominates, or even operates as the sole provider. Large Western media markets have not yet reached the stage of monopoly.

AN OLIGOPOLY exists when there is almost a monopoly. In an oligopoly, four or five companies operate like cardsharps in a poker game. Each player knows what the others are up to, but does not have perfect knowledge. The players organise and control the markets to suit themselves. Others are excluded from the game.

In the United Kingdom, Australia and the United States, the separate major media markets seem to have settled down to four big players per market. Some of these are household names, such as Rupert Murdoch.

A CONGLOMERATE is a collection of diverse companies not bound by common activity or product, but often reinforcing – even promoting – each other's interests. Newscorp, for instance, made use of its ownership of the *Sun* to generate expectation and interest in the launch of Sky TV.

SYNERGY

Merchandising is now a long-established feature of film-making, in Hollywood at least. Often, as much money can be made from the related products marketed alongside the release of a major new film as from the film itself. The merchandising alone from *Batman* (USA, 1989) provided at least $US 200 million. *Jurassic Park* (USA, 1993) cost $US60 million to make, but grossed $US300 million at the box office in 1993 alone. Even more impressive, it is estimated that more than 1000 trademarked products were developed to accompany the film – many of which also appeared in the theme park shop in the film itself. These ranged from the obvious dinosaur kits, through video games, to stickers, toothbrushes and even underwear! These were not directly manufactured by Universal Pictures, the makers of the film, of course: lucrative franchise deals were struck with other companies. Planning, marketing and coordination of release dates are crucial aspects of modern media activity.

In Disney's *Hercules* (USA, 1997), this activity is even satirised, with the merchandising of the hero-figurines occurring *within the film itself*. Although the intention is clearly to make light of this rampant commercialism, in fact, it is a key economic activity in much film and increasingly in television programme making, too.

Enormous queues formed, many hours before shops opened, for the soft-toy versions of the characters from the BBC's hit young children's programme, *Teletubbies*.

Linkage of this kind is described as the process of *synergy* and is crucial to the commercial activities of most modern conglomerates. It is not essential that the same parent owns the companies involved – though it is often the case. The key to its success lies in two or more products being used to promote each other: a hit film makes associated products desirable, then, in turn, the array of merchandise available helps to keep the film itself in the public eye.

Tie-ins and *spin-offs*, where merchandise is closely linked with particular media products, are very much a feature of today's marketing world. So much so that some people even claim that the film is now the trailer for the stream of products that is to follow!

DIVERSIFICATION

Diversification is a process of enlarging a company by taking over or merging with other companies. Sometimes these other companies can be in similar or related areas of business; sometimes they are not. The American NBC network, for instance, is owned by General Electric, which makes nuclear weapons on defence contract. In the United Kingdom, Reed Publishing has a stable of magazines and also makes toilet bowls and shower fittings.

Horizontal integration is when companies expand sideways. The entertainment media sells their products as pastimes in the leisure industry. A film company, for example, may spread its activities into virtual reality technology or holiday resorts. It is still within the leisure industry, but has spread to other parallel activities.

Vertical integration is when expansion up or down occurs. It is made possible because the production process is divided into stages. A newspaper, for instance, begins as a tree, then goes through multiple stages of production and distribution until it finally ends up as stuffing for a padded postbag. In one example of such vertical integration, the Japanese television manufacturer Sony purchased the US film company Columbia in the early 1990s. Sony now controls the production and distribution (via television sets) of some of Hollywood's most famous shows. In Australia, Rupert Murdoch controls 60 per cent of the nation's newspapers and also owns all sources of newsprint.

BENEFITS In the fluid environment of the modern business world, a narrow base of activity is regarded as highly undesirable. Spreading your interests across a range of production activities is the best way of insuring against fluctuations of performance in any particular one.

Diversification increases profits and long-term security. If one part of the firm loses money, the other parts can support it.

PROBLEMS Sometimes, conflicts can arise between the interests of differing arms of a complex organisation. The management of *The Observer* was once famously pressured by its former owner, Tiny

Rowland, not to investigate conditions in mines in South Africa – where Rowland happened to have extensive business interests.

More recently, NBC itself was criticised for giving in to pressure from the nuclear industry over the contents of an adventure drama for television it produced, called *The Atomic Train*. Originally, the programme dealt with the story of a runaway train carrying a cargo of nuclear waste: despite all the hero's best efforts, the train crashes and showers the area with the waste, at the same time triggering a Russian-made nuclear bomb secretly attached by terrorists. In a highly unusual last-minute move, and at great expense, the company decided to re-dub the mini-series, in order to delete all references to nuclear waste. The phrase 'hazardous material' was used instead.

A member of the US Senate Science and Transportation Committee accused NBC of acting out of deference to its parent company, General Electric, which has extensive interests in the nuclear industry.

Media factories

It used to be the case that 95 per cent of television news stories appeared because they happened at the right time (between 11 a.m. and 5 p.m.) or because they occurred close enough for the crew to cover easily and there was enough videotape, according to a study of news-gathering procedures. Today, the means of gathering news have become much more diverse: news reporting has now moved into a 24-hour concept, with a global outlook.

Satellite relays and high-quality portable video equipment have made on-the-spot reports, anywhere in the world, much more feasible now than even a few years ago. Press agencies and the seemingly ubiquitous amateur video cameras can often supply what the organisations' own employees cannot get to in time. It used to be said that television news was very much driven by the availability of quality visual material. With the wide availability of amateur video (and the occasional lowering of technical standards!), there is now very little that cannot be covered.

What makes news has as much to do with institutional practice as newsworthiness. The industrial processes of media organisations are major determinants of the texts. Each organisation has particular values that determine what gets printed or screened.

These values can be divided into two distinct categories: *news values* and *professional values*.

NEWS VALUES

A delegation of Martians, struggling to come to terms with the meanings of words in the English language, might make the mistake of thinking that what was supposed to constitute 'news' were things that were fresh and immediate. With only a little coaching on theory, our extraterrestrial visitors might then assume that only things of importance were to be included under this heading. However, they may still just be a touch confused by some of the items which actually make it into national news bulletins (ITV's famous '… and, finally …' for instance, the upbeat or wryly amusing type of story which was often used to end the news on a more positive note). Almost certainly, they would be dumbfounded by the length of time over which some stories had regularly featured (e.g. Ulster and 300-plus years). Far from being a simple selection of the most important events from anywhere in the world, all news is in fact highly, and necessarily, *selective*.

There are patterns in the selection and presentation of news – whether it be printed or broadcast. Television programmes and newspapers have their own formats, their regular presenters and writers, and, of course, their own *agendas* on how to view the very events which are being reported. The *identity* of the news provider is almost as crucial as the material they present. Audience loyalty, of course, is the crucial target.

A distinct set of criteria has emerged which determines the filtering processes of all the potential events that may be covered in any one day. A study by the Norwegians Galtung and Ruge first identified recurrent factors in the selection of daily news items. Since their pioneering work, others have been added; the most influential now include:

■ **Proximity**

This is perhaps the most important – how close to home does the event occur. There are many old journalist tales about how many Chinese lives equate to British ones for newsworthiness (in this country, that is) and an ongoing debate as to just how interested we are in what goes on abroad. The general feeling is that the further away the location, the larger/more dramatic the story has to be to compete with a natural tendency for audiences to identify primarily with 'homegrown' news. Wars, civil disorder and general upheaval are the staple fare of popular overseas reporting, whereas stories based on the United Kingdom can have a much lower profile.

■ **Predictability**

The coverage given to particular events follows predictable patterns. Media outlets develop certain ways of looking at the world and reinforce this with the way they present new stories. Sometimes this can lead to crass errors of judgment, as in the *Sun*'s treatment of the Hillsborough football tragedy in 1989, when 96 supporters were crushed to death. Used to reporting on soccer fans as hooligans, they made this story fit that stock pattern (without, in this case, bothering to check the facts).

■ **Frequency**

Frequency has to do with the amount of time the story itself actually takes to occur. Events which are completed actions (murders, accidents, economic swings, for instance) are preferred to things which take a long time to unfold (the working through of policies, long-term structural plans, etc.).

■ **Continuity**

On the other hand, once a story has been started, following up to check on developments is regarded as important: police or public enquiries, ongoing trials, industrial action, and so on.

■ **Negativity**

Negativity, of course, has long been one of the prime requirements of all 'good' news reporting. Things that go wrong, trouble, strife and conflict are all regarded as the best sources of story material. If things are going well, the philosophy is, where is the dynamic for an 'angle', or a 'scoop'? A couple of years ago, a prominent BBC newscaster, Martyn Lewis, made a bid for more positive reporting – he wanted to see achievement and good deeds as the staple of television news. His voice has gone largely unheeded within that, or any other, organisation.

■ **Surprise**

Surprise is an element in the selection process, but not as frequent in occurrence as might be thought – nor as random. Too much of the unexpected makes it difficult to impose a pattern on news gathering. Even here, there are broad categories into which items might need to be fitted: for example, natural disasters, and the famine and diseases that often follow.

■ **Celebrity**

This is not strictly on the original list, but decidedly a category which needs adding today. Once confined to national politicians and international leaders, and focused on their public actions: now, however, depending on the nature of the outlet, the figures include stars of screen, pop and sporting arenas, and are more likely to feature aspects of their private lives.

Many other factors can be traced in the selection of news items. Of equal importance, however, is the way in which stories are covered once the initial selection has been made.

PROFESSIONAL VALUES

All institutions have certain ways of doing things, which are built up over time and promoted with a high degree of internal pride. For some, there are *external* constraints, including legal controls, which determine how they do things: this is a very significant area and is dealt with elsewhere. In the media, there are also various *internal* constraints, which are equally important in determining the nature of the products that are generated.

These constraints can be further subdivided into two distinct groups: *formal* and *informal* mechanisms.

FORMAL MECHANISMS exist to guide and monitor the materials supplied to the public. In the case of *newspapers*, there is the Press Complaints Commission (PCC): this body responds to complaints it receives, and reviews published work to determine whether any serious breaches of the Press Code occur. It has no legal powers, and is a voluntary organisation funded by the newspaper industry itself. It can request that editors respond to transgressions which it identifies, but it cannot compel them to do so.

The Press Code is a set of rules governing the conduct of journalists, photographers and their employers (see p. 19 for details); it is designed to ensure fairness and honesty in all news reporting. This code was drawn up by people from within the industry and was considerably strengthened in 1997, following the death of Diana, the Princess of Wales. It was strongly felt at the time that news-papers – and the *paparazzi*, in particular – bore a heavy responsibility for this sad event, flowing from the way in which celebrities were relentlessly pursued for stories about their private lives.

In the realm of *television*, there are two distinct monitoring bodies: one for the BBC and another for commercial television. The Independent Television Commission (ITC) both awards licences to broadcasting companies (such as Carlton or Granada) and scrutinises their output, to ensure that they do nothing to offend public decency – and this applies to advertisements as much as to programme material. In fact, they also check that the companies keep to the terms of the broad-casting provision that they proposed when bidding for the franchise in the first place. This marks the ITC out as very different from the PCC, as it is strictly an *external* agency and has very real control over the ability of the broadcasting companies to function as businesses.

The BBC, on the other hand, has no such *external* monitoring agency, but does have its own Board of Governors, who are responsible for the running of the whole organisation on a solid professional basis. This body is composed of indi-viduals drawn from various positions of eminence in society. They are appointed, ultimately by the government. Their remit includes scrutiny of pro-gramming output, as well as business management.

INFORMAL MECHANISMS are rather harder to see than formal mechanisms, although they may in fact be much more influential in determining the nature of the fare actually produced. All media institutions have their own in-house organisational approaches to their trade and their own particular internal codes about how events are to be interpreted and represented.

In the play *Pravda*, by Howard Brenton and David Hare, there is a scene at the beginning of Act Two where some copy is rewritten by the Duty Editor. The original story submitted by the journalist had been sympathetic to peace protesters camping out around the perimeter fence of an RAF base being used to store US nuclear missiles. The scene shows how the journalist is 'educated' in the outlook of that particular paper: criticism of the police for the brutality of their handling of a largely female grouping is transformed into outright condemnation of the pacifists for violence inflicted on the innocent agents of the law!

In 1984, Joan Smith, a real-life journalist working for the *Sunday Times*, had her report on incidents at Greenham Common – a famous peace camp of the time (see figure 1.6) – altered in a way with which she was not happy. Ultimately, Smith had no more control over what was done to her copy than the fictional journalist depicted in the scene related above.

It is an open secret that newspapers have their own political affiliations – sympathies with particular political parties and their policies. Today, these have become a little more diverse: the *Sun*'s historic shift to support the Labour Party, in the 1997 election, seemed to mark the dawn of this new era. How permanent this shift may prove remains to be seen.

Previously, most national newspapers had been staunch supporters of the Conservative Party. What is not always so clearly understood is the extent to which these organisations are prepared to manip-ulate facts to accommodate this political support.

Similarly, journalists who wish to work for them have to adapt to the perspectives these institutions are prone to take of events they cover. Even at the BBC, there is now a very strong culture of 'referral upwards'. This means that management – and very often senior management – are the judges both of what shall be done and *how* it shall be done. A very tight grip is maintained on the institution's output. This is not, of course, to suggest that this has in any way imperilled its impartiality, for which it has always rightly prided itself. Nevertheless, corporate culture does appear to have spread throughout the entire organisation and suppressed the very possibility of individual employee initiative.

DIVISION OF LABOUR INTO ROLES

Henry Ford used 'assembly-line' techniques to build cars and, by the time the last Model T rolled

Figure 1.5
*Women protesters at Greenham Common in 1983. The British government had granted the US armed forces the facility to store nuclear weapons there. Many people in the United Kingdom felt that this was an infringement of Britain's national sovereignty – quite apart from the threat posed by all nuclear weapons.
(TV Eye, Thames Television, 1983.)*

off the production line in 1926, he had made half of all the cars sold in the United States. Almost all capitalist production followed Ford's mass-production techniques. Each worker performs a single task repetitively on a production line. Labour is 'divided' into component stages.

MEDIA PRODUCERS HAVE SPECIALISED ROLES such as journalist, sub-editor, editor and so on. A consequence of this multiple authorship is that media texts often follow standard formulae.

MEDIA PRODUCTS ARE MADE IN TEAMS so no individual is totally responsible for the meanings communicated. The values of the text are therefore more likely to be those values acceptable to the institution as a whole.

ROUTINES

All media institutions develop routines that can have considerable impact on the shape of the final product. Any institution will do the same: if you have found an effective way of doing business, why look to change it? On the whole, this seems a sensible way to run an organisation.

In news production, however, it does raise some important questions. We have already seen how agendas of news selection are established. If the topics themselves are virtually preselected,

then the means of reporting is increasingly in danger, too. News gatherers return again and again to reliable sources of information. The courts, government offices, local police forces and similar public bodies have always been useful points of contact for information-hungry journalists.

It has been argued that heavy reliance on these sources has led to insufficient objectivity in reporting events involving these agencies. Criticism of the police, for instance, is unlikely to dispose their officers to be helpful to the 'offending' journalist on the next occasion s/he needs information.

NEWS MANAGEMENT

Recognising the power wielded by the holder of information, politicians above all others have now developed sophisticated methods of managing the news. There is a public perception of the media as purveyors of the truth – or of factual accounts of things that happen, at least. Of course, this image is carefully cultivated by news providers themselves. Legendary stories such as the probing investigations by two ordinary journalists into the Watergate scandal in the United States in the early 1970s, which led to the downfall of President Nixon, have helped to consolidate this bold, fearless claim.

Reality is quite another story, however. Even in this notorious case, it was the role of the anonymous supplier of key information – named 'Deep Throat' in the famous film of those times, *All the President's Men* (USA, 1976) – which was probably of the most profound significance in driving the investigation forwards. The tip-offs this source provided gave the journalists the leads they needed to pursue the full facts.

Managing the release of news may not be the new phenomenon many take it for – but it certainly has become a central feature of government in all modern democracies.

Publicly accountable organisations quite naturally need representatives who can deal with the media. It makes sense to appoint to these positions people who have a keen knowledge of what news organisations want, how they operate, and so on. Very often, these people come from within those very organisations: classic cases of 'poacher-turning-gamekeeper'. (Although, given the media's self-proclaimed role of monitoring the activities of government, and the often dubious methods adopted by news managers, that phrase should perhaps be applied the other way round.)

THE SPIN DOCTORS

There is a new breed of news manager in the arena now. Very much a product of the 1990s, the 'spin doctor' is neither an elected member of the government nor even a civil servant, but rather an employee of a political party. These individuals wield considerable control over the way in which information about government activity is released.

The term itself is originally American; it derives from the game of pool and has to do with the techniques of controlling the cue ball. In essence, there is the ball itself, which is a fixed entity and cannot be changed; there is then the manner of its delivery to its point of impact. In terms of government, similarly, there are nuggets of news which have to be presented to the public – not all of them necessarily positive – but there are also various ways in which these pieces of news can be released; these are open to various forms of manipulation, or 'spin'.

You may not be able to change the ball, but you can certainly influence the way in which it is received in the public domain.

The influence of the professionals

Professor John Henningham's 1994 study of the attitudes of journalists has revealed a curious mix. Journalists are mostly in favour of capitalism and free enterprise, but lean towards the left on social

Figure 1.6
The art of 'spin'. The manner in which news is released can dramatically alter the way in which it is received by the public. Modern governments have become highly adept at news management.

issues. They have an 'anything goes' attitude in relation to moral areas and they are often hostile to organised religion.

Whether these views are actually reflected in news output is largely unresearched. So far, only journalists have been surveyed. The social views of other professionals working in the production of television dramas, quiz shows or horror films have not been explored at all.

Huge conglomerate media companies mean that owners must leave much of the day-to-day running of the media to professionals. While it is true that bosses have the power to allocate funds, control policies and to hire and fire, media workers do have operational control over how something will be produced.

GATEKEEPERS

Key personnel within media organisations are designated with some kind of operational control over what passes through the particular institution. The 'gates' are where items of news, for instance, are considered for suitability. The 'keepers' of those gates are those people who determine what gets through and is used: editors and their deputies, chiefly.

We have already seen earlier that owners may have a very direct input on this, too; moreover, journalists themselves may also contribute to the process. Some are asked to cover particular kinds of story – indeed, seek to specialise in certain areas. Others come to know what kinds of material will be of interest to their organisations. This can apply to the kind of item itself, or indeed to *the way in which* it is covered.

INTERNAL CONSTRAINTS

Just as the education system or the police force has a particular 'culture', media institutions develop an ethos of their own about the correct way of doing things. Camera operators have the 'well-trimmed image', while magazine artists have the 'house style'. Formats will, of course, vary widely from outlet to outlet.

Not least among the considerations will be the political outlook of the individual institution. Newspapers, especially, are generally recognised as having preferences among political parties (although these may change) and it is unusual for them to print articles which do not adhere

to these affiliations. Journalists need to be mindful of them when composing their articles.

Journalists are, in theory, also bound by a formal document called the Code of Practice (see p. 19). This is a voluntary code drawn up by the Press Complaints Commission (PCC), the print media monitoring body, funded by the newspaper and magazine industries. On 1 January 1998, following the death of Diana, Princess of Wales, this code was considerably strengthened, as there was widespread concern at the activities of 'certain sections' of the print media – tabloid papers, especially.

However, one leading journalist (Polly Toynbee, then of *The Independent*) wrote shortly before the death of the Princess of Wales of how she had never even read the code, let alone adhered to it. When she showed it to colleagues, they all fell about laughing! If this was the reaction of the more respectable broadsheet press, the responses of the more downmarket publications are not hard to imagine.

Undoubtedly, the new code is much more stringent: whether it is likely to have any greater or more lasting effect still remains to be seen. The *Sun*'s publication in mid-1999 of the 'nipple shot' of Sophie Rhys-Jones, Prince Edward's then-fiancée, tends to suggest that this is perhaps unlikely in the long term (although the editor did subsequently apologise – something of a milestone in itself).

EXTERNAL CONSTRAINTS

The Code of Practice, of course, has no legal standing: journalists and editors can be *asked* to comply with rulings by the Press Complaints Commission, and even asked to desist from future breaches, offer apologies, and so on. But they cannot be *made* to do so.

A range of regulations impact on the final shape of any media text. Some of these are voluntary codes and agreements; others are strictly enforced government regulations. A number of laws also have to be carefully observed, some of which are dealt with below.

Newspapers are traditionally considered to be free from direct government controls. Curran and Seaton give a good account of how, at the end of the nineteenth century, it was only once government *stopped* trying to regulate the press

PCC CODE OF PRACTICE

Figure 1.7
*A summary of the
Press Complaints
Commission
(PCC) Code of
Practice. The code
was tightened up
considerably
following the
death of Diana,
the Princess of
Wales, in 1997.
The right of
individuals to
privacy in their
personal lives was
the main thrust
of the reforms.
Full details can be
obtained from the
PCC's website,
www.pcc.org.uk*

ACCURACY

Newspapers and periodicals should not publish inaccurate, misleading or distorted material including pictures. They should also distinguish clearly between comment, conjecture and fact.

OPPORTUNITY TO REPLY

A fair opportunity for reply to inaccuracies must be given to individuals or organisations when reasonably called for.

PRIVACY

Everyone is entitled to respect for his or her private and family life, home, health and correspondence.

The use of long lens photography to take pictures of people in private places without their consent is unacceptable.

HARASSMENT

Journalists and photographers must neither obtain nor seek to obtain information or pictures through intimidation, harassment or persistent pursuit.

INTRUSION INTO GRIEF OR SHOCK

In cases involving personal grief or shock, enquiries should be carried out and approaches made with sympathy and discretion. Publication must be handled sensitively at such times, but this should not be interpreted as restricting the right to report judicial proceedings.

CHILDREN

Young people should be free to complete their time at school without unnecessary intrusion.

Pupils must not be approached or photographed while at school without the permission of the school authorities. The press must not, even where the law does not prohibit it, identify children under the age of 16 who are involved in cases concerning sexual offences, whether as victims or as witnesses.

LISTENING DEVICES

Journalists must not obtain or publish material obtained by using clandestine listening devices or by intercepting private telephone conversations.

DISCRIMINATION

The press must avoid prejudicial or pejorative reference to a person's race, colour, religion, sex or sexual orientation or to any physical or mental illness or disability.

It must avoid publishing details of a person's race, colour, religion, sexual orientation, physical or mental illness or disability unless these are directly relevant to the story.

PAYMENT FOR ARTICLES

Payment or offers of payment for stories or information must not be made directly or through agents to witnesses or potential witnesses in current criminal proceedings, or to convicted or confessed criminals or to their associates.

FINANCIAL JOURNALISM

Even where the law does not prohibit it, journalists must not use for their own profit financial information they receive in advance of its general publication, nor should they pass such information to others.

VICTIMS OF SEXUAL ASSAULT

The press must not identify victims of sexual assault or publish material likely to contribute to such identification unless there is adequate justification and, by law, they are free to do so.

CONFIDENTIAL SOURCES

Journalists have a moral obligation to protect confidential sources of information.

that it began to become mainstream and respectable.

The Internet is also free from government control because it has developed across national boundaries and enables individuals to virtually set themselves up as media organisations. Radio is said to have a light touch of control.

Television is the most regulated media industry, perhaps mainly because it intrudes into the very heart of family life.

REGULATION AND OWNERSHIP RULES

The precise picture here is quite difficult to pin down. There is a theoretical framework – and then an actual implementation of it. The two do not entirely match up. For instance, under the terms of the original 1990 Broadcasting Act, no broadcaster is technically supposed to own more than one ITV franchise, yet Carlton took over Central in 1994. Equally, no company is supposed to own national newspapers *and* television stations, yet Rupert Murdoch has several of both.

In part, this comes about because of the philosophical commitment of the government of the time to the concept of the free market. They wished to deregulate industries of all kinds – and the troublesome media ones, in particular. If these then fell increasingly to sympathetic, even supportive, wealthy businessmen, this did not present too many problems as far as that government was concerned. The fussy details of (their own) legislation could always be amended to suit, at a later date.

What for many was even more surprising was the attitude of the Labour Party at the time. When a new Labour government was about to be elected, their spokesman on media affairs (speaking on John Pilger's television documentary *Breaking the Mirror*) claimed that his party was actually in favour of even less regulation!

Cross-media ownership is an area that many see as a threat to the very notion of democracy (see p. 10 on Silvio Berlusconi and the perils of multi-media ownership). Yet Labour was identifying it as needing less – not more – restrictions.

TELEVISION

Initially, franchises (licences to broadcast) were restricted to only one for any one company, and a limit set of only up to 20 per cent for ownership of any other broadcasting company. Moreover, newspaper companies were also limited to 20 per cent ownership of British television or radio channels. Subsequent amendments, however, enabled the merger of two television stations.

Regulation is quite complex, given the diverse nature of the provision of television services in this country.

THE BBC is answerable, in the first instance, to its own Board of Governors. They have the power to require a programme to be withdrawn from the schedule, if they deem it unfit for broadcasting, for whatever reason. The board is appointed directly by the government, which also renews the BBC's licence – awarded by Royal Charter every ten years – as well as setting the level of the licence fee.

COMMERCIAL TELEVISION (including all terrestrial, cable and some satellite services), on the other hand, is licensed by the Independent Television Commission (ITC), which publishes codes that these broadcasters must strictly observe. This body also deals with complaints, regarding programme *and* advertising material. Companies are obliged to comply with the rulings of this body: in the long term, their licences can be re-allocated should they fail to do so. Broadcasting franchises are currently determined by auction, with interested companies required to submit sealed bids to the ITC every ten years.

RADIO has proven to be one of the faster developing areas in the past ten years. Regulated by the Radio Authority, there is now a proliferation of new licences operating in this field: national commercial stations, talk radio, specialist music channels are all recent phenomena and have generated a new sense of the possibilities of this medium.

NEWSPAPERS AND MAGAZINES, having their origins in the nineteenth century, have been subject to less regulation than the broadcast media. No licence is required to publish in print – only extensive capital. The last national daily newspaper to be launched, *The Independent*, cost an estimated £21 million. The Press Complaints Commission (PCC), outlined below, scrutinises output for adherence to the voluntary Code of Practice.

BROADCASTING LICENCES

Commercial television and radio broadcasters must obtain a licence before transmission can start. Conditions attached to the broadcasting licences include: the requirement to contribute to an adequate and comprehensive range of services; upholding the 'public interest'; maintaining programme standards; and not broadcasting illegal material (such as pornographic films).

Community television licences are allocated according to whether the broadcaster can prove it can represent the nature and diversity of community interests. Community stations must not be operated for profit.

DEFAMATION AND OTHER LAWS OF RESTRAINT

Defamation consists of two distinct elements: *slander* for the spoken word and *libel* for the written word.

Broadly speaking, the offence consists of three parts: publication, identification and defamation. People who think that their reputations have been damaged by the media may take the matter to court. If found guilty, media organisations may have to pay considerable sums of money. Needless to say, this works as a restraining factor on media texts. In practice, however, any protection the laws of defamation offer is only available to the rich and powerful, who can afford to pay the huge costs involved in such lawsuits.

A number of other laws apply to the nature of reporting that may be carried out for particular kinds of subject, according to where they occur and whom they involve, and the manner in which they may be covered. Restrictions apply to proceedings that are still before the courts that involve young people, as well as to certain specified offences such as rape. Some legislation, moreover, is designed to protect certain information deemed vital to the security of the country. All journalists need to be fully aware of all these limitations to their craft: if not, they could face being the subject of legal action themselves, as could their employers.

CENSORSHIP

Censorship is the removal or prohibition of material regarded as morally, politically or otherwise objectionable. All societies censor in some way, however small. Always a contentious

subject, theoretically censorship is something to which we are nearly all fundamentally opposed, at least in principle; in practice, however, we readily accept it in various forms without demur.

Commentators on the topic will readily cite examples of how, for example, even bad weather was censored in Soviet films of the pre-*glasnost* Brezhnev era. Any sign of drab village life or any evidence of the increasing pollution of the environment was banned. Instead, scenes of pleasant walks in the forest on sunny days were gratuitously inserted into the films to cheer people up!

However, all manner of items are withheld from public view by the media in western societies. In 1996, a group of dockers in Liverpool were sacked: their struggle for reinstatement led to worldwide action, yet was largely ignored by the British media. Journalist John Pilger gives a good account of this in his book *Hidden Agendas*.

Similar treatment was meted out to the peoples of East Timor for many years, after their country had been annexed by neighbouring Indonesia. Their cries for help went unreported in most of the world's media. Other, less critical accounts are put forward to explain these failures of open, honest and comprehensive coverage – but they amount to the same thing, in the end. The fact is that extensive selection takes place about what does and does not get reported.

DIRECT CENSORSHIP of the media does exist, but it is usually moral, rather than political. At times, the British Board of Film Classification has prevented certain films from being shown in the United Kingdom, at least for some time, or until material deemed as offensive has been excised or public taste has moved on.

Commercial television stations often cut scenes from films to suit particular time slots. Scenes of a sexual nature are the most likely to be subject to this treatment.

However, one notorious act of censorship involving the BBC concerned a programme dealing with governmental advice to civilians on how to deal with a nuclear attack. Peter Watkins's film *The War Game* (BBC, 1966) was banned for twenty years for being too graphically *accurate* on how devastating such an attack would be. Other manipulations of what was felt appropriate for the public to be shown occurred under the Thatcher government, most notably concerning its own handling of attacks on it from the IRA, Argentina and other external agencies (cf. *Real Lives* and *Death on the Rock*).

These specific instances may not amount to a concerted policy of state or even corporate censorship, but they do demonstrate how representation of the world around us is subject to manipulation by a variety of vested interests. At the same time, they also serve to remind us how reliant we all are on the media for our understanding of the world in which we live.

SELF-CENSORSHIP occurs when media producers omit material in the belief that it will offend sections of the community. An example of this would be the voluntary abstention of the media from the memorial service for the victims of the massacre of schoolchildren in Dunblane, Scotland. Such sensitivity to the sufferings of the relatives is entirely commendable – if rare.

More typically, and dangerously, self-censorship can protect commercial interests, as well as moral interests. For example, one-time owner of the *Observer*, Tiny Rowland, fought a furious battle with that newspaper over its coverage of stories of corruption and torture by the military in Zimbabwe – a country from which his company, Lonrho, derived considerable profit. Similarly, there is a danger a public service broadcaster such as the BBC may not always be sufficiently critical of the government for fear of cuts, or at least of inadequate increases to the licence fee.

WARTIME AND EMERGENCY CENSORSHIP of the media is provided for in all the major countries of the world. During the Gulf War, in 1991, the US government authorised the banning of all information that could 'jeopardise operations and endanger lives, reveal details of future plans, or the location of forces'. Few would dispute the need to conceal information that may risk the lives of soldiers from our own forces – or civilians of any

Figure 1.8
The Guardian,
Saturday 17 April
1999. Veteran BBC
correspondent
John Simpson was
accused of bias in
his reports on the
Kosovo crisis. Any
questioning of our
own actions in
conflict situations
rapidly leads to
charges of
treachery and
even treason on
the part of the
reporter. Simpson
angrily rebutted
the slur on his long
and distinguished
career in war
reporting.

BBC veteran denies bias

Media: John Simpson counters Downing Street with charge of interfering, writes **Janine Gibson**

John Simpson: 'I know how journalists are coerced'

JOHN Simpson, the veteran BBC foreign correspondent, yesterday angrily denied accusations of Serb bias in his reporting from Belgrade, following reports that government officials have threatened to complain.

Speaking to the Guardian from Belgrade, the BBC's world affairs editor said: "I object very strongly to this accusation of being pro-Serb." He also spoke of his disappointment and anger at the unnamed government official who was quoted in yesterday's Times briefing against him.

Lance Price, deputy to the Prime Minister's press spokesman Alastair Campbell, yesterday attempted to distance Downing Street from the reported comments, saying that no one in Downing Street was giving credence to the quotes. However, BBC insiders believe the briefing came from Mr Campbell, who is close to the Times journalist who wrote the story.

Mr Simpson believes that the briefing, in which a "senior official" accused Mr Simpson of presenting Serb propaganda at face value, was the result of several recent incidents.

"In the first instance I wrote something for the Sunday Telegraph which said that if the purpose of the war was to alienate people here [in Belgrade] from Milosevic then it wasn't working. That provoked a reaction from Downing Street."

One incident cited by the unnamed official took place on Wednesday when the Nine O'Clock News anchorman Michael Buerk asked Mr Simpson during the bulletin about Serb claims that the bombing of the passenger train near Leskovac was down to Nato.

Mr Simpson said he felt certain that the truth would become clear and added that if the Serbs, as they were promising, took journalists to the site then "I think the Serbs will be confident about their side of the story".

Yesterday, Mr Simpson responded to the official's reported accusation of naivety: "I've covered over 30 wars and revolutions. I know how governments coerce journalists, I know the tricks they use. I was in Baghdad and I spent a couple of years in the lobby in Britain. It needs

some one with experience. I'm not doing frontline reporting, I'm doing stuff about how the Serb goverment has approached the war. That takes knowledge and understanding."

He added: "I'm amused by the idea that I'm too simpleminded to understand these things and I'm bamboozled by the Serb government and its tricks. Impartiality of telling what's happening in front of you is bred into me. I've been in the BBC for 34 years now, I know how to have control over what I say or write."

Last week, the Serbian government ejected a member of the crew travelling with Mr

Simpson, a fact which the reporter believes vindicates the BBC's stance. Most seriously, he said, the government briefing runs contrary to the tradition of impartial balanced journalism. "It annoys me that a British government is so willing and enthusiastic about losing the principles of calm and objectivity."

Mr Simpson rejected the suggestion that he has been partisan or simplistic. "I've seen far too many of the crimes that this government has committed in Yugoslavia – I was in Sarajevo. I know what these things are, but I absolutely refuse point blank to put on all that easy chauvinist stuff talking about Nazis, fascists and evil empires. Facts speak for themselves."

On-the-record comments from Downing Street yesterday proffered sympathy with the difficulties that journalists were experiencing reporting from Belgrade and emphasised the importance of a "health warning" on reports explaining that their content was being monitored by Serbs.

Mr Simpson said, however, that he had experienced little interference other than interruption to his telephone calls "just to remind me that there's somebody there listening".

His job would be easier, he said, if the British government stopped interfering.

kind, for that matter. However, blanket secrecy is hateful to media agencies. In some conflicts, such as the Falklands, where the media are dependent on the military for transport to the zone of conflict, almost complete control is possible over news coverage. In other conflicts nearer home, such as Kosovo, journalists can report independently from within the enemy's stronghold.

In this case, of course, as John Simpson of the BBC discovered (see figure 1.8), they may also then be accused of being biased or, worse still, of being duped by the enemy.

▾ ▾ ▾ ▾ ▾ ▾ ▾

activities

1. Some analysts believe concentration of ownership into huge multinationals can no longer be regulated because cunning lawyers always get around the clauses. For example, companies can easily be restructured to give the appearance of independence. Instead, some countries are now moving to regulate for diversity in the *content* of the media, forcing owners to give access to a range of points of view.

Draw up a set of regulations for the media to force greater diversity of content, rather than ownership. Specify how this diversity is to be achieved. Possible means could include:
► equal time regulations for various groups
► right of reply regulations
► access for independent productions/writers.

2. In Sweden, the government gives subsidies to smaller newspapers representing a variety of viewpoints. This allows them to stay in business against their more powerful rivals.

Could this be done in the United Kingdom? Who would pay? Are there sources of revenue available other than taxpayers, such as surcharges on commercial advertising? Discuss.

3. *Star Wars: The Phantom Menace* (USA, 1999) saw the largest merchandising blitz in film history. Research a similar example today. List the merchandise available and describe the ways in which it relates to the media product. How does it promote the media product among its target audience? What are your views on this form of product support?

4. In groups, target a particular audience with an assembly of stories put together from an edition of a national newspaper, or from an on-line source such as Reuters news agency. Describe the audience and outline the appeal of the particular articles you have chosen.

Compare your assembly of stories to those of another group using the same sources, but aiming for a different audience.

5. Collect the annual reports of some of the media organisations in your area. These should provide information about the ownership of the company. Profile the concentration of media ownership in your area and outline any company diversification through the ownership of other companies. If other research methods fail, ring the media organisations themselves.

6. Compare the day's news in two newspapers owned by the same media organisation. Can you find similar stories with similar 'angles'? Or are there any distinct differences?

major assignment

Written assignment

1. Select one of the following tasks and prepare a 600-word response.

Identify the principal owner/s for one of the national media (television, for example). Prepare a personal profile on one of them. To what extent does the medium reflect the interests of the owner?

Research estimates of the percentage of market share that each has accumulated. Research details of other investments each owner has acquired. Conclude with your view on the concentration of ownership in the media. Share your findings with your class.

2. Investigate one of the media industries (e.g. the film industry). Report on the various production agencies (e.g. studio or independent) and the stages of production (e.g. scripting, shooting, editing, etc.). Conclude with an evaluation of the impact that industry practices have on the final product's shape.

3. Select a media organisation and report on the range and type of texts the organisation produces. Explain what effect government regulation has had upon the organisation. Conclude with your view of the implications of your findings.

4. Investigate the institutional context of a media outlet of your choice (e.g. a television or radio station). Outline its corporate structure and ownership and its relationship with other media outlets (e.g. via networking). Conclude with an evaluation of the independence or otherwise of this particular media outlet.

Production assignment

1. In groups, present a live studio news broadcast. You may reuse the text of stories recorded off-air or else refer to television news (p. 250). Allocate production roles to each member of the group. Include a range of stories in the bulletin, such as

an international story, a national story, a local story and a human interest story. Prepare and present the broadcast within a set time span (e.g. two hours of class time).

2. Present a 60-second station promo, showing the characteristics of a particular institutional framework. For example, produce a promo for a government broadcaster with national responsibilities, a commercial organisation with a mass audience or a small independent producer. Explain how your finished promo reflects its context or is typical of a media text from that institution.

Oral assignment

1. Report on the efforts of a media organisation to enter one of the new technologies. Examples could include newspaper ventures into Internet delivery or the investment of a traditional media organisation in pay television. Give your opinion of the effectiveness or desirability of the outcome.

2. Should a media organisation be owned by foreign nationals? Imagine you are presenting a television talk show. Gather class members to represent viewpoints and to debate the arguments for and against.

Audiences

Early studies of the mass media tended to focus on the nature of the items that were generated for publication or broadcast, i.e. the media *products*. Products were seen to be the key to understanding the impact of these new forms of mass communication. As the conveyors of meaning, or values, this was where the main efforts of research were concentrated. If they could be studied closely, broken down and analysed, then the ways in which the media affected populations could be charted, it was felt (see also the section on effects, p. 30). It is still the case that they remain very much at the heart of any serious analysis of media impact on society.

More recently, it has been suggested that the product alone could not be taken as the sole determinant of some magically fixed meaning. Nor would that meaning itself remain constant no matter who watched or read a particular media product, or what the conditions of consumption. Different social, racial, age and gender groups react differently to the same products. The Queen's speech, at Christmas, deeply respected by many in the land as it is, was nevertheless not universally revered. Programmes that may provoke the younger generation into paroxysms of laughter often have exactly the opposite impact on older generations.

STUDYING THE AUDIENCE

Analysts of the media realised that some account needed to be taken of the *consumers* of media products. Audiences would have to be examined as a significant factor in the equation of how meanings were communicated.

Ethnographic studies of how audiences receive media products placed primary emphasis on the consumers. The most radical perspective in this field was that *only* among audiences are meanings generated. Most researchers felt that this was overstepping the mark, however.

▼ ▼ ▼

While a radical 'postmodern' view would dictate that all meaning is locally produced, independent of text or grand theory, popular culture research usually recognizes some relation to the media text. It steers a middle course between text-based and text-

independent interpretations of how media use is meaningful. In fact, much popular culture research is still genre-based, and as a result meaning production is seen as being held together or incited by texts that share a certain set of literary rules of form and content, rather than by how they are used.

Joke Hermes
Reading Women's Magazines

▼ ▼ ▼

CONTROLLING CONSUMPTION

Early studies of audience responses were often driven by fears of passive and non-discriminating reception of media products. The term 'zombie' was widely used (still is, for that matter) to denote a mindless acceptance by viewers and readers of everything fed to them. Watching screen violence, the argument goes, leads people to copy it.

The Jamie Bulger case – when a very young boy was stoned to death by two other boys supposed to have been 'infected' by watching *Child's Play 3* (USA, 1991) and other 'video nasties' – and films such as *Natural Born Killers* (USA, 1994) are widely cited as examples of how screen violence can induce copycat actions among viewers. This feeling persists, despite lack of clear evidence to support it. Many argue the opposite: that no link can be proven; some research seems to endorse this view, most recently in a Home Office-funded study conducted by Dr Kevin Browne in 1997 (see p. 32).

Far from being turned into 'zombies', it has grown increasingly clear that audiences are in fact capable of a high degree of self-determination in the nature of the responses that they made to products offered to them.

Equally, even responses within particular groups may vary according to how, when and with whom the consumption takes place. In one recent sitcom, *The Royle Family*, a working-class family watched *The Antiques Roadshow* not to drool over the value of items presented for their scrutiny, but to *make bets* with each other about their worth. What had been conceived and made as a programme of a (relatively) high cultural order had thus been turned into a kind of interactive

Figure 1.9
Powerful images of desirable life-styles bombard us daily. Adverts constantly try to sell us a range of consumer products. A variety of other programmes also promote notions of glamorous and exciting lives.

game show, *by the people viewing it*. The programme-makers had their intentions in making their product, but the recipients in this instance turned it into quite another kind of programme.

At the same time, it would not be impossible to conceive of individual members of the same family watching the same programme with a more 'reverential', or at least attentive, attitude, when inclined to do so.

ACTIVE AUDIENCES

Attention has turned increasingly to the study of audiences themselves as a key component in the phenomenon of the mass media. Noam Chomsky, the American professor of linguistics who has studied many facets of media manipulation, contends that the real product in the media enterprises of today is in fact the *audience itself*. What has been left out of the equation to date, he suggests, is any recognition that mass media outlets are above all *businesses*. As such, they are engaged in delivering particular audiences to the real drivers of all media activities – the *advertisers*. The general perception is that media corporations use advertising revenue to make programmes to

reach particular audiences. Professor Chomsky proposes an alternative view: that particular programmes are made *so that* particular audiences can be delivered to the advertisers. This perspective calls for a radical rethink of the purposes and especially the nature of the major media corporations of our times.

In the United Kingdom, television has evolved quite differently. The traditions of public service broadcasting initiated by the BBC have established controls of quality in programming that has been required also of commercial broadcasters (see p. 247). However, this has only been applied to *terrestrial* channels; satellite and cable are quite free of these demands and the explosion of growth that is taking place within these spheres looks set to leave us with a system much more like that of the United States in the very near future.

WAYS IN WHICH AUDIENCES CAN 'READ' TEXTS

Everyone has her/his own view of what a media text means. It is also possible to take a number of different viewpoints or 'readings' of a text at the same time. Stuart Hall has suggested at least three main perspectives.

PREFERRED OR DOMINANT READINGS are the readings that are closest to those intended by the producers of the text. If your life experiences and ideas are the same as those in the text, there will be nothing with which to clash. For example, if you were a police officer watching a crime drama, you would probably find it easier to make a preferred reading. In reality, however, a complete and exact preferred reading is impossible.

NEGOTIATED READINGS are made when mental negotiations are needed to overcome some disagreement with the text. For example, a woman watching a film with a male hero has to put herself in his place. This takes a degree of mental negotiation. Someone with a recent speeding ticket may enjoy a crime drama, but still have minor resentments about police officers. Everyone has to mentally negotiate a reading to some extent.

OPPOSITIONAL OR RESISTANT READINGS are made when a person finds their own life experiences are at odds with the views in the text. Crime dramas, for example, are often read oppositionally in prisons. For the inmates, the 'baddies' may in

fact be seen as the 'goodies'. Famously, the Australian soap opera *Prisoner Cell Block H* attracted a cult following for its ham acting and wobbly sets. It certainly was not the intention of its makers that it be revered for its poor production values!

POSITIONING AUDIENCES AND POINT OF VIEW

'Sensitive New Age guys' may want to see men express more emotion on the television screen. They will be waiting a long time according to a study of television fiction. Female characters tend to be shown in tighter close-up than men. Since the close-up allows viewers to see characters expressing emotion, the audience will find it harder to identify with the emotions of male characters.

Texts position audiences to make certain 'readings'. While some audience subgroups can make alternative interpretations, many texts make this difficult in all sorts of subtle ways.

In Disney's film *The Lion King* (USA, 1994), the treacherous hyenas spoke in hip African-American accents. Whoopi Goldberg was one of the voices. There were protests from minority groups, who felt that children watching the film may

*Figure 1.10
An American watching a British soap would understand the programme rather differently from a UK citizen. The American would probably make more of a negotiated reading, entering into more of a fantasy land.*

subsequently be positioned to see African Americans as streetwise, threatening and deceitful.

Whether you like characters or dislike them can also be a way of positioning the audience. Characters with major roles are also more likely to carry the audience along with the beliefs of the text. In traditional Western films, it can be very difficult to make a pro–Native American reading. 'Red Indians', as they were then referred to, appeared as minor characters and extras at best, and bloodthirsty or amoral villains most typically. These films position us to accept the racist credo that 'the only good Indian is a dead Indian'.

MODE OF ADDRESS

No one can be conversational with ten million people. People in the media industries therefore have a problem. Radio announcers have to sound intimate, television newsreaders have to look you directly in the eye and comedy writers have to have a sense of humour that 'clicks'. Yet they have no idea, really, to whom they are talking.

Media professionals are told to address their programmes to individuals. Cadet journalists used to be told: 'Tell it like you're telling your wife or husband!'

It is common for industry professionals to invent fictitious individuals. In the 1970s, radio stations aiming at an audience of housewives spoke to an imaginary 'Marge' or 'Mavis'. Often such characters were demeaning stereotypes that amounted to contempt for the audience. The play *City Sugar* by Stephen Poliakoff charts this attitude very well.

SPEAKING TO YOUR AUDIENCE The mode of address is in fact quite a complex and subtle construction. At one level, it concerns the language the media organisation adopts to communicate with its audience. In the early days of broadcasting, when the BBC was the only source of radio, and with only one channel at that, the announcers (as they were then called) spoke in plummy upper-class voices. This was known as 'RP' ('received pronunciation') – the Queen's English, today. With the arrival of other stations (first, the 'pirates' and, later, subdivisions within the BBC), the first steps towards audience targeting began. With each new station, there is always a further subdivision of audiences – either regionally or between musical genres, or within particular subcultures. It is possible to distinguish particular styles of language for each: the idiom and even the slang of the target group will be adopted. This is most obvious amongst youth-orientated programmes, but is equally the case with *any* broadcast material, and especially so with radio.

Beyond the actual words used, there is also a question of register: the *manner*, or *tone*, in which they are spoken. High-culture stations, such as the BBC's Radios 3 and 4, use a very considered and drawn-out form of speech; popular stations use a much more abrupt and energetic manner of speaking. In each case, appropriate styles are being adopted which are felt to be most likely to succeed in attracting the desired target audiences. This can be readily identified in newspapers, too – most starkly, perhaps, in the tabloids, where a more direct, often 'matey' address is used. The reader is spoken to as if by one of their chums, with the style of speech, and moreover logic, that might be used when setting the world to rights over a pint in a pub.

REGIONAL CHIC

A final, very interesting feature of broadcasting in recent years has been the increase in usage of regional accents. Within a local radio station, of course, this is only to be expected and may seem entirely natural.

In the early years of regional television, this wasn't the case by any means, however. The Queen's English once dominated the airwaves nearly as much as her Navy did the other sort! For a very long time indeed – even predating broadcasting – accents were felt to be evidence of a lack of education, at best, or, worse, of good breeding. Today, it appears that the pendulum has swung a long way. One survey has established that people now see an accent as an indicator of greater trustworthiness.

Even more curiously, the more pronounced the accent, the greater the faith placed in it: hence the proliferation of Geordie and Scottish accents among the ever-expanding phenomenon of the telephone call centres used by banks and other businesses.

This is perhaps a response to the creeping blandness of the standard, universal culture that the media themselves are creating.

Targeted audiences

There is a story that tells of how media magnate Rupert Murdoch once tried to persuade the up-market New York department store Bloomingdale's to advertise in his down-market newspaper, the *New York Post*. He received a very cool response. Looking down his nose, the manager said, 'Mr Murdoch, your readers are our shoplifters!'

SELLING AUDIENCES AS PRODUCTS

Media products are not sold direct to their consumers. Instead, the consumers are sold to other producers. For example, television advertisers buy the audience for a prime-time television programme for thirty seconds so they can show their advertisement. The cost of each thirty-second time slot depends on how high the show's ratings are.

ADVERTISING

Even newspapers and magazines sell their audiences to advertisers. The cover price barely pays for newsprint. The real money is made selling advertising space. It is worth stating again that media organisations are first and foremost *businesses*; and their chief customers are *advertisers*, not their audiences. The crucial role played by advertising in the very foundation of our modern newspaper industries has been well charted (cf. Curran & Seaton, *Power without Responsibility*). Without it, neither the quantity nor the quality of what is available today would be possible. Revenues from sales alone would scarcely cover the costs of printing: advertising is where the bulk of earnings are to be made.

Media organisations aim to maximise audiences. They also aim for particular types of audiences. Some magazines aim only at wealthy professionals and business people. Some television programmes, such as *Seinfeld*, are directly marketed to people who are aged between twenty-five and thirty-nine, with plenty of disposable income.

AUDIENCE MEASUREMENT

Audiences are measured in various ways, some more reliable than others. Considerable development has occurred in this field over the past twenty years; various methods of analysing audience figures *and constituency* are now in constant use. Newspapers have fairly reliable readership figures based on the number of copies sold — and even of copies *read* (see National Readership Survey, p. 405). Free-to-air broadcast media, on the other hand, have no concrete way of knowing whether their programme was being watched.

For them, a system of ratings surveys is used. Audience numbers are calculated from a random sampling of the population, drawn from monitoring devices installed on volunteers' television sets and from questionnaires. The most common agency for this is BARB (British Audience Research Bureau.)

The case has already been put that the media is in the business of selling audiences to advertisers. (French film director Jean-Luc Godard also said: 'Television doesn't make programmes – it makes viewers.') The texts are just the 'bait' to attract the unsuspecting population. Whether through television ratings, for example, or newspaper readership surveys, the media accumulate vast amounts of data about who consumes their products. Profiles of the audiences include their income, their education levels, lifestyle, marital status and age. They even know how many of their households have cats, rather than dogs.

The audience profile is used to convince advertisers they will be getting the right sort of audience. Advertisers will pay a lot of money for a high-income audience, even if it is only small. Low-income audiences are only worthwhile if they are purchased in bulk quantities.

In the 1970s and early 1980s, the US television network CBS had a larger audience than its rivals. However, they were mostly older people, low-income people and country people. Advertisers were not interested and began switching their accounts. CBS had to make changes to its programming 'bait'. It abandoned many of its highest rating programmes in favour of shows aimed at high-income young professionals.

Vulnerable or expert audiences?

Modern audience research started with Nazi propaganda in wartime Germany. It continued in the United States into the 1950s and 1960s during the anti-communist era of the Cold War. There were various media panics at the time, with fears of Russian 'brainwashing' and mass indoctrination. The question researchers asked seemed refreshingly simple: what effect does the media have on people? Asked another way: how vulnerable is the audience?

The answers were not clear. Consequently, from the 1980s onwards, researchers have turned the question around. The question became: what does the audience do with media texts? The audience was now seen as active and diverse. Audience 'pleasure' in a text became the focus of study. The pendulum had swung and the question had become: how *expert* is the audience?

However, the answers seemed to be just as hard to pin down. Some media academics are now calling for the capabilities of both sides of media research to combine in renewed investigation.

THE EFFECTS TRADITION

Effects studies have tried to find out whether the media changes people's behaviour. The question they have often asked has been: 'What does consuming the media *do* to people?' Another question could be: 'Does watching violent films make people more aggressive?'

Effects studies often use social science methods and express the findings in numbers. For example, they could say, 'Ten per cent of the test group showed changed behaviour.'

Studies of film or television violence and political influence have been the main fare of effects research. As a result, the studies have often been funded by governments keen to pass laws of

one sort or another. Effects studies are criticised for regarding the media producer as having all the power and influence.

EFFECTS STUDIES AND THE HYPODERMIC NEEDLE

Early effect studies 'injected' people with a media experience and then waited to see what they would do. A typical study showed violent cartoons to a group of primary school boys and then counted the number of 'violent acts' in the playground afterwards. The number of aggressive acts was then compared with a 'control' group of boys who did not see the cartoons. The intention was to investigate potential links between watching screen violence, and then copying it in actual behaviour in some form.

PROBLEMS The first point that must be made is that the behaviour observed was not 'real', in the sense that it was children *at play* who were studied. What they may do as pretence in the playground is not the same as what they may do for real elsewhere.

Moreover, changes in attitude are not easily measured, because there has to be an external behaviour change to observe. Even if there were an external behaviour change, people do not live in laboratories. Something else could have

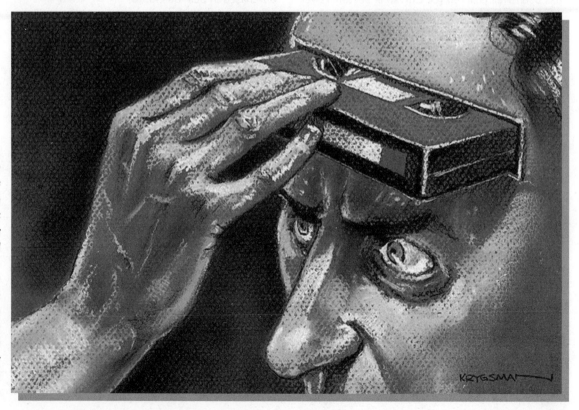

Figure 1.11
Studies in the media effects tradition have tried to show that the media alter our thinking and our behaviour. The results are not clear because it is difficult to prove that the media are the only factor altering human behaviour.

intervened to cause the change. For example, family factors or problems at school could be a more significant cause than the media. In any case, it is quite apparent that film or television violence has not generated external homicidal tendencies in most viewers. It is not actually proven that it has clearly generated these tendencies in *any*!

That does not of course mean it has not changed the way we *think*. Effects studies have not been able to prove or disprove an effect because what people think and what they say or do may be different things (see p. 31 – research study by Dr Kevin Browne).

CULTIVATION STUDIES

The dissatisfaction with simple effects studies led to the development of a more advanced version. Changes in thinking patterns and behaviour are long term. Cultivation studies aim to pinpoint the variable of media consumption in among the complexities of everything else people do.

Typical studies would compare the attitudes of heavy television viewers with the attitudes of infrequent viewers. In one study in the mid-1970s, scores of researchers descended on a snowbound Canadian town. Television was finally coming to the region. The researchers studied life in the town before television and then studied it again after. Comparison revealed significant differences in a range of areas.

PROBLEMS Cultivation studies have found effects that appear to show the media are powerful influences on society. However, they are criticised for their failure to explain how these effects work or ways in which audiences may be actively interpreting media.

RECEPTION STUDIES

Reception studies have tried to find out what sense people make of the media. Researchers have often asked questions such as: 'What do people *do* with the media?' Another question could be: 'How do people *use* the media for their own purposes?'

The tendency in this kind of study is to describe what the researcher observes. The findings are not usually presented as percentages, but are usually descriptive paragraphs. Often they include long quotes from people who have been interviewed.

Reception studies have been strongest in their investigations of the entertainment genres of television. Famous studies have included investigations of audience interpretations of soap operas and cartoons. Many of the most-well known reception studies have been funded by the commercial television networks.

PROBLEMS The main criticism of reception studies has been for regarding the audience as 'all-powerful', with the media influence totally under audience control. They have tended to play down the power of the media as disseminators of meanings and values.

USES AND GRATIFICATIONS

Following the disappointments of the effects studies, some researchers in the 1960s and 1970s went in a totally different direction. They argued that audiences used the media to satisfy certain basic psychological needs.

These included the need for information, a personal identity, social interaction and entertainment. For example, someone talking to their friends about a television show is using the media to make conversation. This is fulfilling a need for social interaction.

Typical studies have looked at how people choose media content according to particular moods or have studied how heavy news viewers like to appear well informed in front of friends. They have also investigated how fans gain certain satisfactions from their favourite shows.

PROBLEMS The viewer is reduced to a set of needs and the meanings in the text become just gratification. A human being is made of much more than, for example, a need for food and a need for social interaction.

The uses and gratifications theorists have also been blamed for ignoring the complexities of the media's influence and giving all power to the audience. They have not explained how needs can be manipulated by advertising agencies. People are shaped by their society, which is in turn shaped by the media and its advertising. The research has not adequately explained how two people with the same need may interpret a programme differently. As well, needs and desires do not explain everything in life.

ETHNOGRAPHIC AUDIENCE RESEARCH

Since the 1980s, reception research has investigated the ways in which audiences make meanings from media texts. Like anthropologists studying traditional tribes or isolated ethnic groups, media researchers observed and interviewed media fans.

Often a researcher will stay with a family and take notes on their media habits. The researcher may also interview family members and ask why they watch certain programmes and what they like about them. A typical study may look at the soap opera audience of teenage girls and the special meanings they receive from the programme.

PROBLEMS Ethnographic studies have provided new information about audiences and their relationships with texts. Nevertheless, they have mainly focused on the entertainment genres such as television soap operas and quiz shows. They have not looked at the political influence of the news, for example.

The descriptive style of ethnographic research can allow the researcher to write a very personal and biased viewpoint. In addition to this, the very presence of the researcher in the living room observing viewers must almost inevitably have an impact on their behaviour.

The Violence Debate

One of the most controversial topics for a long time has been whether the behaviour of audiences is directly affected by what they see on their screens. Strong views are expressed on both sides. Gruesome examples from real life are often used to claim a link between 'media violence' and the awful events that they are said to provoke. The killing of Jamie Bulger (see p. 181) is a particularly vivid example.

In a classic study in the early 1960s, US psychologist Albert Bandura conducted a series of tests that seemed to establish a link between viewing screen violence and imitating it in real life. The tests exposed children to footage of someone treating a large plastic Bobo doll very aggressively. Up to 88 per cent of participant children subsequently imitated this behaviour with a similar doll in the laboratory.

This experiment lent a lot of weight, at the time, to the argument that screen violence is infectious. However, later theorists pointed out that there is a very large difference between what people will do in the laboratory with a doll and what they will do in real life with real people!

Guy Cumberbatch, Senior Lecturer in Applied Psychology at Aston University, cites many investigations into so-called links between screen and real-life violence. Among these were Michael Ryan, at the Hungerford massacre, Ronnie Zamora in Miami and a whole series of other violent incidents examined by Kate Adie and the BBC's

Panorama team in 1988. In no single case was there any hard evidence to substantiate the links claimed at the time. This is a field, he says, where there is a great deal of speculation and assertion – but little or no proof.

▼ ▼ ▼

… there has been a long history of moral panics about the harmful effects of popular culture, such as comics and popular theatre in the nineteenth century, followed by the cinema, video and computer games. These panics are largely fuelled by the popular press and claim that things are getting worse.

In this field, it is all too easy to scaremonger … It is ironic that the media seem largely to blame for the particularly British moral panic about our media.

Guy Cumberbatch

▼ ▼ ▼

Indeed, more recent research has tended to suggest the opposite. In a Home Office-sponsored study conducted by Dr Kevin Browne, in 1998, only a very tentative impact could be detected on young offenders with a predisposition towards violence. There was no evidence of any other groups studied being affected – and even for those who did show some signs of being influenced, the impact was very slight.

More important still, it was experience of violence at home that seemed to be the key factor in generating a preference for violent films. Blaming the media may be easier, but it seems to miss the real explanations for violence in society.

Nevertheless, it remains the case that very many people are highly concerned about the impact of what is screened on how people behave in society.

In his novel *Popcorn*, Ben Elton wittily uses the scenario of a Tarantino-like film director being taken hostage by a psychotic pair of fans who model themselves on two of his own screen 'heroes'. At the end, the audience is offered the opportunity to save the director's life – but only by turning off their live coverage of the stake-out.

In one way or another, the media undoubtedly play a part in the recording of the violence present in our society.

▼ ▼ ▼ ▼ ▼ ▼ ▼

activities

1. Gender can be one factor contributing to the negotiated understanding a person may get from a media text. Explore this with the cooperation of your classmates. With the class, view a film with a strong message about gender, such as *The Full Monty* (UK, 1997) or *Thelma & Louise* (USA, 1991).

Survey class members on their 'readings' of the film based on gender. Discuss their emotional reactions to events. Write a conclusion about the multiple readings it is possible to make from a media text. For example, for *Thelma & Louise*, survey questions could include:

► How did female members of the class feel about the husbands? How did male members react to these characters?

► Which parts of the film did males/females like the best and the least?

► With whom did the males/females identify (see identification, p. 38)?

2. Attempt to make a deliberate 'oppositional' reading of a media text. An oppositional reading is one that is opposed to the view the producers intended. Follow the guidelines set out below.

► Find a media text the point of view of which you strongly disagree. This could be a film from an earlier era that today seems sexist or racist. It could be an article in a magazine for 'over-forties' that criticises your favourite music. It could be a television documentary promoting a negative view of young people and their subcultures.

► Watch, read or listen to the media text. Note your reactions at different places in the text.

► Deliberately try to side with the group or point of view the producer is criticising.

► In 200–300 words, explain how you made the oppositional reading and refer to your reaction to specific parts of the media text.

3. Listen to two or three radio stations and try to determine the mode of address. Who are the fictitious people to which each station is speaking? Name them appropriately and write up brief profiles of these people. Include some extracts from the DJ's patter as evidence.

4. Conduct a simple effects study. You will need the cooperation of your classmates and a tape of a very popular and insistent television programme. Create two groups of class members: a 'control' group and the 'test group'. Have members of the control group quietly count the number of times the word 'of' occurs on p. 35 of this text. Have the test group do the same, only this time, play the tape of their favourite television programme rather loudly at the same time! Collate the results and report on your conclusions.

major assignment

Production assignment

1. Conduct a cultivation study investigating the effects of watching television. Find a small group of people who do not watch television at all (or only very little). This may be difficult at first, since these people are estimated to be only 2 per cent of the population. If you cannot find anyone, use a sample of light television viewers. Compare this sample to a control group of people who are heavy television viewers.

Begin with a description of the project and of the two groups under study. Follow this by devising a questionnaire to give to both groups. Include a short statement saying the results may be imperfect since it has (probably) been impossible to find a total non-television viewer and that there may be other reasons for differences. Interview the two groups and record your answers. Note and collate any differences. Report on your findings and conclude with an evaluation of the results.

Comparison indicators for non-viewers/light viewers and heavy viewers could be drawn from questions based on the following general areas (note that these are not actual questions, only suggested areas in which to develop your own questions):

▶ views on law and order issues, gun ownership, capital punishment etc.

▶ feelings about safety of streets in urban areas, danger posed by unknown people

▶ interest in politics

▶ voting intentions (if they do not mind)

▶ importance of family life and the home

▶ leisure activities, type and time spent

▶ views on fashion and culture, membership of fashionable subgroups, views on local versus US culture, etc.

2. Conduct an ethnographic study investigating the relationship an audience has with a particular media text.

Examples could include: action films and the audience of adolescent males, young people and the new media, television comedy and teenage girls, how a younger family member uses television, etc.

Begin by describing the context or environment of the study (e.g. school in large regional centre) and the people to be studied (e.g. sixteen-year-old girls from farming communities). Follow this with a

short statement saying the findings apply only to this group and no other (generalisations cannot be made). Then describe yourself as interviewer and mention any impact you may have had. Conduct the interviews. While interviewing, record your observations about the relationships that your interview subjects have with the media text. Report on your findings and conclude with an evaluation of the results.

Interview questions could be made up from the following general areas (note: these are not actual questions, only suggested areas in which to develop questions):

▶ gender differences in liked or disliked characters, focus on physical or personality features, who is 'fancied', etc.

▶ how 'realistic' the media text is seen to be

▶ emotional reactions to the text (e.g. fright in horror films, concern in soap operas, etc.)

▶ classification of audience (e.g. fan, regular, casual, etc.)

▶ other leisure activities the interview subjects pursue

▶ viewing/reading practices (e.g. other activities engaged in while watching television, reading magazines, etc.)

Written assignment

Present a 500-word response to one of the following topics.

1. Imagine you are a researcher for a television documentary about the impact of the media on society. Prepare preliminary information in essay form on the effects of the media. Give an account of some of the research findings so far. Conclude with your own evaluation.

2. Research the targeting of audiences by particular media organisations. Recount your findings and evaluate the success of the strategies.

Representation

In the summer of 1999, a series of striking advertisements appeared on billboards around the United Kingdom. With plain white backgrounds, they featured people with a variety of disabilities accompanied by a 'carer'. Beside them was a simple statement in large, bold black type. This text appeared to offer observations that we would expect to apply to the people featured. In one, a man is shown in a wheelchair, with a woman by his side: 'Sex can be a bit of a problem' reads the caption. Automatically, we decode this message as a comment on the difficulties confronting this man, in this most private and fundamental area of human intercourse. However, a further piece of text, in much smaller type, on the other side of the figures, completely reverses our perceptions of what is being said: 'Sarah's a screamer', in this case. The man does have a problem, only not with the act of sex itself!

This particular advertisement works in several ways to subvert our expectations. It leads us into thinking we know what is going on, then artfully pulls the rug out from under us. So, our preconceptions are challenged. At the same time, it also uses sex – a mainstay of all advertising today, it often seems – both to attract our attention and to engage our sympathies. When the twist is revealed, we are surprised – and invited to reconsider our understanding of the original image. Moreover, the warmth and wit of the revelation offers us one last delight: a non-exploitative use of sexuality. It is presented as a universal and positive aspect of human life – just as people with disabilities are.

The ability of the media to manipulate our perceptions is amply demonstrated in this example. On this occasion, the process is a positive one: it is used to challenge our preconceptions and to induce a rethink about a stereotype (see below). The same cannot be said about the majority of media images.

After nearly forty years of feminism, more than 30 per cent of advertising still portrays women as slim blonde 'bimbos' under the age of thirty. A different standard applies to men. At least half the men were allowed to be over thirty, according to a survey by the Broadcasting Standards Council.

Male actors are nearly always dark-haired, in contrast to the typical blonde female. In advertising, only 11 per cent are slim and muscular 'himbos', the remainder being a variety of body weights. While a male ideal definitely exists, men are allowed a greater range of body types.

Women are almost never shown in the driving seat when men and women travel together, says the Broadcasting Standards Council. Whatever the reality of what is taking place in the actual world, media representations continue to follow certain well-established patterns.

It is not only gender analysts who are protesting over their characterisation in the media. Native American Indian Gertrude Minnie-Ha-Ha Custalow had this to say about the Disney film *Pocahontas* (USA, 1995): 'They have her as this beautiful woman when, in fact, Pocahontas was about ten years old when the English arrived. To look at the film you would have thought Pocahontas invented the push-up bra!'

Defining representation

The media do not present reality; they 're-present' it. When things happen, out there in the world, these events are said to 'present' themselves. It is relatively rare for any form of media to capture this first presentation (and, even when they do, they are still mediated to us in various ways: see pp. 6–7). The media are only representing things *once they have occurred*.

This is the theory, at least. The actual practices of many media outlets mean that often it seems to be they *who are generating* the reality on which they are reporting. Many tabloid stories, in particular, have homed in on personal miseries that they themselves have been instrumental in bringing about.

One of the regularly recurring negative images we are exposed to is that of the football hooligan. This social phenomenon has been with us for quite a long time now. Often, it seems to flare up particularly badly during European encounters. It would be interesting to know whether the Romans ever had any problems with unruly crowds after their chariot races – or after the

**Figures
1.12 and 1.13**
*These two film
stills illustrate
changing attitudes
towards the make-
up of the family.
In the older
picture (top),*
**Blow Your Own
Trumpet** *(1958),
the father is a
rather more
formal figure:
although smiling,
he maintains a
distance from the
rest of the family,
and it is clear
they all respect
him, including the
wife. In the more
recent photograph
(bottom),*
**Kramer vs
Kramer** *(1979),
the family is a
much more
intimate group,
physically and
emotionally close;
the sense
of hierarchy
endures, however.*

lion-feeding sessions that early Christians used to suffer. Most media, however, have little concern for what has happened in the past.

In the case of England's public shaming during the Euro 2000 competition, something rather more complex appears to have happened. Following the activities of a tiny number of 'fans' prior to the match with Germany, in the town of Charleroi, numerous television and newspaper outlets in the United Kingdom were very quick to cry 'foul!' Pictures of hooligans and riot police, water cannons and so on were used to cover the sensational story of outbreaks of ugly violence in public places. This is by now a very sad, and very familiar, story. According to one commentator, however, it is just a little too familiar: so much so, in fact, that the media seem to have been predetermined to find it.

▼ ▼ ▼

It was a small fight, some chairs were overturned and a big water pistol was used. Charlie Whelan says television reporting of the football 'riots' in Brussels and Charleroi was staggeringly inaccurate.

Media Guardian, 26 June 2000

▼ ▼ ▼

At least fifty television cameras were counted in the main square of the town, all conveniently poised to capture highly usable images of the 'riots' when they started. Local police had already given out the tip that they intended to make some arrests. When a small handful of inebriated hotheads duly obliged, with a small scuffle involving some chair throwing and chanting, the cannon was turned on and the story was finally written.

Only the broadcasters on BBC Radio 5 Live seem to have reported on the many thousands of fans who had been peacefully enjoying themselves for hours leading up to this incident. That kind of pleasantness, of course, does not make for exciting news.

In a similar vein, faked documentaries and made-up identities/predicaments on chat shows have added to this notion of 'constructed reality'. Members of the public and programme-makers alike, it seems, have become very adept at manipulating the media for their own purposes.

Moreover, it could be argued that, for many people, the 'world' that they perceive through the media is *more real* to them – and certainly a lot

more exciting – than the one in which they actually live. Hollywood, for instance, churns out much more action/romance/fear/danger/sex … than most of us could ever hope to experience first-hand. Even British soap operas offer more incident and intrigue, night after night, than we encounter in our own daily round (or, ironically, than we would probably find comfortable if we *did* have to live through them ourselves).

Therefore, in both *reportage* (coverage of actual events) and *drama* (self-confessed fiction), there are problems centring on our perceptions of what the media reveal to us. There are strong grounds for claiming that the media in fact invent a world – or, worse, worlds! – all of their own, and that these have little to do with the lives that their consumers in fact lead.

The best claim that can be made is that they only present a *selection* of reality. Edited highlights, we might say. This presentation is altered each time a selection is made. In the case of television, the scriptwriter, camera operator, the editor and the producer all make selections and changes. Newspaper stories go through a similar process of selection involving the journalist, the sub-editor and the editor.

Media products are not the same as lived experience, but only consist of a selection of experiences. These manufactured versions of reality are based on the values of the producers and, in turn, the values of the larger society and culture.

A media representation is a depiction, a likeness or a constructed image of something in real life. A representation can be of individual people (e.g. the US president in *Independence Day*, USA, 1996), of social groups (e.g. age groups, gender, racial groups), ideas (e.g. law and order, unemployment), or of events (e.g. a royal wedding or the assassination of US President John F. Kennedy, or JFK, as he was known).

A representation can be a single image, a sequence of images or a whole programme; written words, spoken words or song lyrics.

How representations work

Representations invite audiences to understand them and agree with them in certain preferred ways. Different interpretations are possible to some extent, depending on the audience.

Figure 1.14
Stereotypes allow for quick recognition and humour. In these cartoon depictions of familiar figures, traditional elements have been combined with new ones, to update the images.

■ **A representation is composed of repeated elements**

The more we see these elements repeated, the more the representation will appear natural or 'normal'.

■ **We are invited to either identify with or recognise the representation**

Producers of the media representations may have a view of the world that is similar to our own. If their representation fits in with our view of who we are, we may choose to *identify* with it. This happens, for example, when a film invites us to imagine ourselves in the role of an appealing character. On the other hand, the producers may see a person, idea or event as somehow foreign or different to them. We will be invited to *recognise* the representation from our own experience. A programme might invite us to *identify* with the lawyer hero, for example, but will invite us to only *recognise* the lawbreaking young thugs.

■ **The media make categories of people, events or ideas**

Categories include labels such as 'the unemployed', 'the aged' or 'businessman'. Representations are generalisations about categories and why events, ideas or people belong in them. These categories then become part of our thinking processes.

■ **Representations contain a point of view**

The meaning in a representation is selected and constructed, containing value judgements already in-built. All representations contain the point of view of the people who made them.

■ **Representations have a mode of address**

Hidden behind the apparent naturalness of the representation will be some assumptions about who *you* are. For example, a news item about skinheads will probably address you assuming you are a middle-aged businessman, not a skinhead yourself!

Stereotypes

A *stereotype* is a 'typical' or mass-produced image, repeated so many times it seems to have established a pattern. It is a simplified and highly judgmental type of representation.

One well-known female stereotype is that of the dumb blonde. On the other hand, there is the male stereotype of the foolish sitcom father. Throughout media's history, there has been a long list of stereotypes – the housewife, the nuclear family, the action hero and so on.

The word *stereotype* comes from the printing trade. Printers would make a *papier-mâché* model and then cast a metal printing plate from it. Next, they would ink the plate and hundreds of identical printings could then be reproduced. Just as the image on the metal typesetting plate is fixed and endlessly repeated, so the stereotype is often applied whatever the circumstances.

Stereotypes are an extreme form of representation. Like representations, they are constructed by a process of selection – but the process is excessive. Certain aspects are focused on and then exaggerated. At the same time, an evaluation is made and the audience is invited to make a judgment. The judgment is often on the basis of prejudice. Repetition establishes stereotypes and over time allows them to appear 'natural'.

In the extreme, stereotypes can become an exaggerated caricature resembling a cartoon. In fact, cartoons and comedies rely on stereotypes because they are instantly recognisable. 'Seen one, seen 'em all' could be the familiar cry for all stereotypes.

Many groups in society have stereotypes associated with them. These contain limited and distorted views. For example, in a study of the image of scientists, Dr Roslynn Haynes came up with six stereotypes that have existed since the 1500s. These are: the evil scientist or alchemist (e.g. Dr Strangelove), the noble scientist (e.g. Einstein-like characters), the stupid scientist, the inhuman researcher, the adventurer and finally the crazed scientist whose projects get out of control (e.g. Frankenstein, Dr Jekyll).

Stereotyping is often evident when there is a power imbalance between members of society. Relations between men and women, for example, could encourage the development of stereotypes on both sides. In the same way, disadvantaged minority groups often have stereotypes associated with them.

Ideology

O'Sullivan tells us how, underpinning much of the output of the media, various powerful vested interests operate to ensure particular representations of the world are manifested. Thus, in the West anyway, communism (before it expired) was always presented as inherently bad. Capitalism, on the other hand – by and large, and despite much evidence to the contrary – was always good. Ideology is an organised system of beliefs and values that inform the basis on which a particular society operates.

However, like all else in the media, it is a *construct*. Although it often appears 'natural', in fact it is created.

Noam Chomsky is most forthright on this when he says: 'the media serve the interests of state and corporate power, which are closely interlinked, framing their reporting and analysis in a manner supportive of established privilege and limiting debate accordingly.'

In support of this statement, he goes on to identify five 'filters' that operate in the area of news reporting, which determine the kinds of material that is presented to us:

► the size, concentrated ownership, owner wealth, and profit orientation of the dominant mass-media firms
► advertising as the primary source of income
► reliance of the media on information provided by government, business and 'experts' funded and approved by these primary sources and agents of power
► 'flak' as a means of disciplining the media
► 'anti-communism' as a national religion and control mechanism.

Of course, this latter has been more identified with the United States in its more extreme forms, but British society has not been entirely free of prejudice against this system of government. Where are our thoughts and attitudes on this matter shaped, but through what we see and read in the media?

If this notion now seems a little out of date, we need only to consider whether the collapse of communism has led to a complete absence of national enemies – or whether others have appeared, fortuitously, to take its place? The Iraqi leader Saddam Hussein's role would bear scrutiny for this purpose. George Orwell, in his famous novel *1984*, was very clear about how vital to social control was the creation – and occasional reshuffling – of an external opposition.

Occasionally, as in Margaret Thatcher's unique description of the striking British miners as 'the enemy within', this device can even be turned on a state's own populace.

Questioning representations

To be more critically aware of representations, the following questions need to be asked:
► Who made it?
► When was it made?
► Where was it made?
► What are its social/political/cultural origins?

▶ What are its purposes?

▶ Who benefits from the representation or whose point of view does it support?

▶ Who does not benefit or whose point of view is not considered?

▶ Who or what is not shown?

▽ ▽ ▽ ▽ ▽ ▽ ▽

activities

1. Images, ideas and representations have a history. Search through old television programmes or old magazine advertisements to find representations that are no longer appropriate in today's cultural and social contexts.

2. Modern representations may look as dated and inappropriate in the future as those from, say, the 1950s look today. Question some modern representations using the eight questions on pp. 39–40.

3. Apply Noam Chomsky's five 'filters' to a selection of news items. Try to examine them for evidence of support for, or opposition to, particular forms of government, religion, business or employing organisations.

4. Analyse some representations across different media and compare the results. Representations could be chosen from the list below.

ANALYSIS OF REPRESENTATIONS

People	e.g. politicians, film or rock stars, sports personalities, historical characters, etc.
Groups	e.g. certain occupations, families, youth groups, political groups, etc.
Places	e.g. tourist destinations, city versus country, local regions, overseas countries, etc.
Ideas	e.g. law and order, the future, political points of view, the environment, etc.

5. Select a theme and explore its representation across several different media or over a period of time. Themes could include age, gender, race or social class.

Look through the magazines in your library and find examples of stereotypes. Discuss the way they express their point of view through various features. For example, a 'five o'clock shadow' (darkly stubbled cheeks) on a cartoon character suggests criminal associations.

major assignment

Production assignment

1. Select from the topics below and create an advertisement in a medium of your choice (e.g. magazine, radio etc.).

▶ Create an advertisement based on a selective, positive representation of a group that 'mainstream culture' has so far failed to represent fairly. A model for this could be the recent development of some positive advertising representations of women in positions of power or with successful careers. Try this for another under-represented group.

▶ Create an advertisement for a magazine of your choice based on a selective negative representation of some group that has always enjoyed safe, positive representation from 'mainstream' culture. For example, doctors have often been represented as wise, concerned, self-sacrificing carers. Business people have also enjoyed positive representation. Teachers, similarly, although there are also common negative representations of them.

Note that your advertisement does not have to be for a product directly related to the representation. For example, a television advertisement for chocolate bars used a rowdy classroom of primary school children sneaking chocolate under the desk while a kindly but incompetent teacher attempted to begin the lesson. In this example, a negative representation of a teacher was used to sell a totally unrelated product.

2. Dress up as a well-known stereotype and take a photograph of yourself. Repeat the process for several other stereotypes until you have a portfolio of five or six images. Explain each stereotype and

indicate its defining features. Point out where you have seen the stereotype before.

Written assignment

Choose one of the following assignments and write a 500-word response.

1. Imagine that you have been hired as a media consultant by a community leader from a particular group, such as a gender-specific group, a professional group or an ethnic group. Research the representation of the group and present a broad picture of how they are presented over a range of media. Critically analyse and evaluate your findings. Suggest action the group might take to improve their representation.

2. Select a politician or media star with an image problem. Propose a solution for them to consider.

Outline the problem as you see it, then suggest ways of changing that representation in the media. Conclude with a projected view of the person's new image.

Oral assignment

Prepare a five-minute oral presentation for the following task. You may like to include television or film excerpts to illustrate your points. as you make them. Research the development and changes apparent in a particular representation over several stages in a historical period. Present your findings to the class as a lecture or seminar presentation. Speculate as to the social and cultural contexts that created the representations. Critically analyse and evaluate the representation at each stage over the time period, discussing the viewpoints and ideologies that they contain.

Genre

In essence, genre is a very simple concept. The word itself derives from the French word meaning 'type', or 'kind'. It could in theory be applied to the study of any form of media product, since they all have identifiable categories. In actual practice, however, it has tended to be associated mostly with analysis of film and television programmes.

In essence, genre is a straightforward means of classifying products according to the elements they have in common – most notably narrative form, setting, characters, subjects and themes.

So central is the concept of genre to the study of the media, the organisational approach adopted in this book has been built upon it. Each medium has its own distinctive strands of programme, or article, or visual style, and close examination of these is the chief means used to analyse key features of their production.

A great deal more will be said on this topic in each section of this book. It is not therefore something that will be dwelt on in detail at this point. At least, not in terms of its impact on the products themselves. However, there are some more general observations that are worth making.

Above all else, the point needs making that genre has always been first and foremost an issue

of institutional and production choice, and not least for the satisfaction and pleasure of audiences. It was not something invented for the convenience of study.

Genres and institutions

There is a powerful incentive towards genre-identification for any organisation seeking to engage in media production, in the very obvious area of attracting an audience. Proven interest in particular kinds of product leads inexorably to further creation of more of the same. In the realm of film, especially, where production costs can be extremely high, clarity of genre can be crucial in establishing audience appeal. A certain level of return may be expected, or at least projected, on the strength of previous successes.

Many other factors play a part in securing this, of course: the quality of the script, and of the filming; the actors and the performances they give; the locations used and so on. Working within a genre in itself is no guarantee of anything. However, films which do not have a clear generic identity may find they have even larger hurdles to clear in their pursuit of success.

Attracting production funding – in the world of commercial film, at least – is very much harder if the genre is unclear, for precisely this reason. Television production is not quite on the same scale, of course, but does require the investment and coordination of considerable resources. Commissioners of new proposals want some reassurance as to likely success.

The ability to 'pitch' an idea is crucial. A *pitch* is a presentation that summarises in an extremely compressed form which simultaneously makes the idea sound exciting *and* draws on previous successes. *Alien* (USA, 1979) was apocryphally reported to have been pitched as '*Jaws* in a spaceship'.

At the same time, the marketing of films is very much simpler when the genre is clear. Both posters, with their direct visual appeals, and trailers, with more emphasis on narrative, work much more effectively when audiences can readily recognise the general kind of product that is being sold. Going to see a film constitutes a significant effort, and financial outlay, all things considered: people need to be reasonably certain of enjoying the product if they are to be coaxed into making that commitment.

Although less common today than in the classic days of Hollywood, the multi-picture contract still features with many studios, and particular stars. Actors who can be readily identified with certain kinds of film are reckoned to be 'money in the bank'.

Genres and audiences

Genres are repeated sets of codes and conventions, or systems of signs (see p. 46). Their habitual usage has tended to mean that their structure stays the same, at least for as long as they are a useful way of doing things. Consequently, genres have predictable patterns. There are many well-known media genres, such as the horror film, the newspaper feature article, the situation comedy and so on.

Audiences, too, depend on the notion of genre – and not only for the financial reasons outlined above. Part of our pleasure in watching a film comes from our sense of being able to predict its direction and likely outcome. We like to make informed guesses about what is going to

happen and derive satisfaction or pleasure when we are proved right. We take our clues from a variety of facets that have come to be associated with particular genres: the 'baddie' wears black, the hero has an innate moral sense, the 'vamp' is not to be trusted, the alien wishes to appropriate us or our planet, and so on. Once we can tune into the broad outlines, much fun comes from trying to anticipate the detail.

Of course, there is a fine line here: the script needs to give us enough to engage us, and allow for recognition/anticipation, but not so much that we can work out everything well in advance. We also like, contrarily, to be surprised. Genre simultaneously provides the comfort of familiar outlines *and* the scope for individual variations.

Another important feature of genres is that they are a means of selecting and constructing a certain view of the world. As such, they are closely related to audience 'reading' practices.

The language educator Brian Moon believes the relationship of various genres to people's reading practices can be seen in the David Lynch television series *Twin Peaks*. Released in the late 1980s, it was read by some as a comedy, by others as a soap opera and by a large cult following as a satire. For each of these groups, it appears to have helped their understanding in some way for them to feel they were watching a comedy, or a soap opera, or a satire. The question of which group, if any, is right seems not to matter particularly.

Audiences often find the various genres reassuring. According to Moon, texts are always read through genre and genres 'are like coloured spectacles we can change but never remove'.

Features of genre

Audiences can usually identify genres because they have recognisable features and step-by-step structures. Audience enjoyment of them is often derived from the repetition, with just enough variation to add 'spice'.

■ **Genres have a step-by-step structure**

Genres have a relatively predictable structure of stages that follow each other in a sequence. In terms of narrative, the classic Hollywood formula for musicals was said to be: 'boy meets girl, boy loses girl, boy gets girl'. This is an example of the familiar three-act narrative structure of orientation, complication and finally resolution.

■ **Genres are a development of the cultural context**

In a particular culture, people become used to interacting in certain ways. The rituals of the traditional Maori greeting developed out of the habitual interactions of that culture. Within a culture, people also like hearing stories with familiar subject matter. In Japan, a favourite genre is the samurai story. Respect, loyalty and the importance of tradition are important to this genre.

The values and beliefs of the culture will affect the types of stories they prefer. For example, Western culture generally favours stories where good triumphs over evil. There is little demand for stories where evil is rewarded, or where rewards randomly go to either good or evil. These preferences lead the audience to expect particular characters and familiar plots. The interest lies in the twists and turns along the way to resolution.

The cultural context of the United Kingdom did not call for the development of the Western. With a few exceptions, it has remained a largely American genre. On the other hand, the cultural context of Australia appears to have been favourable to the development of the television soap opera. Australian soap operas are now shown around the world.

Figure 1.15
Many elements combine to generate an identity for a particular programme such as Emma (UK, 1996). Genre is established as much through costume, setting and props as it is through storyline and character.

Figure 1.16
Programmes such as The Bill combine elements of soap opera to create their own format. Current social concerns are also highlighted in this series, as the genres are closely tied to the culture.

■ **Genres can change**

Genres change at about the same pace as the overall culture. Being closely tied to the culture, they reveal the concerns of the time and also who has the most power in that culture. For example, nineteenth-century British novels presented a class-based society that also denied women access to power. This is shown in the film of the novel *Sense and Sensibility* (UK/USA, 1995).

Genres are changing relatively quickly at the moment. Technology has produced a rapid pace of change in the overall culture, changing the previously accepted ways of doing things.

(For more on genres, including hybrid or multi-generic texts, see codes and conventions, pp. 48–9.)

MULTI-GENERIC/ HYBRID TEXTS

Many texts mix and match a range of genres to suit new purposes created by a changing society. For example, programmes such as the police drama *The Bill* combine elements of soap opera in their own format. Documentaries, often regarded as belonging to the larger exposition genre, can also display features of the report genre. Docudrama combines both of these genres with the storytelling features of the narrative genre.

Mixing elements of different genres together draws on formats that have proven popularity. At the same time, of course, they also prevent those formulas from becoming stale.

Genres and codes

There may in fact be many codes linked and operating within the much larger conventional code of the particular genre. For example, the semiotician Roland Barthes suggests that the narrative genre consists of at least five key codes:

▶ **CHARACTER CODES** in which signs relating to personality, appearance and speech are grouped.
▶ **SUSPENSE CODES** in which information is hidden from the reader until the end.
▶ **PLOT CODES** using familiar patterns of story development.
▶ **STRUCTURAL CODES** featuring binary oppositions, such as good versus evil or nature and culture.
▶ **CULTURAL CODES** based on cultural knowledge, beliefs and values.

Barthes argued that, by varying these codes, particular genres such as romances or horror films can be produced.

▼ ▼ ▼ ▼ ▼ ▼ ▼

activities

Written assignment

1. Study a number of films or television programmes of varying genres to see what elements are common within each. Make up a grid to log typical characters, settings, storylines, etc.

2. Examine texts from within one particular genre from different production eras. Identify the elements that have remained constant and also those that have changed. For example, in Westerns, many striking developments have

occurred in terms of visual style, dress, ideology and themes, while settings and even characters have remained remarkably constant.

Oral assignment

Prepare a 'pitch' (see Robert Altman's film *The Player*, USA, 1992) for a new film idea you have devised. You get two minutes with a producer and need to convince him or her of both the essential 'generic' ingredients *and* the innovative qualities of your idea.

Language

Nobody who has an interest in modern society, and certainly nobody who has an interest in relationships of power in modern society, can afford to ignore language.

Norman Fairclough

Linguist

▼ ▼ ▼

Our language can be seen as an old city; a maze of little streets and squares, of old and new houses, and houses with additions from various periods; and this surrounded by a multitude of modern sections with straight and regular streets and uniform houses.

Ludwig Wittgenstein

Philosopher

▼ ▼ ▼

The world we live in, says the linguist Norman Fairclough, is a massive human-created world. This becomes increasingly so as the natural world is transformed to support larger and larger populations. This human world cannot help being a world of values, attitudes and beliefs —or *ideologies*. Ideologies are systems of values. They are closely linked to the cultural and social context. Examples of ideologies include beliefs about gender roles, about the economy (such as economic rationalism, or its opposite – Keynesianism), about the virtues of technology, and so on.

Ideologies are closely linked to power. In medieval times, the Church was the most powerful institution in society and the ideologies of religion predominated.

Today, consumerism seems to be the driving force behind social organisation: stoked up by advertising and serviced by manufacturing industries, our desires and dreams are inspired by media images and controlled by international conglomerates with interests in every facet of leisure pursuits. We may cling to the belief that we are free individuals, distinct and in control of everything we do. In fact, our taste in clothes, in soft drinks, in music, in modes of transport, in food and a in whole range of other aspects of our daily lives are closely scrutinised by the manufacturing and marketing industries. The information gathered is then used to manipulate and guide our subsequent purchase choices. Some influential thinkers, such as Noam Chomsky, would even assert that even in

ideological outlook we are just as much driven by the media as in anything else that we do.

Using language is the most common form of social behaviour in the human world. Fairclough argues ideologies are closely linked to language. This is because language is a tool for thinking and believing. If language carries ideologies, then it also is a vehicle for carrying power.

Consider the many accents of England, for example. The accent of the upper class, called 'received pronunciation' (received ultimately from the royal family) immediately bestows power and status. In its early years, the BBC relied exclusively on this accent, in line with its perception of itself as an institution of authority and influence in public life. Today, of course, a much wider range of accents can be found there, as the nature and purpose of broadcasting has developed. Programmes aimed at young people, for example, would not draw many viewers if the presenters spoke only in the accents of Prince Charles!

Feminists would also agree that language carries ideologies and gives power. The use of gender-specific language, such as 'man' to stand for all people, has helped to exclude women from power.

The concept of 'political correctness' sought precisely to examine assumptions contained within language and to eradicate the in-built biases against minority groups. The hostility and ridicule poured over this term is hardly surprising, given the vested interests it attacks. The attitudes and interests of those hurling the abuse would make for an interesting study in themselves.

Some of the chief characteristics of language and ideologies include:

■ **Naturalisation**

If an ideology or belief system comes to dominate all others it will be seen as 'natural' or 'the only way'. This is in spite of the often arbitrary nature of ideologies. In language, ideologies are most effective when they are invisible. Until the 1960s, for example, it was perfectly normal to use 'he' to mean 'he/she'. This seemed to be common sense and few saw any problem. That is, until women became aware that the language was sustaining an ideology of male superiority at their expense.

Today, a capitalist, consumer-orientated system seems to be the only natural way to organise a technological society. It appears there could be no other way, especially since the collapse of communism. Capitalism has become naturalised.

■ Repetition

The media is a powerful naturalising force because its effects are cumulative. A single media text on its own may have a very minor effect. However, with repetition, a point of view or an ideology comes to appear as common sense. Failure to present or explore alternatives leads to the unchallenged assumption that *this* is the *only* way of doing things.

■ Media texts are often multi-modal

Media texts commonly contain pictures and print in the case of the print media, for example; or voice, sound and visuals on television and film. The language of the media works in a complex mix of modes which can reinforce particular viewpoints. For example, the soundtrack of a documentary can work emotionally while the voiceover can make logical appeals.

The semiotic approach to media language

Within the past century, there has been a profound shift in Western societies from a culture that is based on the written word to one that is increasingly founded on the visual image. The mass media of film, television and advertising especially are now the dominant forces in shaping and controlling social attitudes and aspirations. When we consider that it was not until the latter half of the nineteenth century that the ability to read became universal, the pace with which things are moving becomes striking. On the other hand, it is not that written language is being superseded: supplemented, rather.

The rules of spoken language, or written language cannot be used to understand sound effects or visuals. All that unites these modes is that they are each acts of communication.

However, this uniting factor provides a starting point for analysis. At the most basic level, communication takes place through signs – gestures, sounds, grunts and drawn images.

It is possible to analyse on this level, although it is reducing media language to the plane of sub-atomic particles of communication. However, the reduction to signs does allow all print, sound and visual aspects of media communication to be studied together. This study of signs and sign systems is called *semiotics*.

The genesis of this discipline originates from two influential writers from the early part of the twentieth century, Ferdinand de Saussure and the American Charles Peirce. Another major French philosopher and theorist, Roland Barthes, later made significant developments to their initial contributions on linguistic models. In particular, he developed systems for examining how the abstract models devised by the earlier theorists could be applied to the social context of language, and how usage depended on individual interpretation. He was responsible for devising the system whereby two orders of signification were identified:

▶ the signifier is the sign which refers to an object or concept
▶ the signified is the object or concept to which is referred.

THE SIGN

All communication can be seen as messages created out of signs. A sign can be a smile, a rude hand gesture, a photograph or a letter in the alphabet. The audience for any message gives it meaning by interpreting the signs.

Signs refer to something other than themselves. They work as pointers, giving directions to think in a certain way. For example, the collection of marks on the page that is the word 'apple' bears no resemblance to an actual apple. All the marks do is point us in the direction of thinking about a real apple. While a photograph does bear a resemblance to the object it signifies, it is not the object itself. Therefore, a photograph is only directing us to think the thought, in the same way as letters on a page direct us.

The meaning of a sign depends on the cultural context in which it is used. John Fiske gives the example of an ox. In an English-speaking context, an ox may suggest a beast of burden or something served between two buns with French fries. For a Hindu in India, where there can be a jail sentence for killing this sacred animal, the word 'ox' would

Figure 1.17
Icons (such as a hand, car or person) are signs that resemble the object to which they refer. Symbols (such as a dove, cross or skull and cross-bones) are signs that do not resemble the thing they refer to, but rather suggest ideas that have come to be associated with that thing.

have a very different meaning to that of a European, for instance.

ICONS are signs that resemble the object to which they refer. Photographs are icons because they are images of things that do exist. Similarly, many visual representations adopt an outline resemblance to the objects referred to: road signs of cars and motorbikes are obvious examples. Icons can also be words, however. Onomatopoeia works like an icon because it makes verbal language sound like what it signifies. For example, the word 'crash' sounds like the noise to which it refers.

SYMBOLS are signs that do not resemble the thing to which they refer. The meaning they have is through associations built up over generations of habitual use. The olive branch representing peace or the cross representing Christianity are easily recognised symbols with their roots in antiquity.

DENOTATION is the term given to the naming and describing level of a sign, at its most literal level. This level defines or denotes to what the sign refers. For example, the term 'dove' denotes a small bird from the same family as the pigeon.

CONNOTATION refers to the associated thoughts that any particular sign brings to mind. These may be anything connected, suggested or implied by

the sign. For example, a white dove brings to mind the concept of peace. A turtledove is connected with the imagery of love.

POLYSEMY refers to the capacity of all signs to be 'many signed' (polysemic): i.e. to have more than one meaning. A dictionary is a good place to discover this. The average number of meanings for a single word (or sign) in English is four or five. With seventeen different meanings, the word 'range' is one of the most polysemic. Within a particular culture, signs are not usually regarded as endlessly polysemic. The variations that occur are within limits set by the social and cultural context.

CODES

Codes are systems of signs, put together (usually in sequence) to create meaning. As with a spy code, a set of rules governs the way in which the code is

Figure 1.18
This picture denotes a Mercedes Benz sports car. The Mercedes is a powerful sign, with connotations of wealth, luxury and status. But the Mercedes is polysemous. It can mean a range of things to different people. For some, it could also represent greed and selfishness.

Figure 1.19
This table shows the technical and symbolic codes of the media.

TECHNICAL AND SYMBOLIC CODES

MEDIA	TECHNICAL CODES	SYMBOLIC CODES
Television Film Photographs Computer-based media	Select from: ▶ framing ▶ composition ▶ shot type ▶ camera angle ▶ lighting ▶ special effects ▶ editing ▶ camera movement ▶ sound volume ▶ sound fades and cuts ▶ sound layering ▶ written (structural; e.g. division into parts, words on the screen such as 'later' ▶ computer screen design ▶ computer interactivity ▶ computer sequencing ▶ computer navigation	Select from: ▶ symbolic objects ▶ set design ▶ actors' body language ▶ actors' appearance ▶ lighting ▶ dialogue ▶ sound effects ▶ music ▶ choice of language
Radio CDs etc.	Select from: ▶ fades and cuts ▶ sound volume ▶ sound layers	Select from: ▶ dialogue ▶ music ▶ sound effects ▶ silence
Newspapers Magazines Computer-based multimedia (text) etc.	Select from: ▶ sentence construction ▶ headlines etc. ▶ columns ▶ page design ▶ story placement ▶ layout Also refer to the codes for photographs	Select from: ▶ choice of emotive words ▶ symbolic typefaces or fonts ▶ (e.g. medieval) Also refer to the codes for photographs

assembled and the linkages that will be made. The members of the community using the code consent to the rules and in this way make sense of the communication. Codes are therefore a product of the social and cultural context.

Writing is a code which allows us to represent thoughts on paper. Carefully schooled agreement among users allows the code to be understood. In the same way, sequences of images in a television drama are a code which allows us to participate in the narrative genre. Media academics and educators Barrie McMahon and Robyn Quin have classified the codes of television and film into three categories: technical, symbolic and written codes.

TECHNICAL CODES are the codes of the craft or the profession. They are technical in the sense of being 'techniques' of construction. Examples of technical codes include camera techniques, journalistic techniques, editing techniques and so on.

SYMBOLIC CODES are systems of signs that are embedded within the text itself. These signs have strong associative or connotative meanings connected with them. Symbolic codes include the actors' clothing and body language, music and sound effects, and choice of language.

WRITTEN CODES apply to a range of contexts in which words are used in texts. These may include newspaper headlines, captions attached to photographs, the typography adopted or the house style of a particular publication.

ENCODING refers to the process of making codes. Producers of texts are said to encode their messages using systems of signs. Institutional issues impact on this process.

DECODING refers to the 'reading' of coded messages by the receiver. Issues related to audience have an impact on this process.

CONVENTIONS

Conventions are habits or long accepted ways of doing things. Through repeated experiences, often over generations, audiences become familiar with the procedures of conventions.

The media have hundreds of conventions. Each of them has been built up over so many years that the audience believes they are just 'common sense'. In television and film, for example, a soft dissolve or 'melting' picture is used to signify a flashback; similarly, a fade to black may indicate the passing of time. Had Hollywood developed differently, it could just as easily have been a fade to white (which instead tends to mean death or a dream).

Conventions operate by general agreement with the audience. They are therefore the social and cultural component of signs and codes.

THE COMMUTATION TEST

The meaning of a sign, code or convention can often be discovered by commuting it into something else. Movement, transfer or exchange can often result in vastly different meanings. For example, if the white clothes of the traditional melodrama hero were commuted to black, there would be a change in meaning. This change tells us what the cultural significance of the white clothes was.

▼ ▼ ▼ ▼ ▼ ▼ ▼

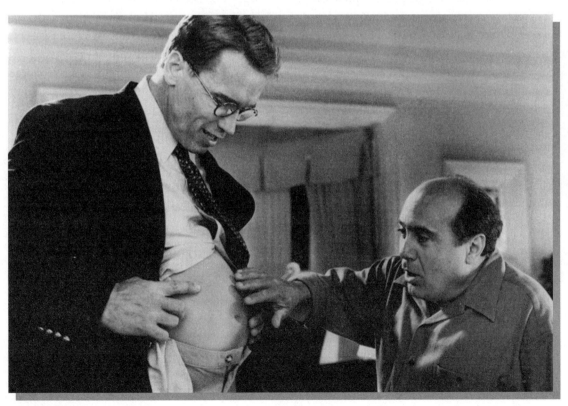

Figure 1.20

In the film Junior (USA, 1994), Arnold Schwarzenegger's character becomes pregnant as part of a medical experiment. 'My baby, my choice', says Arnie, when advised to terminate the pregnancy. The humour comes through the incongruence of the biological commutation. Even today, male and female roles are still divided.

activities

1. Examine a newspaper front page and list all the sources for the news stories – police, government ministers, etc. Consider the following questions:

▶ Which groups appear to provide most of the sources? What is the effect of this?

▶ Which groups are not listed as sources? What is the effect of this?

▶ What is the outcome in the articles? In other words, who is represented as doing what to whom? Who is cast as the hero/villain, perpetrator/victim, reformer/hindrance, etc.?

▶ What adjectives and nouns are used for each set of participants? What would change if these were reversed?

Analyse and discuss the results of your research.

2. Repeatedly record (video or audio) a news report or political speech, varying the accent of the presenter each time. Use upper-class, working-class or broad accents, and perhaps the accent of a disadvantaged minority group. Discuss the results. Are different effects produced, depending upon the accent? If so, why do you think this happens?

3. Isolate an ideology that appears to be have been naturalised, or appears to be just 'common sense.' The ideology could concern the family, work and careers, school, gender or the economy. Examples could include feminism or patriarchy, capitalism, individualism, the work ethic. Examples could also extend to systems of views about social class, ethnic background, race or even child rearing, the virtues of technology, etc. Find media examples of the repetition of your chosen ideology, which works to reinforce its naturalisation.

4. Title sequences of television programmes and films are often rich in meaningful signs, as producers flag the key elements of the programme and the audience to which they are appealing. Analyse a title sequence in terms of the denotation and connotation of its introductory sign systems.

5. Collect images (or words) you believe are clearly more polysemic than most. The meaning of these signs will be very dependent on the context. Use captions to anchor the meaning to a particular interpretation you wish the audience to make. Discuss the results with your class.

Using a computer, change the typeface on a short news article. Try a Gothic font, a futuristic one, a standard one such as Times Roman, and a sans serif, or plain, font such as Arial or Avant Garde. Discuss the connotations of each.

Make a list of well-known visual media conventions and outline their meanings. Include cuts, fades, wipes, split screens, dissolves, etc.

major assignment

Production assignment

Select one of the following production tasks.

1. Prepare the script for a twenty- to thirty-shot video sequence that relies on the powerful connotative effect of selected images to present an emotional appeal. The topic can be of your choice. Specify your target audience as well. Create a column on the side of the script where you explain the hoped-for connotative effect on your target audience of each of your chosen shots.

A topic that allows you to take a strong viewpoint on something may make it easier to think of ways to manipulate associations and images. For example, emotive images are readily available for topics dealing with environmental issues. Advertisements are another suitable choice.

2. Create a magazine advertisement. Cut connotative images from various magazines and assemble them into a composite image, or collage, to sell a product. Explain the totality of the effect, if possible, and give detailed explanations of the connotations of each individual image.

Written assignment

Present a 500-word response to the following topic. Analyse a television advertisement in relation to the following aspects:

▶ denotation and connotation

▶ polysemy where noticeable

▶ technical codes and symbolic codes

▶ use of recognisable conventions.

Media Products: Contexts, Texts and Meanings

So abundant and diverse in nature are the varieties of media product now on offer to us every day, and in numerous ways, that it is quite easy to lose sight of the fact that they are all, without exception, manufactured artefacts with very specific intentions. Once, a long time ago, human beings grew up in a natural world and had to be mindful of all its features for their successful continuous existence: now, especially in the West, it is the 'virtual world' of media manufacture that provides the landscape of our social being. Our dreams, our aspirations, our ambitions are all shaped and driven by the images with which we are surrounded from the moment we are born.

It is useful then to consider the nature of these products: where they come from, how they are generated and what it is they seek to communicate.

Perhaps the first observation worth making concerns the sheer bewildering variety of media artefacts to which we are now exposed on a daily basis. Music and talk on the radio from the moment we wake up; newspapers/television at breakfast; advertisements on cereal packets, bus stops and buses, and a wealth of other sites; television screens everywhere; magazines to browse; CDs; books; films – the list goes on, covering the entire day and even seeing us safely back into our beds last thing at night. In fact, perhaps the most astonishing thing of all, given the blizzard of media images we are exposed to every day of our lives, is how we are *not* bewildered. We absorb them or not as we choose, or as they suit our needs at particular points.

Contexts

There are two broad strands of study concerning considerations of context: first, contexts of *production*, which examine how and why media products are actually made; and, secondly, contexts of *consumption*, which focus on ways in which they are received. The latter is addressed in the section on audiences (see p. 25). Here, we need to take a closer look at the matter of how media products are actually constructed.

When the time of production, the language, the nationality, the organisations involved, the government regulations and all the other factors are combined, the result is called the *context*. Context refers to all of the natural, cultural and social aspects of an environment that help shape the final meaning of a text. Therefore, any media text is very much a part of its context.

THE INFLUENCE OF NATURAL ASPECTS

Natural aspects of a context include the geographical and landscape factors at play in the development of a particular civilisation. Natural aspects of a contextual environment are difficult to separate from the cultural aspects. What makes England, England? Is it the weather? Is it because it is separated from Europe by the English Channel? Or is it the language and culture? Natural and cultural aspects of the context are usually regarded as integrated. The intersection of the two is so difficult to identify and almost impossible to analyse in terms of separate elements.

Consider a Western film such as Clint Eastwood's *Unforgiven* (USA, 1992). An aspect of the context in this Western and all others has been the natural geography of the United States. There had to be a 'West' in the first place, it had to be habitable and it had to support certain types of agriculture. These natural elements of the context excluded Australia (whose 'West' is barren), or the United Kingdom, whose much smaller territory has been occupied and cultivated for much longer periods of time. The natural aspects of the American environment integrated with certain cultural aspects and the Western became possible. At the same time, the concept of 'The West' was used by these films to explore certain key features of the life experienced in those lands: issues of lawlessness, rugged individualism, the pioneering spirit and personal integrity being but some of these.

Of course, these three countries, and various others, do share certain common strands, such as industrial development (and lately decline, too), which make certain other kinds of film more universal. Numerous situations are virtually inter-changeable from one culture to another. *The Full Monty* (UK/USA, 1997), for example, although firmly rooted in the northern English city of

Figure 1.21
Films set in more recent times are likely to have a more universal application. The Full Monty (UK/ USA, 1997), for example, depicts an industrial environment common to the entire Western world.

Sheffield, offers a study of urban and industrial decay, and the devastating impact this has on the role of men in particular, which is recognisable throughout the developed world.

Equally, each country will have distinctive natural features of their own, which make for genres unique to their individual landscapes. In Australia, there is much desert and 'bush', for instance, and, in the United Kingdom, the wilderness of some-where such as Scotland, the rolling downs of the Home Counties and the sea which surrounds them all. In that order, films such as *Walkabout* (Australia, 1970), *Rob Roy* (USA, 1995) and *Shadowlands* (UK, 1993) are unique to the landscapes they depict. Each sets out a distinctive environment that permits a particular kind of representation. The kind of story that can be told in one cannot be reproduced in another.

These landscapes have certain kinds of histories attached to them that suggest a particular kind of story. This is where natural environment interacts with cultural usage.

CULTURAL CONTEXT

The cultural aspects of a context include the language, the history, the values and beliefs, the economic system, the technology and the customs of a particular community or civilisation.

To use the Western as an example once more, the cultural context of this type of film may include the English language, a transplanted European civilisation, a frontier history, a capitalist economy, a certain 'American state of mind', cinema technology and a place called Hollywood. All of these things combine to generate a media product aimed at representing a certain way of life for a particular group of people at a particular point in time. The characters may be imaginary, but the location was real and the stories rooted in a culture which recognisably once existed.

Of course, the nature of what was shown to have happened in the Western 'world' changed dramatically over time. John Ford films presented very different values and concerns from the later ones of Clint Eastwood. Both, in fact, reflect more the nature of their own eras than the actual one supposedly represented. Early Westerns, for instance, traditionally presented Native Americans (so-called 'Indians') as hostile and ruthless savages. *Dances with Wolves* (USA, 1990), coming from a more politically conscious time, attempted to show a more accurate picture of the compas-

sionate, sophisticated society that the more barbaric invaders had systematically destroyed.

Closer to home, Britain's geographical location has given it a very long tradition as a seafaring nation. As an unpredictable and at times wild and savage natural element, the sea as a distinctive feature has provided numerous occasions for dramatic representation, both in literature and in film. The sea as a source of opportunity (piracy), of control (Empire), of threat (invasion by Vikings), of safety (a barrier *against* invasion, in World War II), of employment (fishing/merchant navy), of adventure (running away to …) – all of these have occurred, in various representations, down through the history of these islands. All, of course, have been real options, at different times, for inhabitants of these islands. The same is not the case for a land-locked country such as Luxembourg: culturally, these stories would not hold the same resonance for Luxembourg's residents as they do for Britons. (Although they, of course, will have their own.)

Essentially, there is an environment, or several different ones in some countries, and then histories of interaction with and development within those environments. The most powerful media products will be those which connect with the culture of the peoples at whom they are aimed.

This does not mean that we are unable to enjoy the products of other cultures: from films, through music, to format television programmes, this is manifestly not the case. In many ways, culture is increasingly becoming a global phenomenon. However, when a well-constructed product is rooted firmly within a particular culture which is uniquely our own, its impact is all the more intense. *The Full Monty* may indeed work for an American audience – but nowhere near as powerfully as for Britons.

INSTITUTIONAL CONTEXT

The institutional context describes the interactions of the people around a particular text. For example, the institutional context of ITV television news includes the way that ITV organises its journalists, their work relations, their views of news and the way they target the audience.

For example, ITV chooses television to communicate its news, rather than a newspaper,

because of the institutional context of ITV being organised as a television station. It is not primarily because it happens to have a British cultural context.

SOCIAL CONTEXT

On the audience side, the social context includes audience members themselves, what they do when watching the news and their individual ways of relating to such programmes as ITV news.

Within the cultural context, the social context of a media product includes the nature of the individuals who are communicating and also the medium through which they choose to communicate. The social context effectively describes the social interactions of people around a particular text.

Here we really need to return to our first distinction between contexts of *production* and of *consumption*. For a long time, media products were felt to be virtually self-contained units of meaning, complete within themselves. Study of these discrete texts (see below) would yield all we would need to know about the operations of the media in society. Now, it is firmly established that how a text communicates has a great deal to do with the social environment in which it is received. However, there are also some points to be made regarding the processes of generating media products.

The factors making up the social context might be described in three different ways.

THE SUBJECT MATTER (FIELD) can also form part of the social context. The subject matter is the knowledge or information content of any communication. It tells us who did what to whom, and in what circumstances; or what is being claimed as the benefit of a given product. It certainly helps to determine the shape of the text. Consider human relationships and sexuality as subject matter. Whether it is a music video clip, a news story or a magazine article, such subject matter is sensitive. Moral values and government regulations can be a powerful force in limiting the scope of what is shown, or revealed. No matter what genre or medium is chosen, the taboos of the subject matter at least partially determine the look of the finished product.

Of course, programme-makers – and advertising agencies especially – are always trying to test the boundaries of what is acceptable. Shock value and sex are well known to be important features in the arousal of audience interest. Nevertheless, strict limitations are imposed and transgression of these is actually extremely rare.

The media are often thought to be ruled by fashion. Yet, media genres in fact deal with subject matter that does not age quickly. Soap operas deal with family troubles, while crime dramas deal with threats to law and order. Horror films play upon our recurring fascination with the supernatural and our age-old anxieties about death. These are eternal concerns.

THE ROLES AND RELATIONSHIPS (TENOR) between the producers and the audience give meaning to the communication. Media products are produced and consumed by a variety of different groups of people. These people exist within the one culture, but form different social groups. They all have slightly different ways of relating. Producers belonging to one social group may want to communicate certain points of view. Audience members in another group may get slightly different meanings. Gender, race and class factors also have an impact. Producers and audiences may have varying relationships. BBC Radio 3 and 4 hosts, for example, have a different relationship with their audience than pop show presenters: even the terminology is different. Prisoners watching crime dramas have a very different relationship to the stories than their warders have!

THE MODE AND MEDIUM of the communication is also a contextual factor that shapes its meaning. The mode may be spoken, written, visual, non-verbal or auditory. The medium may be television, radio and so on. A radio broadcast will be different to an Internet home page no matter what roles and relationships exist and irrespective of the subject matter.

Media texts

The social and cultural context shapes the meaning of the text. The products of the media are often referred to as 'texts'. Once, only a book written for study was called a text. Now, the term can loosely include any sequence of communication, such as a music video clip, a radio broadcast or an Internet home page.

■ **A text is a unit of meaning that is complete in some way**

A sequence of meaning, or a story, is the most common media text. News stories, television soap operas, and films are sequenced narratives. In this form, the meanings systematically relate to each other. There is a start, middle and finish.

However, a single image such as a poster or a magazine front cover could also be a text, since it is complete in itself. It has a number of features – such as font size and style, uses of colour, photographic subject selected, how it is lit/made-up/ what angle shot from, etc. – all of which combine to produce a particular identity.

■ **Media texts are created through a process of selection**

What is finally shown on a television programme, for example, is the end result of selection decisions made by the scriptwriter, the producer, the director, the camera operator, the editor and even the actors.

■ **Media texts are said to be 'constructed', rather than natural**

They come with attitudes, interpretations and conclusions already built in. This is inevitable because they come from particular contexts. Institutions such as commercial television stations may have constructed the text or the text may have been aimed at a certain audience, such as 18- to 29-year-olds. The combination of these factors means that a point of view is always there, even in seemingly neutral texts such as the news. Moreover, the nature of the 'construct', or product, and the values and attitudes it reflects, will vary considerably according to the institution presenting it.

CRITICAL LITERACY AND MEDIA TEXTS

Critical literacy is being able to 'read' media texts. This applies as much to visual as to verbal, or indeed aural, matter. People are critically literate if they understand how media texts work, if they understand the social and cultural contexts – and if they can also produce media texts themselves, so much the better.

Critical literacy requires understanding and an ability to question. A critically literate person will ask three fundamental questions of a media text:

▶ Whose story is being told, or whose version is presented?

▶ Who is it for?

▶ Why is it told this way? (What are the organising principles of its composition?)

A critical media literacy also comes from an understanding of the key concepts outlined in the following sections of this chapter.

'COLUMN INCHES' AND 'AIR TIME'

Media texts are geared to suit the space or time available. Newspapers and magazines have column inches, while radio and television have air time.

The pressure for space in newspapers has led to the development of the 'inverted pyramid' presentation of the facts. Sub-editors usually cut space from the bottom paragraphs. However, the story still makes sense as all of the essential information is at the top. On the other hand, filling up space is easy. A national newspaper office is estimated to receive more than a million words of copy a day.

Television programmes are geared for time slots and are formatted to suit the placement of advertisements. A one-hour crime drama is actually more like 48 minutes in length, to allow time for advertisements. The 'set-up' must happen before the initial break, and usually in the first three minutes. The 'wrap-up' comes just after the final advertisement break.

SAMENESS AND REPETITION

Audiences are never guaranteed, no matter how much money is spent. Audiences are disobedient and fickle. This makes media programming a risky business and what works becomes difficult to gauge. Once a successful product has been discovered, the formula is copied over and over again as every other producer tries to cash in. There is, in fact, a highly profitable trade in exporting successful formats. As a result of a desire to guarantee profits in fickle markets, media products often reproduce each other, in seemingly endless variations.

NEGLECT OF MINORITY AUDIENCES

The profit motive of the media works consistently to exclude audiences lacking economic power or

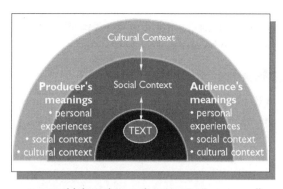

resources. Unless the media organisation can sell the audience to advertisers, there will be no attempt to cater for that audience. The size of the ignored audience can be in the millions.

GLOBALISATION AND WORLDWIDE 'McCULTURE'

Media academic Fred Inglis has written of the 'dumping over the globe of the used-up films and soap operas of three decades at cut prices, so that you can see *Dallas* in Bali, *Kojak* in Finland, and *Sergeant Bilko* in Chile any week of the year'. More recently, remote communities in Russia have become obsessed with *Dallas*. Newspaper columnist Phillip Adams calls this the 'Coca-Colanisation' of culture. He argues that, if biodiversity is important in nature, it is just as important in human culture.

The United States imports about 5 per cent of its media products, while the worldwide average for imports is upwards of 30 per cent of the total schedule. Many small developing countries import more than 90 per cent. Most imports are sourced in the United States, leading to accusations of cultural imperialism.

However, some audience researchers believe there is little cause for alarm in these figures. They argue audiences interpret American media texts in ways unique to the local culture (see 'Audiences', p. 26). Others, such as Justin Lewis, believe this is swinging the pendulum too far. Audiences have *some* power to make interpretation, but the producers still set the agenda in subtle ways.

Producer power depends to some extent on the genre. News is less open to interpretation. Global news networks such as the United States' CNN (Cable News Network) are undoubtedly successful in relaying a US, industrialised world point of view. Entertainment genres, on the other hand, could be regarded in a different light. Soap operas such as *Home and Away* or *Melrose Place* may be somewhat more open to local definitions. When people watch an entertainment programme, they

Figure 1.22
The text (e.g. a television programme) exists within the social and cultural context. Producers and audiences within these context each contribute to the meaning of the text. Certain influences affect the producers and the audience is subject to a whole range of other influences. Put simply, meaning is made on both sides of the text.

enter an imaginary world. In contrast, information genres can be saying, 'This is how it is!'

Meaning

In China, the colour red usually means fortune is shining. As more Chinese buy cars, traffic jams have started to develop in Chinese cities and traffic lights have been imported from Europe and Australia. Yet, accidents haven't been reduced all that much because Chinese drivers have not taken to the lights readily. They are still having difficulty with the Western idea that red means stop, rather than 'good luck'!

Meaning comes from the cultural and social context, just as much as it does from the text. Without prior education, Japanese Noh theatre or Indonesian shadow theatre would have little meaning to a Western audience, because it does not have access to the cultural context.

Even within the same culture, different meanings can be read into the one text. A text provides information-rich sequences that are rather like building blocks. Most people would use the blocks to build similar looking understandings, but each person's ideas would be a little different. Life experiences, gender, race and class may all influence each person's 'construction'. Some people could even build quite unusual structures, yet still be using the same set of building blocks. In the same way, people make different interpretations of the blocks of meaning that are media texts.

▼ ▼ ▼ ▼ ▼ ▼ ▼

activities

Figure 1.23
Context map for the 1980s.

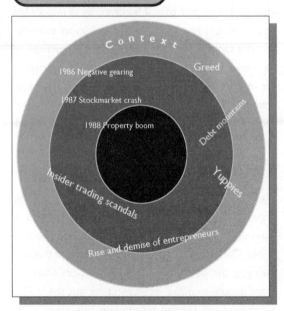

1. Draw up a 'context map' of a decade of your choice, such as the 1960s or the 1990s. A context map could consist of a circle like the one used to illustrate cultural and social contexts, listing inside the landmark features of the decade. As a model, look at the one prepared for the 1980s set out in figure 1.23.

Now list some television programmes or movies that seem to reveal aspects of the context map you have prepared.

2. It is often easier to see aspects of context operating in children's stories, as there is a simplification to suit the target age group. *The Lion, the Witch and the Wardrobe* was made for television in the late 1980s. However, this BBC adaptation of C. S. Lewis's book (which was written in the 1940s) is faithful to the original and therefore largely comes from the context of the 1940s.

View the programme and analyse it for context references from World War II – the time of writing. Find relatively naturalised references to Adolf Hitler, concentration camps, partisans and resistance fighters, the Gestapo, 'quislings' and the Allies.

3. Select a visual text you think is embedded in its context in a significant way. Show excerpts of it to the class and explain the relationship to social, economic, historical or cultural trends. Suggestions could include: *Wall Street* (USA, 1987), economic rationalism and corporate restructuring; *Thelma & Louise* (USA, 1991), feminism in the 1990s; *Easy Rider* (USA, 1969), 1960s counterculture; *Withnail and I* (UK, 1987), for a 1980s revisit to this era; *Strictly Ballroom* (Australia, 1992), multicultural society and individualism; *Batman* movies and the television series from the 1960s for comparative views of crime and Gotham City; *Babe* (Australia, 1995), the institutional context of globalisation and international co-production.

4. Select a movie or television programme. Decide on some aspects of the context of this text you would like to know but which are not clearly visible in the text itself. Examples could include the production house, the costs of production or the salaries paid to the actors. Research these details and present them to the class.

Figure 1.24
The movie **Wall Street** *(1988) reflects the context of the 1980s. The movie's main character, Gordon Gekko, uttered some of the decade's most quotable quotes, including 'Greed is good, greed is right, greed works.'*

chapter two
Computer-based Media

The Language of Computer-based Media

Computer-based media are the amalgamation of a number of different traditional media forms into new digitally based varieties. A process called convergence, where traditional media forms 'converge' into a digital format, accessed via computer, or computerised equipment, has seen the combination of many existing media into engaging and innovative new forms. As a consequence, computer-based language shares elements of many traditional media, particularly those from film, television, magazines and newspapers.

Basic units of computer-based communication

The basic units of computer-based media language are text, images, audio, video and animation (see 'Language of Television and Film', p. 148, and 'Print Media', p. 390). These are combined to create multimedia forms such as the Internet, disc-based multimedia such as CD-ROMs, interactive television and DVDs and video games. These new technologies are continually evolving, developing new ways to combine existing media elements. They can be combined in simple forms such as electronic newspapers – where the text is combined with pictures and video – through to more complex artistic forms – where elements merge or morph into each other, interact with the user or create artistic mindscapes capturing the emotion and feeling of the artist who created it.

Hypertext

Multimedia, at its most basic, is a series of menus and document pages linked together in a weblike structure, allowing the user to access information in a non-linear manner. If a user needs information on a specific subject, they can navigate their way through a multimedia production straight to the information they require, skipping any content not related to their topic of interest. Each page, picture, paragraph or word can be linked to any other page, picture, paragraph or word, and can be viewed in any order the user wishes. This system of navigation is called *hypertext*, and each link, whether it is a word, an icon or a picture, is known as a *hypertext link*.

Hypertext is not a new invention, but is widely believed to have its origins in 1963, when writer Ted Nelson coined the word to describe 'non-sequential writing'. Hypertext author Charles Deemer describes hypertext as being about giving the reader options. '"What do you want to read next?" is the question that hypertext asks again and again.' He sees hypertext in multimedia as: 'What do you want to hear or look at next? Do you want to read the poem, or hear the poem or watch the poet read the poem?'

Working your way through a piece of multimedia such as a CD-ROM, a video game or an Internet site is achieved by 'clicking' on a hypertext link or *hotspot*. A *hotspot* is a link to another piece of information or a multimedia element such as a video clip. A hotspot can be in the form of a highlighted *word*, a button or icon, a menu bar, or part of an image, usually referred to as a *hot spot* within an *image map*. When the mouse pointer is over the top of a hypertext link, it usually changes form. The most common example of this link indicator is when the mouse cursor on-screen changes from an arrow to a hand when it is moved across a hotspot or link. Once you click on the hypertext link, you are transported to new, related materials.

Hypertext is a very efficient way to store information. Multimedia is like a library, but far more intuitive, adapting itself to the users needs by providing the information requested, as well as providing related materials that may be of use.

A library will usually hold a number of William Shakespeare's works in the 822.33 section, each work within its own volume. The library will also hold books about each work, as well as books on Shakespeare himself. It will have information about performances of his plays and the history of the Elizabethan period.

A multimedia production could easily include all of his works on one CD or DVD, linking each work together where there are similarities. It could also link notes about the work with the text itself. This could be achieved by using illustrations and multimedia clips, linking the history of drama, and the historical events of the time with the text, while also allowing the user to view various performances of each work. The CD may even allow you to undertake a virtual guided tour of the rebuilt Globe Theatre where the work was originally performed.

Writer and playwright Charles Deemer concludes that 'hypertext is a web of possibilities, a web of reading experiences … [it] is the language of exploration and discovery – and therefore is the perfect language to become the mother tongue of the Information Age. For writers and readers alike, hypertext may well define what it means to be literate in the 21st century.'

User interfaces

The popular interfaces and appearances of screens will change every year for the rest of history. Every artistic fad you can imagine will be that year's popular way of visualising a document.

Ted Nelson
Inventor of the concept of hypertext

Paul Brown, in an essay on the aesthetics of the computer interface, states that: 'the success of the personal computer revolution was not only due to miniaturisation of components and prices. Far more important was the development of "user friendly" object-orientated and graphical user interfaces (GUI).' The interface is used to navigate around computer-based media. It consists of the icon buttons, menu items and procedures that can be used to operate the product.

Figures 2.1 and 2.2
Hotspots: A button or icon, which is a symbolic or iconic element representing the action, such as an arrow (at left), or an icon representing the material or action that is being accessed, such as a magnifying glass (left) detonating a link to more detailed information.

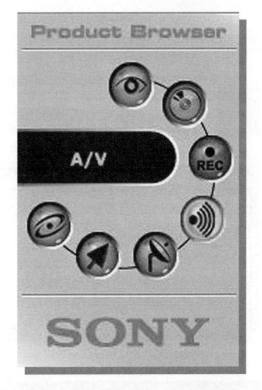

Figure 2.3
An image map: a whole picture with elements within it leading to links, i.e. books on a bookshelf leading to literature, or an illustrated menu or menu bar. Links are accessed by clicking on hotspots actually within the image.

The interface ranges from simple buttons and menus on the screen to more complex interface tools such as 3-D goggles, power gloves and body suits with sensors that allow the user to 'feel'. There is a range of products that provide the sensation of movement. These can include guns that recoil and flight-seats that simulate the movement of a game vehicle. The interface also includes the artificial intelligence built into any multimedia work. This is especially obvious with video games and interactive films. Interactive designer Greg Roach believes that 'the goal of an interface is to create something that is invisible'.

Figures 2.4, 2.5 and 2.6

Symbolic, iconic and indexical interfaces. Symbolic interfaces (top) are complex and are similar to using foreign language. The iconic interface (middle) is very familiar to users, drawing upon the desktop metaphor. The indexical interface (bottom) is harder to use, but more appealing to its target market – the young and technologically aware.

Brown has categorised user interfaces into three categories: *symbolic*, *iconic* and multi-sensory, immersion interfaces known as *indexical*.

THE SYMBOLIC INTERFACE This form of interface is known as *programming*. A user must know the computer language being used and also know the conventions of its use. Programming languages use symbols or characters in the same way that the English language uses words – to represent objects or actions. This interface features few barriers to hinder the user's creativity, but is almost impossible to use without an intimate knowledge of its workings.

THE ICONIC INTERFACE This interface style features icons, which stand for actions, and *pull-down menus* that allow the user to utilise all of the program's pre-programmed options. This interface is extremely productive and easy to use, but limits the user to a range of pre-programmed actions. The most common examples are the *Windows* and *Macintosh* interfaces and their metaphoric *desktop* concept. Using a metaphor that simulates a real-life environment means that users of the product are more familiar with its functions.

THE INDEXICAL INTERFACE This style of interface is richly decorated with images and colour. It is immersive, becoming part of the production and not simply a way in which to use it. It enhances the overall effect and allows the user to become more involved with the product. This is the kind of interface commonly found in many multimedia and video game productions. It provides a variety of navigation options from simple iconic buttons to random artistic patterns or images that transform when clicked. Indexical interfaces allow a computer-based media designer to explore the possibilities of interface design artistically.

INTERFACE GUIDELINES

Apple Computers has released a set of four Human Interface Guidelines to help designers create more usable multimedia, game and web applications.

■ **Unity of style**

Stick to good design practices. Do not clutter the screen with too much content or graphics. Use lots of *white* or free space. Stick with a particular colour scheme and use a balance of design elements.

■ **Unity of metaphors**

Use metaphors to communicate key concepts and features of your application. Use metaphors related to the content to reinforce its use. This leads to intuitive navigation through familiarity. This will be enhanced through their consistent use.

■ **Unity of vision**

Unity of vision is essential to the success of the project. It requires the project to be believable as an experience – for the user to be able to see images instead of characters, or symbols instead of people.

■ **Unity of environment**

Users should feel empowered and in control of the application. They should never feel as if the computer has automatically taken them somewhere. Users' actions should never be changed and their time should not be wasted. Well-designed interfaces are forgiving of a user's mistakes.

activities

1. In small groups, choose and research a topic of your choice, such as an historical event. One half of the group will search for information on the topic and related data in encyclopedias, while the others will use the library's CD-ROM-based encyclopedias. Compare your results. Which method found the best information: which was the easiest to use and which provided the most relevant related information?

2. How has hypertext made information easier to find in multimedia forms, particularity on the Internet? Is the 'web' structure of data on the Internet and other forms of multimedia beneficial for efficient storage and retrieval of information?

3. Analyse a number of different multimedia products. Define which type of interface is used in each, explaining why you think the designer used

it. Examples could include clarity, artistic effect or to enhance the transfer of information.

Is the content's style linked to the interface's style? For example, an encyclopedia may use a very formal iconic interface, while a virtual art gallery may use an artistic indexical one.

4. Locate a couple of nonfiction books of your choice on different subject matters. Explain the type of interface you would choose to use for an electronic version of each book and what elements or navigation tools it may include (e.g. menus, icons, full-page illustrations with hotspots within the image, moving text, animated backgrounds, etc.).

Would you lay it out in a formal manner using headlines and body text, or would you allow the user to experience it more, such as offering virtual tours of art galleries?

New Technology: Issues

We are entering a technological revolution, a revolution that will forever change the way we gather information. According to technology writer Slade Antwar, information technology is creating new means of self-expression and greater independence of thought and action. According to Antwar, these new technologies form part of a newly emerging culture, a culture of technology.

Post-industrial society

We are now moving from an industrial culture to an information-based culture. Today's information technologies have decreased the size of the workforce and created *multiskilled* people in new technology and information-based businesses, while *deskilling* others in traditional industries. Large numbers of people have had to learn new skills to work with the new technology.

The post-industrial revolution has increased profit for some businesses, while bankrupting others. Technology has both increased and decreased customer and client service. We can now access our bank details at any time on line, but we are actively discouraged from dealing directly with another human being over the counter at a bank.

According to the American cultural critic Neil Postman, modern society now worships technology in the same way that the ancients worshipped and sacrificed to various gods. Whereas technology once existed to serve humanity, everyone is now a servant of technology, says Postman. All societies throughout history have used tools. Our society has allowed the tools to take over, he says. Postman calls this new condition *technopoly* – the monopoly of technology!

Technology does not necessarily bring an improvement in everyone's lives. Australian intellectual Barry Jones says: 'For every technological change, the corresponding gain or loss to the quality of life depends on how that technological change is used.'

The current period of rapid change has been termed the *post-industrial revolution*. The last time technology so drastically changed work practices was during the Industrial Revolution (1780–1850). The Industrial Revolution transformed agricultural societies into manufacturing societies. Production became mechanised and cheap; mass-produced goods became widely available. However, the mechanisation of production also led to the devaluing of workers and a subsequent deskilling of traditional abilities. The incomes of working people fell considerably. Many companies treated their workers no better than the machinery on which they worked. In the modern workplace, technology is again being seen as far more valuable than the worker who operates it. Companies invest vast sums of money on technology, while spending less on fewer employees.

The information superhighway

Today, computers are now the basis for vastly expanded entertainment and communications options. The new communication and entertainment device has been termed the *information superhighway* – a massive *datasphere* containing an unlimited amount of information in the form of text, images and sound.

The information superhighway is an interactive medium. The American technology writer George Gilder predicts that choice in the media will better the human race, encouraging self-improvement and reducing the occurrence of 'couch potatoes'. The information superhighway potentially allows such a diverse range of information that it targets niche markets in the same way that magazines do. In contrast, television, radio and, to a lesser extent, newspapers target mass audiences with simple and predictable content. Gilder predicts that the information superhighway will reduce the media's creation of 'lowest common denominator' messages. The new ways of getting information and entertainment will enhance individualism, promoting creativity over passivity.

This new media form is more persuasive than traditional mass media in that it affects not only our entertainment habits, and the way we gather information and form opinions, but also the way in which we live. It is changing everything from the way we work, the way we shop, the way we are entertained and the way we view our culture to the way we are educated and schooled.

Convergence and divergence

Two terms used to describe the impact of the new communications media are *convergence* and *divergence*.

CONVERGENCE The blurring of the boundaries between different telecommunications media is termed *convergence*. The boundary between the television and the computer is already blurring. So, too, is the boundary between the newspaper and the computer. More and more, the computer is becoming the basis of all communication.

Telephone systems, television, radio and newspapers are all converging into a digital domain, where all communication needs are predicted to be delivered door to door through fibre-optic cables or to wireless devices carried with the user. Multimedia represents the convergence of text, pictures, video and sound into a single form. In the same way, the information superhighway is the convergence of television, radio, newspapers, video telephony and telephone services into a single form.

DIVERGENCE The multiplying of the forms of delivery of a media product is called *divergence*. For example, television may be delivered free-to-air, by cable, by satellite and, according to futurologists, via the Internet eventually to handheld devices and ordinary household appliances. All of which will be connected to the same information *datasphere*.

The democratisation of information

But thank God I live in a time when there are entire cable channels dedicated to houseplants, when I can download Serbian protest music composed while B-52s drop my tax dollars on the artists from 40,000 feet, when I can pull up news wires from my bedroom or flip through a magazine for re-marrying brides. Any world without handy Internet resources for Brazilian fingernail fetishists is not a world I want to live in.'

James Poniewozik,
Salon magazine

▼ ▼ ▼

The unprecedented amount of information that can be transferred through fibre-optic cables has allowed for greater volumes of communication, greater user input, more diverse media forms and

Who's Watching The Babysitter?

This Covert Video Clock Cam Will!
Full Line Catalog

Figure 2.7
An advertisement for parents worried about what the baby-sitter gets up to when they are not there. New technology has led to the spread of video cameras throughout society, but has it also led to the creation of a sur-veillance culture?

the expression of a greater degree of opinion and ideas. This has been termed the *democratisation of information*. This means that ordinary people can now take part in the media. People can select individualised programming. They can also create their own programming for others.

Cheaper video technology has meant the general public can create its own programming. Today, the chances are that a camcorder will be there first at the scene of a news event, rather than a professional news crew. Newsrooms scramble to buy dramatic footage from amateurs to increase their ratings. At the same time, the price reductions in video technology have also led to the miniaturisation of cameras, allowing for easier surveillance.

This miniaturisation of cameras has created a whole new genre of voyeuristic 'real-life' enter-tainment. People have been left alone on deserted islands (except for the camera operators) to fend for themselves; they have been locked in houses filled with tiny hidden cameras, which expose every move of the inhabitants to millions of television viewers; some broadcast their most intimate daily routines to hundreds or thousands of Internet users. All seem to satisfy previously hidden voyeuristic audience desires.

Political and environmental groups have also started using the cheaper video technology to document police and armed forces brutality, injustice, pollution and environmental destruction. DIVA, the 'Damned Interfering Video Activists', say the battle is now fought with images in the new *datasphere* and that pictures will become more important than the pen and the sword. Douglas Rushkoff proposes the following scene:

Imagine yourself in the middle of a riot. But, instead of clubs and shields, the police hold camcorders. The crowd they attempt to subdue is also filled with people holding camcorders. Meanwhile, CNN covers the dueling media with cameras of their own, which broadcast their own images over satellites to the rest of the world. Bats, shields and rocks might be tools of the past.

The Internet provides the best opportunity yet for personal expression in the public media. Multimedia presentations tell of average people's experiences and opinions, possibly to millions of viewers. The individual now has the apparent ability to become a 'media giant', in the sense of being able to reach the same potential audience as the established mass media corporations.

The only downside to this, of course, is that so does every other individual with the equipment: in the competing millions of websites, how does anybody know to which one to turn?

The commercial viability of new media has increased as more people gain access to it. As a consequence, mass media corporations are starting to exert a degree of control over what is presented on the 'popular' Internet by transferring the information and entertainment from their traditional media forms such as television and magazines into an on-line format. Because consumers are familiar with their products, their sites become the most popular places to visit on the Internet. While any voice can be heard on the Internet, it is hard for small sites to 'shout' over the top of the content saturation of popular sites, many of which are backed by large corporations who advertise their products to the mass market.

Moore's Law

Charles Moore, the founder of microchip company Intel, once predicted that every eighteen months, the power of the computer will double, for roughly the same cost. This came to be known in the industry as Moore's Law. Moore made this comment in 1965: if anything, the pace of change has accelerated.

Today, computer power doubles more like every *year*. The speed at which technology progresses improves affordability; but it also ensures that expensive new equipment becomes devalued very quickly. Analysts say, within a span of seven years, any computer function will drop to 1 per cent of

its current price, or grow 100 times in power. Dr Doug Kalish, head of Price Waterhouse, compares computers to cars: 'The Cadillac today, if it had twenty years of the same efficiency, would be getting 500,000 miles to the gallon and would cost $2.50 – and you'd fit seven onto the head of a pin.'

Experts have predicted that computer technology will reach 'human' levels of intelligence, or sixty trillion instructions per second, within the next thirty to fifty years. Sony's Playstation II, for example, is currently capable of just five million instructions per second. *Star Wars* creator George Lucas joked that next year's kids will have more computer power than last year's *Star Wars* animators.

New technologies, however, create new problems. Governments around the world are grappling with new issues of censorship and representation.

Ownership of information – information-rich and information-poor

After a recent purchasing spree, Bill Gates, the founder of Microsoft, now owns the digital rights to many of the world's greatest artworks. Every time a digital image of a piece of artwork is used, Bill Gates receives a royalty. This may be despite the actual work being hundreds of years old and perhaps owned by a European art gallery.

INFORMATION-RICH Those who own digital information, those with the money to purchase information and those with the technical skill to access it are termed the *information-rich*. Access also depends on whether people are situated near telephone lines, Internet access providers and optical fibre cables. It is the information-rich who benefit from the changes to a post-industrial society.

INFORMATION-POOR Whole groups in the population could become *information-poor*. The information-poor are those who do not have the advantages that provide easy access to digital information. William Gibson, author of the classic 'cyberpunk' novel *Necromancer*, says the future is already here. It is just that it is unevenly distributed – among those who have the technology. Maria Fernandez, assistant professor at the University of Pittsburgh, states that 'discussion about the Internet and information technologies totally disregards the people of Third World Countries, many of whom don't even have phone lines'.

Privacy

Show me someone who has no financial, sexual, social, political or professional secrets to keep from his family, neighbours or colleagues, and I'll show you someone who is either an exhibitionist or a dullard. Show me a corporation that has no trade secrets or confidential records, and I'll show you a business that isn't very successful. Discretion and tact are pillars of civilisation.

André Bacard
The Computer Privacy Handbook

▼ ▼ ▼

Privacy is the ability to control what, when and how your personal details are provided to other people or organisations. Computers make the control of information more difficult and the transmission, compilation and storage of vast amounts of personal data and statistics far easier.

Computers allow sophisticated data and cross-referencing searches, designed to extract the maximum amount of useful information on any topic from the maximum amount of unsorted data. Computers have the ability to store more information than we have ever encountered before; they can compile data from many sources, building up a detailed personal profile of us all.

Figure 2.8
Anyone with a computer, a phone line, mobile phone or cable access, and an Internet account can search the world for information and entertainment. The variety of information available is so vast as to defy description.

Computers can easily store an individual's credit card and bank transactions, court records, medical records, shopping history and personal details, e-mail correspondence, phone numbers, phone records, taxation records and so on.

Information can be accessed by governments, individuals with authorisation, those who pay for commercial access and criminal elements stealing information. In the information age, personal information becomes commercial data, bought and sold for profit by marketeers, businesses and governments. The future of marketing lies in individualised promotion targeted to each of us based on our personal information contained within databases.

▼ ▼ ▼ ▼ ▼ ▼ ▼

activities

1. Research the Industrial Revolution and report on its effects. Compare these to the effects of the current period of technological change some term 'the post-industrial revolution'.

2. List any examples of technological convergence or divergence you can think of. Research recent developments in these examples using a news-clipping database or similar on-line news resources.

3. In groups, compare the following procedures.
▶ One group type in a paragraph or two of text into a word-processing program, while another group types in a paragraph of text on a

typewriter. Spellcheck the document and correct any mistakes.
▶ Another two groups can work on centring a heading. One group should centre a heading on a manual typewriter, while the other should centre a heading on a computer.
At the conclusion of the experiment, discuss how the computer simplified the process of typing in information. What implication do you believe that this has for the workforce?

4. Think about the way in which you enter text into a computer and the way in which you write on paper. Are you as careful with what you put down when you are typing, or do you structure

and check spelling as well as when you write on paper? Has the computer improved your writing skills? Look at the following points when you construct your answer: efficiency of your writing (length versus content and substance), spelling, planning and grammatical precision.

5. Commentators say that the Internet has democratised information. Use the Internet to visit the home pages of a number of ordinary people, such as other students from around the world. List the kinds of information the home pages present. Evaluate the extent to which the other media can offer such variety.

6. Do you agree with the comment that the 'popular' Internet is owned by the same companies that run traditional media forms? Analyse the sites that you have visited over the past month and calculate roughly what percentage of these are owned by traditional media companies (check the bottom of the home page for details) and which are owned by non-media interests such as individuals, small business and small organisations.

▼ ▼ ▼

The flood of instant information in the world today – at least in the Western industrialised world – sometimes seems not to further, but to retard, education; not to excite, but to dampen, curiosity; not to enlighten, but merely to dismay.

William Shawcross

▼ ▼ ▼

Do you agree or disagree with this comment? Explain your answer and back it up with actual examples of how technologies have either helped or hindered you.

major assignment

Written assignment

Select one of the following topics and prepare a 600-word response.

1. Research the introduction of any new communications technology that has had a significant effect on the existing systems. List the positive and negative changes the new technology has caused. Evaluate the overall benefit. Some suggestions are listed below.

▶ The introduction of sound in movies and the subsequent effect on the silent film industry.

▶ The introduction of electronic news gathering in the early 1980s and its effect on news routines (including deadlines).

▶ The introduction of word processors to the newspaper industry in the early 1980s and its effect on employment in the printing industry.

2. Investigate the movie industry's increasing use of computer-generated special effects. Give a brief history of their use and outline any new developments in the field. Discuss whether special effects creation represents an example of convergence. Evaluate the effect of computer-generated images on the storytelling potential of movies. Conclude with some examples of your favourite effects.

The Internet: The Medium

Sooner or later *everyone* with a computer will be hooked up to the Internet.

Geoff Huston
Internet Society

▼ ▼ ▼

The Internet may be the most 'hyped' communication medium ever to be developed. It has generated more publicity, predictions and controversy than any other mass media. Commentators predict it will be the most influential communication development since Gutenberg developed the printing press in 1450.

The growth of the Internet has taken everyone by surprise. Telephone companies have found their systems straining under the pressure of so many users. Governments have not yet been able to implement any effective regulation or censorship. The business sector has not been able to capitalise and control it through ownership, as they have with other media forms.

The Internet has grown from having very few academic users in the early 1990s to predictions it will top 230 million users at the start of the twenty-first century. A Cyveillance study in mid-2000 showed that the Internet consists of 2.3 billion unique public accessible pages and that five to seven million more pages are being created daily. At this rate, the Internet will double in size every year or two.

Welcome to cyberspace

For more than a century after Alexander Graham Bell invented the telephone, it was thought of it as little more than an instrument for two-way voice communication. Its capacity was measured in how many telephone calls it could handle at once. The telephone system is now measured by how many thousands of millions of gigabytes or 'terabytes' of information can be transferred at any one time. This includes voice transmissions, as well as text, pictures, video and audio information.

More than 50 per cent of the material travelling through telephone lines in the United States is data, according to technology writer

George Gilder. The American organisation once charged with running the Internet, UUNet, has predicted that, in 2002, 90 per cent of all available bandwidth on international telecommunications networks will be Internet-based, peaking at 98 per cent by 2008.

The space taken up on the telephone lines by Internet data has been termed *cyberspace* by science fiction writer William Gibson. The term has now been adapted to represent the Internet as a whole.

The development of the Internet

The Internet had its origins in a 1969 US Department of Defense computer network that allowed military contractors and universities doing military research to exchange information. It was

Figures 2.9 and 2.10
The information superhighway is predicted to work on a user pays basis. Those who can gain access are predicted to become the information-rich. Without skills or unable to afford access the disadvantaged may become the information-poor.

constructed in a *decentralised* manner. This meant there was no central computer in control of the network, but instead all the connected terminals contributed to its overall power. In the event of a military attack taking out part of the network, this decentralisation would allow the rest of the network to function.

In the 1980s, the American National Science Foundation added another network, the Computer Science Research Network, to the global system. This system gave researchers remote access to costly supercomputers housed at large US universities. Each one of the universities then added their own networks to the system, increasing its power.

In the early 1990s, commercial interests were allowed onto the network by the universities and academic organisations. This opened the Internet to the general public. The Internet now runs on networks run by major telecommunication, Internet, computer and media companies, as well as the academic networks. No one organisation in any one country has control, but every server shares access and links to millions of other networks across the world.

How the Internet communicates

The Internet is accessed through an *Internet service provider* (ISP). Subscribers buy access to the Internet through the ISP's *gateway*. This gateway is usually an optical fibre cable linked to the inter-continental telephone and data cables.

The Internet relies on both local and international content and is sent in digital form as tiny *packets* of information. Any text, image, video or audio signal is broken up into small pieces and transmitted one by one from one machine to another, where it is reassembled. Each packet is indistinguishable from another and represents only a tiny part of the information being sent.

The many-to-many medium

The Internet is the first mass media form to allow individual users to select the content they wish to view. It also allows each user to interact with other users. These features have led some analysts to contrast the Internet with the traditional media. Whereas radio and television offer a small number of organisations that broadcast to millions, the Internet has millions of individual people communicating to other millions. Some of this communication takes the form of one-to-one communication, or one-to-several, in chat rooms for instance. However, analysts also describe the Internet as a *many-to-many* medium: millions of individuals create their own websites, hoping to attract the interest of many other Internet users.

The prohibitive entry costs of traditional broadcasting (studios, equipment, transmitters, etc.) are sidestepped with the new technology.

Figure 2.11
The Internet communicates by sending tiny 'packets' of information from one machine to another. Each packet is virtually indistinguishable from its neigh-bours. It is identified only by two elements. The first is the 'header', which contains the delivery destination and sender's addresses. The second is the packet, numbered so that the computer can put everything back together again. Because the packets do not all travel along the same path, monitoring the content entering the country is almost impossible.

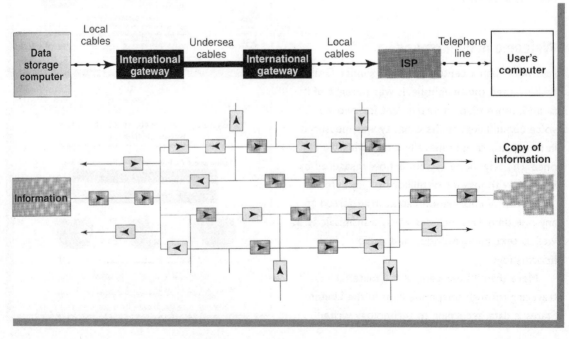

Anyone with a web camera, a computer and a telephone line can turn their home – or bedroom, in some cases! – into a broadcasting centre.

There are two main ways to use the Internet.

■ **As a viewer**

The users explore the Internet, visiting *sites* containing information that interests them. They can use the service much like an interactive newspaper or book. A *site* on the Internet may contain text, images, video, audio and interactive art or games.

■ **As a broadcaster**

The users build their own Internet sites, filling the sites with information they wish to share with others around the world. A user's Internet site is known as a *home page*. The home page is held on the provider's computer. Interactive group discussion through *chat* networks can also allow the users to broadcast their opinions or knowledge to a wide variety of people anywhere in the world.

A completely different media form

American technology writer George Gilder sums up the existing mass media forms such as television as doing little more than 'squeezing the collective consciousness of a country down a few channels'. The diversity of users contributing to the Internet has changed this situation. No other form of mass media has allowed such widespread participation before. Spoken word performer, and ex-Dead Kennedy's member, Jello Biafra now tells his audiences: 'Don't hate the media. Become the media.'

'The impact of giving virtually everyone access to virtually everything will affect society like almost no other form of communication before it', says the electronic pioneer Vern Raburn.

George Gilder has compared the Internet to a car. A car can go down any road you drive it, whether you are allowed there or not, where as the traditional media are like trains, only using a single track and leaving at specific times.

The purposes of the Internet

Today, hundreds of millions of people will use the worldwide computer network known as the *Internet* to communicate with others, to do business,

to complete research, to play games, to watch videos, to view pictures, to do banking, to buy goods, to listen to music and to be educated. Anyone with a computer, an Internet access account and a telephone line, cable access or mobile phone can search the world for information and entertainment.

FULFILLING INFORMATION NEEDS The variety of information available on the Internet is so vast as to defy description. The types of information being distributed on the Internet range from personal opinions, discussions on a wide range of topics, corporate information, and educational, entertainment, and cultural materials.

Surveys have found that the most popular services and sites on the Internet are the directory services, used to locate information on the web. The most popular of these 'yellow pages' type services are Yahoo, AltaVista and Lycos.

PROVIDING A GLOBAL MEETING PLACE The Internet provides the opportunity for cultural exchanges and friendships on a global scale. Everyday people from almost every nation in the world exchange e-mail, 'chat' on talk networks such as ICQ (I seek you), and exchange messages on global bulletin boards.

MEETING A NEED FOR ENTERTAINMENT Surveys have found the primary use of the Internet to be for entertainment and hobbies. A secondary use of the Internet is e-mail related to entertainment purposes.

PROVIDING AN UP-TO-DATE NEWS AND INFORMATION SERVICE The Internet is seen as the world's largest library, providing the latest news from the worlds major news services, as well as links to almost every piece of research, data and information held on every library, educational or university computer system.

ALLOWING INDIVIDUALS TO BECOME CONTENT PROVIDERS The Internet has been termed a *democratic* media, because it allows all of its users to both access and provide information at a personal level. Any user can establish their own *home page*, which can contain any information they desire. As a consequence, it has become a

common lament that '90% of everything [on the Internet] is garbage!'

FULFILLING COMMERCIAL NEEDS Surveys have found that 30 per cent of users have bought materials over the Internet. This is predicted to rise to 38 per cent by the middle of this decade. The most purchased items are music, books, software, magazines and subscriptions. Most of these are inexpensive purchases of between £15 and £30. Many corporations also use the Internet to advertise their products and build brand identity, as well as offering information, services, help and feedback to their customers. The most common commercial use of the Internet by consumers is to research products before they purchase them.

FULFILLING EMOTIONAL NEEDS The Internet has attracted quite a reputation as a meeting place, and many people have met their matches online. The Internet also acts in a more subtle way to fulfil emotional needs. Users can now travel the world and converse with people from all over the world without leaving their chair. For those unable to travel, such as the disabled, it acts as a means to lead an active social life. There have even been reports of 'addiction', and many psychologists offer Internet addiction therapy!

▼ ▼ ▼ ▼ ▼ ▼ ▼

activities

1. If you are an Internet user, or in groups with Internet users, discuss your most commonly used Internet services or the information you access the most. Would you categorise your use of the Internet as being for entertainment, educational or as research purposes?

2. Compare the way in which information is presented in conventional media forms such as newspapers, books and magazines to the way in which it is presented on the Internet. What are the similarities and what are the differences between the two?

3. Organise a class debate on the topic that the Internet will take over from television as the most influential media form.

4. Keep a user's log of the main purposes you have put the Internet to over the past two weeks. Which uses have you tended to favour? Compare your consumption pattern with that of other students.

Structure of Internet Communication

There are several different ways in which the Internet can be used to access data. The most common and popular of these is the World Wide Web (WWW). Many people mistakenly believe the World Wide Web *is* the Internet, but there are a number of other ways of using the Internet, including e-mail, FTP, IRC and Usenet.

World Wide Web (WWW)

The World Wide Web is the most popular of all the Internet applications. It is the driving force behind the popularity of the Net. The World Wide Web is termed the *graphical interface* of the web.

This means that it allows for interaction with text, pictures and animations in a magazine-style format. Websites often include music and video, as well as interactive games and activities. Many sites on the World Wide Web are now entirely animated, mimicking the style of television and computer games.

This Internet application has become so popular that the whole Internet is now nicknamed 'The Web'. This name is derived from the way in which information on the World Wide Web is linked together. The amount of information on the Internet makes it the largest library in the world, spanning all countries and continents.

Figures 2.12 and 2.13
The style of an Internet home page differs depending on its purpose and its owner. Some sites, particularly users' pages, tend to be very informal, while others, normally those of large businesses, are conservative and businesslike.

Hypertext

Wading through the almost infinite amount of data on the World Wide Web is simplified through use of *hypertext*. Hypertext linking is used to join information on many different sites in different countries in a 'web-like' style, allowing almost instantaneous access to related data from anywhere in the world. Hypertext links are in two forms: highlighted words and images or 'hotstpots'.

HIGHLIGHTED WORDS Hypertext links can appear as highlighted or underlined words or sentences describing something, somebody, or a subject title. By 'clicking' on the highlighted word, users are transferred to another site or another page with information about the highlighted topic. Imagine that while reading this paragraph you feel you would like to know more about hypertext. By clicking on a highlighted word, *'hypertext'*, you would instantly be given a new chapter on hypertext, opened to the page with the information you would like to see.

IMAGES OR 'HOTSPOTS' Hypertext links can also appear as images or icons. These can range from simple buttons or arrows, to large menu pictures. For example, imagine a medical page with a menu picture of the human body. Depending on what part of the body you clicked, you could access the related topics.

The World Wide Web consists of tens of thousands of Internet sites, linked together in a dynamic hypertextual form, allowing the viewer to navigate paths through the data. While this is a

very effective way to find information, it is still possible to get trapped in the maze of information or to be misguided. It is easy to spend too much time following links, only to lose sight of the original information. *Bookmarking* your current page before following a link is a good idea so that you can easily find your way back.

Website addresses

Each Internet site has its own unique address. A typical WWW site address reads:

▼ ▼ ▼

http://www.company-name.co.uk/first-page.html

▼ ▼ ▼

Each address starts with http://. This stands for *hypertext transfer protocol*. This instructs the users *browser* how to negotiate the transfer of information from the *server* computer on which it is stored to the user's machine. The next part of the address, 'www', stands for the World Wide Web, while 'company-name' represents the computer on which the information is stored. All web addresses are actually composed of numbers, similar to telephone numbers. When a user types in a name-based address, the request is sent to one of the thousands of *name server* computers around the world. These machines match the name-based address with its number-based equivalent.

The abbreviation '.co' or '.com' states that this is a commercial site, while 'first-page.html' represents the page of information you are currently viewing. The '.html' stands for the computer language the page is programmed in – *hypertext mark-up language*. Other types of pages now used

include the animated '.swf', or Shockwave Flash, and the database-driven '.asp' programming language, which is created by a computer that draws information out of a database and builds a unique temporary page for each user's request.

The address above uses the '.co' or '.com' for commercial site status, but other abbreviations are often encountered. These can include educational (.edu), organisation (.org), network (.net), or government (.gov). There are plans to extend these categories to more specific types as the number of unique names available run out.

The address highlighted above is from the United Kingdom. This is indicated by the 'uk' abbreviation in the address. With the exception of the United States, which has no commonly used country code, all Internet sites, World Wide Web and e-mail addresses have a country of origin code in the address.

SAMPLE COUNTRY CODES FOR INTERNET ADDRESSES

uk-United Kingdom	fr-France	it-Italy
de-Germany	nl-Netherlands	au-Australia
jp-Japan	nz-New Zealand	ch-China
hk-Hong Kong	ca-Canada	fi-Finland
ee-Estonia	se-Sweden	no-Norway
za-South Africa	gr-Greece	pl-Poland

Figure 2.14
This search is looking for the phrase 'media ownership', accompanied by the word 'newspaper', but excluding the word 'television', on a UK-based server. This kind of specialised search helps locate specific information more quickly. When you enter a single key-word or a phrase, a search engine will search its data banks for matching informa-tion and provide you with the title and description of any matching site. The search engine provides a hypertext link to each listed site.

Search engines

The main way in which information is found on the World Wide Web, is through directory services, known as *search engines*. The organisations that operate search engines use super computers to scan Internet sites for keywords and phrases that they store on massive databases. There are many different types of searches available, and they are run by a variety of companies and universities.

Users type in a key word/s or phrase, and a computer on the other side of the world will search its databanks to give a list of sites that may contain the relevant information. There are many techniques that skilled users can utilise to make searching more effective. The use of multiple key words in combination with expressions such as

inverted commas around phrases, and plus and minus signs for including and excluding key words, helps make any search more specific. Most search engines have help pages that give examples on how to best search their databases.

Any user's home page or site can be registered with these search engines, although regular re-registration and updating is required if a site is to be continually easy to find. Most commercial sites pay specialist companies to maintain their top ranking on search engines. This is very important, as studies have found that most users give up after viewing the top thirty matches for any one search.

The sheer number of pages on the Internet makes it very difficult to find the best information available on any home page. With more than 2.3 billion unique pages available, and five to seven million more being added each day, search engines cannot possibly catalogue the entire Internet. Studies have shown that search engines can take up to six months to find a new site and that at least one in every twenty sites linked to by search engines no longer exists.

To further add to the problem of finding information on the Internet, a vast amount of information is now held in databases and not on unique, static pages accessible to most search engines. One study predicts that the Internet is 500 times larger than search engines now show.

E-mail

E-mail is reincarnating the age of letter writing. We're keeping in touch the way the Victorians did, building a personal community connected by a constant stream of letters sharing news and gossip. E-mail is reviving the 'letter' as a forum for wit, style, and personality, as well as serving as an invaluable business tool.

Leslie Schroedor
Silicon Valley PR consultant

▼ ▼ ▼

Electronic mail, known as *e-mail*, allows users to send and almost instantaneously receive messages from any other user in the world. An e-mail

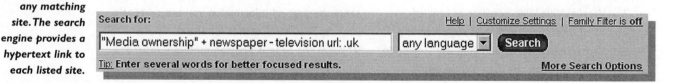

message may also include 'attached' files such as pictures and documents. Each user on the Internet has a unique e-mail address. It is made up of a 'username', the name and type of the Internet provider, and the country code.

A typical UK e-mail address reads:

▼ ▼ ▼

username@providername.co.uk

▼ ▼ ▼

E-mail has become an invaluable business and personal communication form, allowing vast amounts of information, such as whole books, to be inexpensively transferred across the world in a matter of seconds.

E-mail also allows the user to subscribe to on-line discussion groups or newsletters (listservs). Every time someone 'posts' a message to a group, it is automatically sent to the e-mail addresses of all other subscribers. There are thousands of these groups to which a user can subscribe, on any topic imaginable. Subscribing to more than a few groups, however, can mean being inundated with hundreds or thousands of new messages each day.

Many on-line discussion groups are moderated. This means that they have an editor who reads all the messages received and only posts relevant or interesting ones.

Encryption

Since e-mail messages are broadcast across public networks, security becomes a problem for confidential, financial or private messages. The use of encryption software to code the message is a common way of ensuring an e-mail cannot be read by anyone else.

Encryption is based on a simple mathematical equation that scrambles letters or characters into a code. The code is a personalised one based on each user's mathematical 'key'.

It is against the law in the United States to transfer any program that contains high-level encryption abilities outside the United States. This is easily circumvented, as anyone can download these programs from US servers.

The United States and China classify encryption software as a weapon which could breach national security. David A. Lytel from the President's Office of Science and Technology Policy says: 'Cryptography is an enormously powerful tool that needs to be

controlled, just as we control bombs and rockets.' The encryption software PGP is very hard to crack. If a microchip was developed that could try a billion keys (passwords) a second and a billion chips were used to crack the code, it would take ten billion years to try all possible keys.

Encryption is very important for commerce on the net, allowing users to send credit card numbers safely through e-mail or via the World Wide Web. Brad Templeton of ClariNet says when cryptography is outlawed, 'bayl bhgynjf jvyy unir cevinpl!' (a basic ROT13 encrypted version of 'only the outlaws will have privacy!').

FTP

File Transfer Protocol (FTP) sites are places on the net that allow users to both post or 'upload' files, or to download files already on the system. FTP sites usually contain information such as documents, pictures, theses, archives or, most commonly, software.

Most of the software used to access the Internet is free, and FTP sites provide an outlet for its distribution. For example, the Netscape Navigator program can be downloaded from an FTP site. Most FTP sites these days are accessed through a World Wide Web front page that links to the FTP site. All websites are uploaded to the Internet via FTP.

Some FTP sites are for private usage, and require a password to enter. However, most FTP sites are accessed through an anonymous login, allowing users to upload whatever they please. This can lead to potential legal violations.

Usenet

Usenet is a system of public access bulletin boards. There are almost 100,000 different news-groups available, covering almost any interest area, and in many languages. Thousands of these groups are rarely, if ever, used.

Usenet is like a giant global e-mail exchange, with users posting messages to specific news-groups, where they can be read by any other user. These users can then reply to messages already posted or add others of their own.

Usenet is one of the earliest applications developed for the Internet, created in 1979, and brought to its current form with a major update in 1986. Not all providers offer all of the newsgroups, with many censoring controversial drug, crime and sex-related groups.

There are two different types of messages on Usenet.

TEXT Most newsgroups are designed for the posting of text based messages. A posting to a newsgroup is known as an 'article', with hundreds of thousands of new articles posted every day to all the newsgroups.

BINARIES Newsgroups identified by the words 'binaries' or 'pictures' are for the posting of software or images. Images in newsgroups are not seen, but need to be decoded from a textual form and usually viewed in another program.

Categories of Usenet newsgroups

The topic of the each newsgroup is identified by its name or title. There are many different categories of topics on Usenet. The most common is the 'alt', or alternate group. This group was invented when the operators of the large moderated groups would not allow certain content on their newsgroups.

The 'alt' or alternate group is a large, mostly unmonitored list of very diverse topics and discussions. Other newsgroup topics include 'biz' (business), 'rec' (recreational), 'misc' (miscellaneous), 'uk' (UK content), or 'comp' (computer).

These newsgroups are often moderated, edited or censored.

ICQ, IRC and chatrooms

ICQ ('I seek you'), Internet relay chat (IRC) and chatrooms are the ways Internet users communicate in real time. For most people, this is achieved in discussion or social groups using the keyboard to type their conversations. As with the Usenet system of bulletin boards, there are many topics on which to talk. Topics are starting up and closing down all the time. The number of people using each topic or 'channel' can range from two, through to more than one hundred. Each user is known by his or her chosen nickname, codename or 'alias'.

ICQ and chatrooms are seen as the meeting place of the Internet. They are the only places where users can react in real time. ICQ and chatroom conversations have led to a number of on-line romances and even marriages! Internet magazine writer Stuart Ridley describes this form of communication as 'best able, of all the Internet avenues, to give you a real feeling of global community'.

It is possible to have either public or private conversations on ICQ and IRC. ICQ and IRC are also used to swap documents, images, programs or music with other users of similar interests.

Chatrooms are topic based in a way that is similar to ICQ and IRC, but they are run by organisations, companies or individuals. Chatrooms are often moderated and sometimes only available to subscribers.

Figure 2.15
Each topic includes a list of articles, the sender's name (not necessarily his or her real name), the article size, its posting date, and a title. By clicking on the title, it will download in 'binary' (text) form to the user's computer where it has to be decoded.

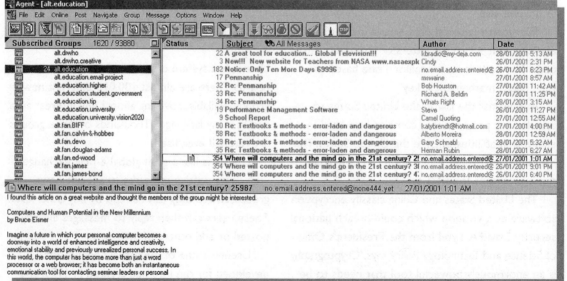

---

activities

1. Assign different groups in the class to find a particular piece of information using each of the above Internet mediums. Which were the most successful methods and why? Take into account the subject used, perhaps trying some others as well. Have a group or class discussion on the most effective way to find information on the Internet. Compile a class list of methods.

2. Choose a popular newsgroup and follow all of the postings to a thread (a series of articles on the same subject, usually denoted by the prefix re: in the title). Comment on the number of postings to each thread, the conventions used (e.g. the way that the original message is quoted), the tone of the replies and postings, and the country of origin of the each author.

3. Type in a popular or current keyword in a search engine and follow a number of the successful 'hits' or matches. Where does most of the information originate from (see the country code on the address – some examples are given on p. 74). Is it balanced or is it all from the one country? Try the same thing on a newsgroup search engine.

4. Research better ways to use search engines to find specific information quickly by using advanced search options such as the ones used in figure 2.14 (p. 74).

Visit several major search engines and document their advanced search techniques. Are there similar methods that can be used across most of the search engines?

Audiences

Technology writer George Gilder has compared the audience for the Internet to the audience for magazines. He says there are thousands of magazines and journals, each targeting a specific audience. Compare this to the television, radio and newspaper industries, where mass audiences with varying tastes are catered for by very few channels. As the popularity of the Internet rises and it becomes increasingly difficult to find information, people are turning to familiar websites linked to existing mass media companies and their television, news and magazine websites.

The Internet provides a more diverse source of information than any media ever has before, targeting specific interest areas. MTV animator and video artist Jon Sanborn predicts there will not be a multiple channel future, but a single channel future – the 'you' channel, programmed exclusively by each audience member. Bruce Sterling, author of *The Hacker Crackdown*, claims that the Internet is already a personalised medium. He states that 'everybody has a different Internet'.

Who uses the Internet?

Information is a commodity, and not all of the UK population can afford it in the Internet age. Those with money have it, while those who do not probably never will, and so the technology divide widens.

Will Knight, discussing an
Office of National Statistics survey,
ZD Net UK

▼ ▼ ▼

Contrary to the teenage hacker stereotypes, surveys show the average age of Internet users is between twenty and forty-four. While the heaviest users of the Internet are professional men, the number of regular women and younger users on the Internet is increasing. Surveys have now shown that the ratio between men and women has equalised, although men are still spending more time on-line. The average Internet user spends 11.2 hours on line each month. Studies have shown that Internet users are now spending less time watching television, making phone calls and sleeping.

The average users are also wealthier than the national average, with a monthly income exceeding £900. More than 50 per cent of households in this income range are connected to the Internet. 66 per cent of users have accessed the Internet from their workplace and a high proportion of them have tertiary qualifications.

The Internet is concentrated in the homes of white, upper income families says US Commerce Secretary William Daley. 'There is a widening gap in computer ownership between those at upper- and lower-income levels and in between urban and rural areas.' Internet usage among those in the poorest third of the UK population has only risen at 3 per cent a year, while usage rates in upper income brackets increases at a rapid pace. The Government is attempting to remedy the situation by providing public access points in schools and libraries.

With the publicity surrounding the Internet, and the invaluable nature of the material found on-line, the audience is increasing at a rapid pace, and is becoming more diverse.

What are the effects?

Even if our kids aren't playing blood-soaked computer games or plotting violence in the dark crannies of an on-line chat room, they are plunging into a whole world of influences and values and enticements that is, most of the time, hidden from our view.

Daniel Okrent
Time magazine

▼ ▼ ▼

The Internet has caused a great deal of controversy over the alleged amount and availability of violent and pornographic materials available, as well as illegal materials such as bomb recipes and crime manuals. Unlike the other media forms, the concern is not based solely on the materials that can be found on-line, but also on the availability of these materials to underage users.

The media have popularised the concept that the Internet is filled with dangerous information

that could persuade people to act in violent and irrational ways. Even though violent crime rates have been falling, especially in the United States, quotes such as the one above lead to public confusion. After one recent teenage shooting spree in the United States, 82 per cent of 660 people surveyed believed the Internet was to blame in some way for the shootings.

Jonathon Wallace, author of *Sex, Laws and Cyberspace* and the *Ethical Spectacle*, is disappointed with the media's portrayal of the Internet. 'Although there are more of them than there used to be, journalists who really understand the Net are still at a premium – and there are too many scare stories out there based on a laughable misunderstanding of the technology and its consequences.'

Others are concerned by the rise of gambling on the Internet. While most legitimate sites require written proof of age, many smaller private operators are more than willing to accept bets from anonymous users who could be underage, or dialling from countries where gambling is illegal.

Some child psychologists are warning that the cult of the Internet is driving kids on to computers too early. Instead of helping advance children's knowledge, the computers are reducing attention spans and hampering language skills. Jane Healy, an educational psychologist from Colorado, says 'they are not talking or expressing themselves. From a computer it's coming at them in a series of stimuli formulated to make them respond quickly.'

INTERNET ADDICTION

A survey of 17,000 users on the ABC news website in the United States concluded that up to 6 per cent of users are 'addicted' to the Internet. The survey concluded that feelings of intimacy, timelessness and lack of inhibition contributed to the 'addictive force' of the Internet. Others are less certain. Journalist Dave Amis wrote in *Internet Freedom News* that 'so-called Internet addiction is in reality a conscious choice to spend a lot of time engaged in on-line activities such as chatrooms. By labelling these activities as an addictive behaviour, it implies that people cannot make rational choices about how they use the Internet'.

▼ ▼ ▼ ▼ ▼ ▼ ▼

activities

1. A study has shown there is little overlap between new pay-TV subscribers and Internet subscribers. What do you feel are the reasons why people subscribe to pay-TV? What are the reasons a different set of people chooses to subscribe to the Internet? What part does the media hype play in the Internet's popularity?

2. What do you think the author means by the following statement? Do you believe it is accurate?

▼ ▼ ▼

TV viewers use their machines to lull themselves into a stupor, while PC users use their machines to become smarter and more productive, better able to exploit further computer advances.'

George Gilder
Life after Television

▼ ▼ ▼

Based on your answer, discuss with the other members of your class what you believe to be the future of the media. Will it be interactive or passive? Is this what you want from the media and will it be to your advantage?

3. More and more corporate control is being exercised over information and services available on the Internet. Do you believe that the ensuing charges for services will hurt those without the ability to pay for access and afford the equipment to access it with?

It has been suggested that the government set up a public information service, acting in a similar way to the one in which the BBC operates for broadcast media. This would allow those who cannot afford to pay for information and services to be provided with the same kind of good, accurate, advertising-free and diverse information that the BBC offers television viewers. Do you believe this to be a good idea for governments?

What else do you believe that a government could do to provide equal access to everybody in society?

4. Discuss whether information found on the Internet could force people to act in violent or irrational ways. Do you think that the information on-line could encourage violence and hate, allow individuals to find validation for their personal violent or hateful beliefs? Or does it force discussion and contemplation about beliefs they hold, as there are so many diverse and opposing opinions voiced on the Internet?

Representation Issues

'The Web is the Great Equalizer' as one of my test users once said. Anybody can put up a site, and increasingly, anybody does. As a result, users don't quite know what to make of information retrieved from the Web. It can be the deep truth, or it can be the ramblings of a nut.

There is no easy way of telling whether a website is reliable. In the physical world, you typically know that certain sources like *The New York Times* are reliable, and you know that if you walk into a Toyota dealership, they will have the specifications of the latest Camry as released by Toyota headquarters.

Jakob Nielsen
Designing Web Usability

▼ ▼ ▼

'Truth', information and data

The traditional media have always regulated who is published and who is not. While this has restricted the diversity of opinion and information that is available, it has also ensured that the information is normally well researched, well structured, accurate and free from plagiarism.

In contrast, Internet providers do not filter the information on their systems in the same way that a publisher filters the content in the books that they publish. A lot of information is not checked for accuracy and not cleared for copyright. It has no guarantee of being well researched and may not be accurate at all. It could merely be someone's opinion.

Figure 2.16
This article can be used as a safe source of reliable information for several reasons: it is from a well-known newspaper, the journalist is listed (on the previous menu page) as being The Times business editor, the article has a clearly marked date, you can contact the author, the page has a copyright message, there is a link to the parent company and the advertising is separated and unrelated to the page content.

Technology commentator Clifford Stoll is critical of the Internet and those who are overly enthusiastic about its vast educational potential. 'The Internet is a perfect diversion from learning … [it] opens many doors that lead to empty rooms.' In his book *Silicon Snake Oil*, he writes that the Internet is sold to us as an information provider, when it actually provides data. 'Unlike data, information has utility, timeliness, accuracy, a pedigree … Editors serve as barometers of quality, and most of the editor's time is spent saying no.'

Internet authors and researchers have identified a number of factors that determine whether information presented on the Internet is accurate and trustworthy.

▶ Is it clear what organisation, company or person is responsible for putting the information on-line? For example: 'EFF is a non-profit, non-partisan organisation working in the public interest to protect fundamental civil liberties, including privacy and freedom of expression in the arena of computers and the Internet.'

▶ Is the author's name and qualifications for providing the information clearly stated (e.g. 'Angus Kidman is the editor of *APC Newswire* and deputy editor of *APC*. *DisGust* is published every Tuesday.')?

▶ Is there a way of contacting the author? This could include an e-mail address, phone number or mailing address. This demonstrates that the author is who they claim to be.

▶ Is there a way of verifying that the author is qualified to write on the subject matter? This would include some indication of their expertise in the subject matter such as membership of professional organisations or professional work and consulting experience. Have they written extensively on the subject matter before?

▶ Is the material on the page copyright and is the name of the copyright holder obvious? Is the date of publication obvious? This ensures that the information is current, and is similar to the publishing information found in the front of any book. Does the page have the official approval of the company, organisation or individual responsible for the site?

▶ Is there a direct link to the home page of the site responsible?

▶ Is there a list of references for the work that can be traced? An example would be a bibliography.

- Is the work free of spelling and grammatical errors?
- Is the page free from advertising? If the page has advertising, is it clearly differentiated from the content, and not related to it in any sponsorship style?

E-COMMERCE AND ON-LINE SHOPPING SITES

E-Commerce and on-line shopping sites that require personal financial and billing details strive to appear trustworthy. There are a number of identifying factors to determine whether it is safe to send credit card details to the site.

- Does the site explain what measures have been taken to ensure the safety of your transaction?
- If the company or individual is requesting information from a user is it clear how that information is going to be used? Many sites state that they will not distribute personal data or sell it for profit.
- Is the site's country of origin apparent? International regulation problems can be a problem with sites that are located in countries with less strict consumer and fraud laws. An address can help you determine whether the site is owned by an existing and reputable store or is simply run from someone's kitchen.
- Are there clear feedback and help mechanisms to help you if any problems arise with any purchased products or services?

PHOTOGRAPHIC FRAUD

Photographic fraud is also becoming increasingly common with the advent of advanced photo-editing programs. Images can be manipulated at high resolutions and either photographically printed, placed on the Internet or published.

Hate Sites

On-line hate is as much a part of the Web as e-commerce, porn sites, and portals. From neo-Nazis and skinheads to the Ku Klux Klan, almost every hate group in America has its own website.

Lakshmi Chaudhry
Wired magazine

▼ ▼ ▼

What is termed 'hate' literature represents a growing presence on the Internet, whether it be the Klu Klux Klan's home page, anti-Holocaust sites, or racist, sexist or homophobic postings to newsgroups. Studies have shown that there are more than 2000 hate sites on the Internet, from hardcore racist sites to joke pages with insensitive content.

The presence of hate sites on the Internet has been shown not to have increased membership of racist organisations. Jordan Kessler from the Anti-Defamation League says the Internet 'has been extremely bad for hate groups. They've been exposed, scrutinised, and poked at.' Hate groups have been traditionally secretive; exposing their propaganda on-line has left them open to public exposure and condemnation. Author Michael Jay Tucker maintains that, '… there is no poison on earth more potent, nor half so deadly, as a partial truth mixed with passion'.

Alan Dershowitz, however, has suggested a solution. 'The best answer to bad speech is good speech.' His proposition is strengthened by the many positive responses to hateful or other inaccurate information posted on-line. There are now numerous anti-hate websites on the Internet, such as the Anti-Defamation League, HateWatch and the Southern Poverty Law Centre.

Membership may not be the only measure of the influence of these organisations. Rabbi Abraham Cooper, an Associate Dean at the Simon Wiesenthal Center, is concerned that 'at risk' individuals could find validation for their hate on the web.

Women and the Internet

The Internet has inherited many values and characteristics of white male American Culture … the influences of its original male designers maintains a strong presence on the net despite the new generations of users.

Rosie Cross and Suzanne Fraser
Geek Girl Ezine

▼ ▼ ▼

Many researchers believe that the male-dominated history, and the large male user demographic of the Internet, acts to hinder female participation in the Internet. This is usually believed to occur through 'flaming' or written or verbal harassment,

the posting of unwanted sexual comments or images, and the difficulty of access for many women not working and therefore not supplied with free Internet access through workplaces.

Under-representation of females

The responsibility of new media use means that each individual should be helping to construct this new global cultural identity incorporating an ethic that does not summarily dismiss people due to sex, race, or whatever.

Rosie Cross,
Founder, *Geek Girl Ezine*

▼ ▼ ▼

The initial lack of female users and the technological base of the Internet contributed to making the Internet a very male domain, dominated by areas most frequently linked with male interests such as computers, technology, privacy and pornography. Over the past few years, the number of female users has rapidly increased. A recent Nielsen/Net Ratings survey showed that, in the United States, 49.5 per cent of Internet users are female. Cyberfeminist Minh McCloy believes that the Internet 'empowers females and presents opportunities for women to achieve individual development and competencies'.

The increase in female users on the Internet has changed the way many websites are marketing and presenting their sites as well as developing their content. It may still take a few years before website creators are targeting the female market as effectively as magazine publishers target theirs, having spent decades fine tuning their approach to marketing.

Sexual harassment

The Internet is seen by some as a new forum for sexual harassment and male domination. Women are being excluded and marginalised from the Internet, it is claimed. This is attributed to men 'flaming', or abusing women personally, rather than accepting their viewpoint. It is quite common for women to use male usernames to avoid this form of harassment.

Australian web publisher Rosie Cross supports the view that harassment exists, saying women can be verbally harassed in electronic messages and in discussion groups. Some women are also offended or intimidated by men masquerading as women by using female usernames and participating in female-orientated discussions, often to disrupt them.

Harassment is widespread on the Internet and is not restricted to women. The tone of much Internet communication is aggressive, and many long-term users treat new users with great disrespect. As women make up a large percentage of this new user group, they are often bear the brunt of aggressive or threatening communication.

Cyberstalking

Cyberstalking is the act of repeatedly threatening or harassing someone over the Internet, via e-mail or other electronic communication device. This phenomenon is similar to off-line stalking. The victim is usually female, while the attacker is normally a male who is known to her. The difference with cyberstalking is that the offence can be carried out in the same room as the victim, or from across the other side of the world. The technology makes it easier for stalkers to mask their identity and disguise their location. The rate of cyberstalking has escalated enormously in the past few years with the spread of the Internet. It provides a new method of committing the same kind of crime.

Pornography

Many researchers, parent and community groups are concerned with the amount of pornography available on the Internet. Some studies have shown that one of the major uses of the Internet is for accessing pornography. However, some recent studies have shown as few as 0.002 per cent of all websites are devoted to sex. Another suggests this figure is closer to 1.5 per cent. This content is more prominent on Usenet, where up to 5 per cent of newsgroup topics are dedicated to sexual discussions and images.

The Internet, as its audience increases, will probably be used less for the viewing of pornography and other adult materials. The increasing commercialisation of the net has also seen much more of the pornography and adult material become accessible only through a pay-to-view system. This is not easily available to those

who cannot prove they are an adult. However, most pay sites still have fairly explicit subscription or promotional pages which are accessible to children.

Cultural imperialism

Traditionally, Third World countries have been concerned with that the free flow will actually lead to a one-way flow of information from Western organisations like news media, which dominate the international flow of information.

Madanmohan Rao, Communications Director,
United Nations Inter Press Service

▼ ▼ ▼

The Internet Society in the United States has found that more than half the Internet's computers reside in that country. The Internet was a US invention and continues to be dominated by American culture. In a study of 350 million links, the Internet survey company Cyveillance revealed that 84.7 per cent of all Internet content is currently American or uses a US web address.

The global nature of the Internet makes it impossible for anyone to monitor from where content is sourced. The existing local content laws have proven to be unenforceable by any nation that has attempted to regulate it. This contributes to what researchers have termed the 'internationalism of culture'.

Internet content originating in the United States, however, is not adapted for markets beyond its shores. It is assumed that, if you are an Internet user, you can speak English and you want American-style products. It is also assumed you can pay for those services with US dollars.

The spread of American culture, already pervasive through the phenomena of Hollywood, fast food and the music industry, grows ever more extensive.

Global participation – the benefits

In most countries, the traditional media are governed by regulations that state how much content must be locally produced. However, the Internet is different. Information on the Internet is not restricted by national borders, unlike the more traditional publications. It sweeps freely in and out of every nation, like the weather.

Amidst the gloom from commentators, some see a positive outcome. In the book *The Electronic Colonialism of the Pacific,* the authors speculate that the Internet also provides a perfect opportunity for minorities to project a global presence. For example, the websites for the Cape York Land Council in northeast Australia and The Centre for World Indigenous Studies in Washington both share the experiences of indigenous people with the world. As the Internet becomes more and more commercially based, the cost of accessing it becomes cheaper. This in turn allows whole new groups of people in many new countries to access it, and to voice their opinions.

The Internet is also extensively used by political groups in countries with dictatorial governments, and it can be used by both sides involved in armed conflicts. This was first seen in the United Nations' action against Serbia in Kosovo, in 1999. Websites and chatrooms were devoted to displaying first-hand reports from both sides of the war.

In the traditional media, nearly everything we read, viewed or heard about the war was filtered, assessed and interpreted by the journalist. Many now believe that the Internet has the capacity to shift this 'balance of power'. Judith Shulevitz, Editor of New York on-line magazine *Slate*, believes that the Internet is very democratising, making it harder to demonise the enemy with both viewpoints in the conflict so accessible.

First-hand reports and personalised contributions added local input, indicating the strength of feeling on both sides of the conflict. The Internet made a significant difference to how the war was being debated, in allowing discussion across a wide range of forums and bringing together people who would never have met in any other circumstance. The traditional media are, of course, still a major source of news and comment; however, the potential of the Internet to offer alternative viewpoints and interpretations of the war was also clearly demonstrated.

▼ ▼ ▼ ▼ ▼ ▼ ▼

activities

1. Scan or video capture an image featuring significant people and events in politics or history. Take this into a photo-editing program and make changes to the image, i.e. use the 'clone' tool to alter facial features, cut and paste in different backgrounds, or delete people from the event. Print out this image. Write a short report on the implications of your actions on politics, law and the court system, and on truth in general.

2. How do you think that 'truth' and 'objectivity' should be guarded on the Internet or in the media? Should images that have been enhanced be labelled even if minor changes are made, i.e. increasing the brightness and contrast so that it prints better? Consider this example: During the OJ Simpson murder trial, OJ was featured on the front cover of many magazines. One week both *Time* magazine and *Newsweek* ran the same photo on their cover. *Time* magazine darkened its copy of the photograph significantly, for 'printing purposes'.

3. How would you go about ensuring that information that you get off the Internet is suitable for use in your assignments? Is there any information you have rejected, or would reject and why? If you have a system of finding good information, or know of a number of reliable information sources, share it with the rest of the class.

4. Women view computers with 'critical distance and ambivalence' in contrast to the typical 'male

techno-evangelism' according to Dr Zoe Sofoulis.

In your experience, do you believe this viewpoint to be accurate? Define how you think women view and use computers; compare this to how you think males view and use computers. Is there a technology gap between the sexes and, if so, do you believe it is diminishing? Discuss this with other members of the class.

major assignment

1. Feminist authors have stated that the Internet is a new forum for sexual harassment and male domination. Do you think that the Internet has changed since this claim was first made a few years ago?

Have any members of the class been harassed on the Internet, i.e. been sent unwanted sexist e-mail or pornographic images, or verbally harassed while engaged in on-line conversations? Discuss strategies for dealing with such situations.

2. It is often stated that 'global culture is American culture'. How do you think that the Internet either contributes to the situation or alleviates it? Is the overall effect ultimately positive or negative? List some of the benefits and problems that this process may bring.

Internet Institutions and Industries

In the traditional media industries, the products on offer are mostly created by large organisations; most of them are driven by the desire to make money (the BBC being the significant exception). It is also the case that businesses and very large corporations have raced to exploit the opportunities available on the Internet. However, there is still scope for the private individual to set up personal sites. This marks the Internet out as fundamentally different from all the other media outlets

Unique features

The exceptionally rapid growth of the Internet has allowed users, organisations and companies to take advantage of the lack of government control over the content.

Traditional media forms are normally under the control of governing or regulatory bodies who decide which content is appropriate. The restricted number of mass media corporations also acts to limit the types of content provided. The Internet is the first mass media form that has ever allowed all of its users to participate without the need to hold broadcasting licences or without the control of a regulating body. This means that Internet content is mostly unregulated, uncensored and unedited.

Ownership and control

The Internet has now become so commercially driven that it has given the existing media giants tremendous advantages over other players. After all, they have the content that can be put on the Internet at no additional cost. They can promote their Internet offerings incessantly on their traditional media, and it's easy for them to bring their standard customers and advertisers over from radio, TV, newspapers and magazines.

Robert McChesney, US media analyst

▼ ▼ ▼

The Internet has offered ordinary citizens their best chance yet to participate in the media. This has been as a result of the simple computer language used and the inexpensive production costs.

However, consumer demand for the latest in technology has led providers of information to adopt new, more expensive technologies, out of reach to almost all private users. Some analysts predict this may effectively put control of the Internet in the hands of the same corporate powers that run the conventional media.

Media theorist Noam Chomsky warns that the ever growing corporate control of the Net has the potential to sidetrack public participation. He has criticised the Microsoft vision of the future of the Internet. 'They want to turn the Internet into a shopping system primarily', says Chomsky. Chief Executive Officer of Time Incorporated Don Logan asks advertisers not to think about the Internet as the 'information superhighway', but as the 'marketing superhighway'.

One of cyberculture's leading authors and original supporters, Douglas Rushkoff, now believes that the Internet has become a hypnotising and corrupting e-commerce tool. 'I realised that the forces attempting to turn the Internet into a marketing machine were actually stronger and better organised than I'd imagined … The Internet has changed, becoming a marketing-driven medium, just like TV.'

Media analyst Robert McChesney argues that the biggest mass media and telecommunication companies are working towards turning the Internet into another branch of their empires by using joint ventures and company mergers as a way of reducing competition and risk. He says that this 'puts an immense amount of political and social power into very few hands.' *Wired* magazine and Yahoo! columnist Jon Katz believes that the overbearing presence on the Internet of the mega-media corporations will make it harder for smaller, more creative businesses to succeed. He believes that the existing media companies and their joint ventures 'will blanket the Net with a blizzard of copyright and patent lawsuits, restraining orders, and other legalistic means of defining turf, identifying markets, and making money'.

Media giants already dominate the Internet. The five biggest and most visited website organisations are America Online, Yahoo-owned sites, Microsoft-owned sites, Lycos and Excite@Home-operated sites. The biggest of the media companies, America Online (AOL), already controls the Internet access of 23 million Americans. This Internet giant merged with broadcaster, film and music producer Time Warner in a £240 billion pound deal. This newly expanded company now has control over both the content on the Internet and the access to it.

▼ ▼ ▼

One huge monolith controlling both content and the means of accessing that content can't be healthy. At the very least, it's likely to result in content that is homogenised and dumbed-down to the lowest common denominator. At worst, it opens the door to the squelching of free expression by overreaching corporate control. If you want to watch TV, use the Internet, see a movie, or listen to music, you'll be an AOL user.

Cnet, Internet-based news and content producing company

▼ ▼ ▼

The Disney corporation also has concerns that the owning of both the content and the means of distributing the content will lead to a situation where preferential treatment could given to its own content while their users are steered away from their competitors' material.

According to Chomsky, the technology has the power to empower or to deskill. Sheila Lennon,

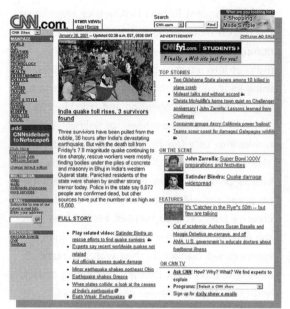

Figure 2.17
CNN offers a free news service on the Internet as an addition to its international cable news service. The site has become one of the biggest news sites on the web. Private home pages cannot compete with the corporate sites of the traditional media. According to analysts, future control of the Internet may slip back into the hands of the corporate owners.

author of *The Global Village Is Finally Wired*, says that we 'empower each other by sharing information … We can create here, together, a society in which everyone has a voice, and everyone's ideas are heard.' This communication model is often referred to as a 'trickle up' form of communication; many ideas 'bubble' up, rather than a few 'raining' down.

Hackers

While many young people with modems and personal computers are innocently exploring networks as they would the secret passages in an interactive fantasy game, others are maliciously destroying every system they can get into. Still other computer users are breaking into networks with

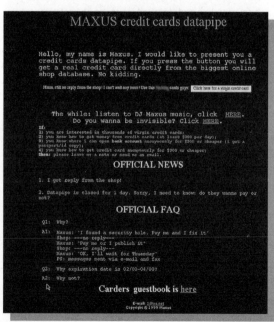

Figure 2.18
The Maxus Credit Card Pipeline site was used to distribute 25,000 credit card numbers to several thousand Internet users in retaliation for a failed extortion bid. This sort of high-profile hacker attack has affected the growth of online sales and e-commerce.

purpose: to gain free telephone connections, to copy information and code, or to uncover corporate and government scandals. No single attitude toward computer hacking and cracking will suffice.

Douglas Rushkoff, media analyst

▼ ▼ ▼

'Information wants to be free' is the catch cry of hackers, crackers and phreakers. *Hackers* are people who gain unauthorised use of computer systems. *Crackers* are users who break the codes protecting software. *Phreakers* are people who gain unauthorised use of telephone systems.

US law enforcer Gail Thackery says hacking, unlike street crime, leaves the victim unseen. 'It's an easy transition from Atari role-modelling games to computer games to going out in the network and doing it in real life.'

Hacking is a very common problem for business and government. An FBI study of Fortune 500 companies in 1999 reported that 62 per cent of them admitted to having computer-related 'security breaches'. The US Department of Defense had 22,124 obvious hacker attacks in 1999. Each attack cost the department one million pounds. The Pentagon and NASA are the primary targets for hackers wanting to test their skills. It is reported that each attracts more than 100,000 attacks a year, most of which are never discovered.

A number of recent high-profile cases have potentially affected the growth of e-commerce and on-line sales. The sheer number of reports and stories in the media and the status of the companies affected has made many users wary of transmitting credit card numbers over the Internet. In one high-profile case, a hacker stole 300,000 credit card records from on-line music store CD Universe. The hacker then demanded US $100,000 for their return. When the company refused, he published 25,000 of the credit card numbers on an Internet site called Maxus Credit Card Pipeline. Before the site was shut down, several thousand users had downloaded the credit card numbers.

▼ ▼ ▼

Media has oversimplified the hacker scene, and many hackers 'feed their developing egos' with the media's overdramatised reports of their daring, meaning that any original cyberian urge to explore cyberspace is quickly overshadowed by their notoriety as outlaws.

Douglas Rushkoff, media analyst

▼ ▼ ▼

activities

1. Who controls the information on the Internet? Draw on the information you have just read, any Internet experiences, or explore the Internet, searching for information on a current news event.

▶ Where did you find the most useful information?

▶ Did you find any alternative views and were these views from corporate, private or university sites?

2. Sheila Lennon says 'we empower each other by sharing information'. The empowerment is gained from the 'trickling up' of diverse information (from users) rather than 'raining' down of limited information (from media corporations).

How do you think that this will alter the nature of global communication, the media and society? Base your answer on the question: who controls the message?

3. Are there any rules governing the types of materials you access or post to the Internet? Make a list of rules and responsibilities from the following sources:

▶ Use the Internet to locate government policy dealing with Internet use

▶ Collect ISP contracts signed by any users in the class detailing rights and responsibilities of using their Internet services.

4. The idea that all information should be free seems a very democratic notion ensuring honest government and corporate behaviour. If all information were free, would you want your personal details, including medical, educational, court and criminal records to be accessible to anyone? Formulate an argument either supporting or debunking the hacker ethic. A class debate could be held as a way to present your findings.

Legal Issues

As technology feature writer Mitch Ratcliffe puts it: 'A computer allows you to make more mistakes faster than any other invention in human history – with the possible exception of handguns and tequila.'

Defamation

Global electronic communication by means of the Internet is clearly challenging legal notions such as defamation. The basis of defamation is that a public statement can harm a person's or a company's reputation. Some users believe that defamation laws should not apply to the Internet. The Internet's openness gives people who have been defamed the opportunity to defend themselves, it is asserted.

Of particular concern are newsgroups, where abuse and aggressive defamation are common modes of communication.

The Internet and the courts

The worldwide nature of the Internet has become a problem for legal proceedings and court cases.

The bigger the case or more notable the crime or defendant, the more publicity it creates. During high-profile cases, a country often imposes a media blackout to prevent potential jurors being biased by media reports and unsubstantiated claims and opinions.

The problem posed for the courts by the nature of the Internet was amply demonstrated during the trial of the notorious sex murderer Fred West. Information about the case was available to people within the United Kingdom through international news sites not affected by the British media blackout.

Privacy and surveillance

Bit by bit and click by click, intimate details of your personal life are piling up in enormous commercial databases – often without your knowledge or consent.

www.consumerreports.org

▼ ▼ ▼

New technology has made it easier for business and government to trace our every move and

gather, compile and cross-reference large amounts
of information about us. The Internet makes this
especially easy. Out of the top fifty websites, thirty
have privacy policies stating their right to
distribute and sell your identifiable information
without your permission. These include The
Microsoft Network, Yahoo!, ZDNet, CD Now,
Geocities, MSNBC, Warner Bros and Netscape.

Jo Ann Barefoot, a privacy expert and managing
director at KPMG Consulting, believes that the
law is about ten years behind the technology.
'There's no question that technology, and its ability
to keep track of all this data, is putting people into
terrain where they don't know what the ethics
are.' She thinks that the monitoring could actually
benefit the consumer with more diverse products
on the market and more niche marketing where it
was too expensive before.

Workplace privacy

When you can catch the worst ones, you'll fire them,
of course; the mediocre ones will find another way
to stick it to you. The best ones will quit and work
at a place that won't spy on them.

Lewis Z. Koch, *ZDNet UK*

▼ ▼ ▼

The American Management Association revealed
that 45 per cent of major US firms record and
review employee communications and activities,
including e-mail and computer files. They estimate
that, by 2001, 80 per cent of large companies in
the United States will be spending $US200 million
on Internet filtering software. Like the Industrial
Revolution, technological developments have not
empowered the employees or workers, but
instead made employers monitoring of them
considerably easier.

While most employers would never listen in
to private telephone calls, very few seem to have
any problem with monitoring and reading private
e-mails. Because the computers that transmit and
store employee e-mail are company property,
most reserve the right to read them. Many
employees, however, feel that this practice creates
an atmosphere of mistrust in the workplace.

Employment consultants point out the adverse
impact this can have on a firm, affecting staff
retention rates, productivity and profit growth.
They also stress that the possible abuse of
technology by staff now requires business to
monitor their staff more carefully.

Cookies

Though the Internet Movie Database can't tell where
else you've been on the web today, the company
delivering its banners [advertisements] knows. That
same company knows if you read *National Review*,
TeenMag, or *Dilbert*. It knows if you're into
professional wrestling or what cruises you were
looking at on Travelocity. It even has some of your
click history through WebMD.com.

Jamie, *Slashdot* contributor

▼ ▼ ▼

Cookies are small pieces of computer code that
are placed on your hard drive by websites and
advertisers. They are usually used to track a
visitor's progress through a website, allowing the
operator to evaluate which pages are the most
popular. They are also used extensively by on-line
stores with 'shopping trolleys' to track your
purchases and allow the addition or subtraction of
items. They are normally unable to expose
personal details to a website operator. Cookies
left by websites that a user visits are called 'first
party' cookies. 'Third party' cookies can have
more sinister implications. These are left on your
hard drive by organisations not associated with
the website being visited, such as the advertising
company that places the banner ads on that site.
These cookies are used to track your movements
across the entire Internet, allowing the advertiser
to build up a profile of your browsing habits and
personal interests. If your profile is linked with
your e-mail address then your data can be merged
with existing consumer databases to build a
profile of your off-line and on-line preferences.

COOKIES

When you visit a website, a small piece of computer code is left on the your computer. Every time you visit a new page on that site, the cookie is updated.

Later, when you return to the website, information about your last visit is extracted from the stored cookie. An updated cookie, still anonymous, is sent back to your hard drive. The website owner now knows that you are a return visitor.

If you give your e-mail address or other personal information to the site, this can be combined with the cookie, which is now no longer anonymous, but linked to your e-mail address. The website operator can now link your browsing activity to your identity.

This can be swapped with other website operators and on-line advertising organisations to build a detailed picture of who you are, where you live, what your interests are, your browsing activity and what you buy. Some operators view other cookies stored on your hard drive to build an instant list of the type of sites you visit.

Doubleclick, the biggest of the Internet banner advertisement placement companies, delivers a billion advertisements every two days. To ensure that it is placing the right advertisements on the right sites for the right kind of person, Doubleclick monitors the web browsing and buying habits of more than 100 million users across 11,500 websites. The advertisements you see on any website may have been selected especially for you by a computer that knows your personal browsing preferences.

These Internet advertisement companies are now merging with consumer record database corporations that track off-line purchases. They can then merge both companies' records, allowing a name and a full personal profile to be assigned to your browsing and on-line shopping habits.

Many advertising companies that position banner advertisements on websites also place parasite 'spyware' on your hard drive. These parasites function by secretly hooking onto your web browser and using its Internet connection for whatever purpose for which the 'spyware' parasite was designed. These range from reporting your Internet usage patterns and tracking your movements across the Internet, to sending a company or individual your e-mail address and reading the contents of your hard drive. The only way to avoid this type of stealth software is to purchase personal 'firewall' security software for your computer, which blocks the operation of stealth software.

Government monitoring

Governments worldwide have been attempting to find ways of monitoring Internet content. All attempts to date have been unsuccessful, and the technology used is usually outdated before the government passes any legislation to enable monitoring. Our own parliament has enacted the RIP, or Regulation of Investigatory Powers, law that grants sweeping powers to the government, allowing it to access e-mail and other encrypted Internet communications without a warrant. The bill requires Internet service providers in the United Kingdom to monitor all data traffic passing through their computers and route any content fitting a certain description to a central government server.

Government surveillance is undertaken for the sake of 'public safety'. The Home Office states that 'the powers within RIP are directed at three specific areas: threat to national security, threat to economic well being and serious and organised crime'.

Despite these assurances, civil liberties campaigners are still concerned that organisations in dispute with the government, such as trade unions, could be targeted through the government's surveillance. 'Anyone organising a demo is open to having their e-mail read', believes Chris Bailey, spokesman for the Association of Progressive Communications. 'It is particularly worrying for international organisations who could have details passed over to regimes without democratic rights for individuals.'

Other campaigners worry that the price of implementing any full-scale government surveillance is too costly, and could damage the country's emerging technology and e-commerce businesses.

E-commerce and marketing

According to an on-line 'e-commerce' clock, the amount of money spent purchasing products from the Internet stood at £2500 an hour in the first year of the twenty-first century – and is now rising rapidly. It is estimated that almost £66 billion was spent on-line over the year as a whole. While this sounds substantial, it actually represented only 1 per cent of the entire amount of consumer spending.

International Data Corp (IDC) predicts that early in this decade, 38 per cent of users will regularly shop on-line. 'This increased likelihood to buy will be driven by greater availability of products, improved buyer confidence in security, and enhanced local language sites for international buyers', suggests David Emberley from IDC.

Consumers can purchase any product they want from the Internet, at a time they want to shop, no matter how obscure the item. A survey by on-line store the Egg Shop found that fossilised woolly mammoth dung, moulds in the shape of private parts, and a Mongolian beard crimper were among more bizarre purchases made over the Internet. The most commonly purchased items, however, are CDs, books, magazines and software.

There are many obstacles to overcome when building a successful on-line store. The biggest hurdle is that people actually like to go out shopping. A survey by London Bridge Software found that 41 per cent of on-line shoppers feel that the Internet makes them feel alienated from the on-line stores.

Media Analyst Douglas Rushkoff believes that this is the major challenge for on-line stores. 'The object of the game for the next century's marketers will be to make the process of shopping and payment absolutely invisible. Our computer programs and networks will guide human behaviour toward the single end of buying more stuff more rapidly.'

Currently, market research techniques seek to classify 'target markets' that comprise millions of consumers organised into easily manageable and understood groups. The processing power of computers enables marketers to keep a separate record for each consumer. As an Internet site visitor, you may be identified when you enter a website. That site would then build customised pages in real time based on your personal profile collected and stored by the marketer's computers. Each time you visit a site, products you want to buy, and ads you want to see are positioned in the most prominent places. Even the design of the page could be tailored to your preference.

E-problems

With its ease of access, massive audience and potential for anonymity, the Internet provides an ideal platform not just for counterfeiters of luxury goods but for unscrupulous businesses or individuals to masquerade as reputable companies.

Howard Cottrell, ArmorGroup

▼ ▼ ▼

On-line sales of counterfeit products are booming. It is estimated that £17 billion of illegally produced goods are sold on line each year through on-line stores and auction houses. Sellers who get caught simply choose a new Internet address and start again. The use of on-line auction sites to distribute goods makes the practice very difficult to police.

Another booming Internet commerce trend is advertising. Jupiter Communications predicts that, by 2005, companies will spend £20 billion advertising their products and services.

The Internet's fifty most popular sites account for 93 per cent of all on-line advertising revenue. Banner advertisements proved the most popular way of advertising, accounting for 58 per cent of the market, while sponsorships accounted for 29 per cent, streaming video ads 6 per cent and e-mail 1 per cent.

On-line culture magazine *Suck* believes that banner advertisements are good for the web because of their 'overt' nature. 'Unlike product placement, paid links, playmercials, customised cursors, and even sponsorship, a banner ad doesn't mix advertising and content.'

Advertising on the Internet is a new field and advertisers are yet to figure out how best to use it. Many companies are beginning to realise the potential for brand building advertising on the Internet. Instead of directly selling to consumers,

companies are spending money on informing the consumer of their existence and building product appeal. Often they use collaborative advertising techniques to send you to a partnered on-line store from where the products are available.

Copyright

The Net has introduced a piracy nightmare for the motion picture, recording, and publishing industries, which have resorted to lawsuits to protect their intellectual property online.

Christopher Jones
Wired News

▼ ▼ ▼

A new generation of young people has grown up assembling vast personalised archives of contemporary culture; collecting music, website bookmarks, films, documents and articles, pictures and text says Jon Katz in a *Yahoo!* feature article. 'Many of these users have no direct experience paying for the pop culture they love, which, until a few years ago was subject to a clear-cut mix of federal theft and copyright laws. Now these people are being called thieves and pirates.'

The structure of the Internet, and the easy reproduction and transmission of digital data will alter the way the next generation views theft, intellectual property and copyright. There is significant potential for copyright infringement on the Internet. The traps for the unwary include the following:

▶ downloading images from on-line services and reproducing them;
▶ copying images, music, films and animations from the Internet;
▶ copying information, then re-selling it – either in print or on the Internet.

The entire premise behind the Internet is the sharing of information. Users often quote the catch phrase: 'Information wants to be free.'

Even the act of using the Internet breaks existing copyright laws. Browsing the Net means copying information from the host computer to the user's computer. It is temporarily stored on the hard disk of the user's computer. Any copyrighted information on the site, such as pictures, texts, sounds and videos, is also copied.

Digital transmission of data reduces everything to a series of ones and zeros, allowing perfect copies to be made of data one time after the other. It is then impossible to tell which is the original piece of data.

Major copyright holders such as the recording, publishing and motion picture industries are fighting what might be a losing battle against copyright theft on the Internet. They are desperately trying to develop ways to make digitally distributed files copy-proof, while reproducible versions of their work, such as music MP3s, spread rapidly across the Internet. Len Kawell, president of e-book publisher Glassbook Inc., states that the 'reality is there's no such thing as an invincible copy protection system. It's impractical to make it both invincible and usable.'

In the digital age, it is difficult to know what is a copyright violation. Anyone buying a magazine or a book from an off-line bookstore is entitled to hand it around, showing numbers of other people. With digital information, it can be illegal to show anyone else information purchased on-line. And, while it is legal to pass around a magazine or book, it is illegal to do so over the Internet, because it then becomes a public broadcast.

Music and film piracy

'MP3' has become the most commonly entered term on major search engines. The music industry stands to lose £66 million pounds to Internet theft in the first two years of this decade. The use of MP3s to distribute music is growing at an exponential rate, throwing up a major challenge to record companies. They need to develop their own way of securely distributing music on line. They then need to encourage users to pay for material they can already source for free.

The record companies have been slow to act against MP3s, resorting to costly court challenges to stop major file-sharing technologies such as Napster. Aram Sinnreich from Internet survey company Jupiter Communications says that 'the labels are absolutely ridiculous to come crying to the courts when they haven't put anything out there themselves that consumers can have an alternative to'.

Jimmy Iovine, music engineer, producer and head of Seagram's Universal Music distribution venture, says that the music industry has lost a big psychological advantage by fighting the MP3 battle in court. 'Our reaction to MP3 and Napster triggered front-page stories everywhere painting the record industry on one side and technology and freedom and kids on the other.'

▼ ▼ ▼

For every site they shut down, a dozen new copy-and-swap technologies – such as Freenet, Gnutella, Gnarly!, Wrapster and !Mesh – pop up. The reality is that the next big thing already is being developed somewhere by some 17-year-old high school student completely off everybody's radar. Technology will continue to evolve.

Hank Barry
Napster Chief Executive Officer

▼ ▼ ▼

Innovative and highly successful MP3 'upstarts' such as Napster and Winamp have made the use and playback of MP3s seem fashionable, by developing software and playback devices that are good-looking, exciting and functional. They have popu-larised their software by building in user-centred and developed features such as chatrooms and downloadable, customisable interfaces and visualisation effects. So popular is this type of software that companies such as Microsoft are appropriating the same visual styles and features in to their software and operating systems.

The major problem that record companies are having is finding a 'bulletproof' way of encrypting copyright files. The first of the new encryption music formats – Microsoft's Windows Media Audio (WMA) – restricted playback to only one machine or a number of plays. This format was cracked almost instantaneously by a hacker who invented a program that intercepted the audio stream as it was being sent from the audio file to the sound card, resaving it without the copyright restrictions. This sort of interception technique has been available for years in the United States, where people use it to copy pay-per-view films and cable programmes. This has been shown to have no effect on consumer film buying, hiring and selling habits.

Increasing numbers of people are gaining access to broadband Internet systems such as cable and ASDL. With these technologies comes the ability to copy entire films off the Internet in as little as twenty minutes. The film industry is

now also trying to find a way of securing their copyrighted materials.

According to a Jupiter Communications study into the effects of file sharing technology, 'all online music activity drives more purchases, not just online spending, but traditional retailers, as well'.

Deep linking

The World Wide Web's killer application is the ability to move from one website to another via a hyperlink. Without linking there would be no Web. Some organisations want to control the way users experience their sites by dictating how they are linked to.

Dave Amis, journalist with
Internet Freedom UK

▼ ▼ ▼

Deep linking is where the author of one site uses a hypertext link to direct their user deep into another website, straight to a piece of information relevant to their own content. This is the basis of hypertext (see p. 73). It provides the user with a straightforward way of accessing a lot of relevant information quickly.

Experts on Cyberspace law are divided on the legality of linking. Many think that anyone who creates a web page explicitly grants the community at large the right to use it. 'The eventual goal of the web is for everything to be linked to everything else. If someone says, "You can't link to my page," well, they are missing the point of the we', says Carl Oppedahl a cyberspace law expert. Maureen A. O'Rourke, Associate Professor of Law at Boston University states, 'site owners should recognise that Internet users want swift access to relevant information without lengthy detours through other pages'.

However, Emily Madoff, an intellectual property lawyer believes that: 'property owners who create the content should have a right to determine how surfers experience their websites. In particular if an owner's home page or another page laden with ads is bypassed by a deep link.' Most opposition to deep linking is based on this commercial assumption. If a user bypasses the front page, a 'hit' is not registered by the site's visitor counter and valuable advertising potential is missed.

The most well-known case of a 'deep linking' copyright dispute was the Microsoft versus

Ticketmaster case. The Microsoft site 'Sidewalk' featured a local event and concert guide that linked deep into the Ticketmaster site – directly to where you could buy the tickets for each event featured on the Microsoft site. With only one click, the user could move from reading about an event, to a page where they could buy the tickets for it. After Ticketmaster had this practice stopped in court, all users had to enter through Ticketmaster's front page and click several times or complete a search to find the appropriate tickets.

▼ ▼ ▼

Linking is what makes the Internet work. It brings together ideas, concepts and information in a way that is easily accessible to Net users. Linking breaks down the barriers between websites making using the Internet more of a seamless and satisfying experience for the user. By stopping deep linking, site owners are effectively denying people swift access to information.

Dave Amis, journalist with
Internet Freedom UK

▼ ▼ ▼

▼ ▼ ▼ ▼ ▼ ▼ ▼

activities

1. Users of Napster software, which allowed users to share digital music files, were more likely to buy more music than non-Napster users, according to a study by research firm Jupiter Communications. Do you agree with these findings or do you believe that Internet users who download MP3s buy fewer CDs as a consequence?

2. 'Information wants to be free' is commonly used to defend piracy on the Internet. Discuss whether you believe that the free distribution of copyright materials on the Internet is the future model of music and film distribution. Alternatively, are file-sharing and distribution companies such as Napster just a 'greedy bunch of corporate raiders trying to make their fortune off others', as *ZDNet UK*'s David Coursey sees it?

3. Do you agree that the nature of the Internet dictates that deep linking into other people's sites is legal or do you believe that the owner of a site

should be allowed to force users to enter only via the front page? Discuss.

4. What view do you take on the discussions around the hacker debate? Do you feel they have a useful role to play? View portions of films such as *Hackers* (USA, 1995) and *Johnny Mnemonic* (Canada, 1995), then discuss the ways in which the characters are set up as role models or anti-role models.

5. If a health insurance company purchases your data from a consumer records database firm that has tracked your Internet viewing preferences using cookies, the company may find out that you have perhaps been visiting many medical sites on a certain disease. If they the health insurance company then refuses you coverage for that disease because of their access to your private Internet browsing habits, is this a breach of your privacy? Discuss.

Censorship

The Internet was designed to withstand nuclear attack. If one of its terminals were to be wiped out, the system would simply route the information around it. There is no central control point. Every user and every access provider in every country has control over the materials that are on-line.

New technology writer Howard Rheingold says it is this decentralisation of control that means 'the delivery system for offensive materials is the same world-wide network that delivers economic opportunity, educational resources, civic forums, and health advice'.

Difficulties in censoring the Internet

According to Rheingold, short of sending the army into foreign countries to prevent users placing offensive materials on the Internet, there is no way in which to censor the Internet. 'The only protection that has a chance of working is to give our sons and daughters moral grounding and some common sense,' he says.

Author Richard Curtis says: 'The great thing about the Internet is that it will not abide by the rules.' The only way to censor the Internet may be to stop it entering the country altogether by shutting off international telephone lines!

Regulation of the Internet raises many difficult issues. There are also a number of technical reasons the Internet may be impossible to censor effectively.

■ The Internet is international

Information does not recognise national borders and is not affected by differing laws in different countries.

■ The Internet is diverse

Sections of the Internet are equivalent to other postal and communications systems that are not subject to significant censorship. For example, personal e-mail between two people is similar to traditional letter writing. IRC chat is similar to telephone conferencing, which is popular in business.

■ Monitoring of content is impossible

Such a vast amount of data is sent down cables and telephone lines that only a tiny fraction of it could ever be carefully monitored. Spot monitoring of data would be the same as British Telecom listening in to random phone calls ensuring that nothing offensive is said. Instituting expensive and ineffective data routers that check the source and destination of every tiny 'packet' of data against a list of banned sites has been suggested as an option. Checking every piece of information for an approved source address, or scanning every word in every document that enters the country, if possible, would be prohibitively expensive and would significantly slow Internet access speeds. Creating a list of 'definitive' banned or approved sites would also prove impossible with 2.3 billion pages to check. There are also numerous methods of disguising the source of information by routing it through an approved computer network.

■ Encryption can code information

Encryption techniques can prevent authorities decoding the information.

■ Offshore newsgroups can be accessed

Restricting Usenet newsgroups is possible; however, access can be gained from overseas newsgroup providers. Dialling internationally to overseas providers and accessing the Internet from there is also another option if measures are put in place to block certain sites.

■ Providers cannot scan

Internet providers cannot guarantee that at any one moment there are not offensive or illegal materials held on their systems. They can scan their users' and corporate home pages held on their systems, but they cannot do this every hour of every day. Many sites containing illegal materials are only open for a couple of hours at a time.

■ Everyone is a broadcaster

There are so many content providers – every user can be a provider – it becomes an impossible task for any agency to monitor the content that they put on line. Attempting to license all providers of content is difficult in a country where so many people contribute.

Views on regulation and censorship

Some studies have suggested that only 0.002 per cent of all websites are offensive or sexual in nature. These types of materials are more common on Usenet; however, out of the 100,000 newsgroups available, only 5 per cent were found to contain potentially offensive materials and most of these groups were unused.

Internet content is currently regulated under the same laws as those applying to a range of other media. If people are caught in possession of materials that are illegal in this country they will face the same criminal charges as if the materials were in any other form. The legislation applies whether the material is on a video, in a book, in the mail, across the phone, or on the Internet.

AGAINST CENSORSHIP

Opponents of censorship claim that many of those calling for restrictions have been misled by the media.

▼ ▼ ▼

Many parents believe that TV bears primary responsibility for violence, that the Internet is awash with dangerous perverts, and that films, videogames, and VCRs have rotted the brains and the values of the weak-minded young, infecting them with a predilection for mayhem. The manipulable media have been all too happy to disseminate such fears.

Jon Katz, *Wired News*

▼ ▼ ▼

Don Tapscott points out in his book *Growing up Digital* that children are 300,000 times more likely to be abused by one of their relatives than by someone they met over the Internet.

Internet service providers express concerns that the difficulty of regulating the Internet will make any attempt extremely expensive, driving smaller companies out of the market, reducing the popularity and potential of the Internet, reducing creativity, and will make it harder for poorer people to pay for access. With broadband Internet now vastly increasing the amount of data entering and exiting the country, analysing every piece becomes a technical impossibility. The Canadian Radio-Television and Telecommunications Commission (CRTC) announced that they would not be attempting to regulate the Internet. 'By not regulating, we hope to support the growth of new

media services in Canada', stated Françoise Bertrand, CRTC Chairperson.

In an early test of the validity of government Internet censorship, an American censorship regime was ruled unconstitutional by the Supreme Court in 1996. In summing up, the judge wrote:

▼ ▼ ▼

The Internet deserves the broadest possible protection from government-imposed, content-based regulation. Some of the dialogue on the Internet surely tests the limits of conventional discourse. But we should expect such speech to occur in a medium in which citizens from all walks of life have a voice. We should also protect the autonomy that such a medium confers to ordinary people as well as media magnates.

▼ ▼ ▼

IN FAVOUR OF CENSORSHIP

At any moment, those same kids exploring jungle fauna or listening to … Baby One More Time are just a few keystrokes away from Pandora's hard drive – from the appalling filth, unspeakable hatred and frightening prescriptions for homicidal mayhem.

Daniel Okrent
Time Magazine

▼ ▼ ▼

In a recent CNN survey 65 per cent of Americans believed that the government should be doing more to regulate 'violence' on the Internet.

Censorship advocates do not believe that the Internet should be treated any differently from any other media form. If television operators are obliged to transmit material that has been classified, why should Internet content providers be exempt?

Those who do want the Internet censored have concerns about materials falling into the hands of children. One of the early advocates of Internet censorship, US senator James Exon, says censorship would protect children from one of the 'pot holes' on the information highway. 'It is not an exaggeration to say that the worst, most vile, most perverse pornography is only a few "click, click, clicks" away from any child on the Internet.'

While pornography has attracted the most media attention, texts instructing on crime have also raised community concerns. Criminal records show homemade bombs have become more common since the advent of the Internet. The Internet also allows the easy distribution of hate literature. Frank Dimant of the Jewish organisation B'nai Brith says that the Internet must be censored or we will have an 'epidemic of hate … You no longer have to lure a kid to a rally. You can feed him hate daily in his own home.' Many fanatical survivalist groups and extreme rightwing organisations make use of the Internet to promote their offensive views on race and gender, and indeed to circulate dangerous information such as how to build bombs.

Three different approaches

Approaches to the issue of Internet regulation have so far taken three directions.

A TECHNICAL SOLUTION There is a range of software parents can buy to restrict known adult sites and newsgroups on the Internet. This software is termed 'censorware'. It also functions to screen incoming information for words and phrases that

Figure 2.20
Filtering software is able to filter out keywords and sites containing offensive materials. Each parent can set his or her own level of censorship.

indicate offensive materials. Other varieties search images for colours that indicate a lot of skin tones in a picture. This software generally acts to remove all pictures containing any form of human subject. It still lets through pornographic images if they are in black and white, or if they are accompanied by other colours.

Censorship at the home level is by far the most effective, filtering out potentially offensive material at the user end.

▼ ▼ ▼

When censorware companies tell you their product 'uses only human review', 'rates individual pages for offensiveness', or 'rates the entire web', or is '100% effective', they are almost certainly lying to you.

The Censorware Project,
censorware.org.

▼ ▼ ▼

Classifying the entire Internet is a technical impossibility according to according to the Censorware Project, an organisation dedicated to exposing the faults in censorware software. Most censorware software companies use computers to scan only parts of the Internet. The bans they apply are almost all exclusively at the server, or host computer level. If one user's site on a domain such as Geocities or Yahoo! contains offensive material, then the millions of other sites on that server are also blocked. Because of the sheer number of sites on line, the search computers rarely rescan the same sites. *Candyland*, an Internet domain once operated by a pornographer, is now a children's board game site. This site was classified as 'off limits' to children for years after the first review.

This censorware software may filter out much offensive content, but there are many drawbacks to its use and its effectiveness is far from 100 per cent. While it may help some families, it is by no means as effective as parental guidance. If whole countries were to operate under this style of software, vast tracts of the Internet would remain off-limits to an entire nation.

THE CHINA SOLUTION In China, all Internet content producers must register with the government. Producers are issued with a licence if their material is regarded as suitable and all Internet access is controlled by government operated Internet providers. Special restrictions apply for

material of a religious or political nature and strict penalties are in place for those who break the rules. Singapore used to have a similar censorship solution but abandoned it when it proved unsuccessful.

SELF-REGULATION Industry bodies, software manufacturers and Internet access and content providers have long discussed the option of self-regulating Internet content. There are two types of self-regulation: Internet provider level and website level.

■ **Internet provider level**

This is effectively the same as government regulation. It requires that Internet providers examine all content passing through their system by utilising some form of censorware software.

■ **Website level**

All Internet publishers, from multibillion pound media organisations to school kids with websites, will be encouraged to assign a certain number of 'keywords' and phrases to their website. These are based on a list developed by industry groups. This would very accurately describe what content is contained on each website, allowing censorware software to operate more efficiently. This method also has its detractors. Describing each site in such detail allows governments to simply mandate that all websites containing political or religious materials should be off-limits to everyone in their countries.

▼ ▼ ▼ ▼ ▼ ▼ ▼

activities

1. The act of possessing information on crime or drug-related topics, if it is instructional, is illegal. Many people argue that information is not dangerous, but rather it is how that information is used that is the problem.

Is it fair to prosecute somebody with bomb or drug recipes if that person is never going to use them? Are Internet users responsible enough to be trusted not to use the information and is prohibiting its possession an effective means to stop people making bombs or drugs?

2. If the Internet is censored, where do you believe the government should draw the line? Should private e-mail messages be subject to censorship and should the use of bad language in chat sessions also be censored?

If it is censored, what effect will this have when e-mail takes over from conventional mail, which is protected from censorship and legal actions such as defamation, or when the Internet is used as the telephone system?

3. Many people are concerned about children accessing adult materials on the Internet. Is it fair therefore, as some pro-censorship groups suggest, to make all content on the Internet suitable for children, banning all adult materials? (Refer to the history of the Internet, pp. 69–70, and studies of who uses the Internet, pp. 77–8, when answering this.)

4. If the international news media had censored information about the Fred West murder trial held in Britain to please the courts, should it then also censor information about other world events such as the Beijing Massacre because the Chinese government wanted it to? Discuss.

5. As the computers that transmit and store employee e-mail belong to a company, most reserve the right to read them. But if a letter passes through and is stored in the company's mailroom it is usually illegal for the company to open it. Discuss whether you think this e-mail monitoring practice is justified or intrusive.

Web Page Design

A media-literate person in the digital age can now not only critique the media, but, through the Internet, can become providers of quality content. Before examining how to design a web page, it is useful to identify what a good website does.

WHAT MAKES A GOOD WEBSITE?

Jennifer Story, from Next Online, states that a good site must be made with a specific purpose in mind. 'It is no longer enough to have a website for the sake of having one. The site must be attractive and innovative in its design, function in terms of its purpose, easy to navigate, frequently updated and fast to download.'

Charlie Fox, director of OmniNet, believes that a site with good interactivity and new technology can also be useful for attracting visitors. 'Net users are usually a jaded bunch with a three-second attention span and you need to make sure they keep coming back.' Many designers warn not to rely on new technology only. People will not return to a site without information or entertainment value.

ELEMENTS OF A TYPICAL WEB PAGE

PAGE TITLE All Internet pages have titles describing their content. A title should be a brief, up to forty characters, and should clearly and understandably explain the pages content. Unless the page title makes it clear what the page contains, many users will never open it. This is especially important when page titles are used out of context in bookmark lists and on search engines. The title should be written so that any user simply scanning the title will still understand it. Simplify the title as much as possible. 'My home page' is more concise than 'Welcome to my home page'.

Figure 2.21
Banner ads are normally long, narrow graphics, featuring a simple 'catch phrase' or simple text designed to make the user 'click' on the ad, which then takes them to a full-page version of the advertisement.

GRAPHICS These can range from banner headings, logos, pictures, navigation menus and other elements designed to give the page an identity. Each page of a site should have a similar use of the same style of graphics. This provides the whole site with a sense of unity.

The use of complex tiled backgrounds is a bad technique as it causes the body text to become hard to read. Any page backgrounds should be simple colours or very simple stylised images. Background images can be applied to an entire page, or can be applied as table or table cell backgrounds only.

BANNER ADVERTISEMENTS The most common form of advertising on computer-based media forms are banner advertisements, which are typically at the top of each page (see p. 105).

HEADLINE TEXT Each different part of a page normally has a headline, in the same way that newspapers or magazines articles do. Like those headlines, an Internet headline should be brief, interesting and act as an enticing explanation about the content that follows it.

BODY TEXT Body text is used to communicate the bulk of any written information. Computer-based media are delivered through a computer monitor, which, unlike newsprint, is of low resolution. Small text on a computer screen is incoherent, so larger sizes are used.

NAVIGATION SYSTEM Page navigation systems are used in two ways. The first is an illustrative form. It usually consists of a picture with 'hotspot' areas called an 'image map', or a series of buttons, each of which takes the user to a different location within an Internet site. As these are constructed as graphics, they should be permanent page elements.

The second type is a text-based navigation system. These are used when navigational links need to be changed often. News sites that have daily changing links are the best example of these. This navigation system also downloads faster than graphic-based styles. New windows-based 'drop-

Figure 2.22
The two types of navigation system: the graphics-based system (top left) and the text-based system (far right and bottom left). The example at bottom left is a text-based drop-down navigation system. This new form of navigation allows a user to go to the exact topic he or she requires with only one click of the mouse, instead of having to navigate through multiple submenu pages.

down' navigation links are becoming popular on sites with many links.

URL ADDRESS/AUTHOR INFORMATION Any Internet page should have contact information on it. This can include its URL (uniform resource locator) address and the creator's identity and e-mail address so that people who require more information or who wish to contribute information can make contact. An Internet page may also feature a guestbook, feedback forms and a date showing when it was updated.

Creating an Internet site

PLANNING OR 'INFORMATION ARCHITECTURE'

Information architecture (also known as IA) is the foundation for great Web design. It is the blueprint of the site upon which all other aspects are built – form, function, metaphor, navigation and interface, interaction, and visual design. Initiating the IA process is the first thing you should do when designing a site.

John Shiple, *Wired* magazine

▼ ▼ ▼

Planning is the most important part of successful web design. There are several stages that an information architect or website planner should define.

■ **Identify mission and goals**

The question needs to be asked, 'Why do you want a website?' Anyone planning a site needs to

know their client's or customer's needs. They must research their products or services, and identify what elements are required on the site to best display them. Do they want information, interviews, interaction, video or audio clips, or other elements? What is the best way to integrate them into their Internet site? For example, do they want the interviews to be the main focus or to be a minor part? Do you need graphics to best illustrate their information or more text-based descriptions?

■ **Define the audience**

What kind of people are you trying to attract? What do they want to do on your site? If the audience visits the site for daily news and current events, then this information must be easily accessible. Determining what aspects of the site will make visitors return is also very important.

■ **Identify the technology to be used**

Is the site going to use traditional static html pages or is it going to be a fully animated extravaganza? Is the site going to feature dynamically generated database-driven pages which are customisable for each user, or is the site simply going to have constant information on pages accessible to all?

■ **Create site maps**

The 'site map' identifies all the possible routes that potential users of the site will travel. You must identify which resources will be available from the front page, and which resources will be deeper in the site.

Organisation of information is an important aspect of the effectiveness of any web page. Good information that is poorly structured will still be unsuccessful. A good model of an Internet site contains information broken into bite-size pieces, and linked by menus and submenus.

■ Design page schematics

After all the content and the structure of the site have been worked out, the information architect must design a layout structure for each page on the site. How is the page going to appear on screen: where is the navigation going to go and where does the heading and body text go? Ease of use needs to be taken into account, as does the nature of the audience and the design style required. Before designing a page, it is useful to examine similar sites. The style of the page will impact on the content and usability of the site.

■ Site construction

Site construction may then begin. If other artists, writers and programmers are building the site,

then a timetable for construction must be built and monitored.

CONTENT

The first step in creating any web page is deciding on the content. People using the Internet are looking for information, goods or services, or entertainment. The site must be useful to Internet users. The last thing the Internet needs is another list of links to other sites. If your page has information on it that the designer is not fully familiar with, they will have to research the topic, either in the library or on the Internet. Once researched, breakdown the subject into topic areas.

NAVIGATION

Web browsing user interfaces must improve enough that it is as easy to navigate the Web as it is to leaf through the pages of a book.

Jakob Nielsen
Web usability expert

▼ ▼ ▼

One of the most crucial aspects of an Internet sites success is its navigation system. The user must feel in control of the experience, but at the

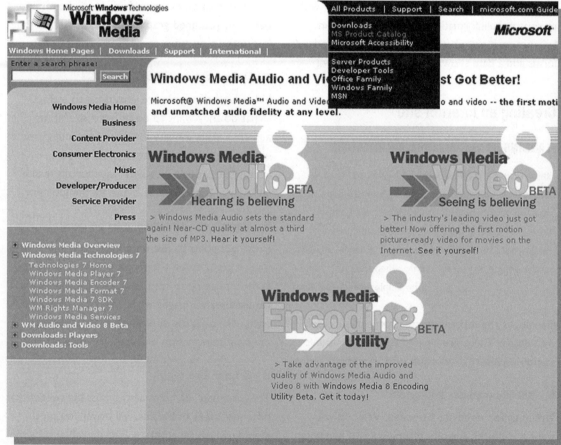

Figure 2.23
With thousands of unique documents, Microsoft's website uses all three navigation techniques to speed up user access. This page features multiple levels menus and submenus grouped into content categories, drop-down text menus, links from image maps, as well as a search facility. The site also features an expandable main menu on the left-hand side of the page.

same time must be led to the information that the sites owners want them to see. This is achieved through the navigation system and the organisation and structure of information on the site.

Good navigation is intuitive and easily understood. A user should always know where a link will take them before they commit to it. Good navigation is not always simple, but a web *de facto* standard has become the simple left-hand side column menu. This has proved to be the easiest and most common way to allow users to navigate around a site. 'Drop-down' style menus, similar to the ones found in Windows and Macintosh operating software, are becoming popular because of the users' familiarity with them, and the potential for users to jump many levels of submenus, straight to the content they desire.

The number of options available on each page needs to be tightly controlled, as overloading a page with navigation links is harmful to the site's principal goals. If many options are required, then submenu pages should be used. There should, however, never be more than three levels of submenus. Sites with hundreds of links now use databases, search facilities and drop-down menus to make navigation easier and quicker.

According to Jacob Neilsen, the navigation should take up no more than 20 per cent of the page as a rule of thumb, while the content should account for 50 to 80 per cent of the page.

The first page, or *home page*, should be the 'landmark' part of the site, and all subsequent pages should link back to it. Most Internet usability experts believe that *splash screens* (introductory screens with no content and with only one link to the next page) should be avoided. The home page should be designed to act as the introductory screen as well as being the main navigational centre of the site.

Navigation controls the user's experience of every website. In the off-line world, a customer buys a product first and experiences its usability and usefulness after they have paid for it. In the on-line world, the user experiences first and buys second. If the user does not understand the experience, or cannot find the product or information they require, they will not buy it – and the competitors are just a click away!

Consistency of the navigation is vital. Each page must feature exactly the same navigation system

and graphics. Users must know at all times where they are, where have have been and where they can go.

GRAPHICS

Graphics on a web page are not just for show; instead it acts as a very important part of the communication medium and the user's interaction experience within a web page. While content is important, the presentation of the overall site will leave a lasting impression of the site's professionalism and authority.

Yale WWW Style Manual

▼ ▼ ▼

Before the advent of the World Wide Web, the Internet was a text-based environment. The Web brought about the graphical user interfaces (GUI) that we now take for granted. When creating a site, good graphic elements are essential. Among the graphics needed include navigation buttons or menu bars, illustrations, photographs, logos and icons.

There are three ways to obtain images. The first, and best, option is to create new images, or have them created by an artist. Another way is to take existing illustrations, images or icons from other sites (after permission has been sought), or use clip art CD's or copyright free Internet sites to find illustrations.

Video or audio clips will have to be filmed, recorded, edited and digitally recorded onto the computer. These should be effectively integrated into the site rather than 'tacked on'.

A well-designed look and feel adds professionalism to any company's or user's Internet site. It presents the information provided or the products being sold by the site as trustworthy and dependable. Good Internet design is a specialised skill requiring knowledge of effective design, as well as knowledge of Internet site page construction techniques.

Special attention should be paid to the first or *home page* of any site. This is the flagship page and should be different from the following pages. While all pages should share the same look and feel, the home page should feature simpler content and have a much larger logo and title.

It is normally a good idea to minimise the amount of graphics on a web page. Pages that take too long to load risk losing the audience's interest. Business communication experts Putnis and Petlin have stated: 'nothing kills interest in a document more than a slow download'. Others argue that long downloads are often worth the wait if the content is of great artistic or entertainment value.

AUTHORING A PAGE

This is the most technically complex part of the procedure. Knowledge of the programming language *html* (hypertext mark-up language) is needed. There are various programs available to make Internet site programming easier, but for a professional result that works on all computers, operating systems and browser types, a program-ming knowledge is required. If complex programming elements such as databases, interactive games, animation, secure financial transactions and feedback forms are needed, a skilled person will be needed to write that part of the site.

Most professional sites now run on databases, while many others are animated for a television-like experience. These types of site require specialist programmers and animators. If the site is fully planned, this aspect of the site construction will be easier and less expensive.

ADVERTISING A SITE

If a site is not advertised, very few users will actually visit it. Before advertising is begun, a short, twenty-five word description of the site is written and a number of key words that relate to it are gathered.

To advertise the site, both its name and a description of the site should be submitted to a number of search engines. In this way, users searching for that topic will find the page. Other ways to advertise include telling others about it in appropriate newsgroups and mailing lists and referring to it at the end of all personal and business e-mail messages.

META TAGS Meta tags are descriptions of your site hidden in the programming code used to build each page. Search engines look for meta tags when the scan the Internet to catalogue its content. The

two most important tags are the 'description' and 'keyword' ones.

GETTING USERS TO RETURN TO A SITE

Jakob Nielson says the key to successful Internet sites is to get users to return through developing a 'relationship' with them. He believes that a site must start treating users as individuals. Some corporate sites, such as Hotwired, allow users to register for free with the site. Users are added to the database and their movements around the site recorded. The computer running the site will inform each user what is new since they last visited and even e-mail each user when changes occur. Other sites e-mail out regular newsletters.

The best way to ensure that people return to a site is first to provide quality information or entertainment, and then to update it regularly.

Writing for multimedia

Multimedia and the Internet require a completely new approach to writing. The style of writing that is appropriate for the on-line world is highly optimised and designed to be able to be quickly scanned by readers. This means text that is constructed in short paragraphs, subheadings and lists. Usability experts Jakob Nielsen and John Morkes found that 79 per cent of all users scanned pages, while very few read word by word. Nielsen also recommends that 50 per cent less text should be written for an Internet site than for a linear document. Any extra content should be linked to via hypertext.

THE INVERTED PYRAMID APPLIED TO INTERNET DESIGN

Jakob Nielsen found that several surveys revealed that only 10 per cent of users actually scroll down a page, preferring to read the top part of a document only, in the same way that many people only read the introduction to a newspaper or magazine article.

Journalists have solved this problem by writing in an inverted pyramid style (see p. 417). When writing the body text for an Internet site, start the document with an introduction that summarises all the information in one succinct sentence. The page is then written with further pieces of information placed in order of importance. Each

Figure 2.24
Example of meta tag entries for a UK-based media education site.

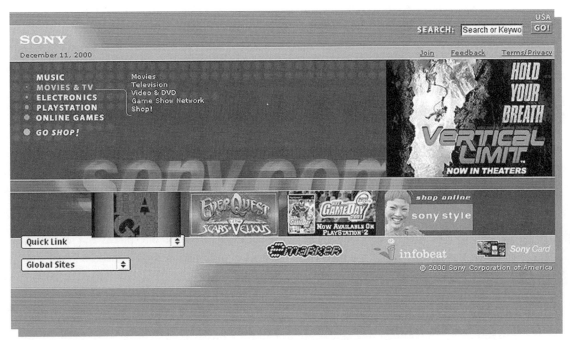

Figure 2.25
Company home pages are one form of advertising on the Internet. The pages are indistinguishable from many other Internet pages and often offer a range of inter-active pastimes to woo consumers. Sony America have adopted a vibrant, colourful and animated design to attract a younger clientele.

page within an Internet site, or within a multi-media document should be written in an inverted pyramid.

PAGE LENGTH

Long pages of information should be avoided states Nielsen. Not only do users not scroll down pages, but lengthy pages can also take a long time to download. He suggests that a designer should avoid putting too much information on one page. It is better to break it up into smaller sections, linked by menus and sub-menus. This will also allow a user to quickly scan the contents of your site, rather than having to wait for a large page. A page twice the length of the computer screen is the optimum size for pages.

Computer-based media are delivered through a computer monitor, which unlike newsprint makes small text incoherent. Information on the web is usually condensed or summarised, and uses larger type than that found in conventional media such as newspapers. Studies have shown that reading off a computer screen is 25 per cent slower than reading off paper.

ELEMENTS OF A TYPICAL CORPORATE PAGE

A typical company home page will have: a statement about the company; a page of infor-mation on each of their products or product lines;

a technical support section where information about their products is stored; an ordering section; a service section, where users can write in with their problems; and a what's new section to let customers know what has been recently released and what is due for release. Simply putting an existing printed brochure on line has been shown to be a very ineffective use of the Internet. A website needs to offer more to a potential customer, and must individualise and engage their interest.

ELEMENTS OF A CONVENTIONAL USER'S PAGE

A typical user's page can vary quite substantially, but the average page usually contains: information about the owner of the site, their hobbies, likes and dislikes; a photograph or two of the owner; personal artwork, music or literature; small amounts of information that interests her or him; a guestbook to gauge others' opinions of the site; and a list of sites which he or she enjoys.

Many users take the opportunity to create a website that says something unique and enter-taining. Some of the most popular Internet sites have traditionally been those of individual users or groups of users who have created works of humour or art that become popular in a cult fashion. Many users who create popular sites put banner advertisements on them to make money.

▼ ▼ ▼ ▼ ▼ ▼ ▼

activities

1. Draw out a map of the structure of an Internet site. Map out how the pages are connected to the menus and the opening page if one exists.

Are the pages in a logical order, in multiple small pages, or one long page, or are the pages constructed in a confused manner? How does the way the site is structured affect how easy it is to get information from it?

2. Print out a number of Internet and multimedia pages and analyse them, pointing out the different page elements. Write what their purpose is and state whether you believe they have used these elements effectively. Does this make navigation of the product easy and informative?

3. On paper, design a simple personal web page detailing who you are, what your interests are, who your friends are and links to their own web

pages. Include lists of websites that you enjoy, a guestbook and photographs of yourself.

4. First, examine a number of web pages, looking closely at the way in which the information is structured and presented on the screen. Secondly, choose a specific business, research it and write a web page for it, integrating text and pictures, and audio or video. Think carefully about how you can break the information into pieces and how those pieces of information should linked on their separate pages.

This task can be prepared on paper, or in *html* format on a disk. If you choose to work on paper, you should include illustrations, logos and button designs, as well as simple page or paragraph references for the hypertext links and a basic overview map.

Internet Advertising

Unlike the traditional media where the message is imposed upon the audience, web advertising must be relevant enough to entice the audience in.

Adam Gosling, *Ad News*

▼ ▼ ▼

'Technology is giving us more and more opportunities to break through to clients,' says David McCaughan from the international advertising agency McCann Erickson. The Internet allows advertisers a whole range of approaches to selling their products or services to the consumer.

WHAT GENRE IS THE INTERNET ADVERTISEMENT?

The Internet advertisement shares many of its features with the newspaper or magazine display ad. It also has many of the elements of the television commercial. Added to both is the interactive capacity common to all Internet communications. Like television advertising, Internet advertising is developing into a medium within a medium. It carries a range of genres in miniature. Particular genres are chosen according to the needs of the product being sold.

Types of Internet advertising

There are two main types of Internet advertising: company home pages and banner advertising.

COMPANY HOME PAGES Company home pages normally provide background information on the company, information on its products and services, consumer help and advice, software updates (if it is a computer company) and often prizes and competitions designed to encourage users to visit the site.

Competitions and prize giveaways work in two ways. Not only does the consumer visit the site and is exposed to the products, but the company normally requests information about the consumer when they fill in their details. Competition forms give the company information about where the consumers saw the advertisements and how effective they were, as well as information about the consumer themselves, such as how much money they earn, how old they are, what sex they are, and what they do for a living.

Underhanded corporate sites often take details of the consumer without permission. The companies have software that can extract an electronic 'calling card' from a consumer's computer (see 'cookies', p. 39). Visitors can unknowingly leave information such as their e-mail addresses, what software they are using, what kind of computers they are using and where they are located. This invasion of privacy has caused outrage among civil libertarians and has debunked the myth about anonymity on the Internet. It has also led to 'junk e-mailing'.

BANNER ADVERTISEMENTS The most common way to advertise on the Internet is to use *banner advertisements*. These are usually on the top of each page and, by clicking on the banner, you are taken to another Internet site belonging to the advertiser.

Banners usually have a clever, mysterious or cryptic hook to make the consumer want to 'click' on them. These advertisements, as part of the World Wide Web, can contain any combination of text, pictures, video, sound and animation, making the presentation an interactive multimedia experience.

▼ ▼ ▼

Your site is not the centre of their universe. Web users are fleeting, and they want information now – not five clicks from now. If, and only if, the destination page provides interesting information related to the ad that attracted the user, may they reward your site with an extended visit.

Jakob Nielsen,
Web usability expert

▼ ▼ ▼

It is critical that a banner ad campaign stands out. The number of users clicking on banner ads has fallen dramatically. A highly successful campaign will have only 1 per cent of users to any site it is posted on click on it. Therefore, it is crucial that the banner's URL is a campaign page or site dedicated to the advertisement, and not just link to the company's home page.

Audience roles and relationships

In the future, the lines of advertising and services may blur, says G. M. O'Connel, the founder of advertising company Modern Media. 'What we've being saying in my company is that advertising

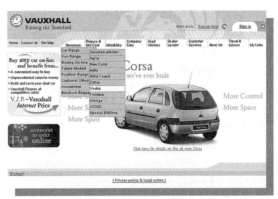

Figure 2.26
This Internet advertising page features a content menu with 'drop-down' text links and a site-based menu featuring contact and site map. The 'drop-down' text menus link the user directly to content deep within the site. From these pages, further product-specific and technical details are available.

should be so good that people confuse it with the product and service.'

Traditional advertising is based on the creation of an image, a form of advertising less suitable for the Internet. On the Internet, user involvement in the advertising and the product is what is important. A consumer may visit the corporate site, may visit user groups and end up developing a relationship with the product.

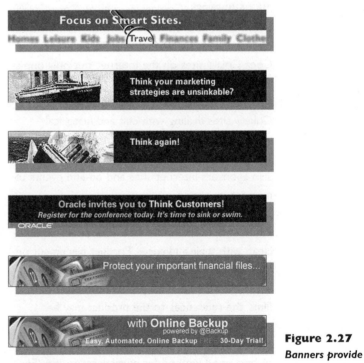

Figure 2.27
Banners provide links to product and service information. They attract the consumer through clever, mysterious or cryptic hooks, strong, bold headlines or statements, or animation.

The Internet is the first medium where the consumer chooses which advertisements they wish to see. This means that advertisements are seen by people who are actually interested in them. They can be more effectively targeted and can contain more product- or service-specific information. From the advertiser's site, direct links can be made to magazine reviews of the product or service, as well as more specific, detailed or technical information, dealer and distributor information, and information about other products or services offered by the company.

The biggest difference between advertising on conventional media, and advertising on the Internet is two-way communication. Kathleen Flinn, editor of *Internet Underground*, says: 'Input from users will likely be a dramatic influence on the shaping of future campaigns, methods, and even the nature of advertising. Internet advertising does not have to be an ugly concept.'

CULT AUDIENCES Companies such as Coca-Cola®, major users of product placement, have embraced on-line and digital media forms. There are lots of Coca-Cola® sites on the Internet, but only one is actually the company's! Working on its cult status and history, it has allowed individuals to set up Coke® sites dealing with cult and historical aspects of its product, as well as sites that allow interaction with real Coke® machines! Coke® also sponsors Internet sites and on-line events to increase its profile.

PRODUCT PLACEMENT Not all advertisers come clean with their audiences. Product placement on the Internet may be more subtle than pictures or links within a page. Like product placement in films, the references to the product may be contained as examples within the text or photographs. G.M. O'Connel concludes that this to be a good method for advertisers to use. 'For instance, you may be about car maintenance at Autosite, not realising all along you're being sold to by Saturn through images of their product.'

Designing Internet advertisements

Internet advertising is a new medium, able to offer a wide range of services and information to a diverse group of people. No other form of

advertising has ever been in the same position of being able to cater for such a mass of individuals.

SIMPLE LAYOUT AND DESIGN TECHNIQUES FOR ADVERTISING

Quite simply, if an ad isn't noticed it may as well not exist.

Nick Souter, senior copywriter,
Leo Burnett

▼ ▼ ▼

The Internet is overflowing with advertising. Major sites often have multiple ads on each page. Of the many ads that a user sees while using the Internet, only a few will stand out. Nick Souter believes that it essential that an advertisement be quickly and easily understood. He says that if the 'simple proposition' of the ad 'is obscured by intrusive and irrelevant imagery and design elements, the message will be lost and the space wasted' (see magazine advertisements, p. 443).

Designer and author Richard Tufnell has identified six stages that make up any design process.

▶ *Identify and analyse the brief.* A brief is a short statement describing the aim of the advertisement or company home page.
▶ *Draw up a list of features and specifications.*
▶ *Think up ideas.*
▶ *Develop your ideas.* Write down the ideas and plan the structure of the page and what the page will look like.
▶ *Realise the solution.* This involves creating the artwork and programming the page.
▶ *Test the solution.* Ensure the page is as effective as it can be, both in terms of accessing the content, and checking that all of the links are functional.

BANNER DESIGN

The most common way to target an audience, and to make them want to find out about a product or service, is through the use of a banner advertisement. These link the potential audience to another site where detailed information about the product or service is held. Only a small amount of information can be supplied on a banner advertisement, so it has to be simple, yet comprehensive, as this is the first contact an audience has with the company, and therefore represents what their products or services are.

Banner advertisements are crucial to the success of any Internet advertising campaign, since an audience member is not forced to see advertising materials as they are on television and radio, but must voluntarily go out of their way to find out about a product a service.

Often the most effective way to target the audience is the simplest. Use of simple, uncluttered arrangements of text and images attracts the eye, as do large bold images or text. The content of the advertisement should appealing, catchy, mysterious, or unusual. The text is the integral part of a banner advertisement. Common copywriting strategies include posing questions such as 'Do you know how many people can fit in a mini?',or using cryptic messages such as 'It's more fun than a barrel of monkeys!', and using directives such as 'click here'. Questions are effective because they initiate interaction with the user.

A basic banner advertisement is 468x60 pixels in size on a computer screen, which approximately translates to 158.5x20.5 mm on a piece of paper. Any combination of text, pictures or simple animation can be used on a banner advertisement.

STYLE

The principle of 'style' is of ever-increasing importance. With the expanding number of similar products and services available, style is often the only distinguishing factor between them. It is the style of the advertisement that also identifies the audience. The use of a visual style identified with the target audience is used to target the ad at its customers. More subtle kinds of advertising, such as product placement on sites popular with the target audience, are also important both in increasing sales and creating a style that will appeal to those likely to pay for the product or service.

Animation remains one of the best ways to augment the impact of an advertisement. Through television, we have become familiar with animated advertisements, while advertisements that pose questions and answer them in further frames excite our curiosity. With the average user looking at banner advertisements for just a second or two, the animation must be basic and the first frames must be the most effective to attract the user quickly.

LOCATION

Properly positioning an advertisement can make or break a campaign. It is no use putting a skate-board advertisement on the website of a financial services company. The actual location on a page can also effect the success of an advertisement. Advertisers are finding that banner advertisements get a higher 'click through' rate when they are placed close to items and links that surfers are used to interacting with, such as a browser scroll bar or a link to download free software.

▼ ▼ ▼ ▼ ▼ ▼ ▼

activities

1. How often do you read advertising on the Internet and what attracts you to it? Are you already interested in the product or service, or is it a clever sales pitch that draws you in? Make a list of good advertising you have seen on the Internet. What makes it effective? Draw up a list of effective adver-tising techniques for Internet advertising, i.e. links to reviews, interactive elements, clever slogans, etc.

2. Do you find advertising on the Internet to be effective and well placed? Is it more informative than advertising in conventional media, and does any interactive elements provide more information about the product or service, or is it normally only for effect and image?

3. Does Internet advertising involve two-way communication more than traditional advertising? Have you ever encountered a situation where you become interested in a product through the advertising allowing you personal experience with the product or service, and other users of the product and service? What do you think would make you want to become personally involved in a product or service, i.e. user groups, cult status, etc?

4. Using the guidelines on p. 106, design an advertisement for a fictional company. Decide on what product you wish to sell, how your banner advertisement will capture the attention and interest of the user, and what information you will

provide them with once they are at your advertising site.

5. Compare the style of a youth-oriented site such as a radio station or record company with a site associated with a political party. Identify the differences in style, and describe why the creators of each site used the different styles.

major assignment

Written assignment

Choose one of the following topics and write a 600-word response.

1. Research what materials are illegal in the United Kingdom in any media form. Follow this by researching current or planned Internet censorship and compare the results. Make suggestions on how you would regulate the Internet, based on information in this textbook, and further research. Regulation does not necessarily mean censorship alone, but could also incorporate such things as a code of practice for users and Internet service providers.

2. Imagine you are a consultant for a women's organisation wanting to encourage females to use the Internet. Produce a report on the matter.

Outline the problem, then suggest a number of strategies that could be incentives to make the Internet more appealing to women in the workplace and at home.

Production assignment

These assignments can be prepared on paper or in html format on a disk. If you choose to work on paper, you should include illustrations, logos and button designs.

The paper assignment should also include simple page or paragraph references for the hypertext links and a simple overview map.

1. Create an Internet page, demonstrating your familiarity with the features of an Internet home page (e.g. a tourist information page, a film page, a club page, a business page, etc.). Follow the layout conventions detailed in 'Designing a Web Page' on p. 108. To advertise your site, create a banner advertisement which provides a link to your page from another popular site.

2. Design an advertisement for a product. Make sure that the banner advertisement will capture the attention and interest of the user. Provide them with information in successive layers of complexity, depending on the user's interest or level of expertise.

Multimedia

Multimedia: Nobody is quite sure what it is, or why it is so sexy, but everybody wants to get a piece of it.

McKenzie Wark

The Multimedia Thing

▼ ▼ ▼

'Multimedia' is a buzz word used with great passion for describing a wide range of products, making it difficult to define exactly what it stands for. Cameron McDonald, in *Macweek*, states that multimedia is used to describe 'an environment in which more than one media type is used; media types being text, graphics, animation, audio and video'.

Multimedia is often considered as being only one technology: the CD-ROM. It is actually present in a number of other different forms, however, including the Internet, information kiosks, interactive television, lectures, presentations and video games. With the convergence of technologies (see p. 61), multimedia can be presented both locally off disks, such as CD-ROMs and DVDs, and equally off updated databases on the Internet. The two blend seamlessly, ensuring the product can be updated automatically, often without the user even knowing or having to intervene.

Some of the first types of multimedia included silent movies. These featured film accompanied by text-based stills illustrations and presentations, often including multiple slide and film projectors, with live commentary or music. The key differences between the old forms of multimedia and the new digital, computer-based ones have been identified by Antwar Slade.

▼ ▼ ▼

The computer environment allows the digitisation of the source material, and provides the ability to *randomly* access this information and to combine any number of media types.

Antwar Slade

Information Technology,

Issues and Implications

▼ ▼ ▼

Slade illustrates the difference between the silent film and a computer-based multimedia version of the film. In a digital computer-based form, the film can be seen in part or in full, in combination with snippets from related movies, commentary and biographies of the stars and film-makers. All of this can be contained within one multimedia product, randomly accessible at any point, and in any order.

Multimedia allows the user to access information under natural inquiry conditions, interactively 'discovering' the information. Studies have shown that, if users have to seek out information interactively, they are more likely to remember it than if they were simply told that information.

McKenzie Wark debunks the 'truism' that multimedia is the only 'active' medium. He states that studies have shown that the audience is an active participant in the production and negotiation of meaning in existing media. 'They accept, resist or negotiate what they see and hear, depending on how it suits what they know of the world and what they imagine in their heads.' Other researchers believe that multimedia is not only an active medium, but an 'interactive' medium.

Wark states that multimedia creators do not really yet know what the public wants from this new technology:

▼ ▼ ▼

To be educated? Why not read a book? To be entertained? Why not watch TV? To be engaged 'interactively'? Well, why not go down to the local bar, coffee shop or Laundromat and chat somebody up?

McKenzie Wark

The Multimedia Thing

▼ ▼ ▼

The features of multimedia

Unconstrained use of multimedia results in user interfaces that confuse users and make it harder for them to understand the information. Not every web page needs to bombard the user with the equivalent of Times Square in impressions and movement.

Jakob Nielsen

Web usability expert

▼ ▼ ▼

There are five main elements used in multimedia: animation, video, audio, text and graphics. Effective integration of multimedia elements is crucial to the success of any multimedia design. These 'multimedia' elements, when well produced and designed, combine to provide an informative and engaging piece of multimedia text.

ANIMATION

Animation can provide a multimedia work with a slick, well-produced feel, both adding impact and providing a more visually exciting interface. Animation is also useful for demonstrations. Presentations can include animated graphs or illustrations of 3-D objects such as machinery or buildings. Animations of complex procedures or machinery can benefit users, as they allow them to discover how something works through manipulation.

Multimedia designers should avoid using animations excessively, as moving images have an overpowering effect on peripheral vision. Jacob Nielsen, web design usability expert, states that anything that moves in the peripheral vision can dominate awareness. This makes it hard for people to concentrate on text. For example, something spinning in the corner of a page makes it hard for people to concentrate on the text in the middle. Animations should usually be avoided on a heavily text-based page.

Animations are good for creating transition effects, particularly when the user is moving between two different parts or styles of a multimedia piece, as the transition will act to define each section. Transitions can also be used for showing direction. A page can animate forwards when you advance to the next page or a zooming-in effect can be added for when more detail about a subject is selected. Transitions should show continuity or be similar for similar kinds of transitions. Most multimedia productions should never feature more than one or two kinds of transition effect.

Animation is effective for enriching graphical representations of objects, actions or concepts. Some types of information are better demonstrated with movement than with still images, particularly when showing actions, mechanics, 3-D environments and structures.

Animation can also be used to attract attention. If you wish to draw the user's attention to a link, provide a briefly animated icon or momentarily animate the linking text. Nielsen warns that the user should be left in peace to read the information without further distraction from excess animation.

The use of animation is rapidly increasing on the Internet through technologies such as Macromedia Flash. Entirely animated websites can look exciting; however, if that animation does not enhance the message of the site, it is bad for its usability. Nielsen warns that animated sites can distract attention from any site's core value.

Web-based animated multimedia productions use various means to minimise the download time of any site. Many navigation, interface and design elements are reused from a common library of shared objects that any page can link to without having to reload them. Animation on the web is often *streamed*, or downloaded bit by bit as the user is progressing through the site. There is no point downloading an entire animation if the user is not going to view the entire work.

To counter the problem of incorrectly applied web animation, Macromedia has released a list of guides to achieve the maximum effectiveness of any animated websites:

■ **Users come to a site with a goal in mind**

Each link within the site should meet with their expectations and lead them toward their goal. When streaming a site, ensure that the navigation loads before the content in case the user wants to go straight to a particular area within a site.

■ **Think about both client and user needs**

The site's goals should reflect business or client needs, while the site structure should reflect the user's needs, leading the user to his or her goal, but bypassing unnecessary content and company jargon.

■ **Avoid unnecessary introductions**

While introductory animations can be exciting, they can also hinder the user's progress towards their goal. Make sure that any introduction can be easily skipped and that the user does not have to see it again every time he or she returns to the site.

■ **Provide logical navigation systems and interactivity**

Guide users to their goals while reminding them where they have been. Give them an exit point from every page back to the home page. Indicate every link's destination clearly.

■ **Design for consistency**

The performance and download time on a site can be enhanced by reusing a consistent set of library

elements. Consistency is also important to create a unified look and feel across the entire production.

■ **Do not overuse unnecessary animation**

The best animations reinforce the site's goals, tell a story or aid in navigation.

■ **Use sound sparingly**

Sound should enhance a website, but not be an indispensable part. Sound can be useful to reinforce actions. Always provide sound on and off buttons and a volume control.

■ **Target low-bandwidth users**

Not all users have high-speed access to the Internet, so ensure that the site or animation loads quickly. Macromedia recommends that the first page of any animated site should be no larger than 40kb.

■ **Design for accessibility**

Make sure that all of your content is available to all users.

■ **Test your site or animation for usability with new users**

VIDEO

Video is a media form with which we are very familiar and comfortable. It is a proven means of effectively transmitting information. As technologies converge into a digital form and broadband Internet access becomes more common, video in multimedia applications will also become common. Presently, both disk- and Internet-based multimedia is limited to the amount of video it can contain. Video used in multimedia productions needs to be highly compressed in order to fit onto a disk or be transmitted through the Internet. Video is compressed by 'stripping' data out that is not required, such as unused colour information and 'out of frame' footage. DVDs have massively expanded the amount of video that can be used in a multimedia production. Prior to this, some productions, especially games, used several disks full of video.

There are three main uses of video:

▶ promoting television shows, films or other non-computer media that traditionally use trailers in their advertising;

▶ giving users the impression of a speaker's personality. The feeling is that a 'talking head' should not be shown unless the speaker has a personality that adds to the user's experience;

▶ showing things that move, such as arts events (e.g. ballet), and product demonstrations, such as car test drives.

Due to bandwidth restrictions on the Internet, video use should be minimised. Excess information can mean that users with slow connections may not want to wait for multimedia elements to download.

▼ ▼ ▼

Under these constraints, video has to accompany text and images more often than it will provide the main content of a website,' says Nielsen.

Jakob Nielsen
Web usability expert

▼ ▼ ▼

With any large file, particularly with those that need to be downloaded from the Internet, it is important that the user is fully aware of exactly what content they are receiving and how big it is. Like animated websites, video on the Internet is also often 'streamed' to the user, downloading bit by bit as the user is watching.

Audio

The main benefit of audio is that it provides a channel that is separate from that of the display.

Jakob Nielsen
Web usability expert

▼ ▼ ▼

Audio can be integrated into a multimedia production in a variety of ways. One of the most effective is narration. Speech can be used to offer commentary without obscuring the information on the screen. Audio can also be used for providing a sense of place or creating a mood. It should be quiet and not interfere with the main information. Audio is effective for creating a dramatic entrance into an individual's or company's home page, or for introducing a disk-based multimedia production.

In the case of the Internet, audio can provide a more efficient and faster method of transmitting a message than video. Because the size of an audio file is so much smaller than a video file, better use of the available bandwidth can be made through using only the audio from a video recording and having only one image to accompany it rather than a full video. Many websites, especially animated ones, use repeated short music clips or samples instead of forcing the user to download long music files.

Good audio can enhance a user's experience. Nielsen cites the example of a video game, where users actually thought the graphics were better when the games manufacturers added improved sound to the game, even though they had not altered the original pictures.

TEXT

Multimedia is a computer-based media form, hence the information presented has to be read or viewed on a computer screen. As the screen is a low-resolution display, it makes it difficult to read large amounts of small text. Generally speaking, until screen technology improves, large amounts of small text should be avoided.

Large amounts of text are, however, quite common. Designers bypass the problem of readability by breaking the text into manageable pieces, connected via menus, and linked via hypertext where related subject matter and issues are raised. This has allowed whole books to be published on-line or on a multimedia CD. As many research materials are large in size, most Internet sites have the document as a separate text file with any graphics embedded within the file. The most popular form of on-line document is the *PDF*, or *portable document format*, file. These files can be downloaded, read off-line, or printed out and read later.

Text for multimedia is normally written in a style similar to that used by journalists. By using the inverted pyramid style of writing (see p. 417), where the most important information is put first, followed by secondary information, a user who does not scroll through each page can still read the most important facts.

Multimedia productions, unlike books, are normally very visual and colourful. Text is often placed on top of background colours or pictures. This sometimes leads to a complete lack of legibility when the background colour or image is a similar colour to the text, too colourful or too complex.

GRAPHICS

Multimedia is a visually intense medium. As so much multimedia is targeted at a youth market, much of it has a visual style similar to that of a music video clip. While this is appropriate for the youth audience, the excessive use of illustrations and pictures can detract from the content of the production.

Pictures, like video, take up a lot of disk space or require a lot of time to download from the Internet. Also like video, pictures are compressed to save space. On the Internet, very large pictures are usually not displayed in full when viewing a web page, but are seen as a small image or icon on the page. When a user clicks on the small image or icon, the picture is then downloaded and displayed on the user's computer. In disk-based multimedia, images are seen at full size on each page and often used for full-page backgrounds. They are often also integrated into the interface, forming a key part of the look and feel of the production.

Other crucial aspects of multimedia include the user interface – the way the user navigates his or her way through the production (see p. 61).

Structuring of information in a multimedia form

The power of multimedia and hypertext lies in the way in which information is linked. When users view a page, they can only view one page at a time. This is in contrast to newspaper readers, who can view the work as a whole. As a result, multimedia users must create a mental model of the information structure.

Patrick Lynch, author of the Yale University's *World Wide Web Style Manual*, maintains that you do not want a user's mental model of your site to be incoherent or jumbled. The site's potential will not be realised if the information in the product is poorly structured and hard to navigate.

Lynch states that users need predictability and structure, with clear functional and graphical continuity between the various components and subsections of your multimedia production. Each menu and document page should keep the same identity. This is achieved by using the same banner graphics, icons or similar graphic devices and style (see p. 98) to establish each page's identity. It also helps to avoid what usability expert Jakob Nielsen describes as 'orphan' pages that do not seem to belong to the same production or site. 'Designing the way the content flows is one of the most difficult tasks facing designers and writers,' write Jon Samsel and Darryl Wimberly in their book *A Guide to Interactive Writing*.

Most multimedia disk-based products and many Internet sites feature an introduction screen, video or animation to create a dramatic opening. This should be avoided on the Internet, as it increases download time and delays users reaching their goal. The main page or home page is next.

This is effectively a global menu page, off which submenu pages or documents radiate. Further documents branch off the submenus. Each page can be linked through hypertext where appropriate (not shown) or, in the case of dual disk/Internet-based multimedia and Internet sites, linked to other sites. The basic model of information organisation allows for ease of use and effective data retrieval. The home page of any multimedia production should always be a landmark, able to be accessed from anywhere within a multimedia piece.

▼ ▼ ▼ ▼ ▼ ▼ ▼

activities

1. Structuring information: map out a segment of a multimedia product, such as a home page of a record company, and document the links leading from that page.

2. Identify the individual media elements in a multimedia product, analysing where they were featured and what they did. Explain whether they had a positive or negative effect on the site's goal

and the way or ways in which they achieved this.

3. Find typical examples of multimedia use. These can include video showing a speaker's personality, such as a Martin Luther King video in a CD-ROM encyclopedia; video or animation demonstrating a product; narration accompanying a picture or video clip; and audio as background music or for a dramatic entry into a multimedia production.

Multimedia Narrative

Hypertext is being touted as a radical new option for fiction. But do we really want the death of narrative?

Pippa Leary and Benjamin Long
21.C magazine

▼ ▼ ▼

George P Landow, author of *Hypertext: The Convergence of Contemporary Critical Theory and Technology*, states that hypertext 'really has the potential to be the next wave of storytelling. The question is, is this total chaos and anarchy, or is it a new reading form that makes the reader a kind of creator?'

For many years now, writers have been grappling with ways to use new technologies in their writing and to create new forms of literature that could not exist without it. William Gibson, science fiction writer, and author of the term, 'cyberspace', was one the first to use technology to create new forms of literature. His book *Agrippa: A Book of the Dead* is written especially for the computer. The story comes on a floppy disk and, due to inbuilt programming, after each line is read it is turned into gibberish, or is deleted completely. Another work, Judy Mallory's *Its Name Is Penelope*, contains the memoirs of a woman. No two readings of this book are the same, as every time the electronic book is opened, all of its 400 pages are reshuffled.

Pippa Leary and Benjamin Long wrote in *21.C* magazine, that hypertext has possible long-term consequences for narrative form, literature and civilisation. 'According to its boosters, hypertext will have the same impact on literature as photography had on painting.'

▼ ▼ ▼

Borrowing from the conventions of print culture, those who view, combine or manipulate text are referred to as readers. Those who create, gather and arrange hypertexts are called writers. Yet hypertext challenges and, many say, obviates these distinctions. Hypertext readers not only choose the order of what they read, but in doing so, also alter its form by their choices.

Jon Samsel and Darryl Wimberly
A Guide to Interactive Writing

▼ ▼ ▼

With conventional written text, the verbal elements, words, sentences and paragraphs are laid out in a fixed, linear order. In hypertext, these elements are connected in a variety of orders. Leary and Long state that, while the author creates all the textual elements and the links, it is the reader who assembles it. They state that the advent of hypertext created the World Wide Web itself, 'a hypermedia text of unprecedented size and accessibilit..'

Analysts of hypertext have defined two different kinds of 'hyperfiction' narrative: exploratory and constructive. While exploratory hyperfiction allows the reader to transform the text, the text retains its fundamental identity. Constructive hyperfiction, on the other hand, allows readers to modify the text and even enter their own words.

Hypertext narrative conventions

Writing for hypertext involves many of the same conventions as traditional 'linear' writing. A story still needs a beginning, a middle and an end, as well as a first turning point and a second turning point (see three-act structure, p. 125). Narratives also require a number of other stylistic conventions, such as 'cliffhanger' elements, emotive content, depth of character and character development, that manipulate the reader or viewer in the same way that conventional media and literature do. Certain information needs to be withheld from the viewer, while other information is revealed at certain times when maximum effect can be gained (e.g. the viewer usually does not want to know the killer's identity at the beginning of a murder mystery).

Authors Jon Samsel and Darryl Wimberly believe that the depth of user interactivity is influenced by four key factors: immersion, exploration, response and satisfaction

IMMERSION

- ▶ Is the belief suspended enough to draw the user into a world of application?
- ▶ How captivating or believable is the application?

EXPLORATION

▶ How much freedom does the user have within the application?

▶ What does the user discover along his or her journey?

RESPONSE

▶ How can the user communicate or interact with characters, objects and activities within the application?

SATISFACTION

▶ What does the user learn from the application?

▶ What can the user take away from the experience?

▶ How pleasurable or satisfying was the experience?

▶ How likely is the user to repeat the experience?

Hypertext narrative uses story conventions to break up the story into different pieces. For example, a hypertext link, offering the viewer a number of choices, may be made just after a major turning point in the story. In general, a hypertext narrative should be broken up when:

▶ a major event has occurred which may alter the story;

▶ the reader or viewer finds out a crucial piece of information;

▶ an emotional event has taken place or is about to take place;

▶ the characters separate, allowing the reader or viewer to follow any one he or she wants to or with whom the reader most identifies;

▶ a cliffhanger point is reached, particularly if the event could affect the narrative or characters. It is a traditional narrative convention to cut to something else, rather than allow the viewer to resolve the cliffhanger situation immediately.

Hypertext links allow the reader to navigate their own way through the work, but ultimately it is the author who is responsible for what pathways can

INTERACTIVE PLAY SCRIPT

(Jack, Polo, Heather and Medalion are in the upstairs bedroom.)
HEATHER: Want to go downstairs for a drink?
MEDALION: Why Not?
HEATHER: Jack? I'm really sorry about your dad.
JACK: Thanks, Hon.
(The women leave to go downstairs)

READER INTERACTION
Do you want to follow the women or stay here with the men? Make your choice below.

(After the women are gone)
JACK: Polo, I know that you …
POLO: Hey man, for the last time, it's not my concern that you got a weirdo old man. Hear what I'm saying? So where's the stash?

(The women head downstairs running into Brown)
BROWN: Hello.
HEATHER: Have you seen Dr Brodey?
BROWN: I think he's in the dining room.
HEATHER: Thanks.

READER INTERACTION
Do you want to go …

New Scene   New Scene

Figure 2.28
Example of part of an interactive play script from Charles Deemer's Chateau de Mort. This play has multiple scenes occurring at once, with the audience choosing what must happen next. This excerpt contains less than one minute of action, in which two 'decision moments' take place. Interactive plays can easily be adapted into 'constructive' hyperfiction works, as the actors can improvise new material.

be taken. This means that the author can still control when a reader finds out information, and controls where a reader goes, making them follow a basic narrative and follow the form of beginning, middle and end.

The role of the author

There is debate about the way in which the role of the author in hypertext works. Many researchers believe that hypertext liberates us from the roles of author and reader. Robert Coover, writing for the *Times Book Review*, promises that hypertext will replace the 'predetermined one-way route' of the conventional novel, liberating us from the 'domination' of the author. In the 1960s, Ted Nelson, father of hypertext, envisioned an electronic publishing media called 'Xanadu'. He states: 'in Xanadu, all authors and readers are considered equal'.

Charles Deemer disagrees. 'Despite the new power given to readers in creating "what happens next", the writer is still in control of the material in a very essential way.' Even though different readers will create individual paths through the 'web' of material, the author still creates the 'universe' in which the interaction occurs and finally determines the outcomes. Authors Jon Samsel and Darryl Wimberly believe that interactive authors are 'experienced architects of narrative construction'. Writer and designer Michael Kaplan says that an interactive author creates narratives that are an amalgam of math and storytelling.

The future of hypertext narratives

The question is often asked as to whether hypertext will take over from traditional media such as the book. Pippa Leary and Brendan Long argue that, to date, hyperfiction novels have not been very satisfying to read, stating that their narratives resemble a video game more than a novel. Robert Coover agrees. 'It is hard to envisage the traditional beginning, middle and end ever being superseded. It just seems too bound into our cultural make-up and history.' Mark Frauenfelder, author of the hypertext work *Beyond Cyberpunk*, states that we want to be entertained and that we want the choices made for us, we want to be surprised.

Multimedia titles have not captured or drawn upon the 'rich soup of narratives that broadly exist in popular culture', laments technology critic McKenzie Wark: 'It would be a shame if the kinds of multimedia were only those "pre-filtered" by cinema and video – completely different media.' Multimedia is a technology in its infancy, similar to film in its early days. Some cultural commentators believe multimedia needs a Sergei Eisenstein (see pp. 155–6) or Thomas Edison to revolutionise the medium in the same way that these men revolutionised film-making. Christopher Vogler, a story consultant for Disney, says 'having all the technology in the world doesn't do you any good unless you do some work to give it meaning'.

Ted Nelson believes that hypertext has a promising future, but does not see it replacing books just yet. 'It has to be better than a book to replace it, it is still much easier to handle paper than it is to handle files, and quicker.'

Leary and Long provide a list of criteria to consider when judging a hypertext work:

▼ ▼ ▼

Are the characters worth following through a labyrinth of hyperfiction? Is the narrative structure engaging? Is its complexity challenging? Is the language fresh? Most importantly does the writer have something new to say in addition to having a new way to say it?

▼ ▼ ▼

▼ ▼ ▼ ▼ ▼ ▼ ▼

activities

1. Search the Internet for examples of interactive and multimedia fiction, poetry, etc. Explain how the author has used hypertext in the work and examine at what points in the story the author breaks the narrative with a hypertext link.

Does it break on 'cliffhanger' points, random points or points where the story could split up? How does this affect the readability, etc.? (Try using these search terms: *hyperfiction*, *hypertext* and *narrative*.)

2. Take an existing short story or film and map out events in the narrative and major complication or turning points in the story on a timeline. Mark on the line places where you feel would be good points to break the narrative where the reader could be faced with a change. Select at least four

places and explain why they are a good points (i.e. crucial turning point) and what choices the reader could be facing.

3. Take a scene from a book or a movie and break it up at a crucial point in the action. Using the hypertext format in the same way that Charles Deemer has (see p. 115), construct two alternative story choices.

4. Create a 300-word hypertext short story, using multimedia elements such as video, pictures and audio with the text to tell a story. For example, pictures could be used in place of a description or a picture or video could be used as a menu, illustrating a range of choices. Within the picture, hotspots could lead to different parts of the story.

Representation and Industry Issues

There are similar representation issues facing multimedia as there are with regard to video games and the Internet.

Multimedia has traditionally drawn from existing media such as television, film and newspapers for the style and types of information it presents. One of the biggest complaints about the multimedia industry is that it is not presenting any new, original materials, but simply re-releasing the same materials seen in other media forms.

Multimedia and culture

> The multimedia industry will be American, the infobahn, for all practical purposes, will be American. It's like the spell-check on your computer; it's American. You lose your national identity hour by hour, word by word. I think we are losing ours.
>
> Phillip Adams
> Cultural commentator and author

▼ ▼ ▼

Cultural representation is a problem that has been recognised by governments around the world. Many help local industries compete against imported materials. Unlike television, multimedia products

are not protected by any local content regulations limiting the amount of foreign product in the local market. The Internet makes content regulation especially difficult, as it cannot be regulated or stopped at a country's border due to its global nature and transmission form (see Internet, p. 69).

Tony Feldman, in his report *Multimedia in the 1990's*, indicated that the vast majority of multimedia titles will be made in the United States, a country he states is known for its parochialism. He gives the example of a title called *The History of Science*. This title ignores many non-US developments and is considered prejudicial by other scientific nations. Another example is *The Encyclopaedia of British Origin*, in which a map of Australia lists only four major population areas in New South Wales, one of which is a non-existent place called Chincester! Feldman believes that the problem is that the non-specialists creating multi-media will have trouble selecting material that is bias-free. There is a lack of editors, researchers and others with traditional publishing experience to ensure accuracy and bias-free information.

As the multimedia audience is so large worldwide, but relatively small in the United

Kingdom, many multimedia productions are geared towards the world's largest market, the United States. Productions pick up American themes, genres and narratives. Games provide the most obvious examples of American culture being portrayed in locally produced products. Games such as *Grand Theft Auto* use American themes of gangster violence acted out by actors using American accents in a game created in the United Kingdom.

Is local content, the story, the location or the artists involved? Technology reporter Chris Nash believes that, while it may be hard to define precisely what local cultural content is, 'unless the line is drawn somewhere, we could easily end up being the cheap backlot for someone else's culture'.

Censorship

Multimedia is grouped with video games in the eyes of the censor. The same regulations that apply to video games apply to multimedia products, although the position of those products or services on the Internet is less clear (see p. 94). Due to the convergence of technologies and media forms on to a digital platform, the boundaries between a video game and a piece of multimedia entertainment are blurred. Consequently, the same rationale for censorship is used – the interactive nature of the product is seen as possibly having a greater effect on the user than traditional media forms.

The Internet, however, is treated differently. While many countries have attempted to censor the Internet, it is a difficult and ineffectual process because of the Internet's global nature and its transmission method (see p. 94). As disk-based multimedia products converge with Internet-based products, it may also become harder to censor the materials actually sold in stores, as only half their content may actually be on disk.

Copyright

Copyright contributes to the expense of multimedia production. Copyright bodies are at pains to inform us that digital transfer of information, including Internet postings and home pages, are the equivalent of book and newspaper publishing and television and radio broadcasts. While individual users of the Internet largely ignore copyright, corporate and business home pages, and any form of multimedia designed to be sold, must not include copyrighted materials unless they have been copyright cleared.

Digital multimedia is providing new opportunities for those wishing to capitalise on copyright. Materials that have largely been in the public domain now cost money to use in a digital form. Business people such as Bill Gates of Microsoft are actively buying the digital rights of information, such as much of the world's art history. Many people who sell the digital rights to their property do not fully understand the consequences of its sale, or the true monetary value of what they are selling.

▼ ▼ ▼ ▼ ▼ ▼ ▼

activities

1. Find examples of locally created multimedia products in a variety of different mediums, such as video games, Internet sites, entertainment CD-ROMs and educational CD-ROMs. Analyse the content, the style and the target audience. Which do you believe are local content and why?

2. Write a short submission to the British Government stating why you believe that funding should be provided to promote UK culture in multimedia products. In doing so, state any examples of traditional and innovative local culture featured in multimedia that you have seen.

3. Research the effects that interactivity has upon an audience. Do the experts believe that it has a greater or lesser impact on the audience and why?

major assignment

Production assignment

Create a short piece of hypertext drama in either an exploratory or constructive hypertextual style.

Allow the audience to make choices or try more innovative techniques such as having multiple scenes occurring at once.

First, write a basic story.

Next, construct a number of alternative endings, after which you can work your way back through the story, writing in the different decision points that lead to each of the different endings.

Finally, cast your play and establish how you will present it. If you try constructive hypernarrative, you will need to be careful that the production does not become solely an improvisational piece. You may want to consider using a director or narrator who can steer the production back to what you have written.

Written assignment

Analyse a multimedia product, making a list of the basic elements used within it. Discuss how the user accesses these elements (i.e. manually or automatically), how effective they are and whether they could have been utilised in a better manner.

Discuss also whether the production chosen presents information from any cultural perspective, i.e. the amount of, or way in which, local information is presented in an encyclopaedia. Also look at whether a standard narrative style or innovative presentation of information is used and how that affects the usability and clarity of the product.

Computer Games

A video or computer game is an entertainment device that is a cross between a board game, a book and a sport. It is delivered electronically, either through a coin-operated machine in an arcade or through a game console or computer in the home. Video games typically place a story or an action inside a purpose-built environment that either simulates reality or creates its own fantasy environment in which to operate.

The video and computer gaming industry has grown from a simple low-key introduction in the mid-1970s to become one of the world's most important industries, turning over about $US15 billion worldwide. A 1999 study showed that 170 million game cartridges and CDs were sold in that year.

What genre is the computer game?

Most computer games work at a rudimentary level within narrative genre. They are often designed as a quest or an adventure, a battle or a race. The *storyline* proceeds from an orientation stage, through various complications and blockages, to a simple resolution.

A MEDIA GENRE

With the rapid convergence of all media types into a digital form, games are also beginning to affect, and be affected by traditional media forms.

'Game-like' narratives have begun to appear in movies, while games with movie-style plots have become common. The visual styles of computer games are also being seen in film. Movies such as *A Bug's Life* emulate the look of a computer game, while computer games are almost always introduced with a film-like cinematic sequence.

Games are the first new computer-based media form to socialise a generation of youth in a way that traditional media forms have in the past. The 'MTV generation' has been overtaken by the 'Nintendo generation'.

In television, the artificially constructed world is beamed into the home, uninvited. Games act in the opposite fashion, with the player choosing to enter the artificial world. Many people are worried that the constructed meanings in video games are more influential than those of the traditional media forms. This is because of the interactive way games present these meanings.

According to video games researcher Vincent O'Donnell, games interact with the audience in a dialogue of emotion, action and reaction. The interactivity means this occurs to a depth that is not possible in the cinema.

But can a video game make you cry? This was the question asked by game producer Electronic Arts in an early advertising campaign. From the industry's point of view, it may not matter. Some of the world's biggest media stars are characters

Figure 2.29
The relationship between computer games and movies moves closer as games spawn movies and vice versa. Lara Croft began as a game character (left), but was then transformed into a model, a singer and, finally, a movie character (right).

from computer games. Lara Croft and the Pokémon characters have become as well known as many of the major Hollywood stars. These are the cult figures for a technological generation, defining 'pop' culture, and selling millions of dollars worth of merchandise.

This new media form has begun to eclipse established media. In 1991, sales of *Super Mario Brothers 3* exceeded box-office takings from *E.T.*, (USA, 1982), the highest earning film to that date. This was just the first of many 'box-office'-breaking games. Pokémon was such a massive film, video, game and merchandising success that there are plans to build a multibillion-dollar Pokémon theme park in Japan.

The relationship between computer games and movies also moves closer as games spawn movies and vice versa. Lara Croft began as a game character, but has since become the basis for a blockbuster movie.

Context

The progress of video and computer games is characterised by how many megabytes of graphics and sound can be transferred per second. The visual and auditory information's complexity and the interaction's believability are what drive the development of the computer game. The genre has created its own market by propelling the consumer to lust after the latest and fastest product.

If a company does not keep up with this consumer culture, it will not survive. Promises of new games with new graphical, audio and interface advances keep the player's fingers firmly on the

keypads and continue to make record profits for game companies.

There are huge profits for the game hardware developers as well. The manufactures of 3D video cards and game console machines push the limits of technology to make the games look and play better, while the game developers rush to keep up with the new hardware advances. The average gamer needs sophisticated and expensive hardware to play the latest games.

The marketing of video and computer games has also become more sophisticated. In an over-saturated market, the games with the biggest marketing push are often the most successful.

Convergence

Convergence has seen an expansion of the way games and games systems can be used. The personal computer and the new console machines such as the Dreamcast, Playstation II and X-Box offer a new dimension to game playing. Over the Internet, games can be played with tens of thousands of other people at the same time. Many console manufactures are creating partnerships with Internet access companies so that users of their machines have to subscribe through specific companies if they want the multi-player capabilities.

While the games console manufactures have designed their machines to access the Internet for multi-player gaming, they have also allowed the players to browse the Internet and use e-mail via their game machine. This saves people with limited money from having to buy a more expensive computer for access to the Internet.

There is also a push by many companies, including Microsoft, to design 'cut-down' computers especially designed and enhanced for game playing and Internet access. This will help to reduce the cost of computer-based entertainment and ensure that the games consoles are updateable with standard over-the-counter computer products, effectively increasing their life span.

Games are now also being exploited by pay-TV companies which allow you to simply attach your computer or console to the television cable system. Instead of going to a game arcade, you can simply download the latest game. These are usually charged on a time on-line basis.

▼ ▼ ▼ ▼ ▼ ▼ ▼

activities

1. Make a list of some of the most readily recognisable media stars today, including video game characters. Have any recent video game characters rivalled the popularity held by Lara Croft and the Pokémon characters? Explain your answer.

2. Explain why you think it is that the consumer is always demanding the latest graphics, sound and interaction advances in games. Are these the criteria you use to judge whether a game is good or not? List any other criteria you might apply, such as genre, plot, characters, etc.

3. Have you ever been influenced to buy a game by slick Hollywood-style marketing? What marketing techniques or features would persuade you to purchase a game?

Examine a couple of magazine, television or Internet advertisements for games and explain how the manufacturer is marketing its game and what the advertisement says about the game. In your opinion, is it a piece of good or bad marketing?

4. Have you ever used computer games you considered educational and beneficial? What aspects made up such games? Did those games encourage deeper thinking, leaving you pondering questions, or were they simply acting as entertainment?

Types of Computer Game

The types of computer game represent various audience tastes, developments in the technology and also differences in the forms of delivery.

ARCADE GAMES

Arcade games were the original form of computer games, starting with simple sports simulations such as table tennis (*Pong*) and hockey, and other games such as *Space Invaders*, *Frogger* and *Pac Man*. Arcade games have simple 'action'-style narratives; simple, easy-to-learn user interfaces; and short play times (more money for game arcades). The most popular of the arcade games were Sega's *Sonic the Hedgehog* and Nintendo's *Donkey Kong* and its sequel *Super Mario Brothers*. Like most games, they consist of a number of levels the player must conquer before the next level can be attained. They have simple key or button-based controls where players have to use special combinations of keys for special moves. Players may also need to use on-screen architecture such as vines or trap doors to succeed in the games.

There is a new range of novelty physical endurance and coordination arcade games being developed where the action is not the manipulation of objects on-screen, but instead the movement of the player on a specially designed platform or with special controls. *Hip Hop Mania*, a simulated DJ experience, requires the players to hit five keys and scratch with a turntable in time to different coloured notes, while *Dance Dance Revolution* uses a video screen and two sets of light-up floor-pads as its interface. The players pick their favourite dance songs, then step on the pads as they light up in time to the music.

RACING GAMES

Racing games are similar to arcade games. They feature a simple action narrative, a simple user interface, and short play times. Unlike arcade games, you have the option to select which course you wish to drive, or which vehicle or character you wish to use. The playing interface is simple, often just consisting of steering keys and gear change keys. However, the cars or spacecraft are usually highly customisable. Most of these games now are capable of using 'force feedback' devices to physically shake the player to further enhance the simulation.

FLIGHT SIMULATORS

Flight simulators are very close to racing games, but normally concentrate on the technical accuracy of the interaction, rather than the narrative of the game. These games range in style. Some are pure simulators imitating the real experience often without other competitors, while others may be war simulations, where the player is provided with targets, and must navigate the plane to its objective. The user interface for these games is often very complex, as they are trying to accurately simulate the real experience and the original craft.

SPORT GAMES

Sports games are unlike any other game type. They often allow the player to control every member of an entire team, as well as manipulating the behind-the-scenes activities. A sport game usually lets you:

▶ be one, or any of the players on the field playing the game

▶ be the coach calling the plays and substituting the players

▶ be the manager of the team, trading and hiring players.

Sports games are held to a degree of accuracy that no other game is. The sports game player is someone who is a sports fan – someone who watches the sport on television and knows the game extremely well. Every rule must be exactly right or the players will leave. The greatest challenges in sports game design is to make the people as credible as possible and to have a very intelligent interface, excellent player behaviour routines and intelligent audio effects.

COMBAT GAMES

This game style is similar to arcade games, having a simple narrative mainly consisting of action, but using very complicated controls. Numerous keys, combinations of keys, and joystick movements, and a great deal of player dexterity are needed to access all of any characters' individual skills and special moves. These games typically have the widest range of characters from which to choose.

The player can normally choose which character they wish to be, with all characters having different skills and special moves. The high level of violence makes these games one of the major targets of the regulators. Games such as *Mortal Kombat* and *Street Fighter* have enjoyed

major successes, spawning movies, television programmes and reaping hundreds of millions of dollars from merchandising.

3D ROLE-PLAYING SHOOTING GAMES

Three-dimensional action games, such as *Quake* and *Tomb Raider*, are similar to combat games in purpose and goals, but have far more complex narrative structures. They also offer the player more interaction with the narrative. Like the combat games, these games are a major concern to those worried about violence. As with the arcade game, a number of levels need to be conquered, before the final confrontation is reached. The way an individual player navigates each level can vary.

The narrative structure of role-play games is very similar to that of an action movie, with the player as the main character. Most of these games use a *point-of-view* (POV) interface. This allows the player to see exactly what the main character does. Role-play games with multi-player options such as *Quake* have become a very popular way to spend time on the office or school network, or on the Internet.

There are other variations of this genre. Some are based on mysteries to be solved, rather than levels to be conquered. Throughout these games, you are presented with a number of clues, and a number of different objects. Combining or swapping the clues and objects solves the puzzles.

ADVENTURE GAMES

These are very similar to 3D shooting games in the way they are normally a role-playing game, but are more focused on the narrative than on the action, and place a high degree of importance on the visual appearance of the game. Games such as *Myst* and *Final Fantasy* are played in rich and detailed fantasy worlds, while others such as *Metal Gear Solid* and *Spycraft* are enacted in atmospheric 'movie-like' environments.

Adventure games were one of the original forms of computer games, originally being entirely text based. Their popularity increased when visuals were added to the text in games such as *King's Quest*. These were the first kind of games to be played across computer networks, and continue to be one of the most popular network game genres. The popularity of this genre has faded since they are generally not as intense as the other genres and tend to emphasise thought over action. This style of game narrative is now being merged with that of the 3D shooter creating games that feature both good stories and a high level of interactivity and excitement.

NON-GOAL SPECIFIC SIMULATION GAMES

There are a number of simulation type games, such as the *Sim City* series and *Virtual Theme Park*, that allow a player to control environmental variables to alter the outcomes of a particular scenario such as the building of a city. By controlling factors such as population, building codes and weather, the player can see the effects of actions they have undertaken upon a particular situation. These games have no story and no single definable goal. Instead, the goal of the game is chosen by the player. These goals can vary as widely as successfully building and maintaining a massive city, to destroying the city through sending a fire through it. There are also a number of educational titles in this genre such as the *Pharaoh* series, where a player can build successful ancient cities based on knowledge of historical social, political and building practices.

INTERACTIVE MOVIES AND FMV GAMES

Interactive movies, also known as *full motion video* (*FMV*) games, are an advanced type of role-playing game. Instead of using computer-generated graphics, they feature movie footage with real actors. These movies, unlike those shown in cinemas, are not limited by any time constraint. They also allow the viewer to alter the story by manipulating the characters.

The 'action/adventure' genre is the most popular for interactive movies since its narrative structure mirrors that of a typical computer game – a number of levels to be completed before the final confrontation and resolution.

Many of the interactive movies on the market are based on existing Hollywood movies. Extra footage is shot while making the movie. This is combined with the footage from the cinema version to create choice for the player. The narrative structure of the interactive movie echoes that of the original movie. However, it offers a number of different paths through the plot, and a few different endings. Scripting and filming the footage for an interactive movie is a very difficult task since so many options have to be taken. Scriptwriters must ensure there is enough footage and story to guarantee there will be no gaps in the narrative. Every scene and every option needs to be fully mapped out so that each choice a player makes actually leads somewhere.

Many games in other genres are now making extensive use of full motion video interludes, becoming virtual movies within games. Games such as *Final Fantasy VII* have more than three hours of video introductions and interludes which act as fragments of narrative and character development. This game cost more than US$20 million to create and employed more than 100 animators and film-makers. FMV allows a player to both watch and become their character.

Feed magazine journalist Gary Daupin believes that many film critics sense the loss of the single 'auteur's' shaping of the aesthetic sense of a film and dislike the video game and interactive form. 'It's almost as if interacting with the story somehow prohibits games from becoming art.'

MASSIVE MULTIPLAYER GAMES

On-line and networked games are the future and that is where we will compete.

Isao Okawa
Sega chairman

▼ ▼ ▼

Many critics see massive multiplayer games as the future of the computer game industry. When *Dreamcast*, the first computer game console with in-built networking capability, was released, it was marketed with the slogan: 'Up to six billion players'.

On-line games are normally adventure games. The game environment is created as a virtual 'persistent universe', still inhabited by players and still developing long after you log off. Thousands of people subscribe to these worlds, where they can interact with other players, fight, learn spells, acquire goods and build their character up through their actions, acquisitions and fighting skills over a long period of time, perhaps even years.

These games do not feature a linear story or a single goal. Instead, players work together to achieve various tasks. The longer you spend on-line and the more skilled you are at the game, the more powerful you will become. This has led to an industry of character and possession selling and trading. There are many auction sites where users with less time or low skill levels can buy characters and game items to increase their standing.

Players' expectations of these games are still based on their experience with single-player games. They still want some form of traditional overall story with themselves in the starring role. Designers of these games have the difficult task of trying to fit a compelling narrative into a totally non-linear world.

▼ ▼ ▼ ▼ ▼ ▼

activities

1. Survey class members to determine their experience of the range of computer games. What proportion of the class has used the full range? What proportion has never played at all? Calculate the average hours users spend per week.

2. Categorise popular computer games within the types listed on pp. 121–4. Are there any which do not fit into these categories? Are there any that seem to exhibit the features of several categories?

3. Survey class members to find out which of them play massive multiplayer games. How do they find these games different to other game forms – i.e. single goal-orientation of normal games versus multiple goal versions of these? Is it that multiplayer games engender a sense of community? Do players have a profile and are the good players of the game known to the other players? Are new, inexperienced players harassed by experienced ones?

The Narrative Structure of Computer Games

The most important aspect of game design is to make an interesting world. You can't just plunge the person into the third act of *King Lear*!

Michael Backes
Screenwriter and video game producer

▼ ▼ ▼

One of the enduring qualities of a movie can be its ability to manipulate our emotions: to make us cry, make us angry or make us happy. The question is, can video games ever hope to achieve this level of emotional attachment within their narratives? As computer writer Steven Levy ponders: 'how can you be involved with a character when you are busy shooting down aliens?'

The fundamental difference between a movie and a computer game is that neither the plot nor the characters are the stars of the latter. In a game, the environment and how you act within that environment is the highlight of an engaging interaction. As a result, narrative structure is often quite rudimentary.

Plot

There's no storyline. Don't let anyone fool you. We will probably hire some scriptwriter right before we launch the game, and they'll come up with one.

Mark Rein
Vice President of Sales, Epic Megagames

▼ ▼ ▼

The plot a game uses depends on its category. Most video games normally feature a simple, straight-forward plot. However, an increasing number of mystery-based adventure games such as *Myst* and *Spycraft* have been made popular through their use of an intricate, 'puzzle-solving' plot.

Arcade games, racing games and flight simulators usually have a brief and simple plot. In most cases, the plot only exists to establish a context in which the action can occur. Flight simulation and racing games often have no plot at all, relying purely on the accuracy and excitement of 'virtually' experiencing the real thing.

The more complex categories of computer games such as role-playing games and interactive movies have stronger plots. However, these are normally highly simplified in comparison to the plots of feature movies.

The three-act structure

Whether they be for movies, television or even novels or plays, most narrative plots conform to a pattern known as the *three-act structure*.

ORIENTATION The first stage is used to set up the story. It is here that the characters are introduced and the context of the story is explained. The introduction or orientation stage ends when the first complication occurs.

COMPLICATIONS There may be several complications or 'turning points' in a plot. The first turning point is where the action in the movie begins. It is the point in the narrative where a major event occurs, causing the main characters to embark on some journey from which there is no turning back. The complications stage is the longest part of any plot. It contains the bulk of the movie's plot action and character development. At its conclusion comes the final turning point. This is the major dramatic point in the story, the event that leads to the resolution.

RESOLUTION The third stage, the resolution or conclusion, serves to tie up any loose ends. It is the shortest stage.

Computer games and the three-act structure

A computer game's plot structure generally follows the three-act structure, but with dramatically shortened first and third stages. The introduction and conclusion sections of computer games have traditionally consisted of just a couple of screens of text or an animation.

Many new games now use complex cinematic sequences to introduce the narrative, to set the mood and intrigue the player. Some games let the player trigger the first complication by extending the orientation stage, allowing the player to first explore their environment and character. Without

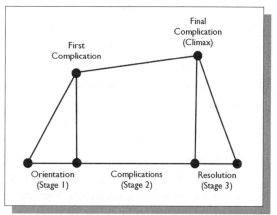

Figure 2.30
The three-act structure is the basis of plot development in the narrative genre, including movies and novels. Computer games also follow this pattern.

first building a player's interest in their character, the game designer is in danger of isolating them from that character.

Half-Life was one of the first games to allow a player to explore their character's identity. This game began with an animated sequence explaining the games environment – a secret research facility. Following this was an exploratory journey through the facility, where the player could interact with other characters, building up a picture of an uneasy work environment, and observing a sense of impending danger. Finally, it is the player that triggers the second stage of the narrative through initiating an experiment that goes horribly wrong.

Half-Life and other similar role-play games such as *Quake* consist of a number of levels or floors to be conquered. At the end of the final level, there is a major confrontation with the all-powerful ruler or demon. The game convention is that this final confrontation requires the use of a special process, power or trick.

THE PROBLEM OF NARRATIVE FLOW

It is the storyteller's role to structure the narrative in such a way that it builds to a dramatic

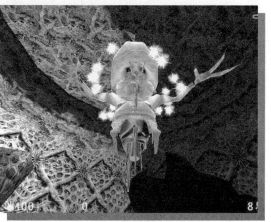

Figure 2.31
The final complication before the third plot stage in the game **Half-Life**: *defeating the alien demon.* **Half-Life** *was unique in that it had multiple types of villains and heroes, both fighting and being helped by humans and aliens.*

conclusion – an action, confrontation or some other events that resolves the story's inner tension. The problem for an interactive storyteller is ensuring that all the characters are ready for the conclusion at the right time. As the player's actions are outside the author's control, there is no guarantee that the player will be ready for the conclusion. This is what is known as 'the problem of narrative flow'.

Most games stick to the simple puzzle-solving, level-by-level approach to game design whereby the players actions are linked to the progression of the plot. The player is unable reach the conclusion until the right puzzles have been solved and the correct weapons have been gathered.

As more complex narratives are written, more sophisticated methods of resolving the plot and directing characters will need to be developed.

MOVIES BASED ON GAMES

The plots of many action movies now mirror the style of video games. Media commentator McKenzie Wark has pointed out similarities between *Terminator II* (USA, 1991) and video games such as *Doom* and *Quake*. In *Terminator II*, a number of confrontations with the liquid metal terminator character occur while trying to escape from each different situation (representing each level). At the end, after surviving all the other confrontations, the enemy is finally defeated after a major 'showdown' in which a special trick is used to melt the liquid man.

Action movies such as *Terminator II* also feature shortened first and third plot stages. Action movie viewers tend to dislike lengthy introductions with lots of character development. They want to get straight into the action, which

normally occurs in the second stage. A movie, like a game, also provides an interesting environment for characters to interact in.

The action movie plot is usually more complex and engaging than that of a computer game. This is due to the use of extra characters, their interaction with the principal character and with the exploration of emotional depth within those characters.

Characters

Video game characters normally follow stereotypes derived from Hollywood-style action movies. Other characters, particularly in fighting and martial arts movies, are based on the Japanese Manga style of animation. Few games have characters any more complex than the simplest of conventional movie characters. This situation has developed because the early game developers were programmers and not storytellers. Writers with experience in creating characters, pacing and plot need to be utilised by gaming companies throughout the course of a game's development if more complex characters are to be created.

Early depictions of characters on-screen were very simple, represented by a few coloured blocks or *pixels*. Rapid technological advances have meant more complex and believable characters have appeared on the screen, but their emotional range has not increased at the same rate. *Tomb Raider*'s Lara Croft is one of the most detailed characters to appear in a video game. *Tomb Raider* ships complete with a detailed description of her upbringing, her family, friends and her life, but little of this character construction actually makes it into the game. It simply serves to make her character and actions more believable, not to drive the narrative.

The next step for games may be to include extra characters actively involved in the game to complicate the narrative. New characters can also be used gradually to reveal more about the main character's personality and background, as is often seen in books and movies. *Half-Life* used its villain character brilliantly. At key points throughout the game, this mysterious villain would appear, helping to develop the notion of a government 'conspiracy' behind the plot, driving the player on to learn more. *Half-Life* was a phenomenally

Figure 2.32
The villain character from the Half-Life series. This mysterious figure appeared throughout the game at key conflict areas to menace the player with its cold 'government conspiracy theory' manner. This conspiracy theory is heightened in this shot when the player sees him leaving the area in an army helicopter.

successful game due to its deeper storytelling and character interaction.

Characters designed so that the player can create their personalities through their actions and interactions with others will also become common. This already occurs in massive multiplayer games, where a character's persona is built over months of interaction within the game and with other players.

CHARACTER IDENTIFICATION

Lara Croft creator, Toby Gard, believes that character interaction can be split into two groups: those with a first-person point of view and those with a third-person point of view.

FIRST-PERSON POINT OF VIEW A first-person game invites players to immerse themselves in the game, playing as though they themselves are in the game. A first-person game should make it as easy as possible for players to believe that they are actually part of the action. The main character must not interfere with the player's 'illusion of immersion'. The character therefore should not act on its own and must remain in the control of the player at all times. It should not speak to other characters unless directed to by the player.

THIRD-PERSON POINT OF VIEW In a third-person game, the player is controlling a character, rather than becoming the character. The third-person point of view allows far greater freedom to tell a more traditional story. This is because the character on the screen is a separate entity and is dissociated from the player. This allows the designer to give characters their own personality and control how they behave.

Environment

There are two main environments for games. The most common is the enclosed world, where the character is bound by walls or some other barrier. This means that the character is limited to areas pre-programmed by the designer. The other type of game environment is the open world, where the character is free to roam forever in any direction. This second type of game is more complex to create and requires the computer to invent new terrain and events, depending on where the player desires to go.

Figure 2.33
First-person point of view: 3-D action games such as **Quake** *allow a player to become the main character. The player sees the action through the eyes of the principal character on-screen.*

Figure 2.34
Third-person point of view: Role-playing games and some 3-D action games such as **Tomb Raider** *allow the player to control a unique character on-screen. Instead of seeing through the eyes of the character, we see the character itself.*

ENVIRONMENTAL STORYTELLING

In many respects, it is the physical space that does much of the work of conveying the story the designers are trying to tell. Colour, lighting and even the texture of a place can fill an audience with excitement or dread.

Don Carson
Gamasutra columnist and game developer

▼ ▼ ▼

The narrative of a game is primarily an environmentally based one. The game's author tells a story through the experience of moving through a real or imagined virtual environment. This is similar to film and television, where any story is played out within a certain environment; however, unlike in film and television, the game player will have choices along the way. Game developer Don Carson believes that the player will make decisions based on their relationship to the virtual world, as well as their everyday experience of the physical world.

Carson believes the three key criteria to good environmental storytelling take the player to a place that:

- ▶ lets them go somewhere they could never go
- ▶ lets them be someone they could never be
- ▶ lets them do things they could never do.

The most important part of introducing characters into a new environment is providing the opportunity for the player to realise where they are, as well as what their relationship is to the environment and what their role within it is. Players navigate through the game world using their knowledge of the real world, so it is important to include familiar elements to which players can anchor themselves. You certainly do not want to alienate the player from your virtual world.

Elements within the environment can drive the narrative. Using lighting to pick out or hide important elements within the game can be an important way to lead the player. Carson believes that the environment and the way that the environment is presented must vary throughout the game. The kinds of spaces, the way they are lit and what is in them must continually change along with the player's reactions towards them.

Carson warns game developers not to make the environment too perfect or similar. Lining up every pot plant with every desk and every chair merely emphasises how fake your world is. It is often the faults in the environment (e.g. a secret passage hidden behind a slightly crooked wall panel) that lead the player to make certain decisions.

Environmental storytelling opens up a wide range of opportunities within a game.

▼ ▼ ▼

What attracts me to computers is the ability to play with hypotheticals and possibilities. Storytelling seems to be a fundamentally linear path through a much larger space of 'potential stories'. If we can present players with a certain level of ambiguity we allow them to take more ownership (and empathy) with what they experience. This also means each player has a different story to tell after playing the game.

Will Wright
Creator of the *Sim City* series
and chief game designer at Maxis

▼ ▼ ▼

CAUSE AND EFFECT

The environment must acknowledge the player's presence, according to *Half-Life* developer Ken Birdwell. When a player performs an action, there

must be a response from the environment. If the character walks into a room, other characters within that room must acknowledge and talk to them; if they fire a shot or set off an explosion, the effect must be visible. 'Our basic theory was that if the world ignores the player, the player won't care about the world.'

Carson believes that one of the most successful ways to draw your audience through the environment is through what he terms *cause-and-effect vignettes*, deliberately created scenes that lead players to come to their own conclusions about what has previously occurred in that area. This can include doors broken open, traces of a recent explosion or a crashed car. These help players learn about what to expect later. Cause and effect can also show the passage of time. A player can return to an area he or she has previously visited to see it completely altered or destroyed.

Having your player follow 'breadcrumbs', such as handwritten notes, graffiti or evidence of fighting left behind by another character or a villain, engages the player's imagination and enhances the drama of your story.

TECHNOLOGY AND ITS
EFFECT ON GAME NARRATIVES

Whenever companies start to give us what we really want – good stories, good gameplay – there is inevitably some major shift on the technological side of things that takes the focus away from these basic foundations.

Brett Todd
Games Domain Review

▼ ▼ ▼

Advances in game technology have both positive and negative effects on game narratives. When CD-ROM based games were released, game developers went to great lengths to ensure that their games featured the most video clips and the biggest-name Hollywood actors. Unfortunately, this had no positive effect on game narratives and game play. Often, most of the development budget was spent on the actors, filming and paying popular bands to create the soundtrack, rather than on developing the best possible story and game.

Advances in 3D technology and its ability to render realistic environments has seen simple two-dimensional games, such as role-playing games, lose much of their popularity to the new breed of 3D actions games and their sophisticated graphics.

Matt Householder, producer for Blizzard Software, also points out that, every time a new games console is released, game developers have to start over from scratch on new hardware and tools.

▼ ▼ ▼

I'm trying to imagine how the motion picture industry would have evolved if camera and film technology were completely altered every few years, and if every movie house had a different kind of projector, and simply watching a new movie would require the audience (or the theatre owner) to make an enormous investment in the newest machinery.

Marc Laidlaw

Designer of *Half-Life*, Valve Software

▼ ▼ ▼

Computer game interfaces

Every element of the user interface is potentially changeable in its shape, location, colour, texture, and size. Designing screens, for computer games in particular, includes the design for backgrounds or scenes, menus, icons, cursors, dialogue boxes, characters, and control panels. At the forefront of interface design remains the computer game. Aspects of interactive game interface design such as: the value of interactivity, enjoyment, choice, ambience, and narrative, current-user requirements and desires are all important elements of interactive computer game interface design.

Marteen Burger

Metro magazine

▼ ▼ ▼

An interface allows a player to manipulate a complex system to achieve their desired outcome. All aspects of the game represented by an interface should communicate their purpose and capabilities. An interface should show the player what they can do with a system, as well as provide feedback from the system. If a gun is capable of only firing once a second, the interface should show that, perhaps by having a recharging symbol built into the gun. If the green liquid on the ground is dangerous, the interface should react and warn the player if they stand in it.

The visual interface creates a single look and feel across all aspects of the game. What you see on the screen does not, however, represent the whole interface. The interface also includes the

tools through which the player manipulates the game, whether it be a joystick, steering wheel or mouse, as well as the game's artificial intelligence (the behaviour of objects within the game, such as computer-controlled characters). The way in which all of these factors work together affects the success of the interface.

The interface should provide the player with the right amount of information needed to make sensible decisions. Importantly, it should not provide too much information or it may slow the progress of the player.

Computer games make extensive use of metaphors and symbolism in their interface design. This helps a player's performance, as the familiarity of the symbols and metaphors used ensures that the player quickly recognises to what each is referring.

SCREEN ARCHITECTURE

There are common language elements featured on the screen of most video games. The most important and common element is the status bar. This can take many forms, but usually features information the player needs to know while playing the game. These can include the character's health, ammunition, objects collected, armour, a vehicle's fuel or damage status, elapsed time, or current level or floor on which the character is situated. These status reports are often reinforced through auditory clues such as heavy breathing or through warning systems on vehicles. Other screen elements can include the weapon being used and a crosshair for accurate firing.

On-screen status objects can take many forms. They can be in the form of separate boxes on the screen or can be integrated into the on-screen action. For example, the status of a vehicle can be displayed on dials on its dashboard, rather than in separate boxes outside the game environment.

Sound

Sound is more immersive than graphics. While graphics will attract you to a scene, the sound playing in the background will create a reality in the player's mind that can never be achieved with graphics alone.

Sound consists of any music or sound effects that are played during a game. This includes the introduction music, the CD-based soundtrack, foley effects (environmental sound) and sound effects. Games now feature sound as sophisticated as feature films, utilising the same kinds of surround-sound technologies.

Sound is a crucial but often overlooked part of a game. Designers are no longer stuck with the beeps of the 1970s and 1980s, but now utilise CD-quality music and sound effects. New games often feature 'intelligent sound', where the artificial intelligence built into the game can apply the right kind of music for the current level of tension in the game. Changes in sound are often triggered through the proximity of a player to an event or character.

Developing a successful game

What computer entertainment lacks most, I think, is a sense of mystery. It's too left-brain … I think there might be real promise in game designs that offer less of a sense of nitpicking mastery and control, and more of a sense of sleaziness and bluesiness and smokiness. Not neat tinkertoy puzzles to be decoded, not 'treasure-hunts for assets,' but creations with some deeper sense of genuine artistic mystery.

Ernest Adams
Gamasutra columnist and game developer

▼ ▼ ▼

With more than 3000 titles being released each year, making a stand-out game is a daunting task. Games manufacturers often simply rely on technology or the latest effects to get their titles noticed, but it is increasingly obvious that, to make a truly successful game, good characterisation, well-paced, believable and engaging narrative and engrossing game play are necessary. This involves avoiding clichés and obvious solutions. The very successful spy game *Metal Gear Solid* was designed as a 'sneak-'em-up' rather than a 'shoot-'em-up', where the player had to avoid guards, rather than storm in, guns blazing. Some of the clever interaction included hiding in cardboard boxes, laying mines and sniping from a distance. If you needed to avoid an invisible infrared security beam, all you had to do was light a cigarette and watch the beam appear through the smoke.

Before design of a specific game begins, the way in which other games feature and use inter-activity, narrative, characters, camera viewpoints,

pacing and graphic styles needs to be studied extensively. Like film-making, game development requires knowledge of the conventions of good game design, as well as good storytelling.

Empowering the player is a technique that builds player dedication to a game series. Providing the player with a number of options and control over the environment when playing the game helps draw an audience and allows the gamer to replay the game multiple times. Allowing the player actually to modify the game is a definite winner. Games such as *Quake* actually allow you to put yourself into the game by constructing your own character from your personal photographs. The Internet allows swapping of game modifications and helps promote the on-line culture of any game.

Testing a game is also vital stage in any games development. The game *Half-Life* went through 200 two-hour test sessions, each resulting in 100 'action' items that required attention or change.

SIMPLIFICATION

Simplification is the vital difference between a game and a simulation. The object of a computer game is to entertain, and other considerations are secondary. Reality is complex and difficult. Games are supposed to be easy and fun. To get from one to the other, you have to simplify.

Ernest Adams
Gamasutra columnist and game developer

▼ ▼ ▼

Simplifying reality is an important part of any game design. While the packaging of many games features the word 'simulation', in reality the games are only a simplified simulation of reality. It takes years to learn how fight in an F-18, drive a Formula One car or accurately shoot high-powered weapons – something that the average gamer will not endure with a game simulation. Paul Jaquays from id Software says that 'only a fragile barrier exists between fun and frustration'.

THE GAMEPLAY OUTLINE

A gameplay outline is a large document that details all the levels within a game, as well as all the interactions, special effects, plot devices and design standards. It shows where every character, monster or weapon is introduced, as well as what skills the player must have or how the player will be taught those skills. This can include seeing another character make a mistake which the player needs to avoid.

The outline of *Half-Life* was more than 200 pages long, detailing everything from how high a button should be to what time of day it is wherever the player may be. It included rough drawings of all levels, as well as a list of requirements that needed creating such as sounds and animations.

WHAT DOES A GAME DESIGNER DO?

Paul O'Connor, senior game designer at Oddworld Inhabitants, defines the tasks of a game designer as:

▶ writing a treatment describing game action in a particular venue

▶ creating technical documentation specifying game controls

▶ formulating a gameplay outline based on required elements of the story

▶ building game environments using 3D modelling software

▶ presenting game ideas and mechanics to upper management

▶ working with programmers to refine game controls and cameras

▶ working with artists to create simple visual means of communicating essential game information

▶ controlling the 'big picture', while experts work on various details (to be the person who knows how everything works as a whole)

▶ writing game manuals and hint materials

▶ keeping an eye on what other companies are doing, and evaluating competing games

▶ creating, updating and maintaining a database containing descriptions of every element of the game

▶ designing puzzles and other game challenges on paper prior to implementing them via the game editor

▶ testing the game and fixing the bugs

▶ modelling the sophisticated interaction of the games climate, creatures, and environment

▶ conceiving original solutions to problems, and fighting with other designers to make your opinions stick.

▽ ▽ ▽ ▽ ▽ ▽ ▽

activities

1. What movies do you know of that have plots similar to video games? Map out the story of one such movie and show how it is similar to a video game. If you do not know of any specific game, base it on one of the game types discussed in this section.

2. Take the plot of a video game and write an outline for a movie that uses a similar narrative. You could try adding new characters and new scenes, and 'fleshing out' existing characters and scenes to give them more depth.

3. Take an existing movie and write the plot for an interactive version, ensuring that you have at least three different endings. Outline briefly the different ways in which you could navigate your way through the story.

4. James Wagner Au wrote in *Salon* magazine that 'it's safe to say today's developers aren't pushing the narrative envelope. Lured by the siren song of ever-improving graphics power, terrified by the risks involved with truly unique ideas in gaming, the industry is collectively stumbling along a path well worn by Hollywood.' Do you believe this statement is true or false? Discuss using game narrative examples.

5. Using a game that you have played recently, or by using a class example, discuss how the environment within the story affected your perception of the narrative. Use specific examples of elements within the environment that contributed to the narrative or drove the player to make a certain decision.

Representation Issues

Game designers are typically male, middle-class Americans. This same group of people also represents the largest portion of the video-game market. As a result, the most commonly cited representation issues for computer games concern gender, cultural issues and the focus on explicit violence.

Gender portrayal

Most computer games are created by males, for males. Traditionally, when females did appear, it was typically in sexist or overtly misogynistic ways: as damsels in distress needing rescue, rewards for successful completion of a game level, victims of violence, and/or sexual objects. Recently, video game companies have started to include more female characters in games, but a good percentage of these female characters continue to be created according to traditional gender stereotypes: the virtuous but passive woman who motivates game action; the evil, sexualised woman who must be overthrown by the male protagonist; the objectified female with huge breasts and lips, and an impossibly small waist.

Dr Kathryn Wright
Gamasutra columnist

▼ ▼ ▼

FEMALES

A common complaint levelled at video games is that they impart very traditional ideas about gender roles – specifically, that they encourage violent and macho behaviour, and are aimed too much at a male market. Games for females, on the other hand, often take a heavy-handed approach to morality. In such games, the morality is

saccharine and preachy – you win if you always make the 'nice' decision.

Some well-known attempts at marketing to young females include 'girl games' such as Purple Moon's *Rockett's New School*, in which the main concern was getting in with the right crowd and making a good impression. This game was widely criticised for its narrow representation of females. In another game, *Tricky Decision*, Rockett gets to choose between 'two cool parties, same night'.

Mattel, in its push to capture the female market, has a number of Barbie games, including the massively popular *Barbie Fashion Designer* and *Barbie Makeover Magic*. While the female market has been identified as uncatered for, attempts to market to girls so far seem to be based on stereotypical notions of girls' interests.

▼ ▼ ▼

Boys get to drive Formula One race cars, fly F-15s, build cities, battle dragons, conquer the galaxy, save the universe. Girls get to … become queen of the prom? Is that really the best we can do for them?

Ernest Adams
Gamasutra columnist and game designer

▼ ▼ ▼

The marketing behind games often presents the biggest problem. Characters such as Lara Croft are strong and independent, even if they have strangely disproportionate bodies. As the game *Tomb Raider* began to become successful, Lara started appearing with less clothing and bigger breasts, being splashed across the covers of books, records and calendars. Models and actors playing her made shopping centre appearances, released music singles and starred in feature films.

By playing computer games, many boys are able to familiarise themselves with computers in a non-threatening way. Some analysts argue that, as long as game programmers continue to ignore females, they are denying girls the opportunity to develop computer skills.

In response to the lack of game titles which appeal to a female market, and in an attempt to get more girls interested in video games, a large number of 'girl games' have been developed using very stereotypical characters, narrative and characters.

Figure 2.35
Screen capture from Epic Megagame's Unreal. 'There's a new girl in town and she's not afraid to kick some ass (or show her own).' C-Net Sneek Peek review.

ARGUMENTS IN FAVOUR OF 'GIRL GAMES'

Proponents of games designed for girls believe that any activity that encourages a girl to use a computer is a good thing, even if it might serve to reinforce stereotypical roles. Interest in computer games can lead to increased computer proficiency, an interest in well-paid technical careers and a general increase in the use of digital media by women.

Others point out how many titles aimed at masculine interests are on the market.

▼ ▼ ▼

I think we're in danger of establishing a double standard here. If Id Software can turn out sex-role stereotyped games for boys, it's unfair to insist that Mattel and others not do it for girls. Games for boys can be about driving fast cars and blowing the hell out of things, but games for girls aren't allowed to be about clothes and makeup? Should games for girls be required to be pure, noble, and above crass commercialism? No way. If we have to have schlock, let's have equal-opportunity schlock.

Ernest Adams

Gamasutra columnist and game designer

▼ ▼ ▼

ARGUMENTS AGAINST 'GIRL GAMES'

'Girl games' offer little hope for greater gender equity in the gaming world. By focusing on popularity and fashion – even if this is what some girls want to focus on – the majority of them reinforce the very same stereotypes they purport to combat.

Rebecca L. Eisenberg

Gamasutra/Ms magazine

▼ ▼ ▼

Critics of girl games complain that they are just as sexist as the macho, male-orientated action games. By focusing on stereotypical female interests such as shopping and popularity, 'girl games' end up reinforcing limited gender roles and polarise the types of game available. They argue that these games reinforce the message that males and females are stereotypically different and that girls require their own games.

Critics also worry that, by reinforcing traditional female stereotypes, these games serve to keep women out of technical fields, the exact opposite of what proponents of these games claim.

Dr Kathryn Wright, a games researcher, believes that gender-neutral games that both sexes

enjoy playing are the solution. Strong male and female characters, as well as a broader range of game experiences, need to be incorporated into games if more girls are to play.

Sega and Sony deliberately design games for the widest possible market. *Sonic the Hedgehog*, Sega's most popular game to date, was designed for both genders and all age groups. Vice President of Marketing at Sony says the most popular PlayStation games are those that have shown 'crossover appeal'.

Games designer and columnist Ernest Adams asks, 'Why make "games for girls"? Why not good games for everybody?'

MALES

Feminists are not the only ones critical of representation in computer games. The way male characters are portrayed also causes concern. 'Action-hero' type characters seem to be the only successful males in games. They are muscle-bound, scantily clad characters, with model good looks. And they almost always speak in American accents.

Recently, programmers have attempted greater diversity. In games where numerous characters are offered, an increasing variety of female as well as ethnic characters are being offered as options. But, where there is only one choice of character, it is almost always going to be an action-hero white male.

Marketers seem to think that using scantily clad women with a sexually suggestive catch-phrase is the best way to sell a game to a male market. Brett Todd, a writer for *Games Domain*, points out how intellectually offensive this is to

Figure 2.36
Are you a SINner? This animated Internet site ad features the character Alexis Sinclair, the main bad 'guy' from the game Sin. *She is a brilliant genetic engineer, but her animated breasts in this advertisement seem to indicate that the game marketers believe that her strengths lie elsewhere.*

men. He believes that this style of marketing implies that male gamers are 'a bunch of hormonal 13-year-olds who would do anything for the sight of a woman naked'.

Farah Houston, also writing for *Games Domain*, says that all this sort of marketing does is reinforce the stereotype held by most women that games are stupid, mindless and childish.

Violence as problem solving

From their earliest days, computer games have been based on violence. Even games such as *Space Invaders* and *Pac Man* required the destruction of opponents to continue the game. Violence in games takes place outside the normal moral universe. What you see on the screen is not a true depiction of death. There is no remorse, there is no pain and sorrow, and the player is not punished for killing; in fact, violence and killing are how you advance and succeed in most games.

Violence is a concern across most types of games. In many games, the player is faced with challenges where the only solution is to forcefully 'blast' or fight your way out. Critics say this effectively rewards violent behaviour and serves to show that there are no other solutions. Some critics want games to offer other solutions or wish to develop more complex and engaging game narratives so that the player has to rely more on intuition and intelligence. Doing so may serve to show that violence is not the only solution. However, programmers say that a game where you sit around a conference table and diplomatically discuss non-violent solutions to a problem would probably never be a hit!

Furthermore, the way in which video games are represented in their own marketing is often misleading. Gamers often seek out provocative content and marketers are all too willing to target this desire. Marketing text such as 'as easy as killing babies with axes' and 'more fun than shooting your neighbour's cats' could not be any more sensational or attention-grabbing, and are usually not a true representation of the actuality of the game.

Cultural issues

The importation of foreign cultures is an established part of a multicultural society. When the cultural imports are dominated as much as they are by a single culture, however, that of the United States, it becomes a concern.

With 3000 new titles being released each year, most of which are from the United States, other cultures are in danger of being swamped with imported cultural ideas. While the United Kingdom has a number of design companies using British characters, such as Eidos's Lara Croft, some smaller European, Asian and Australasian countries have very few locally made games in comparison to a large number of imported ones.

The representation of non-white, middle-class American characters in video games has been traditionally poor, with many racist and stereotypical characters often being developed. Dr Kathyrn Wright, feature writer at *Womengamers.com* and game audience researcher, believes that minority characters in games are often designed to be laughed at, such as black taxi drivers or boxers with huge afro hairstyles speaking in stereotypical slang.

▼ ▼ ▼

Clearly, games are taking the route that television did for years in its portrayal of race. Game developers make games out of their own perceptions, attitudes, and experiences – and that is part of the problem … once more minority and female game developers get into the field, games will naturally change for the better in this respect.

Dr Kathyrn Wright
Womengamers.com feature writer
and game audience researcher

▼ ▼ ▼

Some games unknowingly have an in-built racist message. Steve Brown from *PC Gamer* magazine writes that the game *Soldier of Fortune* has a 'discriminatory and racist message woven into the very fabric of the game, which attributes different values to Iraqi and American citizens' lives'. In the game, a number of US citizens are being held captive in the United States. If you kill a hostage, you are punished; if you kill an American tramp on the subway, you are punished; if you kill an innocent Iraqi civilian, you are not.

activities

1. Discuss whether you think game makers have shown a responsible attitude in marketing towards the largest possible market? Has their focus been too narrow, as critics suggest?

► What are the effects of marketing almost all games towards a single audience?

► Is it easier to market the same type of proven games to the same audience? If so, how can regulators encourage game makers to market good products to a wide variety of potential players?

► Write a short letter to a game company setting out an argument for a greater diversity of games targeted at a range of different people.

2. Sherry Turkle describes the difference between male and female players as the difference between 'hard' and 'soft' masters. According to Turkle, boys are 'hard masters' wishing to control the virtual world, while girls are 'soft masters' willing to play by accommodating, adapting and following the virtual world's rules.

What is your opinion of Turkle's description? Have a class discussion involving both males and females, and students from diverse backgrounds. How do different members of the class treat video games – as a medium to be dominated and conquered, or to be worked through with intuition and stealth?

3. Get together in small groups made up of both males and females, and discuss what particular aspect of video-game characters appeals to each member of the group.

Are there any types of character that you always encounter, any you do not like or any you find to be positive role models. Exchange ideas and discuss each other's preferences. Report back to the class.

4. Would you agree that almost all games are based on violence and the rewarding of violence through success? Explain. What extra non-violent aspects could be incorporated into games to make them more enjoyable? Make a list of your ideas.

5. Based on your experience, what do you estimate the ratio of foreign games to locally made games is? Have any of the popular games released in the past year been produced in this country?

6. Ernest Adams, a columnist at *Gamasutra*, has written:

▼ ▼ ▼

History is full of heroic women whose achievements went far beyond 'making new friends!' Why not track chimpanzees through the jungle with Jane Goodall, or help slaves to freedom with Harriet Tubman, or fly the world with Amelia Earhart, or even, yes, battle the Romans with Queen Boudicca? The problem with the clothes-and-makeup theme isn't just that it's stereotypical, it's that it's *feeble*.

▼ ▼ ▼

Research a famous historical female figure, such as the three mentioned above, and develop a treatment for a game based on her life or adventures.

7. Games researcher and *Womengamers.com* columnist Dr Kathyrn Wright believes:

▼ ▼ ▼

Male gamers see that most male characters are portrayed as unrealistic, muscle-bound Rambo-types, but they simply are not that affected by this. Many female gamers, on the other hand, are irritated when they can not identify with their female character.

▼ ▼ ▼

Discuss this finding. Do you think male game players are unaffected? Do females identify differently in your opinion?

Audience and Institution Issues

There has been little comprehensive study into the effects that video and computer games have upon their audience. Furthermore, those that have been completed are normally outdated quickly due to the rapid rate of game development. However, it is not only religious and other moral groups, but also parental groups, politicians, educators and other professionals such as psychologists that have begun to raise doubts about the effects of video games on young people.

The main concerns revolve around the following.

▶ **AGGRESSION** Do computer games foster antisocial and aggressive behaviour through the glorification of violence and the use of force as a problem-solving device?

▶ **ADDICTION** Are computer games addictive? Are games being played instead of involvement in other more desirable activities such as sports, reading and homework? Does the time-consuming nature of playing computer games impair family life?

▶ **ISOLATION AND NON-SOCIAL BEHAVIOUR** Do games inhibit social development through the non-social nature of the activity?

▶ **PHYSICAL EFFECTS** Are computer games a health hazard: do they cause eye, hand, back and other physical damage including epilepsy?

These concerns are similar to those raised when television, radio and the cinema were introduced. However, even after decades of study, the issue of whether the media influences the viewer remains a complex one (see Audiences, pp. 25–33).

Who plays games?

According to a 1999 Interactive Digital Software Association survey, 43 per cent of PC gamers and 35 per cent of console gamers are female. Of female gamers, 53 per cent play on-line multiplayer games, compared to 43 per cent of males. Adults make up 75 per cent of video game players.

In the year 2000 broadcasting report *Families and Electronic Entertainment*, 5 per cent of children's leisure time was found to be spent on computer and video games. This is small compared to the most popular activity, watching television, which consumed 33 per cent of their time. The same report showed that the most frequently stated reasons for liking games were that 'game playing is fun' (39 per cent) and 'challenging' (17 per cent). In a similar study, participants stated that they sought variety and challenge in the games they play and that they derive satisfaction from developing skills. Games that were perceived as overly simplistic held little appeal. In the same study, gamers felt the most important aspects of a good game were production quality, inherent challenge, multiple player capability, realistic action and sound effects, and lots of levels. No clear link between the presence or degree of aggressive content and market success was found.

THE CORE GAMER AND THE CASUAL GAMER

There are two types of game players according to game developer and columnist Ernest Adams: the core gamer and the casual gamer.

THE CORE GAMER The core gamer plays for the exhilaration of defeating the game. The core gamer is tolerant of frustration because, at the end of the game, he or she wants to have the sense of having achieved something. The harder the task, the stronger the sense of achievement. The core gamer sees playing games as a hobby that requires dedication. Adams believes that too many games are designed for this market. This is because most game developers actually fall into this category themselves, yet this category actually represents only a minority of players.

THE CASUAL GAMER The casual gamer plays for the sheer enjoyment of the game, but is not overly tolerant of frustration brought on by complex puzzles or interactivity that takes too long to master. If a game stops being entertaining, the casual gamer will simply stop playing.

DIFFERENCES BETWEEN FEMALE GAMERS AND MALE GAMERS

Generally, men like games with more action – especially violent action, games with more hand–eye coordination, and games with lots and lots of strategy. Women tend to like games with more story, more character development, and more interaction with characters, games with solving puzzles, games involving the brain rather than the hand, games with a more social aspect.'

> Roberta Williams, creator *King's Quest* series
> Interview by Dr K Wright and Abby Marold
> on Womengamers.com

▼ ▼ ▼

Hi-tech marketing 'think tank' Interval Research Corporation spent four years researching the difference between female and male game players. Broadly speaking, their findings were as given in the table below.

Other research has shown that girls dislike intense competition, find typical computer games boring, dislike violent and aggressive themes, are bored by the repetitive nature of games, complain about a lack of characters to identify with, and are disappointed by the lack of narrative. This is true for a large number of male gamers as well.

Sheri Graner Ray, president of Sirenia Software, a girls' game manufacturer, believes that girls have no problem with violence – as long as there is reason for it:

▼ ▼ ▼

What girls DON'T like is violence for violence's sake. And not because it's 'icky or yucky', but because it is boring! As far as the girls are concerned … why would anyone want to rip someone's beating heart out 15 times in a row??? BORING!

▼ ▼ ▼

A survey on the website Womengamers.com survey showed that women want:

► better female characters and more of them
► more gender neutral games
► a reduction in sexist game contents
► marketing that acknowledges that women gamers exist
► games targeted specifically towards older adolescent girls and adult women, not just pre-adolescent girls
► gaming websites and publications that do not regale them with image after image of scantily clothed women
► on-line gaming atmospheres that are free of gender harassment
► increased female presence in technical fields and the gaming industry.

GENDER DIFFERENCES IN GAME PLAYING

FEMALES	MALES
Assert social influence and structure relationships	Dominate and defeat
Gain social status by affiliating with some people and excluding others	Gain social status through achievement and physical supremacy
Enjoy multi-sensory immersion, discovery and strong story lines	Enjoy speed and action
Succeed through development of friendships	Succeed through elimination of competitors
Like to explore and have new experiences, with degrees of success and varying outcomes	Play 'to win'
Like to know how something works before they try it	Learn how something works by doing it
Girls enjoy 'friendship adventures'	Boys enjoy 'action games'

Figure 2.37
(Source: Interval Research Corporation)

What effect does playing video games have?

Children have shown that when they're playing games they're capable of incredible levels of strategy and thinking, far more than when they're in school.

Nicola Yelland
Senior lecturer in Early Childhood
Studies at Queensland University
of Technology, Australia

▼ ▼ ▼

Video and computer games are distinguished from television by the way the player 'interacts' with the game. The player is directly involved in the game play and the individual's choices influence the outcome of the game. It is unclear whether this interactivity makes the effects of video games more or less serious. In addition, the wide range of game varieties makes any single conclusion difficult.

In contrast to the negative claims made against video games, researchers have found some positive benefits from game play. These have included the confrontation of challenges and difficulties, and the desire to challenge one's skills. Researchers also mention the way games encourage the use of computers and alleviate people's fear of computers in a recreational manner, enhanced educational progress and the development of advanced eye-to-hand coordination.

A study conducted by Dr Tony Liddicoat, head of the Department of Languages at the Australian National University, has found that playing video games involves the use of quite complex skills. 'Gameplaying requires the user to process input from a variety of sources (graphics, text, sound, etc.), synthesising this input and then building a problem-solving response in order to cope with the challenges posed by a particular video game.'

Dr Liddicoat believes that playing video games helps to develop strategic problem-solving skills, enhances high-speed recognition and increases the ability to process language and numeric data rapidly. Players have to learn to solve problems quickly, test hypotheses and decode puzzles. Patricia Greenwood, a psychology professor at UCLA, has studied the relationship between video games and intelligence. Her research attributes an increase in worldwide 'nonverbal IQ' (i.e. spatial skills, the use of icons for problem solving and the

ability to understand things from multiple viewpoints) to the spread of video games.

Dr Liddicoat's study also found that video games tend to promote regular learning, as players practise their skills and take on the game's challenge to reach the next level. Some studies have even shown that children who play video games do better at school than their peers!

One study found that children, through their exposure to computer games as well as other media, have developed ways in which to process a large amount of sound and image information simultaneously. In the research project, a theatre screening two films at once was filled with both children and adults. Most adults were unable to cope and had to leave the theatre. The children, meanwhile, were able to watch all of the presentation and answer questions on all of the films. Many children even noted similarities between the films. The researchers stated: 'you could have added a third film, or even a fourth, and the kids would have kept up'.

A 1990 study found that video games lead to a relatively high level of social and family involvement in the playing of games – up to twice as high as any other form of media. Since that study, however, the nature of games has changed. Older studies deal with simple games the duration of which was limited to a matter of minutes. Today's games can involve intense, individual game play over several days, with relatively advanced narratives and engaging player interfaces.

Dr Nicola Yelland, an early childhood specialist, has criticised any conclusions based on these old studies. 'In many cases, the most violent game during this earlier time period was *Pac Man*, which needs to be sharply contrasted with the versions of *Mortal Kombat* and *Death Trap* now available.' According to Dr Yelland, it would be 'gross generalisation' to conclude that games were not harmful on the basis of evidence reported in older studies.

There are also difficulties with the definition of just who is the audience. According to Tom Zito of Digital Pictures, researchers and policy makers have failed to identify a huge part of the audience for computer games – adults. In many cases, children who grew up on *Pong* are now in their thirties and still like interactive entertainment products. 'If you think everything ought to be appropriate for an eleven-year-old, then your really deluding yourself,' says Zito. Kevin Burmeister, of Sega Ozisoft, says more than half of Sega's game software sales were to adults.

ARE GAMES ADDICTIVE?

One of the major criticisms levelled against computer and video games is that they are 'addictive'. Computer games are specifically designed to be immersive and addictive – just one more hour, one more level.

Studies in the United States have found that, while computer games are popular among the young, actual time spent playing games is low compared to other leisure activities. Playing games becomes a priority for some in the same way as watching television, playing music or playing sport does for others.

However, cases of 'addiction' have been reported. Most of these have been transitory cases, where the addiction is a short-lived occurrence.

The term 'addiction' is a misleading one. Addiction usually refers to a situation where a lack of an additive substance actually denies the body of some essential component it cannot properly function without – either in a physiological or psychological manner. Addiction to games, on the other hand, is usually a sign of an immense love for the media form, a lack of other activities in which to engage or a lack social skills. Analysts suggest these symptoms are not *caused* by video games. Instead, the symptoms are possibly worsened by the games and by the lack of social contact that accompanies their play.

▼ ▼ ▼

It seems that the answer lies in the extent to which your game playing affects other aspects of your life. If your grades are slipping, if you've lost a job because of your preoccupation with gaming, if you're constantly tired from lack of sleep due to gaming, if you never have a meal that isn't delivered to your door in a red car with a sign on top, if you like yourself more as your RPG character than in face-to-face interactions, you might want to take a look at the effect that your game playing is having on your life.

Dr Kathyrn Wright
Womengamers.com feature writer
and game audience researcher

▼ ▼ ▼

DISPLACEMENT EFFECTS

Concerns have also been raised about the possibility of games displacing or taking over from family activities, school performance, peer relations and other more active forms of leisure.

A study conducted in the United States in 1993 has shown that the average game player spends between one and six hours a week playing video games. However, only 1 per cent of girls and 6 per cent of boys spent fifteen hours or more per week playing games.

Television statistics from the same age group show that the average person spends between two and three hours a day watching television. This represents 74 per cent of the total media use by those studied. Video and computer games are the only recreational activity that has ever challenged the domination of television.

Games are also taking over the cultural link with youth once firmly held by rock and pop music. Instead of relating to music idols, game idols have begun to take their place. Sega claims it does not compete against other game companies, but against all other forms of leisure. Games often even come with accompanying music CDs.

The most common location for playing games was found to be in the home, with 77 per cent of all games being played there. Among those who do play games in arcades, 10 to 15 per cent of those surveyed reported high levels of game play.

DO COMPUTER GAMES PROMOTE VIOLENCE AND ANTISOCIAL BEHAVIOUR?

We have movie role models showing violence as fun, and videogames where you kill, and get rewarded for killing, for hours and hours. It is a very combustible mix, enraged young people with access to semiautomatic weapons, exposed to violence as entertainment, violence shown as exciting and thrilling.

Sissella Bok
Mayhem

▼ ▼ ▼

Researchers have raised concerns that games with high violent content may promote aggressive attitudes and behaviour in their players. Sissella Bok, in her book *Mayhem*, writes that young people's lives are saturated with graphic violence in a way that is different and more dangerous than in previous generations. *Feed* magazine journalist Mark Pesce is worried about the way in which

games such as *Quake* detach violence from the usual moral universe that surrounds it: 'there are few limits and no consequences'.

Associate professor and former Army lieutenant David Grossman believes that violent video games such as *Doom* and *Quake* are 'murder simulators' that help break down the natural inhibitions we have towards killing. He states that the US military uses *Quake*-like games to improve 'fire-rates', encouraging soldiers to pull the trigger more readily. Only one-fifth of US soldiers in combat in World War II fired their weapons, a rate that the military pushed to 95 per cent in the Vietnam War, in part through the use of simulations designed to make shooting at humans more routine and 'normal'.

Dr Jeanne Funk, a psychologist at the University of Toledo, believes that the main argument against this theory is that of 'skill transfer'. 'There's a tremendous difference between clicking a mouse in *Half-Life* and hefting a real eight-pound shotgun.' Barry Steinhardt, associate director of the American Civil Liberties Union, has found that there is 'no substantial social-science evidence that shows that entertainment causes violence. The people who commit violence should be held accountable, not the entertainment industry.'

In an examination of the international research on video games, games researcher Kevin Durkin found that, in the few studies conducted on this topic, there were small correlations between the amount of time a person spends playing games and aggression displayed by that person. There appeared to be a slight tendency for either more aggressive children to play more computer games or for games to promote a small rise in aggression in high-frequency players.

A 1996 study, however, found that aggressive content in films had a far greater impact than violence in computer games. This was seen to be because video game players were more interested in beating the enemy than in concentrating on the violent aspects of the games. Dr Jeanne Funk's research shows that players who prefer games with a large amount of violence are more likely to be withdrawn, rather than aggressive.

▼ ▼ ▼

Violence is a normal part of our culture, and having a knee jerk reaction and criticising games is simply not logical or fair. At the end of the day there are a host of psychological, sociological and circumstantial factors that may prompt a person to grab a gun and cause havoc, but if games were really that bad why aren't there more massacres?

Steve Polak
Editor, Playnow.com.au

▼ ▼ ▼

CENSORSHIP

Governments across the world have been besieged by hysterical mass media calls to crack down on violent computer games. While demands for censorship have been made since the early days of game development, it is only since games have started developing a greater sense of realism that governments have acted. Games such as *Mortal Kombat* with its 'fatality tricks' where the player could rip the heart and spinal columns out of their victims have opened the floodgates to new hyper-violent games.

In the United Kingdom, makers of violent video games are supposed to pay the British Board of Film Classification (BBFC) to classify their games under the 1984 Video Recordings Act before they can be sold. BBFC spokeswoman Anna Kemble calls it a 'voluntary' system. Controversial games need to come through the board before they can be legally sold. In several cases, games that were 'particularly nasty or gory' have had to be toned down in order to become 'acceptable' for general release.

The first game to be denied release certification in the United Kingdom was *Carmageddon*, a game where the principal objective is to run down pedestrians on city streets, with extra merit added for the number of deaths and their 'artistic' nature. Before the UK release of *Carmageddon*, game producer Interplay was requested by the board to change the colour of spilled blood from red to green, and to make the human victims look more zombie-like. Fears about computer games such as *Carmageddon II* are based on an assumption that people cannot distinguish between the fantasy of games and reality. The board also failed to see that the game contained violence for humorous effect, rather than for gratuitous reasons. Interestingly, the first game ever to be removed from sale was *Death Race 2000*, a 1976 game where the aim of the game was to run down stick-figure pedestrians. This was the first public outcry about video game violence.

The United States and Australia also classify video and computer games under the same ratings structure as films and video. In the United States, however, many stores are taking censorship into their own hands. Nationwide, M-rated games are not sold in the two major chain stores Montgomery Ward and Sears Roebuck (an M rating in the United States means that sales to a person under 17 can only be made with parental permission). In individual states and cities, local governments are cracking down on game arcades. In Indianapolis, coin-operated video games in which people are decapitated, dismembered, mutilated or maimed are off-limits to children. The game machine must also be partitioned off by a curtain or wall so that it remains out of view of minors.

As a result of the public exposure violent games receive in the media, games' marketers regularly market games by exaggerating the violence within them. *Grand Theft Auto* (GTA), a game in which players can rise through the underworld by performing jobs for gangster godfathers, uses comedic violence and cartoon-like graphics, but was promoted in the United Kingdom as an ultra-violent 'gangsta' game. This game, too, came under the BBFC's scrutiny and was awarded an 18+ certificate.

Simon Butler, general manager of *Grand Theft Auto* game distributor BMG Interactive, says that the game should not fall into the hands of children. He places the blame for this with retailers who sell the game to children and parents who let their children play games targeted at adults. 'It has an 18 certificate and it should not be getting into their hands. *Grand Theft Auto* is not a game for kids. The average PC gamer is aged 26.'

IDENTIFICATION

Identification occurs where there is intense and close involvement with a particular character or character type. In games, identification can lead to the player wishing actually to become that character, leading to the unconscious copying of the character's actions or beliefs. Kevin Durkin summed up these concerns in his study:

▼ ▼ ▼

Players enter new and absorbing, simulated environments in which successful performance demands total concentration on the actions, circumstances and potentialities of a particular entity.

Given that some of the 'star' characters will have violent, often lethal, capacities, the processes and consequences of identification merit careful attention.

▼ ▼ ▼

Identification is a common theme in fiction. Writers want their readers to identify with their characters because it adds emotional power to a story. Games take this effect further. While the character you are playing is not you, you still invest a lot of time and energy in it. In massive multiplayer games, the effect is exaggerated even more, as the role-playing is in a sense a performance for all of the other people you are playing against and your character represents your position in the game.

CATHARSIS

A video game where you pretend to beat someone up is probably preferable to actually beating someone up in the backyard.

Henry Jenkins
Lecturer, MIT, in an interview with CNN

▼ ▼ ▼

Catharsis occurs when the expression of aggressive feelings discharges pent-up aggression. Some people believe this can lead to a reduced desire for violence. In computer games, a player can release aggressive tendencies in simulated combat. Consequently, some researchers believe that playing a video game can reduce the need for violence. Lending some support to this theory, many game players talk about feeling 'drained' after playing games.

Cathartic effects have not been effectively researched to date and remain just theoretical. Some researchers are worried that the cathartic effect of a game may actually intensify the relationship between the release of tension and aggression. Researchers and psychologists Craig Anderson and Karen E. Dill speculate that computer game violence influences behaviour not by inciting aggressive feelings, but by teaching only aggressive solutions to problems.

The history of video games

Historically, video games are the only media form not dominated by US companies. The world's largest game system manufacturers are Japanese,

BRIEF TIMELINE OF VIDEO GAME HISTORY

1951 Ralph Baer conceives the video game.

1958 The first video game is built from a modified oscilloscope.

1961 The first interactive video game is created.

1971 The first commercial video game, *Computer Space*, is released as a stand-alone machine in a bar.

1972 The first text-based adventure game, *Hunt the Wumpus*, is developed.

1976 Game cartridges are developed. In this same year, the first driving game, *Night Driver*, is released by Atari.

1977 Atari becomes a household name with its 2600 system.

1978 The first Japanese game machine is released – the Nintendo Computer Othello. Atari releases the first home computer especially designed to run games – the Atari 400 – and the first vector (line-based) video game is released. Also in this year, the game *Space Invaders* is released. Breaking all known sales records, this game caused coin shortages and riots in Japan and school truancy in the United States.

1979 The first hand-held video game, the Mattel Bradley Microvision, is released, as is the first colour game, *Galaxian*. The first MUD (Multi User Dungeon) is also created in 1979. This is the first networkable multiplayer game

1980 *Pac Man*, originally called *Puckman*, is released. This was the first video game popular with both males and females. The first game with speech, *Stratovox*, is released, as is the first adventure game with graphics, *Mystery House*.

1981 Nintendo creates *Donkey Kong*. A character from this game, Jumpman, was later renamed Mario by US Nintendo staff and went on to become one half of the famous Mario Brothers.

1983 A huge crash in the sales of video games occurs. With too many discount games and game systems on the market sales plummet.

Many game companies, such as Atari and Mattel Electronics, are dumped by their corporate owners.

1986 Three years after the sales crash of video games, the Nintendo Entertainment System (NES) is released. The system debuts with *Super Mario Brothers* and becomes a huge hit.

1989 The Nintendo Game Boy is released.

1989 NEC release the first 16-bit game system with an optional CD player. This is the first time that games are released on CD.

1991 Sega introduces *Sonic the Hedgehog* in an attempt to wrest market domination from Nintendo's *Super Mario Brothers*.

1992 The first 3D shooter, *Wolfenstein 3D*, is released. A whole new game genre is introduced and players are immersed in a game as they had never been before.

1993 The first 32-bit games machines are released. This increase in graphics power led to more sophisticated games with more realistic graphics. As a consequence, in this same year, the first political inquiry was held into video game violence in the United States.

1995 The 32-bit Sony PlayStation is released and becomes a huge sales success. Later in that year, the rival Nintendo 64-bit machine was released. Lack of software damaged its sales. With the sophistication of the home game systems, games arcades suffer a lack of popularity. During the mid-1990s, simulator arcade machines integrating more moving parts to create amusement park ride/video game combinations appear, in order to try to win back players from the home systems.

1996 *Quake*, the first action game designed for multiplayer use over the Internet, is released. On-line gaming becomes mass market.

1998 The 128-bit Sega *Dreamcast* is released. This is the first home games system to allow players to interact across the Internet.

2000 The Sony PlayStation II is released, bringing with it unprecedented graphic capabilities and realism. It, too, allows Internet access for multiplayer gaming.

as are many of the leading game producers. Many video games are influenced by Japanese and not American culture. Many famous video games such as *Space Invaders*, *Pac Man*, *Donkey Kong*, *Super Mario Brothers*, *Sonic the Hedgehog*, *Pokémon* and the *Street Fighter* series are Japanese. The history of video games is characterised by a number of unique and innovative ideas and game styles, and by advances in technology.

The concept of the video game was conceived in 1951 by American television engineer Ralph Baer. He wanted to build a simple game into a television set, but management where he worked ignored the idea. The first working video game was developed in 1958 by physicist Willy Higinbotham, to keep visitors to his laboratory from becoming bored. It was a simple tennis-like game played on a modified oscilloscope. In 1961, MIT student David Rosen developed *Space War*, the first real interactive video game. Played on a supercomputer that was as big as a small house, his game used simple computer text symbols to represent the characters. Seventeen years after conceiving the idea of a television-based game, Ralph Baer finally patented his video game concept in 1968.

The first commercial video game was released in 1971, when 1500 Computer Space machines were released; however, the public, used to the simplicity of pinball machines, found the complex controls too difficult to use. In 1972, the game *Pong*, short for *Ping Pong*, was released. It was a huge success in bars across the United States. In the same year, Magnavox released the first home game console machine.

At first, games machines were capable of playing only one game built into each machine. As technology advanced, portable cassette tape players were used to load the game on to the game console. In 1976, game cartridges became the most popular way to distribute games. However, early computer-based games still used cassette tapes on which to store games. During the 1980s and 1990s, disks and CDs became the best way to store games; however, game piracy became a problem, as these were easily copied. Now the most popular format for games is the DVD, but these, too, present a piracy problem.

The video game market has been traditionally driven not only by technology, money and marketing, but also by each of the major companies 'superstar' characters. The best-known examples of game characters are Nintendo's *Super Mario Brothers* and Sega's *Sonic the Hedgehog*. These characters, and not the games system they were played on, defined which company had market domination.

▼ ▼ ▼ ▼ ▼ ▼ ▼

activities

1. If you are a computer game player, how much time would you usually spend playing games each week? Compare this with others in your class.

► Does the average playing time in the class correspond with the figures below?
Weekly play times
Up to 6 hours per week – average time spent playing games
More than 15 hours a week – 1 per cent of girls; 6 per cent of boys

► How does your class average differ? What may be the reasons for any change? Is the more involving nature of modern games leading to people spending more time playing games? Discuss.

► How would your time be spent if you were not playing games?

2. Do you believe games are becoming a more important media source? To substantiate your answer, find the amount of time you and your friends spend playing video and computer games. Compare this to the time spent on other media activities such as going to the movies, reading newspapers, listening to the radio, watching television or using the Internet.

► Compare your data to that found by the rest of the class.

► Are there any gender or other differences?

3. In a 1996 study, children were asked what media form was the worst for promoting violent behaviour: television and movies, or computer games. Their conclusion was that television and movies had more effect on them than computer games. Do you agree or disagree with them. Why do you agree or disagree?

4. What positive benefits do you think can be derived from playing computer games? What aspects could you add to the games to make them more positive?

major assignment

Written assignment

1. You have been provided with government funding for the development of a computer game. Similar to film funding from the government, one of the conditions attached to the funding is that the game you write is required to be based on UK experiences and use local characters.

▶ Briefly outline three different ideas for games based on a number of different kinds of UK experiences and using a range of stereotypical and non-stereotypical local characters.

▶ Explain why the experiences and characters you chose could be considered to be specific to the United Kingdom.

▶ Develop one of the ideas into a proposal that could be submitted to a government funding body. Include in your submission the game narrative, character descriptions and reasons why your game is worthy of funding (economic grounds alone are not sufficient). Why would your video game be of cultural benefit to the United Kingdom?

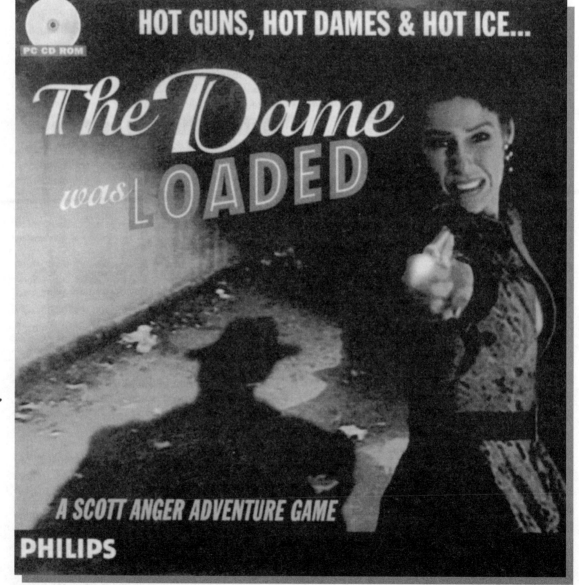

Figure 2.38 The Dame Was Loaded, *an Australian-made American-style CD-based gangster movie, featuring American themes, icons, characteristics and even American accents. The product is supposed to be Australian, but which culture is actually being represented?*

2. Conduct a survey among groups of your peers, both game users and non-users, on one or more of the following topics:

▶ *Violence in video games* Questions asked could include: do video games encourage violence, does the interactive nature of games make the effects of violence worse, does the fact that the player is concentrating on his or her game actions rather than the violence on screen lessen the effects, etc?

▶ *Representation in video games* Questions asked could include: what are the typical characters in video games, are they similar to those in movies and if so what kinds of movies, what characters are least likely to be seen in video games, etc?

Discuss your findings with reference to the arguments in this chapter, as well as further research.

3. Consider Figure 2.38, an Australian CD-based interactive movie. List arguments for and against the idea of UK government initiatives to support a similar UK product that would feature only American cultural idioms.

Production assignment

1. Produce the script to a short (five-minute) interactive movie. The steps you will need to undertake include:

▶ writing a basic story and inventing characters for that story

▶ writing at least three different endings for the story.

▶ planning and 'mapping out' a number of ways through the story to reach any of the three endings, making sure that all paths are resolved. The easiest way to do this is to construct a 'flow chart'.

2. Start with a single beginning point and three endings. Between these start and end points diagrammatically map out three story paths. This way you can see what scenes need to be written, where they intersect, and where they lead. A simple example is shown below.

Next, script the dialogue for each path through the story (some scenes will be repeated on each journey through the narrative, particularly where scenes intersect).

If you need to know how an interactive story works, go to a library and find a 'Choose Your Own Adventure Book'. These books were very popular in the 1980s and have a structure that is very similar to that of an interactive movie script.

chapter three
Film

3 ▶

The Language of Film and Television

The language of the moving image is a complex signifying system, just as complex as our systems of spoken, written and non-verbal communication. Meaning in films, television and other media texts is the result of the conscious choices made by the producers of the text, at each stage of its production, and the knowledge and experience brought to the text by the spectator.

Many of the aspects of moving image language described in the following pages apply to both film and television; however, some uses are particular to specific types of film or television programme and therefore will need to be studied more closely in their contexts in order to explain their particular purposes and effects.

The shot: the unit of visual language

In the visual language of photography, television and film, the *shot* is the smallest unit, equivalent to a very short sentence in prose.

A shot has at least two definitions. Some see it as the interval of time from when the camera is first turned on a scene until the stop button is pressed. This definition includes any continuous movement within the shot. Others define the shot as being the duration of time until the camera is moved to another position. This definition may or may not include continuous camera movement, depending upon how strictly it is interpreted.

Whichever the preferred definition, both contain *picture statements*. Like sentences, picture statements have subjects. The picture statement may be saying: 'Look at these great wide, open plains.' The next shot may make the statement: 'Look at this man on a horse – see what he is doing.'

Picture statements are usually changed for one of two reasons: either a new subject is being introduced or something different about the same subject is going to be shown.

A film-maker or cinematographer faces many choices and decisions when making a film or television programme. He or she can consider five variables when creating a shot: shot size, framing, focus, angle and movement. These aspects are sometimes referred to as *mise-en-shot*, the selection of these five components which are then placed in the shot or frame.

SHOT SIZE

There are eight main shot sizes. Visual emphasis is directly related to the size of the subject in the shot. A big, close subject is more powerful, because it fills the screen. Therefore, the choice of which shot to use is the most fundamental decision every director makes.

The definition of shot sizes depends on just what is the subject of the shot. Most definitions work on a human scale. They define the size of the shot according to how much of the human body can be fitted into the frame.

1. EXTREME LONG SHOT (ELS) is a wide view of the complete setting, such as a cityscape, open prairies with mountains in the background (as in John Ford's classic Westerns) or expanses of desert (as in David Lean's *Lawrence of Arabia* (UK, 1962)). In human terms, a person would be barely visible in the whole scene. The purpose of this shot is to emphasise an expanse of space, showing, isolation, grandeur or spectacle. It is not used in television as often as in film 'which lends itself more to the spectacular' due to the comparatively small size of the television image.

2. LONG SHOT (LS) is somewhat closer than the extreme long shot, but still shows the complete scene. On a human scale, the human figure is clearly visible and the complete person fits easily within the frame. In a typical long shot, the background still dominates the human figure. A long shot is most often used, as an establishing shot, to present the whole scene, often at the start of a film, television programme or a new location. This is so that the audience can understand where the action will take place, regardless of how it is subsequently fragmented by the editing of shots of parts of the scene.

3. MEDIUM LONG SHOT (MLS) still gives a great deal of information about the setting. Human characters can be seen in detail and almost all of the body is in the frame. From somewhere below the knees is the most common framing. French film-makers once called this 'the American shot' as it was very common in classic Hollywood films of the 1930s and 1940s. The medium long shot affords the audience a good view of characters, especially their body language and how they are positioned in relation to another character, and so is often used as a two-shot (of two characters).

4. MEDIUM SHOT (MS) is defined by some as 'not too close, not too far'. On the human body, a medium shot would start at around the waist and include a little space above the head. Gesture, expression and details of physical appearance are now more clearly visible. It is often used, with a medium close-up to link a long shot to a close-up, for example, as one character approaches another who is in the foreground, without which, the change in distance would be over-dramatic.

5. MEDIUM CLOSE-UP (MCU) frames the subject moderately closely. Medium close-ups are the typical frame for a newsreader. The head and shoulders fit comfortably in the frame. Again, this makes the transition between long shots and close-ups and is suitable for conversations between characters and reaction shots, especially in television drama.

6. CLOSE-UP (CU) shows the detail of a subject. A typical close-up might show just the face of a person. The close-up is often used to show the features in greater detail to underline the personality or emotion of a character.

7. BIG CLOSE-UP (BCU) shows almost all of the detail of its subject. On the face, a big close-up includes

from the middle of the forehead to just above the chin. This would show the the *social triangle* of the two eyes and the mouth. Big close-ups are used for extremes of emotion or prop details.

8. EXTREME CLOSE-UP (ECU) shows only a portion of detail or magnifies something that is minute. An example could be a dramatic focusing on someone's eyes or a significant prop detail. Often an extreme close-up is used to create a sense of mystery or tension.

FRAMING

The photographic frame is not just a simple border, according to the American film studies academics David Bordwell and Kristin Thompson. It is not like the margin of a page. The frame produces a vantage point. It gives a point of view, one that is used to select some details and not others. It determines *what* we look at and *how* we look at it.

Extreme long shot (ELS)   Long shot (LS)

Medium long shot (MLS)   Medium shot (MS)

Medium close-up (MCU)   Close-up (CU)

Big close-up (BCU)   Extreme close-up (ECU)

Figure 3.1
The eight shot sizes. The human body is used to define the size of the shot.

Usually, the frame remains on a horizontal axis, with the exception of a *canted* frame, which is one that is not parallel with the horizontal axis. It is often used as an expressionistic device to suggest the point of view of a character with psychological instability, such as madness, or a drugged state. It can also be used in anticipation of a dramatic moment, such as the appearance of a villain down a corridor or a low-angle shot of the exterior of a haunted house.

COMPOSITION

Composing a shot is a matter of arranging its elements to create a desirable effect. Several rules can help with this, many of which originate from the compositional rules of fine art. Indeed, many film-makers have been inspired by the composition and use of colour by particular artists. In addition, it has been said that the way in which the western eye reads a page of writing from top left to bottom right has influenced the ways in which we 'read' the cinema frame of a film, and therefore, the way in which shots are composed.

Robert McKee, a former screenwriter for US television and a theorist on narrative structure, in his analysis of *Casablanca* (USA, 1942), identified

parts of the screen as possessing qualities that affect the way in which the audience subconsciously interprets a character according to where they are placed in the frame.

McKee suggests that the left side of the frame has negative connotations and that the centre of the frame is the weakest part of it. He asserts that both parts of the frame are where Rick Blaine (Humphrey Bogart) is placed for most of the film and that this subconsciously signals his moral weakness and cowardice to the audience. Any character that is placed on the right-hand side has connotations of solidity, balance and strength, which is where Ilsa Lund (Ingrid Bergman), the moral centre of the film, is placed throughout. This is an arguable theory, related to the rule of thirds below, but one that is worth considering in an analysis of composition within the film frame.

LINES AND DIAGONALS Placing elements on imaginary lines can create interesting visual effects. These lines could be horizontally, vertically or diagonally across the image. Diagonal lines build a sense of drama – which may foreshadow the fate of a character – as they increase the sense of depth and movement within the frame.

RULE OF THIRDS Some say the subject of a photograph should never be placed in the centre of the frame. Instead, the focus of interest should be at the intersection of imaginary lines that divide the frame into thirds.

MISE-EN-SCÈNE

The French term *mise-en-scène* translates as 'put in the scene', or frame. It refers to all the visual details a film-maker can include in the screen image. These details could include the props, the setting and the lighting. The term *mise-en-scène* also includes details about the actors' outward appearance (including make-up, costumes, performance), body language and the way in which they are placed in relation to each other by the director (known as *blocking*).

Mise-en-scène is the method of communicating a mass of information in a film, and is equivalent to long descriptive passages in a novel. Some definitions of *mise-en-scène* include mise-en-shot, which refers to how a shot is constructed by the use of the camera (see pp. 152–4).

Figure 3.2
Kept in check, mate! Two framings of a chess game; each has an entirely different meaning. The wider frame (below) gives the audience more information. But even this wider frame is a selection. Beyond the frame could be a prison warder, a lunch trolley or any number of other things capable of changing the meaning of the picture still further.

Figure 3.3
Julia Roberts and Albert Finney in Erin Brockovich *(USA, 2000). Note how the characters are positioned on the vertical 'thirds' of the screen. Also, whilst they are sharply in focus, the rest of the scene is less so.*

LIGHTING

Lighting is another eloquent and complex aspect of film and television language. It is an essential aspect, as film and television need light sources for us to be able to see the image on the screen. Basic lighting consists of a key light, a back light and a fill light; some films and television productions are able to use natural light, enhanced by the use of reflective devices.

The long hours of strong sunlight in California are one of the reasons the US film industry relocated from the East Coast to the West Coast in the early days of the Hollywood film industry. Some lighting, especially for television, aspires to *naturalism*, but many films employ a style known as *pictorialism* (using lighting for aesthetic effect) in order to create more striking and expressionistic (expressing mood and emotion) effects.

Lighting can use colour and manipulate contrast, to create or reduce shadows, in order to suggest associated meanings. For example, red lights are used to convey anger, danger or drama, or any combination of the three, while blue lights are seen as cold, mechanical and industrial. The angle of a light is also important, as the effects of its angle can signify something about a character –

for example, an actor lit from below can look threatening and sinister.

FOCUS

If something is out of focus, you will not want to bother looking at it. Film-makers can use focus to make the audience pay attention to certain details. Selective focus can be used to draw attention to someone's face, for example. The background and other details can be made irrelevant by keeping them out of focus. Out-of-focus shots may also be used to indicate a character losing or regaining consciousness, either due to sleep or injury.

DEEP FOCUS is a stylistic choice, as demonstrated by the director Orson Welles in *Citizen Kane* (USA, 1941) and *The Magnificent Ambersons* (USA, 1942). It allows for the foreground, middle ground and background to be in focus at the same time. This can reduce the need for editing, as the actors are directed to move around the width and depth of a shot and will still remain in focus.

Sometimes the focus is changed during a shot. There are two kinds of focus change.

Film

FOLLOW FOCUS is where the camera follows its moving subject, keeping the focus narrowed on the subject alone, while the background changes. This indicates the importance of the subject being followed.

PULL OR RACK FOCUS is used when the focus is suddenly changed to direct attention away from one subject and towards another. For example, a shot with a wire netting fence in sharp focus may suddenly be pull focused onto prisoners exercising in the enclosed yard beyond. This may be used to draw our attention to another subject, either subtly or dramatically, depending on the pull's speed.

CAMERA ANGLE

The camera angle helps to establish the spatial and emotional relationship the audience has with the subject of the shot. It is also vital to achieve an eyeline match of characters within a sequence, so that we can believe that one character is actually looking at another. This is especially important for the success of the editing process, where, in reality, the original footage may be of an actor talking to a piece of card, as in a close-up, which is often shot without other actors. It is also

important if the character he or she addressing is computer-generated, as in *The Mask* (USA, 1994), and will be added later.

HIGH CAMERA ANGLE This is the angle created when the camera is positioned high and tilted down on the subject. High camera angles tend to put the audience in the position of an adult looking down on a child. The subject looks inferior, or vulnerable; the viewer feels superior.

EXTREMELY HIGH CAMERA ANGLE If the camera is very high, almost overhead, it gives a bird's-eye view of the subject. Sometimes this can create a feeling that God is looking down on events or impart emotional detachment from the drama, such as in the gas station fire in *The Birds* (USA, 1963). In certain cases, it can suggest impending death or punishment. This occurs, for example, at the end of the film *Bonnie and Clyde* (USA, 1967).

LOW CAMERA ANGLE When the camera is positioned low to the ground and tilts upward at its subject, the viewer feels inferior or threatened. The subject seems overpowering. A low camera angle creates the feeling of a child looking up at an all-powerful adult.

Figure 3.4
In the film Psycho (USA, 1960), Marion Crane steals $40,000 and drives out of Phoenix to California. She sleeps overnight in the car, but is awakened by a suspicious police-man. Marion is intimidated by him and a high camera angle makes us feel her lack of power and inferiority. The low camera angle gives the police-man considerable extra power and superiority. The audience also feels menaced when he looks directly at us.

MOVEMENT

Camera movement within a shot directs the audience to where they should look. It can help create dominance and establish visual emphasis. But the movement of the camera can also be like our own movement. When the camera moves in, for example, it is as though we have moved closer ourselves. This increases our spatial relationship with what we see on screen and is intended to increase our emotional response to what we see, whether it is intimacy and empathy, or a predatory or voyeuristic response, for example. The following are types of camera movement.

PANNING means moving the camera in a long horizontal sweep from one side of the scene to the other. Since a long rotation from the left or right like this can be difficult to perform, most camera operators use a tripod. The term came originally from the word *panorama*, meaning a wide, unbroken view. A pan is a good way of setting the scene. It can also be used to heighten the suspense, as the audience scans the scene waiting to be shown something. The speed of a pan can be fast (as in a *swish* or *whip* pan) or slow, depending on the desired effect.

TRACKING shots are where the camera moves along the ground — forwards, backwards, diagonally or from side to side. Originally, the cameras were moved on little railway-like tracks. This method is still used today. However, in a *dolly shot* (a dolly is a tripod with wheels), the whole camera can move in the same way without a track. More recently, Steadicams are also being used.

Steadicam is the trade name for a lightweight, counterbalanced camera fixed to the camera operator's body, which enables smooth and steady hand-held shots to be taken. Its notable early uses were in horror films, such as *Halloween* (USA, 1978) and *The Shining* (USA, 1980).

Tracking shots move the audience through the scene and make the shot seem more three-dimensional. They are also very definite about indicating what is important to the audience: the subject being followed.

CRANE SHOTS are performed by a camera moving up or down on a mechanical arm or crane. The crane can simply move vertically up or down. It can also, however, be raised or lowered at all sorts of angles.

Crane shots are useful for giving a feeling of entering or leaving a series of events. A crane shot up and away at the end of a scene gives an air of finality, as in the last shot of *Much Ado about Nothing* (UK, 1993). It is as though we are returning to a distant universe after having momentarily entered a character's life on Earth.

ZOOM SHOTS are similar to tracking shots in, or a track back. In a zoom shot, however, the camera remains still and so the effect is a little different. A zoom does not have the effect of allowing us to move through the scene. Unlike a tracking shot, it does not add to the three-dimensional feeling. Instead, a zoom enlarges the subject of the image, making it seem more important. Zooming in on a character suggests we should listen to him or her. Zooming out has the opposite effect.

The zoom is a technique that has no parallel in the human eye. Some film-makers refer to it as an unnatural technique because the eye cannot do it. Rather, it is an expressionistic device; whether fast or slow, it can create, intensify and evoke powerful feelings — especially when accompanied by other elements such as music. If realism is desired, film-makers tend to use the zoom sparingly. News filming is an exception to this. Here, the zoom is used to convey a detail or piece of information quickly and directly to the viewer, when time is of the essence.

TILT movement swivels the camera up or down while it is mounted on the tripod. It is like a vertical pan. Like the pan, the tilt gives the impression that something will eventually be revealed. It can also give the feeling of a scene gradually unrolling like a scroll, from top to bottom.

▼ ▼ ▼ ▼ ▼ ▼ ▼

activities

1. Below is a list of four of the main elements of the shot, and types of each of these elements. Create a portfolio of magazine photographs that illustrate each of these. (The fifth element, movement, is obviously excluded from still photographs in magazines).

Place each photograph on a separate page of your portfolio. Title each page with the element and the element type that the photo illustrates (e.g. shot size – medium long shot). Underneath each picture, explain how the image you chose demonstrates the element and the element type in the title. Also explain the effect of the element in each particular photograph.

ELEMENTS AND ELEMENT TYPES OF STILL SHOT

SHOT SIZE: extreme long shot (ELS), long shot (LS), medium long shot (MLS), medium shot (MS), medium close-up (MCU), close-up (CU), big close-up (BCU) and extended close-up (ECU)

FRAMING: lines and diagonals, rule of thirds

FOCUS: selective focus

CAMERA ANGLE: high, extremely high and low camera angle.

2. Below is a list of the elements of movement and focus. Record examples of shots from film or television that illustrate elements and types. On paper, list each shot and the type of movement or focus it represents (for example, movement – pan). Explain how the shot demonstrates the type of movement or focus, and the effect of the element in each particular shot.

ADDITIONAL ELEMENTS AND ELEMENT TYPES OF MOVING SHOT

FOCUS: follow focus, pull focus

MOVEMENT: pan, tracking, crane, zoom, tilt.

Editing: Shot-to-Shot Relationships

A Hollywood film contains between 800 and 1200 shots. For a narrative film, the shooting ratio of filmed *rushes* (original, unedited footage) to final selection is usually about eight to one. However, news and documentary genres, being relatively less tightly planned than films, can have shooting ratios as high as twenty to one.

Editing is often thought of as a process of cutting down. It can also be seen as a means of 'building up' a story. Both are valid approaches. In its simplest form, editing may be defined as the process of coordinating and connecting one shot with the next. Editing is used, most commonly, to reproduce a sense of narrative and spatial continuity (*continuity editing*) that is often referred to as the 'invisible style', used in Hollywood's Golden Age. However, some film and television directors use editing self-consciously in order to create obvious stylistic effects.

The *180-degree rule* is a key aspect of the creation of continuity from the set-up of a shot through to the editing process. Sometimes termed the *imaginary or director's line*, this refers to a hypothetical line drawn between two or more actors to keep the camera on one side of the action so that the audience's perspective is consistent, even if several viewpoints are edited together. If the camera crosses the line, the audience may feel disorientated by the change of perspective.

The use of a *master shot*, the filming of a single scene, usually in a continuous long shot (sometimes by multiple cameras), parts of which are later shot in medium and close-up and edited together, is a classic technique used by Hollywood studios in their heyday. It offered directors and editors a number of choices in the editing process and was another aspect of Hollywood's *invisible style*, whereby the audience was unaware that any editing had taken place. It also offered them a 'safety' shot, if a cutaway or complicated shot did not work or was lost. If this happened, they could always cut back to the master shot.

Editing involves a dilemma. The break between one shot and another potentially interrupts the audience's attention. Each cut is a small jolt for the viewer. Every time a cut is made, there is a risk that the viewer will be brought back to reality. On the other hand, there is no other way of constructing a film. The film-maker's dilemma lies in utilising editing as a tool, yet also controlling its disruptive power at the same time. The negative, unsettling aspects of editing may be controlled and used to advantage using two related elements: juxtapositioning of shots and transitional devices.

The director Alfred Hitchcock produced a film, *Rope* (USA, 1948), which gave the appearance of no editing at all. In fact, the cuts may be identified by close attention to his use of fades and extreme close-ups on dark objects, which momentarily hide the edits.

The *long take* is a shot that is long in duration before it is edited. It is usually combined with deep-focus photography (see p. 151).

Juxtaposition of shots

Juxtapositioning of shots is the placing of shots side by side. The shots interact with each other and create certain meanings. The selection and sequence of shots has an impact on the audience's understanding of the message.

It is said that the Lumière brothers, the founders of film, stumbled upon the idea of editing quite by accident. The camera broke down in the middle of filming. When they got it going again, they found the jump in continuity actually looked good. Juxtapositioning had been discovered.

Traditional Hollywood productions begin with a juxtapositioning of certain shot sizes. The opening sequence usually runs from extreme long shot (ELS) through mid-shot (MS) to close-up (CU), in order to construct the introduction to the narrative from the general (a place) to the specific (a person).

MONTAGE Montage is the process of using a 'collision of images' to create an idea in the mind of the audience. Each image contains ideas and meanings. If separate shots and meanings are placed side by side – even if they mean opposite things – a third meaning can arise. This has been referred to as the *Kuleshov effect*. For example, imagine a shot of a man lying on the ground, holding his stomach. Next to this, place a shot of another man holding a gun. Neither shot on its

own automatically suggests that a murder has occurred. However, the third meaning – that a murder *has* occurred – arises out of the collision of two independent images.

The Russian film theorist and film-maker Sergei Eisenstein developed the theory of montage from this effect (see figure 3.5, p. 156). Montage partly explains the power of music videos and MTV.

Transitions: visual punctuation

The devices used to change from one scene to another are the equivalent of punctuation. They convey certain impressions. They assist understanding by helping to make meaning clear. Audiences learn to make meaning of these visual language conventions because they are constantly repeated in moving image texts.

The following are some of the devices used as 'visual punctuation'.

THE CUT A cut is an instant change to another shot. This is similar to the way our eyes move when we look suddenly at something else. A cut is the least obvious transition because it occurs so quickly and seems to work naturally. A cut can be regarded as the shortest distance between two shots.

MOTIVATING THE CUT There should be a reason for the cut, so that the audience feels that they had wanted to look at this next shot in any case. The motivation could be dialogue or it could be an action from a character. Cutting on action is common because the movement in the shot distracts attention away from the shot change. Cutting on dialogue seems natural because the audience wishes to see each person reply.

THE DISSOLVE During a dissolve, one image gradually blends or dissolves into another. A dissolve is a much longer route between two shots than a cut. For this reason, it introduces greater disruption. Some say it represents a 'dramatic pause'. In a narrative genre, a dissolve can be used to suggest a smooth change in time or place.

THE FADE A fade-out gradually turns the picture to an empty screen (white) or black. A fade-in begins at an empty black screen and gradually reveals a

Figure 3.5
Shots from the Odessa steps sequence in Sergei Eisenstein's The Battleship Potemkin (USSR, 1925). The collision of these apparently unrelated shots of soldiers, guns and a woman creates a powerful emotional response in the audience. This effect is called montage.

picture. The fade is an obvious and disruptive transition. It signals a major change in the progress of the text, such as a change in place or time. The fade is often thought of as being like the curtain in the stage theatre. It opens and closes the show and separates the acts. The fade is the longest route between shots.

DEFOCUS Defocus shots provide transitions by gradually moving out of focus on one scene and refocusing on another. They are similar in character

to the dissolve and are a more gradual way of easing the audience from one shot to another.

THE WIPE A new image 'wipes' across the old one using a defined line. Digital effects switchers allow for a huge variety of wipes, including the flip frame and the page leaf. A wipe is the most unnatural transition and consequently is the most obvious to the audience. It is commonly used in television genres that allow for disjointed presentation, such as news, documentaries and sports coverage.

How editing controls text progress

Bordwell and Thompson maintain that editing offers the film-maker four areas of control over the relationships between shots: picture relationships, rhythmic relationships, space relationships and time relationships.

PICTURE RELATIONSHIPS BETWEEN SHOTS

An editor can make a connection between two scenes if there are any similarities in the actual content of the pictures. These similarities could be in the scenery, in the lighting, in the costumes or in what the characters are actually doing.

One of the most famous matches of picture action occurred at the beginning of Stanley Kubrick's *2001: A Space Odyssey* (UK, 1968). A prehistoric caveman hurls a bone into the air and we watch it spin over and over. The next shot is of a 21st-century space station spinning in space. The spinning bone and the spinning space station connect prehistory with the future.

RHYTHMIC RELATIONSHIPS

Each shot takes up a certain amount of time, or duration, on screen. A shot may range in length from one second to several minutes. Just as variation in the length of notes creates rhythm in music, shot duration can be used to build rhythm in visual texts.

A sequence of rapid shot changes gives an impression of fast, exciting action. On the other hand, a sequence of longer shots may create a reflective, romantic mood. Using cuts speeds up the transition, while dissolves slow it down. Film-makers punctuate fast passages with slow ones, so that the variation in rhythm is accentuated. The acceleration of tempo generates a greater feeling of excitement than a constantly fast rate of cutting.

In the traditional Hollywood style, the rhythm of the shots also depends on the shot size. Long shots are left on the screen for longer than close-ups. This is because it is assumed that the audience needs longer to read the greater amount of detail in a long shot.

SPACE RELATIONSHIPS

With clever editing, a film-maker can make places seem as if they are next door to each other when, in fact, they may be on opposite sides of the Earth. For example, someone can walk out the front door of a constructed set in a Hollywood studio and into a street in Egypt.

Putting shots side by side can suggest that they are in fact taking place within the same space. The traditional progression of extreme long shot through mid shot to close-up was often a device used to create space relationships. An establishing shot would set the scene. All other shots in the sequence would be much closer, allowing the film-maker to return to the studio. The audience would continue to believe the action was taking place within the setting of the establishing shot.

TIME RELATIONSHIPS

The duration of a programme can contain whole lifetimes, or just a few minutes of time in someone's life. Obviously time can be altered in both the filming and the editing. There are several ways this can be done.

COMPRESSING TIME Long passages of time can be shortened to just a few shots. For example, a five-day drive across a continent could be shown with a shot of the starting point, a shot of the road taken in between the journey's beginning and end, and a shot of the arrival at the destination.

EXPANSION OF TIME Prolonging the action can prolong the suspense or draw out the emotional response of the audience. Television soap operas often use this technique, with the emotional response of several characters being shown one after the other.

SIMULTANEOUS TIME Crosscutting from one event to another can give the impression that they are occurring at the same time (simultaneously). In the last-minute rescue scenes of silent-screen melodramas, crosscutting had the audience on the edge of their seats. Classic early silent films have the villain tying the heroine to the railway track, the train steaming around the corner and the hero rushing to the rescue. The excitement lies in the audience's hope that the three events, apparently occurring simultaneously, will somehow end for the best.

FLASHBACK Memories or past events can be shown by juxtaposing shots of the present with

Figure 3.6
*Examples of edits
made on the basis
of the pictorial
content of the
image. The
relationship of
shot A to shot B is
purely visual.*

EDITING BY PICTURE RELATIONSHIP

TITLE	SHOT A	SHOT B
Psycho (USA, 1960)	Close-up of the drain hole at the bottom of the shower. The water swirls down the drain hole, reminding the viewer of the camera rotation in the previous shot	Marion's lifeless eye (the aftermath of the attack in the shower). The camera gently rotates into a close-up of the eye
The Usual Suspects (USA, 1995)	Medium long shot of the mouth of a cave. The cave is the scene of a violent confrontation	Rim of a coffee cup belonging to the man recounting the tale of the events which took place in the cave
Once Were Warriors (NZ, 1994)	Close-up of Beth's face, defiant and proud despite suffering	Close-up of face of carved Maori wooden statue
Baraka (USA, 1992)	Medium close-up shot of monk's head, as he enters into deep meditation	Long shot of natural stone archway on the seashore, as waves break through the gap
Raiders of the Lost Ark (USA. 1981)	Titles showing the Paramount Studios mountain	Dissolve into opening shot of actual mountain where the story begins
2001: A Space Odyssey (UK, 1968)	Tapir bone tossed up into the sky and tumbling over and over	Space station rotating in space
Lawrence of Arabia (UK. 1962)	Close-up shot of Lawrence striking a match	Shot of a flaming desert sun
Titanic (USA, 1997)	Shot of the rusted *Titanic*'s bow under water	Shot of the bow of the ship just before sailing

shots of the past, possibly separated by a transitional device such as a fade.

FLASHFORWARD In visual texts, flashes forwards to the future are rarer than flashbacks to the past. This is because a flashforward is a more obvious break in the logical order of a story.

The soundtrack

If the ear is receiving a reasonably smooth flow of sounds as one sequence gives way to another, the sound will tend to bind the two sequences together and make the transition acceptable.

Karel Reisz
Film director and editing theorist

▼ ▼ ▼

For many years, the quality of sound recording in films lagged behind the development of picture quality. It was not present at all, of course, in the earliest ones!

The main reason for this was that the processes of recording and especially of *synchronisation* posed much greater challenges than simply recording visual images. Initially, the technology did not exist to enable it at all – nor were investors keen to find the money necessary to develop it. When it was introduced, in the late 1920s, the original equipment was very bulky, noisy and hard to manoeuvre on the set. Even with the rapid arrival of portable equipment, it was still expensive to operate and not of very high quality, so that location recording was actively discouraged for a long time. *Singin' in the Rain* (USA, 1952) brilliantly captures the era of the development of sound in the film industry – and the dramatic impact it had on those without suitable voices!

It was not until the arrival of Dolby recording and playback systems that high-fidelity soundtracks became possible. Today, no cinema of quality would be without such playback systems (one of which, THX, has its own trailers in large cinemas) and sound in films has come to play almost an equal part with the pictures themselves.

DIMENSIONS IN SOUND

Sound has three dimensions in television and film: music, sound effects/noise and dialogue. In turn, Bordwell and Thompson, in *Film Art: An Introduction*, identify three qualities of sound used in films that we recognise from our experience of sound in everyday life: *loudness, pitch* and *timbre*.

We are programmed with associations between sound and meaning from our earliest memories and experiences. Most of these associations are universal in any language and therefore account for the translation of the power of many films, regardless of their country of origin.

For example, *loudness* and volume are associated with drama, as in nature, with thunder and lightning, the bangs and crashes of accidents, or raised voices. Silence may be experienced either as peacefulness or as a reminder of loneliness and isolation, or as the precursor to drama or violence.

Pitch, whether high or low, helps us to distinguish between different sources of sounds around us and we make various associations with types of pitch. For example, high-pitched sounds may suggest conflict and tension, again associated with raised voices and anxiety. Low-pitched sounds can be calming or threatening, depending on their context.

Timbre (a musician's term) refers to the properties of harmony that provide sound with colour or tone. It can be used to articulate the mood and meaning of a sound and, in music, it is created by the use of notes, keys and chords. Timbre is also a property of the human voice, in both speaking and singing. Some people possess a rich and rounded timbre; others, a nasal one.

Precise analysis of the interaction of these three sound qualities will reveal the deliberate and elaborate selection of different sound sources and types in order to create mood or establish information. Sound completes the visual impact of the image and creates a sound image for the audience, as well as cueing or confirming their emotional responses.

How sound is mixed and edited in film or television programmes is as precise as the editing of images. The mixing of the levels of different elements of a soundtrack may be used to draw our attention to different pieces of information, such as a door opening, a whisper or a single instrument, just as the various aspects of camera (see pp. 148–59) are used to create meaning.

MUSIC The power of music to manipulate the emotions has always been acknowledged. It is often the music which makes an image come alive, producing an effect in combination that is greater than each in isolation. Whether it is the interweaving of pre-published songs and orchestral extracts or the use of specially commissioned pieces, it is hard to imagine a contemporary film *not* using music. Many films rely more on music than they do on action or even dialogue to establish mood and meaning in the narrative.

Study of the music credits for films, both classic and contemporary, will develop knowledge of the body of work of composers whose work is just as distinctive as the signatures of the directors they worked with, for example:

► Bernard Herrmann with Alfred Hitchcock for *Vertigo* (USA, 1958), *North by Northwest* (USA, 1959) and, most famously, *Psycho* (USA 1960). He also composed the music for *Citizen Kane* (USA, 1941), *The Day the Earth Stood Still* (USA, 1951) and *Taxi Driver* (USA, 1976).
► John Williams with Steven Spielberg for *Jaws* (USA, 1975), *Close Encounters of the Third Kind* (USA, 1977), *Raiders of the Lost Ark* (USA,

1981), *E.T.* (USA, 1982*), Indiana Jones and the Temple of Doom* (USA, 1984), *Schindler's List* (USA, 1993) and *Jurassic Park* (USA, 1993). He was also the composer for the *Superman* and *Star Wars* films.

▶ Hans Zimmer with Ridley Scott for *Hannibal* (USA, 2001), *Gladiator* (USA, 2000), *Thelma & Louise* (USA 1991) and *Black Rain* (USA, 1989). He was also the composer for *Mission Impossible 2* (USA, 2000), *The Thin Red Line* (USA, 1998), *The Lion King* (USA, 1994), *Driving Miss Daisy* (USA, 1989) and *Rain Man* (USA, 1988).

▶ Danny Elfman with Tim Burton for *The Legend of Sleepy Hollow* (USA, 1999), *Edward Scissorhands* (USA, 1990), *Batman* (USA, 1989), *Batman Returns* (USA, 1992) and *Beetlejuice* (USA, 1988). He was also the composer for *Men in Black* (USA, 1997) and *Mission Impossible* (USA, 1996).

▶ James Horner won awards for his compositions for *Braveheart* (USA, 1995) and *Titanic* (USA, 1997).

▶ Ennio Morricone is one of the most prolific composers of film music, including the spaghetti Westerns of the Italian director Sergio Leone.

▶ John Barry is famous for his work on the James Bond films, as well as a whole host of others.

▶ Michael Nyman has made a successful career as a composer of original film scores and is principally associated with the work of British director Peter Greenaway, on such films as *The Draughtsman's Contract* (UK, 1982), *The Cook, the Thief, the Wife and her Lover* (UK/France, 1989) and *Prospero's Books* (Netherlands/France/Italy, 1991). More recently, he composed the score for the film *The Claim* (UK/France/Canada, 2001).

The sales of original and pre-published music used for film soundtracks on CDs is a highly profitable business and is now an essential element of the marketing and subsidiary profit generation of any film. Michael Nyman's evocative soundtrack for Jane Campion's film *The Piano* (Australia/France, 1992) has remained in the radio station Classic FM's classical music charts since its release.

SOUND EFFECTS Sound effects and background noises help to create the sense of reality in a visual text. They also build an idea of a 'real' space in which the action is taking place.

Diegetic sound arises naturally in the action that is unfolding: e.g. music from a car radio, or birds singing. Usually, we can actually see its source. The term comes from the Greek word *diegesis*, meaning the 'world of the story'.

Non-diegetic sound is imported for particular purposes: e.g. a voiceover or the music used to create mood. Although it contributes to the story, diegetic sound is not located strictly within the action that we observe.

Both have roles to play in creating meaning, and audiences learn to accept, and even interpret them, in quite unconscious ways. Sometimes, as with the car radio example, sounds may begin as one type then switch to another. Emotional impact is often greatly enhanced by this technique.

DIALOGUE There are two extremes of television and film dialogue, say media academics and educators Barrie McMahon and Robyn Quin. At one end is highly staged theatrical dialogue. At the other end of the spectrum is mood dialogue where the words are not important, only the characterisation they convey. Modern dialogue has become a compromise between the two. Some Hollywood actors, in particular, are renowned for the clipped speech, even grunts, which they use to express themselves.

However, the delivery of dialogue is an important aspect of the performance of the actor, under the instruction of the director, which brings the screenplay to life. There are various styles of performance, from the classical, theatrical to improvisational, and many actors are cast precisely because a particular performance style, that he or she may be renowned for, is required.

OVERLAPPING SOUND

Just as a brick wall is built by overlapping brick after brick, a visual text is assembled by overlapping sound and image. Cuts to the image are not exactly in line with cuts to the sound. Sound flows over the joins and unites the two scenes.

The overlapping of sound during dialogue sequences is a feature of most modern texts. Cutting to the next speaker for a response shot is usually done before the first speaker has finished. Similarly, background sounds (such as traffic or trains) can be introduced before a cut to a different environment.

The easiest way to bind any sequence together is to use music. This is most clearly demonstrated in music videos and MTV.

TYPES OF SOUND

There are two main types of sound use in the visual language of television and film. Film theorists have come up with a variety of terms. Karel Reisz, for example, uses the terms *synchronous* and *asynchronous*. James Monaco uses *parallel* and *contrapuntal*. He argues that music, sound effects and speech can work with the image, or else comment upon it.

PARALLEL SOUND Parallel sound is logically connected with the image according to James Monaco. The sound comes from within the scene, or emphasises some aspect of the scene. The Hollywood style relied on parallel sound with music, sound effects and dialogue underlining and supporting the image.

CONTRAPUNTAL SOUND (COUNTERPOINT)
Contrapuntal sound provides a commentary on the image and may be unconnected with it. The sound may work against the image to create a third meaning. Contrapuntal sound can come from outside the scene. Stanley Kubrick's *2001: A Space Odyssey* (UK, 1968) and *A Clockwork Orange* (UK, 1971) both used contrapuntal music. In *A Clockwork Orange*, Beethoven's symphonies were contrasted with violent futuristic scenes. Hitchcock used contrapuntal sound in *Psycho* (USA, 1960). Scenes of apparent ordinariness were given high tension using a disturbing orchestral soundtrack: the strident, stabbing strings of Bernard Herrmann's striking introductory score are repeated in various forms throughout the film.

Counterpoint can also apply to dialogue. In one extended sequence in *Apocalypse Now* (USA, 1979), Martin Sheen's voice can be heard over a variety of images as a patrol boat takes him up the river on his mysterious mission. Some of these images relate to the documents he is reading (notes on the four-star general who has 'gone native'); some display the other soldiers' bizarre antics, and brazen disregard for the local people. His tone of increasing bewilderment at what he reads generates a powerful sense of the disorientating impact of the whole experience of their presence in Vietnam.

▼ ▼ ▼ ▼ ▼ ▼ ▼

activities

1. Cut a variety of pictures from magazines or take your own using an instant or digital camera. Place the pictures side by side in pairs, so that you can 'collide' images to create meanings not present in either shot individually. Explore the results of your work by writing underneath what meaning or sense they now convey, or exchange and discuss each other's work.

2. Create a montage of ten or so pictures from magazines exploring a single theme. The pictures should work together to build a strong point of view or a powerful emotion. Possible themes for your montage are:

▶ gender representations;

▶ environmental issues;

▶ political issues;

▶ representation of organisations such as Amnesty International;

▶ broad-based community concerns such as AIDS. Title your work and explain the results.

3. Record some examples of visual language punctuation (transitional devices) and show them to the class, explaining their purpose and effect.

4. Bordwell and Thompson say that there are four basic ways in which editing can control the relationship between shots: pictorial relationships, rhythm relationships, time relationships and space relationships. Look through some films or television programmes and find an example of each type. Show it to the class and explain how the editing works and what effect it has.

5. Find examples of overlapping sound in films or television programmes. Include in your collection some examples of dialogue flowing over a cut.

Pre-production: Scripts and Storyboards

Television and film are primarily visual media. The words and soundtrack are important, but the pictures count for more. Extensive planning and preparation have to go into working out the visualisation of moving image products. Coordination of all the right equipment required for the shoot has to be carefully calculated. Equally, the most effective use of the time of so many expensive human and technical resources must be ensured.

Stages of pre-production

There are several stages of pre-production.

STAGE ONE: THE OUTLINE

An outline is a very brief summary of the programme concept. The legend is that Hollywood moguls insist that, if the outline cannot be given in one sentence, the film will not even be considered. Reportedly, they were most impressed when someone knocked on the studio door and said, 'Danny de Vito and Arnold Schwarzenegger – twins!'

The term *high-concept* is used to describe this kind of film, one that has a single, crystal-clear defining idea at its core (see p. 169). Reputedly, the most famous example is the pitch for *Alien* (USA, 1979): '*Jaws* – in space!'

Often, proposals for new films are delivered in a presentation known as a 'pitch'. Robert Altman satirised this process mercilessly in *The Player* (USA, 1992), where writers and producers are given extremely tight and pressurised spots to present their ideas.

STAGE TWO: THE TREATMENT

A treatment is a broad plan of the proposal, describing each scene in a paragraph or two. Treatments are written in terms of what the audience will see – the first attempt at visualising.

STAGE THREE: THE SCRIPT (OR SCREENPLAY)

Television drama, film and stage-play scripts differ from each other in many significant ways in terms of layout. Each has its own style and it is crucial to observe the appropriate conventions. Many submissions are rejected automatically if they fail to do so. Screenplays may be written from adaptations of a novel or play, or may be written as original screenplays, such as the award-winning one, by Callie Khouri, for the film *Thelma & Louise* (USA, 1991) and the screenplay *The Piano* (Australia/France, 1992).

A common drama screenplay layout has the following features:

Figure 3.7
Alien: '*Jaws in space*' – the perfect pitch.

SAMPLE TREATMENT

Box ...

© Adam Kowaltzke

Box is a short film that asks questions, answers none of them and resolves itself by asking another question, but still leaves you satisfied – almost. In the tradition of many alternative short films, the 'Hollywood' style of narrative structure is abandoned in favour of one which is not designed to tell a story. Instead, it asks questions of the viewer, leaving the story unresolved, but ending with a satisfying twist.

Box features only a few characters, none of whom is important to the story, with the main character being a distinctive cardboard box. The central question (which remains unresolved) is: 'What is in the box?' This line is repeated many times throughout the script. At the very end of the film, the central question changes focus.

Throughout most of the film, the box should stay the primary focus, even dominating the screen at times – i.e. we see things from the box's point of view. The 'human' characters do not have distinct personalities, being fairly unremarkable in order to keep a sense of mystery surrounding the box. The box carriers' demeanour should never give away what may be in the box. Their personalities may change, giving inconsistent notions of what may be inside.

THE NARRATIVE

A box sits on the lap of a young person riding a train at night or in the late afternoon. The person carrying the box is dressed in anonymous clothing (i.e. jeans and T-shirt, etc.) and wears few distinctive items, save for a very decorative ring on the left hand. This is shown in detail when we are given close-ups of the box on the carrier's lap.

The person gets off the train and goes to a friend's house. Here, the question is innocently asked: 'What's in the box?'. This answer is interrupted by a phone call. An arrangement is made to meet that night with the caller.

Figure 3.8

- scenes are numbered, with time and place indicated at the head of the scene
- camera and location directions are in underlined capitals
- acting directions are not underlined
- character names are centred and capitalised one line above the dialogue, rather than beside it (as in theatre scripts)
- dialogue is indented and centred
- generally everything except dialogue is in block capitals

STAGE FOUR: THE STORYBOARD

A storyboard is a series of drawings representing the final images of the production. Cartoon-like picture frames show the action as it happens, in scene-by-scene sequence. Advertising agencies rely heavily on storyboards to present their ideas to clients in order to win contracts. Television and film producers use them less often; however, first time film-makers have succeeded in attracting investment to make their film by showing the storyboard to investors. Storyboards are often used to plan complicated special effects sequences in films. The special edition DVD for *Men in Black* (USA, 1997) has a special feature showing how a spectacular sequence in a tunnel was conceived and executed. There are some variations in storyboard style, but most have the following features:

- shot sizes are written in block capitals underneath each frame
- the action in each scene is briefly described
- dialogue is written in the manner of a stage script. Characters' names are given in capitals, and the dialogue is written in lower case
- sound effects are given last, usually in capitals.

STAGE FIVE: THE CAMERA SCRIPT

A camera script or shooting script is often the result of a final collaboration between the writer and the director. Instructions to the camera crew

Figure 3.9

SAMPLE NARRATIVE SCRIPTS

One Day at a Time

Yes Sir, that's My Baby
Written by: Bud Wiser
© Communications Co.
All Rights Reserved

FADE IN:
INTERIOR: HALLWAY OUTSIDE ANN'S
    APARTMENT – DAY
(BARBARA AND CLIFF ARE ENGAGED IN A KISS,
BARBARA IS LEANING BACK AGAINST THE WALL.)
SFX: DOORBELL (MUFFLED) RINGS TWICE
CLIFF: Do you know, when we kiss, I actually
    think I hear bells ringing.
BARBARA: That could be because you're pushing
    me against the doorbell, Cliff.
(THEY CONTINUE KISSING. ANN COMES JOGGING
AROUND THE CORNER WEARING A SWEATSUIT AND
SNEAKERS.)
    Hello, mother.
CLIFF: Hey, there Ms Romano! What're you
    doing?
ANN: (JOGGING IN PLACE) Same thing you're
    doing, Cliff. Just getting the old blood racing.
(ANN JOGS INTO THE LIVING ROOM.)
CUT TO: … etc.

Lou Grant

Cop
Written by: Seth Freeman
© MTM enterprises

Act One
1. EXTERIOR. STREET – NIGHT
(HUME'S CAR DRIVES UP AND STOPS IN FRONT OF
LOU GRANT'S HOUSE [FOR THIS IS LOU'S STREET IN
SILVERLAKE]. LOU GETS OUT ON THE PASSENGER SIDE.)
LOU: Thanks for the lift, Charlie.
HUME: You're not sore?
LOU: No, no, but next time the Librarian's
    Association needs a guest speaker in a hurry,
    I'm busy, okay?
HUME: It wasn't that bad.
LOU: No, not *that* bad. Come in for a drink and
    I'll tell you this great joke I heard about the
    Dewey Decimal system.
AS HUME GETS OUT OF THE CAR TO JOIN LOU, BOTH
MEN REACT AS A MOTORCYCLE KICKS INTO A ROAR IN
THE DRIVEWAY ACROSS THE STREET, PEELS OUT, THEN
ZOOMS PAST THEM AND AWAY DOWN THE STREET.

are very specific. Of course, for a news script, the shooting has probably already been done. The script is for the editor to cut the pictures while the journalist reads the voiceover. Features of a shooting script include:

▶ all visual instructions on the left side of the page, audio and acting instructions go on the right

▶ shots are numbered and briefly described

▶ lighting sometimes appears in boxes in the centre of the page or sometimes on the extreme right

▶ for news and advertising scripts only, dialogue or voiceover is written in block capitals. Drama scripts use lower case, but with capitals for character names.

Figure 3.10

SAMPLE CAMERA SCRIPT

Note that news and advertising scripts traditionally use block capitals for voiceover text. This is because it is regarded as easier to read. The following script is from a narrative.

VIDEO	AUDIO

SHOT #1
LS OF RAILWAY STATION MOVING IN TO
    TWO SHOT OF RICHARD AND MARNIE
SHOT #2
MCU OF MARNIE
SHOT #3
MCU RICHARD
SHOT #4
CU MARNIE
	RICHARD: What time is this train supposed to
	    come?
	MARNIE: Too late for my job interview, by the
	    looks.
	Richard is becoming somewhat agitated.
	RICHARD: Forget that! You know … you
	    know what I've always wanted to say to
	    you? Marnie …
	    … I love you!
	MARNIE: Oh, Richard … please don't make a
	    fool of yourself here.

activities

1. Write an outline and treatment for a short film about school. The treatment should give a story summary, introduce the main characters and describe the narrative in its main scenes.

2. Storyboard a short dialogue sequence showing two people in conversation. Remember to overlap sound (see p. 160), cutting occasionally during midsentence. Include camera and editing directions under (or beside) each shot.

3. Convert one minute of a television drama or film into about a page of narrative script. Use the conventions of script layout for television and film given on pp. 164 and 165. Include camera directions.

major assignment

Production assignment

Film a short ten- to fifteen-shot video sequence on a topic of your own choice. The sequence should have at least one example of each of the following:

▶ editing to a picture relationship between shots;

▶ simultaneous time created by crosscutting;

▶ at least two different types of transitional devices;

▶ an example of overlapping sound.

Written assignment

Produce a 600-word response to the following.

Write an editor's analysis of a sequence from a film or television programme of your choice. Analyse the major decisions the editor has made, covering montage, transitional devices, and the various means of controlling relationships between shots. Comment on the use of sound. Conclude by evaluating the effectiveness of the editing in the sequence.

Oral assignment

Prepare a five-minute oral presentation on the topic below.

Make notes on the written assignment above and present to the class your analysis of the chosen extract. Use recorded excerpts from the film or programme to illustrate your comments.

Film: The Medium

The audience stampeded in terror at one of the first cinema showings in Paris in 1895. The first films were made in France by the Lumière brothers (whose name, appropriately, means 'light'). One of the films, called *L'Arrivée d'un Train en Gare de la Ciotat*, showed a section of railway station platform, bathed in sunlight. Suddenly, a train comes down the track and heads straight for the camera and also, therefore, the audience. As the train approached, panic broke out in the theatre; people jumped out of their seats and ran for their lives.

Today, we have multi-screen complexes with wraparound Dolby sound – in some cinemas even the chairs move! The quality and capacities of film are now light years ahead of those first ventures. The giant screens of the IMAX cinema offer a scale and clarity, and views of our world, quite unimaginable to those earliest audiences. At France's Futuroscope, near Poitiers, a specially commissioned 3-D narrative film in this format that includes aerial shots of crossing South America's Andes mountain ranges is screened. Technical advances in cinema have been truly tremendous.

In some senses, however, the impulse of film-makers remains the same – to startle, to enthral and to amaze. *Mission Impossible 2* (USA, 2000), although different in degree, is not so far from *L'Arrive d'un Train* as might first appear: thrill and sensation are still very much at the core of much modern film. 'Action and spectacle have been part of film since its inception', says Warwick University's José Arroyo, and to some degree have overtaken the need for satisfying or elaborate narratives (see p. 196 on action/spectacle).

At the same time, audiences are much more film-literate now. They have grown up with film, know the 'language' and are no longer so easily frightened. They also expect more. Yet film still retains the power to transform an ordinary object, such as a train, and make it extraordinary.

The vision of film

Film possesses an amazing power to glorify even the smallest object and make it significant, according to the film historian Brian Appleyard. David Lynch's *Wild at Heart* (USA, 1990) begins

with a fierce explosion. As it turns out, it is nothing more than a match being lit. The ordinary is instantly transformed by the power of the cinema, says Appleyard.

For the Russian director Andrei Tarkovsky, the real magic of film is that it has allowed us to turn time into space. The cinema experience is based on time. The audience spends a certain amount of time in the cinema while the camera creates a recorded flow of real events. In return for spending time, the audience is transported to all sorts of places and spaces.

The cinema is larger than life. It can inflate and exaggerate both the best and the worst in humanity. It has had a powerful role in twentieth-century tyranny, as well as democracy.

Sergei Eisenstein's films were powerful explorations of the repressions of the Tsarist regime and of the joy and heroism of the ordinary people that overthrew it in the Russian Revolution of 1917. Eisenstein is credited with developing the editing concept of *montage*, or the 'collision of images' (see pp. 155–6). Ironically, his films were later coopted by the new tyranny of Stalin's Soviet Union. *The Battleship Potemkin* (USSR, 1925), Eisenstein's heroic film of working-class struggle, was used to support a harsh regime oppressing ordinary people.

The cruel oppression of Nazi Germany was supported by the majestic films of Leni Riefenstahl. Her eulogy of Hitler, *Triumph of the Will* (Germany, 1936), although morally tainted, is still regarded as one of the masterpieces of film.

The films of Hollywood have been just as powerful as military and industrial strength in making the twentieth century the American century. Film's capacity to magnify has sold the American dream to millions, at the same time as exposing its underside.

Film: a primary medium

Jeremy Tunstall has defined three levels of attention that people typically pay to different forms of media: *primary*, *secondary* and *tertiary* attention. First, people can give close, or *primary*, attention (as they might to newspapers). Next, they can give *secondary* attention (as they might to radio or television when doing something else). Thirdly, they can give *tertiary* attention to a medium when it is in the background and below conscious attention (as with supermarket 'musak', for example).

Some forms of media can even switch from one to another: television, for example, may fade from primary to secondary if there are other people in the room with us, or if the phone rings. Film, when viewed in a cinema at least, is virtually always a primary medium – only rarely do we turn our attention away from the screen.

FEATURES OF THE FILM EXPERIENCE

Film requires full audience attention. People make a conscious decision to go the movies. Once there, they enter a darkened cinema that (usually) prevents them from concentrating on anything other than the film. The darkened cinema also makes audiences more ready to 'willingly suspend disbelief' and be a part of the story.

COLLECTIVE AND INDIVIDUAL In the cinema, the audience experiences a film as an isolated individual and also as part of a large and unknown crowd. With such a large public gathering, there is plenty of opportunity for mass behaviour, such as laughing or booing. Yet there is also a chance for private emotion and reflection.

VOYEURISTIC The film experience transforms the audience into 'peeping Toms', according to some film academics. The film events take place while the audience, almost invisible in the dark, observes all the secrets.

QUALITY High-quality sound systems and a large screen reinforce film's power as a primary medium. Television images are made from pixels or electronic dots. In contrast, celluloid film has grain. Being made from light, projected film images more closely resemble the way in which the human eye sees the natural world. New digital systems of recording and projecting will soon, however, be indistinguishable from traditional film quality.

The story-telling medium

The Lumière brothers knew when they showed their early pictures that people were fascinated by pictures that moved. It was not clear what the new invention would be useful for, however. At the time, people thought of film as a kind of fairground attraction, as the early nickelodeons were, or a parlour amusement novelty. The novelty would soon wear off, early critics said.

Cinema could have gone in several directions. It might have become a purely documentary medium, according to Brian Appleyard, moving on from trains at stations to more exotic topics. Or, it might have developed into a kind of television, with a variety of different types of shows, such as games, news and music clips.

Instead, it became a powerful medium for telling stories. Originally, these were short, one-reel stories. Later, they became full novel-length narratives. Documentaries and non-narratives do exist, of course; however, they are in a minority. The novel-length story with well-developed characters and a strong plot has remained the dominant form of the cinema.

Narratology

Narrative is one of the most complex concepts in film study, but one that is rarely considered in complex ways by the audience. There are many theories and books that analyse the often highly complicated narrative structures that underlie even the apparently most simple films.

Those who study narratives are called *narratologists*. One of their most important findings is that narrative is a very deep structure. It seems embedded in human psychology and operates independently of any medium. Even a joke or an anecdote we may tell betrays our implicit under-standing of the need for narrative structure, for, as with our own lives, it has a beginning, a middle and an end.

Narrative is a kind of text organisation, says Seymour Chatman, one of the foremost scholars of filmed adaptations. It is a time-based structure, a sequencing of story events in time. Chatman calls this *story-time*. Story-time is the pure or raw sequence of events as they might exist in time before being retold. In a biography, story-time is that person's actual life span. In *Cinderella*, it is the original essence of the story sequence before it becomes a ballet, an opera or a comic book.

In a similar way, in *Film Art: An Introduction* (McGraw Hill, 2001), Bordwell and Thompson differentiate between the terms *plot* and *story*. *Plot* refers to the sequence of events that occur in the film, while *story* refers to the wider background, e.g. what the audience infers to have happened before and after the events it sees, or those within the plot that it does not see, in the film.

Screenwriters often use the term *backstory* to refer to the parts of the story that we do not see in the plot, which are often referred to in the course of the narrative and aid our understanding of it.

The medium used to tell the story also has its own language of time. This is the time taken by the medium to spin out the story. Depending on the medium, this might be called *film-time* or *book-time*. Chatman calls it *discourse time*.

Discourse time (or film-time) can be different to story-time. Discourse time can be spun out to add tension or dramatically shortened, by ellipsis, to remove less interesting events.

Flashbacks, flashforwards and so on all alter the chain of events that make up the narrative. For example, a film about a person's life story could open with a shot of him or her on their deathbed, flashback to early childhood and then flashforwards to adulthood. A novel might treat events differently because it has a different discourse or language. Both film and novel times are different to the actual story-time. *High Noon* (USA, 1952) is an interesting exception, where the duration of film-time is the same as the story-time.

One of the most remarkable manipulations of these different time frames was in the film *Jacob's Ladder* (USA, 1990). The entire action of the film covers large spans of both space and real time – a soldier's experiences both at home and in Vietnam. Only in the closing sequence is it revealed that the discourse time (i.e. the time frame of the film within which all the events take place) is in fact the few seconds it takes for someone to die when they have been executed.

Only some texts can handle a time-based structure. Not all texts have their own discourse time. Other texts – such as expository essays, for example – use logic-based structures. Or they may operate outside either. Consider Leonardo da Vinci's painting, the *Mona Lisa*. You could spend two minutes or six hours in front of it and still be unsure as to whether she smiled or not. The effect is the same regardless of time. You could not do that with a film or a novel. A painting does not use either a logic- or a time-based discourse.

The two ideas of time explain why a story can be given new life in a different medium, says Chatman. A narrative can be transposed to any medium, as long as it operates with the two systems of time: story-time and discourse time.

At a deep level, the story of a novel or a play can quite naturally be transferred to film. The discourse-time structure will be different, but the story-time structure remains the same.

REALISM

Realism is a concept that can be studied in relation to most media texts, for it is the dominant form of representation in film, television, radio, newspapers and magazines, and in most fictional literature. It is a highly complex topic and many theorists disagree about the precise parameters of this term.

Art forms such as painting and sculpture, dance, music and theatre are often also in the realist mode. However, there are far more examples of non-realist art forms, such as those in abstract art, sculpture and absurdist theatre, than we are used to in the media forms under study in this book.

Realism, then, is the process by which the dominant experience of daily reality (in terms of what our lives look and sound like, the common narratives and ideological perspectives they contain) is reproduced in our media representations. The term *social realism* was used to identify a European movement in novels and paintings in the nineteenth century, which looked at working lives and experience, and exposed social issues. Most of our film and television continues to adhere to this representational tradition, whether they contain a social critique or not. As such, even a science fiction film can be said to be realist.

Realism is a relative concept that tends, in most mainstream texts, to reproduce consensus representations of reality, either directly or indirectly, rather than individual or alternative ones. Realism, the re-creation of physical and emotional reality, is constructed by two processes. First, by the technical processes of recording and editing images and sound. Secondly, by ideological representational processes, by which characters, their narratives, values and beliefs are recognisable to us from our daily lives.

As the dominant mode of representation, realism is taken for granted and rarely considered and it might be easier to explain what it is *not*. It is only when we consider non-realist texts that we fully appreciate the dominance of this mode of representation.

For example, a film such as Luis Buñuel and Salvador Dali's *Un Chien Andalou* (France, 1928) completely defeats our attempts to make sense of the usual constituents of meaning in a film: narrative cause and effect, characters, time and place. The film was an experiment in surrealism (a 1920s movement in art, performance, photography, prose and poetry, of which Salvador Dali was its most famous exponent) and it was extremely influential.

The Spanish film-maker Buñuel went on to experiment with realism in *The Exterminating Angel* (Mexico, 1962) and *The Phantom of Liberty* (France, 1974), finding that he could interweave political protest against the Spanish regime into his films through the use of non-realist techniques such as allegory and symbolism. David Lynch's film *Eraserhead* (USA, 1976) is a more contemporary example of surrealist style and form, as was his cult television series *Twin Peaks*. Parts of Lynch's films *Blue Velvet* (USA, 1986) and *Wild at Heart* (USA, 1990) also experiment with non-realist narrative and imagery.

The Czechoslovakian animator Jan Svankmajer has produced a richly imaginative body of work that is experimental in all aspects of visual narrative, in such films as *Alice* (Switzerland, 1988), based on Lewis Carroll's book *Alice's Adventures in Wonderland*, and collections of short films. Animation can free the creative imagination of the film-maker from the straitjacket of realism, in order to explore creativity or express political protest.

The British film-maker Derek Jarman also made films in a non-realist form, most famously in his moving film *Blue* (UK, 1993), in which, to the accompaniment of voiceover and music, the screen remains an intense shade of blue for the film's 76-minute duration.

Music videos and advertising are accessible and imaginative contemporary examples of non-realist moving image texts. Non-realist film (and television) is on the border between mainstream film and experimental art, and is termed by some as *avant-garde* (ahead of its time) or *alternative*.

Even films as diverse as *The Full Monty* (UK/USA, 1997) and *Notting Hill* (UK, 1999) both resemble particular geographical places in the United Kingdom and are concerned with the reality of human experience, whether that of unemployment or falling in love. They both represent a sense of realism, the credible semblance of reality.

Realism, as a concept, involves a more complex level of theoretical debate than is first apparent, focusing on ideological debates and aesthetic definitions.

Debates about realism in film may include consideration of movements such as: *cinéma vérité*, Soviet formalism (see Eisenstein, p. 155), Italian neo-realism (in the work of Roberto Rossellini, Luchino Visconti and Vittorio de Sica), German Expressionism (Robert Wiene, Fritz Lang, Friedrich Wilhelm Murnau – see pp. 200–5 on the horror genre) and realists (as in the critic and film theorist André Bazin), as well as art cinema.

High-concept films

Sometimes the idea for a film can be proposed in a single word – '*Titanic*', for example, needed no further elaboration. Of course, the names of possible stars count for a great deal, too, in any hopeful pitch.

A high-concept film is one in which every element is highly researched, developed and marketed in order to guarantee as large an international audience as possible, and consequently enormous profits. While the film business always entails an element of risk for investors, as notable expensive flops are testimony to, a high-concept film has been designed in every respect to reduce financial risk.

Typical elements of a high concept film include:

► a single, simple idea at the heart of the plot, often developed from a previous film
► pre-existing central characters (such as a real of fictional figure) or an adaptation from popular fiction or comics, so that it is easy for a mass audience to understand
► a simple, uncomplicated plot
► popular stars to pull in as large an audience as possible
► a universal theme, such as love
► a mainstream genre (or hybrid – a combination – of popular genres)
► a high-profile music soundtrack

► a synergy between film and the increasingly important commercial tie-ins such as CDs and a host of other merchandise, including video games, toys, clothes and themed fast food and confectionery.

Film reviews and other promotional tools

FILM REVIEWS

I go to the films with every experience I can muster – not only in terms of knowing what a particular film is, but also my experiences of life. Once I start watching a film, I let the film happen to me. Then I try to combine myself and the film into my review.

Roger Ebert, *Chicago Sun-Times* and Microsoft *Cinemania*

▼ ▼ ▼

PURPOSES OF THE FILM REVIEW In a daily newspaper, the only thing the reader really wants to know is: is this new film worth seeing? A personal response, with some details on noteworthy features, and comparisons to similar previous films, are all that are called for.

In specialist film magazines such as *Sight and Sound* or *Empire*, the reviewer will be required to do rather more. The readers demand much more information and more detailed critical analysis.

Film reviews have the following basic functions.

► **ANALYSIS** Reviewers analyse a film by breaking it down into its component parts. These might include the film's genre, the actors' performances, the story line and any special effects. The amount of information readers demand depends on the type of publication.

► **EVALUATION** Audiences expect the reviewer to make critical judgments about the film. If they have not seen the film yet, the audience expects a judgment about quality. On the other hand, if the audience has already seen the film, they may expect a 're-view' or a second look. The second look at the film provides a deeper level of understanding. It can also provide a specialist way of looking at the film that may not have been immediately apparent.

► **PERSUASION** Some reviews perform an advertising function for the film. Studios regard positive film reviews as free advertising.

► **ENTERTAINMENT** The average person attends a cinema five times per year. The readership of film reviews is significantly higher. It follows that many of the people reading film reviews do not go to see the films: even so, they want to know about them. This may be in case they do get the chance to go or may equally just be to keep up with what is happening in the film world.

Both the film-maker and the critic are in the entertainment business. Some reviewers deliberately try to write in an exciting 'funky' style to capture some of the energy of popular film.

► **PSYCHOLOGICAL NEEDS** The review also fulfils other purposes, such as the need to appear knowledgeable among friends (see uses and gratifications theories, p. 31).

AUDIENCE ROLES AND RELATIONSHIPS

Once, someone did a study of critics. By and large, they got their jobs by chance rather than studying specifically.

Gene Siskel of the US television review programme *Siskel and Ebert*

▼ ▼ ▼

Many film-makers see the critic as some kind of 'no-talent parasite' who can make or break their films. Audiences, on the other hand, are encouraged to see the critic as a peer. In most publications, the critic writes as if he or she is a member of the audience. The difference is that the critic writes as a member who is much better informed than most.

Equally, critics whose views are wildly different from the majority of readers soon lose their own audience. Over a period of time, readers come to know the style and tastes of individual critics. They learn to look out for the ones who reflect their tastes and interests – and not to bother with those who do not!

Many major film production companies have learnt to tremble over the judgments of some critics. The freelance film site *aint-it-cool-news.com* reaches a huge audience through the Internet. It was widely credited with having caused the flop of *Batman and Robin* (USA, 1997), following a particularly unfavourable review. Nowadays, we can all be a reviewer on a variety of websites from retail companies such as amazon.co.uk to the homepages of private film fans.

With magazines and newspapers, the nature of the publication itself is the key factor in deciding the tone of the review. A broadsheet newspaper may adopt a lofty, considered approach. On the other hand, a tabloid newspaper is likely to encourage a more lively, informal style. A lifestyle magazine may be even more informal. At the other end of the spectrum, specialist journals require the reviewer to adopt a much more erudite, even academic, approach.

For specialist magazines, the reviewer will research extensively. The central exposition or argument may be developed over several pages. The language becomes more complex and may freely make use of critical or theoretical jargon.

Scattered throughout the review is the critic's opinion. Most critics stress that the opinion expressed is personal. They try to make their own tastes and interests obvious to the readers. Some critics even say this is what their readers enjoy most. We may also develop a trust for a particular critic whose opinion chimes with our own, as their past recommendations have pleased us.

FEATURES OF THE FILM REVIEW

The film review is a very flexible prose genre and varies considerably from one publication to another. Some reviews, in specialist magazines, can be well over 1000 words. In some newspapers, however, reviews may be just four or five sentences long. Even a short review will give plot details and an evaluation (usually in the last sentence).

The following are common features of film reviews.

EXPOSITION A review is a personal critical response and therefore consists of a point of view supported by evidence from the film. This use of an argument sustained by proof is called an *exposition*. The reviewer uses analysis and evaluation to carry the exposition to its conclusion.

CLASSIFICATION, CAST AND CREDITS LIST Most reviews provide basic information about the film in a table format near the headline of the article. Although these details are minimal, they still provide evidence for the exposition. They allow the readers to evaluate the film to some extent.

THE PLOT The plot is the storyline or what happens. Reviews give the main details of the plot except the ending, or any particular surprises that are crucial to narrative development. Reviews also evaluate the plot.

THE STARS Cinemagoers are interested in the stars and often choose a film on the basis of who is in it. Responding to audience demand, reviewers give some of the review space to evaluating the performance of well-known actors.

OTHER ELEMENTS OF THE FILM Evidence to support the exposition is often drawn from a number of other film elements as well.

▶ The *theme* of the film is the point it is trying to make. The theme may also be what is learned from the film. For example, the film may be about gender or racial issues, love, courage, etc.
▶ The *script* is a kind of master plan of the film. Reviewers may look at it to assess the effectiveness of dialogue, characterisation and the use of dramatic moments, confrontations, etc.
▶ *Acting* is important to the success of the film and a significant area of comment for reviewers. Even big stars can give poor performances – and critics love nothing better than to point out when they do!
▶ *Setting, costumes, make-up and other details of location* help to create the detail and atmosphere of a film. They are especially important in period films.
▶ *Directing* is crucial to make all the component parts of the film come together. Some film theorists regard the director of the film as similar to the author of a novel. A critic may choose to consider the film in the context of the director's *oeuvre* (body of work). This is called the *auteur* approach – a highly fashionable area of study, at one point (see p. 221 on multiple versus single authorship). Today, the emphasis tends to be on the collaborative nature of film-making.
▶ *Cinematography* is the camera work in the film. Cinematography is regarded as an art in itself and is often evaluated in aesthetic terms. (See film language, p. 154.)
▶ *Editing* of the film is a technique of building the story. (See film language, p. 154.)

▶ *Sound* is crucially important in creating a sense of reality. It also intensifies emotion. (See film language, p. 154.)

STRUCTURE OF THE REVIEW

The film review is most similar in structure to that of a newspaper feature article (see p. 428) or a magazine article (see p. 440).

FILM BLURBS

'One of the top films of the year!' This kind of praise represents the classic *blurb*. A blurb is a short publicity quote. It is often featured on film posters and billboards.

Have you ever wondered how the studios find these ecstatic comments? Very occasionally, they are taken from glowing reviews by well-known reviewers. If a studio is lucky, a respected reviewer will say its film has 'Screen excitement like you've never seen it before'. The publicity staff can then splash this sentence across every poster.

More often, the studio has to go digging for good blurbs. The American film commentator Frank Thompson says: 'You might wonder if publicity dispensers look for a few positive words in an otherwise negative review. You know the kind: "It's a wonder smelly garbage like this can even run through a projector!" shows up in the ad as "… it's a wonder …!"'. However, such practices are increasingly considered as unacceptable.

Figure 3.11
Some film critics earn extra income by writing blurbs for films as soon as they are released. The critics send long lists of blurbs hoping that the studios will buy one or two.

Most blurbs are manufactured especially for the studios. Studio employees often ring film critics and ask them to produce a catchy sentence for their film. Some critics make their living as professional blurb writers.

One professional blurb writer is Jim Whaley, who is based in the US city of Atlanta. Whaley called *Home Alone* (USA, 1990) 'The funniest film of the year!' He later said, 'I honestly thought it was.' As soon as a film comes out, Whaley sends a list of five or six 'raves' to the film studios. One or two will usually be chosen to feature in advertising.

For the film *Die Hard 2* (USA, 1990), Whaley wrote: 'More nerve tingling excitement than any film in memory. You simply haven't seen an action film unless you've seen *Die Hard 2*.'

Occasionally, there is a film every major critic hates, yet the studios can still always find someone to write the blurbs. As Frank Thompson puts it, 'You can always find somebody in some small town who sees his only chance to have his name flash across the country and have his mother see it'.

INTERNET SITES

Most of the film production houses now also have websites. The sites are a kind of advertising. People visit them for information about films, but often spend hours exploring the site and downloading games, gimmicks and promotions.

Teaser clips and trailers are offered by most sites. Often the clips are accompanied by stills, soundbites, production notes and background information on the characters. Competitions and quizzes based on the film ensure that the audience will need to see the film.

Innovative uses of websites began in some style with the famous one produced by the production team for *The Blair Witch Project* (USA, 1999). They cleverly laid the ground with some apparently authentic-looking material on the film's supposedly real-life events, to generate curiosity and advance publicity for the film. The website rapidly became a modern classic in promotional devices.

FILM POSTERS

As advertising for the film, the film poster's main function is to increase box-office sales. At one level, the film poster works much like a display advertisement in a magazine or newspaper. The poster aims to create an identity for the film as a single product different from its competitors.

It also, however, operates in a more complex way. According to television and film theorist John Ellis, one of the key functions of the poster is the creation of a *narrative image*.

The *narrative image* is an idea of what the film might be like. Some of the characteristics of genre, setting and even character can be suggested. It is not a summary of the film or its storyline: more like a tantalising promise of what the film can deliver. Audiences gain an idea of the narrative image of a film and then make a decision whether to attend or not.

HOOKING THE AUDIENCE The film poster is a kind of bait for film audiences. The poster designer aims to create in the minds of the audience a yearning or a desire to know more. It helps to build audience expectations.

The poster poses a question the audience can only answer by attending the film. Stripped to the bare essentials, the question is: 'What happened?' John Ellis calls this question the enigma (or riddle) of the film. Film publicity deepens the enigma to encourage the audience to see the film.

The poster for *Loch Ness* (UK, 1995) creates an enigma for the film using an image of the lake and the tag line: 'Undiscovered … undisturbed … until now!' The audience wants to know what happened. They can only complete this riddle or mystery by seeing the film.

FEATURES OF FILM POSTERS Film posters are similar to the magazine display advertisement (see p. 443). They have a headline, a picture and some very brief *copy* (a publisher's term for the writing). The copy is usually in the form of a caption (also known as a *tag line*) and cast details.

The poster is different to the magazine display advertisement in that it is meant for an audience that is physically on the move – actually walking past. The film poster must capture the attention and interest of the passer-by. As a result, almost all of the message is in the picture, headline and tag line. The audience barely glances at any remaining copy on the poster. This is in contrast to most magazine display advertisements. Although these,

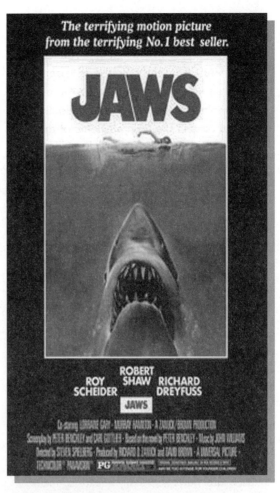

Figure 3.12
The poster for Jaws (USA, 1975) has become one of Hollywood's classics. The narrative of the film is reduced to a simple idea – innocent, unsuspecting swimmer, great big shark! The thematic battle between good and evil is clearly represented, as is the genre of the film. The image is simple and easily remembered.

too, must stop people in their tracks as they thumb through a magazine, the display advertisement often features lengthy copy. This can be read at leisure once the person's attention has been caught.

The design of the poster incorporates some or all of the following features.

▶ **GENRE REFERENCES** The picture in a film poster usually gives an indication of the film's genre. For example, a poster for an action film could suggest a lone hero and high-powered gun violence, while one for a musical may suggest sexual attraction and romance.

▶ **THE STARS** Audiences have expectations for films starring their favourite actors. Many stars are referred to as 'bankable' because of their power to draw audiences and virtually guarantee financial success. Posters focus on stars. For example, the headline from the *Terminator 2* (USA, 1991) poster simply says 'Schwarzenegger'. The lettering for this is bigger than the film title itself.

▶ **THE NARRATIVE IMAGE** Although it is a still

image, the picture on a film poster suggests a story. Sometimes the picture on the poster does not appear in the film at all. More often, a key visual from the narrative is frozen into a single striking picture. This image represents the whole film. Ideally, the frozen visual should contain the main elements of the theme. If the film deals with a battle between good and evil, the poster should represent these elements.

▶ **SIMPLICITY** Simplicity helps audience recall. Film posters aim to create a narrative image the audience can easily remember. Film posters have simple pictures and copy. When designing a poster, the advertising agency often tries to reduce the theme of the film to one or two very short sentences. The poster is then built up from there.

INTERVIEWS AND APPEARANCES

Interviews are one of the key means of promoting audience awareness of forthcoming films. Guest slots for main actors on major television talk shows help to provide some information on content and to arouse further interest.

Such interviews also easily equate to many thousands of pounds worth of free advertising. Talk show hosts are pleased to have big film stars,

of course: studios and film producers even more so! Stars are usually bound by their contract to do the publicity tour interviews for their new film, known as a press 'junket'. A hotel may be booked in a major city and journalists and television/radio interviewers will get a ten- or fifteen-minute slot, rarely longer, with a star, who will in turn promote the film for a television or radio slot, or magazine spot. Magazine feature articles are another source of pre-publicity – also free.

Actors have specific clauses in their contracts governing the number and timing of interviews they will have to give in the run-up to the release of a new film. Appearances at certain functions and public events may also be built into the schedule in the same way.

MARKETING BRITISH CINEMA

… the end of the 1990's sees uncertainty about what the millennium holds. In the UK the number of films produced doubled and the amount of money invested in UK feature film productions rose from £169 million in 1992 to £560 million in 1996. In 1998 the number of films in production dropped but budgets for UK and UK-linked films increased. Print runs dramatically increased with wider launches of films for shorter periods to capitalise on marketing and media interest.

Peter Todd

▼ ▼ ▼

The emphasis that is put on marketing and print runs cannot be stressed enough. In the increasingly diverse wealth of leisure pursuits available today, advertising is crucial to bring a film to public awareness – *and keep it there*, once it has been established. Similarly, the number of copies (prints) that are made, and hence the total number of screens they can be released to, will be key in determining the likely audience size.

Todd points to the interesting differences between promotional campaigns even from within the same company. For *Lock, Stock and Two Smoking Barrels* (UK, 1998), for instance, Polygram used a combination of television advertising and some 1500 poster sites – as well as releasing it on 221 screens. The same company, however, initially used only fourteen screens to release *Elizabeth* (UK, 1998). Television advertising was sustained over a much longer period for this film.

Figure 3.13
The initial advertising campaign for East is East was accused of being misleading as to the film's true nature. Asian faces were conspicuously backgrounded. This poster was used to launch the film in the US.

The promotional campaign will have a profound impact on how a film is perceived. *Four Weddings and a Funeral* (UK, 1994), though made in this country, was released in the United States many months before it was here. It was calculated that its 'heritage appeal' would go down well in the United States and that success there would whip up much more interest back here in seeing a British film that was taking them by storm over there.

Sometimes, however, these calculations can lead to some curious decisions, and even controversies. In the case of *East is East* (UK, 1999), for example, there was a distinct lack of Asian faces on the initial run of posters used to promote the film. Odd, to say the least, in a film that is so much about the experiences of Asian immigrants and their children growing up in the United Kingdom. Leslie Udwin, the film's producer, stressed the marketing decision to 'focus on the fact that it was a universal comedy'. This led to the inclusion of a rather cute shot of the dog on the film posters – although this animal in fact played a rather tiny part in the actual film.

There were criticisms that the advertising campaign was seeking to play down the Asian-ness of the film's subject matter and that, although the film is very funny, it is not primarily a comedy. It in fact deals with some very serious issues, depicts a grim social reality and features some fairly ugly incidents.

▼ ▼ ▼

The main poster, with the dog, was essentially saying to everybody, of all ages, come and see this hysterically funny film. Then they came in to find that it was more than just a comedy, but it's still a comedy, so they weren't disappointed when they got there. Which is great marketing.

Leslie Udwin, Producer of *East is East*,
Black Film-maker, vol. 3, issue 9

▼ ▼ ▼

▼ ▼ ▼ ▼ ▼ ▼ ▼

activities

1. Collect several reviews by the same reviewer. Analyse them according to the following questions:
► What are the most common film elements the reviewer chooses to evaluate? For example, does the reviewer concentrate on stars, or camera work or the director's vision?
► How much of the review is analysis and how much is evaluation? Mark the areas of evaluation with a highlighter pen.
► What seems to be the personal taste of the reviewer. Using the reviews as evidence, try to work out the various viewpoints and prejudices this reviewer has.

2. Collect reviews of the same film drawn from a wide variety of publications, such as newspapers, magazines, cinema journals, etc. Analyse them according to the following questions:
► What audience is each review intended for and how can you tell this from the review itself?
► Which areas of interest in the film are common to most of the reviews?
► Is there a common negative criticism of the film or, alternatively, is one review very different in its criticisms than most of the others?

3. Select a film and tell the story in four to six paragraphs of thirty words each. Do not reveal the ending.

4. In around 200 words, analyse and evaluate one of the common review elements in a film of your choice. For example, concentrate on sound, or editing, or the stars, or the themes, etc.

Some examples of films that are useful for particular review elements are listed below.
► *Editing:* Alfred Hitchcock's films
► *Sound: Citizen Kane* (USA, 1941)
► *Plot:* Action films.

5. Imagine that you are a professional 'blurb machine' who sends blurbs to major studios hoping that they will be used to promote new films. Write some blurbs for several recent-release films. Write five or six blurbs for each film that you choose.

6. Design a website for a film. Plan the quizzes, games and teaser clips you would include on the site. Design a front page for the website, complete with images, links and background graphics.

7. From your favourite film, select a key scene to freeze into a picture for a film poster. Refer to the features of posters before selecting a scene.

Reduce the theme of a film to one or two sentences. Based on these, suggest tag lines or captions for posters advertising the film.

major assignments

Written assignment

Read the task below and prepare a 600-word response.

Review a film for a magazine or newspaper of your choice. Your review should display the main features of the genre. Focus on those elements of the film in which your audience would be most interested.

Production assignment

1. Prepare a poster advertising a film of your choice. The poster should display the main features of the genre. Attach a written description of the advertising appeal of the poster and its target audience.

2. Prepare a comprehensive marketing strategy for a film of your choice. Suggestions for films include a non-Hollywood, non-mainstream, art-house film or perhaps one from Asia, Africa or South America.

3. Prepare an advertising strategy.

▶ Provide a description of any merchandising (e.g. clothing, computer games, toys, food specialities or other franchising arrangements). Following the description of each item, explain the role of the item in the overall marketing strategy and its target audience and projected appeal.

▶ Suggest some marketing stunts or events that would attract large crowds and wide news coverage as free advertising. Briefly explain the role of the event in the overall strategy.

Film Audiences

Figure 3.14
Hollywood's escalating firepower is increasing the potential for violence in the community, say critics. Experts are in disagreement. Does screen violence cause violence in the streets? One cynic has said that the research findings so far are 'yes, no and maybe ...'.

Issues: the violence debate

Do I think screen violence contributes to violence on the streets? Of course, the answer is yes.

Dustin Hoffman, actor

▼ ▼ ▼

A serial killer of children was addicted to *The Sound of Music*. Similarly, Richard Nixon re-ran his favourite film, *Patton*, before ordering the bombing of Cambodia. Literature reports the case of a serial killer whose inspiration was screenings of *The Ten Commandments*. Fortunately such creatures remain few and far between. My principal concerns about violent cinema has not been the turbo-charging of occasional mass murderers. The primary concern should be the deadening effect on the sensibilities of the rest of us.

Phillip Adams, cultural commentator

▼ ▼ ▼

There is no shortage of high-profile movie industry insiders who are willing to break ranks and criticise the cinema's obsession with violence. The legendary director Stanley Kubrick even went so far as to permanently withdraw his own film *A Clockwork Orange* (UK, 1971) from circulation in the United Kingdom. He became convinced that it had been partly responsible for a brutal gang-rape in England. Alan Pakula (*All the President's Men*, USA, 1976; *Presumed Innocent*, USA, 1990) says movie violence is like eating salt. The more you eat, the more you need to eat so that you can taste it at all.

The other side has not been slow to counter-attack. Actor Tom Hanks has criticised 'cheap grandstanding', while leading director Oliver Stone (*JFK*, USA, 1991; *Natural Born Killers*, USA, 1994) has referred to a new 'McCarthyism' (Senator J. McCarthy was the leader of the witch-hunt of supposed communists in Hollywood following World War II).

▼ ▼ ▼

Maybe we need the catharsis of blood-letting and decapitation like the ancient Romans needed it.

Martin Scorsese, film director

(see p. 196 on action/spectacle)

▼ ▼ ▼

THE NEVER-ENDING STORY

Since the beginning of recorded history, violence has been an important part of storytelling. There are violent themes in the Bible, the Greek epics, fairy tales, Shakespearean theatre and nineteenth-century novels. Nor is violence restricted to the narrative tradition. The paintings of Goya and Bosch also depict deep and disturbing horrors.

For most commentators, the issue is not the mere presence of violence, but the context of it. Violence in the Bible, for example, is important to the teaching of lessons about life and the establishment of a moral code. In a film, the context would include the purposes of the violence in the overall meaning and the audience's viewing circumstances.

HOLLYWOOD'S INDUSTRIES

It's the studio executives who decide which movies to make. Hollywood now controls 80 per cent of coming up with a product and then repeating it forever. Those are the people who brought you the Big Mac.

They are run like corporations are run, whether they are making cars or soap. All they talk about is the first-quarter results.

Francis Ford Coppola, film director

▼ ▼ ▼

According to one Hollywood producer, he has seen so many proposals for movies based on serial killers that he is beginning to feel like a victim himself. Most of these proposals are from hopefuls who have been keen to cash in on the violence formula.

FORMULA MOVIES The film and video industries operate in a very competitive market. They will exploit anything that attracts attention and draws crowds. The violence formula can reliably deliver mass audiences and box-office success. For example, the 1992 film *Basic Instinct* (USA, 1991) quickly became the most attended restricted classification film at the cinemas and the next year became the most rented video. Hollywood has built much of its commercial base on a combined sex and violence formula designed to appeal to people less than thirty-five years old.

This has led some critics to believe the concern over violence is at least partly explained by generational differences. According to one survey, 63 per cent of respondents aged eighteen to twenty-four years had seen films in the restricted category. This compared with 30 per cent of those aged forty to fifty-five and 14 per cent of those fifty-five and over.

Some professionals within the industry, however, view violence as essential in creating action scenes. They argue that it is the best tool for maintaining the interest of the audience – both young and old. They claim that violence is limited to scenes where it is appropriate to the context. They also insist that violence is shown to be immoral, unless it was used to enforce the law. According to them, heroes only use violence when absolutely necessary. Many in the industry claim that the violence accurately reflects the real world.

Content analysis produces a different story, however. In surveys between 1973 and 1987, it has been claimed that 88 per cent of all on-screen anti-social acts are rewarded and that the people committing the acts felt justified 83 per cent of the time.

ARTISTIC RESPONSIBILITY

Is the artist solely concerned with art for art's sake, or does the artist have a responsibility to society? At the time you are being an artist, says David Cronenberg, you are no longer a citizen. You

Figure 3.15

MOVIE DEATH COUNT

TITLE	NO. OF DEATHS
Die Hard 2	264
Rambo 3	106
The Wild Bunch	89
Robocop 2	74

have no moral responsibility. Others disagree. According to the early Hollywood director Frank Capra, the film-maker's responsibility is to emphasise the positive side of humanity by showing triumph over adversities and obstacles.

ROMAN CIRCUSES

Many commentators have compared Hollywood violence to the excesses of the Roman circuses. Sir David Puttnam, a former president of Columbia Pictures, says the Roman circuses, where hundreds of thousands of people died, did not start out that way. They started as mild entertainment. But the audience demand for more and more thrills over a couple of hundred years resulted in the circuses becoming more grotesque and more bloody. The end only came when Rome could no longer afford the butchery. Puttnam says it is time now for someone to say: 'Stop – this is enough.'

SOCIAL ECOLOGY

The anti-Hollywood crusader Michael Medved says the death counts are quadrupling and the blast power is increasing by the megaton. Meanwhile, the characters are no longer heroically 'larger than life', but meaner, less decent and less likeable than real-life people. For the conservative campaigner Medved, the Hollywood dream factory has become the poison factory. Others say it is not only the manufacturers of guns, but also the makers of violent films who deal in death.

▼ ▼ ▼

If shoppers are capable of rejecting a brand of tuna because of its links with dolphin slaughter, then surely the public is capable of rejecting base-level splatterpunk if it slaughters our self respect.

I'm not attacking … [artists] … sweating in garrets, but global empires which cynically pander to easy profits, cheap sensations and reversed priorities.

After years of agitation and argument we've finally reached the point where a corporation can be shamed for fouling a river. It's time to tackle a system which fouls another resource – the river of our dreams.

Richard Neville, Australian popular culture commentator and former 1960s free speech campaigner

▼ ▼ ▼

Media research and the effects of violence

Research into film and media violence is as old as the media itself. There have been two main traditions: the effects and cultivation studies tradition and the more recent ethnographic or audience reception tradition (see Audiences, p. 30–2).

Neither tradition has shown a direct and certain cause–effect link between film (or television) violence and increased community violence. The approaches and the findings of both traditions have also been the subject of criticism themselves.

SEEKING EFFECTS

Nearly 80 per cent of all media research has been concerned with violence. For nearly a century, researchers have tried to find relationships with media violence in the following areas.

DIRECT EFFECTS Researchers have sought direct cause–effect relationships between movie violence and increased audience aggression. The results have failed to prove any direct connection. In this regard, research into the effects of media violence is often contrasted with research into the effects of cigarette smoking. These have proved beyond scientific doubt that there are direct causal effects.

COPY-CAT EFFECTS Investigations have been conducted into criminal actions that appear to copy previously viewed screen violence. According to the criminologist Paul Wilson, a significant number of documented examples exist.

DE-SENSITISING EFFECTS Constant viewing of violent material may harden or desensitise audience members to real-life violence. People who watch a lot of violent material may come to believe violence is a normal everyday occurrence. Michael Medved says that people are becoming immune to film violence. The human suffering and pain of the screen victim becomes lost in the process. Research evidence that points to the phenomenon of desensitising does exist.

DISINHIBITION Some researchers have tried to find evidence of a 'loss of conscience' or a lack of self-control among audience members who are viewers of violent films. The studies have sought to prove that screen violence reduces people's inhibitions against committing violent acts themselves. Such evidence as does exist is similar to that suggesting desensitising.

CATHARSIS Watching violent movies is said to help people 'let off steam'. It allows them to release their aggressive urges, according to this line of thinking. The process is referred to in psychology as *catharsis*, a cleansing and purifying liberation (e.g. a sneeze is a catharsis).

Researchers have found little evidence of cathartic effects from viewing screen violence. Most evidence, on the contrary, points to an increase in tension rather than a release.

Like films, sporting events are also said to allow people safely to release excess aggression. In direct contradiction of this notion of catharsis, however, women's refuges regularly report increased domestic violence after major televised football play-offs.

The violence of the Japanese entertainment media is legendary. Some commentators believe that that the cathartic effect accounts for Japan's low level of community violence. Others point to a range of cultural factors that are more likely to be the cause.

THE EFFECTS AND CULTIVATION TRADITIONS

There have been many studies of screen violence in the empirical tradition known as the *effects* tradition. A typical effects study sets out to *prove* something. As with scientific experiments, researchers try to isolate a link between an effect and certain causes.

Effects studies tend to use the social science methods and often express results as numbers or percentages. This is called quantitative research

because the results are expressed as quantities. Quantitative research is similar to that used by advertisers to assess the effectiveness of their sales pitch.

In the 1980s and 1990s, the effects tradition came in for widespread criticism. In 1989, in work for the British Broadcasting Standards Council, Guy Cumberbatch concluded that many of the effects studies had been crudely designed. According to Cumberbatch, they also failed to pay attention to increasing public concern about media violence.

In a 22-year study, Dr Leonard Eron of the University of Illinois found that children with the heaviest exposure to film and television violence were 150 per cent more likely to be convicted of criminal offences when they were adults than those with the lightest exposure.

In a ten-year study, Monroe Lefkowitz found that the more violence an eight-year-old boy watched, the more aggressive his behaviour would be at eighteen years of age. Another study showed that males who watch a lot of violence tended to show a smaller increase in heart rate when shown new violent material than males who did not watch as much screen violence.

Copy-cat effects were analysed in one study. Could violent behaviours be learned and stored in the brain for future reference? Later in life, when a similar situation is encountered, could a person retrieve the violent image and then perform it in real life? The study looked at cases where youths had apparently imitated criminal acts they had seen in movies. In each case, the environment of the real-life crime had definite similarities to the fictional scene.

A few effects researchers have actually put a percentage on the relationship between screen violence and real-life violence. Leonard Eron, for example, believes that 10 per cent of the violence

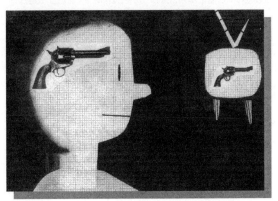

Figure 3.16
Research has so far failed to prove a direct cause-effect link between screen violence and real-life violence. However, certain other, much more complicated effects have been indicated.

chapter three

Figure 3.17
Mickey and Mallory – young lovers on a killing spree. Bestselling author John Grisham lost a close friend in a copycat killing that he says was sparked by the movie **Natural Born Killers.** *Think of a movie as a product, says Grisham, like breast implants or Honda three-wheelers. If a faulty product causes injury, the customer can sue.*

in the community is a result of exposure to violent images.

One of the leading expert in cultivation studies, George Gerbner, believes the focus on whether media violence causes real violence is a mistake. The contribution of media violence to the committing of violence is relatively minor, perhaps 5 per cent, says Gerbner. In contrast, the contribution to long-term perceptions and attitudes towards violence is far greater.

Probably no one in the effects tradition has bettered Wilbur Schramm's summing up of the few firm conclusions about screen violence. Although Schramm spoke only in relation to children and television, his statement has been echoed in findings about adults and film:

▼ ▼ ▼

For *some* children under *some* conditions, *some* television is harmful. For *other* children under the same conditions or the same children under *other* conditions, it may … [have little effect]. For *most* children under *most* conditions, *most* television is probably neither harmful nor particularly beneficial.

▼ ▼ ▼

(See also 'The Violence Debate', pp. 32–3.)

THE ETHNOGRAPHIC OR RECEPTION TRADITION

Ethnographic researchers' main contribution to debate over the issue of screen violence has been to highlight the shortcomings of the effects tradition. Effects studies treated the audience as 'dopes', according to ethnographic researchers. The various ways in which audiences read films were not taken into account (see pp. 30–2). Furthermore, all of the social and cultural factors that influence and explain behaviour were ignored.

There has been a flood of criticism aimed at the effects studies from those in the opposing reception tradition. It has meant that the ethnographic (reception) approach tended to 'write off' the issue of violence. As a result, few studies have tackled the issue and there is not yet a full alternative to the effects tradition. One of the main outcomes, however, has been an understanding that media violence cannot be seen as separate from society as a whole.

Reception researchers point to findings that show that social and economic conditions (such as unemployment, family violence, sexism and racism) are major factors in the committing of violence.

There is a view that the media play a role in community violence because they are central institutions in society. The social and economic conditions of a violent society are therefore represented through the media. The media are a symptom, rather than a cause, it is felt.

Ethnographic studies use group discussions and interviews to build up descriptions of audience behaviour. The results are usually descriptive and are often pieced together from collections of interview quotes. This type of research is called *qualitative research*. This is because it describes the qualities or details of particular subjects.

Ethnographic research commonly has a very tightly focused topic. For example, it may look at the reactions of a group of thirty inner-city migrant women to the violence in *Silence of the Lambs* (USA, 1990).

One important study in the reception tradition was carried out by Hodge and Tripp. The study looked at children's responses to the mid-1980s television cartoon *Fangface*. At least two of its findings are relevant to cinema-going adults.

Hodge and Tripp concluded that, first, media violence is of a totally different nature to real-life violence. Without conflict, art, drama and literature would be almost non-existent. Secondly, they concluded that the meanings gained from screen violence are negotiated and altered by each audience member. The effects of media violence on individuals can only be understood in that personally negotiated form.

However, critics are now taking aim at the ethnographic approach. In the introduction to her book *Living Room Wars*, one of the leading reception researchers Ien Ang outlines some of the criticisms.

The approach exaggerates the power of audiences to make their own meanings, critics say. Instead of being seen as 'dopes', the audiences are now seen as heroes.

Another critic, John Fiske, says the power of the audience is only the power of the weak – the power to make the best of things they cannot change and therefore have to put up with.

The ethnographic tradition has also been criticised for the potential it has to include the researcher's own biases. A researcher can also easily choose which interview quotes and which audience members best suit a personal point of view. In this way, a particular point of view can be 'written into' a reception study.

THE CRIMINOLOGISTS

A lone gunman shot thirty-five people in the world's worst massacre of its type at the convict ruins of Port Arthur, Tasmania in 1996. The owner of the video hire store near the killer's home later told of the gunman's fascination with violent movies.

Three years earlier, in England, two ten-year old boys murdered the toddler James Bulger in scenes reminiscent of an American horror movie and its sequels.

The author John Grisham claims Oliver Stone sparked a killing spree with his film *Natural Born Killers* (USA, 1994) and has called on the victims to take legal action against Hollywood.

▼ ▼ ▼

While I don't think violent videos are the trigger for mass killers, there is considerable evidence to show violent videos can tell a potentially violent person how to express his violence. The copy-cat phenomenon is real – but only with people who have a predisposition to be violent.

And there is no way the experts can predict which one of the viewers will be propelled into murder and mayhem.

Normal people do not turn into violent killers simply as a result of watching a film. The roots of criminal violence are enormously complex.

Dr Paul Wilson
Criminologist

▼ ▼ ▼

MEDIA AS A FACTOR IN CRIMINAL VIOLENCE

The media's role in causing violence has been ranked eleventh out of twelve possible factors, in a report by the National Committee on Violence in Australia. The factors are listed below in descending order of importance.

1. Child development and the influence of the family is the strongest influence on the future committing of violence
2. Standards of behaviour in the general society
3. Economic inequality
4. Cultural disintegration
5. Setting (e.g. a rundown setting can promote violence, a clean setting can reduce violence)
6. Gender inequality
7. Personality factors (two particular characteristics are lack of regard for others and impulsiveness)
8. Substance abuse (including and especially alcohol)
9. Biological factors (male/female and other inherited characteristics)
10. Mental illness (prediction is extremely difficult)
11. Media influences
12. Peer group influences.

The committee concluded that, when it comes to investing limited money and resources for the prevention of violence, the media should be a low priority.

SHORTCIRCUITING THE DEBATE

With no agreement on the outcomes of media violence, government agencies must still find a way to deal with community concern. The dilemma has led to the study of what is termed *community perceptions of violence*.

According to Dr Paul Wilson, the approach may be summed up as 'balancing the views of ordinary people because there is not yet any other way out of the debate'.

▼ ▼ ▼

Society itself will have to act when it senses the limit has been reached. You are not going to end it by censorship, by officially banning violence. My view is there has to be a consumer revolution against it. We will eventually have to say enough is enough.'

Dr Paul Wilson, criminologist

▼ ▼ ▼

The *community perceptions* approach sidesteps the minefield of academic research.

However, the interests of the public are still looked after because the major findings of perceptions research are those very community interests. For example, 60 per cent of one research sample believed that there was too much media violence. Women, parents, people with religious convictions and the elderly were shown to be the most concerned.

On the other hand, 82 per cent of people surveyed believed that adults should be able to watch movies with a restricted classification, if they so desired. Of those interviewed, 65 per cent believed that violence in society was linked to media violence. However, 38 per cent said that they personally enjoyed violent films.

Sexual violence was of greatest concern to the community. Surveys indicate support for more control in this area.

Current trends in attendance

The picture for cinema attendance continues to be healthy at present. A total of 135.5 million people went to see films in the United Kingdom in 1998. Box-office takings were even better,

reaching £514.73 million (Source: *BFI Film and Television Handbook*, 2000). More people are going more often (and paying more!) – especially among the lucrative 15- to 34-year-old market. People aged from fifteen to twenty-four years make up the the age bracket of most regular cinemagoers. They tend to have a high disposable income and spend more money on leisure, in comparison to those in the older age bracket, twenty-five to thirty-four years, who are more likely to spend income on homes and families. However, people aged from twenty-five to thirty-four are more likely to have young children whom they take to the cinema.

In 1998, there was a total of 181 new screens in the United Kingdom – most of them in the forty-seven new multiplex sites, which constitute 58 per cent of the United Kingdom's total screens. So successful has this format been that now 'megaplexes' – with up to thirty screens – are scheduled for early completion. This is because these sites, often attached to a shopping and sports centre, offer audiences convenient one-stop shopping and leisure experiences. They also offer site owners and retailers a chance to maximise profits, from unit rental, retail and food and drink sales, by targeting and providing for their 'captive' audiences.

In addition, there have been some notable UK film successes over the past few years: at the time of their release, *Four Weddings and a Funeral* (UK, 1994) was the most popular film in the country and *The Full Monty* (UK/USA, 1997) was the biggest grossing film *ever* here.

Despite some very real achievements and progress, however, the prospects for British film-making and viewing are not quite so rosy as they might appear. Most of the films shown in the United Kingdom continue to be made in the United States. In 1998, nearly 84 per cent of all films screened in Britain were North American in origin.

UK films accounted for only 12.24 per cent – a disappointing drop of nearly 15 per cent on the previous year (1997). Even then, this figure was only achieved if co-productions (films made with money and personnel from more than one country) with other national sources were included. Wholly UK productions made up less than 5 per cent and 5.76 per cent of all films shown in the United Kingdom in 1998 were

US/UK co-productions. Further, when the United Kingdom does produce a big hit, more often than not the funding comes from the United States – as with the record-breaking *The Full Monty* (USA/UK, 1997).

Moreover, most of the cinema complexes in this country continue to be owned by US companies. As John Hill points out (*The Media in Britain*, Stokes & Reading (eds), Macmillan Press, 1999):

▼ ▼ ▼

… the all-important distribution sector in the UK is even more dominated by US interests than exhibition. Thus, the five largest distributors in Britain (commanding over 80 per cent of the box-office share in 1996 and 1997) are also subsidiaries of the Hollywood majors.

▼ ▼ ▼

It is not that they actively refuse British films; however, there is an almost inevitable preference for the products of their indigenous industries, and of Hollywood especially. More than half of the films made in Britain in 1995 and 1996 did not get a cinema release at all: of those that did, only about 25 per cent received general UK exhibition.

Even with the success of the multiplexes, many people feel that, far from these extending choice, the actual range of films on offer has been slimmed down and standardised. Particular genres of film seem to dominate the film programmes on offer: action movies, romance, comedies and thrillers.

A further unhelpful spin-off of this switch to the multiplex – as with supermarkets and the corner shop – is that the smaller independent exhibitors are increasingly being squeezed out of the frame. This, again, is likely to lead to a reduction in the choice of films available.

THE WAY AHEAD FOR THE UK FILM INDUSTRY

With the establishment of the Film Council (see pp. 189–90) in 2000, there was considerable optimism over the future for film production in the United Kingdom. At last it would be receiving the level of stimulus and support it had long needed. It is a fact of life that American muscle and money dominate in this increasingly global industry. Film-makers have long felt that, if Britain is to produce films at anything like a significant level, it could only do so with subsidy of some kind, to offset the power of the United States.

However, the long-term future is still a long way from being secure.

▼ ▼ ▼

Much future decision-making by the government in the UK depends on the success of the three Lottery-funded franchises awarded to Pathé Pictures, The Film Consortium and DNA Films. These corporations are guaranteed production finance over a six year period and it is hoped that they will provide continuity and stability to the industry. The inclusion of the French-based Pathé was controversial but could be seen to reflect the concerns of Chris Smith [Culture Secretary] to use its unique position 'as a bridge, geographically, culturally and economically, between Europe and the United States.'

Peter Todd

▼ ▼ ▼

MEASURING CINEMA ADMISSIONS

A variety of bodies require reliable and accurate information concerning attendances. Exhibitors of films need to know how well particular films are doing at the box office, so that they can make informed decisions about which films to retain and which to withdraw. Distributors equally wish to know how particular kinds of film are doing – not only ones currently on release, but also previously shown films.

When planning releases, it is vital to have some kind of idea of the likely popularity of a type of film and the length of run it may expect to sustain. It is also important to consider optimum release dates – e.g. 4 July in the United States, Christmas and school holidays – during which producers and distributors will hope to draw big audiences.

Aside from these two bodies, advertising contractors – and naturally their clients! – also like to have information on how many people attend and *what kinds* of people, too. Audience profiles are very important to the companies seeking to promote their products.

METHODS OF MONITORING The main agency involved in gathering information on cinema attendances is the Cinema Advertising Association (CAA), which commissions the poll company Gallup to run the CAA Monitor. Information is gathered on a weekly basis by telephone, as the figures can fluctuate widely in very short spaces of time.

Included in this survey are all circuit and independent cinemas, which make up some 90 per cent of the total. The findings are released on a monthly basis, approximately one month in arrears.

ANALYSING AUDIENCES

Taken altogether, there is a considerable amount of information available to interested parties, on both the scale and constituency of the cinema-going population. It is not, however, necessarily laid out in an easily accessible form. Different sources have different kinds of information.

The CAA Monitor tracks overall numbers attending particular films; however, its figures do not provide any kind of breakdown of the composition of audiences. For this, other sources have to be used.

The Target Group Index (TGI) and the National Readership Survey (NRS – see p. 405) are the sources used for this kind of information. They run continuous surveys on all major media forms and have particular questions on cinema attendances.

In addition, the CAA sponsors CAVIAR (Cinema and Video Industries Audience Research), with support from advertisers, exhibitors, distributors and retailers. Its survey includes video films, cinema, cable and satellite television, as well as magazine and newspaper circulations.

Aside from these, there are also trade magazines and other frequent publications, such as *Screen Finance, Screen International, Screen Daily, Variety Magazine* (for the United States) and of course daily newspapers. The BFI also produces a yearly *BFI Film and Television Handbook*, which lists all kinds of interesting information relating to films screened in the United Kingdom – with the emphasis very much on home-grown products.

Websites are an increasingly useful source of current information, with *bfi.org.uk* providing both a host of features on films produced and shown in this country and many links to other relevant sites. *Britfilmcom.co.uk* and *filmcouncil.org.uk* are particularly useful, too. Many exhibitors/distributors also produce sites with details about films that they are showing (*uci-cinemas.co.uk* is sometimes worth looking at); however, they tend to be rather limited in nature. Film-specific sites are often best – such as *imdb.com*. Whether official or unofficial, they usually carry a wealth of information.

For an independent view of British film, *6degrees.co.uk* is a mine of fascinating material, dedicated to news, reviews and details on what is up and coming.

▼ ▼ ▼ ▼ ▼ ▼ ▼

activities

1. Make a collage of print media comments on screen violence. Below the collage, give your answers to these questions:

▶ What do the comments have in common?

▶ Has a particular movie or criminally violent event sparked concern?

▶ Are there also any calls for a maintenance of freedom of expression?

▶ What is your own opinion of the issue?

▶ Why do you think the print media often run articles on film (or television) violence?

2. Conduct a content analysis of the violence in a selected movie. This style of analysis is often used in studies within the *effects* tradition. The steps set out below provide a guide.

▶ Begin with George Gerbner's definition of violence on p. 317. Count the number of incidents occurring during the movie fitting this definition.

▶ Divide the number of violent actions by the overall length of the movie expressed in hours. This gives the rate of violence per hour (R/H).

▶ The role of violence in the movie may be defined by the portrayal of characters who commit violence or who are subject to it. First count the total number of characters (leave out minor extras if this is too difficult), then count the number of characters seen as either violent or victims of violence. Make this a percentage of total characterisation (%V). Next, count the number of victims of violence, the number of killers and the number killed. Express the results as percentages of the total characterisation.

▶ Some content analysis studies have compiled a violence index. They calculate the index using a more complex version of the following formula: VI = 2 (R/H) x %V.

Calculate your own violence index rating for the movie you have studied.

3. Ethnographic research has shown that the reactions of individual audience members to violence can be complex. Part of this can be whether or not they *identified* (see pp. 127 and 141) with the character committing the violence, or whether they identified themselves in opposition to that person. Design some survey questions aimed at finding out in what way the identification factor has worked for the interview subjects. Interview a small group of people who have recently seen a film containing violence. Record their answers and write a brief report summarising the findings.

4. Take John Grisham's advice, sue Hollywood! Or lead the defence! Conduct a classroom court room in which evidence is tendered for and against the prosecution's claim that Hollywood has sold the world a dangerously life-threatening product. Arrive at a verdict.

major assignments

Written assignment

Choose one of the following and write a 600-word response.
1. Write a review of the evidence for and against any negative social impact from film violence.

Begin with an introduction to the problem. Research the details of several studies and government investigations. Report on the opinions of various academics, community leaders and industry professionals. Evaluate the extent to which movie violence is also gender issue. Conclude with your own evaluation of the issue.

2. Select a movie that has had two versions produced – an early original and a recent remake. Determine if the level of violence has increased. Evaluate the effectiveness of the remake, with the findings of your analysis in mind.

Production assignment

Choose one of the following production projects.
1. Imagine that you are preparing a research project for the British Board of Film Classification (see pp. 21 and 455). Conduct a *community perceptions research* survey of a group of people in your school community. You will need variation in age groups and a balance of gender.

Devise several survey questions designed to find out their views on screen violence and its effects on the committing of violence. Collate the results and present them as percentages. Evaluate the extent to which current movie classifications reflect the community perceptions shown in your survey.

2. Produce a five-minute mini-documentary or current affairs programme dealing with the debate about the effects of screen violence. Your programme should include interviews or panel discussions and extracts from case-study movies.

Film Institutions

Film as a medium may have begun in Europe, but without question it is the United States that has taken a leading role in its development. The overwhelming majority of the films that we are exposed to now originate from Hollywood. Film is a truly international business: production and distribution range right across the globe. Most of the investment, however, comes from the United States – and the profits, of course, return there.

This was not an accidental process and some of the reasons why this happened will be examined later. However, it should be stressed that the making of films continues, at varying levels, around the world. Some European countries – Germany, France and Sweden, for instance – have very long and strong film traditions to which it is not possible to do justice here. Further afield, China, Japan and Hong Kong are notable centres of production, too. In India's so-called 'Bollywood', the centre of its own film production in Bombay, the total number of films produced exceeds even those of the United States.

Hollywood

More has been written about Hollywood than any other topic in film studies – perhaps even any topic ever. There is not scope in this book to do that legend anything like real justice. However, no account of film-making in this country can afford to overlook the impact of this megalith, not least because its power extends far beyond simply the *production* of films.

Distribution (the promotion and availability of the film) and *exhibition* (the scheduling and screening of the film at the cinema) are equally as much determined by the US corporations that dominate the world of film-making.

The classic period of Hollywood is generally agreed to be from 1917 to somewhere in the late 1960s. This was the era of the great studios. Power shifted during this period from actors (formation of United Artists, 1919) to studios (Warner Bros., Paramount, MGM) and back to the stars again – and their agents. The huge sums of money that are commanded by top actors today mean that they have considerable say in how they perform, as well

as in what they perform. Many are able to use their high profile both to produce and direct films, too.

Up until the early 1950s, film attendance saw continuous, at times rapid, growth. During and immediately after World War II, in particular, there was a tremendous boom. Even as the industry was congratulating itself on its unparalleled success, however, a long period of decline began to set in. The arrival of television in the 1950s and the steep rise in new young families following the end of the war were partly responsible for this. So, to some extent, was the complacency of the industry, which felt it could go on churning out films to long-tested but rather tired generic formulae. Right through to the 1990s, audience figures declined steadily, with the cinema industry suffering from the impact of the dawn of the home cinema concept and the increasing availability of the home videocassette recorder throughout the 1980s.

THE 'BRAT PACK' For a brief period in the 1970s with the arrival of the 'Brat Pack' – young, more adventurous actors and directors such as Robert de Niro and Al Pacino, Martin Scorsese and Francis Ford Coppola – there was something of a revival. The latter, in founding Zoetrope Studios, especially sought to take on the studios and show that good films could be made that still made a profit.

Even this, however, turned gradually into the same thing as the system it had sought to kick against. The sheer scale of film-making, the finance required and the competing claims that have to be satisfied meant Zoetrope steadily grew more and more cautious and conventional in its output.

Today, the old studio system of film-making has disappeared, but the emphasis on business continues. Now it is dominated by large corporations and international conglomerates. News Corporation is an example of such a conglomerate, as, under the leadership of Rupert Murdoch, it comprises several related media business interests that are mutually supportive, e.g. the links between BSkyB television and 20th Century Fox film production and distribution.

The television première of *Titanic* (USA, 1997) was aired as a pay-per-view screening on Sky Premier – an exclusive that no other television network would have been likely to afford. This kind of interpenetration of products and markets supports the profitability of the conglomerate as a whole and its constituents. In some way, it harks back to the studios' Hollywood heyday, as other film production companies (such as Warner Bros. and MGM) continue to own cinema chains today; the vertical integration of the old studio system is not completely dead.

Independence in any of the three stages of the film-making process remains a difficult venture. Even if the production of a film is independent, it needs a distribution company behind it to get the film advertised and into cinemas. Independent distribution and exhibition companies are in the minority. As a result, what we see predominantly reflects the output and concerns of the major players in these three areas.

Technical matters

Technical innovation has always been crucial in the success of cinema in attracting audiences. From the 28mm projections of the earliest films, through the 70mm of CinemaScope, to the giant 49mm x 70mm IMAX screenings of today, the actual nature of the film used has been experimented with continually. Quality of film stock and the clarity of the image that results have developed tremendously.

Digital effects, such as the creation of the ship and its sinking sequences in *Titanic* (USA, 1997) and the 'bullet-time' special effects in *The Matrix* (USA, 1999) are examples of the shape of things to come in film production. *Toy Story 2* (USA, 2000) was the first film to be digitally projected, which presents challenges for the current structure of film distribution and exhibition. Mike Figgis's *Timecode 2000* (USA, 2000) used digital technology to produce a film that involved the splitting of the film frame into four, in order to show four points of view simultaneously. Figgis has also predicted that digital technology offers the independent film-maker tremendous opportunities to bypass the usual methods of exhibition, with film-makers taking a portable projector to any kind of public venue to screen his or her film. The quality of the home cinema has improved dramatically recently, with the availability and affordability of DVD players and wide-screen televisions.

Equal advances have been made in the area of sound (see p. 159). The history of the technical means by which sound is both captured and reproduced makes a fascinating study in itself. Numerous methods have been tried and enormous obstacles overcome along the way. The multi-speaker Dolby sound systems that most cinemas feature today make a huge impact on the experience of watching a film. As a result, as much attention is now paid to planning the soundtrack of many present-day films as to the script and camera work.

The multiplex

The organisations and individuals involved in the actual making of films tend to attract most of the attention of fans and critics. However, the contribution of those institutions responsible for screening them should not be overlooked.

The dramatic revival of cinema attendance in the 1990s owes a great deal to the development of the multiplex. Prior to this, most films were screened in city centre sites, often in buildings that had been used for that purpose for a considerable amount of time. Many were no longer the alluring places they had once been. Moreover, city centres had ceased to be the open, accessible places they once were – particularly on weekend nights.

A little-known Belgian, Albert Bert, first recognised the potential for developing a new concept in cinema – the out-of-town site. Make parking easy, even free, put several screens together in one building, invest in the technical quality and the physical comfort of the provision, Bert speculated, and you could change the whole experience of seeing a film.

The current rate of growth of this formula is phenomenal. Bert opened the first multiplex in Europe in 1981, in Ghent. In the United Kingdom, the first multiplex was opened in 1985 and, by 1999, the total number had risen to 142; the number of *screens* in this format went up to a massive 1222 by 1997 (Source: *Screen Finance*). City centre sites have closed all over the country.

Production in the United Kingdom

In many ways, 1997 marked a high point in the history of the film industry in Britain. Audience admissions were at their highest for a quarter of a century, at nearly 140 million for the year, while the multiplex revolution took another major step, with 47 new multi-screen sites opening in 1997.

For good measure, a British film, *The Full Monty* (GB/US 1997), (albeit made with American money) topped the UK box office, taking a record-breaking £46 million, with another British film, *Bean* (GB, 1997), also making it into the top five.

BFI Film and Television Handbook, 1999

▼ ▼ ▼

Britain continue to make films – some of them able to compete on the world market (*Four Weddings and a Funeral, The Full Monty*, etc). Many fine actors and film-makers also come out of the United Kingdom, with a steady stream of them notching up considerable success on the international awards scene. Moreover, we have some of the best technicians and finest post-production facilities anywhere in the world. Generally, the trend for film production in the United Kingdom is encouraging also. Overall output is on the increase and now compares very favourably with the record low of the early 1980s.

What makes this scenario rather less encouraging is that most of those films get very limited releases – very few get national exposure and many suffer from very short runs, too. Distribution is very much dominated by US companies and products.

We have traditionally suffered from drastic under-investment in film production. Film-making is above all a business activity and an extremely expensive one in most of its forms. Vast profits can be made – but so can heavy losses. For the most part, it is financed by private sources and investors in this country have been reluctant to gamble with the large sums involved. The United States, on the other hand, is a society built very much on entrepreneurial activity: they have a far more positive attitude towards taking risks. They also have a very much larger market, of course, and potential for large financial returns.

There are, however, grounds for optimism about production in the United Kingdom. Output did fall to an all-time low of fewer than thirty films in the late 1980s. Against this, the total of 128 made in 1996 is a near record, higher than any year since 1938. There has been a marked overall increase in production over the past decade. More than 500 films were made between 1995 and

2000. With fewer than half that number from 1990–1995, clearly, levels of output are dramatically on the increase.

Nevertheless, due pride in this achievement needs to be tempered with proper understanding of its actual nature. Whereas a total of nearly £550 million was spent on UK films in 1999, in fact only half of that money was spent on wholly UK productions. (Funding from the United States continues to be of major importance in UK film production.) Moreover, average budgets for these films actually declined somewhat.

THE NATIONAL LOTTERY

Recently, the British government has responded to calls from the industry to provide *seed capital* – money to stimulate production – and has introduced tax concessions for the same purpose. A similar move in the Republic of Ireland some years ago is widely perceived as stimulating the very lively film activity there, fuelling a string of successful films that have pulled in foreign investment and fed back into the local economy. *Braveheart* (USA, 1995) and *Saving Private Ryan* (USA, 1999) are good examples of this. The size of crews – cast and technicians – means a considerable amount of money is spent locally on food and accommodation alone. At the same time, there is some generation of local employment, too.

To boost this activity in the United Kingdom, the National Lottery granted some £92 million in 1997 to three companies, to fund some ninety or more films over six years. This fund is administered through the Arts Council of Great Britain.

There was some unhappiness at the funnelling of all these funds into so few hands, and some very respected film-makers were overlooked – Merchant Ivory Productions among them.

It is very much hoped that this substantial injection of new monies will lead to a revival in the industry's fortunes in this country.

THE BRITISH FILM INSTITUTE (BFI)

The purpose of this organisation is primarily to foster education about the moving image – *not* to fund feature film-making. In 1998, a comprehensive review of its activities was begun and a new structure devised to direct its activities. It now has three key departments:

UK Film Production 1999 – Category A

Feature films where the cultural and financial impetus is from the UK and where the majority of personnel are British.

Title	Production companies	Production cost (£m)
Another Life	Boxer Films/Arts Council of England	2.50
Between Two Women	Julie Woodcock Prods/North Country Pictures	5.00
Billy Elliot	Tiger Aspect/WT2/BBC/Arts Council of England	2.80
Blood	Cantor Markham/Loud Mouse/Yorkshire Media Production Agency	1.00
Breathtaking	September Films/Sky Pictures	3.40
Cold Fish	Opus Pictures	2.00
Complicity	Talisman Films/Carlton/Scottish Arts Council/British Screen	4.60
County Kilburn	Watermark Films	1.00
Creatures	Creatures Ltd/DNA/Arts Council of England	4.00
Dead Bolt Dead	It's Alright Ma Productions	1.00
Emotional Backgammon	Corazon	0.01
Essex Boys	Granada Films	3.00
Fed Rotten	Cake Media	0.20
Five Seconds to Spare	Scala/Wildgaze/BBC/Matrix Film and TV	3.00
The Ghost of Greville Lodge	Renown Pictures	0.75
Going off Big Time	KT Films/MIDA	1.50
Guest House Paradiso	Phil McIntyre Prods/House Films/Vision Video	4.00
Hard News Soft Money	Bolt on Media/Atlantic Celtic	1.00
House!	Wire Films/Arts Council of England/British Screen/CFI	2.00
The House of Mirth	Three Rivers/Film Four/Granada Films/Arts Council of England/ Scottish Arts Council/Glasgow Film Fund	7.50
The Inbetweeners	Britpack Films	1.00
Inside Outside Lydia's Head	Coven Garden Films	0.80
It was an Accident	Bukett Pictures/Litmus Pictures/Pathé/Arts Council of England	2.60
Kevin and Perry Go Large	Tiger Aspect/Fragile Films/	4.00
Lava	Sterling Pictures/Waking Point/Orange Top/Ernst and Young	1.00
London Blues	Prince World Ent.	1.00
Love, Honour and Obey	Fugitive/BBC	2.00
Love the One You're With	Palm Tree Prods/British Council/Big Issue Scotland	0.50
The Low Down	Oil Factory/Sleeper Films/Film Four/British Screen	1.00
Nasty Neighbours	Ipso Facto/Glearrines/MPCE/Northern Production Fund/ West Midland Support Agencies	1.50
New Year's Day	Imagine Films/Alchymie/Flashpoint/British Screen	2.50
One Life Stand	Elemental Films	0.50
Offending Angels	Pants Prods	1.00
Pandaemonium	Mariner Prods/BBC/Arts Council of England	3.76
Paradise Grove	Paradise Grove plc/Enterprise Investment Scheme	1.03
Paranoia	Trijbits Productions/Sky/Isle of Man Film Commission	3.14
Purely Belter	Mumbo Jumbo/Film Four	4.00
Saving Grace	Homerun/Wave Pictures/Sky Movies/Portman/Rich Pickings	3.00
Second Generation	Second Generation Films	1.00
Some Voices	Dragon Pictures/FilmFour/British Screen	2.00
Soul's Ark	Weston Union	0.03
Strictly Sinatra	Blue Orange/DNA	4.00
Strong Boys	Cowboy Films/Imagine Films	4.00
There's Only One Jimmy Grimble	Sarah Radclyffe/Impact/Pathe	3.00
The Truth Game	Screen Productions Associates	0.85
Warrior Sisters	Frank Scantori Films	0.01
Whatever Happened to Harold Smith?	West Eleven Films/Intermedia/Arts Council of England	5.64

TOTAL NUMBER OF FILMS	47
TOTAL COST	£105.12m
AVERAGE COST	£2.24m

Source: Screen Finance/X25 Partnership/BFI/British Council

Figure 3.19
'UK Film Production 1999 – Category A', taken from the BFI Film and Television Handbook 2001. This shows the total number of films made in the UK during that year, where the principle impulse for production, culturally and financially, originated from within the UK, and where most of the personnel were British.

▶ *Collections* – houses materials from film, television, computer games, stills posters and museum artefacts, and releases films, videos and DVDs.

▶ *Education* – a new working brief has been drawn up for this area. The BFI adopted a coordinating role in the Film Education Working Group, which set a new agenda for film education. Its intention was to complement the work of other education providers. The film magazine *Sight and Sound* is also produced within this department. It also organises in-service training for media educators in the United Kingdom and publishes books (including this one) and learning resources on the moving image.

▶ *Exhibition* – this has a national exhibition strategy which encompasses film festivals, regional cinemas and the film society movement. It also administers the National Film Theatre (NFT). In addition to the regular screenings of quality films and classics from around the world, the NFT also hosts three film festivals: the international London Film Festival, the Lesbian and Gay Film Festival and the Jewish Film Festival.

In addition to the above, the BFI now also has the new giant-screen IMAX cinema alongside its South Bank complex.

THE FILM COUNCIL

The 80s are behind us. In other words, we do not want to finance socialist-realist art films, nor even Hollywood-scale mega-productions like *The World Is Not Enough*. The Film Council will help to finance popular films that the British public will go and see in the multiplexes on a Friday night. Films that entertain people and make them feel good.

John Woodward, Chief Executive Officer, The Film Council, quoted in *The Guardian*, 25 August 2000

▼ ▼ ▼

Set up to invigorate film-making activity in the United Kingdom, the Film Council is sponsored by the government. It effectively amalgamates the former BFI Productions Board, British Screen, the British Film Commission and the Lottery funds that have been allocated to film production.

It has two distinct arms: one dispensing production funds, to stimulate commercial and new films; the other financing the development of scripts.

Headed by respected figures from within the industry, it has set out with a clear intention to fund commercially viable films. Chief Executive John Woodward says that he sees no difference between their organisation and private financiers: '… the fact that we are dealing with public money should not affect our policy towards providing assistance and finance'.

Critics argue that commercial film-making should be left to commercial operators – subsidies should be used to fund films that are worthy, but may struggle to attract private finance.

However, the Film Council seems to be trying to set a new agenda that will transcend traditional divisions between commercial and art-house cinema. What it is attempting is a wholly new boost to *British* film-making, whatever its nature. Lifting levels of professionalism all-round – whether it be in scriptwriting, production, marketing or financial management – is the ambitious intention. Film production is now a global business and quality products are needed to compete.

▼ ▼ ▼

Global demand for filmed entertainment is expanding massively as digital technology increases the number and variety of delivery outlets. Film is a key engine driving this demand. Meanwhile, cinema-going in the UK and around the world continues to grow, fuelled by investment in new multiplex cinemas. This increase in demand for product offers real potential for the British film industry so long as it is positioned to seize these opportunities as they arise.

www.filmcouncil.org.uk

▼ ▼ ▼

CHANNEL 4

This independent commercial television company was involved in funding film production from the early 1980s. The company itself estimates that it spent more than £90 million on over 250 films up to 1992. Some of the more notable commercial (*Four Weddings and a Funeral*, 1994; *Trainspotting*, 1995) and artistic successes (*My Beautiful Laundrette*, 1985; *Shallow Grave*, 1994) in the United Kingdom have originated from this source. It has long secured its place as the most important supporter of UK film-making.

FilmFour International now operates as a more or less independent production company and is responsible for something like 7 per cent of all UK film production. The associated FilmFour subscription television service has also been a notable success, showing a wide range of films from the United Kingdom and around the world, both recent and past.

THE BBC

A limited amount of film-making originates from the BBC. The emphasis here again tends to be on quality of product, rather than commercial box-office appeal. The BBC has been responsible for a number of distinguished productions, including *Jude* (UK, 1996), *Mrs. Brown* (UK, 1997) and *My Son the Fanatic* (UK, 1999).

▼ ▼ ▼ ▼ ▼ ▼ ▼

activities

1. Explore your local cinema or multiplex for the number of UK-originated films it has shown over a given period. Compare this figure with the US-sourced ones screened over the same period.

2. The soundtrack is now a complex and integral feature of mainstream film production. Using the various types identified on pp. 160–1, log the diverse sound sources used in a film of your choice. Discuss the kinds of impact the different types have on the film's narrative development.

3. Investigate the activities of the Film Council since its birth. How many different films or production companies has it been involved in funding. What about its track record in funding script development – how many of these have made it into production?

4. What other sources of film-making are there in the United Kingdom? Investigate the routes for funding available to independent and short film-makers.

Film Products

Genre

Stories can be categorised into different *genres*, a French term for type or category of narrative (see p. 41). The concept of genre exists across all media forms – in radio, television and music, as well as in magazine and book publishing. It is an organising principle that helps both producers and audiences to produce, package and consume narratives.

In libraries, book and video shops, stories in books are organised in sections according to their subject matter, just as our shopping is organised, either within a supermarket or in separate high-street shops, by categories (fruit and vegetables, meat, cleaning goods, electrical goods, dry cleaners, etc.). The most common narrative genres, whether fiction or non-fiction, familiar to us from books are: biography, autobiography, detective/crime thriller, science fiction, fantasy, horror, war, comedy, travel, etc.

Many of these genres appear in films as well and share common features. The following are the most common film genres and it is fair to say that the boundaries between some of these genres have become indistinct over time:

▶ horror
▶ Western
▶ gangster
▶ science fiction/fantasy
▶ musical
▶ comedy
▶ war
▶ melodrama
▶ romance
▶ documentary/docudrama
▶ biopic
▶ cop/detective/mystery
▶ teenage drama/school films
▶ thriller
▶ spy
▶ action/spectacle
▶ action/adventure
▶ film noir.

There have been many critical debates about whether this last is a genre, a style or indeed a movement. However, recent postmodern, or neo-, films noir and a contemporary variant, tech-noir – as in *Blade Runner* (USA, 1982) and *Terminator II: Judgement Day* (USA, 1991) – have seen its entry in genre lists.

Another area of ongoing debate concerns animation. This is often cited as a genre, but technically it can be considered as a mode of representation, as animated feature films can be in any genre. Also, it would be fair to say that even the divide between 'live' action and animation is becoming difficult to differentiate, as many live action films have computer-generated sequences. *Titanic* (USA, 1997) and *The Matrix* (USA, 1999) are good examples of this, and many contemporary animated films use computer-generated animation, such as *A Bug's Life* (USA, 1998) and *Toy Story 2* (USA, 2000).

Figure 3.20
In Titanic *(USA, 1997), many shots were constructed using computer-generated images – especially in scenes where the ship is sinking. Similar methods were used in* Gladiator *(USA, 2000) to create the crowds seen in the Coliseum.*

chapter three

Figure 3.21
Sean Connery as James Bond – a franchise becomes a sub-genre

VARIATIONS OF GENRE

Some lists of film genres have alternatives, combinations or sub-genres of the above. A *sub-genre* is a type of film that is a variant on the main genre. For example, the spy genre can be considered as a genre in its own right, or as a sub-genre of the war film, action/adventure or thriller. The Bond franchise could, in turn, be considered as a sub-genre of these, because it has particular aspects that have become identified uniquely with Bond films since their first outing with *Dr. No* (UK, 1962).

A combination of two or more genres, such as science fiction with horror in the film *Alien* (USA, 1979), is termed a *generic hybrid*. Romantic comedies are generic hybrids and screwball and black comedies are both sub-genres of the comedy genre.

Hybridisation offers producers creative possibilities from more than one genre and so avoids predictability. It also offers them a wider audience by hoping to attract fans of both genres.

As audiences, we may develop a preference for a particular genre and become, for instance, horror or detective genre fans. Most films are marketed by explicit indications of their genre, either in the design of the poster (see pp. 172–3) or by the casting of a particular actor known for his or her roles in a particular genre, for example, Al Pacino in gangster films and Meg Ryan in romantic comedies.

Every title in a particular genre, in either book or film, tends to share typical elements within the story. In studies of genre, these have been identified as *codes* and *conventions* (see pp. 48–9).

Each genre has its own particular pleasures. These pleasures are created by the tension between the audience's delight in being able to predict what happens next in the plot (from our foreknowledge and expectations of a genre) and the surprise of something new or unexpected. It is essential that a film is never *too* predictable. Genres have become dynamic formulae that change over time. Audiences and their concerns do not stand still and genres have adapted in order to survive and find their audiences.

THE WESTERN

The Western was the earliest film genre, with the production of *The Great Train Robbery* (USA, 1903) as the first Western and the longest film of its day at ten minutes long. It is also considered to be the genre that first attracted a critical debate about film and its cultural status in the 1960s. It is one of the most satisfying genres to analyse because of its clear and consistent codes and conventions. However, the subtle changes in the genre through the decades illustrate how every film genre interacts with, and is evolved by, its context.

RECORDS OF HISTORY? Westerns can be simply read as period dramas that brought to life an important part of North American nineteenth-century history. These films showed the struggles of the frontiersmen who drove westwards, pushing back the frontier of the 'uncivilised' and wild West, along with the lives and times of its famous outlaws and heroes.

The Western also presented enduring and influential myths that connected narratives about such people with the universal and inspiring themes of truth and justice, freedom and democracy. which came to be adopted as its nation's values and characteristics.

However, there have also been many problems with issues of ethics and of representation associated with the Western (see below).

VALUES The genre has always had a strong emblematic connection with the political passage of democracy in North America. Much has been made of former US Presidents, such as Ronald

Reagan (himself a former actor who appeared in Westerns), who have variously aligned themselves with the 'ordinary', 'decent' values of the Western hero in order to appeal to their electorate. Moreover, the Western hero offered a model for male behaviour that became recognised as a universal masculine ideal, to men and women all over the world. Advertisers have used him to sell everything, from jeans to beer and cigarettes.

The Western hero obeyed a strict code of conduct and honour, both in his behaviour towards enemies and those he was duty-bound to protect. Or so the codes and conventions of the films went; he never shot an unarmed man, nor anyone in the back, and the killing of women and children was a cowardly act of villainy. He was a man of few words and suspicious of men with 'fancy' manners and 'fine' words.

This model of unsophisticated but honest values became an ideal for American and European manhood. Even today, this character archetype crops up in different guises. Indiana Jones is transformed from a bookish lecturer of archaeology to a cowboy-hatted hero with a trusty bullwhip, capable of great feats of derring-do – only this time he is fighting the Nazis, instead of 'Injuns' – in *Raiders of the Lost Ark* (USA, 1981). Neither is it a long walk from John Wayne and James Stewart's Western heroes to Bruce Willis's reluctant hero, John MacClane, in the *Die Hard* series (USA, 1988, 1990 and 1995) and Tom Cruise's Ethan Hunt in *Mission Impossible I* and *II* (USA, 1996 and 2000). Different clothes, props and less sophisticated stunts, but essentially the same heroic values and spectacular set pieces, the Western is easily the most obvious precursor of contemporary action/adventure films.

UNIVERSAL APPEAL The genre is not one restricted to American film-makers either. *Once Upon a Time in the West* (Italy, 1968) is a homage to the genre by Italian director Sergio Leone. It is an epic that combines many classic Western subjects and characters. The hardworking pioneer, the 'tart with a heart' seeking redemption and respectability, the greedy railroad owner, the cold-hearted killer and the lone hero appear in many Westerns – all set against the unforgiving expanses of the American West. It has a bravura opening sequence and a haunting musical score by Ennio Morricone. Leone revisited the other classic American film genre, the gangster film, in *Once Upon a Time in America* (USA, 1983). Both films show the influence and iconic status of these two major film genres and America's dominant role in international cinema language and form, as well as in the film industry.

QUESTIONING ETHICS After decades of prolific production from such directors as John Ford and Anthony Mann, the genre steadily declined from the 1950s to an all-time low in the 1960s. The sight of cowboys despatching tribes of 'Red Indians' became outdated in the context of modern life and badly out of tune with the politics of race and civil rights in the 1960s. The softly spoken, *gauche* hero as canonised by the actor John Wayne in his many roles became a figure of fun for the modern sophisticates of the space age Sixties.

The film *Midnight Cowboy* (USA, 1969) shows Jon Voight as a gullible Texan dreamer who wants to make his fortune in New York. However, he ends up as a male prostitute for wealthy women – amused by his quaint, old-fashioned manners and attracted by his 'macho' physique – to earn enough to survive. In *The Electric Horseman* (USA, 1979), Robert Redford plays a disillusioned Wild West rodeo rider who decides to escape the humiliation of being a tame circus act when he finds his horse is being drugged to remain sedate during shows. He escapes to turn his horse free and the film's final scenes show the mythical romance of the land and man's relationship with the horse – two major aspects of the genre's appeal. In different ways, both films illustrate the downfall of the cowboy and the problems for the genre at that time.

The career of actor and director Clint Eastwood is a perfect case study of the evolution of the Western genre and its changing contexts. He moved from his earliest roles in the US television series *Rawhide*, into Sergio Leone's spaghetti Westerns, *A Fistful of Dollars* (Italy/West Germany/Spain, 1964), *For a Few Dollars More* (Italy/Spain/West Germany, 1965) and *The Good the Bad and the Ugly* (Italy, 1966). He then progressed to directing his own films, such as *High Plains Drifter* (USA, 1972) and *Pale Rider* (USA, 1985). Simultaneously, he moved into the 1970s updated equivalent of the Western genre, the cop

Film

Film

Figure 3.22
In Unforgiven,
*director and
star Clint
Eastwood
punctures the
glamorous
myth of the
outlaw and
instead reveals
the cowardice
and violence of
the major
players.*

movie, with its own contemporary gun-toting lone heroes (but with chases in cars instead of on horseback), in such films as *Dirty Harry* (USA, 1971), *Magnum Force* (USA, 1973) and many others.

However, in addition to the guns and chases, it was the character based on a Western archetype first established by John Wayne and Eastwood's stock in trade as an actor that have endured from one genre to the next. In both his Westerns and his cop films, Eastwood played the man with no ties, a free agent, and, as such, a powerfully attractive and escapist character to both men and women for a variety of reasons. Even in *The Bridges of Madison County* (USA, 1995), he is still essentially the same character, a craggy-faced photographer in this case, 'saving' Meryl Streep's restless housewife, but quite resolutely 'just passin' through'.

Eastwood won the Oscar® for Best Director for *Unforgiven* (USA, 1992) – which also won the Best Picture – in what is almost the last word in Westerns, a deconstruction of the genre's myths and legends and of Eastwood's screen persona itself. In it he plays William Munny, a notorious 'killer of women and children' who is forced to go back to being an outlaw to make money to raise his children, as he has not succeeded by peaceful and legal means, as a farmer. The film undermines the glamorous myth of the outlaw and reveals the cowardice, violence and the lies beneath the myths.

NEW REPRESENTATIONS Despite the decline in its popularity and output, the genre is a resilient one, however. Creative film-makers continue to adapt the genre with revisionist storylines and messages, as in *Little Big Man* (USA, 1970), *A Man Called Horse* (USA, 1970), *Dances with Wolves* (USA, 1990) and *The Last of the Mohicans* (USA, 1992). These films explored the damage done by white settlers to the native peoples and their land.

Although a minute fraction of films produced since the 1960s have been Westerns, there have been many attempts to revive the popularity of the genre. *Posse* (USA, 1993) concerned itself with a revisionist narrative about black cowboys; apparently a third of cowboys were black, not that this was apparent from their distinct absence in classic Westerns. Against the backdrop of post–Civil War America and the abolition of slavery, that there should have been black cowboys makes complete sense. Their relative invisibility is a testament to the selectivity of the process of representation in film-making.

Other films have attempted to redress the

inadequate treatment of gender in this genre. *The Ballad of Little Jo* (USA, 1993) looked at the true story of a woman who survived in the West by passing as a man. Sharon Stone starred in (and was co-producer of) *The Quick and the Dead* (USA, 1995). In a nod to 1990s post-feminism, this has a female avenging gunslinger as the hero at the heart of the story.

The film also reveals a playful sense of visual style on the part of the film-maker, Sam Raimi, well established as a director of horror films – most notably *The Evil Dead* (USA, 1982) and *The Evil Dead II* (USA, 1987). *The Quick and the Dead* is a homage to classic Westerns such as *High Noon* (USA, 1952) and *Once Upon a Time in the West* (Italy/USA, 1968), as well as delighting in the use of horror codes and conventions in its set design, use of lighting and canted frames.

Young Guns I and *II* (USA, 1988 and 1990) were a popular series which temporarily revived the genre. *Blazing Saddles* (USA, 1974) and *City Slickers* (USA, 19991) were affectionate parodies and films such as *Wild, Wild West* (USA, 1999) and *Ride with the Devil* (USA, 1999) are more recent attempts to revisit the genre, although with limited success.

THE CONTINUING STATUS OF THE COWBOY The image of the cowboy is an enduring icon in American contemporary popular culture, in advertising as well as in music and literature. The novels *All the Pretty Horses*, by Cormac McCarthy, and *The Horse Whisperer*, by Nicolas Evans, were both quickly made into films. The genre's mark is seen even in films not really about the Wild West, as in *Toy Story I* and *II*'s (USA, 1995 and 1999) cowboy hero, Woody. The setting and outlaw narrative of *Thelma & Louise* (USA, 1991) have many visual and narrative references to the genre, not to mention echoes of another famous Western, *Butch Cassidy and the Sundance Kid* (USA, 1969), in its cliff-top escape.

In Madonna's music video for the track 'Don't Tell Me to Stop' (2000), she slopes along an endless road against a clear blue sky (by Ridley Scott or Gus van Sant?). Then she leaps into a dance routine (part line dance and part *Seven Brides for Seven Brothers?*) with a bunch of choreographed cowboys (Village People meet Bob Fosse?) against a 'wide-screen' billboard on which

a mounted cowboy (Marlboro Man meets *Midnight Cowboy?*) rides a bucking piebald horse. For a while, the cowboy look is 'in', with piebald hide rugs and cushions for the minimalist metro living space and glitter cowboy hats with snakeskin boots for clubbers. Line-dancing clubs abound in the suburbs and Country & Western music continues to provide crossover artists in the shape of Shania Twain and Leanne Rimes.

With such references, the Western and its heroes provide enduring popular cultural and style icons for the rest of the world, as America's cultural imperialism extends well beyond film as a product. Global brands such as Budweiser, Marlboro, Levis, Lee and Jim Beam have all sought to maximise their profits by linking their brands with this part of American history and the values of its heroes because of its global recognition. All over the world, money is exchanged by consumers, for whom these images are still so potent, for a little piece of America.

For *The Claim* (UK/France/ Canada, 2001), the Western genre provided the British director Michael Winterbottom with a new setting for his adaptation of Thomas Hardy's classic novel *The Mayor of Casterbridge*. In his review of the film, *The Observer* newspaper's film critic, Philip French, writes how this is a familiar practice, with two of John Wayne's most famous Westerns being based on older literary sources. *Stagecoach* (USA, 1939) was based on French nineteenth-century author Guy de Maupassant's short story *Boule de Suif* and *Red River* (USA, 1948) on Charles Nordhoff and James Norman Hall's *Mutiny on the Bounty*.

The Claim has resonances of *McCabe and Mrs Miller* (USA, 1971) and *Once Upon a Time in the West* (Italy, 1968). It will undoubtedly bring Hardy to a more extensive international audience, precisely because it was made and marketed as a Western, rather than as a literary adaptation. The relocation from Wessex to the Californian gold rush is not so fanciful a stretch, as both times and places saw men battling the forces of nature to make a living and such tales of fortune and tragedy are common to both the Western and Hardy's novels. Indeed, it could be said that any good story can be relocated and adapted to any setting. Genres go in and out of favour all the time, but great stories never do.

ACTION/SPECTACLE FILMS

The genre of action/spectacle is particularly characterised by American films of the past quarter century. It is a genre that has developed from action/adventure films, which have been around since the invention of film itself. The term refers to films in which there are substantial action sequences and in which the effect of spectacle for the audience is at least as important as their narratives – or arguably more so. The success and popularity of such films led inevitably to more of the same, much the way Hollywood has always been.

It is important to remember that film is a capitalist medium. Although it is an art form, it is one that usually involves a huge financial outlay. Because of the nature of the medium and its production, investors require a return on their investment. However, like most forms of investment, profit – or the amount of profit – is not necessarily guaranteed. Therefore it involves a financial risk for those involved. The reduction of financial risk is a major imperative in the development of a film.

If a film genre is successful once, there is little reason to change the formula too radically, as audiences like to repeat pleasures of previously enjoyed films. That is, until they decide that they are bored with them. Precisely when that critical point is, no one is quite sure. William Goldman, a famous Hollywood screenwriter, once famously said: 'Nobody *knows* anything.' Much as films can be developed in every detail, success at the box office is not necessarily guaranteed.

DEVELOPING CRITICISM As film developed during the twentieth century, the industry utilised technological progress as a means of attracting larger audiences. The action/adventure genre employed more and more spectacle, offering state-of-the-art technology, competing with alternative media such as television, by providing escapist popular entertainment.

Action/spectacle films have not received serious critical attention until fairly recently. They are usually dismissed with such terms as 'blockbuster' and there has tended to be a divide between 'classic' or 'great' films and mere entertainment. However, thirty years on from the rise of the genre, critics and theorists have recently turned their attention to more serious consideration of its qualities.

In *Action/Spectacle Cinema: A Sight & Sound Reader* (BFI, 2000), José Arroyo has collected a wide variety of writing from the film magazine *Sight & Sound* on action/spectacle films and examines various critical debates around the genre.

The first debate is about the definition of the genre itself. It could be said that action/spectacle films are really a mode, rather than a genre. A quick consideration of the types of films grouped under this category show that a wide variety of films in different genres all contain elements of action/spectacle: *Blade Runner* (USA, 1981 and 1991) – science fiction; *Bram Stoker's Dracula* (USA, 1992) – horror; *Saving Private Ryan* (USA, 1998) – war; *Crouching Tiger, Hidden Dragon* (China/Hong Kong/Taiwan/USA, 2001) – martial arts; *Charlie's Angels* (USA, 2000) – 'chick' flick; Bond films – spy; *The Quick and the Dead* (USA, 1993) – Western; *The Godfather Part II* (USA, 1974) – gangster; *Gladiator* (USA, 2000) – historical epic; *Junior* (USA, 1994) – comedy; *Titanic* (USA, 1997) – disaster/romance/period drama; and so on.

Films as various as these defy easy generic definition, but a major part of their appeal is their action sequences and the effect of spectacle created for the audience. Most of the above films could also be described as *high-concept* (see p. 162).

There is considerable overlap between the categories of action/spectacle, high-concept, action/adventure and blockbuster, Arroyo explains. They all refer to slightly different types of films, but share many features, such as similar production profiles, answering to shared audience expectations of their content and sharing similar narrative structures (equilibrium, disequilibrium and restoration of equilibrium) to some extent. What they are not bound to share, unlike other film genres, are their iconography, style and thematic concerns.

SEQUENTIAL PLEASURES Sequels offer us an insight into the successful features of action/spectacle films: the same experience, but different, by 'ideally, an intensification, of the pleasures of the original' (José Arroyo). Action/spectacle films are also seen as the perfect trailer for the merchandise, by which more profit is usually generated than at the box office. With DVD technology, action/spectacle in particular offers the film fan even greater engagement with the film and additional pleasure. Commentaries by cast and film-makers, deleted scenes, trailers, storyboards, games and behind-the-scenes featurettes involve the spectator in the creation of the action and spectacle they enjoyed in the film itself, and thereby seek to forge greater loyalty to future films and their DVD releases. This may be seen in the eagerly awaited special editions for *Mission Impossible 2* (USA, 2000), *Fight Club* (USA, 2000), *Gladiator* (USA, 2000) and *Terminator 2: Judgement Day* (USA, 1991).

Another major debate is a long-running one that exists in many other media and art fields, namely that of 'high' versus 'low' culture and the relative merits of each. Critics, says Arroyo, assert that such films are the mere 'exchange of cash for affect' or that 'the budget *is* the aesthetic'. Both views suggest that such films offer only a functional, transitory and ultimately disposable experience. Others consider whether film, and these films in particular, can really be considered as art, as there is often a critical demarcation between art (improving and ennobling for a privileged *cognoscenti*) and entertainment (ephemeral, cheap and cheerful for the uneducated).

Such critics have missed the point, Arroyo argues – we should not ask whether such films are art, but rather, what *is* art and what is cinema in the current and future context? There are many issues discussed in the book and the collected writings consider action/spectacle films in terms of their authorship, audiences, genre, style, aesthetics, their socio-cultural and historical significance.

GLADIATOR – A CASE STUDY The following commentary on a recent action/ spectacle film, *Gladiator* (USA, 2000), offers a textual analysis of the main aspects of film construction and language in an attempt to demonstrate the defining features of an action/spectacle film:

▶ camera shots (close-up, long shot, etc), angles (high, low, etc), movement (pan, tracking, tilt, etc.)
▶ *mise-en-scène* (set, costumes, landscapes, colours)
▶ special effects (explosions, stunts, CGI)
▶ sound (music, ambient sound, etc.)
▶ editing (cuts, fades, pace).

Figure 3.23
Russell Crowe as Maximus in **Gladiator.** *His gripping performance was central to the overall success of the film.*

Gladiator (USA, 2000) was one of the most popular films of 2000/2001 and was nominated for twelve Academy Awards. Its success lies in a number of features: the gripping central performance from Russell Crowe; the stirring soundtrack from Hans Zimmer; outstanding cinematography and special effects; a highly convincing *mise-en-scène* in both costumes and set; an experienced director at the height of his career (Ridley Scott); and, of course, a great story and a big enough budget to produce it. Many of these depend upon the spectacular aspects of the film and the effect that they have upon the audience.

The aims of the opening sequence are to:

▶ establish the main character – our hero, Maximus
▶ set the scene in both time and place – Germania, AD 180
▶ start the narrative – a battle is about to commence
▶ introduce central themes – strength and honour, freedom and loyalty
▶ move the audience – show them human courage in war

▶ excite the audience – show them the spectacular.

The director's major problem here is to condense the opening battle sequence into just over twelve minutes. Too short and it would not convince us, too long and we may become bored and lose interest.

The desaturated colours of the production logos create the tone immediately. A lone title appears in an appropriate black, hard, chiselled Roman typeface against a background of sepia clouds or smoke, signifying the historical past. Scott then opens the film with a simple technique. He provides us with a legend to give us the facts straight away by telling us the time and the place. This may be seen by some as being a little too cheap, too easy: why does he not *show* us these things rather than *tell* us? The answer lies in Hollywood's style of efficiency and certainty: the narrative must start quickly so as not to lose the audience; it must also establish time and place without doubt in the audience's mind.

In essence, the approach is very much geared towards a mass audience of varying degrees of perception, knowledge and sophistication. But it also gives the audience expectations of the kind of film that it will see by referring to the Roman Empire at the height of its power and the sheer vastness of land that it controlled: 'Over one quarter of the world's population lived and died under the rule of the Caesars.' This suggests the impressive scope of the film and part of what is at stake between the hero and the villain. Although we begin *in medias res*, in the midst of the action of a campaign, the narrative of *Gladiator* begins with one battle – a most decisive one.

The music starts with wind instruments, mysterious but calm, and depth is added with strings and then the haunting voice of Lisa Gerrard. Hans Zimmer, the composer, says that there are nineteen musical themes in this film and most of them are heard in the opening fourteen minutes of the film – in other words, in this battle sequence, almost as in the overture to an opera. The soundtrack is an important signifier for the audience as it provides a *leitmotif* that relates to themes or characters, but it also has an emotional pull on the spectators and can reinforce what is on the screen or prepare them for what is to come. Anticipation is a crucial aspect of the action/spectacle film.

After a fade to black we cut to a close-up slow-motion shot of a man's left hand as he walks through a field of wheat, gently touching the cornheads. The colours are golden, as it is clearly a sunny day; we hear children laughing and playing in the background. It is poetic in both sound and picture as the major theme of freedom is first introduced to us. We do not know who he is or where we are, as we consider the first minor narrative enigma (a question in the mind of the audience).

Cut to a medium close-up of the hero in adorned, warrior garb, broad shoulders, an intense expression on his face. The colours are now cold dark greys as we are in twilight – a stark contrast to the preceding shot which is now clear to us: he was thinking of this scene in a brief reverie (or a premonition?), the full significance of which will be revealed later in the film. He looks serious, strong, determined. He turns to walk away, but catches sight of a bird as it flies away and smiles (at its freedom?). A cut to a long shot of the hero in the background with forest behind him shows him in an otherwise desolate, mud-ridden landscape. Then the spectacle begins as the legion ride into shot in the foreground. The music swells as a pan to the right reveals the size of the army.

It is also worth noting that the large image in the frame of Russell Crowe as star is part of the spectacle of cinema here. Stars are part of the signifying system of cinema as they bring with them many things, for example: expectations of character and action; genre identification; representations of masculinity/femininity; associations of previous films. In Crowe's case, it is a combination of his physicality with gentleness (evidenced in films as wide apart as *Romper Stomper* (Australia, 1992) and *LA Confidential* (USA, 1997). In addition to this, he also looks the part, so starting with a calm and clear close up of him is part of the audience's pleasure.

The slow pace of the opening now gives way to the build-up to the battle. The effect of the style of the opening depends upon the audience being gently lulled into this character's mood and mind-set. We are to be given Maximus's point of view for most of this sequence, so, as he approaches battle, we grow in excitement and anticipation, too.

The next sequence develops the spectacle as Maximus walks confidently down a phalanx of respectful men who are ready for battle. This man is by now clearly established as the hero and central character of the film. As we follow him, in various tracking shots, we see the machinery of war being prepared, indicating how advanced this civilisation is by comparison to the Barbarians. When he stops to talk to Quintus, one of his commanders, a series of questions and answers between the two establishes a number of facts, the most important of which is that he is an expert tactician (when he comments on the range of the catapults and the acceptable risks he will take). It also introduces a hint of conflict between the two characters that will be crucial later on.

The tension then builds as a headless Roman horseman arrives – a message from the Barbarians that war will now commence. The eerie nature of the image, as well as the savagery of the chanting of the Barbarians, indicates the dangerous nature of the enemy. Within the world of the film, the sound is meant to frighten the Romans; in the auditorium, it sets up audience expectations that this battle will be a very bloody one. The adrenalin rush of battle and cinema begins as Maximus informs Quintus, 'At my signal … unleash hell.' At this moment, his loyal, adoring Alsatian dog is also unleashed, a visual allusion to 'let slip the dogs of war' said by Mark Antony in Shakespeare's *Julius Caesar*, which aligns this film with the grandeur and tragic status of its theatrical precedents.

Part of the success of a spectacle is the spectator's involvement in the scene. Here the audience is invited to align itself to Maximus, as we see him as a respectful warrior bringing peace to Europe. The Romans speak in (American) English; the Barbarians in a harsh Germanic one. The Romans are dressed in sophisticated uniforms; the Barbarians in animal furs. The Romans are organised; the Barbarians are huge in number, but less organised. These binary oppositions are part of the structure of a text that helps the audience make sense of what they see.

The director of a battle sequence in a film such as this has three main aims:

▶ to convince us of its reality – it looks like it might have been the kind of battle which did take place

▶ to affect and engage the audience – we must feel something; after all, people are dying here!

▶ to deliver an impressive spectacle and so create awe and wonder in the spectator, by the scale and action of this set-piece

So the director must use techniques that, on the one hand convey a sense of realism, and on the other, appeal to our emotions. The realism comes from a combination of the *mise-en-scène* and the action itself, as well as an assemblage, by editing, of the material in an unobtrusive way. The emotion comes from the soundtrack, the use of the camera and putting together the right sequence of images in the editing process. Both the effects of realism and emotion are, of course, enhanced by the quality of the camerawork; by taking us inside the action, the director makes the action feel real and gives the audience a greater identification with the hero. If we feel part of the action, we will be convinced, moved and excited.

Scott use a number of techniques in the battle sequence to achieve this:

▶ He uses a wide variety of camera shots. Long shots give us the whole picture; medium shots take us into the battle and show us more detail; close-ups show us the intensity of the experience (e.g. Maximus's eyes).

▶ He uses a variety of musical themes. The initial charge is appropriately reminiscent of composer Gustav Holst's *Planet Suite – Mars, the Bringer of War*. The latter melody is in a lower key and is more romantic, yet tragic.

▶ He keeps us in the action, even when the armies are moving at great speed, by using tracking shots that follow Maximus into battle.

▶ He inserts details in the editing – we see close-ups and medium close-ups of blows being inflicted by a variety of weapons.

▶ He shows us the loyal dog fighting alongside his master – always a potential 'tear-jerker'.

▶ He keeps everything plausible and logical – we say, 'Yes, I can see why/how that happened', such as the moment when Maximus backs into one of his own men and turns to kill him.

▶ He switches to slow motion in the latter section when the music changes to a lower key. This is a technique we have seen many times in contemporary films, such as in *Platoon* (USA,

1986), when Samuel Barber's *Adagio for Strings* plays while a US soldier is being graphically gunned down in slow motion, and in *Once Upon a Time in America* (USA, 1983), when a little boy is similarly gunned down in slow motion to the strains of Morricone's soundtrack.

▶ The use of hand-held camera has a very jittery, uneasy effect on the audience and makes us feel as if we are inside the action.

▶ Similarly, he goes in and out of focus, much like it must have felt like in reality as chaos exploded.

▶ The ambient sound of battle harshly reflects the hell of war with the screaming and shouting, clash of steel against steel, the thud of blows, the swish of arrows and flares of flame.

▶ He utilises CGI (computer-generated images) to give the effect of pixilation and a 'grainier' look to the film print to enhance realism

▶ He changes the pace of the editing – we now have much quicker cuts and a vast number of shots.

In many ways, this entire sequence recalls two similar battle scenes in *Braveheart* (USA, 1995) and *Saving Private Ryan* (USA, 1998). The audience's experience of film and how it makes meaning is a continual and cumulative one: we make links between films as we add to our own collection of film experiences.

Scott ends the sequence with two particular punctuation points:

▶ Maximus proclaiming victory
▶ Marcus Aurelius, sighing in relief – 'Thank God'.

We go from one shot of joy, to quite another of relief. After such a sequence, we finish as we began and have a sense of closure. We can now move on to the next scene.

The audience pleasures of this kind of scene are quite varied, from physical stimulation and excitement from the intense action and energy, to a sense of spectacle from the scale and effects of the battle and the sense that this dramatic opening promises a terrific story with a great hero.

THE HORROR GENRE

Horror is another long-serving and resilient genre, and equally one that evolved to incorporate

political and sexual metaphors as every decade has passed. It is rich in allusions to other art forms and is an enormous and rewarding topic of film study. It also has an immense international repertoire.

The genre has survived precisely because it has both very clear generic codes and conventions on the one hand, and tremendously varied departures from the main genre – to avoid predictability – on the other. It is an especially interesting field of research into the representation of women, variously as disposable victims, empowered sexual vixens or avenging angels with attitude.

In *Nightmare: The Birth of Horror* (BBC Books, 1996), Christopher Frayling explores the origins of the horror genre. The first horror films had literary sources and the following titles could be said to contain the essential elements of almost every horror film:

▶ *Frankenstein* – Mary Shelley (1818 and 1831)
▶ *Dr. Jekyll and Mr. Hyde* – Robert Louis Stevenson (1886)
▶ *The Picture of Dorian Grey* – Oscar Wilde (1891)
▶ *Dracula* – Bram Stoker (1897)
▶ *The Hound of the Baskervilles* – Sir Arthur Conan Doyle (1902)
▶ *The Golem* – Gustav Meyrink (1913)

There is not room here to do justice to the work of particular directors and studios – notably Universal Studios in the 1930s and the Hammer Studios in the United Kingdom in the 1950s and 1960s. However, there is a wealth of critical writing on the genre and many films available, with even the earliest and most obscure horror films finding audiences of cult fans and collectors on video and DVD.

A NEW LEASE OF LIFE FOR THE CLASSICS The dynamic nature of horror genre, adapting to changing audience and industry contexts, can be seen in the contemporary synergy of production and marketing of this genre. The classic horror film *Nosferatu, a Symphony in Grey* (Germany, 1922) was issued in a special DVD edition in 2001 at the same time as the release of *Shadow of the Vampire* (USA, 2001), a film about the making of *Nosferatu* itself. Nearly ten years to the day since the release

of *The Silence of the Lambs* (USA, 1991) came *Hannibal* (USA, 2001), previewing on St Valentine's Day with the delicious tag line: 'He's a man after your heart ...' – without the necessity to add '... and your liver, your lungs, your brain and your spleen.'

Close examination of stylistic and structural aspects of both films clearly reveals some of the origins of cinematic horror still present in contemporary texts. Films such as *Nosferatu, The Cabinet of Dr Caligari* (Germany, 1919), *M* (Germany, 1931), *Metropolis* (Germany, 1926) and *Dr Mabuse, the Gambler* (Germany, 1922) were reflections of the times in Weimar Germany of the 1920s and 30s. These were times of poverty, chaos and corruption, but also of radical experimentation in the arts as a reaction to the bourgeois art forms seen in more realist films.

Simply put, the mark of the style of German expressionism – a term taken from fine art and theatre – is that the psychology of character (feelings, sexuality, motivation) is evident in the external manifestations of the text. Distinguishing features of these films include canted angles, chiaroscuro lighting, oblique lines, irregular and fantastic sets and bizarre characters. Put simply, that which is inside is expressed outside, in the *mise-en-scène* and mise-en-shot.

When Hitler came to power in Germany in the 1930s, many of the artists and technicians involved in expressionist film in Germany moved to the United States to flee Nazi persecution. This included directors such as Fritz Lang, Friedrich Murnau and G. W. Pabst. Their aesthetic fed its way into the Hollywood studio system and contributed to a new American genre: film noir. These films have, in turn, influenced contemporary neo-noir and, of course, modern horror.

CONTEMPORARY TASTES IN HORROR Today noir aspects can be seen in horror films such as *Se7en* (USA, 1996) and *Hannibal*, both also classified as crime thriller and serial killer movies. The horror influence is also evident in the dénouement of many neo-noir films – John Dahl's *Red Rock West* (United States, 1992), for instance, the hapless characters of which wind up in a gruesome showdown in a graveyard replete with the stylisation of a Gothic horror film. Canted frames, swirling mist, blue lighting and Dennis

Figure 3.24
Frankenstein (USA, 1931) and many subsequent horror films are indebted to Mary Shelley's novel written more than one hundred years before.

Hopper's star turn, with full Frankenstein's monster stagger, in his death throes – all mark out the influences of the horror genre in this section of the film

The Silence of the Lambs (USA, 1990) was one of only three films ever to win the four top Oscars®. Its eagerly awaited sequel, *Hannibal* (USA, 2001) is a postmodern horror film, in which the eponymous Hannibal is essentially the hero of the film. This is despite the fact that he is a serial killer and therefore more usually represented as the villain of the piece. The victims he despatches in this film are reprehensible characters without his 'redeeming qualities' and therefore, the film seems to propose, they are thoroughly deserving of their Grand Guignol ends:

▶ Mason Verger, a drug-taking paedophiliac monster and Lecter's only surviving victim
▶ Rinaldo Pazzi, an avaricious Italian policeman
▶ Paul Krendler, a corrupt, sexist American FBI agent – so 'rude', comments Lecter.

Lecter is coded here as a 'gentleman' cannibal. He has many qualities that make him attractive to the audience: he is intelligent, educated and sophisticated; in these respects he recalls the magnetic Count Dracula. He is quick-witted and amusing – a master of black comedy; he is a man of immaculate taste in art, fashion and cuisine (with one obvious exception). As such, he is in a strong tradition of 'foreigners' or cultured Europeans (Lecter is cagey about his national origins) created and cast as villains in Hollywood films.

Lecter gets away at the end of the film, probably to the relief of the audience who hungrily await the sequel (as well as a prequel, it is rumoured). In fact, in Harris's original novel Lecter eloped at the end with Clarice Starling – perhaps just a little too far for mainstream tastes. Instead, he escapes with a lingering kiss – a villain who buys his girl Gucci shoes – quite a catch! Apparently, as a character, after the release of the first film, Lecter received vast amounts of fan mail from around the world, especially from women!

Mason Verger appears as the more likely villain or monster, not merely because of his physical disfigurement, but also because he even lives, like the classic horror monster, in the old Gothic house, here surrounded by hi-tech equipment and man-eating pigs. Although Verger lives in the United States, he looks European, again, subtly aligning him with an un-American lifestyle and suggesting his perverse and ghoulish nature.

If the question is asked of what happened between *The Silence of the Lambs* and *Hannibal* to make the change in the prominence of the character so extreme, the answer probably lies in *Se7en* (USA, 1995). From the title sequences alone, we can begin to see the influences of one upon the other: the disjointed images, deliberately poor video quality and minimal titles. The *mise-en-scène* of *Se7en* is an inversion of the horror film; it starts where most end, in rain and claustrophobic darkness. It saves its most brutal act of violence for the final scenes shot in an open rural plain, flooded with sunshine. In a morally ambiguous world, where it is hard to tell who are the heroes and who are the villains, everything in *Se7en* is back to front, just like the opening title sequence.

The fascination with *Se7en* partly lies in its villain, John Doe, being represented as occupying the high moral ground at a crucial moment in the film. He explains that he has killed his victims to

clear society of its human detritus, probably in much the same way that Lecter would, if he were to explain himself. Where the law and the Church are frequently seen to fail modern citizens, it is almost suggested, in the worlds of these films, that such twisted moralists as Lecter and Doe offer honest citizens the only hope of protection.

Many aspects of the characterisation of Hannibal Lecter and John Doe are the same: their articulate and measured expression; their intelligence; ambivalent aspects of their sexuality; their ability to create fear with a glance. *Se7en* treated audiences to a series of gruesome murders, portrayed with all the forensic detail of a coroner's autopsy, bolstered by complex literary references to Dante and the Old Testament of the Bible and its seven deadly sins.

The spectacle served up in *Hannibal* is part European Gothic and part American 'wet' horror, a visceral, body horror and with references to Florentine history and literature. Dante features again in dialogue references and in a scene at an open-air opera where a musical adaptation of Dante's *Inferno* is being performed. These references may also tell us something about the audience for such films and, perhaps, the aspirations of the film-makers themselves.

RECIPE FOR HORROR Genres do not merely exist in their own closed little worlds. They are intertextual and organic; they feed off each other hungrily and expand to include new ideas and themes; they play with audiences' expectations of the codes and conventions already established.

The key codes and conventions of the horror genre have famously been canonised in *Scream* (USA, 1996), *Scream 2* (USA, 1997) and *Scream 3* (USA, 2000). These films were directed by Wes Craven, who is also known for *The Hills Have Eyes* (USA, 1977) and *A Nightmare on Elm Street* (USA, 1984). The *Scream* trilogy, and its followers, *I Know What You Did Last Summer* (USA, 1997) and *Scary Movie* (USA, 2000), delighted in self-conscious intertextual references to *Halloween* (USA, 1979) and *Friday the 13th* (USA, 1980). This delight was shared by audiences of horror fans, who recognised these references; if they did not, the characters obligingly spelled them out for them!

Scream 1, 2 and *3* also spelt out the codes and

conventions, or the 'rules', of horror movies. Their self-reflexivity, together with their intertextuality, were two playfully postmodern aspects of the films' success. It will be interesting to see just how far these film allusions and games can go before the horror genre needs to find another trick to revive it.

The genre of a film (or television) text may be determined by its typical ingredients, or codes and conventions, applied in the table below to two variants of the horror genre:

HORROR SUB-GENRES There are various definitions of horror sub-genres, such as classical Gothic, American Gothic, 'slasher', body-horror, serial killer movies, etc.; the horror writer and theorist, Kim Newman, discusses many of these in *Nightmare Movies* (Harmony Books, 1988).

The horror writer Stephen King delineates two styles of horror in his book on horror fiction, *Danse Macabre* (Futura, 1982). First, there is 'wet' horror, with an abundance of blood, guts, decomposing and shape-changing bodies. Secondly, there is 'dry' horror, which chills and prickles the skin with a sense of mounting unease, often with a

Figure 3.25
Promotional poster for A Nightmare on Elm Street (USA, 1984). Many typical features of the horror genre are utilised in the collage of images.

psychological aspect or dealing with the supernatural or the occult.

All horror films essentially have a monster, whether human or non-human, whether from fantasy or reality. King also discusses four character archetypes: the vampire, the werewolf, the thing without a name and the ghost. Although reductive, most of the types of monster in all horror films can be identified as belonging to one of these and follow, or subvert, the accompanying conventions accordingly.

HORROR CODES AND CONVENTIONS

	DRACULA (UNITED STATES, 1931)	SCREAM (UNITED STATES, 1996)
Sub-genre	Classic Gothic – or Dracula/vampire film	Psychopathic/serial killer or 'slasher movie or 'stalk 'n' slash' movie
Setting	England – nineteenth century Castles, large private houses A foreign country – Transylvania	Suburban contemporary America A community, focusing on school and homes
Characters	Monster – Count Dracula Monster's helpers – Renfield, wolves and vampires Victims – transgressive women, Lucy and male obstacles Hero – Jonathan Harker Hero's helpers – various associates Heroine – Mina Vampire hunter – Professor van Helsing	Monster(s) – serial killers Victims – transgressive teenagers Hero (female) – Sydney Prescott Hero's helpers – friends, police officer, news reporters
Plot	A manhunt – the killing of the monster Dracula	A manhunt – the killing of the monsters – the killers

TABLE CONTINUED OVER PAGE **Figure 3.26**

HORROR CODES AND CONVENTIONS (continued)

	DRACULA (UNITED STATES, 1931)	SCREAM (UNITED STATES, 1996)
Iconography – in *mise-en-scène* (costumes, make-up, props etc.)	Night time and the moon Crucifixes, holy water, candles, bats, cobwebs Dracula's black cloak and pale face Period costume and transport – nineteenth century	Realistic domestic and suburban *mise-en-scène* Knives Telephones Popular culture objects The killers' costume and white mask Contemporary fashion
Music/sound effects	Sound effects of bats, wolves, silence for tension	Contemporary music Original orchestral soundtrack Sound effects for slashing and action sequences, silence for tension
Theme	Good versus evil The power of love	Good versus evil A postmodern lesson in the genre
Representation	MEN: Heroes – are brave and resourceful, sense of honour and decency Victims – become morally depraved Dracula – magnetic and hypnotic power, aristocratic WOMEN: Weak and vulnerable Heroine – romantic love interest, sexually unavailable Victims – disobedient, become morally depraved	MEN: Heroes – resourceful, modest Victims – Stupid, morally ambiguous WOMEN: Heroines – brave, independent, clever Victims – sexually promiscuous, 'bitchy'/stupid ADULTS: Largely ignorant of anything that is going on, arrogant or sceptical
Actors	Bela Lugosi	From a variety of fields, but some may now be associated with horror
Director	Todd Browning – horror specialist	Wes Craven – horror specialist
Intertextuality	The novel by Bram Stoker and the 1927 stage adaptation by Hamilton Deane in London	Halloween and other horror films

FILMS AND IDEOLOGY

All media texts reveal the ideology (systems of ideas, values and beliefs) of the creators as well as that of the audience. The *Scream* trilogy and its imitators are connected to another genre, the teenage drama or school film (see p. 225), and, in much the same way, reveal subtextual indicators of growing concerns and moral panics about the state of America's youth and their lack of sexual and ethical morality. However, riding on the back of 1990s post-feminism and a popular cultural zeitgeist of 'girl power', the *Scream* films portray a strong female hero, Sydney Prescott (Neve Campbell), as indicated by her conventionally masculine name, who outwits the villains.

Yet there are tensions here within her representation. This character shows highly desirable and heroic qualities, such as courage, determination and independence. But her survival, in a self-conscious and direct line of ascendance from Jamie Lee Curtis's Laurie in *Halloween* (USA, 1979), seems to be predicated, as is emphasised at every turn, on her sexual restraint and modesty.

This seems to strike a contradictory and reactionary note against the more radical representation that marks Sydney apart from the conventional female victim stereotypes. In accordance with prevailing ideology, Sydney's sexual restraint is represented as admirable and exemplary, but seems out of touch with contemporary youth culture and experience.

Therefore, what is being proposed here as a viable model of behaviour for young womanhood? Be strong and physical, but be chaste? Is a return to old-fashioned moral values what these films actually propose? In *Men, Women & Chainsaws: Gender in the Modern Horror Film* (BFI, 1992), Carol Clover discusses this character archetype, the 'final girl', and presents other debates about gender representation in horror films.

This is not to say that contemporary films necessarily contain didactic instructions for our behaviour. However, study of these teen/horror films, together with study of gender representation in music, fashion trends, other films and US teenage television drama series such as *Buffy the Vampire Slayer* and *Dawson's Creek*, make for interesting research into popular cultural trends and ideologies.

THE IMPORTANCE OF CONTEXT

Meaningful media research can only be undertaken in context. Any film text, as with a literary text, should be considered in its cultural context, against a background of prevailing and alternative ideologies, trends and other media texts. Such study reveals aspects of the text that might not be otherwise apparent, or appreciated, as well as indicating the nature of audiences' responses to it.

Contexts are many and various and relate not only to the time in which a film was made. The context of an old film re-viewed years later can also reveal interesting aspects of its meaning and reception. There are various contexts and theoretical perspectives that may be researched and considered in order to extend the analysis of any media text, in addition to one's own personal responses. In film, these may include the following theories and perspectives:

► psychoanalytical (e.g. Freud, Jung and Lacan)
► gender studies (e.g. feminist film theory)
► cultural studies (e.g. theories of race and culture)
► structuralist (e.g. Saussure, Lévi-Strauss, Barthes, Metz, etc.)
► Marxist.

▼ ▼ ▼ ▼ ▼ ▼ ▼

activities

1. Determine some of the characteristics of the film audience with a simple survey. Ask students, teachers and family members how often they have been to the cinema in the last month. Collate the responses according to age groups. Use the following categories: 0–14 years; 15–24 years; 25–34 years; 35–44 years; and 45 years and over. Ask for their genre preferences. Analyse the results and discuss any trends or links.

2. Film theorists say that film has subsumed (taken over within a larger category) all of the traditional art forms such as literature, music, fine art and drama. List the elements from each art form that film has taken and used. For example, from literature film has taken and used character (among other elements).

3. Contrast the characteristics of film with those of television (see p. 234).

4. Using the outline of the horror genre above, try to identify the codes and conventions of four other genres, with a list of films for each genre.

What are the distinguishing features of each one, in terms of plots, characters and challenges that they face?

2. Why have some genres thrived and others become less popular over time? Discuss why genre is an important concept in film, on the one hand for audiences and the other for producers.

3. Research a film in its context and look for any subtextual themes or messages that reveal ideological positions and identify their source. Consider your personal ideological position in relation to that of a film.

Production assignment

Plan the opening sequence of a film of your own devising. Look carefully at the analysis of the beginning of *Gladiator* for guidance. You will need to determine the location/s, character/s, events and dialogue that are required to establish your story. At the same time, use of the camera will need very precise planning (see pp. 148–154 on shots, camera angles and movement).

Meticulous attention to detail, in the form of a storyboard will be of considerable benefit. Consider especially how visual features will be harnessed to secure the engagement of audience interest. Intrigue, suspense, mystery and curiosity are all elements that will make people want to go on watching. How can you build these into your opening?

When you have planned all these things, go on to shoot the sequence/s.

major assignment

Written assignments

1. Research the films in a particular genre and study how and why they have changed over a period of time. Analyse changes to costume, settings, characters and storylines. How do these changes relate to developments in the real world of those periods?

Oral assignment

Some see film as a transitional technology, halfway between the live theatre and virtual reality entertainment. Discuss this notion with your fellow students. Do you think that the film medium will be replaced by high-tech screen entertainment, such as virtual reality video games or home cinema?

Docudrama Feature Films

Docudrama is a hybrid of documentary and drama genres which brings real events to life on the film or television screen. What pictures come to mind when you think of the assassination of US President John F. Kennedy in 1963? The presidential cavalcade? Jackie Kennedy in the back seat of the car? Kevin Costner as Jim Garrison? When you think of the Jewish experience of the Nazi holocaust, do you still see the little girl in the red jacket from *Schindler's List*?

Features of docudrama

I think the artist has the right to interpret and reinterpret history and the events of his time.

Oliver Stone, film-maker

▼ ▼ ▼

In the social sciences, the idea of cause and effect is regarded as of prime importance. Social forces produce significant change. Economic data, graphs of community health spending, population trends and so on can be used to show causes and effects.

In docudrama feature films, these forces are shown through the codes and conventions of the visual language (see pp. 47–9). Critics feel that this obliges the audience to judge matters of accuracy and truth by aesthetic standards. Audiences do

not, on the whole, say: 'That was an accurate account'; instead, they tend to say, 'That was a good film.'

Cause and effect, accuracy and truth are each expressed in the docudrama through the elements of character, plot, setting and exposition.

CHARACTER

The classic Hollywood model makes history unknowable apart from its effect upon individual characters.

David Bordwell, Professor of Film Studies, University of Wisconsin

▼ ▼ ▼

One of the central themes of most feature docu-dramas is the relationship between the individual and society. As a result the films tend to highlight individuals, rather than social movements or impersonal processes such as class repression or industrial conflict.

Characters are expanded to represent the individual and collective causes that might be oper-ating in any set of social or historical circumstances.

For example, Jim Garrison in *JFK* (USA, 1991) is a strong, expanded hero figure whose motivation is a desire to solve the unknown and make the world a better place. He holds the

Figure 3.27 *In JFK (USA, 1991), director Oliver Stone intercut actual news footage with dramatised re-creations. What is the effect of this on the public memory of the event? For anyone born after 1963, the film may be the prime source of his or her knowledge about the assassination.*

Figure 3.28
*Julia Roberts in
Erin Brockovich
(USA, 2000).
Elements of
character are
established
through dress,
body posture and
facial expression.*

docudrama narrative together. By overcoming a series of conflicts, intrigues and blockages, he single-handedly brings about a resolution to the film.

However, the real-life Garrison is held in much lower regard by assassination researchers. While the film Garrison is a lone crusader, the character actually stands for about twelve other researchers, including the real-life Garrison. 'We take liberties, make his work larger and make him more of a hero', says director Oliver Stone.

▼ ▼ ▼

What matters is not the re-telling of great historical events, but the poetic awakening of the people who figured in those events. We should re-experience the social and human motives which led people to think, feel and act just as they did in historical reality.

George Lukacs
Historical literature analyst

▼ ▼ ▼

Central characters in docudrama feature films are conventionally employed in one of two ways. They appear either as generalised characters or as great leaders.

GENERALISED CHARACTERS If the focus of the film is on the experience of ordinary people, the scriptwriters may assemble characters to represent their class, or culture, or a social movement. The events in the film may touch upon the lives of these ordinary people and leave them changed in some way.

Generalised characters are similar to the Everyman characters of mediaeval morality plays. One person is meant to stand for everyone. Oliver Stone says of Jim Garrison: 'I was taken with the way a man starts to investigate one small corner of the conspiracy and comes to realise a small-town whodunit has global repercussions. He is darkened and sacrificed, yet he wins his soul in the end.'

GREAT LEADERS If the story cannot be generalised to the level of ordinary people, film-makers tend to deal with the subject matter through a heroic leader. Events are explained as being at least partly due to the psychology of the leader. For example, the events that led to the creation of the Church of England may be explained away as a result of Henry VIII's appetite for wives.

In Richard Attenborough's *Gandhi* (UK, 1982), we see the Indian independence movement symbolised through the heroism of one man. Of course, most mainstream film narratives also require romance to make the story work. Unions between characters can be used to represent the alliances of social groups, political forces or other cause agents.

The chief stereotypes here are of the great leader and the lover. The fate of the lovers points to the underlying exposition. A positive union can mean the reconciliation of conflicting forces, while a negative outcome might suggest that the competing social forces can never be resolved.

Although traditional in most docudramas of today, this reliance on leaders and/or lovers need not be so essential. Alternatives to heroes were explored by Soviet film-makers as early as the 1920s. Sergei Eisenstein (*Battleship Potemkin*, USSR, 1925) searched for ways of treating docudrama without a focus on individual characters. He reduced characterisation to basic stereotypes so that the mass movements themselves could be the heroes. We brought collective action onto the screen, said Eisenstein, in contrast to the individualism of the bourgeois cinema.

He felt that the numbers of visible working-class people and their narratives were an affirmative and politicising statement. This was in contrast to the individualised characters and narratives of conventional cinema at the time, which was derived from traditionally bourgeois forms of entertainment, such as theatre and opera.

PLOT

Feature docudramas are usually centred on a good story in the best Hollywood tradition. This restricts the films to what some historians have scornfully called 'the history of happenings' – a great events, names, and dates approach to the subject.

The traditional narrative stages of orientation, complication and resolution are imposed upon real people and events. The genre chosen to present the story provides a further restriction upon the presentation of real events. For example, the genre may demand a love interest and a strong climax through a personal confrontation.

The director of a docudrama is always torn between two imperatives – whether to be true to the demands of telling a good story, or whether to be true to the facts.

Not all successful docudramas fall into the trap of romanticising history in the Hollywood manner. Some film-makers have more integrity, and respect for the truth. *Land and Freedom* (UK/ Germany/ Spain, 1995) tells the story of the Spanish Civil War of 1936. Or, more accurately, it tells the story

of a young man from Liverpool who goes off to fight on the side of the socialists in that conflict. Director Ken Loach avoids the soft options of happy endings and love interests, and deals instead with a complex political scenario.

One notable scene has a wide number of characters debating their political viewpoints at length in a manner that would be unusual in mainstream film entertainment, given the demands of simplicity. Nevertheless, the story is a powerful human drama that presents the historical facts faithfully.

SETTING

Film is a descriptive medium. The camera records minute details placed within the frame to give the impression of authenticity (see *mise-en-scène*, p. 150). Part of the appeal of the docudrama is the experience of 'being there' at the place where it happened.

The setting of a docudrama has several uses for the film-maker.

SPECTACLE Historical docudramas, in particular, can use the setting to create a sense of grand visuals. The overall spectacle may include any or all of the following:

► period setting, including costumes, buildings, vintage cars and so on
► mass action, such as conquering armies or riot scenes
► environmental spectacle, such as the violent sea, the Scottish highlands, the sweeping plains of the Wild West and so on.

AUTHENTICITY The dramatisation of events can be cut together with shots of the larger setting to suggest the events really are happening at this time and in this place. This is a technique Oliver Stone consistently uses in his film *Salvador* (USA, 1986), based on the experiences of a journalist in war-torn El Salvador.

INTEGRATION OF THE HERO A focus on the settings and their spectacle elements allows the film-maker to suggest that the characters are linked to the forces affecting the larger society. These may be social, geographic, economic or military.

For example, a shot of a young conscript character in a war docudrama as he kisses his girlfriend goodbye can be intercut with footage of crowded wharves and farewell parades. The central character is thereby integrated into larger events.

CONVEYING THE EXPOSITION The setting can express a point of view about the subject of the docudrama. For example, in Eisenstein's *Strike* (USSR, 1924), the factory building represented a point of view about the powerful forces of 'the bosses' in the film.

EXPOSITION

Behind the narrative, at the heart of every docudrama is the exposition. An exposition is an argument supported by evidence (see television documentary, p. 280).

The exposition in Jim Sheridan's *In the Name of the Father* (Ireland/UK, 1993) is that the four Irishmen accused of the IRA bombings of Guildford are innocent and have been wrongfully imprisoned. In *JFK*, the exposition is that there was a conspiracy to kill President John F. Kennedy, with involvement from the highest levels of government in the United States.

The social purpose of docudrama

In the political fallout following the release of *JFK* (USA, 1991), then-President George Bush established an independent five-member committee to review and release some of the secret files stored since the assassination of President Kennedy.

The docudrama is a political genre. The justification for making such films is often 'the public's right to know'. Docudrama shares with the documentary, the privilege of belonging to 'the Fourth Estate' – even if it is at the borderline of fictional genres (see p. 297).

Films set in the past can present a political message to the present. Often the historical subject and setting are just a disguise for a message aimed at contemporary society. *Michael Collins* (USA, 1996) while dealing with events in Ireland surrounding a popular leader of the same name, in fact also seeks to offer some comment on the violence that has continued to trouble Northern Ireland until very recently.

Present-day film-makers might have a variety of motives when they propose historical docudramas. There could be a desire to search for national origins, for example. *Braveheart* (USA, 1995), for example, took as its subject the life of the Scottish folk hero, William Wallace. It was no accident, however, that the time of its making coincided with a strong resurgence of national pride and a renewed push for political independence among the Scots.

Figure 3.29
In the docudrama **In the Name of the Father** *(Ireland/UK, 1993) Gerry Conlon and his lawyer, Gareth Pierce, go over the evidence that will eventually lead to his release. The basis of every docudrama is an exposition. In the Name of the Father argues that Gerry Conlon has been wrongly imprisoned for an IRA bombing.*

Docudrama and traditional documentary

The genre of docudrama developed as a result of three problems film-makers found with the traditional documentary genre. These problems are as follows:

■ **Traditional documentaries are selective**

Traditional documentaries claim to deliver the truth, but they can never present more than a very selective view of reality.

■ **Traditional documentary methods excluded re-enactments and scripted dialogue**

This meant that they could never penetrate beyond the surface or show thoughts and inner feelings.

■ **Vast areas of subject matter are closed to traditional documentary makers**

Nothing can be shown that occurred before the 1890s, when film was invented. No secret deals behind closed doors can be shown. Events that turned out to be important but were not filmed at the time would be off-limits. Excluded would be some of the most significant events of the twentieth century. For example, no filmed record of the actual operation of the Nazi extermination camps has survived (if it ever existed).

■ **Traditional documentaries cannot provide the same level of understanding as docudramas**

The makers of docudramas claim that audiences gain a deeper understanding of people and events. Traditional documentaries cannot provide this, it was asserted, because they can never get beneath the surface of the people involved. Dramatisations also have the power of narrative to absorb the audience. Many film-makers of documentaries, however, would argue this point!

DOCUMENTARY MODES

Documentary is a form that is used in television and radio, as well as film. It involves as much construction as any fictional narrative and cannot simply be defined as filming what is seen and heard. In *Representing Reality: Issues and Concepts in Documentary* (Bloomington & Indianapolis, 1989), Bill Nichols identifies five modes of documentary (summarised below) that can be usefully applied to the study of any documentary text:

EXPOSITORY uses a disembodied and authoritative voiceover commenting on what is seen and heard.

OBSERVATIONAL tries to offer 'a slice of life' by being 'a fly on the wall'. Both of these popular phrases suggest that the film-makers try not to alter what they are recording – an idealistic and impossible aim.

INTERACTIVE emphasises the presence of the film-maker, either as director or camera operator, and may be indicated by questions to the documentary's subjects from off-camera.

REFLEXIVE reveals the processes of construction themselves to be as much a part of the subject of the documentary itself.

PERFORMATIVE tries to focus on the poetic or aesthetic processes of film expression, while distancing itself from references to the outside world.

In another among many attempts to define documentary and its variants, such as in the writing of John Corner. Richard Barsam, in *The Non-Fiction Film* (Bloomington & Indianapolis, 1992) has identified the following categories of documentary: documentary, factual film, films of exploration, direct cinema, *cinéma vérité* and propaganda film.

The following are the titles of some notable film documentaries for further research:

► *Nanook of the North* (USA, 1922) – Robert Flaherty
► *Man with a Movie Camera* (USSR, 1929) – Dziga Vertov
► *Drifters* (UK, 1929) – John Grierson
► *Coal Face* (UK, 1935) – Alberto Cavalcanti
► *Night Mail* (UK, 1936) – Harry Watt and Basil Wright
► *Fires Were Started* (UK, 1942) – Humphrey Jennings
► *The Thin Blue Line* (USA, 1988) – Errol Morris
► *Roger & Me* (USA, 1989) – Michael Moore
► *Hoop Dreams* (USA, 1994) – James, Marx and Gilbert
► *When We Were Kings* (USA, 1996) – Leon Gast and Taylor Hackford.

▼ ▼ ▼ ▼ ▼ ▼ ▼

activities

1. List some real-life events of interest to the public where there is a strong storyline to lend itself to docudrama treatment. The events could be from the present day, the recent past or some earlier historical period.

2. Analyse the characterisation in a docudrama of your choice. Comment on whether the film uses generalised 'Everyman' characterisation or relies on the great leader approach.

3. Describe the use of setting in a docudrama. How is it used – as spectacle, to integrate the hero, to lend authenticity and/or to convey the exposition? Explain.

4. Suppose you were planning a docudrama of a suitable subject. Select several narrative film genres you could possibly use to convey the subject matter. What variations to the treatment would be required? For example, how would the treatment change if it was presented as a romance as opposed to a thriller?

5. Compare a docudrama and a traditional documentary dealing with the same subject. Evaluate the presentation of the information. Which do you think has a more valid claim to 'truth'?

6. List the expositions of several well-known docudramas you have seen. Write a paragraph explaining the argument and presenting some of the supporting evidence.

7. Explain why it could be asserted that television, rather than film, is the best medium for the documentary, for both the producers and the audience.

8. Study a variety of documentaries, on either television or film, and try to categorise them according to Nichols's five documentary modes (see p. 211). How are the distinctions between each mode demonstrated in your chosen text(s)?

Docudrama Representation Issues

The docudrama and truth

The arguments for and against the use of docudrama are based on differing ideas of what is 'truth' and what is 'accuracy'.

CRITICISM

The central criticism levelled against docudrama is that it is incapable of telling the truth. Quite a major accusation, obviously. However, we must always remember that all media texts are representational and therefore 'the truth' is most certainly a relative concept.

Even if an event had already been recorded on film, a docudrama attempting to deal with this event would have to mimic the original exactly to be in any way truthful. There would be no point in this. Neither could any film possibly capture the whole truth about anything. Therefore, the argument goes, any change to the portrayal of events *as they actually occurred* is a reduction of truthfulness.

If an event was not filmed, of course, then actors are required to give a rendition of what happened. This puts the truth equally at a disadvantage, it is claimed. Even if the language

used in the re-creation is 'authentic' and based on court records, for example, drama still alters the truth. Accents may be different, inflection, volume, gestures, stance and so on could all help to change meaning, according to how they are delivered. What results is a *version* of the original event, not the actual thing itself.

Aside from the actors speaking the lines, there are also the directors who orchestrate them, and scriptwriters, camera operators and editors who all contribute to construct a version that moves further and further from the truth.

At the heart of traditional documentaries lie claims to be dealing with the truth. These claims are based on argument and evidence, assembled from research, interviews and filmed footage. One critic has pointed to a famous incident concerning former USSR President Krushchev losing his temper during international negotiations. This incident was captured on film and shown widely on television. Critic Jerry Keuhl asks how can we tell if Krushchev ever lost his temper in public? Film of him banging his shoe on a desk at the United Nations Assembly exists and is very strong evidence. Film of Telly Savalas dressed as

Figure 3.30 *Actor Denzel Washington in a scene from Spike Lee's* Malcolm X *(USA, 1992). Screen biographies are a form of docudrama that has always been popular with feature film-makers. (The issues of truth are further complicated when an actor with a huge public following lends some of his own 'image' to a filmed interpretation of someone else's life.)*

Krushchev and banging on a desk somewhere in Hollywood, on the other hand, is evidence of nothing and will convince no one.

Or will it? It could be argued that Hollywood's various versions of history are believed, especially by those brought up with this 'history'. This can be seen in the furore that accompanied the reception of Spielberg's *Saving Private Ryan* (USA, 1998), which angered many European spectators due to its overwhelming Americanisation of this version of a historic event, the D-Day landings on Omaha Beach.

IN DEFENCE

'Getting it right' does have validity in journalistic terms. Not against the standards of an elusive absolute 'truth', but against the standards of evidence as they might be understood in a court of law.

Leslie Woodhead

Docudrama pioneer

▼ ▼ ▼

According to Leslie Woodhead, much of the heat in the docudrama debate is generated by arguments over accuracy versus absolute truth.

Woodhead's docudramas have been regarded as authoritative enough to be tendered as court evidence. His 1979 production *Collision Course*

contains a second-by-second reconstruction of the last few minutes before the world's worst mid-air collision. It was used as evidence in an inquiry into air safety.

Docudrama and history

The great stories of history have always captivated film-makers. Now, they are starting to engage historians as consultants to the productions. Using the experience gained through their involvement with films, some historians are speaking out about the role of history on the screen.

▼ ▼ ▼

Traditional written history is too narrow in focus to render the fullness of the complex, multi-dimensional world in which humans live.

Only film, with its quick cuts to new sequences, dissolves, fades, speed-ups and slow motion can ever hope to approximate real life.

Only film can provide empathetic reconstruction to convey how historical people witnessed, understood and lived their lives.'

R. J. Raack, historian

▼ ▼ ▼

Films cannot fulfil the basic demands for truth and verification that historians demand, argues

Figure 3.31
Warren Beatty as John Reed in Reds (USA, 1981). Biographical docudramas can alter the truth for the story's sake. In a generally fine and stirring film, however, there are inaccuracies. John Reed makes a train journey from France to Petrograd in 1917 – impossible at the time.

Professor Robert Rosenstone. Films insert fictions to improve the story. They also tend to confuse memory with history – if someone remembers something, then it must be true. This means they ignore the possibility of faulty memory, exaggeration or even lies.

Worst of all, says Rosenstone, they create a closed world with a single linear story. This denies alternative points of view and banishes all complexity.

However, to argue against this, history itself, is just that – a series of stories, versions and interpretations of events. Just as the camera most certainly can lie, so the human eye, or our perception of what we saw or heard, may be misled or mistaken. Even a document from an eyewitness or an interview with a famous leader is subject to memory loss or biased points of view and can never be entirely reliable on its own. As in law, fact needs the corroboration of evidence from a variety of reliable sources.

However, for most people the emphasis in history is on the story. Academic historians are few in number and, according to Professor Rosenstone, they are in danger of becoming even fewer.

Film is capable of dealing with the past and can attract huge audiences. This is the medium historians can use to again create narrative histories that will touch large numbers of people and give meaning to the past.

On the one hand, films such as *Robin Hood: Prince of Thieves* (USA, 1991) clearly romanticise history: apart from anything else, the lush soundtrack is clearly contemporary. However, the film-makers do not set out to give a history lesson and nor do the public go expecting one. Nor, either, a geography lesson, as the film betrayed an inaccurate knowledge of British geography, with Hadrian's Wall, on the Scottish borders, a stone's throw from Dover, on the South Coast of England. However, the United Kingdom was not the film's primary audience and Hadrian's Wall provided a visually spectacular location opportunity.

On the other hand, film is at least *capable* of giving *some* idea of what life was like for people living in different eras – and occasionally makes conscientious efforts to do so. *Rob Roy* (USA, 1995) is a good example of a film that tries hard for authenticity, both in its account of the events it deals with, and in the realisation of the living

Figure 3.32
Details of costume and location are crucial in establishing authenticity in films such as **Rob Roy** *(USA, 1995).*

conditions for people in that time and place.

Not all historians agree, however. The great danger of film, says historian David Herlihy, is that it makes the viewer an eyewitness. In order to accept the dramatisation of the film, the viewer must also suspend disbelief. In history, this is a dangerous thing.

▼ ▼ ▼

Doubt is not visual. Warnings of any sort, appeals to maintain critical detachment, cannot be easily photographed. Warnings require a retreat from the visual to the written word.

David Herlihy, historian

▼ ▼ ▼

Film representations versus the written word

Historical docudramas on film present information in a different way to written histories. Some of these differences are listed below.

▶ Film highlights individuals, rather than focusing on the underlying structures that produce change.

▶ The amount of traditional information is significantly less than can be conveyed by written accounts.

▶ Film can cram hundreds of tiny details about life in the past into a single frame. The biggest advantage film has over the written word is its use of *mise-en-scène* (see p. 150). Antique objects, furnishings, costumes and so on can all convey an idea of what it was like to live in a certain period.

▶ Historical docudramas virtually always sacrifice complexity for action. Their plots must be in continual movement from orientation to climax. Any aspect of history that is too complex or is not visual will be ignored.

▼ ▼ ▼ ▼ ▼ ▼ ▼

activities

1. Can drama be used as a method of presenting real-life material? Discuss the docudrama's claim on truth.

2. From a history book, find graphical or tabular evidence of some structural causes for historical events – statistics on unemployment, population, famine, etc. Think of a way of transposing this information into a film scene. Discuss film's effectiveness as a means of communicating this data.

3. Analyse the usage of *mise-en-scène* (see p. 150) in a sequence from an historical docudrama covering any period. Identify the meaningful objects included in the scenes, such as landscape, period architecture, costumes, transport, etc. Evaluate the effectiveness of these elements in conveying information about the period.

4. How can an audience be encouraged to critically evaluate evidence presented within a docudrama? One historian has suggested subtitles be displayed on the screen outlining alternative points of view. Suggest other ways of solving the problem.

▶ setting – as spectacle, integrating device, authenticating device or vehicle for conveying exposition
▶ exposition
▶ representation of the topic.

2. Select a docudrama film and a traditional documentary dealing with the same topic. Compare the representation of the topic made by each form. Evaluate the relative accuracy and the justification of any claims to the truth.

Production assignment

Make a thirty- to sixty-second promotional trailer for a docudrama film on a topic of your choice. The voiceover in the promo should express the exposition of the programme as a question the film will answer.

For example, the exposition of *JFK* could be expressed as 'Who really did kill JFK and what was the involvement of the US government?' The promo shots should give an indication of plot, character and the use of setting.

Oral assignment

Prepare a five-minute oral presentation for the following task.

Make a comparison of two docudramas dealing with the same topic. Analyse the variations in viewpoints they contain and illustrate your comments with excerpts from the films. Advance reasons for differences.

Suggested films include: historical docudramas made in different eras; filmed versions of Shakespearean historical plays such as *Henry V*; biographies such as *Malcolm X* (1972 and 1992) and *Shadowlands* (1985 and 1993); and docudramas relating to the Jewish Holocaust of World War II.

major assignment

Written assignment

Write a 600-word essay on one of the topics set out below.

1. Analyse and evaluate a docudrama of your own choice. In your response, discuss the aspects set out below. You may find it easier to use headings.
▶ plot
▶ character – generalised or great leader; romantic interest

Film Adaptations of Literary Texts

There is a basic conflict of visions. The author of the novel has seen in his mind's eye for many months, or for years, the faces, the gestures, the mannerisms of his characters. Then on the screen appear total strangers displacing those images, asserting new characteristics, outward and inward. The writer almost can't help being outraged.

John Hersey
Novelist

▼ ▼ ▼

Film's reliance on textual sources is profound and enduring. The use in one medium of materials that originated in another is certainly nothing new. Shakespeare did it, and the tradition goes back even before him. However, the degree to which the particular medium of film is dependent on others is quite unique.

Novels provide the basis of much of the world's film production. More than 30 per cent of all films ever made are derived from novels, according to estimates. Adaptations from plays and short stories bring this figure up to some 5 per cent. Shakespeare remains an ongoing success story for many modern film adaptations. There have also been many major feature films based on poems, including *Ulysses* (Italy, 1954), *The Charge of the Light Brigade* (UK, 1968) and *The Man from Snowy River* (Australia, 1982).

The trade in stories is now turning back the other way. It is reasonably common for successful films to be turned into books. Moreover, much novel writing has in turn been deeply influenced by film's methods and narrative structures. It has shaped the way in which writers approach their craft (not least because many hope to see their work turned into a film!). While literature has been a powerful influence on film, the reverse is also the case. For example, Dashiel Hammett, the American crime thriller writer, was heavily influenced by early gangster films. The novels he subsequently wrote went on to influence films that were made later.

The modern narrative would not be what it is without the precedent set by films. Several changes in literature appear to be the result of film's influence, especially the following:

▶ Changes in the storytelling point of view can be traced to the film technique of moving the camera from one position to another. The postwar novel *Catch-22* by Joseph Heller, for example, uses this technique. The perspective shifts from one character to another. Every so often it returns to the viewpoint of the main character, Yossarian.

Novels and film both have always used this technique for following the *action*. Film, however, can use it for *characterisation*. Multiple perspectives become possible, even necessary.

▶ Closely related to this is the nature of the story that is being told. Film is much more bound up in showing the story from an *exterior* perspective. Since the arrival of film, literature has tended to move away from realism. Instead of focusing on the external world, it has become increasingly concerned with the realities inside the heads of its characters, which has also coincided with the popularisation of psychology. The invention of photography in the 1830s had much the same effect on modern art, as painters were freed from the constraints of realism, representing the world in a recognisable form.

The features of filmed adaptations of novels

Film is a multi-sensory communal experience emphasising immediacy, whereas literature is a mono-sensory experience more conducive to reflection.

William Jinks
The Celluloid Literature

▼ ▼ ▼

The features of filmed adaptations of novels are best highlighted by making comparisons of the different ways literary texts work. Many academics have attempted this task. Their findings centre on differences in six areas: narrative, methods of description, uses of imagination, differences in authorship, point of view, and aspects of artistic interpretation.

THE NATURE OF NARRATIVE

Like the novels and plays they are based upon, film adaptations belong to the narrative form. A narrative is often a causal chain of events. This is the most common type of narrative and it has a step-by-step series of happenings where one thing leads to another.

An important element of narrative is character, because events and actions must be performed by someone – or at least be relevant to them. Moreover, much modern story telling likes to see character *causing* the action. (This has not always been the case – the ancient Greeks saw people as *subject* to events often initiated by the gods).

Film is a comparatively new kind of narrative medium, but the need to tell stories has been with us since the beginning of human history. Until the widespread use of print, stories were told in the oral tradition. The novel had its beginnings in the eighteenth century, but did not reach its maturity until the nineteenth century. In the twentieth century, film and television have taken on the role of chief storytellers.

APPROACH TO THE NARRATIVE

Alfred Hitchcock is reported to have remarked that the length of a film should be directly related to the size of the human bladder and no longer; perhaps this explains the extremely abrupt endings to most of his films! While a book can be put down and then picked up later, a film is usually viewed in one sitting, although videos and DVDs now allow for repeated and episodic viewings. An average book may take eight to ten hours to read, whereas a film is rarely longer than two hours.

Films of novels have to be selections of the story, rather than the whole thing. Wayne Wang's *The Joy Luck Club* (USA, 1993) did not include all the stories featured in Amy Tan's novel. Even so, the rough cut is reported to have been four hours long. With the release length of the film being just over two hours, even more was cut.

As film is a medium that requires action, it is often only the story action that is selected. The inner motivations and thoughts, which make up much of a novel, are usually eliminated in film.

▼ ▼ ▼

Film is found to work from perception (sight) towards signification (meaning), from external facts to interior motivations and consequences – from the given world to the meaning of a story. Literary fiction works oppositely. It begins with signs (words) which attempt to develop perception. It elaborates a world out of a story.'

Dudley Andrew, film theorist

▼ ▼ ▼

Mary Shelley's Frankenstein (US, 1994) is a good case in point. When the final scenes are played out on the Arctic ice, film is able to make a much

Figure 3.33
A dismal visit to the countryside in Trainspotting (UK, 1996). Features of landscape and weather have long been used in novels and films to convey moods and predicaments of main characters.

Figure 3.34
Still from **Room
with a View** *(UK,
1985). In the
novel, the author
often dwells on
descriptions of
costume and
setting: details
that the film has
to be careful to
re-create, but
that are delivered
at a glance.*

more direct appeal to the senses than the novel can. The savage grandeur of the backdrop is shown in all its glittering fierceness. The novel of course has words to prompt the reader's imagination; but the film can actually show the grieving Creature as it destroys itself on Frankenstein's blazing funeral pyre. With film, the terrifying scene is presented to us in sparkling light and sound.

Film is more direct in its storytelling approach than the novel. The audience sees a filmed construction of events as they happen. In a novel, they must imagine it. Some say this greater directness accounts for film's larger audiences.

On the other hand the directness of film tends to limit it to realism. Film cannot easily avoid a sense of the factual or the realistic – even in fantasy. Fantasy, psychological studies, feelings and emotions are much easier in a novel.

DESCRIPTION

People often say that the film version of a novel is not as descriptive as the original. All the describing power of the prose has been lost.

Nothing could be further from the truth, says Seymour Chatman. Film possesses a vast array of descriptive detail in each frame. It has so much detail that some art critics even refer to it as overspecified.

Film uses the power of *mise-en-scène* to describe even the minutest details (see p. 150). Descriptive information can be delivered from within the frame to show details of costume, props, landscape and weather that would be beyond even the lengthiest novel.

Yet, no one notices apparently. According to Chatman this is because of a unique property of film's language.

In Jane Campion's *The Piano* (Australia/France, 1992), there is a scene featuring Ada and Alistair's wedding photograph which shows the sham of their marriage, as there was no real wedding ceremony – just a legal contract between Ada's father and her prospective husband, given the lack of rights women had in Victorian times. Ada (Holly Hunter) is made to wear the sodden wedding dress over her usual dress; the rain beats down mercilessly, not auguring well for their future together.

The backdrop of the photograph reinforces the artificial and staged nature of the proceedings and their relationship itself. In stark contrast to the wild and untamed New Zealand bush where the characters live, it shows a painting of a pleasant and orderly rural scene located, from the look of the thin cypress fir trees, in an Italian landscape, to suggest a romantic European tour.

Alistair (Sam Neill) looks stiff and formal in his tight, wet clothes, anticipating how uncomfortable and ultimately unsuccessful he will become in his role as patriarch.

In the context of the film, this single frame both indicates the doomed nature of the central relationship and satirises the pretensions and artifices of the settlers, their aspirations to Victorian middle class lifestyles and the moral debates that will be explored in the film. There is more in this single frame than would appear in even the most descriptive novel. Audiences barely notice these tiny details because of film's unique narrative pressure; however, films can now be easily watched again and again on video tape or DVD, facilitating closer attention and analysis.

Descriptive passages in most novels come as interruptions to the narrative. Critics have spoken of 'blocks' or 'chunks', and even 'islands', of descriptive writing inserted into the story.

Some people skip a long section of description just to find out what happens next. Description in a novel is often the author's way of suspending story-time (see p. 167) and putting plot, characters or setting under the microscope. Everything is frozen until we have finished looking. Some readers find this frustrating – they want to get on with the action! This use of description is a unique aspect of the novel's discourse time, says Seymour Chatman (see p. 168). It is part of the novel's special language that allows it to tell the story.

Film has another discourse time. It operates in a different way. In film, you can never stop the action. The pressure of the narrative in film is so great that the audience does not want to stop and contemplate things for a while. Events must move along.

The descriptive details in a film are mixed in with the narrative and we barely notice them. During the course of the novel *The Remains of the Day*, by Kazuo Ishiguro, many paragraphs are given over to describing Darlington Hall, the focal point of all the action. In the opening shots of the film, we see the house and simply say to ourselves, 'Oh, a big country mansion in the 1920s or 1930s. What is going to happen?'

In a novel, description often contains evaluation. The author judges the scene and the people in it as well as describing the visual details.

Film does not readily evaluate what it describes. This has led some critics to say film merely *presents* descriptive information. There is no easy way for the audience to know what the director thinks of a character. There is often no judgement. However, other critics have pointed out that judgment can be strongly hinted at through camera angles or lighting. Symbolic codes such as clothing or body language can also express judgement and study of more imaginative directors, such as Jane Campion's work in *The Piano* (Australia/France, 1992), can reveal a sophisticated use of symbolic codes, such as weather, costume and landscape.

Film is not lacking in descriptive power, or emotional charge, it simply works in different ways from other kinds of literary texts.

IMAGINATION AND THE AUDIENCE

At a very basic level of communication, both words and images are signs. Communication takes place by arranging these signs into systems (see signs, codes and conventions, pp. 47–9).

Words are signs that are a long way removed from what it is they refer to. For example, there is no way that the black letters on this page forming the word 'London' have any resemblance to the city itself.

However, a filmed image is much closer to that which it signifies. A filmed image of a street in Hackney, East London, may not have been what most people thought of with the word, 'London'. But it is definitely a version of London and much closer than the alphabetical symbol for it. (Nevertheless, it is important to remember that it is still only a *representation* of London, and not the actual place itself.)

The greater gap between the word and what it signifies means there is a greater role for the imagination in the novel. The novelist has less control than the film-maker over how the created sign system will be received, says Brian McFarlane in his book *Words and Images*. The novelist can choose the words, but is unable to prescribe what each reader will make of them. (See types of readings, p. 27.)

On the other hand, the film-maker has less opportunity to create fantasy or other-worldly images because films tend to realism. Computer-generated special effects have freed film-makers from this limitation to some extent, but it is still easier (and much cheaper!) in a novel to conjure

up the unreal. However, the film-maker has more control over how the audience *receives* the images. The visual sign is closer to the actual than the alphabetical sign. People's interpretation of a visual image does vary, but only within certain limits.

MULTIPLE VERSUS SINGLE AUTHORSHIP

A novel, poem or play is usually the work of a single author. Editors and other advisers certainly have input, but the author has sole control over the vast bulk of the work. In percentage terms, the input of the author is probably around 99 per cent.

A film, on the other hand, is the product of a collaborative effort. The director must rely on the camera operators, editors, scriptwriters and a whole host of other people to create the film.

The director must also rely upon the actors. Even if the director can completely dominate the cast, the gestures and movements of an individual actor remain the personal product of that individual. They can never wholly be the property of the director's imagination, which accounts for the preferences for a certain actor in casting decisions. In some cases, the actor is given immense freedom with the re-creation of a character or even, as in the case of British film-maker Mike Leigh, the narrative itself.

A result of film's multiple authorship is the dilution of the strong individual vision that often characterises a novel. A great deal of debate has ranged around the topic of whether the single author – or *auteur* (see p. 449) – is likely to produce better films. Directors such as Alfred Hitchcock and Orson Welles are used to suggest that they would. In particular, Hitchcock's long and distinguished career serves as a model of the high point of individual artistic vision.

However, there are also countless films where individual directors have unarguably ruined films. It is very rare indeed for them to have absolute control. The auteur view of the director under-estimates the power of the producer and in fact many a director has been fired from a film project and replaced.

POINT OF VIEW

A novel can be told from varying perspectives. The author can be an all-powerful storyteller. The novel can be in a first person narrative, or it can be told from the viewpoints of several different characters. The narrators can be authoritative, or they can be unreliable. The reader can decide whom they believe. In the case of famous American novel of teenage angst, *The Catcher in*

Figure 3.36
A scene from Howards End (UK, 1992), an Ismail Merchant and James Ivory film. This adaptation of E. M. Forster's novel cost millions to produce and needed mass audience appeal to recoup the expenditure. In contrast, the novel was inexpensive. Merchant/Ivory films are noted for their richly descriptive mise-en-scène.

the *Rye* by J. D. Salinger, the narrator, Holden Caulfield, is unreliable, as he tells us from the start that he is 'a terrific liar'.

In Salinger's cult novel, although Holden tells us an unreliable story, the reader can work out the true story and eventually comes to know more than the narrator himself, an immensely skilful narrative technique. This complicated use of narrative point of view may be one of the reasons that a film adaptation has never been attempted.

With film, you tend to believe what you see. Film seems to present the world objectively. The illusion of reality in film is so strong, that it is difficult to represent the world from a subjective point of view. However, films may be narrated either by omniscient narration (all knowing – the equivalent of third-person narrative in a novel) or by restricted narration (the equivalent of first-person narrative) – or sometimes in a combination of the two points of view. While a novel can be told from the point of view of someone gradually going insane, this is almost impossible in a film.

The film and literature critic Stuart McDougal has described some attempts that films have made to overcome this hurdle. Jack Clayton's film *The Innocents* (UK, 1961) tried to put into film terms

some of the subtlety of Henry James's novel *The Turn of the Screw*. Henry James's narrator is not very reliable. The film uses sound to highlight the subjectivity of what is being seen.

INTERPRETATION

A faithful translation is often a betrayal of the original.

René Clair
French film director

▼ ▼ ▼

The film-maker is not a mere translator for the author of a novel or play, says the film and literature theorist George Bluestone, but a completely new author. The film-maker is an independent artist in his or her own right. For René Clair, the film-maker's role is to make a new story from the elements of the old – the plot, characters, settings and themes. This should be instead of simply copying a product constructed with the writer's tools.

THE SOCIAL CONTEXT OF FILMED ADAPTATIONS

The Hollywood producer is governed less by the laws of aesthetics than by the laws of the marketplace.

George Bluestone
Novels into Film

▼ ▼ ▼

Some of the most important differences between literary texts and their film counterparts are due solely to the context of the industry.

The cost of production is one of the most important considerations. An average literary novel costs a great deal less to produce than even a small-scale independent film. Even more so with a poem.

In contrast, the film adaptation of Rose Tremain's novel *Restoration* (USA, 1996) cost $19 million. Francis Ford Coppola's Vietnam classic *Apocalypse Now* (USA, 1979) used Joseph Conrad's book *Heart of Darkness* as its inspiration. The film cost $23 million at the time.

A novel can be judged a financial success if its sales reach 10,000 copies; poetry is scarcely ever judged in financial terms at all. In contrast, a mainstream film must record attendances in the millions to recoup costs. As a result, commercial films must aim at mass audiences. Commercial films cannot appeal to special interest groups unless the mass audience can be attracted as well. On the other hand, literary texts can afford to cater for much

smaller segments of the reading public.

The need to be responsive to a mass audience explains at least two other differences most people notice between the film versions and their sources. Romance is often expanded in the film version. A good, strong 'love interest' is seen as crucial in driving the narrative. This element of the story may even be emphasised beyond the weight given it in the original. At the same time, as advertisers have long known, sex sells.

Today, films are often quite explicit in their depiction of intimate relationships. The television adaptation of William Thackeray's *Vanity Fair* in 1999 attracted much criticism for its frank depiction of flesh and sexual activity. There are no passages of this kind in the novel, it was argued. Maybe not, went the reply, but that was only because the values of Victorian society would not allow them to be printed: this did not mean that people were not *doing* it! A contemporary audience would expect to see relationships to be shown in terms that they are used to.

▼ ▼ ▼ ▼ ▼ ▼ ▼

activities

1. Read a novel (or play) of your choice that you know to have been made into a film. View the film version and obtain the screenplay (often available via the Internet movie database), then try the following tasks.

▶ Write an outline of what Seymour Chatman calls the 'story-time'. This is the basic sequence of story events as it might exist in time, without yet being either a novel or a film.

▶ Next, outline the 'discourse time' arrangement of this story in each medium. This is the particular expression of the story in the novel and also in the film. For example, the film may start later in the story while the novel may not dwell for long on exciting action scenes. Or, the novel may be divided into chapters, whereas the film is a single unit, etc.

▶ Compare the three versions as interpretations of the deeper sequence of story events. How have events been presented in each medium? Has the novel or the film chopped up the sequence to a greater degree?

2. From a novel, find sections of block description. What purpose do these fulfil in that particular novel? Do they interrupt the narrative? How would they be dealt with in a film?

3. Conduct a survey designed to discover the different reading experience people have with novels as opposed to films. Read William Jinks's comments on p. 217. Devise several questions aimed at exploring the differences he describes. Survey a range of people and collate the results.

4. According to Dudley Andrew, film has trouble showing the inner thoughts and moods of people. List some ways in which a director could use landscape to indicate the mood of a character.

5. View an extract from Merchant/Ivory adaptation such as *Howards End* or *The Remains of the Day*. What descriptive data can you discover from the film extract's *mise-en-scène* (see p. 150)? Compare this with a passage of description in a novel.

6. Select a novel/play that has had a film adaptation made of it. When you have read a novel, but *before* you view the film, write down descriptions of the main characters and the landscapes as you imagine them to be. Describe what *you* see in your mind's eye, rather than repeat the author's vision. Discuss the descriptions with other class members. Now view the film and compare. Discuss your findings in class.

7. Find examples of filmed adaptations where the original novels have told the story from the perspective of a variety of characters. Analyse the methods the film-maker has used to overcome the problem in particular extracts. For example, compare extracts of the film *Catch-22* (USA, 1970) with extracts from its written counterpart.

major assignment

Written assignment

Write a 600-word response to the task below.

Make a detailed comparison of a novel and its film adaptation. Analyse and evaluate each using the following as areas of investigation. Conclude with an opinion on the overall effectiveness of each version.

► the basis of the story and its treatment in each medium (consider Chatman's 'story-time' and 'discourse-time' – see pp. 167–8)
► description: audience reception and imagination; the effect of the context of production (including multiple authorship); storytelling perspective (e.g. first-person, multi-character, omniscient narration, etc.)

Production assignment

1. On video, produce a two- to three-minute extract from a novel or short story of your choice. Write a screenplay or storyboard it first to help to organise and visualise your ideas. The extract should include a suitable mixture of dialogue, action and description.

Write a short paragraph to accompany the video explaining some of the choices you were faced with and the reasoning behind the decisions you made.

2. Either script or storyboard an extract or scene from a novel that was not shown in the filmed adaptation. For example, consider scenes in the novels and films of *Kes* (UK, 1969) or *One Flew Over the Cuckoo's Nest* (USA, 1975). Write a short paragraph to accompany the script or storyboard explaining some of the choices you were faced with and considering the possible reasons for the scene's exclusion from the filmed adaptation.

Oral assignment

Prepare a five-minute oral presentation for the following task.

Make a comparison of two filmed adaptations of the same novel. Analyse the variations in interpretation they contain and illustrate your comments with excerpts from the films. Advance reasons for differences. Suggested films to analyse are: *Little Women* (1933, 1949, 1978 and 1994) or films of Dickens's novels, including *Oliver Twist* (1922, 1948 and 1982).

Films about School

In the middle of the mayhem that passes for normal in the current crop of US high-school films – zitty geeks lusting after their teachers, pushy kids fixing the school elections, would-be prom queens killing their rivals, space aliens invading the minds and bodies of their teachers – along comes a British film with nothing so deranged going on in the classroom: just the usual bullies and sadists, and a stand-out teacher with a heart of gold.

John Cunningham
The Guardian, 24 September 1999

▼ ▼ ▼

The unnamed film referred to here is the (re-released) all-time classic British film about school – *Kes*, by director Ken Loach. First made in 1969, this film still shines above all others made in this country – and possibly anywhere else – for its simplicity, its pathos and its honesty about the largely grim lives of its characters. There is compassion, and tenderness, and beauty in the film: but it is all steadily crushed by the harsh social environment of its northern industrial setting. Despite this, it remains a profoundly stirring film whose resonance may be seen in the film *Billy Elliot* (UK, 2000).

Cunningham goes on to observe that there has been a distinct absence of serious attempts to deal with schools as a subject in this country ever since. This is in clear contrast to the steady stream of high school films issuing from the United States, as well as the many US television series focusing on school and college life. This is very odd, he says, given their rich potential:

they can legitimately be portrayed as microcosms of the larger world into which pupils are debauched; their hierarchies invite conflict as well as consensus; the way teachers use or abuse their unique power is intriguing; their treatment of youngsters who assert their personalities –either as rebels or geniuses – is the essence of drama.

Certainly, numerous American high school films have proved this to be the case. *Dazed and Confused* (USA, 1993) shows a very clear-eyed picture of the brutality of adolescence, as does *The Breakfast Club* (USA, 1985) and *Heathers* (USA, 1988).

Figure 3.37
Main character Billy Caspar, in Kes (UK, 1969). In a harsh northern environment, the brutal realities of life are brought home to him through the fate of his beloved pet kestrel.

Cunningham suggests that the reason may partly be because our writers have gone on to choose different subjects, for reasons of their own. However, he notes that US studios have been adept at recognising and exploiting the ongoing fascination with this period in people's lives – after all, it is the one thing that absolutely all of us have in common. Perhaps the lack of such films is more to do with the failure of commissioners, than of writers.

In fact, there has been another notable contribution to this field, which did a great deal to explore the social tensions in schools, and the larger society surrounding adolescents, too. This was a quartet of films under the title *Made in Britain*, by David Leland, screened in 1983. Powerful, explosive and shocking, with a bravura debut from Tim Roth, the series made a big impact at the time – but they were made for television. This is not to lessen their achievement, but rather again to question why such material is not commanded for the big screen.

What genre are films about school?

There have really only ever been two films about school: *Goodbye Mr. Chips* (UK, 1939 and 1969) and *The Blackboard Jungle* (USA, 1955). Everything else has been a remake of one or the other, says one film commentator.

Audiences were shocked by the violence and social tensions exposed by *Blackboard Jungle*. In the film, an idealistic teacher is assigned to a New York City school that resembles a battle zone. Bill Haley's classic single 'Rock around the Clock' opens the film. The use of new rock music also challenged audiences. However, they could be reassured that by the end, the heroic young teacher had finally broken through to at least one of the students.

Goodbye Mr. Chips, on the other hand, is set in a traditional English grammar school. Mr Chipping is a shy schoolmaster who overcompensates by acting as a stern disciplinarian. Marriage softens him a little. Tragically, his wife dies in childbirth, along with the baby. He then devotes his life to 'his boys', seeing several generations through to manhood. The film concludes with Chips in his eighties, on his deathbed uttering his last words of love for his students.

Features of films about school

PLOTS

As with most narrative films, school films follow the traditional narrative pattern of an orientation stage, a complications stage and a resolution stage. Certain films place an evaluation stage just before the resolution. These three narrative stages have various names according to the narrative theorists being considered, from Tsvetan Todorov to Christopher Vogler. Essentially, however, they all refer to a three-act dramatic structure originally identified by the Greek philosopher Aristotle in his treatise, *Poetics*.

ORIENTATION STAGE The first stage of the narrative sets up the situation and illustrates the problem. In *Blackboard Jungle*–style films, the problem is drastic and requires drastic solutions. The school is in crisis and a strong hero is required to restore order. The methods may be unusual. Often the problems at the school can be taken as a symbol of the sickness of the larger society. Some critics have described this type of film about school as an urban Western. The arrival of the teacher is similar to the arrival of the Western hero at the frontier.

In *Goodbye Mr. Chips*–type films, the orientation begins an awakening. The students (or, in some cases, the teacher) must come to terms with the meaning of their own lives. The teacher arrives as a guide and conducts the students through to the turning point of adulthood.

COMPLICATIONS STAGE The path to fulfilment is a rocky one. In each case, the teacher and the students must take 'the road less travelled'. The teacher is often at war with the authorities. In *Mr. Holland's Opus* (USA, 1995), obstacles are provided by the cost-cutting short-sightedness of Vice Principal Wolters. But the teacher may just as often be at war with the students. Principal 'Crazy Joe' Clark's first act in *Lean on Me* (USA, 1989) is to call together 300 of the school's drug dealers and troublemakers and expel them.

CLIMAX In *Principal* (USA, 1987), James Belushi has a *High Noon* (USA, 1952) style confrontation with the leader of a gang of school thugs. In *Blackboard Jungle*, the classroom teacher confronts a student who is wielding a flick knife. The climax is the high point of excitement in the film. Those parallels that film critics have made with the Western are often very apparent at this point.

Sometimes the climax comes as the students overcome a major obstacle. A class of tough East LA students sits the Advanced Placement Calculus Test and passes with flying colours in *Stand and Deliver* (USA, 1988).

In *The Prime of Miss Jean Brodie* (UK, 1969) and *Dead Poets' Society* (USA, 1989) the climax comes as the unconventional and inspiring teachers overenthuse their students. In both of these films, there is a student death which leads to an evaluation stage.

EVALUATION STAGE In a real school, the final matriculation ceremony offers a chance to evaluate school careers for many students. Final grades are themselves another evaluation. Perhaps as a result of this frequent focus on judging performance, the evaluation stage is a relatively common feature of films about school.

Often it is the teacher's career or their style of teaching which comes under scrutiny. Despite the disapproval of the authority figures, in *Dead Poets' Society*, the students stand on their desks to offer their own verdict in the parting salute, 'Oh, captain, my captain'.

THE RESOLUTION Few films have offered such a rousing conclusion to a teaching career as Glenn Holland received in *Mr. Holland's Opus*. One of his students, now respectably grown up, offers this: 'We are your symphony, the music of your life.' There are echoes of the conclusion to *Goodbye Mr. Chips*, the story of a teacher at an English grammar school for boys. The doctor is at the deathbed of the eighty-year-old Mr. Chipping. He murmurs to another teacher, 'It's a shame he never had any children of his own.' Chips replies, 'You're wrong. I have … thousands of them, thousands of them, and all my boys.'

In *Blackboard Jungle*–style films, the resolution comes as the hero restores order (and learning) to the strife-torn school.

CHARACTERS

It is a characteristic of all feature films that they tend to elevate individuals (see Docudrama, p. 207). But each character in a film has an explicit and precise function, a purpose for being there, whether it is major or minor. Film is far too time-consuming and expensive a process for superfluous characters to be included (as they represent a source of costly expenditure).

The functions of characters have been studied in depth by many narrative theorists (again, far too many to do justice to here). Vladimir Propp's analysis of the similarities between stock characters of Russian folk tales in *The Morphology of the Folktale* has been adapted and applied to the roles of characters in films. It is clear to see that there are characters who have similar roles and functions in all films, regardless of the genre. Any character who has dialogue has a function that relates to other characters, for example, either assisting the hero or creating obstacles and conflicts for the hero. Changing definitions of the roles of hero and villain in themselves make for interesting study in films across several years, as our definitions of these roles have changed tremendously over the past fifty years, in particular, since World War II, with its various, and relative, incarnations of heroes and villains.

Conflict is a necessary ingredient for any narrative; it is the engine that propels the narrative forward, which is essential for it to reach its conclusion. Conflict is usually provided by clashes between opposing characters. The work of Claude Lévi-Strauss, the anthropologist, on binary opposition has been useful in analysing the structural functions of characters and themes in films. Binary opposition is an element of our daily lives and experience, such as man and woman, darkness and light, hot and cold and love and hate.

Many narratives, in any medium, on any topic, have been found to contain opposing pairs of themes or characters; good versus evil being the most common, with characters being representative of either side. Study of Westerns has revealed thematic oppositions, such as domesticity and independence, or desert and cultivation, or savagery and civilisation.

Contemporary films such as *Batman* (USA, 1989) have explored the possibility that, in an increasingly complex, morally ambiguous world, the distance between extremes of right and wrong and hero and villain are not so very far or unrelated.

Films about school are no exception and have their share of larger-than-life characters who all have specific roles and opposing relationships. This is the case, even when the story is based on facts, as are *Stand and Deliver* and *Lean on Me*.

THE MASTER TEACHER In many films about school, the hero is an inspiring teacher who is prepared to throw away the traditional approach. He or she gets through to students by sheer force of personality. This teacher, says the French cultural critic Jacques Rancière, is the revolutionary teacher of the popular imagination. The master teacher is the great leader everyone wishes they had at school.

These film teachers are more than mere teachers, says Rancière. They are grand masters. They are not bound by the curriculum or the rules of the school. In many cases they break rules and challenge traditions. Master teachers in the films use the classroom as a theatre. The teacher is the only actor, the students hear only the master, says Rancière. In many ways these teachers are like pied pipers or cult leaders. The students are the adoring throng.

THE STUDENTS In *Dead Poets' Society*, Robin Williams seems to hypnotise his students. The students in films about school seem totally focused on the master teacher, according to Jacques Rancière. While they are challenged to be themselves as individuals, they also seem to be dangling on the strings of the master teacher, he says.

THE FUDDY-DUDDIES A proportion of the teaching staff are portrayed as fossils. These are people whose teaching practices are seen to be suffering from *rigor mortis*. Their role in the film is to block the energies of the students and the young-at-heart master teacher.

THE TROOPERS Whether shell-shocked or battle hardened, the majority of the staff seem to have lost the will to do anything but go through the motions. Jacques Rancière calls these characters 'the troopers'. Staff in *The Blackboard Jungle* are under siege, but lack the courage and the leadership to carry on. A turning point for them comes when one of the teachers has his collection of jazz records smashed.

SETTINGS

Some school locations are more worthy of being filmed than others. In films about school, the most common locations are those that express the battle lines of the conflict. The washroom, the lockers, the gym and the secret 'hang-out' (e.g. the cave in *Dead Poets' Society*) belong to the students. The staffroom is the site of the teachers' discontent. The central conflict usually takes place in the classroom. It is the place where teachers and students come together. The conflict may be between different teaching styles or between the teacher and uncontrollable students.

The context

Everybody can relate to a film about school because it is the one place everybody has been. The teenage audience, especially those who fall into the fifteen to twenty-four age bracket, are big spenders at the cinema and films with a student point of view can be very popular.

Meanwhile, the adult audience looks back on their own experience of school with a sense of nostalgia for 'the best days of their lives'.

Just under half the population has children in an educational institution. As parents, they are worried about their children's future. Films about school can play upon these concerns, showing an education system in decline. Problems in the education system may also stand for problems in the larger society.

In the press and on television, concern about the state of schools and teenage drugs and violence is represented as an increasing moral panic and reference to films and real events, such as the occasional high school massacre in the United States, are almost indistinguishable and fuel concern.

Films reveal the ideologies of their contexts and their audiences (see p. 51). Films about schools can fuel concern, but may, in the film's final moments, provide a reassuring resolution when the rebellious teenagers have been tamed or banished and equilibrium restored. School or teenage drama films also often contain ideological messages of hope, of overcoming class or gender obstacles, for example, to succeed academically or to achieve self-actualisation.

▼ ▼ ▼ ▼ ▼ ▼

activities

1. Watch the climax in a *The Blackboard Jungle*–style film and compare it to the climax in a Western. What similarities and differences can you find? Record your answer in a short paragraph.

2. Select a film about school and analyse its plot stages. Is there an orientation stage, a complications stage, an evaluation stage and a resolution? Does the film deviate from the typical narrative pattern?

3. View the evaluation stages of those films about school that seem to make a judgment about a teacher, a school or even the meaning of adolescence or adulthood. In a few short paragraphs, record the evaluation that you think the film is making. Compare it with the evaluations of other films you've watched on this topic. What similarities or differences can you see?

4. Re-read Jacques Rancière's ideas about the recurring characters in films about school (see pp. 227–8): the master teachers, the troopers, the rapt students, etc. Select a film about school and evaluate the characters according to Rancière's stereotypes.

5. Imagine you are the locations officer for a film support company. Film some suitable school location shots for a film from around your school. These would be shown to film directors who are selecting ideal settings. Accompany each location shot with a summary of its possible uses.

Representation and Audience Issues in School Films

The study of representation in films tends to focus on ideological analysis and interpretation of how people, places, eras and ideas are represented within the films, either directly or indirectly. It should be remembered that our personal perspectives inform our judgements of what we see on screen.

▼ ▼ ▼

FREDDY SHOOP:

Look, I ain't no English teacher. See, double negative. I hand out basketballs and check for jock straps. I'm like real challenged. The only reason I got into this teaching gig was to get my summers off.

VICE-PRINCIPAL:

That's okay. These are real students. They're unmotivated, irresponsible, not too bright. They relate to you.

Summer School (USA, 1987)

▼ ▼ ▼

Representing the problem: changes since *Goodbye Mr. Chips*

Communications academic Steven Thomsen has completed a study of more than fifty years of films about schools. There have been big changes in the way in which the plots and characters have been shown over that time, he says.

Films about school are driven by the same forces of 'good versus evil' that propel almost all narrative films. In school films, one teacher hero is established as 'good' and is then pitted against some form of 'evil' within the school or its community.

EARLY FILMS

Until the 1950s, the forces of 'evil' in films about school tended to come from the community beyond the school gate. Teachers were represented as liberators in a world of ignorance and schools were often portrayed as havens of enlightenment. Students were tightly controlled and often needed encouragement to 'be themselves'.

In *The Corn is Green* (USA, 1945; re-made for television in 1979), a headstrong English woman arrives in a Welsh village to find only one person in the town can read or write. She sets up a school against strong opposition from the villagers. Despite threats from village saboteurs, she then succeeds in getting one of her students to Oxford.

MODERN DEPICTIONS

Following on from *The Blackboard Jungle* (USA, 1955), films increasingly represented 'the enemy'

egotist. Look at what a monstrous, trite, overstuffed set-up you get – a school principal who looks like a travesty of Thomas Arnold. The type hasn't been seen since Dickens. You get a Hitlerish papa who screams about his son's career …

R.B. Heilman,
American educator

▼ ▼ ▼

There are two kinds of teachers in the films about school, says educator David Hill. In films specifically about them they are portrayed as heroic, dedicated and inspiring. When they are used for comic effect, they are buffoons and self-serving idiots, says Hill.

Rancière's master teacher is not shown as a typical teacher in the films. Instead, the ordinary teacher is portrayed as being far from competent and often a blockage to the hero. In addition, nearly all the master teachers in the past thirty years have been men. This, despite the actual proportion of males in teaching being lower than 30 per cent.

A recent exception to the trend was Michelle Pfeiffer's portrayal of LouAnne Johnson in *Dangerous Minds* (USA, 1995). Although a woman, she is rendered as an ex-marine, to establish her toughness. (Interestingly, the role of her boyfriend was cut out – perhaps to avoid conflicting with her quasi-maleness, and saintly dedication to her work!)

as being within the school, says Thomsen. 'Discipline is not the enemy of enthusiasm,' says Joe Clark in *Lean on Me* (USA, 1989). In modern representations of school, students need to be civilised, rather than set free. The new 'evil' became predatory students who were out of control, incompetent teachers and fuddy-duddy administrators.

In *Teachers* (USA, 1984), Nick Nolte is a burned-out humanities teacher at war with both the school management and his delinquent students. At the start of the film, scenes of chaotic violence establish the negative atmosphere. One student is stabbed, but the management makes him sit bleeding in the school office. A teacher is beaten up and a psychotic student bites another teacher on the hand.

The curriculum

At a crucial dramatic moment in *Lean on Me*, Clark 'gives in' and magnanimously allows the school anthem to be given a soul-gospel treatment, whilst all throughout rap is disqualified as purely 'delinquent noise'. (See particularly the scene of the rowdy school assembly.)

Adrian Martin
Film critic and writer

▼ ▼ ▼

Depictions of teachers

First, you've got this guy on a white horse charging in to save the place. So you need some set-up black hats to make him look like a hero instead of a moral

In films about school, it is often the role of the master teacher to inspire students to discover the value of learning. The curriculum they are inspired to take up is usually an old-fashioned one based upon the classical 'great works'. The curriculum can be loosely defined as all the learning that takes place at school, including the subjects offered. In films about school, the subjects shown are the most traditional ones. English and mathematics are the two most likely to appear.

In *Good Will Hunting* (USA, 1997) the unschooled hero is a natural genius in the latter. Similarly, in *Stand and Deliver* (USA, 1988), students gain access to the world of higher mathematics and pass their exams. Meanwhile, in *Dead Poets' Society*, Robin Williams as Mr Keating quotes from the poets Tennyson, Thoreau and Whitman. The culture being passed on is the most classical, manageable and conservative that is available, says Adrian Martin. Newer subjects or innovative approaches to old ones are not shown.

The films seem to offer little evaluation or criticism of the curriculum itself, or its methods of assessment. This is rather curious, given the expertise and self-conviction of so many others in them – politicians especially.

The School as Metaphor

Whether the school is a public school or a private school depends upon whether the film is a *Blackboard Jungle*–style film or more in the style of *Goodbye Mr. Chips*. Scenes of chaotic violence and out-of-control students are invariably shown as occurring in the public sector schools (*Made in Britain*, UK, 1983). *If* (UK, 1968) is the classic rare exception to this. For once, mayhem and murder break out in a private school.

The films also suggest that public education (and perhaps society at large) is in a state of long-term decline. In *The Election* (USA, 1999), the dirty tricks and hostility of a high school contest for student president are a clear metaphor for the real presidential elections. Ruthless ambition, calculated seduction, adultery and even a touch off lesbianism are all thrown into the pot. The leading female will not let anybody stand in her way.

Films about schools and teenagers may be seen as symptomatic of our fears about the state of our society, the future and deteriorating moral values. They often reinforce the view that society's progress is always negative – what hope have we for the future, if our youth are not in a fit state to look after it?

Given that the audience for such films is primarily young people themselves, such negative representations of young people shocking their parents and communities are popular precisely because they feed into the need for often very cooperative and reasonable teenagers to be rebellious and to delight in adult outrage. Films offer all of us, whatever our age, whatever the film, opportunities to fantasise and experience vicarious sensations and emotions, in the safety of the cinema or sitting room.

▼ ▼ ▼ ▼ ▼ ▼

activities

1. Select an early film about school (or a film set in an earlier time such as *Dead Poets' Society*) and compare it to a modern school film. Re-read the findings of Steven Thomsen's research (p. 229). Do your selected films set up a 'good versus evil' opposition? If so, where is the negative force located: within the school or outside (or both)?

2. Canvas your teachers' opinions about their fictional representations.

3. Compare the students in some school films to the students in various classes with which you are familiar. How true-to-life do you find these fictional representations? Do you feel they are as diverse as real students?

4. What popular subjects are available in the curriculum at your school that have not been shown as worthwhile and inspiring in the film curriculums? Suggest reasons for this.

Discuss Adrian Martin's criticism that the film curriculum is too conservative and focused only on the great classics (including mathematics 'classics' such as calculus).

5. Explore the similarities and differences between representations of schools in US films and UK television series, such as *Grange Hill*, and try to account for these similarities and differences.

major assignment

Written assignment

Choose one of the following topics and write a 600-word response.

1. Prepare an analysis that examines the representation of teachers, students, the school and the curriculum in two different types of films about school. Following the analysis, make a comparison of the two depictions. Conclude with an evaluation of the representations in relation to your actual experience of school life.

2. Have films about school affected the public's perception of students, teachers, schools and the curriculum? Conduct a 'cultivation' study in response to this question (see cultivation studies, pp. 31 and 179).

To conduct something resembling a cultivation study, devise some questions designed to find out what people think about school. Base the questions on aspects of school that have been covered in the sections on school films in this text. Then present the survey questions to regular filmgoers who have seen a number of films about school. Present the same questions to people who rarely go to the films and have not seen recent films about school. Collate the results.

Analyse the results of your survey and conclude with an evaluation of the effect of films (and television) about school on public perceptions of schooling.

Production assignment

Choose one of the following tasks and produce a short (two to three minutes) video.

1. Storyboard or film two versions of your school: first, as a *Goodbye Mr. Chips*–style institution; and, secondly, as a *Blackboard Jungle*–style school in crisis. Include stereotypical scenes that indicate each category. Both could include scenes with a master-teacher and class, school gate and corridor scenes, washroom scenes and staffroom scenes, etc.

2. Rework the usual images of teachers, students, schools and the curriculum commonly seen in films about school. Present alternatives to the 'master teacher', the 'students from hell' and the 'great classics' curriculum.

When you have completed your film, attach an explanation of the ways in which you have challenged stereotypes. Evaluate your success in doing so. How difficult was it to change the conventions?

chapter four
Television

4 ▶

Television: The Medium

In just 50 years, television has stripped away our sociable natures. Cocooned in the glowing world of the cathode tube, people no longer know their neighbours. It has dammed the natural flow of human contact that builds friendships, neighbourhoods and ultimately nations. Millions of modern, well-educated people barely speak to strangers outside work and shopping trips. As a result, one of the most precious resources – simple human trust – has been all but eradicated. We don't trust one another as much simply because we don't know one another as much.

Television has made our communities wider and shallower.

Dr Robert Putnam
Dillon Professor of International Affairs
Harvard University

▼ ▼ ▼

Television is the first mass-produced symbolic environment. The significance of that can be reflected in the word that sums up the most distinctive element of human life, the most crucial distinction between humans and other creatures – story telling. We experience the world through stories. Whoever tells the stories of a culture defines the terms, the agenda and the common issues we face.

Television has replaced most stories told by parents and has either replaced or organised what we learn in schools or in church.

We need a new environment movement, addressing the environment that is most crucial to our humanity – the environment of the stories we tell; the environment that shapes so much of what we think and do in common.'

George Gerbner
University of Pennsylvania

▼ ▼ ▼

On the one hand, television has always attracted criticism for being an adverse force in people's lives – sapping their energies, substituting for imagination and sociability. On the other, it is claimed that it offers stimuli far exceeding any leisure activity that has ever existed before.

Television has been called 'the most awesome godless force' in the modern world. It is a force many people reckon they cannot do without. The US state of New York has enacted a law declaring the television set to be 'a utensil necessary for a family to survive in this society'. Should a New York family go bankrupt, the television – along with clothes, the water supply and kitchen utensils – cannot be taken from them.

Surveys say the average person watches about four hours of television a day. This is one-third of a typical person's waking hours. It is almost as much time as is spent in the classroom – except that it continues over a lifetime. The impact of television on human civilisation may yet prove greater than any other invention, except perhaps the wheel!

Why is television so powerful? The eyes are superior to the other senses as information receivers. Hearing is the second best. Their impact is formidable when combined. But above all else, it is television's *apparent* re-creation of actual life that makes it the most influential of all the media. We are led to believe that television is a 'window on the world', showing us a supposed objective reality. Even in fiction-based programmes, there is a carefully constructed illusion of normality, of recognisable locations and characters, and of course believable incidents.

In fact, everything about it is completely artificial. What television actually shows to us is an endless parade of highly selective images of what goes on in the world – and that includes the news and documentaries. The process of selection is charged with ideological and other filtering mechanisms. Television could be said more accurately to *create* our picture of the world than merely to reflect what is already there.

The runaway success *Big Brother*, by Channel 4, goes even further by generating its own mini-reality, with its own, highly artificial rules and values. Not only has the station created its own environment, but also the contestants enter knowing that they, too, can add their particular outlooks to the programme – as indeed, in the voting, can the audience.

A domestic medium

'Anything on telly?' 'No, nothing!' This is a common household exchange, according to the University of Westminster's Paddy Scannell. He argues people really mean that there is nothing out of the *ordinary* on television – only the usual programmes on the usual channels at the usual times. This ordinariness is precisely the intended effect of broadcast television, he says.

Television needs to be ordinary because it is present in everyone's living rooms. It is a domestic medium that is viewed while people are doing a variety of other things. Television is a regular part of day-to-day life.

INATTENTIVE VIEWERS Research shows that people pay attention to the television screen only 65 per cent of the time. By installing a small camera behind the television screen, researchers found viewers involved in a whole range of activities apart from watching the television set.

Even when they were watching, many people constantly switched channels – often in rapid bursts. The research also showed that many people do not bother to watch programmes all the way through. The average amount watched was 80 per cent of the whole programme.

PROGRAMMES Television programmes contain different and unrelated items, just as a newspaper or magazine does. Almost all programme material on television, however, consists of series formats. A series is a group of thematically related programmes – such as *Friends*, *The X-Files* or comedy series such as *Absolutely Fabulous* and *Mr Bean*.

The series format developed in the first half of the century as a way of answering the need for a ceaseless supply of programmes. The content of a

show could vary from episode to episode, but the format remains the same and can be repeated over and over again. As a result, television became a medium of 'difference within sameness', churning out repeated patterns of programming.

MULTI-CHANNELS The rapidly growing number of channels is likely to bring profound changes to the way we all watch television. In digital, cable and satellite formats, there are now many channels that are dedicated to single programme genres. MTV, UK Style, Discovery Wings, and Carlton Food, for example, all have particular topics that form the basis of the programmes that they offer.

We are unlikely to watch any one of them for the whole evening – but we will turn to them when we want that particular kind of programme. This in turn will create much more dedicated forms of advertising, as marketing strategies will be able to identify niche audiences.

TIME SLOTS

On the more traditional terrestrial channels, the viewing day is divided into a number of time zones. The most important time zone is peak time, or prime time. Prime time is from 7 p.m. to 10 p.m. and it is at this time that the television audience is largest. Prime time gradually tails off until most viewers have left at around 10.30 p.m. Specialist programmes with small audiences are shown after 10 p.m.

Early morning programmes tend to be a combination of news, interviews and light enter-tainment. This time slot has not so far attracted a large audience. Early afternoon programmes feature soap operas, quiz shows, cooking, gardening and old films. The late afternoon (after 3.30 p.m.) concentrates on children's shows, comedies, youth and pop music shows and cartoons.

A dream-like reality

A recent American Surgeon-General's report on television and violence reported that those who watch more television tend to dream less. This has led some television scholars to contend that, if television can affect the dreaming of individuals, then maybe it is dream-like in itself. Television may therefore represent the collective dreams of society as a whole.

Peter Wood, of Duke University in the United States, believes television shares six basic similarities with dreams.

■ **Television and dreams are highly visual**

According to the founder of modern psycho-analysis, Sigmund Freud, most dreams consist of visual material.

■ **Television and dreams are highly symbolic**

Both television and dreams transform experience into visual symbols.

■ **Both television and dreams involve wish fulfilment**

Many people have the experience of dreaming about something they greatly desire. Whether it be quiz shows or prime time violence, television performs the same function.

■ **Television and dreams contain disjointed and mismatched material**

The editing practices of television, for example, offer the chance to 'collide' images the same way that dreams do.

■ **Both television and dreams are forgotten in the same way**

The content of television is enormously powerful, yet like most dreams it is pushed under the consciousness and forgotten except for a few memorable fragments.

■ **Television and dreams make use of recent experience**

Critics accuse television of having no past. Television news, in particular, seems to report

endless streams of events but never asks why these things happen. Dreams also tend to repeat what is known and has happened recently.

Television as a bard or town crier

Fiske and Hartley have developed the idea of bardic television.

TELEVISION AS A MODERN BALLADEER Whenever there was a battle, a noble wedding, or a murder, the balladeers of 200 or 300 years ago wrote songs and verse about it. The ballads were sung in every town and village and the ideas of the time were passed along from person to person. The verses of the balladeer showed what were the central concerns of the society.

Today, television fulfils this function, telling society at least one version of the concerns of the present day. When television was first introduced, this town crier function was very evident. Most people did not own sets and so they gathered outside electrical retail shops to watch 'the bard'. Television told them, and is still telling us now, of the world outside. As the home becomes a greater focus for leisure activities, the 'town crier' role of television will become ever more important.

TELEVISION AS MODERN FOLKLORE Folklore is the traditional beliefs and tales of oral cultures. It allowed individuals to be part of a group, a culture and a heritage. It promoted social solidarity. Television works in the same way. It presents a view of the current morality of society. It shows a selection of achievements, problems and meanings of life within the group of 'folk' in the 'global village'.

Other purposes of television

Theorists have commented on a range of other purposes television fulfils in the most people's lives.

■ **Television can fulfil the need for information**

All people have a desire for knowledge and understanding. Television can be a great educator on a huge range of topics. The reporting of current events is one of its duties as well. It therefore has a responsibility to be truthful.

■ **Television can provide entertainment**

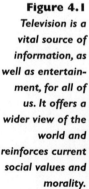

Figure 4.1
Television is a vital source of information, as well as entertainment, for all of us. It offers a wider view of the world and reinforces current social values and morality.

Television has taken over the role of the circus, the theatre, the concert hall and the cinema as the chief provider of mass entertainment. It has borrowed heavily from all these and created a great deal that is unique to itself.

The results of this survey (figure 4.2) show that entertainment is seen as the main purpose for most peoples' viewing.

■ **Television can fulfil emotional needs**
When the preschool child is sat in front of the television set, when the parent watches a midday film to relieve boredom, when the tired office worker switches on the set after the evening meal, the television is being used to fulfil emotional needs. It may be the need for love, for

REASON FOR WATCHING TV	
RESPONSE	**% OF GROUP SURVEYED**
Information	31
Entertainment	61
Half and half	7
Don't know	2

Figure 4.3
In a survey of television audiences, viewers were asked what, for them, ranked as the most important reason for watching television – information or entertainment?

company, for diversion or the release of tension, or for escape. The ability to fulfil these needs is one reason that television is so powerful.

▼ ▼ ▼ ▼ ▼ ▼ ▼

activities

1. A survey of television viewers in 1973 gave the following results. Have times changed? Conduct a class survey on this question and present your results in percentages. Compare the results of both surveys in a paragraph.

HOURS OF TV VIEWING	
How many hours a week do you watch television?	
Less than 12	30%
Between 12 and 20	28%
More than 21	42%

Figure 4.2

2. The television set does not get the undivided attention of its viewers, much to the dismay of television executives. Research has shown a remarkable range of viewer activities while the set is on: reading, eating, squabbling, etc. Observe your family for an evening. What other activities do they engage in while viewing? Do these interfere with their pleasure in and/or engagement with viewing?

Alternatively, write a short paragraph outlining the range of things you do while watching television. Do your habits differ according to whether you are with family or friends?

3. Compare a traditional ballad with a television drama using the guidelines below:
► What is the main subject of each? Compare the subjects.
► Why would people listen to or watch them? Compare the reasons.
► What does each tell about the society it came from? Make a list.
► What (easily understood) rules govern the making of these formats?
► Do you think they are similar? If so, what are the similarities? Explain your answer.

4. Make a list of some of the more interesting things that television, like a bard or balladeer, has told you about the outside world that you would not have been able to see in any other way.

5. Television is like folklore – it allows people to belong to a group. Have you witnessed any great achievements or tragedies on television? List as many as you can. Earlier generations might say the shooting of John Lennon or the assassination of JFK. Your examples could include the discovery of the possibility of life on Mars, or the death of Diana, Princess of Wales. On considerably less of a global scale, the triumph (or failure) of your favoured football team will probably be the focus of much discussion.

Did your reactions to these events confirm your membership of a particular group? Did you identify with the people involved at the time?

6. Study the television viewing guide. Count the number of 'information' programmes and the number of 'entertainment' programmes. Write down the findings and provide an analysis of the result in a short paragraph. Try to identify the different 'needs'

satisfied by watching each type of programme.

7. The quotations which open this section describe a society where there has been a profound loss of 'neighbourliness', and where television has taken over the traditional role of the 'storyteller' in the community. What evidence can you find to support either of these claims? How much of an adverse effect has this had on society, in your opinion?

Measuring Audiences

Reasons for monitoring

The need to establish the size and nature of audiences has been recognised since the earliest days of television. For commercial television, this obviously relates to the broadcasters' ability to reassure advertisers that they are reaching their potential customers. As ITV depends almost totally on this source of revenue, the need to provide clear and accurate information is crucially important. It is not simply a question of *numbers* of viewers, but also of *who exactly* is watching *when*.

Although the BBC does not depend on advertising for income, it does have to justify the monies it receives from the licence fee. If its audience share were to fall significantly below its rivals', it would find its funding being questioned. The government would find it hard to continue supporting with a universal fee an organisation that might be seen to be a minority broadcaster.

With the present increased number of new channels available through cable and satellite, of course – and even more so with the further expansion promised with the new digital delivery systems – this does seem to be an increasingly likely event, in any case. How the BBC will cope with the pressures on its core funding that this will bring, is one of the hot issues for the corporation in the immediate future.

Raymond Kent identifies four principal bodies of people who need information on audience composition:

▶ programme makes and schedulers
▶ media owners
▶ advertisers
▶ advertising agencies and media buyers.

PROGRAMME MAKERS AND SCHEDULERS need to know exactly what kind of audiences they are likely to attract on particular days and at different times of the day.

The allocation of resources for types of programme is closely related to likely audience-share. Equally, development of new material will require key information on most suitable times to attract the designated audience.

MEDIA OWNERS need to be able to offer proof of access to manufacturers of products to the right kind of audiences for the goods they wish to sell. Nobody wants to advertise at times when their target market is not going to be watching.

THE ADVERTISERS wish to know about both size and composition, or constituency of audiences. They will have allocated a budget to advertise their particular products, and will naturally want to make their outlay effective.

ADVERTISING AGENCIES AND MEDIA BUYERS will want to compare the costs of access to target markets across a range of media outlets, so that they can advise their clients on the most appropriate medium, or combination of media, for achieving their objectives.

Methods of monitoring

Data on television audiences is currently compiled by BARB (the Broadcasters' Audience Research Board). This is a private company, jointly owned by the BBC and ITV. Its work is governed by committees made up of representatives from all the major broadcasting organisations, including satellite, and advertising agencies.

In 1984, it introduced the AGB Peoplemeter, a set-top device for monitoring who was watching what programmes, and for how long. In addition, a selected sample of 40,000 households are surveyed throughout the year to gather more detailed information on individual viewer profiles, and their viewing habits and preferences.

RATINGS

Television rating (TVR) is the term used to describe the size of audience for a particular programme. It is calculated by expressing the actual numbers of people who watched as a percentage of the relevant population size for a given area. 'Teenagers rating for *Buffy, the Vampire Slayer* in the London area', for example, is the proportion of all the teenagers in that area who tuned in to a given episode of that programme. If three-quarters of this target group had done so, then its TVR would have been 75 – or 75 *ratings points*.

With advertisements, of course, these points can accumulate according to the number of times the advertisement is shown. This gives *gross ratings points* (GRP).

RATING THE RATINGS Ratings points were initially devised as a system of gauging audience sizes in order to supply advertisers with information. This was to assist them in selecting slots that would suit their budgets and target audiences. However, an entirely new usage is taking over within the industry: programming itself is increasingly being determined primarily by ratings success.

Programmes that gather big audiences are continued; those that do not are axed. No real surprises here, perhaps. There seems to be a clear commercial logic to this approach. However, there is also a danger in this appeal to populism. Size alone is no guarantee of merit. Many people feel that the 'lowest common denominator' factor often means that populist programmes are inherently lacking in content. They are 'easy viewing', providing entertainment only – there is never anything in them to challenge audiences or make them think. Should programmes that appeal to smaller numbers be squeezed out, simply because of their audience size? Documentaries on important social and political topics rarely appeal to large audiences: does this mean that they should not be made?

Of course, there is a very large debate around the notion of what constitutes 'quality'. It is

Viewing Figures

Viewing figures are currently available for the following productions:

Supply and Demand, Supply and Demand 2, Trial and Retribution 1, Trial and Retribution 2, Trial and Retribution 3, Trial and Retribution 4, Mind Games, Killer Net

Supply and Demand
Feb 9th 1997

	Start - finish		Individuals	Adults	Men	Women
Part One	2102-2200	TVR	18.92	21.74	19.90	23.36
		000's	10273	9722	4151	5571
		% Share	43	43	42	44
Part Two	2245-2341	TVR	12.92	15.29	15.17	15.39
		000's	7013	6835	3164	3671
		% Share	47	47	46	48
Source: BARB/TNS						

Supply and Demand 2
Sept 1 - Oct 6 1998

	Start - finish		Individuals	Adults	Men	Women
Episode One 01/09/98	2100-2156	TVR	16.23	18.27	15.91	20.49
		000's	8889	8322	3515	4807
		% Share	40	40	37	42
Episode Two 08/09/98	2102-2159	TVR	13.03	14.88	13.36	16.31
		000's	7132	6775	2950	3825
		% Share	32	33	31	34
Episode Three 15/09/98	2100-2156	TVR	12.64	14.53	11.39	17.48
		000's	6923	6617	2516	4101

Figure 4.4
Viewing figures for two Lynda La Plante dramas. These tables come from La Plante's production company website to attract potential programme buyers to any future La Plante productions – though the figures themselves are sourced from BARB.

impossible to get a universal definition, simply because people have very different priorities in terms of their programme preferences. Indeed, the same individual may have different requirements at different times of their day/week.

Apart from all the arguments that might be had on that topic, there is also a question about diversity in the schedules: shouldn't broadcasters be obliged to maintain a range of programmes? Minority audiences pay the same licence fee/ subscription rates as everyone else, and their tastes should surely also be catered for.

Moreover, what do you do about commissioning new programmes? If you use the proven success of a particular format as your only criterion of success, how do you ever bring in new ones? Many critics feel that a dire consequence of a ratings-driven policy for programming is that creativity is being slowly but surely strangled.

The future of audiences: globalisation

What we are seeing is the creation of a global oligopoly. It happened to the oil and automotive industries earlier this century; now it is happening to the entertainment industry.

Christopher Dixon,
Media analyst for Paine Webber

▼ ▼ ▼

A profound shift is taking place in the ownership patterns of media companies: previously they were primarily national in character, but now they are increasingly global operations.

A similar transformation is taking place in the nature and composition of audiences for television. The arrival of digital technology has ushered in two separate but distinct developments in television production. On the one hand, the number of channels available has been vastly increased; on the other, dramatic technical improvements have led to CD-quality of sound and the introduction of widescreen. Three significant developments are predicted as a result of these advances.

■ **There will be increased fragmentation of audiences**

Viewers already have access to a wide range of channels. The tendency will be for people to pick and mix their programmes, drawing up their own individual schedules, perhaps storing them on

extended digital recording devices. They can then 'time-shift' their viewing to suit themselves. Loyalty to any one station will simply disappear.

■ **There will be a much greater thrust towards globalised production**

Economies of scale and the pressures to create hit programmes will lead to greater standardisation; this in turn will have a huge impact on world culture. Hollywood films already dominate the world: fast-food culture has rapidly followed, with sitcoms, chat shows and confessionals in hot pursuit. Cultural colonisation of this kind is likely to continue, with the United States leading the way. So, does global culture really mean American culture? Do we really have nothing about our own society that is not worth representing?

■ **Greater interactivity will emerge as a significant feature of the new digital era**

Home shopping is already here, and increasing rapidly, as is the wealth of information services, such as films on demand, on digital television. The greatest leap, however, is likely to be in the growth of two-way communications facilities. As the technologies of broadcasting and the Internet converge, merely accessing content may not be sufficient to satisfy consumers: the opportunities for individuals to turn into broadcasters may well be what drives the next generation. Personal websites, often with cameras attached, are already commonplace. The next logical step could be for individuals to start generating their own content for transmission.

Analysing audiences

Broadcasters and advertisers have their own pressing reasons for wishing to know more about the people who consume their products. Media academics, of course, have an equal enthusiasm to study these groups, but a quite different agenda in relation to purposes and, especially, to methods.

The general history of developments in media audience analysis is outlined in chapter 1 (see pp. 25–32). The current trend is towards a much closer focus on the way that the people who make up the audience actually conduct their lives.

In a curiously striking way, this trend chimes in rather neatly with the possible scenario outlined in the last section. With the advent of greater opportunities for two-way communication, the ways in which people communicate with each other will be the natural place to study the social and cultural forces that are shaping their lives. Discourse analysis has flourished in recent years as a new and exciting approach to tackling precisely these areas.

DISCOURSE ANALYSIS

Deriving in part from traditions in literary studies, discourse analysis is concerned with the analysis of modes of communication. It seeks to identify social beliefs and shared cultural values through studying the ways in which people talk and write. All human communication, it suggests, is composed of complex structural processes. If these can be clarified and scrutinised carefully, the underlying assumptions can be traced, and the processes of ideological transmission laid bare. There is in this discipline a particular fascination with social control, and the persuasive potential of dominant interest groups.

The French theorist Michel Foucault developed a sophisticated theory of social processes, which has been especially influential in this field. He saw society as a complex series of overlapping, but separately developing discourses.

Martin Barker, of Sussex University, makes the observation that language is never 'innocent'. The very ways in which we talk and write are shaped and determined by the activities and interests of particular groups in society – to which we do not even need to belong, ourselves, for them to be influencing us. All language uses 'contain forms that structure the contents of what we say'. What we say is laden with meanings that are predetermined, beyond our control, and above all 'create and maintain relations between people'.

Discourse analysis is especially interested in *intertextuality*: the ways in which media texts relate to each other. No text exists in isolation in our media-rich world. We are all so steeped in the images of the texts that have gone before, that we cannot help but draw from them as we encounter a new one: in the same way that the creators of that text anticipate and expect that we will do.

Institutions and Policy

The television broadcasting environment

In the past ten years, there have been important changes in the regulations and operating environments of television in the United Kingdom. Similar changes have occurred in those of Australia, Canada and New Zealand. The operations of the media are closely bound to the currents of political thought in any given era. A profound revision took place in politics during the 1980's and beyond, and the impact it had on the media is significant and enduring.

Since at least World War II, most Western democracies have carefully regulated the television broadcasting environment. Regulations were based on several justifications.

BROADCASTING AS A NATIONAL RESOURCE The airwaves were seen as national property to be used in the national interest for the good of the public. The 'public service' notion of broadcasting was established at the outset, with the BBC being the first and only broadcaster in the United Kingdom for a long time.

SPECTRUM SCARCITY The television broadcasting spectrum is limited and therefore a scarce resource. There could only ever be a limited number of television channels. Spectrum usage therefore required regulations at least in part as a rationing measure.

TELEVISION'S POWER Unlike newspapers, television has constant access to every living room in the country. This is felt to give it an influence that is potentially far greater than any other medium. At the same time, in view of its intrusion into the heart of the family home, careful limits must be set on the nature of the material that is transmitted.

CONFLICTS OF INTEREST Commercial profit motives were seen as often being in opposition to the needs of democracy and the principles of quality broadcasting. External regulation was the only possible way of ensuring quality provision.

PRESENT TRENDS

By the 1990s, political, social and technological changes meant earlier justifications for regulation no longer had widespread support from government. These changes included the following:

■ The 'free market'

The dominance of the idea of the 'free market' as a solution to *all* the nation's economic problems was also applied to broadcasting. This in turn brought a desire for less regulation. In Britain, especially, the government led a crusade against the interference of the 'Nanny State'. The market would sort its own problems out, this philosophy asserted – it did not need the interference of government.

■ Multi-channel television

Cable and satellite systems became capable of delivering hundreds of new channels. Instead of everyone looking at the same few channels, there was suddenly the potential for a bewildering choice. This weakened the idea of spectrum scarcity and the need for regulation to ration resources.

■ Globalisation

The worldwide intermeshing of television is called globalisation. Globalisation has its recent history in the development of multinational corporations. These huge business empires, such as Rupert Murdoch's News International, have capital resources larger than the entire economic output of many small and medium-sized nations. Movements to encourage freer world trade have also encouraged trade in media products and the spread of multinational media corporations. Satellite and cable technology have contributed to the process by opening up the airwaves.

The idea of globalisation has an earlier echo in the work of Marshall McLuhan, who wrote of the 'global village' in the 1960s. In the 'global village', the instantaneous nature of modern communications broke down the barriers of time, space, national or geographical differences.

■ Localisation

Many analysts believe that globalisation is being accompanied by the opposite trend of localisation. They use the word 'local' in the sense of regional and also to cover a range of narrow groupings of people across individual societies or even across the world. Local could therefore mean people living in the Midlands – or, in the case of the new Restricted Service Licences (RSLs), which are much more specific as to location) Asians living in Leicester. It could also be used to mean everyone around the world interested in the music of U2, for example. Multi-channel television is capable of narrowly targeting like-minded subcultural audiences who may find the mainstream channels irrelevant.

Localisation may occur as the 'social glue' provided by the old national media gradually loses its strength. Some analysts see the trend as positive because it allows more media rights for subcultural or local groups. Others believe it is a two-edged sword, with as many potential negatives as positives.

LOSS OF A NATION?

In between the two extremes of global and local, the importance of the nation may be under threat. In the past, we worried about a world where society was dominated by a handful of media outlets. However, the problems of creating some sort of consensus in a society where people will no longer be sharing the same sort of media experiences may be still greater. This could pose a threat to the very notion of democracy.

Some analysts have even wondered whether the forces of globalisation and the forces of localism will need the surviving nation more than ever – to mediate between them!

Public service versus commercial television

In public service broadcasting, television producers receive the money to make programmes. In the commercial sector, it is the reverse. They make

Figure 4.5
Some analysts see pay television as the beginning of a larger movement known as 'convergence'. Convergence is the merging of forms of delivery. Pay television, the Internet, telephones and computer-based media will combine in the near future.

They call it CABLE TV ... but until they settle which channel out of the twenty they'll watch ... I call it INTERACTIVE ...

programmes in order to get the money.

For a number of years now, there has been ongoing debate as to whether there is still a place for public service provision in broadcasting. Or, more specifically, how it should be funded and how big it should be. The licence fee, in particular, is a source of ongoing controversy. The BBC naturally wishes to see it continue – and continue to increase, annually, to help meet rising costs and future development plans. Commercial companies, on the other hand, resent the fact that these revenues are so readily available to their chief rival. This rival does not have to do anything to secure these funds – the government simply delivers them to the BBC. The commercial companies, of course, have to work to get their income, by selling advertising space.

Having an equal competitor such as the BBC lessens their own revenues, as their income depends on the size of the audiences they can attract – the amount they can charge for their advertising services is directly related to this.

The nature of the media reflects the nature of society. Therefore, the debate is really over what kind of society people want. Both sides seem to agree that they want a television environment that promotes freedom; however, both sides in the debate do not mean the same thing by freedom. Public service television argues for 'freedom from …'. Commercial television argues for 'freedom to …'.

PUBLIC SERVICE TELEVISION

In public service television, the core belief is that it is free from the pressures of commercial television – which is driven by the need to maximise revenues at all times. As its income is guaranteed, public service television is freer to explore, innovate and invest in quality provision.

This does not mean that it can become complacent and forget about the need to maintain healthy audience sizes. Were it to fall behind the commercial companies significantly, there would soon be a serious challenge to the continuance of the licence fee.

In the United Kingdom, Australia, Canada and New Zealand, public service television has been organised along broadly similar lines. Michael Tracey, of the University of Colorado in the United States, has studied a range of public service

broadcasters around the world and developed a number of principles. These form the basis of the public broadcaster's definition of freedom.

1. UNIVERSAL AVAILABILITY Public broadcasters tend to make sure their signal is available to as many people as possible. This is not to maximise the audience, but as a right of citizenship. The aim is to serve the *whole population*.

2. UNIVERSAL APPEAL Programmes are produced with a real concern for quality *and* to appeal to a wide range of tastes, not just to 'high culture' elites (such as opera lovers). The populism that leads to cultural mediocrity, however, is also to be avoided.

3. DIVERSITY AND PROVISION FOR MINORITIES Public service television provides access to the media for disadvantaged or minority groups. In a multicultural society, public service television should be pluralist and diverse.

4. SERVING THE PUBLIC SPHERE A vital principle of the work of public broadcasting is that addresses, and helps to foster a sense of national identity. It must also motivate viewers to recognise their roles as *citizens*, possessing certain obligations as well as rights, in the society that they inhabit.

5. EDUCATION OF THE PUBLIC Educational programming ranging from school to university material demonstrates the public service broadcaster's view of the audience as a citizen with certain needs and rights, and of its own role in nourishing broad social and political literacy – vital to the health of a modern democracy

Figure 4.6
Globalisation means ever more television programmes aimed at a world audience. The Simpsons is an example of an effective global programme. One reason for its success is the fact that it is a cartoon and can therefore be dubbed into any language. Critics say that globalisation actually means Americanisation.

6. INDEPENDENCE Public service television can best serve the public when it is independent of both the government and commercial interests. Of equal importance is the encouragement of independent-minded programme-makers.

7. PROMOTION OF GOOD PROGRAMMING A full commitment is needed to making programmes of high quality, whatever the size or nature of their intended audience. The pressures of advertising organisations to allocate most resources to greatest audience numbers are to be resisted.

8. LIBERATE THE PROGRAMME-MAKERS Despite a continuing need for regulation of the broadcasting industry, those who make the programmes should be empowered to explore and develop the most original and interesting work of which they are capable. Even when this sometimes means challenging received ideas of what is acceptable. Managers have a crucial role to play in this.

CRITICISM The market opponents of public service television argue that it is funded as another, indirect, form of taxation. This was perhaps reasonable enough, when there was little alternative provision. With three terrestrial commercial channels, the arrival of satellite and cable, and especially the new multi-channel era, this is no longer reasonable, they assert. Many people pay considerable sums for these new services and are not interested in the public service channels: if they are not using them, why should they have to pay for them?

David Elstein, when head of BSkyB, pointed out that the ultimate sanction for non-payment of the licence fee is imprisonment! Even if rarely used, this is a poor reflection on the core idea of Public *Service* Broadcasting.

COMMERCIAL TELEVISION

In commercial television, 'freedom to …' tends to mean freedom to maximise profits. The undisputed purpose of industry is to make money. This sector argues that it can only do so by making good-quality, popular programmes.

In addition, they often cite the following points to support their arguments:

DIVERSITY Commercial broadcasters argue that the market creates the best chance of diversity of choice. People will only watch what they are interested in: commercial operators will cater for those tastes.

CONSUMER SOVEREIGNTY Commercial operators see the audience as consumers, rather than as citizens. The consumer is 'king', or sovereign, and rules by casting a vote for a particular programme through the ratings system (in the case of free-to-air television) or with cash (in the case of pay-TV). Of course, consumers with big wallets are worth more than the less well off.

CONSUMER CHOICE The contemporary consumer wishes to be exposed to as wide a choice as possible, supporters of the market argue. The consumer does not need educating or regulating.

CRITICISM Opponents of the market approach say that the only freedom it gives is to large multinational corporations. They dominate production and reduce the range and quality of programmes, only catering for big spending majorities. This also gives rise to the 'lowest common denominator' factor, where certain basic fascinations with sex, quizzes, chat shows, rows and celebrities are relied upon. Critics argue that diversity is reduced and national culture is impoverished. *Quality* and *popular* are largely incompatible concepts when it comes to programme-making.

In 1997, for example, ITV was severely criticised for its diminishing production of serious documentaries – a certain level of which it had promised in its licence application (*ITC Overview of ITV Performance*, March 1997). In their place, a rash of the new 'docu-soaps' had appeared, such as *Neighbours from Hell*. Although the argument may be that these programmes are very popular, they can in no way be seen as of the same kind as, or an equal replacement for, serious documentaries.

Deregulation

Deregulation stems from the belief that the 'free market' is the answer to all problems. Society, so the theory goes, had become too bogged down with rules and regulations: governments should adopt a more 'hands off' approach and allow the producers of goods in society to get on with doing things how they saw best. The television industry was no different.

For quite different reasons, the government was also very keen to 'reform' the BBC, in particular. Its declared intention was to make it more commercially minded and more responsive to its customers. In reality, more complex political and ideological goals were driving its actions. Devising alternative methods of funding was one important factor; reducing its independence and objectivity most certainly was another. Assisted by various voices in the right-wing press – especially that large chunk of it which belonged to Rupert Murdoch's News Corporation – it set about squeezing the BBC financially, and attacking it directly and indirectly.

REVIEWING TELEVISION PROVISION

The Peacock Committee was set up to investigate television provision in the United Kingdom. Ironically, this body actually turned its attention mainly to ITC and left the BBC largely alone. Its report, in 1986, recommended that the licence fee should continue to be the main method of funding. Most importantly, it also said that there should be no advertising on the BBC. It did introduce the notion of quotas of independent production, which was to have a significant impact on internal organisation and management of the BBC.

One of the most significant outcomes of this review was the decision to replace the old IBA (Independent Broadcasting Authority) with the ITC (Independent Television Commission) in 1990. This body had a much less demanding remit for monitoring output and practices: a 'light touch' form of regulation was required.

In addition, a new system of bidding for franchises was introduced. There had been complaints that the old method was opaque and unclear in its selection criteria. In the new one, interested companies were invited to submit sealed bids, with the award going to the highest. Bidders had to pass a 'quality threshold', guaranteeing a minimum standard of quality in the nature of the programming they would produce.

Overall, however, this new system of bidding did not produce any significant changes to the nature of the provision itself. Nor, indeed, did the experience make the participants any happier that a fairer process had been found. Moreover, the

ITC proved itself quite capable of interpreting its duties in a way that was more concerned with preserving the traditions of broadcasting than overturning them. This certainly had not been the intention of the government.

In the end, the BBC managed to survive more or less intact. Certainly, privatisation had been avoided – although many have questioned at what cost.

The BBC

The British Broadcasting Corporation was initially a broadcaster of radio only: when television arrived, it was regarded as a very poor relation to the all-powerful radio. Within the corporation, people were very snooty indeed about this new upstart and gave it little credibility or status. Many felt it would never catch on at all!

HISTORY The BBC was established by Royal Charter in 1926, after a brief identity as a private company. Although John Logie Baird had made his first successful television transmission in that very same year, it was not until 1936 that a regular service was offered – the world's first public service television channel. It did not last long, as the service was suspended when World War II broke out. Not until 1946 was a permanent service established; even then, it only had a range of forty miles (sixty-five kilometres) from its base in Alexander Palace, in North London.

Its first Director-General was John (later Lord) Reith. His influence on the identity and qualities of the institution was very profound. A stern Christian, he was demanding in his expectations of himself and of others. He saw from the outset the crucial role that the BBC could play in the life of the nation. He was determined that its guiding philosophy should be primarily concerned with social priorities, not financial ones.

It was Reith who coined the statement that the BBC's mission was 'to inform, educate and entertain (and to offer) the best in every sphere of human endeavour'. These are the core 'Reithian values' that are still taken to constitute the basis of public service broadcasting to this day (although many now find them rather paternalistic in their self-important view of what the public *should have* in their viewing).

One of the points on which he was firmest was that the BBC should be neutral in politics. He had a profound personal disdain for politics himself; however, beyond that, he also felt that impartiality was critical if they were to achieve *national* credibility. Too close an identification with party politics could soon tarnish the BBC's reputation, and lead to accusations of partisanship. Reith was undoubtedly authoritarian, even a bully, however, he was also enormously successful in setting up from scratch what was to be one of the most prestigious broadcasting organisations in the world for the remainder of the twentieth century.

THE VOICE OF THE NATION Some have questioned whether the BBC entirely deserves this reputation for impartiality. Curran and Seaton detail how, in the very year of its birth, it tamely accepted government restrictions on coverage given to the General Strike. This set a pattern that was to recur throughout the troubled times of the 1930s and was consolidated during World War II. Overt censorship has never been applied – it has never had to be. The BBC has always been careful to court the goodwill of government and avoid any too direct opposition to the line it takes.

It has always cultivated a role as a full, active and important member of the Establishment of this country. As such, it is naturally supportive of its central institutions. For many years, it served as a kind of voice of the nation. On major State occasions (royal weddings, the Coronation) and other significant national events (such as the FA Cup Final), it was the first choice of preferred television coverage – from public and participants alike. It has established a unique place in the heart of most people's sense of what Britain actually is.

Governments, nevertheless, have never been shy of reminding the BBC that it is dependent on them for the renewal of the licence fee. This system of funding is intended to make the BBC more independent – the famous 'arm's length' principle, whereby public institutions are funded out of public monies, but allowed to run themselves. It is clear, however, that the arm remains connected to the body of government and that the hand that doles out the money still has considerable clout.

THE FUTURE Britain is quite unique in having had a public institution such as the BBC lead the development of broadcasting. In most other countries, commercial operators have assumed that role. With the explosion of new channels arriving in the digital era, however, it is debatable whether the BBC will be able to continue in its present form. Today's, media incur huge business costs in keeping abreast of contemporary developments. At present, the trend is towards merger and concentration of businesses in fewer and larger enterprises. In the United States, Disney has already bought ABC, News Corp the Fox film studios, and Viacom have recently taken over CBS – this latter to form a company worth £80 billion! These organisations dwarf the BBC and, on the basis of the licence fee alone, it is inconceivable that it will be able to remain a significant player in this spiralling market in the United Kingdom, never mind the rest of the world.

The implications of this for the current licensing system are serious. Without a reasonable market share, it is unlikely that the current licence fee will be able to survive – if the majority of viewers are watching other things, the pressure to abolish it will be enormous, from viewers and commercial operators alike.

One way or another, it seems likely that some other method of funding – whether through a form of privatisation or some mixture of private and public funding – is inescapable and likely to come in the very near future, at that.

ITV

In September 1955, the ITA (Independent Television Authority) began transmissions. This was a wholly new venture in this country – a system where funding derived entirely from advertising. Considerable debate had taken place over whether it should be allowed at all. Commercial pressures won out, however, and the steady expansion into provision of a new, alternative service was under way. In fact, it was to take almost until the end of the decade to make it a truly national one: a series of separate operating companies were gradually established, covering different regional broadcasting areas. Some programmes would be transmitted in common – 'networked' – and others would be chosen for the different regions, with some made specifically for particular regions. This is broadly the pattern that remains today, with various changes of operator.

From the outset, it was also announced that a specialist news service would be provided by the Independent Television News Company (ITN) and that this service would be offered across all the Independent Television (ITV) companies.

Clearly, a good deal of this structure remains intact. However, much has also changed: not only the companies running the services, but also even the services being offered.

In 1982, Channel 4 was born, probably one of the most innovative and exciting developments in the entire British television industry. Breakfast television, cable and satellite were soon to follow.

Channel 4

The way in which this new service was to be administered was new and quite unique. A wholly owned subsidiary of the IBA, it was financed by a subscription levied on the ITV companies. These, in turn, were enabled to sell the advertising space it brought with it within their local regions.

It has to be said that the channel got off to something of a shaky start and, in the early days, there were often many gaps where insufficient advertisements could be found to fill the time allocated. This slow start was not aided by the remit of the new channel to 'encourage innovation and experiment' (Broadcasting Act, 1980). The core philosophy of Channel 4 has always been to target minority audiences and develop new kinds of programmes. Its first Chief Executive, Jeremy Isaacs, took this challenge to unprecedented, often startling heights. For a time, it developed a certain notoriety as the 'sex and swearing' channel.

Despite this, Channel 4 steadily established a very favourable following among the young, in particular. By 1992, it had narrowly overtaken BBC2 in its share of the total British television audience. Innovations in funding of films, which were also released to cinemas overseas, and many controversial programmes dealing with daring and difficult topics, soon gave it a clear identity. The crucial eighteen- to thirty-year-old audience firmly identified with the new channel. This group is now a highly desirable target for advertisers because of its lucrative levels of disposable income. Competition for advertising space grew, as did revenues from it. So much so that, in the early

1990s, under its next chief Michael Grade, it was to lead a campaign to have the advertising space brought under its own control – completely reversing the source of complaints about the system which had initially been made. In 1998, although some changes had been made to the funding formula, it paid £90 million to the ITC for distribution to the ITV companies.

One other unique feature of this channel is that it is the only one to offer dedicated minority

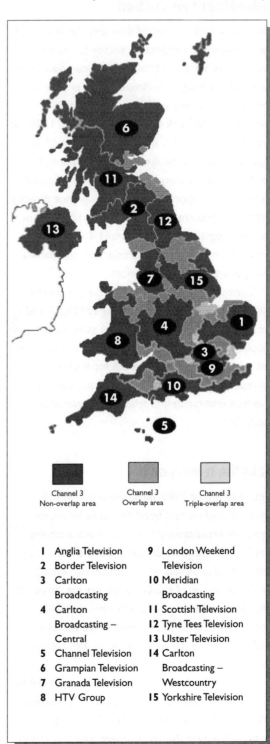

1	Anglia Television
2	Border Television
3	Carlton Broadcasting
4	Carlton Broadcasting – Central
5	Channel Television
6	Grampian Television
7	Granada Television
8	HTV Group
9	London Weekend Television
10	Meridian Broadcasting
11	Scottish Television
12	Tyne Tees Television
13	Ulster Television
14	Carlton Broadcasting – Westcountry
15	Yorkshire Television

Channel 3
Non-overlap area

Channel 3
Overlap area

Channel 3
Triple-overlap area

Figure 4.7
Map of the fifteen regional Channel 3 (ITV) franchises and their licensees, in 2001. (Source: ITC)

language broadcasting. S4C is a Welsh-language service, providing a range of programmes for people in that community. Initially, government proposals backed away from a manifesto promise to establish a full service. Coordinated and sustained protest from Welsh-language campaigners, however, led to a policy reversal and the dedicated channel was established as originally outlined.

Independent production

The creation of Channel 4 also saw the advent of the independent production sector for British television. A number of voices had been clamouring for this for a long time. Broadcasting production was very much tied up in the 'comfortable duopoly' (cf. Peacock Committee Report, 1986) of the BBC and ITV. This had led to charges of weak representation of the diverse communities of contemporary society – and moreover of scant employment opportunities for anyone not directly employed by them. From the outset, some 30 per cent of programming for Channel 4 was commissioned from independent production companies, giving this area a massive boost.

Curiously, it had been mainly people on the political left who had been calling for this – and yet it was very much a right-wing government that supplied it. Its reasons for doing so, however, were not in order to answer the call for increased representation of minority voices, so much as to give free enterprise a foothold in the television industries.

Satellite television

Until the end of 1989, most television in the United Kingdom had been delivered by means of *terrestrial* broadcasting (a series of transmitters and booster stations dotted around the country, using *analogue* signals and received via aerials). With the arrival of *satellite* broadcasting, however, the older method had a brash new rival. This system relies on a *dish* to receive transmissions, as well as a *decoder* to turn the signal into pictures and sound.

In part, this development had been spurred by the 1977 World Radio Administrative Conference (WRAC) allocation of five DBS channels to Britain. However, the government also saw the key

opportunity for 'possible industrial benefits' (W. Whitelaw). The construction of satellites themselves was seen as a useful way of boosting Britain's aerospace industries. Setting up a UK broadcasting service using this technology would be a crucial part of establishing a reputation in this field.

In December 1986, the IBA awarded the franchise to British Satellite Broadcasting (BSB): it took nearly another four years to get its system operational. Meanwhile, the feared launch of a rival service finally occurred in February 1989, when Rupert Murdoch's Sky took off. By the time BSB began, people had already begun to invest in the dishes for the earlier system. The publicity that Murdoch had been able to generate for his service – greatly aided by his ownership of several national newspaper titles in this country – meant that the momentum needed to match this could never quite be achieved.

In fact, start-up costs for both these operations had been so heavy that *both* were running heavy losses. By November 1990, a plan for merger was agreed and BSkyB was born.

In the end, none of the ambitions that had been laid out as reasons for establishing a satellite broadcasting service had actually been achieved:

► no UK technology had been used either to establish or to run the service
► there was no UK control
► UK material was only a small portion of the programme output.

Cable television

Cable television has actually been in existence for quite a long time in this country, beginning its life well before satellite. Recently, there has been a great deal of activity delivering the new fibre optic cable to the majority of UK homes.

Prior to 1979, cable services had been on a very small scale only – a 'narrowband' facility, largely devoted to supplying existing terrestrial programmes and mainly in areas where reception by aerial was poor. In the early 1980s, however, its fortunes began to improve. New 'broadband' capacity was introduced, greatly expanding the number of channels on offer.

What brought about this transformation was a combination of political and technological factors.

In the United States, the cable industry was booming, with some ten million subscribers already signed up and a steady flow of new ones joining daily. This service offered a range of other facilities, such as Home Box Office, and the call was for Britain to offer something similar. The arrival of the newer, high-capacity fibre optic cables had opened up the possibilities in terms of the range of services that could be offered. Here, the inclusion of telephony perhaps more than anything else made the business an attractive one to investors. Deregulation of the telecommunications industry in particular made it a target for US money, for this was still rigidly separated from television services in that country.

The 1984 Cable and Broadcasting Act put in place a very loose regulatory framework – there were no 'quality programming' restrictions such as applied to the terrestrial companies, for instance. The need to 'liberalise' British broadcasting policy and lift constraints so that business could flourish had been clearly spelt out. The government responded fully to this call, only stipulating limits to levels of foreign ownership, and programme content.

Despite all this, however, British investors were very slow to get involved. Out of twenty franchises awarded in 1983, only seven were in operation by 1986. Taking stock of the problems, the 1990 Broadcasting Act removed the restrictions on foreign investment. Shortly afterwards, things began to develop much more rapidly. Strangely, despite fears of the opposite effect, the launch of satellite television actually helped to boost business for cable. The publicity it generated helped the general public to become much more aware of the alternatives to the terrestrial diet on which they had been brought up.

The key features that were used to promote cable an attractive option were:

► the inclusion of telephony, particularly with the growth in telecommuting
► the facility for home shopping
► the possibilities of video-on-demand.

In reality, cable has actually developed mainly on the facilities it offers in additional television provision. Telephone services have played a significant part, but the much-vaunted interactivity that has long been promised has yet to materialise. Take-up as a whole has not been as high as forecast. .

Moreover, the two big boosts for Britain that were identified as prime reasons for setting up the entire cable industry have not been realised either:

► significant levels of British investment/ownership have not occurred – of 127 franchises allocated by 1993, only four were wholly British
► neither has British industry benefited much. BT was the only company even to attempt to get involved and it withdrew from any serious activity quite early on.

Channel 5

Some have speculated that the decision to approve the establishment of this new channel came about, politically, because of the Peacock Report's failure to recommend advertising on the BBC. Certainly, there was considerable commercial pressure from advertisers to find some way to break the stranglehold that ITV had over this field, and especially to bring down the high prices it was able to charge.

In 1992, bids were invited for this licence. Only one was forthcoming, however, and that was rejected as unsatisfactory by the ITC. The general economic difficulties of the late 1980s were clearly still affecting business confidence. In 1995, following an upturn in the economy, a second round of invitations brought forth bids from four consortia. In the end, Channel Five Broadcasting was awarded the licence – but only after the ITC had exercised some discretion in its assessment of the relative qualities of the bids. Two of them had been ruled out, including the highest bidder. Once more, the original conception of the bidding process had been deftly sidestepped.

High start-up costs and doubts about the likely levels of advertising revenue dogged the birth of this channel. Today, it seems quite firmly established and has certainly succeeded in carving out a distinctive identity for itself.

Digital television

The entire future of broadcasting resides in this development. In essence, digital is a form of technology that transmits television signals in a different way. Its chief advantage is that it compresses sound and visual information far more than the old analogue system. This allows for many more channels to be broadcast. Some of the possible benefits of this may include:

▶ staggered starts for key programmes, such as feature films, allowing consumers choice in viewing times
▶ more control over the *nature* of the viewing (e.g. choice of camera angle in a sports programme)
▶ better quality of sound and pictures
▶ home shopping
▶ Internet connection.

Many of these diverse functions can already be based around the common facility of a television set – and the plan is to add in electronic games facilities, home cinema, and so on. Multi-function screens are the development target for manufacturers and service providers alike.

The government has already announced the end of analogue transmission. All new television sets now have in-built digital capacity. Although digital transmission is available as an option for viewers now, it will shortly become the only means of receiving a signal.

▼ ▼ ▼ ▼ ▼ ▼ ▼

activities

1. The beliefs that led to a heavily regulated television broadcasting environment after World War II still have value for some analysts. Discuss their relevance in terms of today's television. To what extent was the old 'duopoly' useful and productive?

2. Can you find any evidence of the idea that television works as 'social glue'? Identify large-scale events that have occurred in the past few years and discuss the ways in which they were picked up and responded to by the media at the time, as well as the audiences the programmes covering these events drew.

3. Examine the case for the continuation of public service broadcasting in the United Kingdom. With the advent of hundreds of new channels in the digital age, will there still be a place for it? What about funding: should this continue to be via the licence fee or should some other method be found? If so, what possibilities for doing this fairly can you think of?

4. To what extent have the United Kingdom's commercial television companies lived up to claims of promoting freedom of choice, diversity and consumer sovereignty?

Television News: Purposes and Functions

The world view of the middle-aged, middle-class male is being challenged by those who do not want to be patronised, or told what is really meaningful. We can make our own minds up.

Suzanne Moore, *The Independent*
7 November 1997

▼ ▼ ▼

NEWS FROM THE FRONT DESK

Only a short while ago, television companies were being criticised for their over-reliance on male journalists and presenters. Today, the imbalance appears to have been addressed: all stations now have a range of women in key positions (although

this still does not mean that they are represented in equal numbers). Now it is even possible to have a female presenter addressing female correspondents. The only surprise is in how long it took them to remedy this shortcoming.

The arrival of Kirsty Young on Channel 5 in the late 1990s helped to shake up ideas about the way in which the news could be presented. Perching *on* the desk, rather than sitting behind it, walking around a bright, busy newsroom, conversational rather than lecturing, she brought a new informality to the craft of newsreading. Other channels were not long in making changes of their own.

Some critics have accused television of 'tabloidising' the news, arguing that these changes have tended to trivialise and dumb down the contents – Channel 4's *Big Breakfast*, for example. Others have welcomed an overhaul they felt was long overdue, claiming that a less Westminster-dominated, more consumer-focused programme is more appropriate for the mood of the times.

Certainly, there has been much rearrangement of the whole business of news presentation – not least with the historic shift of ITV's flagship, *News at Ten*, to the later time of 11 p.m. Subsequently, there was a tense confrontation over this move between the companies and the ITC, the regulator for commercial television. An early suggestion that the BBC might like to move into the vacant time slot was initially angrily rejected. Later, it did precisely that.

THE NATURE OF NEWS

Media analysts J. Galtung and M. Ruge say that all news is actually 'olds'. The regular structure of the story, the kinds of people interviewed, the sorts of pictures and so on – all are part of a pattern. The stories and topics that make the news today are just the same ones that have always made good news stories. They have become traditional: politics, murders, disasters, crimes and accidents are really endless repeats.

Even new and unexpected events are shown in terms of traditional and regular patterns. The old ways are not examined with new perspectives. Rather, the new is constantly evaluated using old perspectives.

THE SOCIAL PURPOSE OF NEWS

Coverage of the day's events has always been one of the key public service functions of television. Now up-to-the-minute and round-the-clock, it has also become one of its most keenly contested areas. CNN, the US-based news service, has turned itself into a global industry, from quite modest cable origins. News gathering is big business, too.

THE NEWS AS MYTH

The television news is probably the first programme an adult viewer sits down to after a hard day at work. The events of the individual's day at work are still spinning in his or her memory. The television news presents the main outside world events of the day – the 'big picture' to match the viewer's 'little picture'. In some indefinable way, it helps the individual to know it has been a 'big day' for everyone!

Entertaining as much as informing, the news programme is divided into short dramatic 'stories'. Many of these 'stories' are similar in nature to the police dramas and situation comedies that follow later in the night. Just as ancient societies used myths to pass on the tribal identity, attitudes and beliefs, the television news passes on modern society's view of the day's events. Social and cultural identity is generated around the events that are selected for presentation – particularly so in the ways in which they are reported.

It is this mythical aspect of the news that the individual uses to make sense of his or her world.

Figure 4.8
Discussion should reflect the true weight and diversity of opinion on any given topic. In practice, vested interests and 'experts' are usually given more coverage.

Figure 4.9
*Television news
programmes have
their own way of
reporting stories,
just as much
as newspapers
do. Usually,
the differences
are rather
more subtle.*

THE FUNCTIONS OF TELEVISION NEWS

The essential features of news coverage can be summarised as follows.

FAIRNESS AND BALANCE The news should offer a balance of opposing viewpoints. The weight of differing opinion in the community should be reflected in the news services so that the community sees more than one viewpoint from each channel.

INFORMATION Television news should present an accurate and factual account of the events of the moment. It should broadcast all issues of public importance, including the most controversial.

EXPLANATION More than bare facts are needed. Events need to be explained, placed in perspective and analysed. News and current affairs programmes should examine issues from the variety of viewpoints that exist in society. Discussion should reflect the true weight of opinion in the community.

ENTERTAINMENT Television is an entertainment medium. News and current affairs should be prepared in an interesting and appealing format. At the same time, entertainment should not undermine the community's right to knowledge and information.

INDEPENDENCE The news should be 'reasonably' independent from the commercial pressures that apply to other sections of the television station. It also should be free of government manipulation.

THE SUBJECT MATTER

Although news on television is often thought to be about the unexpected and new, it is easily divided into routine categories. Anything that falls outside the categories or is too unusual does not appear.

- **POLITICS** covers government, parliament, politicians and policies.
- **THE ECONOMY** features the stock market and the national economic performance, including trade, unemployment, interest and exchange rates, and inflation.
- **FOREIGN AFFAIRS** presents news on international relations and also shows events in other countries.
- **NATIONAL AFFAIRS** concerns major crime, industrial relations, the environment, the law and so on. Conflict is an essential ingredient for audience interest.
- **HUMAN INTEREST STORIES** concentrate on entertainment, rather than information. Celebrities make regular appearances, along with extraordinary animals and amusing 'and finally …' stories.
- **DISASTERS** appear regularly on the news and, if the pictures are dramatic, the story could go right to the top of the bulletin.
- **SPORT** nearly always appears at the end of the bulletin. Conflict is the essential ingredient and competitive sport the main focus.

This order does represent a rough hierarchy of

importance, although position within it can vary according to the precise nature and scale of the particular story.

So what is it that we do not get? There are vast areas of social life that never appear on television news. Little is said about the lives of ordinary people. Men appear more than women. Public life is shown, while private life is seen as unimportant. Personal relations, sexuality, family life, working conditions and so on are all invisible.

Moreover, the point of view in the topics that are covered tends to favour the official and the managerial. Very little attention is paid to those without some kind of status. Locations used for interviews endorse and support the authority of the figures consulted – or lack of it!

Roles and relationships in news

The news ranks both people and events according to their significance or power. This gives them a position of importance in the bulletin. Further to that, the structure of the news story itself is also a hierarchy. Important facts go first, less important facts are stated later in the story.

THE NEWSREADER The all-knowing news reader speaks directly to, and looks directly at, the audience. The newsreader is shown in mid close-up and dominates the screen. He or she appears to be in command and delegates stories to the reporters.

THE REPORTERS The news reporter also looks the audience directly in the eye. Reporters are usually shown in a medium shot of head, shoulders and upper body.

AUTHORITY FIGURES Reporters ask questions of people with authority in a given organisation. These leaders are never given access to the news-reader. While talking, they look at the reporter. In fact, advisers often tell them not to look directly at the audience as it makes them seem shifty.

Figure 4.10
The autocue allows the newsreader to read the news from the lens of the camera. Angled glass over the lends acts as a mirror. The autocue faces upwards and projects the script onto the angled glass and into the newsreader's line of sight.

THE VIEWERS Those people at the bottom of the hierarchy are never seen (except in the ratings). They are the viewers.

THE NEWSREADER

Television news is a series of disjointed reports. The newsreader is the only link between them. The newsreader is also the only link between the reporters, the events and the audience. He or she appears to know how everything happening in the world has fitted together. This position of authority corresponds to that of a priest behind the pulpit or a schoolteacher at the blackboard.

Newsreaders aim for authority and credibility. The reporters are in the field and the newsreader is almost like a ringmaster, coordinating reports and calling for them from all quarters of the globe. They have to have an air of authority and a suitably serious manner; however, they have also to project an image that is warm and human

To give the viewers the impression that their presentation is 'just for them', newsreaders must constantly look the viewer in the eye. They avoid looking down at their pages by using the autocue.

▼ ▼ ▼ ▼ ▼ ▼ ▼

activities

1. On the news, new events are defined using old patterns and perspectives.

A radio telescope has received coherent signals indicating signs of life in outer space. Few details have been deciphered, except that the life forms are at least as advanced as humans and are relatively nearby.

The world is at once overjoyed and panicking. Make sense of the event by planning a news report using the traditional patterns. Use the questions below as a guide.

▶ Who would you interview? What would you ask them?

▶ What other film would you take?

▶ What graphics or maps would be used? Describe some examples.

▶ Are there any people or scenes you would *not* include?

2. Study the introduction sequences for national and/or local news programmes. Describe and compare the visual images, the music and any graphics used. What effects are they being used to try to generate? How does this differ from one station/programme to another?

3. The news has a hierarchical structure. This can be understood by acting out the opposite. Form small groups and prepare a dramatic script for one of the following scenes. Act out the scene, video it, then ask the class to comment on the effects of the reversal.

▶ A reporter interviews an ordinary member of a crowd of protesters, ignoring a leader and spokesperson.

▶ A community leader forces a reporter to justify his or her actions and explain his or her opinions.

▶ A group of reporters sends the newsreader out to do his or her own stories.

4. There are more than just a few points of similarity between newsreaders, priests and teachers. Make a list of them.

5. The job of the newsreader is to reassure the viewers. This can be understood by acting out the

reverse. Form a group and prepare a news segment as follows.

▶ Prepare a collection of disturbing and serious news reports. Delegate them to members of the group who will act as reporters.

▶ Have a group member act as newsreader. Instead of reassuring viewers, this newsreader is unfriendly, prone to depression and sometimes aggressive.

Present the news segments and ask for class comment. Now act out some other unusual behaviours for newsreaders. What is the class reaction?

6. Suppose you are a news journalist seeking fairness and balance. List the range of opinions you would seek, or the main community groups, you would need to interview, on the following news events.

▶ an accident at a nuclear power plant

▶ a proposed woodchip industry in an historic forest area

▶ increases in taxation

▶ immigration cutbacks.

7. Pick an important story that interests you on the television news. Jot down all the facts. Now compare your list with the coverage in a major newspaper. Write a brief report on your findings.

8. Compare the evening news bulletins on different television stations. To do this, you will need to allocate different class members or groups to each of the competing programmes. As you watch the news, fill in a table similar to the one shown on the opposite page.

Collate your findings, documenting the following:

▶ overall number of stories

▶ degree of similarity between stations

▶ differences in the order of priority given to the same story

▶ differences in amount of time devoted to stories.

Considering the needs of several selected audience groupings, recommend the best television news for each that is available in your area.

Figure 4.11

EVENING NEWS BULLETIN COMPARISON

TV STATION	STORY TITLE	FOREIGN DOMESTIC OR BOTH	POSITION IN BULLETIN	TIME TAKEN
Politics				
Business and the economy				
Industrial relations (unions and management)				
National affairs	Ozone hole	Both	5	30 seconds
Disasters				
Human interest				
Sport				
Foreign affairs				

9. Write a short paragraph explaining the meaning of the cartoon at right (figure 4.12). Give an indication of the nature of television news that may have inspired the cartoonist to draw this cartoon.

Comment on the meaning of this cartoon and its relevance to recent news bulletins.

Figure 4.12

The Structure of Television News

Most news programmes begin with short, one-line summaries of the key news items. These serve as appetisers, or 'hooks' both to *engage* interest and to *retain* it once the programme has begun. If interest in the immediate item begins to wander, curiosity about the remainder should help to keep the viewer watching the programme.

On commercial television, the process is repeated just before the commercial break. The intention, again, is to keep the audience watching, to capture people's attention so that they will want to know the detail behind the headlines. The BBC news has a similar midpoint refresher, even though there is no formal break in its bulletins. Television news is constantly stretched between the need to keep things moving and the obligation to go into sufficient detail to do the story justice.

Television news reports begin with a lead of about twenty-five words. This is similar to the newspaper intro. The remainder of the report tends to be structured conversationally. As in a conversation between two people, the events naturally unfold in chronological order.

In contrast, a newspaper story is structured using the inverted pyramid model. Newspaper stories are much more inclined to ignore chronological order and jump all over the place (see p. 417). This structure is forced on newspaper reports because editors cut stories from the bottom paragraphs upwards.

Television news reports are not shortened by leaving out the last few scenes. Instead, scenes can usually be cut out from any point in the report, except the lead.

The lead

The first sentence (or sometimes two) of a television news story is called the *lead*. In television news, the lead is the equivalent of the intro in a newspaper story.

Television news is written for people who are probably not paying attention. Leads must catch and hold the viewer's attention and summarise the important parts of the story.

FEATURES OF THE LEAD

A lead is written in a conversational or narrative style. It is designed to highlight the most dramatic part of the story. The exciting and important parts of the news story should follow, just as they would if you were telling them to a friend.

To tell 'who', 'what', 'when' and 'where' is the aim of all news stories. Broadcast news leads tend to emphasise a couple of these aspects, rather than trying to force them all into the lead at once.

Figure 4.13
A newswriter's decision to use a certain type of lead can depend on the personal style of the newsreader.

WHO is the most important element because the news is about people. Identifying the subject prepares the viewer for the likely nature of the item to follow. In television news, titles are often combined with the names of important or well-known people. Prime Minister Y of Israel, for example. Often first names will be left out if the name is familiar to listeners. Ordinary people are usually given labels such as 'a woman' or 'an unemployed labourer'.

WHAT is the next key element. Unless something has happened, there can be no news. Important new developments, or unexpected events for the people involved, are the most favoured. The hierarchy of importance will shift according to the scale of the particular story.

WHEN can be indicated with the verb tense. If the verb is in the present tense, the news is assumed to have happened today or else still to be happening. Otherwise, the time should be stated. A fresh story is always more interesting than an old one. 'When' also determines the importance of the news event.

WHERE the story is located is also important. It will determine the importance of the news. Faraway disasters rank lower in importance than nearby disasters. National stories take priority over local ones. However, local ones can go up the league of importance if sufficiently dramatic.

TYPES OF LEADS

There are four main types of leads and the choice is up to the writer. A number of factors can influence the writer's decision to use a certain type of lead. Some stories demand certain types of leads. News stories breaking right at the moment, for example, cannot be given leads suitable for feature stories.

HARD NEWS LEADS are used for first release stories and updates. These stress the immediacy of the event and rely on information that is timely. Hard news leads diminish in value as time passes. A hard news lead is shown below.

▼ ▼ ▼

TWO PEOPLE ARE DEAD AND 40,000 ARE HOMELESS TONIGHT IN THE WAKE OF

HURRICANE ANDREW, WHICH RIPPED THROUGH THE BAHAMAS LAST NIGHT.

▼ ▼ ▼

FEATURE LEADS are used for background stories if 'when' is not a main factor. For example, a story on a terrorist group planting a bomb is hard news. A story about the growth of terrorism in the Middle East is a feature story and could be held for several days without losing its importance. A feature lead is shown below.

▼ ▼ ▼

THOUSANDS OF TOURISTS COULD BE HOLIDAYING IN SPACE IN THE NEXT 30 YEARS UNDER A BOLD NEW AMERICAN SPACE PROGRAM.

▼ ▼ ▼

SOFT NEWS LEADS introduce a story with a human-interest angle. Soft news focuses on celebrities and the unusual antics of ordinary people. A soft news lead is shown below.

▼ ▼ ▼

LOLLIPOP LADIES IN LIVERPOOL – THE LATEST VICTIMS OF ROAD RAGE – ARE SIGNING UP FOR SELF-DEFENCE TRAINING TO LEARN HOW TO COPE WITH AGGRESSIVE DRIVERS.

▼ ▼ ▼

THROWAWAY LEADS were developed with the understanding that people are not paying full attention to the television set. They may be involved in any number of distracting activities.

To help the audience, the facts are repeated later in the story – often in the second sentence. Viewers do not notice, however, because the wording is different and detail is added. The throwaway lead simply cues them to listen to the story and catch the details on the second time round.

A throwaway lead is shown below, with the repetition underlined. Note that a few extra facts are added to hide the repetition in this case, although many throwaway leads simply repeat the same details in a different way.

▼ ▼ ▼

THE BRISTOL HEADQUARTERS OF A BIKERS' GROUP WAS BLOWN APART EARLY THIS MORNING. THE FRONT OF THE HELLS ANGELS' BRICK HIDEOUT IN THE ST PAUL'S AREA WAS BLOWN OUT BY THE BLAST AT ABOUT 8.30 A.M.

▼ ▼ ▼

UMBRELLA LEADS are used to connect two or more stories to give the appearance of a flow of stories. A shared theme is found to tie them together.

▼ ▼ ▼

This is the umbrella lead:

<u>THE NATION'S ECONOMY DOMINATES THE NEWS TONIGHT</u>.

This is the lead for story one:

BUSINESS HAS GIVEN THE THUMBS DOWN TO TALK OF FURTHER INTEREST RATE RISES …

Story one follows on from here.

This is the lead for story two:

THE JOBLESS RATE HAS GONE UP MORE THAN I PER CENT THIS QUARTER …

Story two follows on from here.

▼ ▼ ▼

▼ ▼ ▼ ▼ ▼ ▼ ▼

activities

1. Making use of a national news programme, identify the components of 'who', 'what', 'when' and 'where' in each of several leading stories.

2. Scan a bulletin for examples of hard news, soft news, feature, throwaway and umbrella leads. Are any of the leads a combination of more than one category?

3. Write a throwaway lead for the story below. Cue the audience by simply restating the facts in another way and finding synonyms for the key words.

You may wish to give a monetary value for 'expensive'. Avoid repeating particular words such as vandals or excavator (consider 'heavy machinery', 'diggers' or 'bulldozers', for example).

▼ ▼ ▼

USING AN EARTHMOVING EXCAVATOR, VANDALS SYSTEMATICALLY DESTROYED EXPENSIVE BUILDINGS AND EQUIPMENT AT A SEWERAGE PLANT NEAR IPSWICH BETWEEN 10 P.M. AND MIDNIGHT LAST NIGHT.

▼ ▼ ▼

4. Write an umbrella lead for the two historic stories below. The stories were top of the bulletin at one time during the 1999 Kosovo crisis. Find the common element and use it as the basis of the lead. The umbrella lead should combine both stories under one group heading. Note that in the first story there is a rudimentary umbrella lead in the first sentence. This needs to be expanded to make an umbrella lead to cover both stories.

► NATO CHIEFS IN KOSOVO APOLOGISED FOR THE BOMBING OF THE CHINESE EMBASSY LAST NIGHT, BUT CLAIM IT WAS AN ERROR CAUSED BY FAULTY INFORMATION.

► IN CHINA, THE US EMBASSY IN PEKING IS BESIEGED BY THOUSANDS OF DEMONSTRA-TORS, PROTESTING AT THE UNPROVOKED IMPERIALIST HOSTILITY.

Television News Grammar

Television news has developed its own grammatical conventions in the half century or so since the first broadcasts. Both functional grammar and traditional grammar can explain how the news message is structured.

Traditional grammar

VERB TENSES

Television journalists write in the present tense or the present perfect tense. This is because these tenses go naturally with the pictures on the news clip, showing events as they are actually happening. Newspaper journalists, on the other hand, write in the past tense.

PRESENT TENSE says something *is* happening now. The immediacy of the present tense can be used to impress viewers with a sense of urgency. For example:

> The government is launching a major new initiative in its fight against the drug trade.

The present tense should be used sparingly, however, as it can sound ridiculous at times. A comedy team once satirised the use of present tense on television news with the following lead:

> Hitler, still dead tonight …

PRESENT PERFECT TENSE says something has just happened. It sounds almost as up to date and recent as present tense. Present perfect tense suggests the action has been completed or perfected. The finished event is then seen from the viewpoint of the present.

Present perfect tense is made up of two verb parts. One part is a present tense verb such as *is*, *are* or *being*. The second part, the main verb, is in the past tense – the action is completed. The past tense verb combined with the present tense gives a feeling of greater urgency and immediacy than straight past tense.

> Three people are dead tonight following a freak storm in Salisbury.

PAST IMPERFECT TENSE refers to something that *was* happening. It describes the action as still happening, but in the past. It is as effective as present perfect in conveying a certain sense of urgency and immediacy.

> A man was riding down the street on a bicycle with a purse between his teeth, and a woman was running after him shrieking, 'Stop, you'll not get away!'

FUTURE TENSE is commonly used since prediction is a part of the news service. Future tense says something *will* happen.

> A government minister says free public transport will provide the answer to congested cities.

PAST TENSE is not often heard on broadcast news. Past tense says something *has* happened. Past tense uses a single verb alone, such as 'killed', or else combines two past tense words, such as 'were killed'. Past tense is often pushed towards the end of the sentence or story by present verbs at the beginning. In the following story, past tense does not appear until the second sentence.

> The nation is in mourning tonight following the deaths of nine people in an horrific accident on the M1 at Nottingham. The victims died when …

ACTIVE VOICE

Journalists usually write stories in the active voice. The active voice makes news more dynamic by focusing attention on the action. Consider the sentences below.

> *Passive voice:* The man's car was struck by a train.
> *Active voice:* A train struck the man's car.

The active voice sentence focuses attention on the train, which was the cause of all the action. The passive voice sentence focuses on the man's car, which was simply receiving the action. Action makes for interesting news, so news writers prefer active voice.

The key to writing in the active voice is the word order. The subject must control the action.

In other words, someone or something must do the action, rather than have it done to them. A simple way to recognise passive voice is to look for the word 'by'. A passive object has something done to it *by* an active subject.

News writers use the passive voice when using the active voice would sound ridiculous. For example, 'A man was killed by a car today' would not be written as ' A car killed a man today'.

Putting the news first

People watch the news so that they can find out what happened. The television news lead must try to summarise what happened and put it towards the front of the lead. The aim is to attract the audience away from whatever distractions they may be involved in while watching the news. In the television news lead below, the news is clearly towards the front.

> A helicopter was used in a daring daylight escape from a Paris prison today.

In this lead, the most newsworthy item is that a helicopter was used in the escape, rather than the escape itself.

However, putting the newsworthy information first in the sentence can change the meaning, as it tends to remove considerations about who carried out the event and why. For example, in the lead above, the focus is on the means of escape, rather than the escapees. We are prevented from thinking about the motives that may have caused the escape – or the implications for prison security, among other things.

Functional grammar

In functional grammar, the first chunk of meaning in a sentence is called the *theme*. It may be a *participant* (who or what), a *process* (the action occurring) or a *circumstance* (where, when, why or how). Journalists decide whether to make a participant, a process or a circumstance the theme of the story depending on which is more interesting to the audience.

Participants who do something are called *actors*. Participants who have something done to them are called *goals*. In news writing, the actor

usually comes first. This means the sentence is in the active voice. If the goal of the sentence comes first, then that sentence is in the passive voice.

News writers aim to put the most interesting part of their sentences at the beginning. This means that it will become the first chunk of meaning, or the *theme*. As journalists attempt to turn the most interesting details into the theme, they sometimes resort to the passive voice.

> Protesters were thrust aside today when bulldozers moved in to the last remaining trees on the route for the new bypass at …

The theme of the sentence is the protesters. But the journalist could well have made the actors the theme (or the focus) of the sentence. It might then read like this:

> Police and workmen thrust aside protesters today when bulldozers moved in on the last …

Television journalists are very careful about their use of processes (verbs). They choose processes with a strong action meaning and a sense of urgency.

News writers want the public to feel as though the news is still happening or has only just happened.

Attribution

A news writer has to make it clear who said any quoted statements in the news story. Failure to do this will lead the public to think the statements belong to the writer, drawing accusations of bias. Statements that lay blame, voice an opinion or may be disputed all need to be attributed to someone. Even first reports of disasters, often sketchy and open to question, must be attributed to someone in authority.

The listener needs to be warned beforehand if what he or she is soon about to hear is a quote or a summary of a quote. Later may mean never to the viewer. Something may cause a distraction and a quoted opinion may be remembered as a fact. For broadcast, attribution goes at the head of the sentence.

Usually the person's title is given before their name, so that the audience can be *prepared* or 'teed up' to catch the name. An example is shown below.

The Feed the World Foundation president, David Beckmann, says Britain has the second highest level of child poverty in the industrialised world.

Tight writing

Stories must be told in the fewest number of words. At the same time, they must be concise and informative. Being brief does not mean leaving out the facts. If there are, for instance, ten main points people need to know about a story, all of these should be mentioned.

American journalist Bill Small relates how, if Moses were to give out a modern Ten Commandments, the television news lead would start out: 'Today at Mount Sinai, Moses came down with Ten Commandments, the most important three of which are …'. His point was that stories should be simplified, but not at the cost of basic elements. Simple words, simple sentences and simple explanations make for tight writing. One sentence should equal one idea.

▼ ▼ ▼ ▼ ▼ ▼

activities

1. Identify the verb tenses used in the leads below. The verbs are in italics. Notice that some leads have more than one verb tense. Identify each tense used in the lead.

▶ A catastrophe of monumental proportions. That *is* how Western experts *are describing* the Soviet nuclear power station disaster.

▶ As we *were telling* you earlier, a shop owner has appeared in the magistrates' court *charged* with *planting* four bombs in a convenience store yesterday.

▶ Australia *has airlifted* emergency supplies to the Solomon Islands in the wake of Cyclone Namu.

▶ A spectacular midair collision between two vintage air force jets at an air show in Suffolk *claimed* the lives of two men.

▶ In London, a block of flats for homeless families, near Hyde Park, *was destroyed* by fire.

2. The leads below are all written in the passive voice. Convert them to the active voice so that they are stronger and more interesting.

▶ Military action against Israel will be increased by guerilla groups following this week's raids.

▶ Two suspects were charged with murder by court authorities.

▶ Reductions in bus services were discussed last night by the city council executive.

▶ A man was devoured by a lion at an African game park yesterday.

3. Change these leads into present perfect tense.

▶ A three-storey block of flats fell down today in Sydney's western suburbs.

▶ In Sweden, the government took imports of fresh fruit from Eastern Europe off the market.

▶ He came back.

4. Convert the leads below into past imperfect tense.

▶ Parents lined up outside clinics and drug stores hoping for more.

▶ The government told parents not to worry.

▶ Six hundred workers threatened to leave.

5. Rewrite these leads so that the news comes first. (See the notes for the second item.)

▶ Leicester Royal Infirmary reports that three pedestrians run down by an out-of-control car are in a critical condition.

▶ A charted jet carrying orphans on holiday has crashed on take-off in Sri Lanka, killing all eighty-eight on board.
(*Note*: if a total of eighty-eight people were on board, this would include an unknown number of crew. Write the lead without actually mentioning the words crew or passengers. The most important detail is that eighty-eight were killed, the second most important detail is that among them were orphans.)

▶ Refuse workers have been terrorised by a sniper today and Glasgow police are searching for him right now.

6. Decide which items on the list below should be given some sort of attribution. Some items may require attribution because the television station may not wish to say as fact what is said in the leads. Briefly write down why you consider attribution necessary.

- ▶ Pilot error caused the crash of the Japan Airlines plane in which all sixty people died.
- ▶ The prime minister will face a hostile electorate if he calls an election now.
- ▶ Gun battles between police and underground Muslim groups were fought in the streets of Beirut today.
- ▶ This just in, a bomb has gone off in a Welsh supermarket. Two people are dead and 100 are injured. Ambulances are now on the scene.

7. Rewrite these newspaper intros as leads for television news, changing the position of the attribution. Remember to change the verb tense of the attribution (e.g. 'said' becomes 'says').

- ▶ MUNICH: The go-ahead has been given for the demolition of a nuclear power station, the first such operation in history, West German authorities said earlier today.
- ▶ Unjust bus fare rises would mean that Birmingham pensioners would be prisoners of their suburb, Councillor Dean Wells (Labour Party) said this morning.
- ▶ TOKYO: Buildings of the future may bounce their way safely through major earthquakes, according to a Japanese tyre company which says it has developed a shock-absorbing rubber for use in construction.

Writing a Television News Script

The script format

Television news script is always written in block capitals. This is because block capitals are easier for the newsreader to see. The television pictures are listed on the left-hand side of the script, and the short 'grabs' of speech to go with the pictures are written in block capitals on the right-hand side. Sentences do not have to be completed before the change of picture. A sentence can run over several pictures without being difficult to read.

Putting the picture in the script

Television news appeals to two senses – sight and sound. Words are lost as soon as they are said, so they must always be kept simple. They must also complement the pictures. Pictures are in fact probably more important than words, as television is primarily a visual medium. Pictures and script should reinforce each other; however, they should not compete for the viewer's attention. The script should not tell the viewer what he or she can see already.

The pictures are listed and numbered on the left-hand side of the script, directly in line with the short 'grab' of speech that is to go with it. Often the journalist describes the picture in brief detail so that the editor can form an an idea of what is to go with each short speech. The shots are numbered from one to however many shots are in the story.

▼ ▼ ▼ ▼ ▼ ▼ ▼

activities

1. Record a television news story and make a list of each of the shots. Transcribe the verbal report (the voiceover). Combine the two into the format of a television news script.

2. Find a short newspaper report and lay it out in the style of a television news script. Imagine the pictures that you could use and set out details of these on the left-hand side of the script, numbering them appropriately.

Remember to change verb tenses where necessary. The past tense may be acceptable in some places.

Writing a Lead

A good lead sets the tone for the whole story. The basic rules for writing leads are set out in the news structure and news grammar sections of this book (see pp. 256–8 and 259–61). There is no one single way to introduce a story. The leads below (in italics) refer to the same story, but they take different approaches.

▼ ▼ ▼

ACROSS AMERICA, FROM THE WHITE HOUSE TO THE DESERT, MILLIONS FORMED HUMAN CHAINS TO RAISE MONEY TO FIGHT POVERTY IN THE UNITED STATES. IT WASN'T THE UNBROKEN LINE FROM COAST TO COAST THAT ORGANISERS WANTED, BUT US CORRESPONDENT ROBERT PENFOLD REPORTS, HANDS ACROSS AMERICA IS BEING HAILED AN OUTSTANDING SUCCESS.

IN THE LAND OF HOPE AND GLORY, THE UNITED STATES, ALL IS NOT AS IT SHOULD BE. THE PROBLEMS OF THE POOR AND HOMELESS THERE ARE MINOR COMPARED WITH THOSE IN AFRICA, NEVERTHELESS, MILLIONS OF PEOPLE HAVE TAKEN PART IN A UNIQUE EXERCISE TO HELP THEM, TOO. THEY PAID TEN DOLLARS EACH TO JOIN HANDS ACROSS THE NATION.

▼ ▼ ▼

Where possible, the lead should include whatever it is that makes the event newsworthy. In the story of a prison escape shown below, it is the devil-may-care boldness of the operation that both channels have considered the newsworthy element. Each has taken a different approach to the same event.

▼ ▼ ▼

A HELICOPTER WAS USED IN A DARING DAYLIGHT ESCAPE FROM A PARIS PRISON TODAY. FRENCH AUTHORITIES BELIEVE THE AIRCRAFT WAS PILOTED BY A WOMAN.

A PRISON BREAK IN THE HEART OF PARIS HAS EARNED GRUDGING TOP MARKS FROM THE FRENCH POLICE FOR AUDACITY. THE MAN, WHO GOT AWAY FOR THE FOURTH TIME, USED A HELICOPTER FLOWN BY A WOMAN.

▼ ▼ ▼

▼ ▼ ▼ ▼ ▼ ▼ ▼

activities

Use the information below to create leads for television news items. Include almost all of the information in the lead. The story to follow will contain additional information not given here. Note that each story neglects to say when the event occurred. This is because the event itself is so newsworthy that words cannot be wasted on the time factor.

► The story takes place in Atlantic City in the United States.

A man puts three 25 cent coins into a poker machine. On his final pull, he wins $1.3 million.

He said that last week he lost $217 in 'that damn machine'.

His name is Anthony Lattanzio.

► Hugh Peskett is a London genealogist. He has been asked to trace descendants of a Texas rancher named Pelham Humphries.

Humphries was shot dead in a bar in 1840.

Oil was found on Humphries property after his death.

Royalties have accumulated for 150 years.

His heirs are entitled to $2.9 billion.

► Diane Hunt is a cleaning lady. She works at an exclusive department store.

The store is Nieman-Marcus in Dallas, Texas.

She stole 343 designer gowns by hiding them in her vacuum cleaner.

She did this during her nightly rounds.

A total value of $1 million was placed on the gowns.

Writing the Rest of the Story

Here is a telephone call.

Is that you Kevin? Barry here. Listen, I just witnessed a disaster! Tonight, I'm driving along. Suddenly this massive great explosion happens on the motorway. A busload of people just about got killed. Yeah, listen! This petrol tanker crashes into a truck. Petrol everywhere! Anyway, this stupid jerk in a Ford stops and lights up flares to warn oncoming cars. What an idiot! One of the flares lit the petrol and KABOOM! Luckily, no one was hurt. But this big National Express bus was caught in the flames and everyone had to jump out the escape window …

The television news for that night is shown below.

The sample television news story shown here closely resembles the telephone conversation about the event. This is not a coincidence. An informal narrative structure is best suited to the needs of broadcast news reports and also to telephone recounts. Barry's telephone call has a lead the same as the television news story. He was attempting to grab the listener's attention. The rest of the story in both cases is in step-by-step chronological order.

If anyone had been killed, Barry would have announced it to Kevin at the beginning of his story. The television news would also have mentioned it in the lead.

STRUCTURING A STORY FOR TELEVISION NEWS

The story should be structured in chronological order after the lead. The lead should feature the story's most important event in a brief summary.

The rest of the story then expands on what happened and to whom. Interviews with experts or eyewitnesses may be included from time to time. Chronological order is most common in television news stories because it best matches the progress of events as shown in the pictures. Newspaper reports are not constrained by this.

The story should be conversational without being too chatty or wordy. It should not mention irrelevant details.

WORD COUNTS AND TIMING The number of words can be checked against the allocated time for the story by reckoning on a reading speed of three words per second.

NEWS SCRIPT

Shot of newsreader with 'Motorway Disaster' chroma-key	Newsreader: A MOTORIST WANTING TO BE HELPFUL LIT A PETROL EXPLOSION ON THE M25 EARLIER TONIGHT. NO ONE WAS INJURED. BUT FOR A BUS FULL OF PASSENGERS, IT WAS CLOSE.
Shot 1: Charred truck and tanker	IT BEGAN WHEN A LOW LOADER COLLIDED WITH A PETROL TANKER, SPILLING 10,000 LITRES OF PETROL.
Shot 2: Fire-blackened guard rails	A MOTORIST LIT FLARES TO WARN ONCOMING TRAFFIC OF THE ACCIDENT. ONE FLARE WAS TOO CLOSE AND SET THE PETROL ABLAZE. THE FLAMES RACED 500 METRES DOWN THE ROADWAY.
Shot 3: Police cars and ambulance	THERE ARE NO REPORTED INJURIES …
Shot 4: National Express bus	… BUT A BUSLOAD OF PEOPLE HAD TO SCRAMBLE FOR THEIR LIVES …
Shot 5: Open fire-escape window at back of bus	… THROUGH THE BACK WINDOW, AS THE ROAD IN FRONT OF THEM WAS ENGULFED IN A SEA OF FLAMES.

activities

Set out below is a partly completed news script. The journalist had prepared the lead, assembled the vision and completed a conclusion, but was then called away urgently. A quote from an interview had also been placed with the matching pictures.

The news editor has asked you to complete the story for tonight's news. The original journalist has left all the necessary facts. They are listed in the fact sheet on p. 266. The news editor reminds you about three more things:

▶ Time limits are strict. Calculate length using the three words per second rule.

▶ Sentences can run from one picture to another – just use dots to indicate a break. For example, in shot 1, you need six words before the picture changes to shot 3, where you need

NEWS SCRIPT

Shot of newsreader with chroma-key graphic 'War Toys' in the text box	EVER WORRIED ABOUT CHILDREN PLAYING WITH WAR TOYS? WELL, IN TEL AVIV, A FORMER ISRAELI FIGHTER PILOT DECIDED TO DO SOMETHING ABOUT IT.
Shot 1 (2 seconds): Children smashing toys	
Shot 2 (3 seconds): Toys thrown into box ready to be smashed	
Shot 3 (1 second): Close-up of war toys, guns, etc.	
Shot 4 (2 seconds): Small boy with toy gun	
Shot 5 (4 seconds): Crowd scene	
Shot 6 (5 seconds): Toy tank is smashed	
Shot 7 (20 seconds): Abbie Nathan, former fighter pilot	Abbie Nathan: 'WE ARE TRYING TO CREATE A NEW GENERATION OF CHILDREN, WHO WILL STOP PLAYING WITH WAR TOYS, TRYING TO GIVE THEM SOME OTHER CREATIVE THINGS. MAYBE ONE DAY WHEN THEY GROW UP, AND THEY REMEMBER THE DAY THEY DESTROYED THE TOYS, MAYBE THEY WILL TRY TO DESTROY THE REAL THING, IN TIME TO COME.'
Shot 8 (8 seconds): Trestle where war toys are being exchanged for other types of toys	
Shot 9 (2 seconds): Boy eating ice cream	
Shot 10 (10 seconds): More toy smashing	

FACT SHEET

- People were invited to Tel Aviv to wage war on war toys.
- About 5000 people turned up.
- There were long queues at the smashings.
- The children came to smash the toys with hammers provided by the organisers.
- The crowd was made up mostly of children and their parents.
- The campaign is the brainchild of Abbie Nathan.
- Abbie Nathan is flamboyant, a former fighter pilot and restaurateur.
- He is now a peacemaker, he says.
- Psychologists say it is debatable whether smashing toys would actually decrease violence.
- The children seemed to enjoy it.
- In return for their smashed tanks and M16s, the children were given peace toys such as building blocks and books.
- Ice cream and chocolate were handed out in large quantities.

three words. Use dots to show the break in between.

- The newsreader's intro is not the lead of the story itself. The story has its own separate lead, which needs to be different again.
- Remember to change the facts so that they are in the broadcast style of writing. They will need rewording.

Planning the News Bulletin

In selecting items for inclusion in news bulletins, there is always a tension between the sense of the importance of particular stories and the competing sense of what makes good viewing. Many news editors start with the pictures that they have and build from there. Others have a keener concern for the 'ought to know' factor: how much the stories are about things about which the public *should* be informed.

Bulletin flow

The most important news stories go up the front of the news bulletin, just as a newspaper puts them on the front page. However, similarities with newspapers end there. Viewer tune-out would be a serious problem if the bulletin started with important stories and finished with dull ones. The aim of television news editors is to keep a balance of interest throughout the programme.

The news bulletin must have flow. There should be a good mix of important but visually dull stories with the visually grabbing. It is like 'sugaring the pill'. Getting the right mix comes with practice. It is a balance between show business values and news values.

Bulletin segmentation

Basic divisions into news, sport and weather are common to all stations. However, some stations divide the bulletin into more segments. A segment of international news is quite often used to add interest to the middle of the bulletin. Lighter stories or human-interest stories are used to brighten up the end of the news segment before the sports news. Some stations finish the whole bulletin with a human-interest story before the weather. Nearly all stations recap the main news headlines at the end of the newscast.

▼ ▼ ▼ ▼ ▼ ▼ ▼

1. Watch the evening news on a commercial channel, and then on the BBC. Draw up a chart like the one below and list the first three stories on each. Write a paragraph pointing to any similarities or differences.

STORY NUMBER	COMMERCIAL TELEVISION	BBC
Story 1		
Story 2		
Story 3		

2. Try to discover the system of segmentation used in the news bulletins of commercial stations serving your area. Watch the news and jot down the story topics through to the weather segment. Show the pattern of divisions either on a diagram or in a paragraph.

What sense of 'flow' can you discover in a news bulletin? Watch the news and fill in a table like the one listed above. Decide which stories have strong visuals and which are visually dull. Which stories do you find most interesting overall? Use the results of the survey to write a short paragraph on news 'flow'.

Representation Issues in News, Current Affairs and Documentaries

The representation of events, ideas, people and places in news and documentaries naturally delivers a point of view. The point of view in a representation can be regarded as a bias – a kind of favouritism or preference for one side over another.

Bias in television news, current affairs and documentaries can be treated as a by-product of the basic processes of newsgathering: selection, language, visuals, time and sequence.

Selection Processes

As the clock ticks away the minutes to the opening broadcast, news and current affairs editors work frantically, sifting and selecting stories for broadcast. It is a process so habitual and speedy as to be almost instinctive. Material is selected using four main institutional processes.

ROUTINES of newsgathering mean some news is selected and other news ignored. A story breaking at 5 p.m. has a greater chance of appearance than one breaking at 9 p.m. A story with easy access, a story close by, or a story with strong visuals may all be preferred over other stories. Reporters also have regular places they visit to gather news. These are 'rounds' or 'beats', such as the police, the courts, parliament, etc.

TRADITIONAL NEWS VALUES decide what is news and what is not news. This tradition carries on from newspaper values and is part of the institutional culture of media organisations (see newspaper representation issues, p. 414). Selection procedures are often institutional. Commercial television may choose differently to a public service broadcaster.

VISUAL SELECTION is necessary because television is a visual medium. A story with no pictures may be passed over for a lesser story with strong pictures.

CULTURAL SELECTION is probably the most powerful filter. Society believes some things can be said and others cannot. The ordinary citizen is the target of the news and current affairs, and assumptions are made regarding a common sense view of the world that most people will support. This viewpoint is the one used to select the stories. Other viewpoints are rarely selected.

Selection of facts

Bias can occur when some facts are selected while others are ignored. Consider the profile of Fred Smith, shown below. Then look at the selection that was made.

FRED SMITH	FRED SMITH FOR PRIME MINISTER
Father	Father
Violent drunk	Charity worker
Charity worker	Lifeguard
Volunteer lifeguard	
Chain smoker	
Drink driver	

Language

The Glasgow University Media Group has conducted exhaustive research into the language used on television news. They found that the language itself can lead to significant bias.

Its study concentrated on the reporting of industrial news such as strikes. The 'who', 'what', 'when', 'where' structure of stories was found to neglect the *causes* of strikes. Stories focused on strikers as the group causing disputes, yet all industrial action involves two sides. Industrial news always sees unions 'demanding' and employers 'offering'. The Glasgow analysts point out that to talk of employers 'demanding' and unions 'offering' seems absurd. Repetition normalises the bias created by the language used.

Putting the news first in a sentence also creates a distortion. The focus is on the 'what'. Television news stories, in particular, never seem to get to the 'why'.

Visuals

Further bias can be generated through the nature of visual material gathered. The camera may record the truth, but it can also be highly partial in the bit it chooses.

Bosses tend to be filmed as individuals in close-up, wearing formal clothes and in the authoritative locations of their offices. Workers, by contrast, tend to be filmed in groups, on-site, in mid-shot or long shot, and in their working clothes. The effect of this is to lend greater importance and weight to what the managers say, while casting workers as unruly troublemakers.

Camera angle can also indicate a point of view (see pp. 148–53).

Editing adds a further process of selection. The picture sequence shown on the television screen may be a rearrangement of the original footage. Editors may have changed the order of the pictures to suit the story.

Time

The short time span of a news story creates a 'bias against understanding', according to some analysts. Typical news bulletins, with a large number of stories in a short time work against a deep understanding. A famine in Ethiopia is shown as a group of starving people. The general problem of world food resources is too complex for the time allowed.

Certain viewpoints may be given more time than others. The Glasgow group report that: '… in the first four months of our survey there were 17 occasions when the news showed viewpoints against the government's policy of wage restraint. There were 287 occasions when views supporting these policies were broadcast.'

Story placement

The position of a story in a news bulletin can help to generate our sense of what is important and even cause bias. For example, the two stories below appeared one after another in a news programme.

Story one
AND NOW THAT CONTROVERSIAL GOVERNMENT GRANT OF £10,000 TO A GROUP OF FEMINIST SKATERS FOR THE DESIGN OF A WOMEN'S SKATEBOARD.

Story two
TODAY, A HANDICAPPED BOY GOES WITHOUT A WHEELCHAIR BECAUSE THE GOVERNMENT SAYS THERE IS NO MORE MONEY AVAILABLE.

The impact of one story on the other is considerable. Together they make a powerful statement that could not be said to be objective or unbiased.

▼ ▼ ▼ ▼ ▼ ▼ ▼

activities

1. News and current affairs directors select stories in response to their own cultural background and that of their audience.

► Suggest some unusual backgrounds that might change a news director's view of what makes news and current affairs.

► Suggest some of the stories you would then include if you were broadcasting to an audience of similar backgrounds to the editor's.

2. From the facts below, produce a biased report. The report could either be in favour of management, or unfavourable to them. Write a lead and about 200 words of story. Remember to change verb tenses.

▼ ▼ ▼

Gigantic cars recorded a loss of £98.4 million in the year to December 31, due to the fall of the pound and high interest rates, the company said today.

The sharp drop was the second consecutive year of poor performance. Last year, the vehicle manufacturer recorded a loss of £51.3 million. It increased its share of domestic car sales from 20.8 per cent to 22.2 per cent.

The strengthening domestic performance was paralleled in exports; which rose 10 per cent to £218 million, consolidating it as a leading exporter of manufactured goods.

The Minister for Industry, Ms Lowe, said the poor showing could not be attributed entirely to the weakness of the pound, or to interest rates.

'I think a lot of this loss had accumulated before the full effects of the recent economic downturn, for example.

'I mean, it's not for me to deny what Gigantic is saying, but I really think there are other factors as well.' Other car companies have reported record profits, she said. 'Maybe the management of the company is not as good as it should be', Ms Lowe said.

▼ ▼ ▼

3. Suppose there are two main parties in Parliament, Blue and Yellow. Decide which party is favoured in the following statements. Briefly

explain why. Suggest an alternative way of wording the statement.

▼ ▼ ▼

THE BLUE DOMINATED PARLIAMENT REJECTED PLEAS FOR A CHANGE IN POLICY FROM THE YELLOW MAJORITY IN THE UPPER HOUSE.

▼ ▼ ▼

THE YELLOWS HAVE DRAWN UP A SET OF DEMANDS AND HAVE SO FAR REFUSED COMPROMISE OFFERS FROM THE BLUES.

▼ ▼ ▼

THE YELLOW PARTY HAS STOOD FIRM AGAINST A THREATENED RECRUITMENT DRIVE AMONG ITS OWN MEMBERS BY THE CONTROVERSIAL BLUE PARTY.

▼ ▼ ▼

4. Look at the cartoon below and consider the selection the camera operator has made. Suggest a reason for this and say what you think the point of the cartoon is.

Figure 4.14

5. Suggest some 'story pairs' that could have an impact on each other's meaning. For example, a story on alcohol advertising followed by a story on a drink driving accident would change viewers' ideas on alcohol advertising.

Television Documentaries and Current Affairs

Documentaries

Pioneer film-maker John Grierson first coined the term 'documentary' in 1926 to describe a film made about life on a South Sea island. In so doing, he defined documentary as the 'creative treatment of actuality' (or reality).

Argument has raged ever since as to just how creative the treatment may become. At the close of the century, severe problems arose over the issue of authenticity. In the case of Carlton Television's *The Connection*, an award-winning investigation of the international drugs trade, creativity extended too far: large sections of the programme were subsequently proven to have been faked and the company was fined heavily.

Many film-makers, however, argue that all film is 'faked', essentially – in the sense that it is impossible to capture all events raw, as they happen; the use of reconstruction is inevitable. Moreover, any attempt to record reality is in any case bound to suffer from the impact the very presence of the film crew has on its subject.

▼ ▼ ▼

I think the truth is what you actually come away with at the end of seeing the film. I mean it's your truth that you're seeing. Everybody who makes a film is putting their own truth on the screen.

Diane Tammes, film-maker

▼ ▼ ▼

Creative development over the years has meant that the term *documentary* now covers a huge range of different production methods and forms. It is getting harder to find agreement among film-makers on just what a documentary is. Some analysts have argued for the term to be replaced with a new phrase such as *non-fiction programming*. *The Thin Blue Line* (USA, 1988) is a film that sets out to prove the innocence of a man found guilty of murdering a policeman in Dallas, Texas. Director Errol Morris borrows heavily from conventions of film noir to make his exploration of a miscarriage of justice all the more emphatic; for all this, as well as its being feature length, his film remains firmly non-fiction.

Despite the lack of agreement about styles, the common thread across all types of documentaries remains the use of the recorded images and sounds of actual reality or lived experience. Documentaries are not just about facts, though. Instead, facts are used to create socially critical argument, thereby inviting the audience to draw conclusions.

Broadcasting professor at the University of Nebraska, Peter Mayeux, says that documentaries present facts about a subject using real events, persons or places. He says that documentaries then creatively interpret or comment on those realities and people's concerns about them.

Current affairs

Current affairs programmes are midway between documentaries and the news. Britain has a long and respected tradition of reporting of this kind: ongoing programmes such as BBC 2's *Newsnight*, and Channel 4's *Despatches* offer serious and searching analysis and commentary. They offer a more in-depth probing of what's in the news.

Items on these programmes generally range in length from a couple of minutes only, up to as much as fifteen minutes. Current affairs features of thirty minutes or longer then move into the realm of the documentary.

For a long time now, the current affairs format has been an important one for exploring weighty issues and important social developments. However, there is a growing concern at the tendency for some programmes of this kind to edge towards ratings-driven, populist issues. ITV's *Tonight with Trevor McDonald* has been accused of choosing items for the broad nature of their appeal, rather than any real weight or importance. The series was launched with extended interviews of some of the youths widely suspected of murdering Stephen Lawrence. This attracted accusations of sensationalism from many quarters. The programme could do nothing to resolve the problems of that case – but was guaranteed to attract a big audience for itself.

In its report *Television Industry Tracking Study* (1999), the British Film Institute identified widespread belief *from within the industry itself* that quality of output had fallen in the previous five years. Many of those surveyed believed that ethical standards had also declined, due to the pressure for ratings. More pointedly still, over half of those working in news and current affairs said that they had been pressured to 'distort the truth and/or misrepresent the views of contributors' (Sue Quinn, *The Guardian*, 24 May 1999).

Features of documentaries and current affairs

There are five central elements of the documentary, according to John Corner, of the University of Liverpool. These are observation, interview, dramatisation, *mise-en-scène* and exposition. Different styles of documentary concentrate more on particular sets of elements from the five. Some of the basic elements also apply to many current affairs stories.

OBSERVATION Most documentaries contain sequences of observation. Usually, the programme-makers pretend that the camera is unseen or ignored by the people taking part in the events. This 'unseen' observation places the audience in the role of eyewitnesses to the realities portrayed. The observation sequence then works as witness evidence for the documentary producer's argument.

One criticism of this approach is its tendency to turn participants into objects, rather than subjects. They are treated only for their functional use to the film-maker.

INTERVIEW Television documentaries rely on interviews, which can be used to make a contrast with the observation sequences. The interviewer is either seen or unseen. The speaker is questioned and addresses the interviewer and not the audience. Sometimes pictures are dubbed over the speaker's replies in support of what is said.

Documentary makers structure interviews in two ways. They can intercut fragments of the interview with observation and other material. Or, they can allow the interview to run uninterrupted. The tendency here is to use participant witnesses for recent history, and experts for more distant events. All must of course be good on camera. Once again, the question of performing for the occasion arises.

DRAMATISATION All documentaries use a sense of drama through the observation element. The audience is an eyewitness to dramatic events. These seem to occur naturally in from of the camera. As well, all programme-makers build in a sense of dramatic conflict to heighten audience involvement.

Some documentaries use dramatisation to portray people and events the film-maker cannot gain access to in real life. These fictional sequences are said to be 'based on fact'.

MISE-EN-SCÈNE In the language of television and film, *mise-en-scène* refers to things 'put into the shot' (see p. 150). Documentary makers carefully compose shots so that they contain the images they want the audience to see. These are used to advance the argument of the exposition.

EXPOSITION The line of argument in a documentary is called the *exposition*. An exposition is made up of description combined with commentary. The exposition is what the documentary is 'saying'.

John Corner believes that the exposition in a documentary may be either plain and direct, or indirect and hidden. It always exists, nevertheless. For example, some styles of documentary rely heavily on the observation element. A narrator does not tell the audience what to think, but they are shown sequences that lead them to make conclusions. These highly observational documentaries can be said to have strong evidence, but weak exposition. Other programmes can be the reverse of this.

Post-Grierson: a New Wave breaking?

Former film-maker, journalist and academic John Marshall has identified a 'New Wave' of European film-making. This new approach consists of 'authored films which replace the observational approach ... with work that is telling an overtly personal and constructed story'. Making use of strong narrative lines, distinct points of view and strong characterisation, he urges films that are committed, clear and purposeful.

The Gulf Conflict, he argues, as the first digital and video war, has probably had as much impact on younger documentarists as Vietnam – the first television war – had on an earlier generation.

▼ ▼ ▼

Since the Gulf War we have moved to a more complex world: from a wish for immediacy to an awareness of mediation – a suspicion that appearance may bear little relationship to meaning. When the footage is supplied by an Air Force and the commentary comes courtesy of Generals then what, exactly, are we experiencing? A shared reality or the most expensive video game in the world?

John Marshall
Secretary-General of DOCUMENTARY,
European Union MEDIA Programme

▼ ▼ ▼

Betrayal (UK, 1982), by Frederik von Krusenstjera, is cited as an example of this new mode of committed investigation. A 'journalist' researches the story of a former Berlin activist-turned-Stasi agent, Sacha Anderson. Gradually, the very identity of the man fades away into a series of mirages that eventually call into question more widespread collusion in the work of the secret services.

In *Child of the Death Camps* (ITV, 1999), Binjamin Wilkomirski is exposed as having faked reminiscences of a childhood supposedly spent in a Nazi death camp. Challengingly, its director Christopher Oligiati, had allowed his protagonist to set out his seemingly authentic tales before

Figure 4.15
Humour forms part of the point of view or exposition in the documentary Canetoads: An Unnatural History (Australia, 1983).

proceeding to pull them apart. The sense of devastation the audience feels is all the more intense for having been taken in by the protagonist's lies.

A strong feeling now exists among film-makers that the time has come to abandon the conventions of assumed objectivity. Frustration with the constraints imposed by this role extends also to matters of style and approach.

▼ ▼ ▼

Documentary must abandon its limited, and always serious, tone ... Audiences know full well that Grierson's public education purpose, however much glossed and disguised, is a virtual guarantee for boredom.'

Brian Winston
Dean of Communications
University of Westminster

▼ ▼ ▼

Commitment, Brian Winston also points out, has always been seen as 'a species of deviancy'. But the objectivity so insisted on by Grierson concealed, in effect, his production of 'editorials for the established order'.

Moreover, the sermon-like nature of many documentaries, however worthy the subjects, are precisely the qualities that are alienating audiences – younger ones especially. Perhaps the greatest challenge to producers lies in the pressing question of how to make programmes that are about serious topics, yet are also accessible and attractive to audiences.

One successful alternative to the usual serious approach can be found in a new breed of satirical documentary. Two outstanding examples of this kind of humorous approach include: Michael Moore's *Roger and Me* (USA, 1989), which details the social impact of a major car producer moving its operations out of a US city, and *Cane Toads* (Australia, 1983), which deals with a very real problem of a growing infestation of a particularly repulsive species in Australia.

In the United Kingdom, a number of notable programmes have perhaps generated a whole new fictional sub-genre in itself – the 'mockumentary'. In the BBC series *People Like Us*, by John Morton, various significant social figures – head teachers, solicitors, estate agents, etc. – are gently sent up, by apparently 'straight' documentaries that manage to signal the true intentions to their viewers. This is achieved by a carefully crass series of blunders in the filming, together with unfortunate interventions by the all-too-human figure of the film-maker himself! Channel 4's *Brasseye*, similarly, used presenter Chris Morris to deceive various celebrities and experts into thinking they were participating in a serious programme, when in fact the purpose was satirical.

Differences between current affairs and documentaries

Chief differences between current affairs and documentary programmes centre on the pressure of deadlines and the view of the audience. Where a documentary maker may take months to produce a programme, a current affairs producer must have several stories ready each night.

The depth in which a topic can be explored is determined by the amount of time available to the item. A full-length, single-subject documentary (usually around one hour) can obviously get to grips with much more complex issues than can a five- or ten-minute slot on a magazine-style programme.

▼ ▼ ▼

The problems about documentary are not to do with whether you can actually go in and film something. The problems are to do with what you do with it afterwards.

Life doesn't come in thirty-minute, ninety-minute or hour-long segments. The whole business of documentary film is to take material shot from life and mould it into stories.

Brian Winston

▼ ▼ ▼

The audience for current affairs programmes is a varied one. Some switch between programmes and make comparison across a range of news sources. However, many audience members watch for pleasure as well as for information. Current affairs programmes, more clearly than documentaries, are aiming to provide 'info-tainment' – information and entertainment in a highly watchable package.

Social purpose, values and representation

The public's right to know is one of the most important claims in support of democracy and free speech. The public's right to know is also the main justification of the documentary maker.

Documentary programmes gain much of their authority from the connection they have with the democratic processes. Like news reportage, documentary production is seen as the belonging to the 'Fourth Estate' (see p. 401) of democracy. The other three national 'estates' (or centres of power in society – parliament, the public service executive and the legal judiciary – are kept in line with the publicity provided by the fourth estate of the news media.

Telling the public about it has definitely made a difference at times. Documentaries have resulted in changes to legislation and, at times, even thrown out governments. There are many well-known examples. In Britain, Ken Loach's *Cathy Come Home* (BBC, 1966) resulted in action to improve the condition of the homeless. *Cathy Come Home* was a hard-hitting documentary, revealing the devastating effects of homelessness on families. Its impact on viewers led to the establishment of the housing charity Shelter. (Interestingly, in a BFI survey of the 100 television programmes of all time, published in September 2000, this film was ranked *second*).

In the United States, *No Harvest for the Reaper* was successful in bringing about legislation to help migrant farm workers. In Australia, the *Four Corners* documentary *Moonlight State* about official corruption led to the fall of the Bjelke-Petersen state government in Queensland.

In many Third World countries, documentary provides a vital – sometimes the only – source of reliable information outside of the State-dominated news sources.

Cause and effect

Some analysts have criticised documentary makers for failing to look at the causes of events. They feel that most documentaries glory in the sensationalism of the problems, but never examine the deeper origins. As a result, the programmes merely gain sympathy for the symptoms and effects.

This explains the acceptability of many controversial issues as subject matter, says commentator Brian Winston. The worst that can happen is that the audience will dip into its pockets and donate money for homeless shelters, for example. Documentary makers rarely question the deeper organisation and fairness of society.

Truth

It is critical that film-makers be rid of the fantasy that the documentary can be an unproblematic representation of reality and that 'truth' can be conveniently dispensed and received like Valium.'

Dennis O'Rourke
Documentary film-maker

▼ ▼ ▼

Now, with regard to the matter of truth, in the natural sciences, for example, no-one hesitates to talk about truth and among ordinary people no-one hesitates either. But among sophisticated people, you're supposed to question the notion of truth.

It is a truism that your point of view on the world is going to colour the way you approach things.

But by no means should it lead us to question the belief that we're trying to find out the truth about the world. The denial of the urge for objective reality, that's a tremendously effective propaganda weapon. It fully incapacitates anyone who accepts it.

Of course, wealthy and powerful people are never going to accept it, but they're delighted to have everyone else accept it.

Noam Chomsky
Professor of Linguistics
and media theorist

▼ ▼ ▼

Since the beginnings of the documentary, people have struggled with ideas of 'truth' and 'reality'. And sometimes documentaries have attracted the counterclaims of 'lies' and 'fabrication'. John Corner believes that everyone would be better off using the idea of 'evidence', rather than truth. He

says recording technologies produce only traces of the physical world. These traces can be used as evidence of actuality or reality. This evidence then supports the exposition.

On the other hand, reporters can easily do what lawyers are often seen to be doing in court – finding only those experts who support their own point of view.

The documentary is created out of the actual or real by a series of transformations. These include scripting, filming, editing and transmission. The documentary therefore represents a 'transformed world' and not the whole truth.

The social context and institutions of documentaries

Unlike current affairs programmes, documentaries are not good ratings boosters for the commercial networks. They are the first programmes to be cut if money is tight.

General public interest in documentaries seems to extend only to programmes based on sex, violence and law and order. The highest rating documentary ever broadcast in the United States, for example, was called *Violence in America*. In listings of the top 700 programmes broadcast in America, documentaries on other subjects usually fall in the bottom 100. Commercial networks often see documentaries made in the public interest as non-profit items of little interest to advertisers.

Commercial interests also affect the subject matter of documentaries. John Culhane, in a *New York Times* article, listed a number of taboo

Figure 4.16
Each stage in documentary production involves selection and takes the programme further away from complete 'actuality' or even 'truth'. The audience is presented with a limited amount of evidence upon which to make an interpretation.

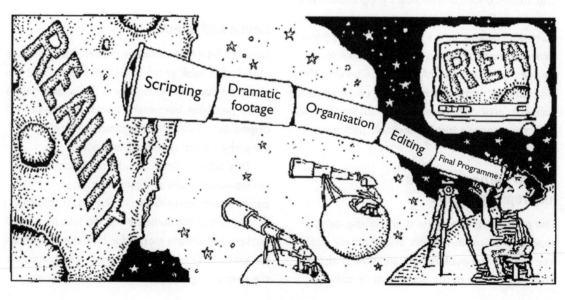

Figure 4.17
The docudrama
Death of a
Princess (1980),
caused an
international
diplomatic furore
with its exposition
of Saudi Arabia's
harsh system of
criminal justice.

subjects on commercial television. They included controversial investigations into big business, the networks themselves, the military industrial complex and nuclear power.

Controversy is not popular with commercial television networks. It offends advertisers. Here in Britain, an international political furore blew up over *The Death of a Princess*, a docudrama which sought to examine the harsh punishments doled out by the Saudi Arabian system of justice.

Public service television features many more documentaries than the commercial networks. However, public service television can also operate under pressures that affect the subject matter of programmes. Too much offence to the government of the day can result in restrictions to increases in the licence fee.

Roles, relationships and audience

A Vietnamese peasant said, 'First they bomb us as much as they please, then they film it.' Film director Peter Davis understood when he commented, 'The second confrontation of the Vietnamese with American technology is only slightly less humiliating than the first.'

Calvin Pryluck

▼ ▼ ▼

There is a complex relationship between the people who are shown in the documentary, the documentary producer and the audience. The complexity comes from three directions. First, there is the importance of the public's right to know in a democracy. Second, there are the rights of the individual being filmed. Third, there remains the question of the audience reaction.

Current affairs and documentaries are often about society's 'victims' – people who have been unable to defend themselves. A classic example of this would be ITV's *7-Up*, which took a group of children of that age and explored differences that location and social class made to their lives and expectations (and revisited them at seven-year intervals). Unfortunately, this has also included an inability to defend themselves against film-makers.

Documentaries use human beings as evidence in their expositions. They exploit and expose people's lives. This may be for the best of motives, but sometimes the results can be disastrous. Two documentaries concerned with people's experience of poverty were made in Canada in the 1960s. They both turned out badly for the people in the programmes. The subjects of the documentaries felt humiliated and degraded after the screenings. They were mocked by their neighbours and eventually felt they had to remove their children from local schools. In England, more recently, some participants in *The Dinner Party*, an experimental gathering of diverse people for food and talk, felt they had been set up and badly represented in the film that was transmitted.

Later variations on this theme might include *Castaway 2000* and *Big Brother*. Here, though, there is no pretence of 'studying' these people and trying to get a view of their real lives. The latter, in particular, seems to have generated a whole new set of behaviour patterns!

When documentary producers talk of the 'public's right to know', they are making an assumption about the audience. Producers are suggesting that if the audience is shown something is wrong, public opinion will move to correct it. There are many cases where this has occurred. There are equally as many where it has not. Modern audience research has shown media effects and therefore audience reaction to be highly complex (see pp. 25–32).

Types of documentaries

Changing ideas of truth and different understandings about the audience have produced at least six main documentary styles: fully narrated, fly-on-the-wall, mixed, self-reflexive and docudrama, with the possible addition of docusoaps.

FULLY NARRATED Direct address documentaries use an off-screen voiceover to convey the exposition. The voiceover is used to make sense of the visuals and dominates their meaning. The full narration style is often used in nature documentaries and was also popular in the cinema newsreels of the past.

The narrator often gives such an impression of authority about the topic that critics have dubbed the style 'the voice of God' documentary.

FLY-ON-THE-WALL Documentaries of this type draw from both the *cinéma vérité* (France) and

direct cinema (US) styles, and rely almost totally on observation. There is no commentary or narration: the cameras are left to record the subjects without interference, and viewers come to their own conclusions. Sometimes the camera and its movements can themselves convey a chilling commentary. This happened in *The Battle for Chile*, for example, when the camera suddenly falters and drops to the floor, recording the moment when the cameraman was shot.

Critics of the *vérité* documentary say that the fly-on-the-wall style hands the control of the exposition from the documentary maker to the subjects. Moreover, the very presence of the cameras affects the behaviour of the subjects. Exponents reply that this may be a change of control, but does not alter the relationship to truth – you cannot necessarily believe what the subjects of the documentary say either!

The process of editing in itself, of course, creates meanings too. The extracts chosen, the order in which they are assembled, any other material that is used to surround 'fly' extracts – all combine to offer a particular kind of commentary.

MIXED Many documentaries use a combination of interview, observation and narration to advance the argument. In contrast to the 'voice of God' style, the narration is often from within the frame (and therefore the action). Narration from within the scene is also the style adopted in modern news reporting. The journalist speaks to the camera and then pictures of the action continue over his or her voice.

While this style uses aspects from most of the others, critics say it is still bound to present itself as representing objective reality and not just a selective construction.

SELF-REFLEXIVE When the subjects of a documentary acknowledge the presence of the camera and often speak directly to the film-maker, the style is said to be self-reflexive. Self-reflexive documentaries make a point of drawing attention to the film-maker's role in constructing a view of reality. For example, in Dennis O'Rourke's documentary *Cannibal Tours*, the subjects actually talk to O'Rourke while he is behind the camera. He replies and asks them further questions.

Critics say self-reflexive documentaries can be

confusing and may fall into empty narcissism. By drawing attention to themselves as film-makers, they are seeking self-publicity. The film is about the film-maker, rather than the subject.

DOCUDRAMA A docudrama is a re-enactment of events as they are supposed to have actually happened. In this style, the elements of argument and exposition are combined with those of the fictional narrative. The resulting story is then said to be 'based on fact'. Oliver Stone's film *JFK* (USA, 1991) is an example of a docudrama. The format is particularly popular with television companies, and many striking examples have succeeded in vividly re-creating dramatic and often tragic events. *Hillsborough* (ITV, 1996), which dealt with the catastrophe at the football ground of that name, was one of the most outstanding instances of this genre, helped in no small part by the presence of writer Jimmy McGovern on the team.

Critics say that docudramas claim to represent truth, but can only ever hope to deliver fiction. The programmes are not filmed 'actuality'. In passing themselves off as reality, they are at best misleading and at worst positively dangerous in their inevitable partiality.

DOCUSOAPS A phenomenon of recent years has been the explosion of programmes that follow the daily lives of particular individuals within a designated occupation. These originated in the United Kingdom and for some time were unique to it.

They began grandly with Andrew Bethell's *The House*, which took a bird's-eye view of the internal workings of the Royal Opera House. Later, they expanded rapidly to include employees on a cruise liner, in an airport and in a host of other, sometimes quite mundane, environments.

Many dispute whether these programmes are really documentaries in any sense: they seek, after all, not to explore topics so much as to eavesdrop on them. However, many of them have proved to be enormously popular – thirteen million viewers was the highest recorded. This alone guarantees repeated use of the format. An additional attraction for producers is the relatively low production cost. A minimal film crew and no cast fees to pay mean that they can produce material of this nature for a fraction of the cost, for instance, of a new drama.

The appeal for audiences seems to come from strangely opposite impulses. On the one hand, they wish to see 'exotic' places – ones they are unlikely to get to themselves. On the other, there is an equal fascination with seeing places that they *have* been to – but revealed from behind-the-scenes. In either case, the biggest fascination is with the *people* who are involved: these shows need distinctive personalities (they do not have to be likeable!) for the audience to latch on to.

Disneyfication

Steven Barnett, of the University of Westminster, has blamed programming of this kind for the 'Disneyfication' of British television culture. He claims that pressure from broadcasters for 'bright, safe, glossy and formulaic guaranteed ratings successes' is driving out programmes that challenge and innovate. In a report compiled for the charity-based campaign for quality television, a dramatic decline is traced in the volume of current affairs produced over the last twenty years. Moreover, even in those that remain the focus has softened, with the more difficult subjects of political, industrial and foreign news stories giving way to 'ratings-friendly domestic and commercial topics'.

▼ ▼ ▼ ▼ ▼ ▼ ▼

activities

1. Watch a documentary to identify its use of the five central genre elements described by John Corner (p. 271). Briefly describe the sequences in the documentary that illustrate particular elements, including the exposition or argument (what the documentary is saying). Draw up a table to record the results of your analysis. On one side, make a list of the different types of documentary you have identified; on the other, give a brief summary of the sequence/s that help you identify it as such.

2. Identify any documentaries that you believe have made a difference in national affairs. Study at least one of them and determine what it was that made an impact.

3. Review a documentary on a controversial topic to see if it examines the problem's deeper causes or merely sensationalises the symptoms or effects.

4. Debate whether there is a place for the search for 'truth' in the modern documentary.

5. View a documentary and select some significant shots for analysis. Does the framing or shot size affect the meaning in any way? Would different points of view have been implied with different framings? Suggest framings for different effects.

6. Storyboard a sequence of about ten frames for a documentary on a topic of your choice aimed at a specific audience. For example, you could aim at teenagers, middle-aged people, etc. Show the results to the class and note any variations in the 'reality' that is presented.

7. Compare several documentaries dealing with the same subject. Discuss the differences in the exposition.

8. Some analysts argue that the documentary makers have a 'duty of care' to the people who are the subjects of their programmes. What do you think? Discuss this issue in class.

9. Watch a selection of documentaries and classify them according to the main style they adopt: fully narrated, fly-on-the-wall, mixed, self-reflexive or docudrama. Make sure you can justify your decisions about the classifications.

10. Watch some older documentaries and discuss any variations you perceive in the view of 'reality' compared with that presented in modern programmes. Documentaries dealing with nuclear power, the environment or transport are good for comparison.

Developing the Documentary or Current Affairs Concept

The topic

Out of the vastness of actuality or reality, the documentary creator chooses a topic. The topic does not just come out of thin air. It is not objective and neutral. The topic a film-maker chooses will be influenced by a range of factors, including the person's own life experiences, personality and political beliefs, as well as the nature of the institution in which he or she works.

The documentary-maker Michael Rabiger suggests choosing manageable topics that match the producer's budget and capabilities. Newspapers, magazines, books and even notice boards can be the sources of documentary topics. Rabiger then proceeds to ask a number of questions:

▶ Do I already have some knowledge and opinions about this topic?
▶ Is this a subject I have a strong emotional connection with?
▶ What is unusual or interesting about it?
▶ How narrowly can the programme focus its attention?

Think small. Think local, Rabiger advises. A film about inner-city life might be too large and unwieldy. However, twenty-four hours in the life of one particular café in the city may say a great deal. Experience in the small world can represent the larger world around it.

Representing and visualising the topic

Once the topic has been settled upon, the film-maker can plan to use certain people, places and events to present the point of view about the topic. These are carefully selected, but are shown as being somehow typical of the way things naturally are. This planning process involves research, visualisation, arranging interviews and developing the central idea.

RESEARCH In large production units a team of researchers works on a documentary. In contrast, small-scale independent production means individual film-makers and writers must often do it all themselves. However, all tend to follow a concept development scheme, which includes the following considerations.

▶ **VISUALS** What can be *shown*? Television is a visual medium and documentary uses what can be *seen* as its main evidence. Action-based pictures, or static ones if they are expressive in other ways, are preferable to lots of shots of people talking.

Archive footage, street scenes, open countryside and close-ups of faces are just some of the stock materials used to suggest the intended meaning, or emotional qualities of particular themes.

▶ **INTERVIEWS** In a documentary, either the researcher or the producer arranges the interviews during the planning and development stage. In current affairs, the reporter arranges the interviews. Before filming, some general questions are asked of the interview subjects to see if they will make 'good television'. The most interesting questions are left until the actual filmed interview to keep the discussion lively and spontaneous.

An interview can be held anywhere, but the setting does affect the meaning. In the home, the interview subject may be more relaxed and friendly. In the park, the subject may feel more anonymous – being just one of a crowd. Unusual settings can add drama to the interview. The setting can also provide a comment on the interview.

Planned questions for interviews usually begin with the factual questions first. These put the interview subject at ease. The more taxing or emotionally gripping questions are asked as the interview develops.

▶ **VOX POP** can be used as light or humorous relief from serious narration or in-depth interviews. Vox pop is short for *vox populi*, or 'voice of the people'. The technique consists of street interviews of the general public with

Figure 4.18
An unemployed man is interviewed in the swimming pool for the Channel Four documentary **When the Dog Bites.** *Planning for unusual settings can add drama to the interview.*

each person being asked the same question. The replies are then strung together in a fast sequence. Vox pop are good for suggesting that there is general agreement, or else the opposite – that there is a diversity of opinion.

The exposition

Once research has made the exposition possible, many documentary-makers attempt to write it out as a single sentence. The supporting evidence is then listed in point form under the statement of the exposition. Interviews and footage of action are included in the plans.

The exposition is often modified as the programme's production continues. This is a unique aspect of the documentary. The full expression of its ideas may not be finalised until the last moments.

▼ ▼ ▼ ▼ ▼ ▼ ▼

activities

1. Think of three or four topics you believe could make effective documentaries. Now consider the questions Michael Rabiger asks when choosing the topic for a documentary. Apply them to your topics and write down your responses.

2. Using a documentary topic as the starting point, develop a planned exposition based on research, visuals and interviews. Follow these stages in the development process:

▶ Begin by listing all possible interview subjects for the topic.

▶ Make a list of supporting resources (e.g. library references, magazines and newspaper articles).

▶ List some visuals that illustrate the topic. Aim to include as many shots of action and movement as you can.

3. As the basis for an exposition, develop a point of view on a topic of your own choice. Follow these stages:

▶ Research the topic using at least three or four sources. Take notes.

▶ Once you have knowledge and understanding, develop the point of view you will take on the subject.

▶ Express the point of view as a single sentence.

▶ Present the single sentence viewpoint on a page supported by notes from the sources as evidence.

4. Conduct a vox pop (see pp. 279–80) in the class on a topic of general interest or amusement. Limit each person's response to a few sentences. Edit the comments together in a way that lends support to a point of view. As a variation, try to edit another version that suggests differing opinion on the same topic.

5. Watch a documentary and note down the length of time devoted to interviews. How long does each speaker have to give their point of view. Are some allowed more time than others? Do you think some people should have been given more time? Explain.

6. Suppose you were planning to film a documentary about your school or college. Make a list of interview subjects and noteworthy events you could film that would express some of the conflicts you believe exist. Select one from the list, then work out a sequence of shots/materials/interviews you could use to cover the topic. How would you ensure that a particular point of view was represented?

Scripting and Structuring the Documentary

After initial development work on the documentary, the material must be organised into a logical pattern. This framework should show the relationship of all the ideas and all the supporting evidence.

Narrative conventions

Documentary relies heavily on the traditional conventions of narrative.

In other words, there is a definite beginning, middle and end. There is also strong focus on character and conflict. Other conventions of narrative forms are also used, including music, special settings and lighting.

THE BEGINNING The orientation stage has to capture audience attention as quickly as possible. There are many ways of doing this. The central question of the documentary can be posed at the beginning in an intriguing way. The most dramatic piece of action footage can be placed at the beginning or some quick interview cuts in conflict with each other can get audience attention.

THE MIDDLE The complication stage should be the most compelling. The middle section often examines the issue in human terms, with a focus on people and their opinions. Conflict is strengthened in the middle section of the programme. The script may even develop this conflict to provide blockages to the fulfilment of the exposition. For example, just when the exposition seems to have 'set out on its way', a piece of apparently conflicting evidence may be introduced. However, all complications must eventually support the exposition, just as the narrative hero triumphs in the end. An example of complication built into the narration is shown below.

▼ ▼ ▼

Narrator: ... AND THE STREET KIDS' PROBLEMS ARE THE RESULT OF INCREASING YOUTH UNEMPLOYMENT, A POVERTY CYCLE AND THE BREAKDOWN OF THE FAMILY.

BUT FOR SOME THIS SIMPLY ISN'T TRUE. SAMANTHA IS 16 AND FROM A WELL-TO-DO NUCLEAR FAMILY UNIT. SHE'S A 'STRAIGHT A' STUDENT AND A PRIVATE SCHOOL RUNAWAY ...

▼ ▼ ▼

THE END The documentary makes the exposition fully apparent by the resolution stage. Any complication built into the exposition must be resolved. At this point, the audience is in no doubt as to what the programme is saying. There may even be a course of action the audience can take to address the problem.

CONFLICT Issues make good documentary topics because there is some kind of conflict in them. Conflict can be between people with different beliefs, different goals, different circumstances or ambitions. The conflict can also be within individual, with the surroundings or between the generations or social classes.

Conflict is often shown developing through several stages. This allows the documentary to use the narrative technique of complication and tension.

The conflict must be shown in action. Otherwise it remains an invisible concept in the mind of the film-maker. Usually some kind of confrontation is orchestrated for the cameras so the audience can see the conflict for themselves. For example, a programme may be about a young woman's battle against long-term unemployment. The conflict can be shown if she is filmed visiting an employment agency or at a job interview. Clashes with parents or meetings with luckier friends and successful classmates may also show the conflict.

A SENSE OF MOVEMENT Additional strength can be given to the narrative elements of a documentary if the action has a sense of development or movement. According to the documentary-maker Michael Rabiger, this can take at least three forms.

▶ physical movement represented, for example, by a journey, a change of job, a change of city.
▶ movement in time represented, for example, by the natural seasons, the growth of a child or change over an historical period.
▶ psychological change represented by, for example, an athlete overcoming fear of failure, an ex-prisoner adjusting to the world outside.

MUSIC AND SOUND EFFECTS Sound is effective in producing an emotional response in the audience.

DOCUMENTARY ORGANISATIONAL PLAN

'Trip to Nowhere'
PRODUCED BY NBC

TOPIC: DRUG USE AMONG SCHOOL CHILDREN

CENTRAL IDEA OF THE EXPOSITION Although the use of drugs among school children is widespread and dangerous, steps can be taken that will alleviate the problem.

THE PROBLEM
I Student drug users come from all parts of society.
▶ They include the poor and those who suffer from discrimination.
▶ They include wealthy students.
  1. Some school leaders use drugs.
  2. Some athletes use drugs.
▶ They include young children, among them fourth and fifth graders.

II Drugs are available to students everywhere.
▶ They can obtained on the streets.
▶ They can be obtained in schools where every child is approached by a drug pusher at one time or another.
▶ They can be obtained at parks and music festivals.

III Children use drugs to escape various types of problems.
▶ They try to escape faulty home relationships.

▶ They try to escape what they see as a betrayal by society.
▶ They try to escape insecurity.

IV Drug use has serious consequences.
▶ It brings on dangerous 'trips'.
▶ It causes illnesses.
▶ It sometimes results in death.

THE SOLUTION
I Finding a solution to this problem is difficult.
▶ Parent–child relationships create problems.
  1. The parent's first impulse is to punish.
  2. The child often suffers from alienation.
▶ The law creates problems by requiring that minors treated by doctors for drug use be reported to legal authorities.

II There are a number of possible approaches to the use of drugs among school children.
▶ The young can help.
  1. They can speak out at school assemblies.
  2. They can participate in rehabilitation units.
▶ Various groups can be formed to combat the problem.
  1. Physicians can organise.
  2. Parents can assemble to obtain mutual advice and help.
  3. Civic groups can be formed.
▶ Therapy centres can be set up.
▶ Adults and children can help drug users find alternatives to a drug-orientated world.

Sound can also work either to support the image or to conflict with it and create an alternative meaning (see p. 161).

In the Dennis O'Rourke documentary *Half Life*, about nuclear testing in the South Pacific, the sound conflicts with the images. Hawaiian guitar music mocks the idea of a South Pacific paradise. Meanwhile, beeping noises mixed over the interviews create the impression of background radioactivity.

Structuring the exposition

Edgar Willis and Camille D'Arienzo have suggested five commonly recurring patterns used to structure documentary expositions:

▶ chronological order of events by time
▶ an order based on the location
▶ classification order, such as effects of a problem on different groups of people or different environments

▶ cause-and-effect order

▶ problem and solution order.

The narration

Narration is an important binding element in the structure of the documentary, providing links between segments. Narration is a means of controlling the flow of information. On television, narration serves to make things clear. It can also be used comment upon and reinforce what the pictures already show. Professor of broadcasting at the University of Nebraska, Peter Mayeux, suggests the following techniques for writing effective narration:

▶ Keep the narration sparse and concise. It should not dominate the programme. Narration should not tell the viewers what they can see already.

▶ Give a mixture of on-camera and off-camera narration.

▶ Keep the style conversational.

▶ Relate the narration directly to the progress of the exposition.

▶ Use narration the same way all sound can be used – either to support the image or to conflict with it to create another meaning. Mayeux gives the example of pictures showing a war-torn city while a poetic voiceover describes the city as it once was. The narration is in opposition to the image and together with the pictures creates a sense of great loss.

BROADCAST STYLE Like news reports, documentaries use the specialised writing style of broadcast journalism (see pp. 259–60).

TIMING Documentary makers sometimes write the narration and cut the pictures to suit; at other times they may write the narration to suit already edited sequences. In either situation, it is important to know the exact timed length of the narration. A rule of thumb for most readers is a speed of three words per second.

Scripting

Scripting for the documentary normally progresses alongside the production stages. Aspects of the narration may not even be written until right at the end of production.

There are usually three stages in script production. These are the treatment, the outline and the full script.

THE TREATMENT is an explanation of the basic topic and exposition. It describes the purpose of the programme, the audience, aspects of the content for major sequences and the overall style of the documentary.

THE OUTLINE sets out most of the main ideas and shows the relationship between the main points and supporting evidence. It also suggests the final structure of the programme. The outline is a 'living' document that changes as the documentary proceeds.

THE FULL SCRIPT is often not completed until near the end of production. A variety of script styles may be used. However, news journalists often work on documentary projects, so many continue to use the news script style (see pp. 259–64).

▼ ▼ ▼ ▼ ▼ ▼ ▼

activities

1. Analyse and evaluate a documentary focusing on the following key aspects of its structure.

- ▶ **THE BEGINNING** – how has audience attention been gained?
- ▶ **THE MIDDLE** – how does the programme use people to focus on the problem?
- ▶ **COMPLICATIONS** – list any complications in the middle section. Explain how these are introduced (e.g. in the narration or via interviews, etc).
- ▶ **CONFLICT** – list the main conflicts and evaluate one or two scenes where the conflict is actually shown rather than described.
- ▶ **MOVEMENT/DEVELOPMENT** – how has the programme created any sense of movement, progress or development to add to the narrative elements?

2. Storyboard several scenes showing the conflict behind some issue at your school or college. To begin, think of some current issues that would suit the documentary-makers' criteria of 'conflict'. Write down one topic and then picture how you could show the conflict 'in action'. Draw the scenes.

For example, the conflict could be as simple as an individual's struggle to gain a good academic result. A few scenes before and during a stressful exam would show this conflict.

3. View a documentary and note down how the programme moves from one sequence to another. Is the linkage made by narration, sound or visual means? Is the linkage made through time or location connections? Is it made by cause and effect, or problem and solution? Suggest other ways the linkage could have been made.

4. Discuss the use of sound in a particular documentary. In general, does the sound support the image or work in conflict with it in some way? Explain your answer.

5. Record a non-interview section from an existing documentary. With a topic not connected to the original, write narration and record it onto the tape. Present it to the class and compare the results with those of other class members. Discuss the various effects.

6. Select an issue you feel strongly about. What structuring pattern, of the five listed by Willis and D'Arienzo, would you use to explore the topic? Rough out some ideas organised under the pattern you have chosen.

major assignment

Production assignment

1. The style of a documentary can have a significant impact on the meaning. Make two documentaries on the same topic with the same exposition. Each documentary should be three to five minutes long. One documentary should be in the self-reflexive style, acknowledging the presence of the film-maker. The second may be in one of the other styles, such as full narration, mixed, fly-on-the-wall or docudrama.

2. Make a documentary about your school or college with a very clear exposition. For instance, you may wish to present it as either an ideal learning centre or a prison.

Written assignment

Produce a 600-word written response to the following topic.

Analyse and evaluate a documentary of your choice. Your report should deal with the aspects set out below. You may find it easier to write the report using headings from the following sections:

- ▶ Describe the style of the programme.
- ▶ Investigate the use of the generic elements (observation, interview, *mise-en-scène*, exposition).
- ▶ Provide an outline of the structure. Use the outline on p. 282 as a guide.
- ▶ Analyse the use of elements from the narrative genre (beginning, middle, end, conflict, movement, music and sound).
- ▶ Analyse the use of narration.
- ▶ Evaluate the effectiveness of the programme and also its particular representation of 'reality'.

Soap Operas

The 'soul of the nation'?

The modern, socially aware soaps … are more powerful than politics in influencing attitudes. Governments come and go, policies change … But soaps provide the constant in our lives. They set out to reflect society, but end up affecting, gently changing, the way we think about our lives, and those around us.

Mal Young

Head of Drama Series, BBC

▼ ▼ ▼

Substantial claims are made for the role and significance of soap operas in the cultural life of the nation. Mal Young stresses the cohesive qualities of soap – the 'sole remaining shared experience' available to the population that '[does] more to break down social and class boundaries than any government could ever do'.

After years of scorn, they are receiving praise from some unexpected people. Stephen Logan, of Cambridge University, has highlighted the cultural snobbery that tends to condemn works because of their very popularity. Even Shakespeare suffered from this, in his time. While avoiding a direct comparison, he suggests that 'popularity that lasts … remains the most reliable criterion of artistic merit'.

Style

Some analysts say soap opera styles fluctuate between the polar opposite of melodrama and realism. The British soap opera tends towards the pole of realism; the American soap opera towards the pole of melodrama. The Australian soap opera, with its emphasis on suburban life, alternates between the two.

MELODRAMA Soap operas share many of the features of melodrama. In melodrama, the focus is on the emotional aspects of the narrative and mild to high suspense. Good and evil exist in extremes. The good are persecuted, but finally rewarded.

REALISM The social issues and dramas faced by ordinary people has always been the mainstay of soap operas. This places them within the realist approach to narrative.

Julia Smith, creator of the BBC soap opera *EastEnders*, said the show owed much to the style of Charles Dickens, the great social writer of the nineteenth century. He rooted his stories firmly in the actualities of life for people in his time and focused closely the living conditions of the day. Smith says that, from the beginning, she wanted *EastEnders* to have 'documentary realism'.

Beginnings on radio

Soap companies and breakfast cereal companies in the United States sponsored hundreds of serialised dramas on radio in the 1930s and 1940s. The serials would hook huge numbers of housewives, who would then be a captive audience for advertisements from Colgate-Palmolive, Procter and Gamble, or Kellogs.

Advertising promoted more than just soap and breakfast cereals, of course; however, the term 'soap opera' had been coined quite early on – and it stuck. When television came, serial dramas such as *The Guiding Light* easily transferred to the new medium. This particular serial has been going for more than seventy years in the United States now and is the longest running soap opera in the world.

In the early days, the tone of these programmes was heavily moralistic: the indulgence of tuning in to the television during the day had to be offset by some very clear and worthy lessons in social conduct. They were also deliberately static in their action – to allow the largely housewife audience plenty of opportunities to look away and attend to their household duties.

Television soap opera

Television is a domestic medium, watched at home, informally and often inattentively. Unlike film, television does not offer the feeling of a special event. People often just collapse in front of it and let the programmes flow over them. Soap operas are ideally suited to this sort of viewing. Plots and characters continue indefinitely. People identify with the characters and that encourages audience involvement.

Figure 4.20

Daytime soap operas are slower, while prime-time soap operas have more action. Both types can go on for years, allowing for considerable audience involvement.

SOAP OPERA LONGEVITY		
FIRST AND LAST EPISODE	**SERIES**	**COUNTRY OF ORIGIN**
1960–	*Coronation Street*	United Kingdom
1978–89	*Dallas*	United States
1981–89	*Dynasty*	United States
1982–93	*A Country Practice*	Australia
1984–	*Brookside*	United Kingdom
1984–	*Neighbours*	Australia
1985–	*EastEnders*	United Kingdom
1988–	*Home and Away*	Australia

Soap operas are famous for their huge following. They are using the characteristics of television in a unique way, according to television critic and academic Horace Newcomb. At least in this sense, they could be seen as the furthest advance of television art.

Figure 4.21

Bet Lynch, a larger-than-life character from Coronation Street, television's longest-running soap opera.

DAYTIME SOAP OPERAS At one time, television soap operas were broadcast only between 9 a.m. and 3 p.m. The daytime soap operas tended to be slow moving, with a style that emphasised the emotional. More recently, daytime soap operas have been influenced by the prime-time shows.

PRIME-TIME SOAP OPERAS Since the 1980s, soap operas have moved into evening time slots – a space previously reserved for crime dramas and films. Prime-time soap operas usually have much more action. The emphasis moves away from the home and family to include more of the outside world.

At times, there is an almost cinematic quality to this – as, for example, in the notably dramatic plunge of the Mitchell brothers into the River Thames in the BBC soap opera *EastEnders*.

DIGITAL SOAP OPERAS

The success of the soap opera on both radio and television has led some producers to experiment with the genre on the Internet. 'Cyber-soap' producers believe the web will become increasingly colourful and interactive. They say that more and more people will turn to it for entertainment as well as information. In readiness, several Internet soap opera sites have been set up. One of the advantages digital soap operas offer is cost. One whole year's worth is said to cost only as much as just one week of television soap.

Social functions

As well as the traditional narrative purposes of entertainment, comment, information and persuasion, soap operas have fulfilled another purpose.

Concentrating on relationships and emotions, soap operas offer a style of narrative Tanya Modleski says is feminine. In her book *Loving with a Vengeance*, she calls for a feminist narrative style to be developed from the lead given by soap operas.

Far from being escapist, says Renata Adler of the *New Yorker* magazine, soap operas present 'the most steady, open-ended sadness to be found outside of life itself'.

Context

The factory was a vast, dark concrete box of a building, sixty metres long. More than seventy people slave away here, working anything up to fifteen hours a day. The goods were sold in eighty countries. This was the *Dallas* factory. UK soap operas tend to use more outdoor locations. Otherwise, similar conditions apply. To create a long-running serial, it is necessary to use assembly line techniques.

The product itself is very profitable. Soap operas are relatively inexpensive to produce. A week of a daytime soap opera can be produced for the cost of just one episode of a prime-time crime drama. Sets and even costumes are fixed and can be used over considerable periods of time.

Soap operas also bring in huge advertising revenues for commercial networks. A single advertisement break can earn as much money as it takes to produce the entire episode.

The soap opera close-up

The conventional camera styles of a soap opera require close-ups that bring us right up to the character, where we can see their tears or hear their breathing. Often it is only the audience that is able to see the character's expression.

A face in close-up is what, before the age of film, only a lover or a mother ever saw. Feminist critic Tanya Modleski says 'soap operas appear to activate the gaze of the mother – in order to provoke anxiety about the welfare of others.'

▼ ▼ ▼ ▼ ▼ ▼ ▼

activities

1. Make a list of the products promoted during the advertising breaks of a modern television soap opera. In a paragraph, report your findings and comment on any changes in sponsorship since the 1930s.

2. Set up a classroom television talk show, complete with host, where panellists can debate the main critical viewpoints on soap operas. Film the presentation and, if possible, edit in example footage to illustrate some of the points the panellists make.

3. Female characters were once always used to provide the main focus and plot action in soap operas. This was an industry rule in the early days. Discuss whether or not it still holds true today.

4. List the emotions shown in close-up in one episode of a soap opera. Then try filming some comic 'soap opera close-ups' of your own. Form groups and think up some storylines that could end with the camera focused on the contorted face of one of your classmates. Film the scenes and show the funniest ones to the class.

Soap Opera Plots

To watch real life on a television screen would be a very boring exercise indeed. A serial takes a real-life situation and condenses the time span of it, which in turn heightens the drama. The criterion for plotting a good serial is always 'Is it telling a good story?' If not, then don't use it.

Story almost invariably takes precedence over character. It doesn't matter how interesting the characters are, if the story is weak then the show will be dull. And a dull show means the viewers switch off.

Peter Pinne,
Grundy Television, Australia

▼ ▼ ▼

A US study found eight divorces, two bigamous marriages, four separations and six planned divorces in six months of viewing a daytime serial. Soap opera plots centre on relationships and personal problems. The frequency is well above that of real life.

Plot structure

Soap operas are 'open' texts, unlike most narratives which are said to be 'closed'. An open text is one allowing multiple interpretations. Open texts such as soap operas contain many characters and therefore points of view. There is usually no single hero. Characters often experience changes. The plot is rarely resolved. Any resolution is simply to allow for the next conflict.

The structure of a soap opera is different to most other narratives. The Greek philosopher Aristotle argued that drama has a beginning, a middle and an end. Detective stories aim for the solution – the end. Soap operas or serial dramas, however, consist of an infinite middle that offers no suggestion of ending. Apart, that is, from when characters leave the series – when a sudden injection of high drama is needed or when the actors receive better offers elsewhere!

Plot features

EMOTIONAL COMPLICATIONS AND CLIMAXES

Actions and climaxes are usually of secondary importance in a soap opera. Catastrophes only provide convenient occasions for people to come together to vent their intense emotions and work out solutions. The emphasis in soap operas is not the significant event, but its build-up and aftermath.

PLOT EXPANSION As more and more people react to significant events or climaxes, the plot is said to expand, rather than progress. In a hospital drama, plot expansion may begin when a patient is found to have a fatal disease. First, doctors and nurses expand on the crisis, perhaps as they hold up the tell-tale X-rays. Then the story expands outwards even further as the patient is informed, relatives react to the news, friends and neighbours are included, and so on.

ROTATING PLOT LINES Another feature of soap opera plots is rotating plot lines. The plot shifts from one set of characters and their story to another. The serial's plot line rotates in this way through to the end of each episode. One soap opera writer has compared the multiple plots to a series of rolls of toilet paper, each with greater or lesser amounts of paper still on the roll.

CLIFF-HANGERS A standard feature in all serial dramas is the cliff-hanger – named after the predicament many matinee idols seemed to get into at the end of each episode. High-tension cliff-hangers are relatively rare in soap operas. Instead,

at the end of an episode, viewers are left pondering emotional options. A character may have received bad news or made an unexpected discovery. The audience can speculate on the future direction the story will take.

In *EastEnders*, the actors speak of turning to the last page each time they get a new script, to see who gets the 'dum-dum, dum, doosh!' – the dramatic high point with which the programme ends.

Plot styles

There are two styles of soap opera plot commonly in use: serial plot style and block plot style.

▶ **SERIAL PLOT STYLE** is the traditional format, as used in shows such as *Brookside* and *Neighbours*. The stories build to a cliff-hanger at the end of each episode; some plot lines can go on for months.

▶ **BLOCK PLOT STYLE** is a hybrid, which combines the self-contained story of a series drama with the continuing story of a serial. This form was created in Australia and is now familiar from a number of series, such as *The Bill*.

Programmes can be single one-hour blocks or multi-part. Each has a central story or issue which is resolved within the two hours. At the same time, the serial element is used as a background to the episodes, sometimes with ongoing stories, or at least character detail.

COMMON THEMES

LOVE is at the centre of many plots. Soap operas are a kind of romance and the emotions springing from love provide a reservoir of stories. Love makes people ambitious, jealous, bitter, vengeful – and even happy, sometimes.

CONFLICT is of course the basis of all drama. However, the focus is very much on *personal* relationships. Although many characters are shown in a place of work, there is scarcely any reference to difficulties they may be having there. *Industrial* relationships are definitely off the agenda.

SECRETS AND CONFIDENCES have afforded soap operas some of their very best moments. The exchange of information between characters sets up conflict and dramatic irony (where the audience know more than some of the characters), and secures audience attention to find out what happens when the secrets come out.

SICKNESS AND INJURY are common problems on soap operas. Some soap operas are even set in hospitals. Characters rarely die from disease, however – most die because of accidents or violence. The banalities of diagnosis and patient treatment do not make for useful drama – the melodramatic potential of this setting is much more the focus of interest When soap opera characters do die from disease, it is usually a rare and sensational affliction with a glamorous name.

SKELETONS IN THE CUPBOARD emerge with startling frequency. Old lovers, business acquaintances, spouses, so-called friends, errant parents and even children turn up, to threaten the calm of the current situation.

PLANS GOING WRONG are another recurring feature. Despite the best efforts and intentions of the instigators, problems occur and nothing quite works out as intended. Usually, these also ripple outwards and affect others in various ways. The impossibility of ever doing anything right seems to be an enduring feature of life for characters in soap operas. The negative nature of this message is offset, however, by the fact that very little permanent or serious damage ever seems to result from this.

Writing for soap operas

On our serials, we have a team of four storyliners and one story editor who create the plot

progression of the programme. Once the storylines have been created they are farmed out to a team of freelance writers who then develop the script from there. The team numbers about ten or twelve. Once written, they are then edited by the script editors. There are usually two to a show.

The writer gets one week to write the script and the editors have to edit two half-hour episodes per week. It's all based on how many episodes are made of the show on a weekly basis. Serials are usually produced at the rate of two hours per week (or five half hours). The writers work six weeks ahead of studio production.

Peter Pinne,
Grundy Productions,
Australia

▼ ▼ ▼

Every soap opera has a 'bible'. This is an enormous reference book outlining the past, present and projected future of the programme. A page is added to the book each episode. With a team of writers working separately on different episodes, it is vital that they remain informed of both previous and future developments.

▼ ▼ ▼

Different executive producers have different styles but generally, as with other soaps, writers attend occasional story conferences. Here stories and character developments are suggested and discussed with script editors and producers. Anything said is filtered back to the script department, where the story editor may or may not take it on board.

Sean Day-Lewis,
Talk of Drama
(on writing for *EastEnders*)

▼ ▼ ▼

▼ ▼ ▼ ▼ ▼ ▼

activities

1. How many crises have threatened to overwhelm your favourite soap opera character? Select a character and draw up a dramatic profile of events.

2. Look at the table reprinted below and then answer the questions.

▶ How would you explain the increase in family and marital problems?

▶ Why has the percentage of social and romantic problems declined, do you think?

▶ 'Soap operas seem to have narrowed in scope since 1941.' Would you agree or disagree? Use the figures to support your answer.

PROBLEMS IN US SOAP OPERAS

PROBLEM	1941	1987
Family	18%	28%
Marital	10%	22%
Medical	9%	16%
Social	22%	11%
Romance	16%	11%
Crime	9%	11%
Other	16%	0%

Figure 4.22

3. Identify the plot rotation in an episode of a soap opera. Note down each change of character group/setting/plot as it occurs. Comment on the degree of advancement of the plot – would you say much happens in each segment?

Outline any examples of soap opera plots involving love, sickness or confused identity.

4. When an actor has to leave, writers may be forced to use even the most unlikely stories to 'write out' the character.

Suppose you are a scriptwriter. Choose a famous soap opera character and suggest ways to 'write them out' of the series. Set out a brief plot line that matches up with the character's expected behaviour.

5. Many production houses start off a story with a conference of writers. Act out one of these conferences. Use the following steps as a guide.

▶ Form groups of four to five people.

▶ Decide on the general story. It could be an original idea or it could be based on an existing soap opera.

▶ Allocate a point of view about the progress of the story to each member. For example, one writer wants the hero to marry while another wants him to die tragically.

▶ Hold the conference and try to bring the group to agreement on the outline to the whole story.

Soap Opera Characters

For a good soap, good writing is absolutely essential. Believable characters of different age groups and behaviour patterns so that you're going to get a natural conflict of ideas. Some characters slightly larger than life so that people will either love them or hate them.

Julia Smith
Creator of *EastEnders*

▼ ▼ ▼

Original patterns

In the early days of soap operas, casts – and costs – were much more limited than they are today. This was due largely to their scheduling as daytime viewing: the big investment has always been in programmes for the evening.

One of the major consequences for characters in early soap operas was that they tended to fall into stock 'types'. All narrative needs certain roles to be fulfilled to drive the story forwards. The following could be found, in one form or another, in most soap operas:

▶ **THE SCHEMING VILLAINESS** Often the star of the show, the scheming villainess was also sometimes presented as a victim – an unhappy child, an abused wife or unlucky in love. Unlike the good characters, however, she used and manipulated people to save her own skin. While everyone had problems, the villainess connived to work her way out of her disadvantages through ruthless scheming.

► **THE LONG-SUFFERING WOMAN** The female victim is the character the majority of the audience feels for the most. They tend to put themselves in her shoes – they identify with her. Watching her through daily crises several days a week, some viewers know her better than their own friends and neighbours. The long-suffering victim must have some obvious strengths. She must be caring and loving, and she must have great amounts of willpower. Above all, she must be seen to be a creative force, rather than a destructive one.

► **THE HELPFUL PROBLEM SOLVER** This was a person of great experience and sound judgment. Often with a regrettable past, he/she is thus protected from accusations of being a 'do-gooder'.

► **THE ROMANTIC HERO** If it were a fairy tale, he would be a handsome prince. In soap operas, the romantic hero is single, handsome and available. Often tearaways or rebels, they are never allowed to be too wild. They must be available for the stable wedded life. The romantic hero walks a tightrope between an attractive sense of danger and boring sturdiness.

► **THE RUTHLESS VILLAIN** Like the villainess, the villain was popular with fans. This is not so much because they liked him as a person, but because they appreciated his importance in dealing up a good story. He despoiled all the pretty girls (except the heroine). He spent money extravagantly, he got drunk and insulting, and he ruined his rivals. Whatever he did had an evil motive: that made things very simple.

Many of these characteristics derived from even earlier melodramas, popular at the beginning of the century. Some have survived into our current soap operas, although today characters tend to be more rounded, complex individuals.

Complicating the cast

One of the major consequences of transferring into the prime-time slots has been the big increase in the size of casts. Most soap operas have a cast of fifteen to twenty regular characters, although not all of them will be 'on deck' at any one time. Soap operas always have many more characters than other programmes such as crime drama or situation comedy series. This is because soap operas must have enough characters to populate the various rotating plot lines. As well as the complement of regular characters, there must be provision for new entrants. These characters can introduce fresh story lines.

Regular characters will have certain defined aspects to their personalities that will need to be observed at all times. However, a distinguishing feature of modern soaps is the possibility of *development*. They may go through experiences that cause them to change in some way. Phil Mitchell in *EastEnders*, for example, had a problem with alcoholism for some time. The problems this caused him in his personal life were considerable. Slowly, painfully, he learned to overcome this dependency: the struggle then and the constant vigilance thereafter show the character learning from his experience and changing his behaviour as a result.

The roles of trouble-maker, gossip, liar, cheat and so on tend now to be picked up by different characters at different times. This produces much more complex, interesting and credible characters.

Figure 4.23
Pat and Roy from **EastEnders**. *Sometimes characters are 'rested' from the programme for a while, only to return later and continue casting their spells.*

Attracting audiences

For any programme to be successful, it has to have across-the-board appeal, i.e. to children, teenagers, young marrieds and the older bracket. The twenty- to thirty-year-old age group is the hardest to attract, as most people in this group do not watch television on a regular basis. In order to maximise a serial's potential, the age range of the characters tends to reflect the age range of the viewers. People like to identify with their own peer group. They also like to watch attractive looking actors. Therefore, a conscious effort is made to find and cast the best-looking talent available.

▼ ▼ ▼ ▼ ▼ ▼ ▼

activities

1. Choose a soap opera and draw up tables similar to those below. Either by watching several episodes, or remembering those of previous weeks, consider characters as they are involved in two separate plot incidents. Fill in the table, then answer the questions below.

PLOTLINE 1		
CHARACTER	PROBLEM	CHARACTER'S REACTION

PLOTLINE 2		
CHARACTER	PROBLEM	CHARACTER'S REACTION

▶ Was there any change or development in the personality of the character? Did he or she appear to learn anything from the experience of plotline one?

▶ In your opinion, does character development make scriptwriting of plots easier or more difficult? Explain your answer.

2. If scriptwriters allowed characters to be totally stereotyped, the shows would become boring. Select a soap opera character and explain what it is that adds depth to him or her.

Outline the basic role that he or she has and then expand this with the features that extend his or her character: vulnerable points, soft spots, any examples of a capacity to love, good and bad points, etc.

Explain what motivates the character. What aspects of the character are not stereotyped?

3. Imagine that you are an executive of a television production company selling serials in a foreign country. Prepare an advertisement for one of the well-known soap operas, including an introductory guide to the main characters.

Outline each of their personalities and their place in the overall scheme of things.

4. Soap opera characters now do develop and change. Outline any significant changes that have occurred to one or more characters with which you are familiar and describe the events that brought about that change.

5. In a group, script a short soap opera segment showing a major crisis. Choose well-known soap opera characters and write them into the script as characters involved in the crisis. Allow plenty of scope for them to show their best-known characteristics.

Avoid using the character names and then act the segment out to other members of your class. Ask them to identify the characters from your portrayal.

Film the most popular segments as a further extension of this activity.

Soap Opera Settings

The strong melodramatic plots of soap operas are sometimes called 'potboilers'. The setting is like the 'pot' or the cauldron – it holds all the ingredients within it. The setting of the soap opera creates the sense of community and provides the opportunity for the characters to become involved in each other's lives.

Setting requirements

All soap opera settings several have basic features in common.

MEETING PLACES Ideally, the setting should have a variety of meeting places or at least provide a reason for the characters to meet each other. Cafés and bars are good for this purpose, with their ever-changing flow of customers.

PRIVATE LOCATIONS For the more personal, and often intense, encounters, private locations are best. Individual homes provide the bulk of these, although places of work can also be called upon – but only when conveniently empty of customers or colleagues.

A LIMITED WORLD The soap opera setting should have clearly defined limits. Geographically, all the locations used tend to be in close proximity. The soap opera world is a somewhat closed one – a small pond with a mixture of big fish.

REGULARS AND NEWCOMERS A good setting allows for a number of main characters, as well as the arrival of newcomers on a regular basis.

A MIX OF AGES Characters of mixed age ranges must be able to interact naturally. The mix of ages is needed to guarantee broad target audiences, as people naturally identify most readily with their own peer group.

Real communities

Since the arrival of post-industrial society, people have been told that the only constant is change. Soap opera viewers are members of a society that has been in a state of constant transformation. Increasing commercialism, lack of security in employment, geographic mobility and the loss of extended families have all taken their toll. Most analysts believe there is now a yearning throughout the Western world for the secure communities of a 'golden past'.

Possibly the most appealing aspect of soap operas and serials is that people are always connected to each other, whether through love or hate. They have time to drink cups of tea, to gossip, speculate and interfere in each other's business. This can be reassuring in a world where most people would not have a clue whether or not they are living next door to the Yorkshire Ripper.

'Homey' soap communities

Many people find solace in the secure communities of soap operas. After all, some have lasted for more than thirty years. In this small world, people have time to care.

▼ ▼ ▼

As real-life communities and the traditional family group have deconstructed, so our reliance on the virtual communities of soap has become more important in our lives. The television audience may be going through massive change as the viewer is confronted by choice, but the soaps are the remaining shared experience.

The traditional family gathering around the glowing box every evening is a thing of the past. But although the viewing experience may be physically separated, the emotional one remains stable as the family all unite around one common slot each night. The Soap.

Mal Young
Head of Drama Series, BBC

▼ ▼ ▼

A close-knit community that also has a sense of connection with the outside world is not easy to find. When the BBC began planning a soap opera in 1983, they received dozens of ideas for settings before they finally settled on the East End of London.

▼ ▼ ▼

They just wouldn't have worked. There was one about a mobile home site, which wasn't a starter – far too limiting and restricting in the way it could be

Figures 4.24 and 4.25

A trick of editing can create an instant soap opera community. The studio interior of a house from **Neighbours** *is edited with an external shot of a house in a suburban street, many kilometres away. The connection is fictional. The result is Ramsay Street.*

presented. There was another about a shopping arcade – nice idea, but too expensive with all the extras that would be needed. There was just one part of London that seemed right – the East End. It appeared to have absolutely everything – vitality, community spirit, ethnic minorities, strong family ties, young people, the right atmosphere and, of course, all those larger-than-life Cockney characters.

Julia Smith
Creator of *EastEnders*

▼ ▼ ▼

Soap opera producers have a liking for certain types of 'homey' physical settings. These are listed below.

THE SUBURBS are often used in soaps. Safely away from the world of work, this is where all the dramas of personal life take place. Close enough to big towns or cities for their problems to intrude occasionally, but far enough away to enable the domestic to dominate. *Neighbours* and *Brookside* are good examples of this.

THE INNER CITY is very rarely used, except where it can offer a closed world, somewhat isolated from the full complexity of modern life, yet still with potential for interaction with the larger world. An inner city area with a high proportion of minority

groups or a strong class culture can provide this kind of setting, such as *EastEnders* or *Coronation Street*.

THE COUNTRY TOWN provides the necessary interlocking relationships. *Emmerdale*, along with the radio serial *The Archers*, offers a variety of locations both within the town itself, and out among the surrounding farms.

Australian soap operas have chosen small country towns, small beach communities and close-knit streets in anonymous suburbs. All are safely away from the evils of the city and the isolation of the outback. Yet refugees from these threatening places can still provide story lines.

Families

All soap operas rely on the family as the basis of character relationships. Most focus on the family in the community. Some realist soap operas see the community as a declining force. The level of support offered by local busybodies and next-door neighbours is seen as likely to provoke audience disbelief. Soap operas in the realist style have tended to narrow the focus to the family alone.

Caring workplaces

The caring professions make an excellent basis for soap opera settings. Certain of them – medical practitioners, nurses, vets and even the police force – have been used time and time again. The distinctions between 'true' soap operas and other drama series, such as *Casualty* and *The Bill* have tended to blur over the years.

Standing like a great brick and concrete outcrop in a sea of anonymous suburbia, the general hospital is the perfect world within a world. This bustling community offers its own social system of doctors, nurses and patients. Ready-made plots with life and death climaxes are lying in every bed. That love should spring easily seems only natural in such a place of everyday miracles.

Like the hospital, the police station is a refuge of safety in a heartless world. And veterinary practices in small country towns combine people's fondness for animals with that most basic feature of soap operas – that everybody should know everybody else.

activities

1. The creator of *EastEnders*, Julia Smith, thought a mobile home site was too limiting for a soap opera. Can you think of any limitations with this idea? Do you agree with her?

2. Criticise these possible settings and titles for a soap opera. What limitations do they have?
▶ *Guiding Beacon* – the story of a lighthouse keeper's large family and their lives together on an island in stormy seas.

▶ *Twilight Days* – the laughter and the tears of life in an old people's home.
▶ *Flight Deck* – ups and downs in the private lives of the pilots and flight attendants who keep our planes in the air.

3. Suggest some fresh 'small world' settings for soap operas that have so far been ignored by the producers. What advantages do they have? What are their limitations?

Representation on Soap Operas

The media have replaced religion as the chief means of spreading moral values, according to some media analysts. These moral teachings are quite apparent in soap operas. With large and loyal audiences, soap operas are at liberty to explore social issues and present a range of viewpoints. Quite often, a soap opera has helped to modify community attitudes.

Scriptwriters are approached by all sorts of groups eager to portray their message to the community – not least the government, who wish to encourage educative storylines on topics such as safe sex, cancer, drug abuse and so on. They want to use media power for positive purposes. Media commentators suggest that it is time for television to recognise two things. First, that it has social responsibilities and, secondly, that it can replace ignorance and prejudice with informed community awareness and friendship.

Realism

Soap operas aim for a feeling that their world is similar to real life and lived experience. Family-centred, focused on relationships and with familiar domestic settings and plots, their aim is to reassure, rather than to challenge. The audience is encouraged to believe they are watching a parallel world – similar to their own, but separate.

Soap operas also deal with the social issues and the concerns of the time. Since both the real world and the soap opera world are dealing with

similar issues, the realism of the programme is further enhanced.

What sort of real world?

The world of *Neighbours* is the world of the detergent advert; everything from the kitchen worktops to the S-bend is squeaky clean. Everyone's hair and underwear is freshly laundered. No one is shabby or eccentric; no one is poor or any colour but white. *Neighbours* is the Australian version of the American dream, owner-occupied, White-Anglo-Saxon-Protestant paradise.

Germaine Greer
Writer and academic

▼ ▼ ▼

Figure 4.26
Scriptwriters are often asked to manipulate the social conscience of the audience. Soap operas can portray messages from all manner of organisations, government or otherwise.

Critics of the representation of the world offered by soap operas focus on a variety of areas. Not all will apply to every programme.

DISTORTED WORLD According to American critic Ruth Rosen, soap opera characters rarely eat except at restaurants; motherhood is glorified, but no one is ever glimpsed caring for the offspring; family life is praised, but divorces occur at twice the real frequency; amnesia is a common disease; lots of people have split personalities; and once, a woman spent seventeen days in a revolving door having flashbacks!

REACTIONARY IDEOLOGY As a form, soap opera tends to be reactionary in its ideology. Characters are caught in a kind of moral time-warp: nobody is allowed to change or develop in any real sense. Any character that does anything radical is obliged to leave. Anyone attempting to do anything to try to improve the small world they inhabit is punished, ridiculed or villainised. *EastEnders* is a classic example of this.

PROBLEMS ARE PERSONAL No attempt is made to link the problems characters have to larger social causes. For example, in *Neighbours*, Brad was a happy-go-lucky surfer. He was also unemployed, but unemployment as a social issue was only presented as a matter of Brad's personality. Unemployment is also usually seen as a male problem only.

CONFLICT IS RESOLVED The inner circle of the family is seen as the solution to all problems. Quite difficult social problems are resolved through family love, courage and tolerance. Absence of family support is repeatedly shown as a distinct shortcoming in the lives of key characters; one that they are keenly aware of. How reflective of today's world this is – when families are increasingly dispersed geographically – is open to question.

LEAD FROM BEHIND It could never be said that soap operas are important catalysts for social change. They follow from a safe distance, rather than lead. They do not commit themselves to progressive solutions to problems. Instead, they aim for the 'middle ground' or the consensus viewpoint. *Brookside* may have pioneered the first lesbian screen kiss, but this came only after social recognition of lesbianism had become much more widely established. The pressure for high ratings means most soap operas never go beyond mild reformism. To create an identity of being socially progressive, of course, there is quite a lot of competition between soaps to be the first to introduce 'daring' topics.

UNREALISTIC MINORITY CHARACTERS Minority characters often have to stand for the whole of their population, as so few of them are given important roles. Consequently, the soap opera producers have a problem. Minority characters are unable to be villains for fear it will promote racism, but there is no room for them as heart-throbs or heroes either. As a result, they often end up as 'wishy-washy'. *EastEnders* is the one clear exception here. Recently, it has introduced a number of new characters from different ethnic minority backgrounds. They are neither 'token' (merely there to fill an obvious gap) nor marginalised, but are well-rounded, complex personalities in their own right.

▼ ▼ ▼ ▼ ▼ ▼

activities

1. List some difficult social problems that you have watched soap operas wrestle with recently. How would you rate the soap operas' stance: ahead of public opinion, level with it or safely lagging behind?

2. Can you work out the overall moral standpoint of a particular soap opera? Start by listing the broad view it has taken of issues recently. Does an overall philosophy/point of view emerge? Write your answer in a paragraph.

3. Soap operas can express their morality as much by what is left out as by what is shown. Make a list of taboo areas that a soap opera could discourage by never allowing them to appear.

4. Apart from various charities and benefits, which groups would most like to portray their messages on soap operas? Consider which groups would have the best chance. Which groups would have little chance? Explain.

5. Recent studies have highlighted differences between British, US and Australian soap operas regarding morality. What differences can you see in the following areas? Mention specific dramas.
- ▶ money (and greed)
- ▶ family life
- ▶ marriage
- ▶ single parents
- ▶ male–female sex role

6. Many media academics say that soap operas concentrate on the personal, instead of the larger social meanings of problems. Find examples to either support or refute this criticism.

Where you agree with the criticism, list the examples and explain how the programme could have dealt with the issue differently. Where you disagree with this criticism, show why.

The Soap Opera Audience

Fans of soap operas get very involved with the characters. The stars tell hair-raising stories of fans who confuse them with their character roles. The 'Free the Weatherfield One' campaign (when Deirdre was duped by her boyfriend and imprisoned for credit card fraud on *Coronation Street*) gathered a lot of momentum – attracting even the support of the prime minister, Tony Blair. The tendency to get immersed in the fiction does not end with the viewers. In South American soap opera *Cuerpo E Alma*, the leading man murdered his leading lady *in real life* when their on-screen relationship ended.

While those who confuse reality are a tiny minority, most people get involved in what they see as television. Lionel Tiger, an anthropologist, says: 'Our sense of community apparently may include fictional television characters.' Relationships with fictional characters are not new. The Ancient Greeks believed in the literal reality of their myths.

▼ ▼ ▼

There are an awful lot of lonely people in the world who live in bed-sitters. If we can give them something they can discuss over their shop counter the next morning then it's worthwhile. Soaps aren't only for families, they're important to a lot of people living by themselves, too.

Julia Smith
Creator of *EastEnders*

▼ ▼ ▼

Who watches?

A surprising number of people watch daytime soap operas. The US audience, for example, is estimated to be more than fifty million. Around 80 per cent are women.

The swelling of the ranks of the unemployed and under-employed since the 1980s has increased the number of daytime viewers. Even though more people have jobs today, the flexible or part-time nature of much employment means that many are still able to tune in during the day. Increases in the numbers of university and college students have also altered the traditional audience profile.

For prime-time soap operas, the bulk of the audience is still female. but a large minority is male. Apart from this bias to one sex, the other aspects of the audience are the same as for television audiences in general. Similarly, the levels of education amongst soap opera viewers are the same as in the community as a whole.

A spectator sport

Sports fans talk in a language of tactics and principles that outsiders find hard to follow. Soap operas work in a similar way: knowledge of the internal workings of the cast greatly enhances the pleasure to be had from watching.

In soap operas, of course, characters are heavily interrelated – either directly, through family, or indirectly, through relationships and dealings that go back a long way. While one purpose of this is to rule out the need for outsiders to create action, another reason is to encourage audience involvement. Viewers know the ins and outs of every relationship and follow characters often until death – and sometimes beyond! The more complicated the background, the more those viewers who know what is going on can enjoy being spectators. The more the spectator knows, the more likely he or she is to wait and see how everything turns out.

Why we watch

Some researchers say the elderly, for example, watch soap operas for friendship and company. Other researches have found soap operas are often discussed among friends and so give viewers something to share. A major thrust of the BBC's advertising for *EastEnders* has plugged the notion that 'it's the one that everyone's talking about'.

Brookside's producer, Phil Redmond, says we watch because soap operas give us a sense of belonging and identity.

One of the main findings to come out of audience research into soap opera viewing is that viewers are capable of complex judgments about the programmes. Morality and ethics feature highly in people's responses; audiences hold very forthright views, and are swift to respond to on-screen events.

However, what they respond to can sometimes be interesting in itself. *Brookside*'s highest ever source of complaints was the episode when Barry Grant appeared to be about to kill a dog that he had kidnapped. The actual rape of Sheila Grant, in another episode, provoked nothing like so much audience fury.

Uses and gratifications

Richard Kilborn, of the University of Stirling, has examined uses and gratifications research (see p. 31) and noted seven main reasons audiences find soaps 'gratifying'.

► Soap opera scheduling provides a regular encounter.
► Sharing opinions provides social interaction.
► Soap operas fulfil person-centred needs (viewing pleasure).
► People identify and get involved with the programmes.
► Soap operas provide escapism.
► People learn from the programmes.
► Watching a soap is like watching a game.

▼ ▼ ▼ ▼ ▼ ▼ ▼

activities

1. Recognition of soap opera characters is said to be higher than for other television programmes. Test this assertion. Make a list of prime-time soap opera characters. Identify them by some aspect of their personality, or by incidents that have occurred that involved them. See what percentage of your class recognises each one. Do the same for a prime-time crime drama, then compare the results.

2. Plots are complicated so that viewers in-the-know can enjoy being knowledgeable. Soap operas are a kind of spectator sport. Demonstrate this by forming a panel of soap opera fans. Write a quiz on the fine details of plot and character in one soap opera, and award points according to how much each fan knows.

3. Survey the reasons for soap opera watching amongst viewers you know of. Write down their reasons in short paragraphs. Sort all your answers

into categories of reasons and briefly summarise those reasons.

For each category, find the best quote from your answers and include it in your summary. Write up the results in about 200 words.

major assignment

Written assignment

Choose one of these assignments and write a 600-word essay.

1. Watch several episodes of a well-known soap opera. Discuss the plot in detail. Examine any rotating plot lines, outline what common stories are dealt with and discuss the treatment of action climaxes.

2. How stereotyped are the characters on your favourite soap opera? Watch several episodes and search for any clear-cut character types, such as the busybody, or the schemer. Analyse how these character types are used in the soap opera. Is there anything that prevents the character from being a stereotype? Evaluate the overall level of stereotyping in the programme.

3. What social issues have you seen examined on soap operas? Evaluate any differences you see in the treatment compared with the treatment on a current affairs programme. Conclude with an opinion on whether you think it is right that a soap opera should examine social issues, or whether it is too much like an attempt to preach to audiences, and tell them what they should think

4. Contrast the pace of a day-time soap opera and a prime-time soap opera. Compare the amount of action in each rotating plot line. Analyse the use of outside shots. Compare the use of close-ups. Conclude with an opinion on which you think is the more interesting programme.

Production assignment

Choose one of these assignments

1. Film a sixty-second advertisement or trailer for a new soap opera of your creation. The action can be shot with the aid of role-play, drawings, sketches, and pictures from books, models and footage you take on location. The trailer should give some idea of the following:

- ▶ title and theme music
- ▶ small-world setting
- ▶ characters who adopt the roles of heroine, villainess, hero, helpful problem solver, etc.
- ▶ possible plot developments showing at least glimpses of two rotating plot lines.

2. *Minutes of Our Lives* is the title of a comedy sketch you are filming. In two minutes of pot-boiling anguish, you will use all the conventions of soap operas.

You can introduce all the characters, make them thoroughly miserable, give them exotic diseases and then dramatically kill them off in a heart-wrenching big close-up.

Television Comedy

Traditional performance comedy styles

Over its long history, performance comedy has settled into several basic categories.

FARCE is mad comedy with a crazy, exaggerated plot. Anything can happen. Characters in a farce are usually outlandish and odd rather than believable people. The focus is on an increasingly frenetic action and how far a picture of reality can be distorted.

BLACK COMEDY takes what would normally be tragedy and makes a savage, cruel humour out of it. It deals with realistic situations and characters, and manipulates them in order to expose inherent weaknesses or contradictions.

It is meant to be taken as both serious and funny, at one and the same time. Black comedy can also be known as *tragic farce*.

BURLESQUE is a take-off of the serious, formal styles of tragedy or romance. A modern, comic version of Shakespeare's play *Romeo and Juliet* would be a burlesque.

Burlesque depends on a wide gap between the mundane, day-to-day subject matter and the grand style. Many humorous advertisements use a burlesque style.

COMEDY OF MANNERS uses a clever, witty character to poke fun at all that is awkward, stuffy and boring.

SATIRE uses humour as a weapon of criticism. Alone of all the types of humour, it has an essentially serious moral purpose. Its ultimate intention is to expose shortcomings in people, and help push them towards better ways of doing or seeing things. The attacks that are made can be quite vicious, and highly personal. For it to be true satire, it has got to hurt the victim.

Comedy on television

In its earliest forms, comedy on television consisted mainly of variety shows, in a pattern set largely by radio, and probably harking back to the days of the Victorian music halls. A series of separate items – sketches, solo stand-up slots and duets – would be interspersed with songs, and dance routines. In many respects, even a show such as *Monty Python's Flying Circus* followed in this tradition: more manic, perhaps, but essentially the same format (although excluding the musical turns!).

That style of programme has now effectively disappeared from our screens.

Only three basic styles of comedy appear as television series with any regularity: the situation comedy, the sketch comedy and stand-up comedy.

SITUATION COMEDIES, or comedy dramas, place regularly appearing characters in funny situations. Just as you have to 'be there' to see the funny side of some things in real life, so in situation comedies (sitcoms) you have to know the characters and watch the mess they get into to derive enjoyment. Seeing how they get out of things is half the humour.

Since they are usually short thirty-minute dramas, the basics of plot, character and setting are very important. Situation comedies are a distant relative of the comedy of manners. Both are comedies of character and personality.

The United Kingdom has a very long tradition of programmes of this kind – extending back to examples such as *Steptoe & Son*, with others still being shown (*Reginald Perrin*, *Dad's Army*), and yet others still being made (*Only Fools and Horses: Xmas Special*).

Sitcoms have formal settings, are highly structured and are unvarying in the principle ingredients of the show. We get pleasure primarily

from seeing the embarrassing happening to someone we feel we know – and like!

SKETCH COMEDY is made up of a series of separate items, normally with no real linking theme. Topicality is often a feature – people and events in the news are favourite targets. However, ongoing human foibles are just as likely for inclusion. Unlike satire, there is no intention to provoke improvements – the emphasis is simply on making fun. Traditional farce, burlesque and black comedy provide the essential material for sketch comedy, as demonstrated by *French and Saunders* and *Goodness Gracious Me!*

STAND-UP COMEDY has been around since perhaps the dawn of time. A large part of its appeal is the sheer simplicity of a single performer who holds us with nothing else but the power of his or her material – and their style of delivery, of course! The solo comic has always had a special place in British culture.

In the mid-1980s, however, stand-up comedy underwent a significant shift of emphasis. Where previously performers had held our attention with the complicated, the bawdy or the erratic inventiveness of their stories, now the distinctly political began to feature at the heart of the routines. Performers such as Ben Elton began to make a concerted attack on the politicians of the times. Others, such as Jo Brand and Jenni Eclair, followed with challenging material on sexuality and many other former taboo subjects. In many ways, these performers were coming up through the late-night comedy circuits that were booming then. Changing tastes in audience social activities meant shifts in the nature of the material broadcast. Towards the end of 1999, Frank Skinner was in negotiations with the BBC for a £20 million deal. (It collapsed, but he did just about as well at ITV.)

Features of comedy

Most comedy follows basic conventions or traditional ways of doing things. There are three central elements. Different styles of comedy favour some of the elements over others.

STEREOTYPES Comedy deals in stereotypes and caricatures because the audience needs to

Figure 4.27
Ali G introduced a unique form of alternative comedy by going out on the streets to interview his 'victims'. He rapidly became mainstream with his own television series.

Figure 4.28
Some say the basis of humour is triumph. Trips, slips and stumbles (and squashings) are funny because they make us feel superior. In the cartoon, we naturally believe David will win against Goliath. When he gets his comeuppance, it is amusing, not least because it is unexpected.

recognise the humour quickly. There is no time for them to get to know a well-developed character and then see the funny side of this person. The character needs to be immediately funny. Physical characteristics and mannerisms, and ways of speaking can help to establish identity.

STARTLING EVENTS Comedy often begins with a startling announcement or event. The beginning of a comedy plunges the audience immediately into a world of humour. A general rule says, the more startling or difficult the beginning, the sweeter the ending.

Even the first lines of jokes follow this basic rule. Consider this first line: 'A man swallows his glass eye and goes to the doctor for advice …'. This surprising mishap sets the scene. We have entered a strange, funny world where anything can happen. Whatever conclusion follows the opener, it has to satisfy all our expectations for a sweet ending.

SNOWBALLING ACTION The action in comedy snowballs towards a conclusion. Comedy requires a simplification of the world so that everyone can understand and see the joke. Simplified characters plunge into a startling world, then accumulate one set of troubles after another. Repetition of confusion or absurdity also creates a snowballing effect. The comedy then accelerates to its conclusion. This works in a similar way to the climaxes in drama. The excitement of the audience rises and the desire for the resolution mounts. There is great relief when it finally comes, heightening audience pleasure.

The subject matter: what makes us laugh?

Television is a medium of entertainment which permits millions of people to listen to the same joke at the same time and yet remain lonesome.

T.S. Eliot

▼ ▼ ▼

The companionship of laughter is one of its most important elements – laughter is not often a solitary experience. After all, that is why comedies on television have laughter tracks (canned laughter).

Humour has a number of other important elements that are present in some form in all television comedies.

TRIUMPH

Primitive laughter is said to spring naturally from the throats of the victors after a battle. It expresses their joy and also releases the emotional strain of combat. The losers demobilise in the opposite way: they weep.

Someone slipping on a banana skin is greeted by a chorus of laughter. The audience has triumphed. The more dignified the victim, the more humiliating the defeat.

A number of theorists now believe laughter can be traced back to aggression and even hatred. Racism thrives on making fun of its victims: ridicule can be used to dehumanise peoples, paving the way for further, more physical assaults. Generally a great boon to humanity, laughter has often been manipulated – through jokes – to attack specific targets.

A battle can be fought with words alone. New York society wit Dorothy Parker was famous for her verbal triumphs. When informed that a certain actress was always kind to her inferiors, Parker replied, 'And where does she find them?' Bette Davis once described an ambitious and flirtatious starlet as 'the original good time who was had by all'. To ridicule someone or something is to triumph through language.

INCONGRUITY (UNLIKELY MISMATCHES)

Linking two elements that usually do not belong together will often provoke laughter. Comedy is created when the usually serious logic of most events is broken up and something unlikely appears. Sometimes even a contrast can make us laugh. A thin Stan Laurel and a fat Oliver Hardy; a short Ronnie Corbett and a large Ronnie Barker – these pairings prepare audiences to be ready for comedy.

EXAGGERATION

EXAGGERATION If a situation is blown up out of all proportion, the usual rules of logic no longer apply. Exaggeration is a common way of introducing incongruity. Comic possibilities then arise naturally.

ANIMATION When inanimate objects are brought to life, the result is also an incongruous situation. In one episode of *The Young Ones*, the refrigerator door opened and a tomato began a conversation with the other rotting vegetable matter inside.

SURPRISE

A man sits down, but someone has snatched the chair away and he falls on the floor. When something is expected but does not happen, the result is comedy. A bucket of water finds an unsuspecting victim. It can be equally funny for something to occur when nothing is expected. The element of surprise can be defined as the absence of what ought to be.

SURPRISE IN LANGUAGE is sometimes all too easy to achieve. The huge number of English words with more than one meaning are constantly ambushing the unwary. *Malapropism* is the term that describes this tendency – from a famous character in an eighteenth-century play, who aspired to use long, fancy words, but often got the wrong ones! Mrs Buckett (*Keeping Up Appearances*) is an equally amusing modern exponent of this pretension.

PUNS are one form of surprise in language. We are expecting one meaning but receive another. A riddle based on a pun begins, 'Why was there no card playing on the Ark?' The answer is, 'Because Noah sat on the deck!' The humour is based on the two meanings of deck.

DOUBLE ENTENDRES lurk everywhere in English as well. From the French word for double meanings, *double entendres* are puns of a sexually suggestive type. Any vague use of 'it' and doubtful use of 'do' almost automatically becomes sexual.

Primitive tribes are said to have a highly developed sense of humour based on surprise in language. Because there is no written spelling to indicate the meanings, there is a much greater chance of puns and double entendres.

Surprise in language can also be introduced by switching a listener from one logical train of thought to another, less logical one. Stephen Leacock once wrote, 'The Legendary Bulbecks were a fabulous race; half man, half horse, half bird.' At first he seemed to be serious, until the absurdity of what he was actually saying dawned and the whole logical structure collapsed into nonsense.

▼ ▼ ▼ ▼ ▼ ▼ ▼

activities

1. Categorise the comedies now on television under the three main headings shown in the table set out below. Include the country of origin for each comedy.

2. Do certain television channels have a programming preference for one type of comedy? Consult a television guide for scheduling information. Report back to the class on your findings.

3. Set up a classroom television talk show, complete with a host, where panellists can debate the merits of their preferred comedy type. While panellists discuss which type of comedy they think is best, have somebody film the presentation and later edit in some example comedy footage.

4. The Monty Python picture below has a stereotyped character and a startling event. Identify and explain the effect of each of these. What elements of humour are in use here?

Figure 4.29

5. Write down the first lines of as many jokes as you can think of. How many of these make a startling announcement or plunge the audience into an unreal world? Explain how this is achieved in one of the lines you have thought of.

6. Watch a comedy on television, making sure you pay attention to the following:

▶ Count the repetition (or snowballing) in the action. The repetition could be a continually mistaken identity, a repeated fault (such as snobbery) or a repeated phrase or line.

▶ Try to find examples of the elements of humour: triumph, incongruity and surprise.

7. Here are some famous insults from the early days of Hollywood.

Groucho Marx: 'I never forget a face, but in your case I'll make an exception.'

Anonymous: 'I can't bear fools!'

Dorothy Parker: 'That's funny, your mother could.'

Now write down some of the funniest insults you have heard. If you cannot remember any, try making them up.

8. Traditionally, we have laughed (in triumph) at the unlucky or the foolish. What television characters have replaced the Roman fool, the village idiot, the court jester and the sad sack?

TELEVISION COMEDY CATEGORIES

COUNTRY OF ORIGIN	SITUATION COMEDY	SKETCH COMEDY	STAND-UP COMEDY

Situation Comedy

The situation comedy, or sitcom, has been the longest lasting style of entertainment on television. Other genres, such as Westerns and variety shows, have come and gone. It seems the sitcom has a special appeal to television audiences.

Part of the charm is in the situation itself: a regular and stable situation allows audiences to experience the special sense of 'being there'. It is undoubtedly the characters, however, who provide most of the appeal. Their quirks and eccentricities are what drive the humour and the audiences look for these qualities with predisposed affection.

The situation or 'comic trap'

'All successful situation comedies have some trap in which people must exist – like marriage', says scriptwriter Barry Took. The perfect situation for a sitcom, he believes, is 'a little enclosed world where you have to live by the rules'.

THE FAMILY The most popular of the enclosed worlds is the family. The family is seen as the source of individual strength. Family support is based on respect and love for the individual and this is confirmed at the end of each episode. Episode plots are built on the minor ways in which family members annoy or hurt each other.

OTHER COMIC TRAPS There are other comic traps. The army is an enclosed world and has provided many a sitcom series. *Porridge* was set in a prison. Flat-share comedies are another variation on the enclosed world format. *Men Behaving Badly* followed in this tradition.

Figure 4.30
Men Behaving
Badly, *a classic*
example of a flat-
sharing sitcom.
The enclosed
world that the
characters inhabit
is the comic trap
from which all
the humour flows.

Flow of humour

Once the situation has been established, the humour comes from the characters. The flow of humour in sitcoms can be uni-directional or multi-directional. Uni-directional comedy allows just one person to make all the jokes.

Rowan Atkinson in *Mr Bean* has total comic authority. The only truly funny character in the programme is *Mr Bean* himself. However, the same comic's *Blackadder* series was different. The humour is multi-directional. Many different characters are allowed to be funny.

In programmes with a comic duo, the humour is shared between them, often at the expense of other characters. Eddie and Patsy in *Absolutely Fabulous* shared all the laughs. A host of 'straight' characters, such as Eddie's daughter Saffron, are regularly humiliated.

Social comment

The situation comedy differs from parody or sketch comedy in that it maintains a 'surface reality'. The world of a situation comedy at first glance appears normal. It reflects a recognisable location, with features that are appropriate to it.

In an attempt to show society as it is in reality, American sitcoms in particular, have taken to making social comments. *M*A*S*H* ran from 1972 until 1983. Although it was set in Korea, few viewers can have failed to relate it to America's involvement in Vietnam. In some episodes, *M*A*S*H* abandoned humour altogether in favour of harsh criticism.

Copycat formulas

If one sitcom succeeds, it is followed by a score of similar ones. The success of one formula in capturing a certain audience results in the formula being applied again and again.

In the 1960s, there was *Bewitched* and *I Dream of Jeannie* (a genie). Towards the end of the 1960s, a family of ghouls in *The Munsters* competed with a similar *Addams Family*. Repeats of the shows are still popular today. *The Addams Family* reappeared in film form in 1991 and again in 1993.

Working-class families facing hard times was the copycat formula of the 1990s. The model was developed by *The Simpsons* and the unruly *Roseanne*.

In the United Kingdom, there has been a whole spate of situation comedies about dodgy but endearing working-class characters, from *Steptoe & Son* to *Only Fools and Horses* and, more recently, *The Royle Family*.

It is interesting to ask whether we are laughing *with* such characters or *at* them. Many British sitcoms base their humour on observing characters as they struggle to make themselves better than they really are – and failing. This in fact cuts across class lines, whether it is the working-class Del Boy, the middle-class Mrs Buckett or the (tending towards) upper-class Basil Fawlty.

▼ ▼ ▼ ▼ ▼ ▼ ▼

activities

1. Make a list of current situation comedies. Beside each one explain the 'trap' or 'enclosed world' that provides the comic action.

2. The humour in situation comedies can be unidirectional or multidirectional. Describe the flow of humour on one sitcom. Give some examples to illustrate your report.

3. Watch some American situation comedies, such as *Friends* or *The Simpsons*. What social comments, if any, are being made? List them and decide

whether any particular point of view is being promoted.

4. Make a list of social issues that would be likely to displease advertisers and corporate sponsors.

5. What audiences *should* sitcoms be written for, that are at present being ignored? Explain your answer.

6. Examine a selection of sitcoms for the ways in which they represent people of different social, racial, gender and regional origins.

Sitcom Plots

Figure 4.32
Set in a veterinary practice, Beast depended on visual humour and 'wacky' events.

They may be just ordinary families living in quiet urban/suburban/inner-city streets, but in each episode the most trying events befall them. The only thing that separates sitcoms from soap operas is that, in sitcoms, the problems are all resolved happily, every episode.

The sitcom plot is the story outline of the 'funny things' that will happen to the characters in each episode. Plots are sometimes fairly slight. This is not a problem because the plot is mainly there to carry the fifty or so gags and one-liners that make up the humour. We do not expect them to address serious issues, and do not criticise them for being unrealistic. Only for not being funny.

Figure 4.33
Blackadder broke new ground for a sitcom when the last series ended with a shockingly sombre finale that suggested the deaths of its main characters.

The situation

Situation comedies tend to be long-running. The situation, or 'comic trap' itself must be sufficiently stable to withstand the continual minor upsets that begin each episode. Unlike a serial, there must be no threat of change at the end of each episode. They always end happily and no one gets killed.

The situation comedy is a series that must be capable of endless reproduction. Whatever happens, each episode must not change the characters or the overall situation. The next episode must also be able to start with the same basic series ingredients.

The importance of this rule can easily be seen when it is deliberately broken. Final episodes often introduce some plot line to destroy the series. In the final episode of *The Young Ones*, they commandeered a bus and drove it along a dangerous winding road. Neil called out, 'Look out for that cliff face!' But his warning came too late. The bus crashed through a giant billboard picture of Cliff Richard's face and rolled over in flames to the bottom of a rocky cliff. The sitcom formula has been broken. The characters have gone the same way as the bus. Too much has now changed and the series can no longer be reproduced.

A similar profound change of mood signalled the final end of the *Blackadder* series: when the team rose to go 'over the top', the only sound that could be heard was the sudden, ominous chattering of machine guns. There were no more laughs.

Stages in the sitcom plot

The plot of a sitcom is made up of three basic parts: the establishment of the problem, the complication and confusion and, finally, the resolution.

ESTABLISHING THE PROBLEM takes up several scenes at the beginning of the show. In each episode, the characters need to face some comic difficulty.

COMPLICATION AND CONFUSION are the result of the problem, and so the story line develops. Complication usually develops out of some sort of human error or mistake. In the resulting confusion the humour builds up. Characters interact with each other and heighten the confusion. The snowballing confusion has a similar effect on the audience of a comedy that suspense does in a thriller.

Quick scene changes build a frenzied pace. It is rare for a scene to last longer than two minutes. Some scenes only last ninety seconds.

RESOLUTION OF THE CONFUSION comes just when it seems things could not get any further out of hand. All the errors are quickly put right. Everything soon gets back to normal. The audience breathes a collective sigh of relief. This 'sigh of relief' contrasts with the audience response at the end of a crime drama or thriller. In a thriller, as the last jigsaw piece is put in place, the audience is more likely to say 'Aha!'

Sitcoms tend to resolve themselves by resorting to proverbs, sayings or common-sense folk wisdom. Simple remedies allow the characters to solve their problems and even learn to laugh at them. Everyone delights in the restored companionship when it is all over – even the audience feels reassured.

▼ ▼ ▼ ▼ ▼ ▼ ▼

activities

1. Choose a situation comedy that is familiar to you. Briefly explain the overall situation, then outline some of the funny things that have happened to the characters in the series episodes. Deal with at least two episodes.

2. Think up a plot setting for a situation comedy – an enclosed world for the characters. Now suggest a number of story lines for some episodes in the series. Base these plot lines on small upsets to the stability of the 'comic trap'.

3. Suppose you wanted to kill off a situation comedy now popular on television. How would you introduce change in a final episode that would prevent it from returning to normal.

4. Count the number and duration of the scenes in a popular sitcom. How many scenes are there? How many are longer than 90 seconds?

5. Identify the three main parts of a sitcom plot as they occur in a comedy with which you are familiar. For each stage (i.e. the problem stage, the complications stage and the resolution), provide a brief summary of events. Time the duration of each stage and record the results on a programme time line.

The Crime Drama Genre

Crime dramas or police shows make up approximately 20 per cent of prime time programming in all television markets throughout the English-speaking world.

Every night, civilisation comes under threat from murderers, muggers, blackmailers and petty thieves. In television-land, however, crime never pays. It is always unsuccessful. Just before the last advertisement, the cops catch the criminals. The audience is reassured. If the law is broken, law enforcers will track down the offender. Society will be protected. The fact that this bears little relation to real life appears to have no bearing on the public's appetite for more.

Defining the genre

One critic has referred to crime shows as 'comedies of public safety'. The demands of series programming mean the main characters can never be killed off.

In traditional tragedy, the death of the hero is always likely – usually through his or her own weaknesses. In traditional comedy, everything ends happily and no one is killed. The conventions of television series writing mean that the crime show is closer to a classic definition of comedy than it is to tragedy. Not that there is anything remotely resembling humour in them.

Traditionally, melodrama has been the most powerful stylistic feature of crime drama, just as it has in soap operas. The happy endings, the moralistic tone and the exaggerated sense of community threat are all classic melodramatic features.

However, the usual melodramatic battle between good and evil is not really a battle at all. Everyone knows what the outcome will be. The television crime series rarely comments on the universal eternal struggle between good and evil, law and chaos. This is not why audiences watch. They watch to see just exactly how the cop will finally catch the criminal. The identity of a show is determined by the personality of the law enforcer going about his or her business. The interest comes from the interaction with others and 'lifestyle' factors.

Over the past ten years, notably, there has been a wholly new breed of crime drama, where much more difficult material is tackled. Sometimes, the police themselves *are* the criminals – or at least as morally ambiguous as them. Psychotic criminals, serial killings and mutilations seem to be increasingly the audience-pullers of today.

Origins of crime drama

Crime has been a fascination at least since Wilkie Collins's *The Moonstone* (1871). It was the first best-seller crime novel. Conan Doyle's *Sherlock Holmes* novels are more widely known and provided early material for transcription to radio and television.

The first programme to foreground the police themselves, *Dixon of Dock Green* (1950–1974), featured a stereotypical British bobby. His trademark friendly greeting to camera ('Evening all') seems to have entered the language, if only as parody. That and his equally informal farewell at the end of each show were intended to reassure the audience that all was well – the problems had all been sorted out.

In much the same vein, the United States series *Dragnet* (1952–1959) finished each episode with a report on the culprits' prison sentences. In the United Kingdom, *Z Cars* introduced a tougher, more challenging range of criminals and crimes they committed. In the 1970s, a much more hard-hitting series, *Gangsters*, took a Hollywood-style look at Birmingham. Gritty and shot on location, it

Figure 4.34
Helen Mirren as DI Tennison in Prime Suspect. The character's personal struggles are almost as big a part of the story as any crimes they have to work on.

pioneered many of the enduring features of current crime drama.

Types of crime drama

The historical development of the crime drama has been towards the form of the soap opera. A parallel trend towards the sitcom has not produced long-lasting success. Action shows with an injection of humour did appear in the late 1970s. Mostly, the humour was built around smart wisecracks and police station banter. A small number of characters provided the plot lines. Often the show centred on a partnership. Plots usually had a high level of fantasy or improbability.

Three main variations of the crime drama genre are currently represented on television.

TRADITIONAL CRIME DRAMA Early shows followed the conventions set up in the 1952 series *Dragnet*. These shows were not unlike urban Westerns. The novels of Raymond Chandler and Dashiel Hammet were major influences.

A small number of hard-boiled detectives were central characters. They confronted a crime every episode and it was always resolved. The plot was carried by the action of the detectives, who were clearly heroes beyond reproach. Most of them lived to fight crime and their personal life was non-existent. Criminals were remote from the audience. They were never developed as characters. Instead, they usually died on the streets as they had come – alone. Programmes such as *A Touch of Frost* and *Prime Suspect* continue this tradition. Despite many other changes, it is interesting to note the troubled personal life of the 'hero' remains a key feature of most crime shows. *Cracker* is a particularly fine example of this.

In the traditional crime drama genre, the camera takes no particular point of view. The 'well-trimmed image' of most camera work gives a neat look. Like a magazine photograph, the subject matter appears more orderly than in real life. Shots clearly establish setting with obvious signals such as street signs. Dramatic lighting and camera angles build up the excitement.

SOAP OPERA-INFLUENCED CRIME DRAMA Less attention to crime itself and a greater focus on character became one fashionable development

during the 1980s. In Britain, *The Sweeney* had earlier set the pace in the mid-1970s, followed by *Inspector Morse* more recently. *Hill Street Blues* began the change in the United States in 1981. Many others have followed since.

The soap opera influences can be seen in several aspects. A large number of central characters (thirteen principals in *Hill Street Blues*) share the focus of the plot between them. Private lives and personal problems account for important subplots in the overall story. Sometimes several story lines operate in a similar way to rotating plots on soap operas.

The world view of the soap opera–influenced crime drama is different to that of the old 'cops and robbers' shows. The police are shown to be caught between savage criminal violence and a set of procedures that are no longer working. They sometimes break the law themselves if it means catching a law-breaker. They are trapped in a system.

The Bill is a good example of this kind of drama. We never actually see any crimes being committed. The programme is about the police, not crime as such: we arrive with them, later, after the deed has been done.

In the soap opera-influenced crime drama, the scene often feels tight and cramped. Working conditions are often shabby and constricted. The camera is kept close in on key characters, and personal stories dominate the agenda.

PSYCHO-CRIME DRAMAS Television has always taken its cue from developments in the world of film, and crime shows have done so more heavily than most. One noticeable strand in crime that became big box office during the 1990s was the theme of gruesome murder and the attendant forensic detection process – in particular, the

Figure 4.36
*Familiar faces from **The Bill**. The emphasis on personal challenges facing individual officers identifies this show more with soap operas than other police dramas.*

world of the serial killer. *Silence of the Lambs* (USA, 1990) introduced this to the big screen; Lynda la Plante to the small. Her succession of *Trial and Retribution* dramas for ITV pursued a growing obsession with a very dark side to the human psyche. With its distinctive split-screen techniques, it has established itself as a virtual monopoly purveyor of psychotic crime.

Increased preoccupation with crimes of this kind inevitably required a specialist equipped to solve them. Interestingly, although *Cracker*'s Fitz shares many of the law enforcers attributes (personal life a mess, attached to alcohol, generally shambolic), he is not a member of the police force. Instead, he works alongside them, as a forensic psychiatrist. The emphasis in this series is not so much whodunit, as why-did-he: how has the mind broken down to bring about such desperate acts of (usually) violence against others? Fitz, of course, understands because he is himself so close to those dark workings of the tormented soul.

Although not directly connected in terms of format (especially not in the nature of the crimes tackled), the BBC's *The Cops* has at least a loose allegiance with this broad development. More in line with the soap format, generally, with its focus on personalities and the internal workings of the police force, there is nevertheless in its vision of society a comparable downbeat and broadly negative view espoused. More often than not, each programme ends with a very bleak outlook.

The rundown area of Manchester where the series is set is infested with drugs and their associated problems of violence and theft. Poverty is endemic and social problems seem hopelessly incapable of resolution. When residents do offer information about pushers to the local force, their homes are targeted and their lives threatened. Officers themselves are scarcely positive role models – the very first programme in the first series began with a female taking cocaine in a club, then hastening to her shift at the local 'nick'. The 'canteen culture' of macho male behaviour, sexist derision of female colleagues and general antagonism towards superiors does little to engage our respect.

Considerable criticism from the police themselves (they withdrew cooperation from the second series) has tended to obscure the fact that, for all this, a strangely sympathetic picture emerges. Characters are not attractive, either physically or especially in their personalities, but they do have to deal with individuals and situations that are even less so.

Tony Garnett, the producer, has talked about the difficulty of dealing with political issues in an overt manner on television today. In response, he has developed what he terms 'Trojan horse' drama, which seeks to subvert traditional genres. This series, he insists, is not documentary, but a form of 'distilled naturalism':

▼ ▼ ▼

I say to the team: 'We're going to do research, research and research. Then we're going to go home

and make it all up', because in the end we're in the fiction business.

Tony Garnett
Series Producer, *The Cops*

▼ ▼ ▼

The programme uses many of the techniques first developed by *NYPD Blue*. With jerky, hand-held camera and snatchy zooms to catch characters talking that often miss, the audience is positioned as the eager, perhaps naïve newcomer, straining to get in on the action.

Curiously, all the carefully composed shots that used to be taught as the basis of the film craft have been abandoned. Instead, authenticity now appears to derive from the raw feel of home video production.

▼ ▼ ▼ ▼ ▼ ▼ ▼

activities

1. Make a list of the first nine or ten shots from the title sequence of a crime drama. Often these are standard shots that do not vary from episode to episode. Now answer these questions:

► How is the setting suggested? What does the setting mean? For example, is it glamorous or squalid?

► Do any shots suggest action or violence to come?

► Do any shots suggest emphasis on character or lifestyle?

2. Police reports indicate that the clean-up rate for murder and other major crime is not nearly as successful as the rate for television crime. Try to explain television's preference for crime that does not succeed.

3. Consider the variations in crime dramas from different nations. Discuss the questions below.

► What variations are there in style? Are the traditional, soap opera and sitcom influences equally evident?

► What variations are there in the view given of

the police? Are they portrayed in a positive or a negative way?

► Does one nation favour cops over private eyes, or vice versa? What are the differences between them?

► What variations in fast car chases are there – the frequency, the speed, dramatic smashes, etc? Can you think of any reasons for these variations?

► Is violence more important in American shows?

4. Use the guide questions below to comment on the camera work of one of your favourite crime shows.

► Is it a well-trimmed image (i.e. well set out and balanced)? Is it a hand-held look (jerky, cluttered and natural looking)? Explain using examples.

► How often are establishing shots used (street signs, familiar scenery, building names, etc.) before the action moves on? Give examples.

► What use is made of dramatic or unusual shots and angles (high above, floor level, across car bonnets, etc)? What is the effect of these?

Crime Drama Plots

'Whodunnit?' is not the important question in most crime drama. The outlaw is usually obvious enough, even if the lawbreaker is not revealed in the first minute. The main problem in television crime shows is the pursuit and capture of the criminal. The story is about the way he or she is bought to justice.

Most plots in Western society's narratives follow a traditional pattern. Greek tragedy has given us the idea that a character comes to a tragic end through his or her own fault. From the Old Testament comes the idea that life is a series of tests and temptations. These can be overcome only by following the law of God. The history of drama pushes us towards the sort of plots that end in good defeating evil.

The structure of the plot

Crime dramas follow the traditional narrative structure of an orientation stage, a complications stage and a resolution. Crime show scriptwriters often refer to the first and final stages as the *set-up* and the *wrap-up*.

THE SET-UP The first scenes should grab the attention of the viewer. Usually enough is revealed to let the viewer know what the rest of the programme will be about. The main problem is 'set up' within the first five or six minutes.

THE COMPLICATIONS Once the main problem has been set up in a television drama, the plot proceeds with a series of small problems or tests. The main characters are threatened with more crises every step of the way until the capture of the lawbreaker. Scriptwriters say each new crisis

should seem more difficult than the one that went before. Each should seem to put the main character even further from the moment of victory. The tension progressively builds up to the main climax.

THE CLIMAX Just before the end, the climax is reached and the outlaw is caught. The climax is the most important scene after the first scenes. The climax is the high point of excitement. A car chase, a brawl or intense confrontations ending in the capture of the lawbreaker are the most popular climaxes.

THE WRAP-UP The final scenes are the next most important in the programme. All the loose ends of the plot must be satisfactorily tied up. The audience must be able to accept the solutions, no matter how far-fetched they are. Usually some kind of preparation has been done earlier in the plot. A character may behave strangely; a clue may be dropped.

This sort of preparation is called *foreshadowing*. In one episode of a crime drama, an anonymous figure in a black motorcycle helmet is murdering police sharpshooters, one after another, outside the local bar and games room. In the wrap-up, the motive was almost beyond audience belief. The cops kept beating the motorcycle 'tough' at a video game called *Sharpshooter* – so he murdered them. However, the audience was carefully prepared for this far-fetched conclusion. Several times, the motorcyclist is shown challenging anybody who will accept a game, and then being a violent bad loser.

Foreshadowing of some kind is present in all crime dramas and whodunnits. This is why some people are able to guess the outcome: they have recognised the carefully planted clues.

▼ ▼ ▼ ▼ ▼ ▼ ▼

activities

1. Compare the television crime drama genre with the traditional whodunnit novel in which the identity of the criminal is withheld until the last moment. Consider the differences in terms of the following:

- ► character of both hero and criminal
- ► clues and hints to the solution within the plot
- ► red herrings (false clues) to confuse the audience.

Write up your conclusions in a brief paragraph.

2. Some crime shows have a standard way of presenting the main problem or the set-up. For example, the superintendent calling the detectives in to parcel out the assignments, is a common format. Make a list of shows that follow a routine style. Beside the title of the show, describe how the problem is always set up.

3. Look at the plot diagram below for one episode of a soap opera-influenced crime drama.

THE SET-UP On a routine visit to a railway yard, the female police officer and central character is taken hostage. Her kidnapper locks the officer and himself in a railway freight wagon. He demands ransom and safe passage.

MINOR PROBLEM ONE The temperature in the freight car rises intolerably. The kidnapper threatens to kill the policewoman then and there. She talks him out of it and tries to calm him down. She finds out his name is Boyd.

PROBLEM OVERCOME – BUT HOW WILL SHE GET OUT?

MINOR PROBLEM TWO Police special squads arrive and begin bargaining. The kidnapper wants to move out of the scorching wagon into an air-conditioned shed nearby. He again threatens to shoot the main character. Police agree as a tactic.

PROBLEM OVERCOME – BUT HAVE THE POLICE GIVEN IN?

MINOR PROBLEM THREE Police snipers take position, while the police officer's partner creates a distraction. The partner must walk out to the shed to turn on the air conditioning. The kidnapper is covering the partner and does not notice the special squad snipers. MISSION ACCOMPLISHED – BUT CAN THE POLICEWOMAN BE SAVED?

THE WRAP-UP The climax comes when the police marksmen burst through the door of the shed and 'blow away' the outlaw in a hail of gunfire. The female police officer is unharmed and collapses quietly in her partner's arms.

Now watch an episode of a crime drama. As in the example above, set out the stages of the plot. Provide details on: the set-up, the build-up of minor problems and the wrap-up.

4. Watch an episode of a crime show that has a far-fetched ending. How has the scriptwriter managed to get the audience to accept it? What examples of preparation or foreshadowing can you find?

5. Count the number of scenes in one episode of a crime drama. Time the shortest scene and the longest scene. Write a short paragraph commenting on the pace of your chosen crime show.

Figure 4.37
The wrap-up on **The Bill** *In TV-land, it is rare that crimes are not solved or criminals not arrested. Critics have questioned success rates of television police compared with their real-life counterparts.*

Crime Drama Characters

Traditionally, the police have had generally positive representation on television shows. One of the most popular ongoing series, *The Bill*, has been criticised for its too-supportive coverage: a 'mouthpiece for the Met' is how some describe it. It is very popular with the police themselves and, in its fifteen years of production, it has never received a single complaint.

However, some of the newer shows, such as *The Cops* and *Liverpool 1*, have been taking a rather different view of the force.

▼ ▼ ▼

All cop shows except *The Cops* are good PR for the police. But I am not in the PR business.

Tony Garnett
Executive Producer, *The Cops*

▼ ▼ ▼

Adverse reaction by the police to the way they are portrayed on the small screen is no new thing.

In the early 1960s, they did not at first approve of *Z-Cars*. Strange though it seems to us now, their reason was that it presented them as too human! Showing officers suffering from the problems and pressures of everyday life would, it was felt, undermine public confidence in the force.

It is interesting to note the similarity of reaction to *The Cops* – nearly forty years later. Though here there may be felt to be rather more grounds for complaint. Characters are revealed doing all sorts of things, both on duty and off, that are distinctly dubious, including trying to chat up one victim of a crime and setting up a complainant for a particularly nasty beating. Eric Coulter, Series Producer to the show, maintains, however, that the portrait is broadly supportive: 'The Cops shows the police in a positive light. We showed it's not all car chases. It can be a difficult, shitty job and, like doctors, the police have to have a sense of humour to deal with it.'

Times have changed. Now, programmes are much more likely to question their authority. Characterisation on crime dramas reflects the changes in society: both attitudes towards the police, and the attitudes *of* the police themselves. Today, diverse personality types are the heroes of crime dramas. The character type of the hero depends on what style the crime show adopts.

Stereotyping

Each week when you tune into your favourite crime drama, you can be sure that you will meet the same people. In the more traditional series, a character does not start off with one set of personality traits and finish an episode having learned some lesson or changed behaviour in some fundamental way. This does not mean that characters are completely static or unchanging. They do have personalities; however, these operate within strict limits.

The Law Enforcers

Only the law enforcers are allowed to have identifiable personalities in most television series. Villains are chiefly there to enable the qualities of the hero to be tested and demonstrated anew. It is rare for them to receive sympathetic treatment of any kind.

Three main kinds of programme can be identified, each with their own stylistic formulae: the traditional genre, the soap opera-influenced crime drama and the psycho-crime drama.

TRADITIONAL GENRE Law enforcers are like soldiers enlisted in the war against evil. They are single-minded in their goal: the eradication of crime. These hard-boiled detectives are men and women of virtue in a sinful and corrupt world. Toughness and cynicism hide a heart that is noble and honourable. In a civilisation under threat, television encourages the detective to take over the basic moral functions of capturing, and even passing judgment on those who commit crimes. The general approach of this type of programme has largely faded now, but it is interesting to note how much it has informed subsequent shows.

SOAP OPERA-INFLUENCED CRIME DRAMA This genre encourages audience involvement in the private lives of the law enforcers. Often the story gives more attention to personal dramas than to crime fighting.

PSYCHO-CRIME DRAMAS These concentrate on human weaknesses in the law enforcer, as much as on the darker side of the criminal mind. The troubled/non-existent personal life, the consequences of too many hours spent confronting the evils that men do and grappling with the impulses that could prompt them, the corrosive effect on personality – all prove too much for an existence outside of the job itself. In *A Touch of Frost*, this takes the form of wryly humorous, at times wistful recognition of the limitations imposed; in a show such as *Taggart*, the tone is altogether darker.

The Lawbreakers

The villains on television crime dramas are almost characterless. While regular law enforcers appear week after week, the criminals make are fresh each episode. There is no time for character development and so the lawbreakers appear as crude stereotypes. Clothing, physical characteristics and accents are used to brand the criminal and make him instantly recognisable. Antisocial behaviour such as violence, disloyalty and cowardice complete the picture.

As in most television genres, there is little attempt to relate characters to larger social concerns. The criminals in crime dramas are really caricatures who are motivated solely by their own personal failings. The criminal is a weak character, who commits crimes because of personal weaknesses. There is a large imbalance in the social backgrounds of the criminals portrayed – the overwhelming majority are working class. Moreover, the types of crime depicted are from a fairly narrow range, concentrating mainly on the personal and the violent.

Crime shows are in fact much harsher in their judgments than the courts where real criminals are tried: there, at least, they have some scope for pleas of mitigation. On television, little allowance is made for the circumstances that lead up to crime.

Identification

Viewers forget their own lives when they become absorbed in a drama. They put themselves in the place of the leading characters. If these are handsome or glamorous the viewers may even wish they *were* the main characters. This is called identification with the main characters (although physical beauty is not always a necessity – witness Robbie Coltrane in his portrayal of Fitz, in *Cracker*). Other endearing qualities, of persistence, intelligence and determination are also used to promote the lead character as a sympathetic if flawed hero.

▼ ▼ ▼ ▼ ▼ ▼ ▼

activities

1. Imagine you are a writer on the production team of a crime drama series. Writing is running about six weeks ahead of the shooting. More plots are needed and so more 'baddies' are required. Draw up a list of stereotypical television villains you could use. Include details of motivation, dress and behaviour.

2. Give a description of the kind of criminal you *never* see on television. Give him or her a believable motivation or background reason for pursuing a life of crime.

3. You are a series creator who has to create the basic personality details of a detective team you would like to see in a new series. The series will be soap opera-influenced and will encourage audience involvement in 'human' side of the team

as well. Prepare an outline of the series to present for a network vice president's consideration.

4. Watch a selection of crime shows. Then answer the questions below.
► What similarities and differences can you see between the main characters of each the shows surveyed?
► Choose one of the characters and write down as much personal information about him or her that you have built up over several episodes.
► What kinds of crime are dealt with and what kind are *not*?

5. What reasons are offered for the crimes committed on television crime shows? Describe the personality and motivation of the villain in several of the crime shows you have seen.

6. Women's roles in crime dramas have undergone a dramatic change in the past fifty years. In the 1950s and 1960s, women were usually pretty 'decorations' or else they were housewives. Even in the 1970s, programmes such as *Charlie's Angels* relied heavily on sex appeal.

In today's post-feminist crime dramas, female police officers and detectives can be at the centre of the action. Watch an old crime drama and compare it with a modern show featuring a female lead. Write a report on your comparisons using the areas of investigation listed below.

▶ character of the female lead versus that of the male lead in a 1960s show

▶ types of stories that feature female lead

▶ effect on violence or mode of action

▶ progress of women as shown by changes in the roles played by women

▶ the extent to which women play central roles today.

Crime Drama: Issues

The personal is never political

Crime is in reality a very political topic. General elections usually feature prominent 'solutions' to the 'problem' of crime. Politicians of all parties recognise the need to take a strong stand on this issue. Crime dramas, however, generally avoid dealing with political, social and economic issues, because they are complex, and contentious.

Few traditional television crime dramas ever seriously analyse the reasons for crime. Problems in society that breed crime, such as the divisions between rich and poor, or unemployment are rarely mentioned. Traditional crime dramas have offered little understanding of the overall situation. There is a tendency for the traditional television crime drama to suggest that lawbreakers are born, not made.

In one episode of *The Bill*, a streetwise copper asks himself why a childhood friend has turned to armed robbery – 'I just don't understand it.' His hard-boiled partner replies, 'Don't even try, George, it's just human nature.'

There are differences between the traditional and the newer crime dramas in their approach to social problems. However, most programmes play it safe when it comes to social criticism.

Newer soap opera-influenced programmes such as *The Bill* and *NYPD Blue* do tackle social issues and do not always resolve them neatly. The shows that do analyse the reasons for crime still rarely lead the viewer to think that anything could be or should be done about significantly changing society. They are even less likely to suggest that the viewers themselves could take personal political action.

Commercial programmes must make sure that advertisers or other powerful groups are not offended. At the same time, the television companies are themselves major corporations with commercial interests of their own to protect.

Computer crime, white-collar crime and the corporate crimes of big business, in particular, are also rarely mentioned on television crime shows. They are perhaps a much greater threat to society and certainly cost the community vast sums of money. They offer little in the way of exciting action, however, and no readily identifiable victim. The television crime drama series concentrates almost exclusively on murders, assaults, drug abuse and robberies.

Television violence

The average rate of violent incidents across all television programmes is 7.5 per hour, according to Professor George Gerbner, an American researcher from the cultivation studies approach (see Audiences, p. 31). Gerbner maintains that the average teenager will have seen 10,000 murders by the time he or she reaches sixteen years of age. The typical television cop kills around forty-eight people a year. However, real-life police in the United States fired their guns on average only once every twenty-seven years.

For American crime dramas, the rate of violence is almost eighteen incidents per hour, according to one study. This is exceeded only by children's cartoons, where the rate is said to be twenty-three per hour. The difference is that no one gets killed permanently in the cartoons.

British crime dramas are less violent than the American shows, a BBC study shows. The incidence of violence on British crime dramas averaged eight incidents per hour.

George Gerbner's definition of violence may consist of one or all of the following.

▶ the expression of physical force (with or without weapon) against self or other;
▶ forcing action against one's will on pain of being hurt or killed;
▶ actually being hurt or killed.

There is no disagreement over the amount of violence on television and, in particular, on crime dramas. But the jury is still out on whether the level of violence negatively affects viewers (see The Violence Debate, pp. 32–3 and pp. 178–82).

The anxious audience

Is television making us more anxious, or are we already anxious before we switch on our favourite crime show?

CULTIVATING ANXIETY George Gerbner's cultivation effects studies have led him to argue heavy television viewing increases anxiety. The violence on the screen leads the viewer to think the outside world is equally as violent, says Gerbner. Crime dramas cultivate an image of a 'scary world'. Reactions to this may actually increase distrust and eventually contribute to more crime.

In an attempt to counter this, *Crimewatch* regularly carries a disclaimer at the end of the programme. The intention is to reassure viewers that incidences of violent crime, especially, are actually very low in number, taken across the country as a whole. Many feel, however, that there is a discernible effect of programmes of this nature –

and dramas such as *Taggart*, described as a 'film noir cop show' – of encouraging a *fear* of crime.

OPPOSING VIEW Richard Sparks, in his book *Television and the Drama of Crime*, argues against this point of view. It is not likely, he says, that television crime shows actually cause significant amounts of fear and anxiety. But it is possible they play on fears, exploiting them or reassuring them. Viewers may be reassured when order is restored at the end of the programme. They may also experience a cathartic release (see p. 179) by playing out some of their real-life fears in story form.

Ethnographic researchers (see pp. 180–1) have argued, along with Sparks, that viewers have complex motivations for watching television, and various degrees of involvement in particular programmes. Audience members could, for example, regard a crime drama as totally unrealistic and boring. They may only be watching because their friends do. On the other hand, they may be deeply engrossed in the conventions of the genre and may only be interested in the sense of threat because it makes a good set-up and wrap-up.

REASSURING ANXIETIES Television cop shows introduce crimes precisely in order that they can be solved. The set-up exists for the purpose of leading us via complications to the wrap-up. Everything is back to normal at the end. The resolution comforts the audience and restores the moral order, says Ellis Cashmore, Professor of Sociology at Staffordshire University.

A LITTLE THRILL OF PLEASURE Most people live routine and safe lives. Their most dangerous activity is driving to work, statistically speaking. Cashmore says viewers like to see heroes who always live in danger. The audience can share the thrill, but from the safety of their living rooms.

▼ ▼ ▼ ▼ ▼ ▼

activities

1. Watch an episode of a crime drama and count the number of violent incidents using Professor Gerbner's definition (p. 317). How does this relate to your own perception of violence in society?

2. Most research shows that people's reaction to violence on television changes according to who does it, how realistic it is, how close to home it is, as well as other factors.

One study used a chart on which viewers circled their answers in each category after watching a crime show.

Study one viewer's table as set out in the chart below, then carry out the activity following.

Make copies of the chart. Watch a selection of different crime dramas, circle the appropriate information and give your reaction to the violence. Compare your reaction with other members of the class. Is there any pattern? Does a particular sort of character, or form of violence disturb people the most? What form do people find the least disturbing?

3. Discuss whether you think television crime dramas increase social anxiety or provide a safety valve for community boredom and frustration.

major assignment

Written assignment

Choose one of these assignments and write a 600-word report.

1. Make a comparison of television crime dramas of different styles. Consider the conventions of plot, character and setting. Which style do you prefer?

2. Analyse the progress of the plot in a television crime show of your choice. Discuss the set-up, the build-up of problems, the climax and the wrap-up. Outline the probable reaction of the audience to each stage. What evidence of foreshadowing can you find before the conclusion? Evaluate the overall storyline.

3. Evaluate the characterisation on television crime dramas. Consider both stereotyped and rounded characters. What improvements would you like to see?

4. Analyse the representation of society, law enforcers and lawbreakers on a popular crime

VIEWER'S CHART

Fictional setting	British crime drama	US crime drama	Australian crime drama	Other
Character involvement	Law enforcer	Criminal	Male	Female
Form of violence	Shooting	Stabbing	Explosion	Fist fight
Degree of harm caused	Fatal injury	Non-fatal injury	No observable harm	
Physical setting	Indoors	Outdoors	Day time	Night time
Effect	Very disturbing personally	Could disturb others	Not disturbing at all	

show. Support your analysis with particular incidents and characters from the show. Speculate as to the possible effects of these representations.

5. Is the television crime drama helping to increase our anxiety levels? Analyse the arguments for and against the question using aspects of current crime shows and the evidence of your own surveys to support your argument.

Production assignment

Choose one of these assignments

1. Some magazines create send-ups of popular television crime dramas. Try producing one of these yourself – either in script or cartoon form. Your production should clearly make comic reference to the set-up, the build up of problems and the wrap-up. Remember there is also plenty of

potential for humour in stereotypical characters, exaggerated violence and extreme moral viewpoints.

2. Film an advertisement or trailer for a new crime drama of your creation. Role-play the characters and key scenes. Additional scenes can be shot with the aid of drawings, pictures, sketches, book illustrations, etc. The promo should be sixty seconds long and give some idea of the following:

► title and theme music
► setting
► style (e.g. soap opera-influenced)
► characters
► possible plot developments – e.g. glimpses of the crimes to be solved.

Your production should show your familiarity with the crime drama genre.

Crime Drama Settings

The city

The menacing and dangerous city is the setting needed to match the threat of the crime. The action happens 'out there' – on the wrong side of town. The viewer is made to feel that the naked city is a monster about to break out. Only the heroes offer protection.

Crime dramas began as urban Westerns and detectives needed the city just as much as cowhands needed the wide, open spaces. For some shows, the actual city is unimportant. A menacing inner urban environment is all that is needed. The city is not necessarily specified. The opening shots can be taken in one city and the action scenes could be shot in another. In the era of television globalisation (see p. 242), the anonymous setting appeals to importers. The show is set everywhere but nowhere.

In other shows, the setting and the specific city plays a more important part. This may be in one of several ways.

■ **The travelogue setting**

Some cities have scenery and weather that offer the citizens of the big population centres a sense of being on holiday. Hawaii and Miami, for

example, can boast spectacular scenery that adds zest to even the weakest of plots.

Miami, in particular, is also a believable location. The glittering pleasure capital is the entry point for one-third of the illegal drugs coming into the United States. On television, the dream-like landscape of white sands and hotel towers makes a dramatic contrast with the nightmare underworld of the drug trade.

■ **The 'specific is universal' setting**

Locating a drama in a specific city may be a means of safely commenting upon the problems of the larger world outside. This usage of setting is often reserved for minor cities off the well-worn crime trails. The same effect can be gained by using a specific time period to comment on the present.

■ **The 'capitals of crime' setting**

New York, with its dangerous subways, vast areas of urban decay and extremes of wealth and poverty, has always been the model setting. Likewise, London can be a dangerous place, even for the heroes. In one episode of a crime show, a cop says: '... each time I stop a car, I don't know if I'm going to get my head blown off or not.' Los Angeles, once a travelogue and lifestyle setting, has now joined the ranks of the crime capitals to become a favoured setting. Los Angeles also has the advantage of being the centre of US television production.

The office

Back at the station or office, a regular flow of characters can provide story lines for main characters to take up. Suspects can be shuffled in and out. Private lives can be discussed with colleagues.

To establish the feeling of a cramped police

station or private eye's office, plenty of tight shots are used.

The time setting

Perhaps to increase the feeling of threat, crime dramas are usually set in the present. The results of events in the past are known. The present does not offer that safety. A present-time setting makes the capture of the lawbreaker more urgent and the need for reassurance more heartfelt.

▼ ▼ ▼ ▼ ▼ ▼

activities

1. Make a list of crime shows where the specific setting is very important to the plots. Make another list of crime shows that could take place in any major city.

2. What suitable settings for a television crime drama can you suggest apart from New York, Los Angeles, Miami and London? The setting must offer the possibility of plenty of believable crime.

3. Your production company has negotiated with the networks to create a crime drama set in the past. This unusual concession has been granted because the programme can safely offer comment on present-day problems (not necessarily law-and-order problems). Provide a selection of eras that would make good settings. Explain their believability and relevance to today's audiences.

4. What kind of action is reserved for the office setting? Survey several episodes of a crime drama and report on the results.

5. Film some moody establishing shots for a crime drama. Suppose the story line concerns an undercover detective team sent to your school. The programme represents youth crime gangs as a serious problem. The undercover police act as students and gain the confidence of gang leaders.

Film ugly or dangerous-looking settings around your school or college to create the mood shots. If the programme were to be made, these would then be intercut with indoor studio scenes. In a few paragraphs, explain the impact of each shot and how it could be used in the programme.

The Television Advertisement

Today, you are probably going to see about seventy television advertisements. Watching average amounts of television until you are seventeen will expose you to more than half a million advertisements. Advertising is now a normal – if sometimes irritating – part of life in a post-industrial society.

It is estimated that nearly two pounds in every hundred generated in the economy of the United Kingdom is spent on advertising. In 1997, this amounted to just over £13 *billion* in total.

What genre is the television advertisement?

To some, the advertisement is a parasite, feeding off all the other genres of television in the search for novelty and cleverness. The process, however, also works in reverse. The advertisement is a powerful influence on mainstream genres. Many television programmes (and films) have reworked their formats to reflect discoveries first made in advertising. The US sitcom *Friends*, for example, is made up of a series of tightly composed mini-narratives, rather like a number of advertisements strung together.

As production values – and budgets! – have grown to equal those of feature films, and distinguished actors and sporting personalities have been recruited, so the status of television advertising has risen, too. Columnists discuss, comedy shows parody – the flow between mainstream programmes and advertisements is two-way. Intertextuality is very much a feature of the modern television advertisement: references to other cultural products, especially cinematic films, are increasingly common.

The advertisement is probably television's most intense moment. According to John Corner, of the University of Liverpool, the tight time constraints and the need to get the message across make the advertisement an extraordinarily compressed form of television.

Television's routine and domestic nature is the very element used in advertisements to woo the viewers. They are repeated regularly and, depending on the circumstances, they are dramatic, comic, personal, frantic or relaxed. Just like television at its best.

John Corner sees advertisements as being worked up into a variety of 'micro-formats' or mini-genres. Commentator Philip Adams once referred to them as little thirty-second pieces of cultural baggage. Indeed, it is possible to see many advertisements as mini-musicals, thrillers, Westerns, soap operas, and so on. Often, the micro-format advertisements contain all the key elements of the larger genres.

The variety of formats within television advertising has caused some analysts to ask whether advertising might be better described as a medium. Television advertising is like a medium within a medium and carries a range of genres in miniature. All advertisements do not have the same step-by-step genre structure: each takes its own structure from the particular genre chosen to sell the product.

Hard centre, soft exterior

Each advertisement has two parts, says advertising analyst John Thompson. First there is a rational and logical core. Around this is spun a decorative and often irrational outer coating.

The *core* of the advertisement is the central message giving knowledge about the product. Advertisers have become very cunning at working just inside the laws of truth in advertising (see pp. 334–5). Consequently, this core of product information is getting smaller and smaller.

The *soft exterior* of the advertisement is the image the advertiser wishes to give the product. This provides the entertainment value of the advertisement and the attractive lure to the consumer. Unlike the core, the decorative periphery is not governed by any laws on truthful representation. Probably as a result, the decorative lure of advertising is increasing in size as the core diminishes.

Features of the television advertisement

Ninety-five per cent of all advertisements broadcast are thirty seconds in duration. Fifteen-second and sixty-second advertisements are also made. The shorter advertisements are increasing in popularity, partly due to rising advertising costs. Forty-five second advertisements are rare because they are hard to place.

Advertising is a communication aimed solely at promoting the purchase of products. The television advertisement has several basic communicative elements, suggests John Corner.

REAL TIME Advertising on television places a greater burden on consumers than does advertising in other mediums. Advertisements demand that the viewers both listen and watch. As well, advertisements take up real time, and viewers must wait until they are finished before they can go back to the programme.

REPETITION The need to repeat advertisements to increase the chances of reaching the audience is a factor in the design of the advertisement. They are made for multiple viewings, with layers of meaning. There should always be something extra for the viewer to notice, copywriters say. Advertisements are also made to be viewed in fast-forward mode. Advertisers are only too aware many people videotape programmes and later zip through the advertisements with the remote VCR control.

SPEECH The direct address voiceover can control the meaning of an advertisement. Voiceovers can also personalise the advertisement, assuming a relationship with the viewer. The television advertisement also gains dramatic qualities from the use of speech that it shares with other television drama genres. This sets it apart from newspaper and billboard advertising.

DRAMATIC ACTION Many advertisements with a 'micro-format' structure follow the traditional structure of the dramatic narrative. They have an orientation stage, a complications stage and a resolution stage – all in thirty seconds.

DEMONSTRATIVE ACTION Television advertisements are the next best thing to the door-to-door salesman – the break in the main programme is their foot in the door. They offer the chance to demonstrate the product in action right there in the consumer's own home.

SYMBOLISM A symbol is anything that is used to suggest or stand for something else. A dove is the

symbol of peace, for example. Advertisements rely on symbols more heavily than any other media form. This is because of the symbol's ability to communicate quickly, emotionally and powerfully.

MUSIC AND SOUND Advertisements are brief and intensive television events. Music and sound are very important parts of message. Music, for example, can provide the mood and establish the plot, characters and action. Music also links scenes and can lead the advertisement to a strong conclusion. Jingles are a special combination of music and words in advertisements. Jingles increase product awareness, making it surface in our minds without conscious effort.

Sound effects can also increase product awareness and heighten its desirability. The fizz of a soft drink and the crunch of a breakfast cereal are examples of sounds that create a heightened reality around the product.

The social effects of advertisements

Many commentators suggest that advertising is a kind of 'anti-news'. Its purpose is not to inform, but to mislead. Advertising aims to promote selfishness, instead of democratic involvement in society. People are constantly given the message that the quality of life is measured by the possessions they buy. It is consumerism at its worst.

It has also been argued that advertising raises the price of goods and encourages people to buy more than they need. Between £4 and £5 per head for every member of the population of the United Kingdom is spent on advertising.

Naturally, advertisers themselves see plenty of benefits to advertising. They argue that advertising is an information service that promotes greater competition among producers of goods and services. Competition helps to keep prices lower, they claim. Advertising is an efficient means of distributing goods to mass markets. Advertising encourages a greater variety of goods and acts as a spur to invention.

Advertising has become much more complex in recent years. Advertising is now a chain of interlocking activities that connects politics to sport to celebrities to toys and so on. For better or worse, it now commands a powerful and central position in society.

Social context and institutions

Extravagance is common in the advertising industry. The US computer company Apple once made a sixty-second advertisement for $300,000 and then paid a television station $1 million to show it once only during the Superbowl, a football match watched by the whole country. The advertisement was never screened again. It was judged to be a big success.

Advertising is the fuel and lifeblood of commercial television. If it runs out, so do the production budgets for television drama. Advertisements are the price consumers have to pay for 'free' television.

▼ ▼ ▼ ▼ ▼ ▼ ▼

activities

1. Find examples of advertisements on television that seem to have been created as 'micro-formats'. The micro-format advertisements follow the key conventions of the mainstream television programmes they interrupt. Describe the scenes that represent the main stages of the progress of the mini-genre.

2. Advertising analyst John Thompson has argued there are two parts to advertisements: a core and a decorative periphery. Analyse some advertisements and identify what is core and what is decorative. In each advertisement, explain how the decorative aspect appeals to the viewer. Evaluate which aspect is the most powerful selling agent.

3. Until 1989, Russian television did not carry advertising. Russian people got word of what was available in shops from friends and by window shopping. What are the benefits and disadvantages of a society without advertising? Explain.

4. Can you think of an advertisement which stands up to repeated viewing and yet still seems enjoyable (or at least tolerable)? Analyse the advertisement to identify the features that permit repetition.

For example, a comic advertisement must have more to the humour than the punch line, if it is to remain entertaining after one or two viewings. Other advertisements may rely on the continuing pleasure associated with a particular song.

Types of Television Advertisement

Television advertisements can be divided into a number of general categories – or combinations of categories. The main categories are dramatisation, testimonial, demonstration, spokesperson/sales pitch, documentary, song and dance productions, and analogy.

Dramatisation

Television advertisements that involve the product in a story are referred to as *dramatisations*. The story structure usually follows a simple plot with a beginning, middle and a close. Within the time of the advertisement, the plot develops in a step-by-step, logical order.

Until recently, in most dramatised advertisements, the product was the hero. As advertising becomes more sophisticated, however, the product is beginning to take a back seat. The focus has moved to the decorative periphery of the advertisement. The story is used to create a

Figure 4.38
Advertising is a compelling form of communication. It works by generating powerful images of desirable lifestyles, looks or feelings. Consumers are seduced by the association between these states and the products they buy.

Figure 4.39
Demonstration advertisements are much favoured by some advertisers. They have been used to promote laundry products since television advertising first began.

lifestyle image statement, which just happens to contain the product.

Slice-of-life advertisements are dramatised situations in which the product saves the people from their real-life problem. 'Big date tonight – but what about my breath?' 'Don't worry Charlie, gargle with this …'. The product is introduced, praised and tried. At the end of the advertisement, it is revealed that the user is now a better and happier person for having used the product.

Testimonial advertisements

When someone uses a product, is satisfied and tells others about it, the advertisement is known as a *testimonial*.

AVERAGE CONSUMER TESTIMONIALS are created with very ordinary people singing the praises of the product.. Viewers are expected to relate to these people as peers. Advertisers usually choose people who are not too beautiful or too handsome, and with faces full of character that can quickly win over viewers. It is said that the more amateurish the performance, the more believable the audience finds it.

FAMOUS FACES are also used to give testimony to the worth of a product. Getting a celebrity to move the merchandise is a technique as old as advertising. Gary Lineker, John Cleese and Denise van Outen have all added their talents to advertisements for everything from beef burgers to computers. When John Cleese did advertisements for the computer company Compaq, only 2 per cent of the population knew that Compaq existed. After John Cleese's advertisements, nearly 50 per cent were aware of the company. The fame of the celebrity rubs off on to the product.

Demonstration advertisements

Demonstrations get to the very heart of television's impact. Probably no other medium can provide a demonstration of the product actually in use. This is where television comes closest to the idea of a door-to-door salesperson.

Spokesperson/sales pitch

The use of an on-camera announcer speaking directly to viewers dates from the earliest days of television and was a carry-over from radio. This type of advertisement is generally just talk, although it may be accompanied by selling aids such as charts and demonstrations. The hard-sell advertisement is usually short because the viewer's attention wanders if the sales talk is too long.

Documentary

Advertisements in the style of a documentary or a news bulletin can be used. The advertisement may show a new way to use a product or explain its processing or testing. Another technique is to show the product being used in a newsworthy situation.

Song-and-dance productions

Advertisers of soft drinks, cars and other products aimed at young people often use advertisements with original music and dancing. With fast movement, intricate dance routines and rapid shot changes, this type of advertisement is expensive to produce. On the other hand, the generation of a sense of lifestyle, as in the Pepsi® and Coke® advertisements, can be considerable and can play a powerful part in creating exactly the right image for the product.

Analogy advertisements

An analogy is similar to a metaphor or a simile. It shows the likeness between two things. An analogy advertisement will take a product and show its relationship to something else. In one advertisement, for example, a stampeding herd of horses was compared to the performance of a car.

▼ ▼ ▼ ▼ ▼ ▼ ▼

activities

1. Consider a dramatisation advertisement currently showing on television.
▶ Outline the structure of the advertisement, showing the orientation, complications and resolution.
▶ Does the opening sequence arouse curiosity? Explain.
▶ Is the product crucial in providing a solution to the situation, or is it merely placed within a lifestyle or image context?

2. Watch an advertisement that uses a spokesperson to speak directly to the viewers about the product. Use the guidelines below to evaluate the advertisement.
▶ Describe the announcer/spokesperson. Consider descriptions such as overbearing, funny, weak, irritating, warm, likeable.
▶ Consider the speech. Is it sincere? Long? Too many ideas? Simple? Short? Decide whether you think people are prepared to listen to the speech.
▶ Evaluate the backdrop or setting. Does it add interest?
▶ How effective are the demonstrations? Do they show the product in use?
▶ How prominent is the name of the product? Is it mentioned many times?

3. Analogy advertisements compare the product to something else. Make a list of products and think of suitable analogies that would appeal to consumers (e.g. bathroom cleaner – pine forests and sparkling streams).

4. Demonstration advertisements are said to be among the best at holding viewers' attention, proving the product's superiority and persuading them to buy. Look at the demonstration advertisement shown below from David Ogilvy's book *Ogilvy on Advertising* and then answer the following questions.
▶ How believable do you find this advertisement? Comment on the believability of other demonstration advertisements you have seen on television.
▶ Demonstration advertisements often use close-ups. How many close-ups are there in this one? Watch other demonstration advertisements on television and count the number of close-ups and extreme close-up shots.
▶ The message of this advertisements is easily understood without the soundtrack. Watch some demonstration advertisements on television with the sound turned off. Can you still understand the message of the advertisement? Evaluate the power of the visuals compared with the sound.

Figure 4.40
A French advertisement showed the strength of a glue by applying it to the soles of the announcer's shoes and gluing him to the ceiling.

Writing the Television Advertisement

Getting the idea

Although the 'flash of inspiration' has its place in advertising, the process of composing an advertisement involves many considerations.

The usual procedure is for the advertising team, including a writer and an art director, to be supplied with a range of information about the client and the future advertisement. This could include details about product, the potential consumer, the time and length of the advertisement and the size of the budget. Armed with this information, they can then begin to formulate their ideas.

▼ ▼ ▼

Ideas can come at any time. On a plane. In a bath. Whilst making love. At the football. Drunk. Sober. And occasionally … sitting at a desk in the office.

Once a creative person has the input of a brief, it's a challenge and it doesn't go out of his head because the big hand is on the twelve and the little hand is on the five.

But there needs to be discipline. Creativity does not come out of a vacuum, but is the end result of a mind being programmed with all the component parts of the problem (marketing objective, product benefit, consumer attitude, competitive activity). To honour all these disciplines in one simple and memorable idea is not so much the result of dreaming as of sweating. And the only end definition of advertising creativity is that it sells. Originality is often creativity's biggest enemy.

(The late) Peter Heathwood, Creative director, George Patterson Bates, Australia

▼ ▼ ▼

The product

Knowledge of the product is the first stage in writing a television advertisement. The copywriters of the television advertisement repeatedly ask themselves several questions about the product. How new is the product? How is it made? What is it used for?

■ Is it new?

NEW INVENTION A new product may open up a market that did not exist before.

NEW MODEL This could be a refinement of an existing product.

NEW FEATURE An existing product could have an added feature.

■ How is the product made?

THE INGREDIENTS The product may have some special ingredient that would appeal to people.

THE MANUFACTURING PROCESS How the product is made can be something that appeals to consumers. Rolls Royce's appeal is in its largely hand-crafted vehicles.

THE REPUTATION OF THE COMPANY Many people will buy a product because they have faith in the company.

BRAND RELIABILITY This is allied to company name, but relies on the established belief in the quality of a particular product.

■ Where is it made?

An unusual place of origin can become a selling point. Imported products often take advantage of this. Some make use of exotic associations; others of reputations for reliability, efficiency or ingenuity.

■ What are its uses and features?

Copywriters ask themselves the following about a product:

▶ What is its main use?
▶ How is it versatile?
▶ What is its convenience?
▶ Does it represent quality?
▶ Is it economic to buy or use?

The unique selling point

The unique selling point (USP) is an aspect of the product that makes it different from its competitors. The difference can be real or imagined. One advertising agency once wrote a toothpaste slogan: 'Gets rid of film on teeth.' All toothpaste gets rid of film on teeth – even just a brush will do that. This agency said it first, however, so it appeared to be a special feature of that particular product.

The unique selling point can be highlighted by either creating a problem and allowing the product to solve it, by showing the results of using the product or showing the results of not using the product. It is most common for an advertisement to show the good things that happen when the product is being used. Detergents get out stains or drinks provide satisfaction. Some advertisements reverse this and show the bad or amusing things could happen when the product is not used. Collars are still grey, hair is still stringy and so on until the product is used, with amazing results.

Advertisements must establish a feeling of need in their audience. The consumer must be made to feel they need the product. With a product that is not essential, or a product line where there are many competing brands on the market, the advertisement writer appeals to basic human desires. With toothpaste and soap advertising, for example, the need to be clean is often passed over in favour of the desire to be attractive to the opposite sex.

The people

Advertisers need to know the customers and their hopes and aspirations. Who uses the product? Where? How often? Why? Research can provide a lot of the answers. The right audience can be a bonanza for the advertisers.

▼ ▼ ▼

We now ask: where is the gold so I can go dig there? The older style approach was to just dig holes somewhere in the middle of anywhere.

Ian Elliot
George Patterson Bates

▼ ▼ ▼

The aim of advertising is to help make products appear as pleasing as possible, regardless of whether or not they are actually of use or benefit to anyone.

Most products face competitors that are much the same as they are. This is especially true of petroleum products, for example. To survive, the product must be given an identity or personality.

One way to achieve this is through the use of signifiers, or objects that have a special significance for the audience. For example, a yacht can signify wealth and leisure.

▼ ▼ ▼

'Identity' or 'personality' are better words than 'image', which has about it connotations of unreality and lack of substance.

First, use market research regularly to establish what the most favourable identity should be and what the current one is. Then use creativity as the tool to turn the one into the other.

(The late) Peter Heathwood
George Patterson Bates

▼ ▼ ▼

The process commences with market research when groups of people in the target market are questioned in order to find out their attitudes, emotions, likes and dislikes.

The next step for the advertising agent is to find aspects of the product that can fit into that system of belief or emotions.

The creation of the 'image' is stimulation to get a response from the potential consumers and working out what response you want so people but the product.

Geoff Wild, Chairman and CEO,
Ogilvy and Mather advertising agency

▼ ▼ ▼

Types of signifiers

THE BRAND NAME Even though constant repetition can be irritating, most advertisement writers repeat the brand name as often as possible. A thirty-second advertisement can contain anywhere from five to fifteen mentions of the product name. The main purpose of this is to burn the brand name into the listener's brain.

SLOGANS Catchy slogans are a good way to make the audience remember the advertisement. Techniques of poetry are useful in slogan writing. Poetry is easier to learn than prose and this is used to advantage in advertising. Rhyme, onomatopoeia, rhythm, alliteration and so on – all help to strengthen the message. For example, advertisements for Kit Kat always include the slogan 'Have a break. Have a Kit Kat'. Here, there is the alliteration of the Ks and there is also onomatopoeia as the 'K' sound suggests the crisp snap of the breaking biscuit.

USE ORDINARY LANGUAGE Advertisement writers mostly use words and phrases the audience is sure to understand. The main ideas are always expressed simply and in familiar terms.

ADJECTIVES AND VERBS Writers often use double adjectives to add extra power to their statements while keeping them short. Bread becomes 'oven-fresh' and grapes are 'sun-ripened'. The choice of verb in an advertisement is very important because verbs suggest action. Advertisement writers substitute strong action verbs for weak ones (see p. 447).

Humour

Research shows that humour attracts attention and helps the audience remember the message.

Humorous advertisements also create a positive mood and this may increase the power of the advert to persuade.

▼ ▼ ▼

Humour must come out of the brand. It can't fit a dozen other products. Humour has to create a point of view about the product.

Manning Rubin
J. Walter Thompson Co. advertising agency

▼ ▼ ▼

▼ ▼ ▼ ▼ ▼ ▼ ▼

activities

1. Find a product that you have not seen advertised on television. Ask yourself the three questions about it, as listed on p. 326. From your answers, make notes that might be used to create an idea for a television advertisement.

2. Below is an advertisement for Volkswagen, shown in the United States at the time of the 1974 oil crisis. Identify and explain the unique selling point. Explain how almost every line in the advertisement reinforces the unique selling point.

3. Watch several television advertisements. Note the names of the products and identify for each the unique selling point of the advertisement.

4. Analyse a television advertisement that attempts to build up an identity for the product, using the following questions:
► What is the favourable identity the advertiser is trying to create?
► What group in society is the image aimed at?
► Make a list of signifiers that help to build up the image and are a clear indication of the appeal to the target audience.
► What aspects of the product fit the image created by the advertiser?

5. View several television advertisements and count the number of times the brand name is mentioned. Some advertisements mention the

Figure 4.41
Veteran advertiser David Ogilvy believes this advertisement to have been one of the most successful uses of humour in advertising that he has ever seen. At the time, American cars were 'extravagant chromed gas guzzlers'.

Open on funeral procession of limousines each containing the benefactors of a will.
Male voice over: I, Maxwell E. Snavely, being of sound mind and body do bequeath the following:

To my wife Rose, who spent money like there was no tomorrow, I leave $100 and a calendar . . .
To my sons Rodney and Victor, who spent every dime I ever gave them on fancy cars and fast women . . . I leave $50 in dimes . . .

To my business partner, Jules, whose motto was 'spend, spend, spend' I leave nothing, nothing, nothing. And to my other friends and relatives who also never learned the value of a dollar, I leave . . . a dollar.

Finally, to my nephew, Harold, who oft time said: 'A penny saved is a penny earned'. And who also oft time said 'Gee Uncle Max, it sure pays to own a Volkswagen' . . . I leave my entire fortune of one hundred billion dollars.

name only once. Compare the effectiveness of these with the advertisements that repeat the brand name several times.

6. Imagine you are working for an advertising agency and you have just been handed a contract to create an advertising campaign for Unilux Tyres. Your brief is set out below.

THE PRODUCT Unilux has just begun local manufacture. Until now Unilux had only offered a limited range of imported tyres and consumer awareness of the brand name is low.

MARKET RESEARCH Research has been carried out on the reasons people select certain brands of tyre. The findings are listed below.

► Consumers favour recognised brands.

► They want quality, reliability, performance and safety.

► Tyre advertisements usually feature well-known racing drivers talking about wet weather, road conditions and the tyre. Research shows people simply become confused after watching such advertisements. Tyres are a low-interest product and are a 'grudge' purchase.

THE PEOPLE The primary target audience is men aged twenty-five to fifty-four. There is a secondary audience being everyone aged over eighteen.

YOUR BRIEF Create the wording for a thirty-second advertisement that will build consumer awareness of the Unilux range of tyres. The advertisement should build a positive attitude to the brand name. Refer to p. 330 for details of script layout.

Television Advertisement Pictures: Scripts and Storyboards

Pictures tell the story

When television first began it was thought of as radio with pictures. The dreams of radio listeners had been answered – they could now see as well as hear their favourite programmes. Advertisers still relied on words to do the selling. Pictures were thought to be of lesser importance.

Today, advertisers rely on pictures to tell the story. What they show is often more important than what they say. Words are still important, but because there are often so few of them they must be chosen carefully. However, more than half the weight of the message is carried by the pictures.

Try watching an advertisement with the sound turned down. It is more than likely that the pictures will still tell the story and the advertising message will be conveyed almost as clearly.

Editing

Advertisements are rarely made up of just a few shots and scenes. A feature of advertisements is the large number of different shots crammed together in a very short space of time. A thirty-second advertisement may have as many as thirty or forty separate shots, and five or six scenes.

The opening seconds of an advertisement are vital. These either grab and hold the viewers' attention, or send them off to the bathroom. A visual surprise in the first shot is often used to grab attention.

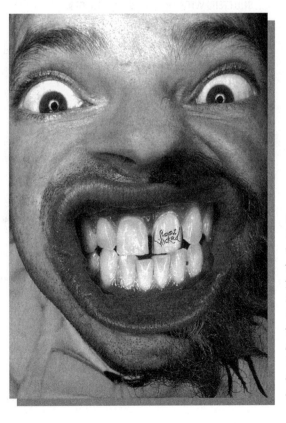

Figure 4.42
Even if the sound were turned off in this commercial for Roadshow Interactive's CD-Rom games, the message remained clear. The pictures carry the weight of the message.

Figure 4.43
*A section of the
script for a
Coke®
advertisement
devised by
McCann-Erikson*

ADVERTISEMENT SCRIPT

VIDEO	AUDIO
SHOT 1: OPEN ON BEDROOM IN BIG OLD QUEENSLAND COUNTRY HOUSE. IT IS THE MIDDLE OF A HOT AND STEAMY TROPICAL NIGHT. THE ROOM IS DRAMATICALLY LIT BY A FLICKERING GOLDEN LIGHT DANCING ACROSS THE WALLS. SUDDENLY A GUY JERKS UP INTO A SITTING POSITION IN CU – AS THOUGH HE HAD BEEN AWAKENED FROM A BAD DREAM. THERE IS SWEAT ON HIS BROW. HE BLINKS RAPIDLY.	<u>MUSICAL INTRO</u>
SHOT 2: CUT TO ELEVATED WIDE SHOT – WE ARE LOOKING THROUGH THE SLOWLY ROTATING BLADES OF A LAZY CEILING FAN. DOWN ONTO THE GUY IN HIS BED. HE SWINGS HIS LEGS OFF THE BIG BED AND ONTO THE FLOOR. HE IS HOT!	I think I hear the sounds of then …
SHOT 3: CUT TO ANOTHER BEDROOM IN THE HOUSE – GUY 2 IS SITTING IN A WICKER CHAIR HOLDING AN ELECTRIC FAN TO HIS FACE. A GIRL IN ANOTHER CHAIR IS HOLDING HER LONG HAIR OFF THE BACK OF HER NECK, SEEKING RELIEF FROM THE OPPRESSIVE HEAT.	And people talking … The scene's recalled …
SHOT 4: CUT TO CU OF OUTSIDE OF LOUVRE WINDOW SHUTTERS WITH THE FLICKERING GOLDEN LIGHT, THEY ARE THROWN OPEN BY GUY 1.	By minute movement …
SHOT 5: CUT TO A BATHROOM IN THE HOUSE. LYING IN A COLD BATH FOR RELIEF FROM THE HEAT IS GUY 3. HE HAS A FACE CLOTH OVER HIS FOREHEAD, ONE LEG IS HANGING OVER THE SIDE. HE IS LISTENING TO A CASSETTE.	And songs they fall …
SHOT 6: CUT TO ECU OF GIRL'S CHEST AS SHE RUNS AN ICE CUBE OVER IT.	That certain texture …
SHOT 7: CUT TO ECU OF GUY'S FOREHEAD. HE WIPES AWAY PERSPIRATION WITH A TOWEL.	That certain beat …
SHOT 8: CUT TO ANOTHER BEDROOM. GUY 4 IS SITTING UP IN BED, TAKING OFF A DAMP T-SHIRT. HE FLINGS IT AWAY AND PICKS UP A CAN OF COKE FROM HIS BEDSIDE TABLE. HE SHAKES IT, TURNS IT UPSIDE DOWN – EMPTY!	To lie in a sweat, on familiar sheets …
ETC.	Etc.

Close-ups are a feature of television advertisements. Details they can show provide an answer to the consumers' demand to examine the product. In advertisements for food, the closer the shot, the more people's mouths water.

Jingles and music

'When you've got nothing to say, sing it!' is an old saying among advertisers. However, there have been some very effective jingles and some lyrics have even entered our daily vocabulary. Two popular ways of using jingles are as a simple sign-off or as a full jingle soundtrack – e.g. Coke's 'It's the Real Thing!'

Music in advertising is not restricted to jingles. With television air-time so expensive, advertisers want music with instant impact. Well-known pop songs are often used in advertisements to take advantage of the good feelings they generate in the target audience. It may cost four times as much to buy the rights to an old hit as to write an original jingle, but advertisers do not mind the price. Songs full of memories do not take time to grow on people. Original jingles cannot produce the same impact.

Music recording companies have whole departments devoted to recommending and finding tracks for advertisements. One company has a computer classification of more than 20,000 song titles cross-referenced to contain every word an advertising agency could need. If, for example, a real estate company wants a song with the word 'house' in it, a list of at least fifty songs can be provided.

The script

The advertisement script is typed onto a page divided in half. Audio (words, music and sound effects) goes on the right-hand side of the page and video (shot listings and instructions for settings and action) goes on the left-hand side. Everything spoken by someone is typed in ordinary upper and lower case letters. Everything else – such as character names, sound effects, music and so on – is typed in capital letters.

The storyboard

The storyboard is an illustrated script (see pp. 162–3). Cartoon-like picture frames are sketched to show the action as it happens in scene-by-scene sequence.

Only the key moments and key scenes are drawn for a storyboard. This means shot descriptions and detailed descriptions of the action are essential. A sketch may show a close-up of a man's face, but this may actually occur at the end of a short scene. The beginning shot may be a longer view and the camera may gradually move in. Video directions would explain this: 'MOVE FROM LS TO CU OF MAN'S FACE'. The number of frames in a storyboard should be the minimum number necessary to tell the story.

▼ ▼ ▼ ▼ ▼ ▼ ▼

activities

1. Count the number of times the shot changes on a television advertisement. Do this while watching the advertisement with a piece of paper in front of you. Each time there is a shot change, make a mark or tick on the paper. Count up the total at the end.

2. Editing can be an important way of influencing the emotions of the audience. Watch a number of television advertisements and look for an example of two shots that have been carefully placed together to produce an emotional reaction. Describe the shots and explain the intended effect.

3. Many jingles have become part of our everyday vocabulary. Make a list of well-known jingles that come immediately to mind. Discuss the impact they are intended to have: how is this generated?

4. Music is used in advertising to build the appeal to the audience. Listen to the music used in an advertisement and comment on the contribution it makes to the advertising message. The questions below may give you some idea of the likely appeal.
► How does the music create warm memories (nostalgia)?
► How does it add to the lifestyle or the image

the advertiser wants to portray?

▶ Does the music contain key words that relate to the product (e.g. music for a car advertisement may contain lines such as 'takes your breath away').

5. Imagine you are working for an advertising agency and you have just been handed some work for a new client, 'Deep Seas'. Your brief is set out below.

THE PRODUCT Deep Seas Fish Fingers are made from whole fish as opposed to minced fish found in the majority of fish fingers.

MARKET RESEARCH Research has shown that ads

for fish fingers have to overcome several obstacles. The findings are set out below.

▶ Most of those people surveyed believe fish fingers to contain less than the highest quality fish.

▶ Many people have reservations about serving convenience foods.

THE PEOPLE The target audience is women with families.

YOUR BRIEF Create a thirty-second advertisement that will persuade people to buy Deep Seas Fish Fingers. Sketch out a storyboard showing key images from the advertisement, together with details of shot sizes and dialogue.

Representation Issues in Television Advertisements

In 1995, the naked mid-torso of a pregnant woman was featured in a US advertisement for the new wide-bodied Toyota Camry. 'There's nothing more comfortable than being inside a wide body' was the slogan. After cries of outrage from women's groups, the advertisement was hastily withdrawn.

While a US survey shows that only 16 per cent of people had actually complained about an advert, approximately 50 per cent said they had wanted to, but had not done so. What moves so many people to become annoyed about advertisements? More than half of all complaints allege offensiveness, discrimination or sexism. Most of the remaining half are complaints about ethics and truthfulness.

Added together, this means 97 per cent of all complaints about advertising concern representation and charges of misrepresentation.

Representation through stereotyping

Have you ever thought how much an advertiser could save by using real-life characters instead of professional models? For a much smaller fee, a real-life nurse could be persuaded to appear in a hospital scene. Advertising agencies have actually tried this approach, but got very unsatisfactory results.

Real-life workers do not make good stereotypes. The actual nurse, for example, would probably not be convincing on television. It is

quite likely the real-life professional would not be recognised as a proper nurse by viewers who have become accustomed to the stereotype. Instead, advertisers believe it works much better to get models who fit the stereotype to pose in completely make-believe scenes.

Stereotypes (see pp. 38–9) allow an advertisement to communicate instantly and non-verbally. As most advertisements only last thirty seconds, the viewers must instantly recognise and accept the stereotyped image as 'believable'. Like comedy, advertising as we now know it could not exist without the use of stereotypes.

The stereotype harnesses the cultural knowledge of the viewer. A person's cultural knowledge might include all the comics, all the television shows, all the books and each prejudice and belief he or she has ever encountered. Tapping into this long built-up cultural knowledge, stereotypes often include the most extreme and exaggerated characteristics of groups, ideas or events.

The views of the dominant and most powerful groups in society tend to be reinforced by stereotypes in television advertising. This is because non-dominant groups (who also hold stereotypes) usually do not have so much spending power.

Women

Getting the representation right for women has been one of the most difficult balancing acts advertising agencies have had to face. Women are the most lucrative audience for television advertising, but they also make 65 per cent of all complaints about advertising.

Statisticians were aware of greatly increased numbers of women in the workforce as early as 1966. However, up until the 1980s, the typical woman on television advertisements was presented as a housewife. She was usually young, with an executive-type husband and two children. The meaning in her life came from discussions about the benefits of miracle washing powders, oven and toilet cleaners and modern appliances. She won her husband's approval with good household management, lots of cosmetics and impeccable grooming.

In the mid-1980s came the new stereotype of the supermum. She managed all the tasks of the traditional stereotype, as well as holding down a high-powered job. Feminists were strongly critical. Gillian Dyer, for example, said that the new stereotype still did not criticise the basic power structures or the continuing male dominance of the workplace and the family.

By the mid-1990s, the supermum stereotype had been partly replaced by the busy career mother. The new super-stressed mum was now desperate for the product to provide relief from the hectic demands of the double shift. Advertisers seemed keen to be sympathetic to women's increasing stress levels as they tried to juggle their dual roles in the workforce and the home.

However, a recent survey of 150 advertisements found that the representation of women was still out of touch with reality, even today. When women were portrayed, nearly 60 per cent were young and beautiful, 26 per cent were obsessed with body image and 18 per cent were housewives. Nearly 90 per cent of the women viewers surveyed believed advertisements did not show home life as it really was. The survey clearly showed advertisers still have a long way to go.

Men

Men are shown as weak and pathetic in nearly 11 per cent of advertisements, according to a 1996 survey. The same survey found 'muscle men' (or 'himbos') were the representations of men shown in 27 per cent of advertisements. Other common stereotypes of men included 'Mr Fix-its' in 9 per cent of advertisements and sensitive new age guys in 17 per cent of ads. Powerful business-men appeared in 18 per cent of the surveyed advertisements.

Until recently, few men have complained about the depiction of males on television advertising. The main reason for recent complaint has been the broadcasting of a number of advertisements seen as demeaning to men. If the gender roles were reversed in the advertisement, the depiction would be banned. Advertisers would not dare treat women in such a demeaning manner, most complainants have argued. So far none of these complaints has been upheld. Authorities argue that what the community will see as acceptable in the portrayal of women is currently very different from what is acceptable for men.

Ethnic minorities

Whereas women have made significant gains in advertising representations in the past two decades, the representation of ethnic minority groups has hardly changed. This is despite a focus on multiculturalism in the broader community. When ethnic minorities appear in television advertising, it is usually to promote food products such as curries and sauces.

In one notorious case, the car makers Ford actually airbrushed several black faces out of a promotional photograph that had been taken of some of their staff. After furious protest, an apology was made and an attempt at an explanation – but the message was clear. The company had not been comfortable with the level of minority representation in the photograph, however much it might reflect the actual composition of their actual workforce.

Part of the reason for the stereotyped portrayal of ethnic groups is that, unlike women, advertisers have not so far identified them as separate big-spending target audiences.

THE AFRICAN-AMERICAN EXPERIENCE

Following the mass civil rights demonstrations in the 1960s, American black organisations pressured the government and corporations to use more African-American models in their advertisements. Content analysis surveys in the 1990s showed the battle had been won. Their representation in television advertisements has been found to be just slightly higher than their percentage share of the population.

However, research shows African Americans are usually seen endorsing products of lower value than those endorsed by white Americans. The sex of the black model is usually male and is less likely than white models to be have a highly skilled occupation. African Americans are three times more likely to be portrayed as sports stars, but only half as likely to be shown in business roles.

Occupations

Nearly everybody in 'Adland' has a high-paying professional job. After a content analysis study of almost 320 advertisements, a US survey has shown that 87 per cent of people are shown as having highly skilled occupations. Only 13 per cent of advertisements feature people in low-income or unskilled occupations.

Globalisation and representation

The globalisation (see p. 55) of advertising is increasing. As a result, advertisers are beginning to look for appeals that work on a global basis. Visual representations are the common denominator. There is no need to speak any language to understand the visual, says Phil Dusenberry of the New York–based agency BBDO Worldwide. Visual concepts driven by global needs will be the future of advertising, he says.

The shift to global advertising could mean an expansion of the 'decorative periphery' of advertising and a move away from the lists of claims and product praise. The 'rational core' of advertising may wither away, as international advertisers skirt around various national laws pertaining to truth in advertising. Accompanying the trend could be the global penetration of stereotypes from the dominant cultures, particularly the United States.

Reflecting or shaping reality?

Should the representations of advertising simply reflect the real world or should they influence it? Many groups such as feminists and consumer groups believe that today's advertising relies on outmoded stereotypes and is socially irresponsible.

Marketing professionals disagree. They see the industry as a business. The aim is to communicate messages that sell their clients' products. Advertisers say their marketing simply reflects the world as it is. Otherwise, consumers would not buy the advertised products.

As advertisers aim to make money, they only ever present 'safe' images that follow, rather than lead, public opinion. More than anything, they fear a consumer backlash to their images that could lead to a drop in product sales. Their client's reaction would be to immediately cancel the account.

Representation and society

There are two ways the representations of advertising interact with society. The first is by drawing in something desirable from the wider culture and attaching it to a product. For example, love can be attached to chocolates or the power of feminism can be attached to insurance products. The second interaction advertising has with society is in an outwards direction – it is the 'spin-off' effect of advertising. The commercialism of ads may be extended to a greater commercialism in other walks of life. For example, since the 1980s some schools have been referring to students as 'clients'.

John Corner, of the University of Liverpool refers to these two effects as the centripetal and centrifugal forces of advertising representations.

The US literary critic Wayne Booth calls advertising representations 'pornographic'. Advertising seeks to arouse appetite and desire, he says. Booth outlines a number of properties of advertising representation which he says make advertisements a depressing cultural event.

► Advertisements do not permit other ways of thinking and suggest moral values that are taken for granted as normal.
► Advertisements link the noblest human emotions with greedy demand for products.
► Advertisements depend on stereotypes.
► Advertisements show that the only goal in life is material success – there are no losers in Adland.

Truth in advertising

'All Aspirin is not alike. In tests for quality, Bayer proves superior.' To most people, this would mean that Bayer Aspirin is better at relieving headaches than other aspirin. However, later study revealed that the 'tests for quality' were conducted by Bayer themselves and showed that their aspirin was superior because the tablets were whiter and less breakable than the other aspirins tested.

In advertising, as in war, truth is the first casualty. In advertising, there are two standards of truth – what might be called the *literal* truth and the *suggested* truth. The literal truth is what exactly is said. Statements are carefully constructed so that they do not actually contain a lie. The suggested truth is what most people could be expected to understand by what is said. The suggested message relies on people using the logic of conversation, rather than legal logic. Toothpaste manufacturers commonly say that their product 'helps to prevent tooth decay'. This is literally true, as even brushing your teeth with your finger would help to prevent tooth decay. However, most people understand this statement to mean that the toothpaste *will* prevent tooth decay.

Advertisers can be expected to make the strongest claims that they are able to defend. Therefore, the advertiser who can justify saying

statement one is not likely to make statement two.

1. Most people who use Painfree get immediate pain relief.
2. Many people who use Painfree get immediate pain relief.

Sentence two is weaker than sentence one. Suppose the manufacturer of Painfree were to have sampled twenty million people and asked who had and who had not had immediate relief from taking Painfree. Suppose they discovered that 200,000 got immediate pain relief. In this case, the manufacturer would be right in saying that many people who used Painfree got immediate pain relief because 200,000 is certainly many people by anybody's standards. However, 200,000 is just 1 per cent of the total sample.

Advertisers also use verbs like 'may', 'can' and 'could' to protect themselves in case they are asked to defend the literal truth in court. Advertisers usually treat the word *can*, for example, as meaning 'to be possible'. This makes claims containing 'can' quite weak, as anything at all is possible.

▼ ▼ ▼ ▼ ▼ ▼ ▼

activities

1. Perform a content analysis on a selection of advertisements to score the incidence of various stereotypes of different groups. A content analysis counts the occurrence of certain representations within the content of the advertisement.

Calculate the incidence of the stereotypes as a percentage of the total number of advertisements containing the target group.

2. Research the historical development of the representation of a selected group in television advertising (e.g. housewives).

3. Create an advertisement based on a 'reverse stereotype' of a selected group. A reverse

stereotype changes the common depictions of a group into opposite ones, or takes on the stereotypical elements of more powerful groups. A reverse stereotype, for example, could be of a powerful Asian businesswoman.

4. Find examples of advertisements that appear to be using the two standards of truth, the literal and the suggested truth. Make a list of the claims that they make.

Question somebody else who has also seen the advertisement to find out whether they have taken the literal truth or the suggested conversational truth to be the meaning of the advertisement.

Television Advertisements: Audience Issues

The target audience

Advertisers have turned to the social sciences such as psychology and sociology, in order to understand consumer behaviour. Techniques of predicting consumer behaviour have now become very precise and very expensive. Advertisers believe consumers can be 'sorted out', grouped together and delivered to sponsors as neatly packaged groups. For example, in the United States, a research organisation has divided the entire US population into 121 different socio-demographic groups. The company believes it can predict the behaviour of each of these groups.

Advertising psychology has one basic belief: each group in society has deep-seated needs, fears and weaknesses. Advertising agencies then make it seem as if ordinary, everyday products can cure these weaknesses.

Appeals to instincts and emotions

Television advertisements aim to create the feeling that an instinct can be satisfied or an emotion soothed through the use of the sponsor's product. The range of human instincts and emotions provides plenty of scope.

The *acquisitive* instinct has been with humanity since cavemen days. It causes us to save, collect and hoard all kinds of possessions. From it we get a satisfying feeling of ownership.

The *sexual* instinct is one of the strongest in the make-up of human beings and therefore is the most widely used appeal on television advertise-ments. Sex appeal can be used to sell anything from cars to shampoo.

The *herd* instinct draws people together and makes them want to be part of a group or a crowd. Advertisers link their products to the basic human need for friendship and can therefore lead people to believe that the use of the product will overcome their loneliness. McDonald's, Coke and Pepsi have all used appeals to the herd instinct. Their advertisements are warm and friendly. McDonald's stresses the family aspect of together-ness, while Coke and Pepsi stress peer group togetherness.

Love is the most important human emotion. When lovers are shown using the product, the magic of love is attached to the product.

Maternal love is another favourite emotion with advertisers. According to the advertisements a mother shows her love only when she uses certain products.

Fears are present for each of our instincts and emotions and these are exploited by advertisers as well. Love as an emotion has many fears associated with it – loneliness, rejection and so on. Advertisers play on these to frighten people into buying the product. They suggest failure to use the product will cause some dreaded result, such as rejection by the opposite sex.

Demographic appeals

The term *demographics* is derived from the Greek words *demos* for 'people' and *graphics* for 'writing' (or mapping). Advertisers have built up huge numbers of people maps of the population based on their social class, their age, sex, education, religion, family size and so on. These people maps are constantly changing as society changes.

Advertisers buy time in advertisement breaks from television stations. They are very definite about who they want to target before they buy the time. The television station has a demographic breakdown of the audience for each programme it broadcasts. The advertiser matches this data with his or her target audience.

THE DEMOGRAPHICS OF GENDER Women are the group most sought after by television advertisers. This is because they spend more money than any other group. For example, 60 per cent of twenty- to thirty-year-olds buying property are women. Women also make more than 70 per cent of all household purchases.

Researchers have divided women into four categories:

► women at home who do not plan to work in the future
► women at home who plan to return to the workforce

- women for whom work is an economic necessity
- women for whom work is a career.

Men still make 64 per cent of business decisions and may be targeted by business advertisers. Yet males as a group are in a state of change and upheaval, advertisers say. One advertising research agency has divided males into two intersecting segments. The first aspect is based on the degree of success achieved. The second is based on the balance between modern and traditional beliefs – i.e. 'new' men versus 'old' men.

THE DEMOGRAPHICS OF SOCIAL CLASS Money talks as far as advertisers are concerned. The most desirable audience is the audience with the most cash. Accordingly, advertisers have devised a scale of relative spending power.

- *'A' households* are successful upper professionals or business people. They include surgeons, barristers and company executives (including television and advertising executives). Only 2 per cent of the population is in this category.
- *'B' households* are below the top, but are still well off. They include doctors, dentists, directors of small companies, and so on. These households comprise around 10 per cent of the population.
- *'C1' households* are the lower middle class and make up a quarter of the population. They include trades people, various skilled white-collar workers and the owners of small businesses.
- *'C2' households* are skilled manual workers, such as lorry drivers and craftspeople on building sites.
- *'D' households* are unskilled manual workers such as labourers, traffic wardens, factory workers, cleaners and so on.
- *'E' households* are people receiving welfare, including the unemployed and retired pensioners.

FAMILY LIFE CYCLE The family life cycle is seen as divided into nine categories:

- **SINGLES** – young single people not living at home

- **NEWLY MARRIED COUPLES** – young with no children
- **FULL NEST ONE** – young married couples with youngest child under six
- **FULL NEST TWO** – young married couples with youngest child six or older
- **FULL NEST THREE** – older married couples with dependent children
- **EMPTY NEST ONE** – older married couples still in the workforce, no children living with them
- **EMPTY NEST TWO** – older married couples retired, no children living at home
- **SOLITARY SURVIVOR IN WORK FORCE**
- **SOLITARY SURVIVOR, RETIRED.**

THE YOUTH MARKET The youth units of the advertising research companies have identified at least five subcultural groups of teenagers. Music remains a powerful influence on each of these. But technology is also something with which many teenage subcultures identify. Researchers believe today's youth are far more divided into 'tribes' than previous generations.

There is a diversity of people out there, but advertising agencies are happy with that. They do not want everyone to be the same.

Some things, however, never change. Advertising strategy planners believe there are three timeless appeals to teenagers.

- 'My parents don't understand me', which has been a stage for all generations.
- The issues of 'today' have affected every generation. The most important to teenagers are currently the environment, unemployment and crime/drug abuse, according to one report.
- The various ways in which teenagers represent themselves to their peers.

Attitudes and beliefs

The Stanford Research Institutes Values and Lifestyles Programme (VALS) in the United States has organised people's attitudes and beliefs into five groupings. People have been put into categories according to how they spend their leisure time, what they consider important in the world and what they think of themselves and the world around them.

- **BELONGERS** – traditional, conservative conformist; family-orientated, like security, hate change and like a strong community
- **EMULATORS** – young people searching for an identity, desiring to fit into adult world, but can be discouraged about prospects
- **EMULATOR-ACHIEVERS** – successful, enjoy acquiring things and buy brand names
- **SOCIETALLY CONSCIOUS ACHIEVERS** – inner peace and environment more important than financial success; want personal fulfilment, lovers of outdoors and fitness, like to experiment
- **NEEDS DIRECTED** – survivors on incomes that only allow needs and not wants to be fulfilled; pensioners and those on unemployment benefits, for example.

Do advertisements really work?

'I know half the money I spend on advertising is wasted … but which half?' said Lord Lever of Lever Brothers, the detergent manufacturers. Since Lever's famous comment was made in the 1920s, things have probably improved. Television audience surveys conducted by companies such as A. C. Nielsen have improved the science of advertising.

Only a quarter of the money is wasted now, says Ian Elliott, manager of George Patterson Bates. The trouble still is knowing which quarter.

It cannot simply be coincidence that the biggest-spending brands promoted *just happen* to be the biggest-selling.

Will they watch it?

An advertisement must be seen before there is any communication. The television viewer is not breathlessly waiting to see the advertisements. The viewer could not care less – and may have better things to do.

About 1 per cent of the advertising budget goes into testing whether or not the advertisement appeals to its target audience. The most popular method of testing is through group discussion. A group of people is assembled to represent the target market. They are then shown the advertisement and afterwards discuss how they feel about it.

Remembering the advertisement

Almost all of the persuasion that takes place occurs among those who remember the advertisement. Recall of the message is the most important factor in persuasion. The advertiser must put the consumer through the four stages of the memory process, so that he or she will remember the advertisement.

- attention to the advertisement
- storage of the advertisement in long-term memory
- remembering the advertisement over days, weeks or years
- retrieval of the advertisement at the point of sale.

Advertisers have found several factors help consumers to remember their advertisements. First, they try to play on people's emotions because people remember emotional experiences. Also, key elements of the message are often set to music because jingles or poetic rhymes are more easily remembered. Finally, a key picture or main image is more easily remembered than words and advertisers try to include the product in this key picture.

Has it boosted sales?

Although many factors can influence the sales of products, most manufacturers believe that advertising is a large factor and so they encourage market research into the effects on sales. This is done in several ways.

CONSUMER INTERVIEWS A sample group of consumers is taken and they are asked questions about their purchases. This same group of consumers is again surveyed after the advertisements have been shown.

STOCK ON THE SHELVES Quantities of stock on store shelves are noted before the advertising campaign begins and again after it has finished.

TEST MARKETS An advertising campaign may be conducted in one city, or one region, and not held in another. Consumer purchases in the two markets are compared for the effects on sales.

Vulnerable or expert audience?

The early studies of advertising asked the question, what does advertising *do* to people? They began searching for the answer using a simple stimulus-response method. If an advertisement were shown, the natural response would be to go out and buy the product.

Such studies did not credit the viewer with very much intelligence. The idea that advertisements brainwash us came from a view of advertising as a giant syringe, injecting us with messages. The viewer was like a zombie, having no control over things.

Later, researchers took the view that advertisements are just one influence among a host of others. They have also seen a greater role for audience intelligence and expertise.

Some academics, such as John Corner, question whether people pay serious attention to advertisements. If they do not, the power of advertisements would therefore be less than that of the mainstream programming.

In post-industrial society, young people especially often enjoy advertisements for their entertainment value. Some may collect favourite advertisements and some even enjoy them as an 'art form'. Yet, they may have no intention of buying the product. This has led some academics to conclude that advertising has very little effect in the short term.

One of the most serious-sounding criticisms, if valid, would be the oft-expressed charge that particular advertisements are ridiculous. A good example of this would be the action-film manoeuvres Volvo put one of their cars through recently: a series of high-octane explosions on a runway, in pursuit of some unexplained goal. The car swerves and weaves round various obstacles, and – marvellous! – comes through entirely unscathed. Not the scenario most commuters have to confront in their daily gridlock. No doubt many viewers felt that the whole thing was hilariously funny. However, the company recognised that, although they had a quality product, it had attracted a reputation of being rather staid and boring. *To the audience being targeted*, the advertisement was intended not so much to be taken on a literal level, as to provide some reassuring images of the product that counteracted this image problem.

Are advertisers right to spend all that money? It may well be that most advertisements wash over the majority of the audience. Advertisements are only aimed at those who are thinking of buying and nobody could possibly be thinking of buying everything that is advertised. However, sales figures suggest that advertisements can definitely persuade the smaller group of people who are thinking of buying to choose a particular product when they do.

If the emphasis on brainwashing was exaggerated, so, too, is the emphasis on the totally immune and expert audience, says John Corner. Businesses do not spend more than £13 billion a year without being reasonably certain they are getting some return.

▼ ▼ ▼ ▼ ▼ ▼ ▼

activities

1. The advertisement below appeared in a trade magazine aimed at advertisers themselves. The humour in the advertisement comes from satire – as advertisers would know many advertisements play on people's desire to be like someone else. Read through the satire and then answer these questions:

▶ Can you think of any television advertisements that suggest a consumer can be a better person if they use the product?

▶ Explain how these ads play on fears that ordinary people may have.

▶ A satirical advertisement such as this pokes fun at people who fall for this advertising

technique. Why do you think such advertising has proved to be so successful on television? Does the audience really swallow the appeal, or is the audience more expert? Does the audience really think their emotional needs and fears can be solved by the use of a product? Explain your point of view.

2. Describe some television advertisements that make obvious appeal to the sexual instinct. Are these advertisements aimed exclusively at men or are there also advertisements exploiting sexual instinct that appeal to women?

3. Chocolate advertisements often feature images of love to help sell the product. Describe some of these advertisements and explain how the images work. What other products also use images of love?

4. Peer groups are very important to teenagers. Products that are aimed at a teenage market often use fear of rejection by the peer group or images of belonging to a strong peer group to help sell the product. Describe some television advertisements that use the peer group to sell the product.

5. Advertisers might study the demographics of the family if they wish to advertise products that are purchased for family consumption, such as food and household equipment and supplies.

▶ Which of the nine categories in the family life cycle (see p. 337) would be most profitable for advertisers? In other words, which groups have the highest income?

▶ Choose three or four of the life cycle categories and make a short list of food or household products that could easily be sold to people in the categories.

▶ Imagine you were asked to produce a series of advertisements for frozen food aimed at each of the life cycle categories. Explain how each advertisement would differ from the one before.

6. Advertisers group people according to their socioeconomic status. There are six groups commonly referred to in television advertising (see p. 337). Watch some television advertisements

Figure 4.44

and assign each to one of the categories. Outline the factors that influenced your decision. Are there any gaps? Try to offer possible reasons for this.

7. Stanford University's VALS demographic programme identifies five groups according to values and attitudes (see p. 338). Certain kinds of advertisements suit certain categories, but most advertisements focus on the three groups likely to spend most on consumables: belongers and emulator/achievers.

Watch a number of television advertisements and decide whether you think they appeal to belongers, emulators or emulator/achievers. Give reasons for your choice.

8. Research into whether or not people remember television advertisements often begins with phone calls to a sample group of people. Interviewers ring during the evening and ask questions such as: 'Thinking about the very last advert that was shown just before I called, can you tell me what product was being advertised?'

The interviewer scores an answer as correct if the person recalled any of the brands or companies in the last cluster of advertisements aired before the call. In the past thirty years, the percentage of people who remember the advertisements has dropped from 18 per cent to 7 per cent.

Try this research experiment with your class. Watch a commercial television programme, stop the programme sometime after an advertisement break and then answer the question posed by the television interviewer in the paragraph above. Convert the results to percentages.

major assignment

Written assignment

Prepare a 600-word report on a single advertisement, or a collection of two or three advertisements.

Report on the key selling point of the advertisement, the decorative periphery and the rational core. Discuss the representation of people, ideas, places or events. Report on the apparent target audience and discuss the appeal the advertisement makes to this audience. Conclude with your own evaluation of the advertisement's effectiveness.

Production assignment

Make a television ad storyboard for a client of your choice. On a separate sheet include a description of the product you are advertising, explain the key selling point, the image you are trying to project and the market to which you want to appeal.

Talk Shows

There are many types of talk show, but one type provokes the most interest, the most outrage and the most … well, talk! The daytime issue-based talk show has come to dominate discussion and influence all other talk shows. The first of these shows to make it big were American and they are notorious for being sensational and bizarre (such as *The Jerry Springer Show*). Others followed here (*Vanessa*, for a time, and *Trisha*), although they do not tend to be quite so excitable. One critic describes them as 'a whole degraded landscape of schlock'.

To others, talk shows are 'classical popular culture', the roots of which go back to the sensationalist newspapers of a century ago. One hundred years ago, the tabloid newspapers ran articles on murders, sex crimes and disasters. Termed *yellow journalism*, the writing style focused on human-interest stories with shock value. The papers were purchased by a newly arrived urban working class.

The American sociologist Joshua Gamson, of Yale University, offers a further explanation of the programme's roots. 'Talk shows are built from middle class traditions of rationality-driven discussion on the one hand and urban and rural working-class traditions of emotionally driven participation and spectacular mass entertainments, on the other.' Talk shows have mixed polite 'high' society and unruly 'low' culture.

Whatever their origins, they have become big business. The *Oprah Winfrey Show* is seen in sixty-five countries. Before the host's retirement, *Donahue* was seen in fifty-one countries.

Features of talk shows

There are a number of defining characteristics of the issues-orientated daytime talk show.

■ Issues orientation

The subject matter for talk shows focuses on social problems or personal issues that are currently public concerns. Typical topics could include, for instance, drug or child abuse or family breakdown. In essence, the shows are a kind of 'fleshing out' of the personal impact of what is currently newsworthy.

■ Audience participation is encouraged

Audiences are involved in the show and are often called upon to provide comment on the issues. Audience involvement is a valuable back-up for the producers of the show if the guests or hosts appeal begins to flag.

■ A host provides moral authority

The host provides the structure for the show and mediates between the participants. The host leads the show to a satisfactory and often uplifting moral resolution or a call to action.

■ Experts give specialised comment

Invited experts in the chosen field provide educated knowledge to balance the host's moral authority.

■ Females predominate in the audience

Although significant numbers of males do watch, the daytime talk show sells advertising space on the basis of a majority female audience.

■ Private non-network companies produce the shows

Most of the talk shows are produced cheaply by independent companies and then sold to syndicators for network distribution. Oprah

Winfrey's show, for example is produced by her own company, Harpo ('Oprah' backwards).

The structure of the talk show genre

It is the game show that is most often compared to the talk show. Both genres use a regular host with ever-changing guests and include the audience as eager participants in the overall performance. However, the daytime talk shows are often placed on the programme between the midday news and afternoon soap operas. Perhaps as a result, the talk show structure borrows key elements from both. The result is a hybrid genre that is part game show, part news and part soap.

'Much of the appeal of the genre is its claim that audiences are witnessing something non-fiction,' says sociologist Joshua Gamson. The goal of the talk show is to be like a soap opera, but real at the same time. Research shows that viewers can be prevented from switching channels if a programme is either very familiar or very unusual. Gamson believes the challenge for television executives is to design a show that is both. 'The talk show, in its combination of the familiar-yet-different – its constantly shifting, news-oriented focuses and its highly charged ad-libbed performance – seems calculated to meet this challenge.'

The talk show genre is a complex one containing elements of the report genre from news combined with the exposition genre that is common in documentaries. While the news focuses on events and looks at broad social experience, talk shows use the same events to focus on the individual and personal experience. Frequently, talk shows use the problem/solution structure that is also a standard way of organising documentaries. Yet the programmes also operate within the narrative genre. The orientation, complication and resolution structure of narratives is typical of talk shows as well. And talk shows share with narratives a deep involvement with characters and events.

Melodrama is the dominant narrative form used in talk shows. The stereotypes of victim, victimiser and hero in melodramas make the talk show producer's job easy. 'Producers can pattern an hour's drama around an age-old social or personal issue,' says Jane Shattuc. But more than this, says Shattuc, the melodrama is also a female-centred narrative. The key character or protagonist is often passive and is rescued by a secondary, active character. The rescuer then teaches the victim about the secrets to his or her heroic power. Talk shows use the melodramatic form to present the host as a hero seen to be helping those without the power to solve their own problems.

Conflict and pain are highlighted in talk shows, creating the impression that something important or 'real' is occurring. To be chosen, a topic must have clear conflict in it. These are commonly sexual, marital, or generational conflicts; however, topics can be based on class or racial conflicts as well. A good topic or 'story' has a strong, aggressive antagonism between viewpoints or between people.

▼ ▼ ▼

We watch as a young girl describes in lurid detail how she was neglected by her alcoholic mother, whom she has not seen for years. The girl's pain appears great. Then the host tells her, and us, that the mother is in the studio. The mother walks on the stage and says, 'I'm sorry' and the daughter replies 'I love you.'

That's it. That's the resolution.

We all know that is not how real problems are solved, but a more appropriate treatment would never fit the show's format.

Jeanne Heaton and Nona Wilson
Tuning in Trouble

▼ ▼ ▼

Resolution is usually managed by the host and constructed by the programme's narrative. For most of the show, the topic or problem might have been presented as serious and even life-threatening. But then, just at the end show provides a quick and easy solution.

THE HOST

Oprah Winfrey is the embodiment of the American Dream – the poor girl who worked hard, got straight As in school, overcame the obstacles of racial prejudice, obesity, sexual abuse as a child and crack cocaine abuse as an adult and became one of the most famous women in the world.'

Vicki Abt
Coming after Oprah

▼ ▼ ▼

Topics come and go and there is a constant parade of guests, each new one more outlandish than the last. The host, however, always remains there, like a beacon of familiarity.

Indeed, because the talk show topics are often duplicated by other talk shows, the personality of the host is often all that distinguishes one show from another. According to Jane Shattuc, talk show hosts have become the major form of product differentiation. 'Winfrey and the other hosts are like brand names on labels, devices to attract women buyers.' She goes on to say that the most obvious sign that they are of central importance is that the shows are almost always named after them. And usually the show is known just by their first name – a sign of the friendly intimacy the audience has with them.

Development of this sense of intimacy with the audience is vital if the shows are to develop a loyal following. The shows depend on some people's willingness to confide their secrets and on other's eagerness to listen. Much of this support depends on whether the viewers like the host.

The talk show host's role is a complex one, encompassing the following tasks.

■ Welcoming and reassuring

The host welcomes both the guests and the audience into a reassuringly familiar format. First names are used as the host puts everyone at ease so that an open discussion can flow.

■ Being a focus point

Unlike a news anchor person, the talk show host has to be someone with whom the audience both at home and in the studio can identify. The host must be someone with whom we would like to talk or argue.

Jerry Springer says, 'the studio audience is often fearful. There's a lot of anxiety there.' The host has to get people feeling safe enough to speak. Either that or stir people up so they will want to stand up and call out.

■ Being non-judgmental

Regardless of how bizarre or horrific the revelations are, the host is always non-judgmental and apparently objective. The host continues to appear interested concerned and knowledgeable without being critical.

■ Sharing the pain

Somehow guests have to be encouraged to talk freely about painful subjects. The host is often someone with a troubled or difficult past themselves. For instance, Phil Donahue was a single father when he raised his sons. Hosts need to build a common bond with their guests and the audience based on a shared experience of suffering. Life has been hard for them, but they have overcome their adversity. People like to talk to someone who really understands what it is like.

■ Being a therapist

Since the talk show is often like a confessional, the host acts somewhat like a priest or psychologist. 'My show is really a ministry, a ministry that doesn't ask for money. I can't tell you how many lives we've changed – or inspired to change,' says Oprah Winfrey.

■ Uncovering all the secrets

The audience wants to hear the most scandalous revelations. The role of the host is to probe for details and express interest in finding out more. Oprah Winfrey believes: 'It's okay to titillate if in the process you help someone.' Often disclosure is encouraged with gentle words of support from the host such as, 'I don't know how you coped'.

■ Provoking conflict

Because the format demands dramatic conflict, hosts have to be skilful in creating it. Whether provocative questioning to get a rise out of a guest, or to encourage outrageous behaviour the host often plays to the audience's desire for a brawl of some kind.

■ Providing resolution

Having stirred things up, the host must also be able to bring about a resolution in the last minutes of the show. One way to do this is to for the host to act as a 'gatekeeper'. The host selects the questions from the audience so that there appears to be some sort of majority rule about which is the rightful side of the issue. However, the audience likes to leave the show with the feeling that somehow, they put things right or saw justice done. If the show finishes with an educational message or appears to be socially responsible in some way, the home audience will feel less like peeping toms and more like concerned citizens. A 'feel-good' resolution has been obtained.

According to research done by Heaton and Wilson, talk show hosts take up about 30 per cent of the total on air programme time. Since most of their role is involved with engaging others in conversation, however, the average length of their comments is only about seven seconds.

The job of the camera operators and programme director, on the other hand, is to skilfully weave the host into the visuals of the show. They must select just the right moment to cut to a reaction shot or when to move to a close up during intense questioning.

THE GUESTS

Daytime talk shows are transforming television into a three-ringed circus of the lurid, grotesque and dysfunctional. In the free market of pop culture only the most daring – that is the most salacious – survive.

Susan Crabtree
'Talking Trash'

▼ ▼ ▼

While psychologist Jeanne Heaton has called them a 'passing parade of pathology' and Neal Gabler says they 'exhibit their deformities for attention', the guests are the raw material the talk show transforms into its product. Without their personal stories and private pain, there would be no talk.

Why do they do it? While research has been limited so far, two main motivations have been shown to exist. One motivation is a noble one: individuals who had suffered wanted to educate the public and improve things for others. The second motivation was for the thrill of appearing on television.

The guest's role on talk show programmes is much simpler than the host's. The guest is there to supply the following.

TALK Whether it is to talk provocatively, to confess, to argue or to express feelings, the guest is the centre of controversy. Talk is good, but not wide-ranging talk. The guest has to stick to the set topic. And a guest can never say, 'It's none of your business!'

STEREOTYPED EXAMPLES OF THE TOPIC Guests are there to represent viewpoints or to provoke discussion about issues. To make them fit into the narrative, guests are often chosen on the basis of stereotypes, such as 'the unfaithful wife', 'the abusive husband', etc. Each show is based around a theme and guests are treated as illustrations of the theme. They are not shown as complete, rounded personalities with a variety of strengths, weaknesses and interests. Sometimes during the show, captions are used to label the guests, further stereotyping or narrowing them. Sociologist Vicki Abt refers to this process of stereotyping guests as 'flattening the round'.

ENTERTAINMENT AND CONFRONTATION It is said that guests are encouraged to be unique and take advantage of difference. The primary factor in booking a guest is their entertainment value. According to Gamson, one show's producer says, 'When you're booking guests, you're thinking, "How much confrontation can this person provide me?" The more the better. You want people just this side of a fist fight.'

Heaton and Wilson's research shows that guests get about 39 per cent of the programme time and the average length of their responses is thirteen seconds. They conclude: 'guests need to reveal all, but quickly!'

THE EXPERTS

The shows would have us believe that the primary role of experts is to provide expertise. But producers prefer experts who can provide succinct, pithy answers that give the impression of expertise without all the bothersome and time-consuming details.

Jeanne Heaton and Nona Wilson
Tuning in Trouble

▼ ▼ ▼

Newspaper advice columns began in the early years of the twentieth century. Jane Shattuc argues that the talk show expert descends from the women's help pages and 'agony aunt' columns in newspapers and magazines.

The most commonly appearing experts are psychologists, social workers and relationship counsellors. Next in frequency of appearance on talk shows come the writers of self-help books. Appearing less often, but still quite regularly, are officials from welfare agencies, education authorities and health organisations.

Experts fulfil the following functions.

■ **Providing the voice of authority**

Using external voices of authority is a tradition derived from the news and documentary genre. As political, social or economic events unfold, various experts in the field tell us what it means and what to expect as a possible outcome. The talk show uses experts to support the moral authority of the host.

■ **Providing answers**

Experts have to be able to use their knowledge to give useful formulas and uncomplicated advice.

■ **Summarising and clarifying**

Audiences hear the guests' pain and relive the events as they recount them. But they are somewhat at a loss to know what it all means. The role of the expert is to make sense of the little 'slice of life' that the viewers have seen.

■ **Being a cooling element**

Emotions run high on talk shows. Guests can break down or even resort to fist fighting. The expert is the voice of rational and impartial 'science'.

■ **Providing resolution**

Most talk shows say they aim to educate and inform their audiences as well as entertain them. While viewers may have been fascinated 'peeping toms' for most of the show, the expert can provide the educational element. Experts can tell us what to do about the problem and so finish the show on a positive note.

Heaton and Wilson's research shows that experts get about 9 per cent of the total programme. They say: 'Compared to the host, the experts have very little opportunity to present their points of view. The average expert comment is about thirteen seconds long.'

THE STUDIO AUDIENCE

Like the ancient Greek chorus, they comment on the action. They function like the fans at a ball game or participants in a new-age therapy group.

Vicki Abt
Coming after Oprah

▼ ▼ ▼

Daytime talk shows have various ways of selecting their studio audiences. Some give away tickets in selective mail-outs after interested people ring the studio. Other shows are much more open and take whoever turns up on the day. On occasion, production staff have even gone out into the street to haul people in!

Audiences tend to be from certain groups in the community because they are the only ones available for daytime filming sessions. They have to be able to take time off work (or be unemployed/not working) and they have to be able to plan ahead to be free of commitments.

Most shows invite organisations and social issue groups to attend. Women's groups were often sought after, but any group related to the topic of the day is usually contacted.

Once in the studio, audience members are seated randomly according to clothing colour and also randomly according to their stated viewpoints about the topic of the day. The following are the key roles that the audience play:

■ **Add emotional intensity**

Audiences are warmed up before the shows start. Often this can be with a comedian or some kind of interactive performer. The idea is to 'egg' them on or even to make them angry. During the show, the audience has to provide excitement at similar levels to that of fans at a sports stadium.

■ **Provide reactions**

Visible and audible reactions are required. Cheering and jeering are encouraged.

■ **Act as adjudicators**

Audience members are called upon to ask questions, give advice, to tell their own stories and ultimately sit in judgement like a jury.

■ **Stand for the millions watching at home**

Studio audiences represent 'the people' and so they stand in for the viewers at home. Like game show audiences, the talk show audience helps to build the involvement of the home audience. Viewers at home get a 'charge' or excitement and feel part of the performance when they see audience members call out or get up and speak. It is almost as if they are sitting in the audience themselves.

Social purpose of talk shows

Post-industrial nations are made of overlapping communities, often with little real connection with each other and sometimes ill at ease with each other. Television has become one way of building agreement through a shared experience.

Television (and all media) helps build a sense of community by creating involvement in what some analysts refer to as 'the public sphere'. The public sphere is the realm of mass meetings, political debate, citizenship and involvement in the democratic processes of the nation. In television, the public sphere is apparent in news programming, current affairs and documentaries. At least until the second half of the twentieth century, the public sphere was seen as traditionally masculine while the private sphere of the home was seen as traditionally feminine.

The contribution of talk shows, argues Jane Shattuc, is bringing what was once private into public view, thereby creating an alternative – a new 'counter public sphere'. Thanks to the television talk show: 'the private has become public. The personal is political.'

The talk show, says Robin Anderson, Professor of Communications at Fordham University in New York, promised to be a kind of televised town hall meeting. So far, however, she says that the shows have failed to be a forum for public discussion because of their commercialism.

Nevertheless, some analysts argue talk shows allow minorities and disadvantaged people a voice on television that they have never had before. Sociologist Joshua Gamson sees the shows as offering an opportunity for 'big shot visibility and media accreditation. For people whose identities go against the norm, this is the only spot in mainstream media culture to speak on their own terms.'

Michael Harrison, the editor of the US *Talkers Magazine*, which covers the talk media industry, has this to say:

▼ ▼ ▼

Talk shows serve the simple need for connections with other people. People don't know their neighbours any more and they wouldn't have time to talk over the back fence if they did. But there's still a need for a human community, so it's a virtual, electronic, global media community.

▼ ▼ ▼

However, says Vicki Abt, before television people could not easily act as voyeurs or peeping toms without risking their reputations in the community. Now, with talk shows, it is all available in our lounge rooms completely conscience-free. The global communities do not have any of the social and personal responsibilities that are attached to real life.

Talk show audiences

MAJORITY FEMALE AUDIENCES According to a survey of media markets, daytime television talk show audiences are made up of 58 per cent females and 42 per cent males. Almost half are aged forty-five or older and a majority come from groups with lower levels of both education and income. About 45 per cent are not employed and a further 10 per cent work part-time.

As audiences are sold to advertisers, the talk show has constructed a majority female audience that will represent a certain type of consumer.

WHY PEOPLE WATCH The talk show offers and 'empowering kind of therapy', says Jane Shattuc. 'They offer connections to other people and the outrageousness of it all is entertaining. People are critical of these shows and they're media savvy enough to know when they're being had!' says Shattuc.

Vicki Abt argues that talk shows are comforting because they typically showcase individuals who are worse off than the viewers at home. 'Very often we benchmark our own experiences against and take solace from the plight of those less fortunate – or in this case, less respectable – than ourselves.'

Her comments are borne out to some extent by research conducted by Cynthia Frisby. Respondents recorded thoughts and feelings as they watched talk shows at home. Those who watched shows where the guests were worse off than themselves felt better about their own lives. Frisby goes on to say: 'Feeling better about oneself may be one of the primary reasons people watch the "trashier" talk shows'.

Representation issues

Talk shows generate social tolerance and give much needed visibility to non-conformists. The shows are

about talk: the more silence there has been on a subject, the more 'not telling', the better talk topic it is.

Joshua Gamson
Yale sociologist

▼ ▼ ▼

While talk shows have opened up television to minority groups and groups with special interests based around their identities, it is debatable whether this has deepened media democracy.

Their focus on conflict, as well, tends to work against a deeper understanding of the issues and favours extreme viewpoints and simple remedies. Media critic and journalist Howard Kurtz says: 'Talk culture is spectacularly ill-suited to dealing with complicated subjects. It is far easier to stop something – a health plan, a pay rise – than to forge a consensus among competing interests.'

Political analysts sometimes claim the talk shows are having a negative effect on voter confidence. Says Richard Leone: 'The tabloid issues have muscled their way into the political agenda. Our popular culture relentlessly portrays political life as dominated by corruption, sexual escapades, deals – everything but the substantive work of governing. This may attract viewers but it also alienates voters.' Meanwhile, many of the real issues facing society are completely ignored.

Some of the assumptions behind the simplistic talk show view of life are outlined by sociologists and cultural commentators Vicki Abt and Leonard Mustazza.

► A few minutes of advice can overcome a lifetime of struggle. There are quick fixes to complex problems.
► Talk therapy is useful for all problems.
► Personal confessions of individuals can solve the similar problems of thousands of others.
► Huge social injustices such as economic deprivation and educational inequality can be overcome by an expert's few words of advice.

Psychologists Heaton and Wilson offer their own concerns about the view of mental health problems portrayed in talk shows.

► All problems are presented as equally urgent and solvable (from a bad date to murder).
► The view of mental health problems and of 'normality' is distorted.

- A 'That's me!' copycat syndrome can develop as viewers overidentify and 'discover' they, too, have (for instance) multiple personality disorder.

- The public's compassion is exhausted by overexposure to attention-seekers.
- Simple solutions leave viewers frustrated as to why their own problems are not so easily solved.

activities

1. Hosts are one of the key points of product differentiation between similar shows. Make a list of the different hosts and write down the key characteristics that make them different from each other. Include such attributes as physical features, personal histories, on-camera style, whether they are supportive or contemptuous of guests, etc.

2. Watching the host respond to the guests is an important aspect of viewer involvement in the programme. Record a talk show and then list all of the cutaways the director in the control room has made to the host responding to guests. Provide a description of the messages these reaction shots give to the viewer at home.

3. Some commentators have compared talk shows with ball sports games. Make a comparison between a major sporting event and one of the talk shows. If possible, use segments of recorded tape and present your findings to the class.

4. The mood of the show tends to set the style of camera work. For instance, an emotional show will have the camera operators on the run looking for the 'criers'. A fun show might spend a lot more time on the audience and cut quickly between different members for an energetic feel. Analyse one talk show and see if you can make out the intent of the camera operators and the producer.

5. Look over the concerns Abt and Mustazza, or Heaton and Wilson have about the view of the world portrayed by afternoon talk shows. Select two of their concerns and provide an illustration from a talk show. If possible, record a segment and present it to the class.

6. Try your hand at writing the television guide 'teasers' for a talk show. For example, 'You can't get a date? You're off to Ricki's dating boot camp!'

(*Ricki Lake*). Invent some new shows and try to capture the feel of them in the teasers.

7. Debate whether talk shows actually allow minorities a voice on television or whether they give them air time only to ridicule them.

major assignment

Production assignment

Create your own talk show programme based on the following steps. You may decide to film the production, or it may be that the plans of the programme will be acceptable.

Select a topic of current social interest from the newspapers, magazines or television. The topic should allow people to easily take sides and express strong viewpoints.

- Research the main points of view within the topic.
- Decide on one or two guests who will be living examples of the issue under discussion.
- Select a suitable expert to provide commentary. Provide reasons for your choice of expert.
- Draw up a list of relevant groups you might contact to provide audience members. Prepare a seating plan for representatives of the different points of view.
- Write the host's introductory speech.
- Give a list of options for a possible resolution to the discussion.

If time allows, hold a simulation talk show and film the proceedings. You could try filming with several cameras (*The Oprah Winfrey Show* uses up to seven!) and editing live to tape, as the professionals do.

Written assignment

Produce a 600-word response to the following topic.

Analyse and evaluate one episode of a talk show of your own choice. Your report should deal with the aspects set out below. You may find it easier to write the report using headings.

▶ Outline the details of the show such as title, time shown, host, etc.

▶ Provide a description of the topic.

▶ Outline the participants, such as the guests, audience members as you perceive them, experts, etc.

▶ Describe the main points of view.

▶ Analyse the progress of the discussion showing the development of the conflict and moments of climax. This could be further illustrated graphically.

▶ Describe how the resolution was brought about.

▶ Evaluate the coverage of the topic and the likely impact of the programme on a wide audience. In doing so, discuss the representation of the issue and any likely implications of this representation for the viewers.

chapter five
Radio

5▶

The Language of Radio

The ear is not a very intelligent organ. It processes information relatively slowly and even then it only sometimes gets it right. Radio broadcasters are often advised to use the principle of KISS when they are doing their job – 'Keep It Simple, Stupid.'

Unlike film, television, computer-based media or the print media, radio cannot be seen. Unlike a newspaper, it cannot be held in the hand and read over and over again. Television can signify meaning through images. Radio has only sounds.

Workers in the industry do not, however, regard this as a limitation. To them, the power of the human imagination liberated by radio is far greater than the visual stimuli of the other media

Basic units of radio language

Radio communication exists in *time*. Radio takes time to be heard and it is impossible to go back in time. You need to hear it right the first time because it will not be repeated. This is different to newspaper communication, say, which exists in *space*. A newspaper devotes space to stories; it takes up space at the breakfast table and, like the table, it is a physical object. The reader can range backwards and forwards freely over material he or she wishes to check or re-read. With video recorders, viewers can do the same with television. Radio, on the whole, tends to be heard only *once*.

The codes (see pp. 47–9) of radio language consist of words, sound effects, music and silence. These are shared to some extent with television and film, but radio uses them in rather different ways.

WORDS Words are signs that stand for something else. The word 'apple' does not look anything like the fruit that grows on trees. It is a sign within the semiotic language of signs (see p. 46). Radio relies on collections of these word signs as symbolic codes to communicate meaning.

Words on radio are spoken. This makes them different to words printed on a page because extra layers of meaning can be added. The tone of voice or the inflection can communicate meaning. The person speaking the words is therefore an additional sign. The personality of the DJ or the accent of a character in an advertisement can add to the meaning of what is being said. For example, an American accent or an upper-class English accent in a radio advertisement can convey extra meaning beyond the exact word meaning.

SOUND EFFECTS Words are a human invention, but there are many other sources of sound, too. Many of these are indirectly caused by people – e.g. vehicles, construction work or the beeps at traffic lights. There are many more that occur naturally in the real world – birdsong, trickling streams, various forms of weather.

Sounds do not exist as themselves, however: they are always caused by something. In a very real sense, they can be said to stand for something. Therefore sounds are signs, just as words are (see pp. 46–7 on semiotics). In radio, a very wide range of sounds is used to generate a variety of different meanings.

In the same way that television and film producers select certain images, radio producers select certain sounds. They construct these in logical orders to create meaning. Some sounds are included or stand out because the producer believes they are important. Other sounds are softer or left out altogether. Ships' fog horns, whistles that rise in pitch, bells and horns are some examples of sounds that can be used to generate meanings or moods.

There are a number of ways in which sound can be used. The American academics Edgar Willis and Camille D'Arienzo classify sound into three main functions.

▶ *Action sounds* are created by some kind of movement, such as a car racing by or a jet passing overhead.
▶ *Setting sounds*, such as the twittering of birds or the crashing of waves, indicate the surroundings or the setting. Some go even further to suggest particular details such as the time – the hooting of an owl is used to signify night.
▶ *Symbolic sounds* are meant to suggest an idea, particularly in a fantasy. Willis and D'Arienzo give the example of a rising note on a slide whistle representing Pinocchio's lengthening nose in a radio adaptation of the children's story.

(For other ways of classifying sound, see also Sound Effects in 'The Language of Film and Television', p. 160.)

MUSIC Music can signify something beyond itself, in the same way that sounds and words do. For example, a saxophone solo can stand for city nightlife. However, music is also just itself. It is very difficult for anyone to say what a piece of music means. It can build up emotions; it can move people to tears. Music can never be said to mean something, however, in the way in which the word 'apple' means the fruit of a tree. Unlike words, music can be enjoyed as complete meaning in itself, without having to refer to anything else.

Of course, a great deal of music also makes full use of words. Songs deal with a very wide range of emotional and even intellectual expression. However, music alone also has its own unique way of communicating.

SILENCE The American comedian Jack Benny cultivated a reputation for being a penny-pinching miser. In one famous radio comedy skit, Benny was confronted with a mugger on the street. The mugger says, 'Your money or your life!' There is a prolonged silence from Jack Benny. Then, as the studio audience responds to the silence, they begin to laugh and applaud. It is dawning on them that Benny must be thinking hard about which to choose.

Just as sound effects can signify meaning, so, too, can their absence. In this usage, silence can actually function in the same way as noise. The sudden blanking of all sound sources can be used, in a drama for example, to signify a switch to a character's internal thoughts or the passage of time between two scenes.

The main radio code

Radio relies mainly on the verbal codes of the spoken word. This may seem strange for the medium that gave the world the Top 40. Andrew Crisell says that it is speech on radio that sets music and sounds in context and gives them their final meaning.

Most of the radio stations aimed at younger audiences depend on the same pop music to provide the attraction. It is the nature of the DJs that makes all the difference in the success the stations achieve. Chris Evans built up a huge following for his breakfast show on Radio 1. When he left, audience figures plummeted – and did not recover until the appointment of Zoe Ball. The kind of music played throughout this time varied hardly at all. What DJs generate is a sense of *atmosphere*, or even *attitude*, which is crucial for engaging this audience.

At times, in some shows, the music seems almost incidental to the ongoing banter of the DJs and their guests. Indeed, the studio crew members themselves – Zoe's 'zoo', as they were known – have been increasingly drawn in, to help generate a sense of the lively, fun lifestyles led by those involved in the music industry in some way.

Radio scripts and semi-scripts

Radio stations use a variety of scripting formats. Some of the common ones are shown below.

PROGRAMME FORMATS Most programmes on radio are regularly scheduled and do not require detailed scripting. The shows have been produced so often that the routines are clearly set up. These shows may use a programme format. A programme format is a 'bare bones' script used when programmes are produced regularly. The programme format relies upon everyone being familiar with the basic routines.

Figure 5.1
An example of a formal radio script.

RADIO SCRIPT

CALLARD & BOWSER DESSERT NOUGAT: 'THE PAPER'

MUSIC:	THEME FROM 'AN ENGLISH COUNTRY GARDEN'
SFX:	BIRDS TWITTERING
BRITISH VOICE:	(PRINCE CHARLES SOUND-ALIKE) You know, one of the questions one is most often asked in life is … Does one eat the paper? One invariably replies, not if it's *The Times*. (CHUCKLES TO SELF)
	But if it's the paper on Callard & Bowser Dessert Nougat, one most certainly does … because it's a rice paper. And it's very nice. And it's simply there to protect one's fingers from becoming sticky … and leave them free for waving … or shaking hands … or … or … gardening/
AUSTRALIAN VOICE:	Callard & Bowser. That's English for nougat.

SEMI-SCRIPTS Some radio programmes are semi-scripted. The opening and closing segments and commercial cues may be fully scripted. The remainder of the programme is then ad-libbed or assembled informally.

RADIO SCRIPTS The formal radio script is similar to the television drama script – although it pre-dates this by several decades, of course! There are various styles, but most follow these conventions.

► Everything except dialogue is in block capitals.
► Acting directions are placed in brackets.
► Music directions are underlined.

▼ ▼ ▼ ▼ ▼ ▼ ▼

activities

1. Analyse the use of the basic units of radio language in an advertisement.

Comment on the proportion of the advertisement devoted to each element: the use of accents and voice inflection to convey meaning and the effectiveness of the music, as well as any other sound effects employed. What do each of these features add?

2. Investigate Andrew Crisell's statement that the voice gives meaning to the music on radio. Listen to several local and national stations; try to express what kind of atmosphere is created on each. How do the DJs generate this atmosphere?

3. Transcribe an advertisement from radio using the formal radio script style.

The Medium of Radio

STRETCHING THE IMAGINATION

MAN: Radio? Why should I advertise on radio? There's nothing to look at … no pictures.

GUY: Listen, you can do things on radio you couldn't possibly do on TV.

MAN: That'll be the day.

GUY: Ah-huh. All right, watch this. (AHEM) Okay, people, now when I give you the cue, I want the 700-foot mountain of whipped cream to roll into Lake Michigan which has been drained and filled with hot chocolate. Then the Royal Canadian Air Force will fly overhead towing the 10-ton maraschino cherry that will be dropped into the whipped cream, to the cheering of 25,000 extras. All right … cue the mountain …

SOUND EFFECTS (SFX): GROANING AND CREAKING OF MOUNTAIN INTO BIG SPLASH!

GUY: Cue the air force!

SFX: DRONE OF MANY PLANES.

GUY: Cue the maraschino cherry …

SFX: WHISTLE OF BOMB INTO BLOOP! OF CHERRY HITTING WHIPPED CREAM

GUY: Okay, 25,000 cheering extras …

SFX: ROAR OF MIGHTY CROWD. SOUND BUILDS UP AND CUTS OFF SHARP!

GUY: Now … you wanta try that on television?

MAN: Well …

GUY: You see … radio is a very special medium, because it stretches the imagination.

MAN: Doesn't television stretch the imagination?

GUY: Up to 21 inches, yes.

▼ ▼ ▼

Figure 5.2
With radio, it is not so much what goes in the ears as what comes out of the imagination. 'The pictures are better on radio' is an old saying from the early days of television.

The 'blind medium'

Sometimes radio is said to be a blind medium because it involves only one of the five senses – hearing. The messages of radio consist only of sounds and occasional silences. Things that may be self-evident or clearly visible on television have to be described carefully on radio. A great deal of the talk on radio is devoted to exploring people's thoughts, ideas and opinions; however, where activities are the focus, questions are framed in such a way as to encourage guests to *describe* what they are doing.

The great strength of radio is that it is said to involve the imagination more fully. In television, the action takes place on the screen – the scenes are the same no matter who is watching: little or no interpretation is needed. In radio, the images are all in the listener's mind, so that each person becomes creative.

This use of the imagination is not limited to radio plays and comedies. When we listen to radio news or weather reports, we are also forced to imagine the *real* world.

The Canadian media philosopher Marshall McLuhan says radio is a 'hot' medium, while television is a 'cool' medium. Radio heats up the imagination. It stimulates, while television relaxes.

The companion medium

Radio is also called the companion medium. The presenter's voice gives a strong sense of personal communication – providing company for each individual listener. Some of the pleasure the listener gains from the company of radio comes from a sense of being anonymous. The radio companion does not demand to know anything about the listener. The listener has no obligation to talk back to his or her electronic friend.

Many do, however! Talking to your radio, as with a television set, is not an uncommon phenomenon. This can cover a range of reactions, from appreciation to hostility.

Listeners have always been encouraged to respond to programmes, via the post or, more recently, by telephone. With fax and e-mail, they can even make a direct and instant contribution.

The intimate medium

While radio can still be regarded as a mass medium, the appeal to the imagination of each person makes it a very personal medium. The process of listening to the radio is 'inward' and intimate – like reading a book.

Radio encourages intimacy by directly addressing itself to the individual. DJs and other broadcasters are told never to imagine their audience as a group. Instead, they must talk to someone quite specific and real – and appropriate to their target audience, of course. Even microphone etiquette promotes intimacy. Presenters sit just 30–40 centimetres away from the mike and speak confidentially to it.

Radio's intimacy has increased over the years. Families once used to sit around the kitchen table or the fireside listening to radio from a Bakelite receiver. Now, people listen to radio individually, in their cars, on personal stereos and even at work. The experience of listening to radio is now largely an individual one.

The flexible medium

The biggest advantage radio has over television and newspapers is the speed at which it can be produced. There is no need for the printing and distribution that holds newspapers to strict deadlines. Reports can be phoned in and updated hourly, or even sooner. Unlike television, there is no need for expensive and heavy camera equipment and no delay as videotape is edited. Radio is a flexible medium.

Radio's flexibility becomes most apparent during times of crisis. Audiences can turn to radio for the most up-to-the-minute news. By and large, radio is still the most accessible medium to people during the working day.

Of course, radio *stations* can be set up fairly quickly, too. The history of pirate broadcasting in the United Kingdom is traced later (see pp. 360–1). More recently, during the conflicts in the Gulf and Kosovo, local radio stations were set up for either the indigenous peoples or the serving troops.

The undemanding medium

Most of the action on radio takes place in your imagination. Even the music is a personal and emotive experience. The advantage of this is that it leaves your hands free for driving, doing the ironing or a host of other secondary activities.

Listening to the radio in the car is now one of the primary uses listed in audience surveys. Listeners can carry a radio with them wherever they go. Radio does not demand exclusive attention in the way that a newspaper or television does. As a result, radio has become the background in locations as varied as hairdressing salons, factory floors and shopping centres.

▼ ▼ ▼ ▼ ▼ ▼

activities

1. A competition was held in 1969 for the best radio advertisement on the theme 'Radio Stretches the Imagination'. Below is the winning entry. Read it and then answer the questions.

VOICE 1: About 380 years before Christ was born, Plato philosophised:

VOICE 2: The true size of a city is indicated by the number of people who can hear the voice of a public speaker.

VOICE 1: By the number of people who can hear the voice …

ACTUALITY: APOLLO 12 Houston. Tranquillity Base here. The Eagle has landed.

VOICE 1: The world is getting smaller. The world is getting faster. People, who 100 years ago never met each other, now are forced to meet each other.

SFX CROWD SCENE: (INDISTINCT SHOUTING) … Let's go.

VOICE 1: The public speaker talks and the world listens. Radio is the message. Radio is the public speaker today.

SFX MUSIC: CONTEMPORARY MUSIC

VOICE 1: Radio is heard because the world listens, and waits, and learns, and sees. Radio is the public speaker – their guide in a world of conflict. Radio makes you think and care. Radio stretches the imagination.

- Do you agree with the final comments of Voice 1? Explain.
- The radio link-up with the first men on the moon is used here to demonstrate how radio keeps people in touch. Voice 1 states that radio has other roles as well. Can you think of some types of radio broadcasts as examples of radio's other roles?
- Do some people use radio for the opposite reasons as well (so they do not have to think or care)? Explain.
- Try writing your own advertisement on the theme 'Radio Stretches the Imagination'.

2. In class, choose a station, turn the radio on and listen for a few minutes. Write down the impressions that occur to you as you listen. What kinds of voices do the presenters have: are they warm/friendly/lively/confiding? What atmosphere is generated? What means other than voices are used and how do these contribute?

Compare your impressions with those of other class members. Does everyone receive the same message from radio?

Radio Audiences

There are more radios in this country than people. Every household has at least one radio and the average number is three. Some 58 per cent of the population live in households with more than four radios. Radio has the widest penetration of any media, even more widespread than television.

The popularity of radio looks set to increase, due to a number of factors. The Henley Centre for Forecasting says there may be an increase in radio listening and a decrease in television viewing. The causes include more car ownership, the growth of single-person households, increasing time pressure and a growth in leisure pursuits outside the home.

Figure 5.3
Radio is often referred to as the 'companion' medium. The listening experience is often individual and highly personal.

Characteristics of the radio audience

A MORNING AUDIENCE Before the arrival of television, radio drew its biggest audiences in the evening. Families would sit down in their living rooms to listen to the sorts of programmes they now watch on television. When television arrived, it drove radio out into the kitchen and the car. Breakfast time became the big listening period, followed by drive times – when people are travelling to and from work, both in the mornings and from approximately 4 to 7 p.m.

With increasing 'portability' – first transistor radios and now personal stereos with radio features – radio has taken on more the role of a companion medium. Today, it is available in virtually every situation.

DISTRACTED AUDIENCES Radio is lifestyle, biological clock, information provider and 'music on tap'. It is the unthinking background to the events of the day, the BBC's Aubrey Singer once famously claimed.

People listen to radio while doing something else. Television, on the other hand, requires immobility and most of their attention. This difference has led analysts to call radio a 'secondary' medium. It is often in the background of the audience's minds and is of secondary importance to them.

Most people can give only a short span of attention to the radio. They tune in while driving to the shops, for example, and the radio is turned off with the ignition. In the opinion of the radio analyst Andrew Crisell, this means radio is 'appropriated' or 'borrowed' by the listener for his or her own purposes. Some say this makes it different to television that tends to 'appropriate' or take over the audience instead.

CREATURES OF HABIT The success of radio stations is built on the listener's desire to tune in to the same station, at the same times every day.

The times people tune in are not so much a result of the programmes as the routines and schedules of listeners' lives. Broadcasters are aware of this and plot the nature of their programmes around audience availability. In other words, certain styles of programme are offered according to the likelihood of audiences tuning in at that time of day.

'Drive-times' (when people are on their way to and coming back from work) are recognised as highly desirable audience availability times; hence big-name DJs are promoted at these times.

DAYTIME AUDIENCES The peak listening time for radio is from 7.00 to 8.30 a.m. Women spend more time listening to the radio than men. The peak morning listening times are dominated by females.

OLDER AUDIENCES Teenagers are often thought to be the biggest audience for radio. In strict numerical terms, this is true. However, they actually listen to the radio *less* than other groups. Part of the reason for this is that they spend less time driving than do adults.

A growing concern for commercial broadcasters in particular is how they have overlooked the older audiences. The over forty-fours are recognised to be a growing niche and are forecast to make up more than 40 per cent of the total market within the next ten years.

▼ ▼ ▼

Older listeners like a more grown-up style of presentation. They want quality news and information, not inane banter, or lists of who's shagging who around the world. There's no doubt that there's a strong market opportunity among the 45-plus age group. Commercial radio doesn't serve that audience.

Jason Bryant
Managing Director of New
Development, TalkSport

▼ ▼ ▼

After a number of years of virtual level-pegging, the BBC edged ahead of its commercial rivals once more in the overall listening figures at the start of the millennium. Figures for October – December 1999 showed its share at 51.3 per cent, compared to 46.7 per cent for commercial stations. This was due largely to its provision of a broad variety of output, appealing to older audiences, according to the Radio Advertising Bureau.

The target audience

These days, radio stations do a lot of market research. Radio is not hit and miss any more; targeting audiences has become a precise science.

FROM BROADCASTING TO 'NARROWCASTING' Before the arrival of television, radio stations tried to be all things to all people. Now, stations are 'narrow-casting'. Rather than putting on air programmes of broad appeal, they are targeting an audience and zeroing in on that group's interests.

Each station tries to give itself a unique 'brand' identity to attract the kind of audience it desires. The specific audience may be defined as a locality audience, an age group, an audience for a certain music type, a socio-economic group and a group with a certain self-image.

Figure 5.4

ADULT LISTENERS

LISTENING TIME EACH WEEK

Housewives	21 hours 10 minutes
All women 18-plus	22 hours 59 minutes
All men 18-plus	21 hours 18 minutes

Figure 5.5

TEENAGE LISTENERS

LISTENING TIME EACH WEEK

All-group average	21 hours 10 minutes
Teenagers	15 hours 50 minutes

Ratings

Research shows that almost 89 per cent of people listen to the radio at least once a week. Audience measurement is conducted by RAJAR (Radio Joint Audience Research), a body which is jointly owned by the BBC and commercial radio. The methodology used is to place a weekly listening diary with some 650 households throughout Britain and Northern Ireland, recording all radio usage by everyone in them from the age of four upwards. A revision of this system led to 'RAJAR 99', which simplified the format of the listening diaries and personalised them to each participant, set up additional interviews with one member from each household, and introduced new three-monthly reports on findings.

In part, the need for improvements was driven by the complexities of the ever-growing services – especially with the launch of Digital Radio.

Why people listen

Many analysts say that radio's special audience characteristics make it well suited to the 'uses and gratifications' approach to audience research (see also p. 31). This is because the radio audience seems to use radio at their convenience and for certain purposes. Listeners tune in and out as it suits them.

Analysts have identified the following uses and gratifications for radio audiences:

Figure 5.6
The talk-show host as portrayed in **Talk Radio** *by Oliver Stone (USA, 1988). Most radio stations in the UK are music-oriented. Apart from the BBC, only one other station, TalkSport, offers entirely speech-based programmes. An earlier experiment with 'shock-jocks' imported from the US, designed to provoke lively discussions, was rapidly abandoned when audiences failed to tune in.*

- ▶ Radio gratifies certain psychological needs, such as the need for companionship and a sense of community.
- ▶ Needs can be fulfilled without giving up other activities when somebody listens to the radio, whereas television demands more of the audience's attention.
- ▶ Radio provides the information for conversations.
- ▶ People use radio to 'structure' their day.

▼ ▼ ▼ ▼ ▼ ▼ ▼

activities

1. Conduct a survey that investigates the amounts and/or times of people's radio listening habits. Set your findings out in chart form and explain the key reasons for the peak listening times that you discover.

2. Extend your survey into differing age groups: what do you find about the kinds of stations that are preferred by each age group?

3. Do a comparative study of the viewing times for television. What do you notice about the respective peak audience times and how do you account for these?

4. Make a list of the places in which you have listened to the radio in the past week. Also list the activities in which you were engaged. What kind of function did radio perform: was it in the background or were you concentrating on your listening?

Radio Institutions

The prospects for radio seem to be on the up at present. Its status as a major medium has fluctuated widely since it was first established: at one time it was very much the 'voice of the nation', listened to by millions the length and breadth of the land – indeed, around the world! Later, it appeared to be in decline. Radio audiences have always been large, but were affected seriously by the arrival of television.

Today, with huge improvements in the quality of broadcast sound and new digital developments, audience figures are healthy once more. Broadcasting companies claim that the range and diversity of services offered by radio has never been so extensive. The recent growth of new and diverse stations covering everything from classical music to hip-hop and dance would appear to confirm this.

Many critics, however, are very worried by the repetition of standard formula formats in what are claimed as new stations. As with the sprawl of new television channels, the tendency is towards replicating proven successful formulas, rather than trying out new ones.

Early days

The BBC *was* the history of radio for the first fifty years of its life. From its birth in 1922, right up until 1972, the BBC was the sole authorised broadcaster in the United Kingdom. Even then, when commercial radio finally arrived, it was only in the form of *local* radio (the BBC itself had begun broadcasting in this form back in 1955). We have to wait right up to the 1990s to see a *national* commercial licence be granted.

The prime reason for this was the birth of commercial television in the mid-1950s. This expansion had soaked up much of the investment interest available for private broadcasting at that time. In addition, the technical superiority of television – and cinema, too – soon left radio lagging far behind. It rapidly came to be regarded as an inferior medium

It was left largely to the BBC to carry this field. There were important competitors, broadcasting from abroad: Radio Normandie and

Radio Luxembourg, from virtually the outset. For many at the time, they provided vital and much-cherished alternatives. There was only one national provider, however, and it had only one station, for a long time! The current division into first four (later five) national BBC radio stations did not occur until 1967. This was just after the Marine Offences Act had been passed, to outlaw the pirates such as Radio Caroline (a hugely successful station that had attracted a million listeners in only three weeks!)

Until the arrival of stations like this, radio had been declining in popularity. It had been enormously influential before World War II, but began to lose out badly to the resumption of television broadcasting after it. The arrival of cheap transistor radios in the early 1960s, however, along with an explosion of new styles in the pop music being broadcast by the pirate stations, brought about a dramatic change in popular interest.

From its launch, Radio 1, especially, was hugely successful – although this is not so surprising when one considers that many of the popular pirate DJs were brought in to run it!

The pirates

The history of popular radio in the United Kingdom – appropriately for an island nation! – has been very much dominated by pirate broadcasters. The great opening up of the airwaves that took place during the late 1950s and early 1960s was driven by illegal offshore stations, such as radios Caroline and Veronica (the very first), operating from static ships in the North Sea. They supplied the music that the young wanted to hear, but could not get from the BBC, the only official broadcaster of radio in Britain at that time.

Going back to the very beginnings of radio, some have called Marconi himself – the inventor of radio – the very first pirate. He set up his equipment on Salisbury Plain in 1896, without official permission, and made the first broadcast. As there was no legislation covering this new medium at the time, this description of him perhaps stretches the facts rather. Nevertheless, his action could be seen as representative of the direct action that would be taken time and again by unlicenced individuals, when it proved impossible for particular groups to find the music they liked on the airwaves.

Hind and Mosco have detailed how it was another wave of pirate stations – pumping out new and exciting forms of black music chiefly, and working from inland sites this time – that reinvigorated music broadcasting in the 1980s, after a long period when it had seemed to be in decline again. Radio Invicta (1970), devoted to soul music and only broadcasting for a few hours at a time, had been the pioneer. Others followed, beaming out from record shops, festivals and even back bedrooms! Stations such as Mastermind, JFM and DBC (Dread Broadcasting Corporation) specialised in different musical styles, worked from incredibly cramped conditions and had to move on regularly to evade the government's detector vans.

Others still ventured into areas quite unrelated to music. Politics was one favourite, with Radio Enoch broadcasting right-wing material in the Midlands and Radio Arthur sending out propaganda in support of striking miners in the north Nottinghamshire area – cheekily supplanting Radio Trent's airspace with a stronger signal. Perhaps one of the most unusual was Breakfast Pirate Radio, set up by stand-up comic and actor Keith Allen, which went out seven times only on alternate Sundays in 1983. It ran all sorts of items – news-related, topical and provocative – mostly speech-based and, by his own admission, most of it made up.

In all sorts of forms, pirate radio has been around for a very long time. Made up of a bewildering variety of material, personality, intention and efficiency, it is highly mobile, intensely local and, by its very nature, hard to count on. The one sure thing about it is that still with us today; whatever the restraints imposed upon it, in one form or another, it is bound to continue.

Often, the shows pioneered on pirate radio have given the lead to the official stations, which have then copied their styles and even employed their DJs. It is beyond question that the present composition and style of many mainstream broadcasters owe a great deal to their illicit forebears. Even where they have not been taken up in some form directly, pirate broadcasters have contributed a great deal to the diversity and development of radio provision in the United Kingdom.

Present fortunes

With radio once more showing significant increases in audience figures, it seems extraordinary that it should have developed in such an almost haphazard fashion. With the eventual arrival of FM broadcasting, however, and more recently with the development of text services, radio has firmly re-established itself as a significant component of the media world. Considerable excitement has been generated around the prospects that 'multiplexes' (bundles of digital frequencies allowing more than six stations per licence) will open up. Radio could be set to play a full and challenging part in the future that is unfolding.

With highly successful launches in the early 1990s of national commercial stations such as Classic FM (the first and now the largest) and Virgin, and then – admittedly less successful – Talk Radio (now TalkSport), commercial sponsors and advertisers have become much more interested in participating in this medium generally.

In addition to these national broadcasters, there are now more than 242 local and regional stations. Moreover, recognition of the growth of the older market finally appeared with the launch by Capital of *Life* (aimed at women) and the proposed One World Radio, aimed at challenging the BBC's dominance in speech-based provision.

Niche marketing has become the speciality of commercial broadcasters: targeting very specific social groupings, based on identification with particular musical styles. With high audience loyalty, and especially with their comparatively low production costs, they make themselves highly attractive to advertisers.

The BBC

Not only is it the *oldest* of all the radio broadcasters, but also today the BBC continues to dominate the market as the *largest* of all the producers of radio in the United Kingdom. Its market share may have declined in the past few years, but, nevertheless, it still outstrips by a very long way any other *single* broadcaster. According to RAJAR (Radio Joint Audience Research – see p. 358) at the start of the millennium it was still attracting just over 51 per cent of the total audience for radio.

Moreover, with a network of local, national and international services, the sheer range and reach of its output dwarf that of any other company anywhere in the world. It must be remembered that many, many kinds of programmes *only occurred* on BBC radio until very recently: including quiz shows, comedy, documentary, dramas and features. Not until 2000 was there any commercial station built around anything other than music – apart from TalkSport.

In any other medium, it is inconceivable that exclusive responsibility of this kind would be left to a sole provider.

BBC World Service

Widely regarded as perhaps the world's most trusted broadcaster, the BBC World Service attracts a regular weekly audience of more than 140 million people. Its reputation rests solidly on the reliability and impartiality of its news and current affairs coverage. Hundreds of news bulletins, covering events all over the world, are put out each day. It maintains a network of correspondents – some staff, others freelance – across the globe.

In addition to its news output, a wide range of other programmes is also produced: science, the arts, classical and new drama, the environment and religion feature regularly.

The service makes use of a streaming system (i.e. available on the Internet), time-shifted to ensure that its programmes are received at times that are appropriate to the host countries. One stream serves Europe and North America, a second covers Africa, and a third the whole of Asia and the Pacific.

BBC national stations

Following the banning of pirate stations in 1967, the BBC was divided into four separate stations. With some development and refinement, these retain essentially the same character today.

RADIO 1 is mainly devoted to pop music. Created in response to the recognition of the success of the pirate stations, it has always been firmly rooted in chart music and is mainstream in the bulk of its output. Specialised slots for minority tastes do occur later in the schedules. For much of the day, however, the playlist (pre-selected

singles, no matter who the DJ) dominates.

Touring roadshows, at various spots around the country, often attract large outdoor audiences; the station has always striven to maintain itself in the forefront of popular styles. Its audience size has varied wildly, mainly depending on its lead DJs. Some have been hugely popular (Chris Evans, Zoe Ball), others less so.

Today it faces growing competition from an expanding private market.

RADIO 2 is still essentially music-orientated, but is dedicated more to 'easy-listening' music. Initially it was established for an older audience, but it also succeeded in drawing disaffected Radio 1 listeners when that station tried to develop its formats in the mid-1990s. (As their initial audience aged, in any case, they needed somewhere else to go). New presenters such as Steve Wright and Michael Parkinson helped to achieve this increase. It is in fact one of the most listened-to stations in the United Kingdom – if not the world! Figures from the start of the century indicate that 12.8 per cent of the population (21 per cent of total audience) listen for thirteen or more hours per week.

RADIO 3 is primarily dedicated to the broadcast of classical music. In addition, it also produces a range of other cultural shows, such as talks, drama and documentaries. In recent years, it has suffered somewhat from the success of its new commercial rival, Classic FM (although, embarrassingly, much of this audience was created anew – something the BBC had maintained could not be done!).

RADIO 4 is an entirely speech-based station. A very wide range of material is produced – from in-depth news and current affairs programmes (including *Today* and *PM* – much feared by politicians for their rigorous questioning), to features, magazine and comedy shows, more drama, book readings and so on. An attempt to recast the schedules in the late 1990s also lost it quite a chunk of its regular audiences, without attracting any new ones. A number of shows that had been axed had to be brought back and key personnel responsible moved on to pastures new.

A considerable part of the BBC's public service obligation in radio broadcasting is to be found in the output of this station. Its audiences are typically older, professional and educated, and mostly middle-class.

RADIO 5 LIVE was a very much later addition and is dedicated mainly to sports coverage – live wherever possible.

Local radio

Like so much else in this medium, local radio broadcasting was developed initially by the BBC. The first station was Radio Leicester, which began in 1967. Today, there is a network of stations across the United Kingdom, and the BBC is justly proud of its community involvement.

Local commercial radio commenced in 1972 and, before the end of the century, the Radio Authority had issued the 200th licence. In addition, the new phenomenon of regional radio reached into double figures.

However, much as with television, independent local radio (ILR) is ever more characterised by consolidation of ownership. The range of companies that now dominate British radio broadcasting is very narrow and consists of three main players: GWR (Great Western), EMAP and Capital. Many listeners complain that this leads to a uniformity of output, with middle-of-the-road music dominating. The great strength of local radio is supposed to be that it can reflect the needs and character of its local audience – something that is in danger of getting lost in the creeping conformity of format broadcasting.

Commercial radio

Commercial radio operators, of course, run essentially as businesses. Their prime intention is to make money. The original commercial radio broadcasters did have some public service obligations written into their licences; however, this has largely disappeared in the later expansions.

Profits, as with all the other commercial media, are made by selling its listeners to advertisers. Radio has one advantage here over other media: it has the greatest proximity to shopping. Whether it is heard as listeners leave home or when they are in the car, radio has the last say before the shoppers buy!

CLASSIC FM Classic FM was the first of the national commercial stations, starting in 1992, and now has the largest audience of all the independent national radio stations. Its output is entirely dedicated to classical music and opera. Many felt this was an unlikely prospect when it was first proposed. Used to the advertisement-free, uninterrupted broadcasts of whole works on Radio 3, lovers of serious music doubted the station's ability to do justice to this area.

However, the commercial station developed a new approach, concentrating on much shorter pieces and extracts (where Radio 3 played longer, complete works). Moreover, they would play several 'back-to-back', thereby countering the charge that the advertisements would intrude on the atmosphere needed to listen to music of this kind. At 4.3 per cent (RAJAR, February 2000), Classic FM had at this point more than tripled the audience of its BBC rival.

Commercial logic has shown once more that, where there is a market, a formula can be devised to suit the needs of both audiences *and* media producers/advertisers.

VIRGIN RADIO Established in 1993, Virgin Radio was the second national commercial licence to be granted and was yet one more venture by the entrepreneur Richard Branson. In May 1997, it was acquired by Capital FM, with the Radio Authority's approval, but its purchase was then referred to the Monopolies and Mergers Commission. Chris Evans was taken on later that year to present the breakfast show, to offer direct competition with Radio 1 – and then ended up buying the station himself!

TALKSPORT One of the more adventurous – and controversial – stations, TalkSport started in 1995 with the intention of offering a more upbeat 'talk only' service. Where the BBC's was broadly devoted to high culture, however, this one was determined to be populist and provocative. So-called 'shock jocks' from the United States were brought over to get the concept off the ground. They were notorious for their aggressive, at times rude treatment of their phone-in callers and were not shy of venting their opinions on any topic that came up for discussion. It was hoped that this new style of broadcasting would shake up the more cosy traditions of British broadcasting.

However, it rapidly became obvious that this was not a style that was going to gain much of a foothold on this side of the Atlantic. Audience figures remained very low. In 1998, Talk signalled a move into sports coverage, and a direct challenge to Radio 5 Live, when it took on Danny Baker after he had been fired from that station.

The appointment of Kelvin McKenzie, one-time boisterous editor of the *Sun*, instigated this new direction. He made sweeping changes to the staff, including most of the presenters. Audiences declined sharply. A necessary first step, he argued, in laying the ground for a new identity and gradually building up a wholly new following. Early in 2000, however, a heavy blow was dealt to the station when coverage of Test cricket was lost to the BBC, despite TalkSport having put in a higher bid.

▼ ▼ ▼

Losing the Test match bidding betrays how one-dimensional the offering that is TalkSport is. It only has money to offer. It certainly hasn't got diversity of audience.

Eugen Beer, Media Consultant,
Beer Davies

▼ ▼ ▼

Positioning and identity are critically important features of a station's chances of success in the growing field of radio. However, they are not the only factors – access to audiences clearly counts a great deal, too. At only 1.5 per cent, TalkSport's share is evidently felt to be too low to carry an event of such national significance.

Narrowcasters

Radio broadcasts to categories of people. The population of listeners is divided into groups according to their age, socioeconomic groups, tastes in music and the sorts of products they like to buy.

Radio stations prepare a programme format that will appeal to a certain group. Advertisers then buy advertising time on the station. Commercial radio now broadcasts to a range of specialised groups, rather than the whole public.

The ratings

The ratings are a kind of popularity poll to tell radio executives how many people are listening to their station (see the section on Audiences, p. 357).

The Radio Authority

Established in 1991, the Radio Authority licenses and regulates all independent, commercial radio, including restricted service licences (RSLs), hospital radio and student radio. Appointed by the Secretary of State for National Heritage, its responsibilities are threefold:

▶ to plan out frequencies
▶ to appoint licensees, and enforce ownership rules
▶ to regulate programming and advertising.

It is paid for by a levy on all the commercial companies, calculated according to size, and makes no demand on government spending.

▼ ▼ ▼ ▼ ▼ ▼ ▼

1. Select one of the national BBC radio stations. Make a lifestyle profile of your idea of a typical listener to that station (e.g. age, career, interests, income, etc.). Give a brief list of what you would imagine to be that person's favourite programmes on particular days. Now find someone who actually does listen to the programmes you listed. How do they compare to your idea of the typical listener? Is there a stereotypical view of a BBC listener? How accurate is it?

2. At set times, sample programmes on any three BBC stations – national or local – by flicking across the dial or by consulting a programme guide. Explain who you think those programmes are trying to reach. Define your audiences by age, social class and personal interests.

3. Describe and compare the musical styles available on a national and a local commercial radio station. How do they differ?

1. Outline the role the BBC plays in British culture. Evaluate its effectiveness in carrying out this role. Refer to particular stations and programmes in your outline. What specific contributions do they make that are unavailable from other sources? What future provision should be made for BBC funding?

2. Evaluate the extent to which commercial radio serves the public. Who is the real consumer of commercial radio: advertisers or the listener? Analyse radio formats and narrowcasting in your response to provide support for your point of view.

3. Are the real frontiers of radio with the public radio stations? Discuss particular programmes and specific stations to argue your position.

4. What provision is there for minority programming on either local or national radio stations? Review particular programmes to support your statements.

Production assignment

Select a radio station and prepare a set of survey questions aimed at finding out what sort of people listen. Prepare another set of questions you think advertisers would like to use on these listeners. Now try out the survey questions around your neighbourhood and collate the results. Prepare a brief report summarising your findings.

major assignment

Written assignment

Choose one of these assignments and write a 500-word essay.

Radio Music Formats

Pop music's job is to get you through the day. A profoundly important thing ... like fresh bread.

Pete Townsend, The Who

▼ ▼ ▼

There is a strange contradiction in modern radio broadcasting: that part of it dedicated to pop music, anyway. While the past ten years have seen a significant increase in the number of stations operating, some critics believe that they sound more and more alike. Diversity appears to be shrinking, they say, the more stations we get.

Each format represents an attempt at *narrowcasting* – reaching a particular target audience. Consistency of sound has been created with music formulas, designed to attract certain age groups (and repel others). Network owners such as GWR make a virtue of this and put forward their 'brand' of radio as one that the listener can rely on to be precisely the same, wherever they happen to tune in around the country. All the stations in their chain are local, but they broadcast to the same formula.

The negative outcome of all this, it is claimed, has been to promote a bland end-product. Rather like the much-maligned modern-day tomato, stations end up uniform and rather tasteless. Media consultant Guy Hornsby (founder of Kiss 102, Manchester), however, maintains the exact opposite: constant experimentation has produced a much greater variety of tomatoes on supermarket shelves now, each with distinctive qualities of taste. In the same way, he points out, research endlessly refines the radio product. 'It's just like the perfect Big Mac radio: when you know you've got a quality product, you make it available everywhere, and people know they can rely on the brand.'

The main formats

CONTEMPORARY HIT RADIO (CHR) Contemporary hit radio (CHR) began in the 1980s as a development of the Top 40 format. Fewer hits are rotated more often. The result is a streamlined Top 40. A limited selection of titles from the previous five years will also be included. The audience targeted is primarily teenagers. Capital is a good example of this format, and Radio 1 the most successful.

Adult CHR is targeted at the twenty-five to forty-four age group. For variety, some hits of the early 1990s are often included in this format to appeal to the older listeners.

NEW HIT RADIO (NHR) A variation on CHR, new hit radio (NHR) tends to concentrate on largely dance and indie music. Nothing over five years old will be used. These stations are much more aggressive in their sound and are usually commercial. Their strengths lie in spotting gaps in the market and filling niches – especially among the younger audiences.

ADULT CONTEMPORARY (AC) Adult contemporary (AC) stations play soft rock aimed at the thirty-five to fifty-four age group. Familiarity is important to adult contemporary stations and they rely on a mix of hits from the past and more recent songs that have already been proven hits. Adult contemporary means no rap and no heavy metal.

Radio 2 has been the phenomenal success story in this category over the past ten years. Where it used to be seen as the 'housewives' station', with a programme of easy listening/'beautiful music', now it is much more orientated towards classic

Figure 5.7
Radio 2 has traditionally been associated with an older audience. Once this meant a diet of MOR and light classical music. As the 1960s generation has aged, however, the 'new generation' of older people has required a much livelier range of musical styles.

rock and pop. As the 1960s generation has aged, they have moved on from the chart-based Radio 1 and sought out alternative providers of their preferred musical styles.

Record rotation and the playlist

In the early days of pop radio, it was the DJs who dominated. More recently, with the standardisation traced above, the personality of the presenter came to count for much less. Computer-generated lists of tracks led to loss of individuality. Automation of the studios led to a button-pushing functionality. However, today the situation has recovered once more. Playlists are carefully researched and material recycled much more efficiently.

▼ ▼ ▼

The role of the jocks has changed dramatically. They were very good, originally, but then declined. A 'run the list' mentality grew up. Now, they are much more alert and responsive once again.

Guy Hornsby,
Media Consultant

▼ ▼ ▼

Selector

It is in this area that most of the debate around quality centres. The formulaes adopted by individual stations are key in establishing station identity. They are all created by a computer system known as Selector, created by a US company, Radio computing Services (RCS).

On this programme, every single track that the station owns is recorded – as well as all its jingles, station idents and other regularly occurring items. It has a sophisticated cataloguing system, which allows titles to be entered according to their mood, pace, energy, era and even beat. On a five-point scale, tracks are carefully evaluated for whether they come towards the top, bottom or somewhere in the middle. This job is crucial, as it will ultimately generate the whole identity of the station. It would normally be done by the programmes director, or head of music. For consistency, it is absolutely crucial that only one person does it – and that it is regularly updated. Certain other functions then also come into play:

DAYPARTING is the division of the day into segments or time slots. Each day part has a particular

character. For example, many radio stations become more teen orientated after 3 p.m., but aim for an older audience in 'drive-time' after 5 p.m. Once all the music is catalogued, it can then be tagged with a code to appear in certain slots in the day or even the shows of particular DJs.

RECORD ROTATION refers to the number of times a particular record is played. This depends on its popularity and the time of day that its mood and style would suit. FM stations rotate records more slowly than AM stations. The highest rotation on a station is typically every four hours. The longest rotation is usually five or six weeks.

THE PLAYLIST is the list of music tracks the radio station plans to broadcast. The list varies from week to week. Most stations have a current playlist of about forty songs and a longer rotation of around 600 to 700 tracks. NHR stations would change their list every day; others less frequently. Radio 2 has an active playlist of more than 3500 titles.

Restricting creativity

Format restrictions do not affect new rock music alone. Whole musical styles such as world music, jazz, blues, folk, New Age and so on get little airplay on mainstream commercial radio. Some BBC stations do offer programmes that cover some of these, however.

Another audience group not catered for by formats is the ten to seventeen age range: they have little money to spend and are of minimal interest to advertisers. It used to be that the number-one selling hits got plenty of airplay in all cities. Now, it depends on the formats available in a particular city. On several occasions, the national top-selling hits have not received any airplay on commercial radio stations. The songs were teen hits and not liked by the main target audience of 25- to 40-year-olds.

The reluctance of programme directors to let in new or unusual music comes from a fear of losing the advertising. Radio audiences are creatures of habit. Commercial radio stations cannot afford to let their target audience switch off. A loss of a single ratings point can mean hundreds of thousands of pounds in lost advertising revenue. Programme directors dare not play anything likely to irritate or offend their listeners. As a result, format playlists can become very predictable.

Critics say the format system has made it all but impossible for really new music styles to break through. Radio discourages large areas of modern music, including music with a social conscience, says Clive Davis the president of Arista Records.

Programme directors disagree. Radio's job is not to educate the population, but to reflect what is popular, they say.

Audiences

Most advertising money is spent chasing the 25- to 40-year-old audience, as they have the disposable cash and are flexible enough to be persuaded into making new purchases. Advertisers say younger consumers are willing to try new products, but do not have the money. Older audiences have the money, but are too set in their ways.

AUDIENCES NOT SERVED A tight selective format creates a loyal audience. Radio stations can then deal advertisers a market of like-minded people in the same age category. However, a tight format has another effect. It repels those it does not aim to serve, leaving them free to move to another format or else remove themselves entirely from the radio audience. The group not served can be quite large. Commercial broadcasters will select whatever format maximises profits – even if other stations are also using that format. The format will be duplicated as often as is profitable. It is not necessary to have the largest audience. The size of the audience does not determine how much money can be made – that is determined by the size of audience income.

▼ ▼ ▼ ▼ ▼ ▼ ▼

activities

1. Create a sixty-minute playlist for one of the major radio station formats. List about –ten to fifteen song titles and allow twelve minutes for advertisements. Outline the target audience you have in mind and identify the features of your choices designed to appeal to them.

2. In the United States, many radio stations get their programmes by satellite. Shows are put together to appeal to certain formats and then sold to radio stations that have satellite links. Look at the advertisement for a satellite programme below. Now design your own advertisement for a format show of your choice.

3. Make a list of the formats playing in your nearest city. Try to identify the likely audience for these, then say whether you feel there is any duplication.

4. In your class group hold a radio station management meeting. One of the radio stations in your city is going to change formats. The question is what should the new format be? The demo-graphic information below may get you started.

▶ 18–24 years – consumers of tomorrow, but mainly students

▶ 25–39 years – prime target of advertisers – home establishers

▶ 30–45 years – largest group – families, many with two incomes

▶ 35–54 years – large group, high income

▶ 55–64 years – smaller group, highest income of all, no dependants.

5. Critics believe that the current format system prevents a lot of music getting to air. Radio stations, on the other hand, say that, if their audience wants it, they will play it. Which point of view do you think is closer to the truth? Debate.

major assignment

Written assignment

Briefly describe the radio formats available in your city, then evaluate them from your perspective as an audience member. Discuss the positives and negatives of radio station formats.

Production assignment

Imagine that you are to attend a meeting of radio station executives with a proposal for a new music format aimed at a target audience that is currently being ignored.

Prepare a complete submission containing presentations in the following areas:

▶ *Format* – name and define.

▶ *Audience* – define age range, tastes, etc.

▶ *Music* – prepare a playlist of 100 titles and for some of these, give notes to explain the appeal to the target audience.

▶ *DJs* – outline the personalities you would seek.

▶ *Advertisers* – list a large range of potential advertisers interested in the target group.

▶ *Image* – design a publicity poster to promote the format.

Radio News

It is not easy to give a universal assessment of the nature of radio news. Different stations give different emphasis both to the amount and to the selection of what is covered. Even where news appears in the schedules is not standardised. Most stations tend to give it in hourly bulletins – usually on the hour, although some do it on the half-hour.

On music-dominated stations, news tends to be delivered in the form of hourly bulletins and consist of a series of short summaries. It is often geared towards the interests of the particular audience that the individual station attracts. Items concerning pop stars and celebrities, for instance, are likely to occur frequently. Political and other serious topics are usually treated in brief outlines of key points.

On the BBC's Radio 4, on the other hand, news is normally give much more extensive coverage, with some programmes allocating an entire hour to the news, in some cases.

A possible shortcoming of radio news is that it lacks the pictures that television can supply. Yet,

this supposed television advantage can also turn into a liability, when the *need* for good pictures can dictate the items that get covered. Radio has one distinct advantage over television in that it is free to choose items for their essential worth and interest to their listeners.

Another, much more important, advantage is to be found in the fact that radio goes on issuing news bulletins throughout the day, keeping up with developments on breaking news stories *as they occur*. Radio tends to be the source people will turn to if they want an update on something – whether it is the latest cricket scores or information on major crimes, disasters and so on. It is recognised as the 'now' medium.

The time when this is most important is first thing in the morning. When people wake, there is a tendency to turn on the radio. The news contained in the morning newspaper is anything from six to twenty-four hours old. Although the popularity of breakfast television has grown considerably in the past few years, there is still a massive audience for radio. Quite simply, you can

Figure 5.8
Audiences for different radio stations have different interests and expectations from their news programmes. Where some are keen to keep up with the latest celebrity gossip, others want information on more serious topics. Stations select their material to suit what they feel is right for their particular target audience.

listen to it while you move around, eating, washing, dressing, getting ready to go out; moreover, even when you do leave the house, you can still tune in in the car or on personal radios.

Structure and features of radio news

According to pioneer radio journalist Edward R. Murrow, radio news takes its style from the special qualities of the medium. Radio offers instantaneous response to the news, the chance for the voice of the reporter to reflect the drama of the situation and the opportunity for the reporter to be a participant in events. But radio is a 'blind' medium. The radio news reporter must also describe the news. Unlike television, the pictures must be created in the listener's mind.

THE LENGTH OF RADIO AND NEWS STORIES

The attention span of the average radio listener is about thirty seconds, research shows. For radio news, this means the story needs to be short and to the point. Listeners do not have the chance to hear it again, unlike newspaper stories, which can be read over and over again.

A basic rule is the better the story, the longer run it gets. Thirty seconds is long enough for a scripted story that is to be read by the newsreader. Four paragraphs basically equal thirty seconds; eight paragraphs a minute. The journalist should be able to tell the story in four paragraphs, incorporating the old rules: who, what, where, when.

In brief: be bright and tight.

WRITING THE NEWS STORY

Both television and radio use the broadcast style of news presentation (see pp. 256–63).

The old advice was to write the radio news as though it was being told to someone running to catch a bus. Journalists were taught to ask themselves what would he or she want to know quickly? What were the most important facts? They would then write the radio news accordingly, as they would only have thirty seconds to grab the listener's attention and tell them what they wanted him or her to know.

PUTTING THE STORY INTO A NEWS BULLETIN

Radio bulletins are far more frequent than television news broadcasts. A faithful radio listener can tire

very quickly of hearing the same news stories over and over again. Radio stations often prepare a variety of news bulletins and rotate them.

Individual news stories within bulletins may also be given several different treatments. The facts remain the same, but the news angle is varied.

TELEVISION WITHOUT PICTURES

The television news reporter looks for 'the picture that is worth a thousand words'. The radio reporter needs to create that picture in the listener's mind. One way is with verbal description. Another is to use sound. The click of a rifle bolt, the barked commands of an officer, the rhythmic sounds of soldiers drilling for war – sounds can evoke vivid pictures.

Steve Wadhams, of the Canadian Broadcasting Corporation, toured notorious ex-President of Uganda Idi Amin's torture chambers in 1979. With him was the Reverend Lukwiya, who had been held there for three months. The Reverend Lukwiya had just been released following the Tanzanian invasion of Amin's Uganda. Wadhams manages to capture some of the horror of the torture chamber by creating a sound picture of the place.

▼ ▼ ▼

SOUNDS OF FOOTSTEPS DESCENDING … DEVELOPING AN ECHO.

WADHAMS: We're descending some stairs into a very dark area …

REV. LUKWIYA: The smell is so bad it makes me sick.

WADHAMS: It's very dark, we have a small torch, come on through and be careful where you tread. Do you think they have all the bodies out now?

REV. LUKWIYA: I think all the bodies are out now, because as you can see with the torch … there is nothing now.

VOICES HAVE NOW SUNK TO WHISPERS. THERE IS THE SOUND OF WATER DRIPPING. IN THE DARKNESS WADHAMS KICKS AN OLD TIN CAN. IT RATTLES EERILY.

WADHAMS: What's on the floor? Let's have a look.

REV. LUKWIYA: Pieces of shoes, and I think they broke this door. This was where the killing was done.

WADHAMS: Just look at this; people were killed in this room up to how long ago?

REV. LUKWIYA: Well, up to when I was released they were being killed … about two weeks ago, since the Tanzanians came …

▼ ▼ ▼

Formats and the representation of news

The idea of 'something for everybody' programming is a thing of the past in commercial radio. Stations now try for target audiences. Music formats are designed to appeal to these groups. To some extent news style is also altered to suit the tastes of the target groups.

News on pop music stations

For the 18- to 39-year-old age groups targeted by pop music stations, news tends to be a lower priority. As a result, stations usually target news to the interests and desires of their youth audience. The big stories are covered, but bulletins may also feature lifestyle articles such as health issues and cultural news. Often the style of presentation is chatty and informal.

News can be an important part of programming for older listeners, however. They tend to like a broad coverage and traditional

STAND BY NOW LISTENERS 'COS FIREMAN BOB SNOW IS GONNA RATTLE OFF HIS FIVE FAVOURITE BANDS.....

Figure 5.9
People's desire for news tends to increase with age. Formats that aim at younger audiences may give news a lower priority.

delivery styles. The core audience in this instance is from forty to fifty-four years of age.

▼ ▼ ▼ ▼ ▼ ▼ ▼

activities

1. Try to assess radio's role in bringing in the news on an unfolding story. Choose a major story, if possible: if not, at least choose one that seems to develop as the day goes on. What kinds of changes are made? What details are added? Are any dropped? What may the different reasons be for each decision?

2. Listen to some of the great radio newscasts of the past. Try to find a recording of the declaration of World War II or the first eyewitness report of the Hindenberg disaster (a chilling account that begins in celebration, but ends in tragedy). Do you still find them powerful and even moving? What is it that comes through? Explain.

3. Both television and radio use the broadcast style of news presentation. Converting from one to the other can be useful in understanding the differences between the two mediums.
▶ Transcribe a television news story with good action pictures. (See Television News, pp. 264–6.)
▶ Now prepare the story for radio, giving brief

descriptions where necessary.
▶ Compare and contrast the ways news is presented on television and radio.

4. Commercial radio often tries to find stories with an upbeat ending: this is because it wants to maintain a generally cheerful atmosphere for its programmes. Look through the newspapers and find an example of a 'happy ending' story. Write it up for commercial radio using this principle. Then try writing it again in the more formal style of a public service broadcaster.

5. Record the news bulletins of a number of different radio stations. Choose one major news item and compare the treatment of the story across the different stations. Use the checklist below as a guide for comparison.
▶ *Style* – is the broadcast formal, or chatty?
▶ *Length* – is the news item thirty seconds long? Twenty seconds? Ten seconds?
▶ *Emphasis* – does the item represent the majority view? Or does it have a youth angle?

Written and production skills

Compile a radio news bulletin for a youth-orientated radio station. Choose stories that would appeal to the target age group and write a script for each story.

Along with the script, provide an explanation of each story's appeal to the target audience. (For guidelines on preparing a news bulletin, see Television News, pp. 256–8.) Make a recording of your bulletin.

Radio Documentaries

A documentary is any programme based on 'documents' – or factual records. Documentaries are about facts, not fiction: real people, real issues and actual events. The aim of a documentary is to explore a subject and, in some cases, to present a point of view.

The social purpose of documentary

Producers say that one purpose of documentaries is 'to rock the boat'. Certainly, documentaries that deal with social or political issues often try to change people's attitudes. These documentaries educate as well as inform. They will be found more on television than on radio. The BBC does produce sometimes controversial radio investigations; on the whole, the commercial stations do not. (See Television Documentaries, p. 273.)

Types of documentary

Radio documentaries come in two basic forms: narrative and non-narrative.

THE NARRATIVE FORM uses a narrator to drive the programme forward in a logical, informative way. The narrator can provide facts, link the viewpoints of various speakers and allow the programme to cover a lot of ground in a short time.

THE NON-NARRATIVE FORM allows the people in the documentary to speak without interruption. Segments are edited to give a feeling of a forward moving, well-linked programme.

SUBJECT MATTER

News documentaries may deal with social issues and politics. Cultural documentaries may deal with lifestyles, history, art, etc. Whatever the topic, the real subject matter is people. People are interested in people. While facts are important, the human stories keep people listening.

The human story is said to have three basic, classical patterns in a documentary. These are:

► human courage, strength and nobility in a hostile environment
► problems facing society and the ways they can be solved
► ordinary, everyday lives whose details are presented in an artistic way.

DRAMA

Although it is based on fact and not fiction, a documentary needs to be dramatic. Its purpose is to present facts and events, but in a way that will engage its audience. So while a documentary should be dealing with the truth, it is never just the plain, unadorned truth. Editing and narration can make things seem much more compelling and often quite different to the reality being represented.

Writing documentaries for radio

To write a documentary, take the real words of real people, include the sounds of related events and combine them together in a dramatic script. Organisation is the key to success.

DEVELOPING THE IDEAS is the first step. A statement of the main idea is a good focus for a plan. Supporting ideas can then be listed so they reinforce the central idea. 'Sub-supporting' ideas should be listed underneath each larger point. Keep the number of main points (supporting the central idea) to a reasonable number. Most documentaries have more than two main points, but fewer than five.

ORGANISING THE PROGRAMME is a matter of working out which style suits the subject matter. The American writers Edgar Willis and Camille D'Arienzo suggest the following patterns, but there are many more:

▶ a chronological order of events (by time)
▶ a classifying order – noting, for example the effects of some particular problem on different age groups of people
▶ a cause-and-effect organisation
▶ a problem-solution structure.

VARYING THE SOUNDS FOR RADIO is an important way of keeping the listener interested. The documentary material may consist of interviews, narrator's links, music, discussion and recordings of actual events. This material should be organised to provide variety. All the interviews, for example, should not be kept together. Male and female voices should be interchanged for variety. A short musical phrase may prevent boredom.

INTRODUCING CONFLICT is one way of capturing audience interest. Conflict is vital to drama and also, therefore, to dramatic documentaries. Clashing points of view provide conflict. Documentaries about social and political issues have conflict built in.

WRITING THE LEAD is often the hardest part. The lead must gain the attention of the listener straight away. There are several ways to do this, for example:

▶ beginning with sound effects
▶ beginning with a sensational statement
▶ asking a question.

This is how BBC producer John Herbert opened a documentary on prison life:

▼ ▼ ▼

Sound effects of footsteps coming out of the distance, coming closer, with the crunch of gravel underfoot. The footsteps stop, a key is put into a very large echoing lock and, with a dull, boomy metallic sound, a heavy door is opened. Then the footsteps continue into the distance, fading under a voice saying: 'The Men Inside: a look at life in prison.'

▼ ▼ ▼

THE MIDDLE should seek to explore the topic in more depth – teasing out issues, seeking a variety of points of view from relevant people and working through the important features in a clear, logical manner. The main intention should be to take the listener on journey, which introduces them to new ideas, or insights, yet which also avoids the pitfall of overcomplication.

THE ENDING of a good documentary should provoke the listener into thinking about the issues in the programme. Some of the more usual types of ending are listed below.

▶ a summary of the main ideas – often done by the narrator
▶ a return to key statements by the people who made them
▶ a repeat of a single, significant phrase
▶ sound effects
▶ questions about the future of matters raised in the documentary.

▼ ▼ ▼ ▼ ▼ ▼ ▼

activities

1. Make a list of the radio documentaries going to air this week. Listen to as many of them as you can. Analyse their form and subject content by following the steps set out below.

▶ Decide whether they are narrative or non-narrative documentaries.

▶ Categorise their subject matter according to general concerns (e.g. courage, society, ordinary lives).

2. Select a documentary topic. Planning for a five-minute programme, write an organisational plan for the topic based on the one shown in Television Documentaries (p. 282). Follow these steps:

▶ Write down your purpose.

▶ What is the central idea?

▶ Decide on a structure (chronological, classifying, cause/effect, problem/solution).

▶ List the supporting ideas.

▶ Underneath each supporting idea, list sub-supporting ideas.

3. Create a production plan for the documentary topic you selected for the previous activity. Each idea must somehow be explained in the documentary. To achieve this, the production plan should show how each idea will be put across to the listeners. Choose from the following techniques:

▶ interviews

▶ narration

▶ dramatisation

▶ vox pop (street interviews)

▶ panel discussions

▶ news item extracts.

major assignment

Written assignment

Choose one of the following assignments.

1. 'While a documentary can be true, it is never the whole truth.' Evaluate several examples of radio documentaries in relation to this statement.

2. Listen to a radio documentary and make notes on its organisational structure in the manner of Willis and D'Arienzo on p. 282. Evaluate the effectiveness of this structure.

What other organisational structures could have been used? Discuss whether or not using these structures would have changed the meaning of the documentary.

Production assignment

Record a five-minute radio documentary on a topic of your choice. Follow these steps:

▶ Select a title and prepare research data.

▶ Create an organisational plan.

▶ Build production notes from the organisational plan.

▶ Record raw material.

▶ Assemble the material and edit the documentary on to the final tape.

Radio Comedies

British radio comedy, as so much else, really began on the BBC. The truly astonishing thing is that that is where it *exclusively* continues. Quite simply, nobody else does comedy shows on radio.

Comedy had featured on a number of programmes from the early days. However, it was after World War II that it took off. The mad world of *The Goon Show* was an instant hit in 1951. It built on the postwar mood of dissatisfaction and the desire to break down the old rules. In the process, it stood the supposedly real world on its head. *The Goon Show* continues to be influential even today. No comedy programme has managed to capture the public imagination so strongly – except perhaps for television's *Monty Python's Flying Circus*.

Figure 5.10
*Meera Syal and
Kulvinder Ghir
from the hugely
successful Asian
comedy series*
**Goodness
Gracious Me!**
*Like many other
hit BBC television
comedies, it
actually began life
as a radio show.*

Today, radio would be hard pressed to pay for major new comedy shows with star performers. Television has stolen all the big shows. But radio has become the home of experimental comedy and up-and-coming performers. Young performers and writers from university revues or the fringes of the arts festivals are often invited to work in radio.

A long tradition in the BBC is that radio acts as a 'nursery slope' for television. New comedy acts and programme formats 'cut their teeth' in radio, where the costs are very much lower. Those that prove popular may then graduate to television. *Not the Nine O'clock News*, *The Hitchhiker's Guide to the Galaxy* and *Goodness Gracious Me!* (the hugely successful Asian comedy show) – all began their very successful lives on Radio 4. Writers and performers learn their craft here, before moving on when they are ready.

Types of radio comedy

Just three basic styles of comedy are used with any regularity on radio: variety or stand-up comedy, situation comedy and sketch comedy. **QUIZ SHOWS** are one of the most regular, and popular, formats. Some take current affairs as their subject (*The News Quiz*); others are a series of guessing games with the panel (*What's My Line?*, *The Music Quiz*).

SITUATION COMEDIES place a set of characters in a funny situation. The humour comes from the way the characters handle the situation. Situation comedies are really short dramas and so plot, character and setting are very important.

SKETCH OR ABSURD PARODY COMEDIES make their humour out of a series of skits or sketches. Usually they are unconnected and the show jumps from one topic to another. Sound effects, plot characters and setting are usually very exaggerated. Shows such as this are sometimes presented by a duo, who use loosely scripted or improvised dialogue to build quips and gags into social commentaries. The humour comes out of the way each member of the duo plays off the other's comments. *Mel & Sue* (which very quickly went to television) was a good example of this.

The features of radio comedy

Radio is the theatre of the imagination. No other medium has the freedom to operate entirely in the minds of the listeners.

In comedy, this allows the absurdity to have double the effect. Things that are illogical, exaggerated or irrational take off in the imagination. When they have to be pictured, as on television, the limits are set by reality.

This distinction from television comedy is illustrated by the success of another radio show *The Hitchhiker's Guide to the Galaxy*, which failed when it was transferred to the screen. By not picturing its characters, *Hitchhiker* could remain a satire of modern travel and people's cosmic wonder, yet also develop on the levels of fantasy, imagination and the unconscious.

▼ ▼ ▼

On television, it simply became another space epic.

David Berry
The Listener

▼ ▼ ▼

Sound effects are a great source of humour in radio comedies. Exaggerated loud bangs, ground-shaking footsteps, whistling bombs and so on are all part of the humour. For *The Goon Show*, the sound effects almost became a show within a show.

▼ ▼ ▼

Supposing the scene was about the French Revolution with the hated aristos being guillotined. To establish the atmosphere, the phonograms operator would have sorted out a disc of crowd noises. Then, for the actual effect of the guillotine blade descending, I'd scrape a sword down a piece of metal; then for the blade decapitating the victim, I'd cut a cabbage into a basket. Then the grams man would bring in a disc effect of crowds cheering their appreciation.

Vernon Lawrence
Studio Manager, *The Goon Show*

▼ ▼ ▼

Writing radio comedy

BUILDING FOR LAUGHS Dramas build from crisis to crisis until they reach a climax. Comedy builds from joke to joke. Radio comedy, in particular, needs to be very fast paced. Unlike television, there are no pictures to keep the audience's attention. Humour is piled one joke on another, barely leaving time for the laughter to stop. The old radio comedies had the gags coming at four or five a minute when they got moving. Some went even faster. The number of jokes per programme put a lot of pressure and responsibility on the gag-creating abilities of the writers.

▼ ▼ ▼

They worked from eight o'clock in the morning turning out jokes, choosing a subject – wife jokes, etc. – until they and it were exhausted. They began

to sell gags and patter sketches – it used to take 35 to 40 jokes to sustain five minutes of patter – to most of the radio comedians.

Peter Black
The Listener

▼ ▼ ▼

In the extract below, from *The Goon Show*, the gags have been underlined. Notice how many there are in such a short space of time.

▼ ▼ ▼

ORCHESTRA CLIMAX ... THEN DOWN ... NOW BEHIND:

BILL: The English Channel 1941. Across the silent strip of green-grey water – in England – coastal towns were deserted, except for people. Despite the threat of invasion and the stringent blackout rules, elderly gentlefolk of Bexhill-on-Sea still took their evening constitution.

FX: EBB TIDE ON A GRAVEL BEACH.

CRUN: Ohh - it's quite windy on these cliffs.

MINNIE: What a nice summer evening – typical English.

CRUN: Mnk yes –- the rain's lovely and warm – I think I'll take one of my sou'westers off – here, hold my elephant gun.

MINNIE: I don't know what you brought it for – you can't shoot elephants in England.

CRUN: Mnk? Why not?

MINNIE: They're out of season.

CRUN: Does this mean we'll have to have pelican for dinner again?

MINNIE: Yes, I'm afraid so.

CRUN: Then I'll risk it, I'll shoot an elephant out of season.

BOTH: (GO OFF MUMBLING IN DISTANCE)

BILL: Listeners who are listening will, of course, realise that Minnie and Henry are talking rubbish – as erudite people will realise, there are no elephants in Sussex. They are only found in Kent North on a straight line drawn between two points thus making it the shortest distance.

▼ ▼ ▼

Characters

The characters in radio comedy are often stereotyped. A stereotyped character is not a fully developed character. Instead a stereotype is a pattern character – always the same and constantly recycled to take advantage of the fixed mental images in the minds of the audience (see stereotypes, p. 38). The Goons used many stereotypes: blithering military idiots, senile pensioners, private school bullies and so on. The point is that these characters are all instantly recognisable.

Most radio and television comedy relies on stereotypes because the purpose of the shows is not to understand the characters, but to laugh at them. For the laugh to begin immediately, the characters need to be instantly recognisable as funny. Only with a stereotype is this possible.

Sound Effects

Dialogue is not the only source of humour in a radio script. Well-planned sound effects can get a lot of laughs. They are also useful for setting the scene and introducing action. Sound effects make good transitions from one point to another in the plot – especially in illogical plots.

The Plot

Comedy plots do not need to be logical. In fact, illogical plots or events are what radio comedy thrives on. Illogical thinking makes exaggeration, incongruity and surprise all the easier to achieve – and comedy is made up of these basic ingredients (see pp. 300–2).

Most comedy plots begin with a startling announcement or event. The audience is immediately plunged into a world of humour. From here confusion and illogicality snowball as characters accumulate one set of problems after another. The excitement of the audience mounts with the desire for a resolution and there is great relief when it finally comes. (See p. 307.)

Many radio comedy plots are built from parodies of other types of shows. A parody mimics or 'takes off' something else. Detective stories, adventure stories, romantic love stories and so on can all be parodied to provide plots for comedies.

A good checklist for building the plot of radio comedies has been suggested by the American broadcast writers Daniel Garvey and William Rivers.

▶ Separate each segment of the show into blocks. The breaks could be variety or musical acts, or advertisements.

▶ Decide where the funniest lines should go. Some writers advise the beginning or middle. Others say the best should go near the end.

▶ Within the segments build the humour to a climax. The gags should get increasingly funny. This is the snowballing effect.

▶ Come up with little gags to lead into the big gags. Try not to let a minute pass without something funny.

▼ ▼ ▼ ▼ ▼ ▼ ▼

activities

1. *Goon Show* sound effects were, for many listeners, as funny as the dialogue. Look at the script extract below, then answer the questions following.

VOICE 1: Male hormones forever! Ahhh … hha (collapses) Ahhhh … mr …

FX: THUD OF BODY & BITS OF BODY SCATTER-ING. BALL BEARINGS, MARBLES ROLL ALONG FLOOR. HANDFUL OF FORKS. METALLIC RESONANT. NUTS & BOLTS FALLING.

CRUN: Oh dear, he's disintegrated Min … I'll have to take over his trousers.

▶ Would you say the humour is based on incongruity? Explain.

▶ What does Crun's comment contribute to the understanding of the sound effects?

▶ Does the sound effect build to a climax or does it start at the climax and gradually

diminish in effect. In other words, is the 'thud' or the 'nuts and bolts falling' the best part? Would the sound effect be as good if the order was rearranged? Why?

2. Listen to a three- to five-minute segment of a radio comedy, then undertake the activities below.

▶ Count the gags in this segment. How many are there per minute?

▶ Discuss each of the jokes and the way they work. Are they based on surprise, incongruity, exaggeration or puns? How often is the audience switched from one meaning to another?

▶ Summarise the plot (or the exposition if there is no plot) as it develops in the segment. Does it take illogical turns? Are there places (especially introductory sections) where the plot (or exposition) is seemingly normal before taking an illogical twist? Can you discern any purpose for this normality?

3. Choose a subject or theme. Hold a class brainstorming session. Think of as many jokes on your subject or theme as you can. Once it is exhausted, try another subject.

4. Make a list of stereotypes you think would provide enough humour to be used in radio comedy.

5. Try creating your own detailed sound effects descriptions. If possible, include a little dialogue before and after to show how you might use it. Possible situations could be a visit to the dentist or doctor, a haunted house or a time machine.

6. Write your own script for a radio comedy on a topic of your choice. Refer back to the checklist provided by Garvey and Rivers (p. 377) for guidelines on starting your script.

major assignment

Written assignment

Choose one of these assignments and write a 600-word response.

1. 'Radio comedy can be funnier than television comedy.' Explain how someone could make such a statement and then evaluate its worth. In your answer, use examples from actual radio and television programmes.

2. Listen to or read a script from a radio comedy classic such as *The Goon Show*. Comment on the following:
- startling first scenes
- building for laughs/snowballing confusion
- sound effects
- stereotyping
- resolution.

3. Compare the basic comedy types on radio – variety, stand-up, sketch comedy and situation comedy. Alternatively, you could compare modern radio comedy with examples from the past. Evaluate which you think is the funnier. Use examples to support your point of view.

Production assignment

Script and record a two-minute radio comedy sketch, with sound effects. The following guidelines could help you:
- Brainstorm for ideas and gags.
- Build for laughs.
- Use stereotyped characters to allow quick humour.

Radio Dramas

In the English-speaking world, Britain produces most of the radio drama. With about 1500 original plays on air every year, British radio drama even exceeds Hollywood's film output. Australia and Canada both produce a limited number of plays, but their smaller resources mean that they cannot equal the volume of British plays. In the United States, the impact of television has made radio drama a scarce commodity. In fact, the US output is negligible.

Radio drama relies on the spoken word. As a result, it is said to be a 'writer's format'. Certainly, many famous playwrights began their careers in radio drama or owe a great deal of their success to it; some playwrights have depended on radio drama for ongoing support.

Alan Ayckbourn, Harold Pinter, Samuel Beckett and Tom Stoppard have all written for radio. Many writers of importance delight in the opportunity to explore the potential and challenges of this distinctive medium. Beckett, for instance, wrote one play in which one of the characters was a musical instrument; in *Cigarettes and Chocolate*, Anthony Minghella set himself the unusual challenge of having his main character give up speaking! It was the Welsh poet Dylan Thomas who wrote probably the most famous radio play ever: *Under Milk Wood*. Set in the Welsh village of Llareggub, Dylan Thomas's play created a kind of music out of the spoken work.

Types of radio plays

SERIAL DRAMA OR SOAP OPERAS are considered to be part of radio's gift to modern culture. Soap operas began as a radio form, originally in the United States. In the United Kingdom, *The Archers* has been drawing audiences in the millions since 1951 and is the world's longest-running soap opera.

SINGLE RADIO PLAYS draw smaller audiences than the serials. However, they also provide some of the most innovative and challenging new drama anywhere. Radios 3 and 4 both produce excellent work in this field. The range of subjects tackled is enormous, and the styles used diverse and constantly evolving.

DRAMATISED FEATURES are mixtures of fact with fictional dialogue. Some call this 'faction'. Recreations of historical events or dramatised biographies come in this category. They may also be classified as docudramas (see p. 207).

ADAPTATIONS OF CLASSIC NOVELS and book readings make up a large proportion of radio's total drama production. Radio 4's *A Book at Bedtime* is a long-standing favourite with listeners, although other, longer adaptations also occur earlier in the evenings – e.g. *The Classic Serial*, aired on Sundays.

ADAPTATIONS OF STAGE PLAYS add to the output of single plays. While not written for radio, many stage plays in fact work well on air. Shakespeare plays are regularly broadcast with great success. Modern classics, too, are regularly broadcast, providing many people with their only means of encountering these works.

Radio drama and stage drama – the differences

Radio and stage dramas may both have the same aim of communication, but there are differences in their approach.

▶ The actors are invisible in a radio drama. Techniques of gesture and facial expression cannot be used. The actor must rely on voice alone. But this also means that physical appearance plays no part in casting: a fat actor can play a thin man, a petite actress can play an Amazon and a bald man can play Samson.

▶ Actors do not need to project their voices. They usually stand quite close to the mikes. Their voices may actually be softer in the studio than they are coming out of the speakers. Opportunities for intimacy or emotional intensity may actually be much greater in this medium.

▶ In a radio play, the actor can hold the script and work from it. There is no need to commit lines to memory. With less preparation time, very well-known actors can be persuaded to participate, in spite of their very busy schedules.

▶ A radio play can be produced in three to four days, as against a month for television or the theatre. Production costs are therefore very much lower, enabling more diversity of output.

▶ Scenes and scene changes are invisible. Radio drama therefore has greater freedom. However, all scene changes must be suggested by dialogue or narration.

▶ Radio has no means of showing if anyone is present other than by letting them speak. Characters cannot be present but silent, unless they are constantly referred to.

▶ Listeners are usually alone and so there is no audience crowd to provide group reactions.

▶ The audience is domestic and almost always doing something else as well. They may be just relaxing in an armchair, or quite possibly attending to chores in either house or garden.

▶ In Britain at least, radio plays draw audiences in the millions. It has been calculated it would take a London West End theatre two and a half centuries to reach the audience of one of the feature dramas on the BBC.

The features of radio drama

SOUNDS Sounds are the building blocks of radio drama. Radio relies on only one of the senses: hearing. Variety of sound is what will hold the audience's attention. Naturally occurring background sounds, atmospheric music, special effects – all combine to create a unique aural

Figure 5.11
Radio can take the listener inside a character's head or let inner- most thoughts be heard. For the writer, asides and soliloquies seem more natural in a radio script than in the theatre.

landscape. The final effect is not unlike a musical performance with its changes in instruments, volume and tempo.

▼ ▼ ▼

There is one simple and vital fact governing radio form. The radio act comes out of silence, vibrates in the void and in the mind and returns to silence, like music.

Donald McWhinnie
BBC Radio Drama Department

▼ ▼ ▼

WORDS Words are the most important factor in the creation of a radio play. On television and on the stage, visual effects and gesture can do a lot of the talking. Dialogue or narration, however, must convey the bulk of meaning in radio drama. No matter how good the imagination of the listener, the success of the radio play depends upon choosing the right words to express the drama in an engaging manner.

Changes in scene, distinctive voices, changes in the number of people speaking and changes in speed will all create interest. Audiences rely on their innate ability to distinguish voices in order to make sense of the unfolding action.

IMAGINATION Imagination provides the pictures on radio. As a result, each listener will create for themselves a different performance of the same play. The extent of his or her imagination is the only limit. This means radio drama has greater freedom from the restrictions of time and setting than drama in any other medium.

Despite this freedom, some critics say most radio drama only asks the listener to imagine that with which he or she is already familiar. The popular plays and serials, especially, go over the same sort of ground again and again.

Writing radio drama

It is very difficult to judge how a radio play will sound from the script. The play may look completely different in print from the way it sounds on air. Similarly, a play that may take only twenty minutes to read can take up to an hour to perform. After writing the first draft of a radio play, it is a good idea to make any adjustment after it has been heard in a test performance.

Techniques of presentation

Using a narrator is one way of compensating for the lack of pictures on radio. All settings, scene changes and even the actors themselves are invisible on radio. The narrator can be used to create the 'mind pictures' for the listener. The narrator's part often begins after the announcement of the title. S/he explains the dramatic situation and gives indications of the characters. The narrator then allows the characters and action to take over. Whenever some bridging explanations are needed, the narrator reappears. The narrator's role therefore becomes similar to the use of subtitles in a silent film. A related technique is to use a character as a narrator. This avoids the disadvantages of an impersonal and unidentified voice.

Many plays do not bother with the device of a narrator. Action is self-contained and self-explanatory. All indications of setting, scene changes and character movement are given in dialogue or sound effects. In most cases, it is felt that events have a greater feeling of realism if presented as if they were happening *at the time*.

ASIDES AND SOLILOQUIES are confidential comments characters make that only the audience can hear. A soliloquy is a long speech in which a character reveals his/her thoughts. An aside is just a quick comment to the audience. These devices work well on radio because it is such an intimate and com- panionable medium. Radio allows the play to take place inside the listener's head. Here, the secret thoughts of a character do not seem out of place.

SETTING AND SCENE CHANGES

A journey through the human psyche, encounters with submolecular life forms or adventures in space are all possible on radio. Most of these can be created on screen too, of course: however, not without elaborate and costly special effects. The writer for radio can conjure up the settings with just words and sounds. To avoid too much description, the setting can be shown in the dialogue. Look at the examples below. The listeners can tell it is a tropical setting on a hot day:

TOM: (CALLING FROM DISTANCE) Where are
   you?
KATHY: Over here, Tom, under the mango tree ... in
   the shade
TOM: Best place on a day like this ... (CLOSER)
   What are you doing?

The setting descriptions and scene changes in radio plays are often written in this kind of shorthand. This allows writers to make plenty of scene changes. Quick scene changes are a feature of radio plays. Some may have as many as twenty changes in thirty minutes.

DIALOGUE

Dialogue carries most of the meaning of the play. While sounding natural and lifelike, dialogue can be used for a number of basic functions.

► The first speeches should give indications as to setting of time and/or place, to help the listener understand where the drama is located, and the likely nature of the action.
► Most people do not talk in complete sentences all the time. They use snatches of speech, phrases, and half-finished sentences just as often as complete ones. Therefore the rhythm of speech can show a lot about a person and serve to develop character portrayal.
► Speech styles, accents and manner of speaking can be used to give instant clues about a character's class, status and possibly even previous history. They can also be used to distinguish characters from one another.

While dialogue is the most important element of radio drama, it must not ramble on too much. Audiences will soon tire of the same character talking for extended periods of time. Dialogue needs to be economical as well.

SOUND EFFECTS

As with dialogue, the writer needs to be economical in the use of sound effects. The veteran BBC writer and producer Felix Felton has suggested four simple rules for the writer to follow when planning sound effects.

► The ear cannot follow and understand a complex combination of sounds. If, for example a racetrack is the background, there is no use having roaring crowds, thudding horses' hooves, bookies' cries and all the other noises all on together.
► Often a simple sound, just on its own allows the listener to choose his/her own picture. This is better than forcing the imagery over and over again.

▼ ▼ ▼

There was a beautiful example of this in a radio play called *The Country Mouse Goes to Town*. The mouse and his wife find themselves in a vast metropolitan pantry where the holes in the Gruyère cheese are as big as railway tunnels. The problem was to make the listener see the scene through a mouse's eyes. It was swiftly done. One mouse said, 'It's so quiet in here you could hear a pin drop.' And immediately a large iron crowbar was sent crashing down upon a slab of concrete.

Felix Felton
Writer, actor and producer

▼ ▼ ▼

► Footsteps and slamming doors are best kept to a minimum. The entrances and exits of characters are also best indicated through voice alone.
► The value and meaning of sound effects depend on the dialogue or the story. They are of little value in themselves.

MUSIC

Music in a radio play can work in a similar way to lighting in a stage play. It creates moods and atmosphere and helps to establish settings or scene changes. It is mainly used in brief excerpts, between scenes, either to summarise the mood of what has just happened or to signal a change of mood in what is to come.

More extended pieces may also be used as background to ongoing dialogue, to underscore or emphasise the events taking place. In this case, it will be set at a lower volume level.

Characters

Characters are often created from a writer's own knowledge of people. New writers are encouraged to draw on their first-hand experiences. To make characters live for the reader, they must first live for the writer. Knowing how people speak, how they sound is the first step in making effective characters.

Next, it is essential to understand a character's motivation. What makes them do what they do? What is it that they want – and what prevents them from getting it? When the motivations of different characters come face to face, there is conflict. All drama is built out of conflict.

The plot

The plots in most modern dramas still follow a pattern set down in the dramas of Ancient Greece. The main character faces a series of increasingly demanding obstacles while struggling to solve the major problem of the drama. The crises build up until at the point of highest dramatic tension, the climax comes.

In radio, the tension is lost quickly after the climax. There are no pictures to hold the attention of the audience, who may be about to return to the washing up. As a result, radio writers usually tie up the loose ends quickly once the major problem is resolved.

▼ ▼ ▼ ▼ ▼ ▼ ▼

activities

1. What range of radio drama is available? Using a programme guide, make a list of the titles under each of the major categories. Use a table like figure 5.12 below.

▶ Why do you think the radio dramas have been programmed into those time slots? What sort of audiences would be available to listen at those times? Has television programming been a factor in the choice of time? Discuss.

▶ Is radio drama available on commercial radio stations? Advance some reasons to explain your answer.

▶ Investigate audience figures for the different kinds of drama identified in the above table. What conclusions could be drawn regarding either times of types of drama broadcast?

2. Listen to a radio drama. Now jot down your impressions of the following:

▶ main male character's likely appearance, dress and personality

▶ main female character's likely appearance, dress and personality

▶ features of the setting

▶ appearances of selected scenes.

Compare your impressions with those of the rest of the class. What have you used to generate those impressions? Discuss.

3. British playwright and radio critic David Wade cites the following dialogue as an example of good radio. Dot is a nurse-housekeeper and Sybil is a very old lady. Read it through, then answer the questions.

RANGE OF RADIO DRAMAS

TYPE	TITLE	COUNTRY OF ORIGIN	STATION	TIME
Soap opera				
Single radio play				
Dramatised feature				
Novel adaptation				
Stage adaptation				

Figure 5.12

▼ ▼ ▼

MORE CHERRY CAKE by Jehane Markham

SYBIL: Thomas and I with the boys on the beach at
Seaford … before the war. Thomas is wearing
white flannels. The wind blows the cloth against
his legs. It is hot. We sit with our backs to the
breakwater. Tar melts between the cracks of the
bleached wood. The children drink lemonade out
of bottles with straws.

PAUSE. TITLE OF PLAY ANNOUNCED.

DOT: (MURMURING) Butter in curls in butter dish.
Jam in a pot with long-handled spoon. (OPENS
DOOR) Did you have a nice rest?

SYBIL: I heard that baby again.

DOT: Have you been worrying?

SYBIL: Not really worrying.

DOT: You've been upsetting yourself again. What's
the problem?

SYBIL: I heard a baby crying quite distinctly.

DOT: There aren't any babies for miles around here.
I've already told you. It's your ears playing you up
again. You know what Dr Williams said.

SYBIL: If only his father were still alive, he knew how
to put everything right.

▼ ▼ ▼

► Who is the old lady talking to before Dot
enters? Is there a word for this dramatic
device?

► 'Thomas and I with the boys on the beach at
Seaford… before the war.' What is the old lady
looking at?

► Dot's first speech gives the listeners a clue to
the setting of the play. What sort of house is
it? How does the morning tea show this?

► Much of the action in this play takes place in
the form of memories and wanderings inside
Sybil's head. Find two or three comments in
the dialogue that suggest this will be so.

4. Try writing short sections of dialogue from
your own ideas for radio plays. Include brief
suggestions of setting in the dialogue to give
listeners an idea of the scene.

5. The rhythm of their speech can be used to
distinguish one character from another. Rhythm
can be varied with pauses, usage of long or short
words, use of complete and incomplete sentences
and so on. Accent is another means of
distinguishing between characters.

Write a short section of dialogue that will
distinguish between the following characters.

► an educated woman/uneducated man
► a farmer/young city person
► old person/young person
► a gossip/victim

6. Write a short (five-minute) radio play based
entirely on sound effects and music. First think of
a plot that can be told with sound effects. Add
characters that can be identified by sound. Be sure
to build to a climax towards the end of the play.
Thrillers, mad car chases, clownish musical
competitions and animal stories are all possible
with sound effects.

Before you start planning, read about a recent
play based on sound effects.

▼ ▼ ▼

The Revenge was a wordless sequence of noises.
Twigs crackled. Lumps of earth crumbled underfoot.
There was a great deal of heavy breathing. Doors
opened and closed. Someone, it became apparent,
was on the run. Grunt. Grunt. Aargh! (SOUND OF
FOOTSTEPS ON STAIRS, BOTTLE FALLING FROM
TABLE, NOISE OF BOOT, ETC.) Its characters were
necessarily limited to 'the pursuer' and 'the pursued';
its plot was just a chase …

Jonathan Raban
Radio dramatist and author

▼ ▼ ▼

7. Suggest music styles or individual titles that
could be used to identify some settings.

8. Script and record a short play of your own.
Choose your own subject, but try to base it on
people you know and have it deal with situations

Figure 5.13
*A few radio plays
have relied
entirely on sound
effects and music
to tell the story.
The idea is seen
as a novelty,
however, as words
are a far more
effective way to
tell a story. Sounds
and music alone
severely limit the
complexity of
the drama.*

of which you have first-hand knowledge. You do not have to be an expert, but you should try to give your piece some direction and work towards a resolution of some kind.

major assignment

Written assignment

Choose one of these assignments and write a 600-word essay.

1. 'Stage drama remains superior to radio drama'. Explain how someone could make such a statement and then decide whether or not you agree with it. At the same time, provide some details on the differences between the stage play and the radio play.

2. Write a review of a radio play. Use the following as a guide:
- plot
- character
- setting
- use of sound
- use of audience imagination.

Production assignment

Script and record a thirty-minute radio play. Show your familiarity with the genre in handling the following for radio:
- plot
- character
- setting and scene changes
- use of music to create atmosphere
- use of sound to create pictures in the listener's mind
- stimuli for imagination.

Radio Advertisements

Radio may be an invisible medium, but, in the words of London Capital Radio's Philip Pinnegar, a radio advertisement is 'inexpensive, personal, targetable, selective, immediate, intrusive … and you don't have to fly to the Bahamas to make the thing.' The American advertisers Bert Berdis and Alan Barzman compare radio advertising to television advertising. They say radio allows them to play different characters, visit far off lands and make up monsters. In television, creative thinking is restricted by the size of the budget.

In spite of these advantages, advertisers reckon on a radio advertisement having to be repeated three times to have as much impact as a single television commercial. A radio advertisement, they say reaches only about 47 per cent of the target audience. Television or newspaper advertisements are said to reach 80 or 90 per cent. Radio is able to compensate to some extent with two other factors. Radio does not lend itself to remote control 'zapping', as television does. People cannot, therefore, escape the commercials as easily. Also, radio is also the last thing people hear as they jump out of their cars to go into the supermarket.

More about advertising

In 1999, the total spend on radio advertising in the United Kingdom was £464 million. Throughout most of the 1990s, its market grew faster than any other media outlet and increased over the whole period by some 240 per cent.

Nearly 80 per cent of all 15- to 24-year-olds listened to commercial radio each week, as did just under 60 per cent of all listeners aged 15 to 44, and 70 per cent of children (source: Radio Advertising Bureau, December 1999).

The 'Commercial Radio Generation', as those under forty-four years of age have been dubbed, would seem to have a clear preference for commercial radio. However, it should also be remembered that BBC radios 1 and 2 between them account for nearly a quarter of *all* listeners (statistics can always be used in a number of different ways!).

(For information on the social purpose and contexts of advertising, the types of advertising, audience demographic appeals and ad music, see Television Advertising, p. 321.)

Figure 5.14
*Radio stations
simply cannot
afford to play
music with no
advertisements.
Their revenues
come almost
entirely from
advertising.*

Advertising time zones

Prices for advertisements vary according to the time they go to air. An advertisement in a breakfast time slot may cost ten times the price of an advertisement in the late evening. The time slots are usually breakfast, morning, afternoon, drive time and evening.

Radio advertisements and the audience

Radio does not aim for a mass audience in the way that television does. Radio narrowcasts, it doesn't broadcast. Specific groups – usually age groups – are targeted and attracted by the station's music format. Research tells advertisers all about the station's audience: their age, sex, income, education level, etc. If a product is advertised across several different music formats, it is not unusual for the advertisement to be reworded for each group. In the capital cities, where formats are often duplicated, advertisers after a certain audience may need to advertise on several stations to be sure of reaching most of the target group.

Writing radio advertisements

ATLANTIS POOLS

SHE: (HALF ASLEEP, GRUMBLING) George, I have to get some sleep.

HE: Hold still.

SHE: I can't hear you, George.

HE: Of course you can't hear me. I just filled up your ear with plaster of Paris.

SHE: What?!

HE: If we want Atlantis Pools to build us a pool that's shaped like your ear, we have to show them the shape of your ear.

SHE: Huh?

HE: Your ear is the perfect prototype for our swimming pool. It should be set by now … hold still.

SOUND EFFECT: SLURPY 'FLOOP' AS HE REMOVES PLASTER OF PARIS FROM EAR.

SHE: (WHIMPERS)

HE: Look at that fabulous detail? The diving board goes there and – see your earlobe? …

SHE: Eh?

HE: … that's where the patio'll be! … and here, where you had your ear pierced – guess what goes there?

SHE: What goes there, George?

HE: A built-in barbecue!

SHE: (GROANS)

ANNCR: Atlantis Pools can build almost any shape pool you want. And Atlantis will pay a hard-cash penalty if construction isn't finished when promised. Drive out to the Atlantis Display Centre at 9 Woodvale Road, Woodvale. Seven days a week.

SHE: Get away from me, George.

HE: But your left ear won't do – we have a right-hand back yard!

SHE: (THROUGH GRITTED TEETH) Don't touch me, George …

▼ ▼ ▼

Award-winning advertising copywriter Street Remley believes the above advertisement is a good example of radio copywriting. First, it concentrates solely on the key selling point of the product. Secondly, it builds up entertaining visual images in the mind of the listener. According to Street Remley, the aim of a radio ad writer should be to plant the seeds of mental pictures; pictures that show the product in a positive light.

Getting the Idea

Knowledge of the product is the starting point for all radio advertising copywriting. The product must be interrogated (see p. 326). Is it new? How is it made? What is it used for? Writers try to find a 'unique selling point' in the product – something to make it different from its competitors. The difference can be real or imagined.

Once the unique selling point has been established, it often suggests the story. The American radio advertisers Bert Berdis and Bart Barzman say they help things along with a 'what if' game. 'The agency brief might say our product has two doors. Okay, what if it didn't have any doors – or what if it had nine doors?'

The persuasive techniques

There are five basic stages in the radio commercial, copywriters say:

▶ getting attention
▶ holding interest
▶ showing the existence of a problem – real or imagined
▶ giving a solution to the problem
▶ getting action on the suggested solution (purchasing the product).

THE OPENING LINES – getting attention. No one turns on the radio to listen to advertisements. Ads are an annoyance – an intrusion. Therefore, the first couple of lines must immediately grab the listener's attention. The dramatic advertisement makes even more demands on the writer. The basic situation must be explained in the first few lines as well. But even testimonial or straight-sell advertisements must create a need to listen in the first few lines.

DIALOGUE – holding interest. Dialogue is to radio advertising what pictures are to television. People talking is what most advertisements use as their primary selling tool. Advertising copywriters try to keep dialogue sounding natural. Short phrases and plenty of interjections help create the feeling of real-life talk. A character will usually only have one or two lines of copy before another character replies or interjects. If there are long blocks of talk from one character, others usually comment or interject at regular intervals. Often they may just say something as simple as 'Oh yeah' or 'You can say that again!' But even that will serve to remind listeners that other characters do exist and are still there.

Characters should seem to be real people. Dialogue that simply provides long exchanges of product benefits works against the advertisement in the long run. People cannot bear to listen to it more than once. The basis of dialogue is probably best left to just one (or two) unique selling points.

In the following advertisement, music, sound effects and dialogue combine to make the ad effective. Notice that no character speaks in long blocks of copy without an interruption.

▼ ▼ ▼

McDONALD'S AD
MUSIC: LONE RANGER THEME UP
COWBOY HERO: (AMERICAN ACCENT) Hold it!
MUSIC: THEME PLAYBACK SPEED COMICALLY SLOWED UNTIL IT GRINDS TO A HALT.
HERO: What in the Sam Hill is happenin' here?
'JERK' VOICE:(EXCITED) It's McDonald's Beefsteaks Bonanza!
HERO: (SLOWLY) Oh, I kinda remember that show. There was a big guy …
'JERK': No, no, no, no, no … Beefsteaks Bonanza. (COWBOY THEME UNDER)When you buy a McFeast or Quarterpounder from McDonald's, they give you a game card and they …
HERO: Take it easy, kid.
'JERK': … scratch only three spots and if they match you win a McFeast or Quarterpounder, french fries or Coca Cola!
HERO: Well, what're we standin' here for?
SFX:BULLET RICOCHET
MUSIC: LONE RANGE THEME UP THEN UNDER.
VOICEOVER: Get straight into McDonald's for the Beefsteaks Bonanza.

▼ ▼ ▼

Music, sound effects and dialogue combine to make this an effective advertisement. Notice no character speaks in long blocks of copy without interruption.

ADVERTISEMENTS WITH A STORY – identifying and solving the problem. The unique selling point of a product is often highlighted in a story. Advertising copywriters dream up a problem and allow the product to solve it – the product becomes the hero. To complete the five steps of advertisement copywriting, an announcer's voiceover may be added. The voiceover suggests the action – immediate purchase of the produce.

CLOSING LINES – getting action. Closing lines require a strong finish to leave some lasting impression in listeners' minds. A sound effect, a hard-selling voice-over, a high point in the humour are all common solutions to the problem of audience inattention.

Music

'When you've got nothing, to say, sing it' is an old advertisers' saying. The word for sung commercials –

jingles – reflects this attitude. *Jingle* suggests an empty, meaningless, jangling rhyme. But many radio jingles have been very effective and some of the lyrics have entered our daily vocabulary. A jingle can be used as a sign off at the end of a commercial, or as a full jingle sound track.

On radio, brief snatches of music are also used to suggest settings or amplify moods that can add to the dialogue. This use of music demands sound tracks that the public can recognise in an instant.

Since radio is a music medium itself, some care has to be taken with the choice of music in an advertisement. The station format has to be a consideration.

▼ ▼ ▼

If I know what I'm going to write is going to run on a rock station, I will very carefully avoid using anything that borders on rock music. I might use barber-shop quartet – or something. The last thing I can have happen is to let my commercial bleed into the programming that surrounds it.

Street Remley
Advertising copywriter

▼ ▼ ▼

▼ ▼ ▼ ▼ ▼ ▼ ▼

activities

1. Listen to a number of radio commercials and divide them according to the main categories: straight sell, dramatisation, testimonial and musical (see Types of Advertisement, pp. 323–5).

2. Read the advertisement below, then answer the questions and try the activity. (*SFX* is short for sound effects.)

▼ ▼ ▼

SUBURBAN MAN: Grunt

GUY: Good morning.

MAN: Morning.

SFX: <u>BIRDS TWITTERING</u>

GUY: Chopping down the pine tree?

MAN: Oh yeah. The wife wants some genuine pine furniture.

SFX: <u>BIRDS</u>

GUY: Pine Cottage.

MAN: Pine Cottage?

GUY: (FIRMLY) Pine Cottage. First quality real pine furniture.

MAN: Yeah, but it costs a fortune.

GUY: Nah. Use their latest savings catalogue. I'm surprised you haven't got one in your letterbox.

MAN: Mmm. You're right! Here's everything we've been looking for and we'll save a bundle.

RANGER: Good. You can use the money.

MAN: Eh?

SFX: <u>BIRDS</u>

RANGER: I'm the warden and here's your fine for chopping down the tree.

VOICEOVER: Pine Cottage, the natural place for pine furniture. Their catalogue of savings out now.

▼ ▼ ▼

► What category of advertisement is this: straight sell, testimonial, dramatisation or musical, or some combination? (See Television Advertising, pp. 323–5.)

► Explain how the product is the hero.

► Count the number of times the name is mentioned. Why so many? Look at how many times the idea of *real* pine is reinforced. Would the listeners find this annoying or not? Why?

▶ Read and record this advertisement with two classmates. Vary the expression until you arrive at something that sounds natural.

3. Record an advertisement with effective dialogue. Transcribe the advertisement (so that you get to see how it looks on paper after you have heard it). Now write a paragraph explaining why you think the dialogue was effective.

4. Many jingles have become part of our everyday vocabulary. Make a list of well-known jingles that come immediately to mind.

5. Music is used to build the appeal to the audience. Listen to the music used in an advertisement and comment on the contribution that it makes to the advertising message. The questions below may give you some idea of the likely appeal.

▶ Does the music create warm memories – nostalgia?

▶ Does it add to the lifestyle or image the advertiser wants to portray?

▶ Does it contain key words that relate to the product, for example money in a banking commercial?

6. Make a list of songs you think could contain useful key words. List the title, the key word and a possible related product.

7. Copywriters say that there are five steps in persuasive advertisement writing:

▶ getting attention

▶ holding attention

▶ showing a problem

▶ showing a solution

▶ getting action – i.e. a purchase.

Analyse a radio advertisement and discuss its use of the five steps.

8. Try writing an advertisement that uses a famous personality to present the product. Write the advertisement in the style you would expect of the person selected.

Would it be serious or would it be straight? What kind of product might they allow themselves to be associated with? What category of advertisement do you think would be most effective? (See 'Television Advertising', pp. 323–5.)

major assignment

Combined written and production assignment

Prepare a radio advertising campaign for a client of your choice. Create a series of advertisements to be run on the same radio station with the one target audience. Alternatively, create a series of advertisements where each one is for a different station and a different target audience.

Include a submission giving a description of the product, an explanation of the unique selling point, an outline of the image you are trying to project and the market to which you want to appeal.

Make a sample recording of one of the advertisements outlined.

chapter six
Newspapers and Magazines

6 ▶

The Language of the Print Media

'I know my ideal newspaper,' said the American newspaper baron William Randolph Hearst, the man upon whom the movie *Citizen Kane* (United States, 1941) is based. 'It's one where the reader looks at page one and says, "Gee Whiz"; turns to page two and says, "Holy Moses"; turns to the middle and says, "God Almighty!"'

The language of the print media is a specialised one based on immediacy (critics might say sensationalism) and multi-modal presentation (see multi-modal, p. 5). The print media are multi-modal because they rely on photographs and other visual material, as well as text.

Basic units of print media language

The *codes* (see pp. 47–9) of print language consist of the printed word, location and page layout, and story length. To these, still photographs add some of the codes of the visual image.

The printed word

The language of newspapers and magazines has developed particular characteristics over the last century and a half. Really, we should speak of their *languages*, as wide variations exist in terms of purpose, subjects, tone and outlook. It is impossible to summarise *all* publications in the same way, but the following are some general observations.

A NEUTRAL CODE? Words printed on a page are signs that stand for something else (see pp. 46–8). The word 'earthquake', for example, does not resemble the actual event in any way: it is merely an agreed series of symbols that represents the *idea* of the event. On one level, these symbols provide the means for describing the world in an objective way.

The print media rely on collections of word signs as *symbolic codes* (see pp. 48–9) to communicate meaning. However, they do not always employ them in a strictly neutral manner. Emotive words and descriptive, action-orientated language are the symbolic codes of the print media.

Although newspapers are *meant* to report events in an impartial manner, in fact they rely heavily on the emotional charge that certain kinds of words can bring to the coverage they offer. Refugees are 'crooks' and 'dole cheats' in some papers, for example, and 'asylum seekers' in others.

SENSATION 'When a dog bites a man, that's not news. But when a man bites a dog, now *that's* news!' said the American newspaper editor Charles Dana. Newswriting styles favour action and excitement. The unexpected twist is another favourite (see pp. 13–14 and 267–8). Intensity and urgency in one sector, careful evaluation and analysis in another are often the keys to the organisation of their products. In both, the construction of individual sentences and the structuring of whole stories are designed to put the most important facts first.

ECONOMY Never use two or three words when one will do, young journalists are advised. Ever since the telegraph and telegram put a cost on words, economies of language have also meant economies of production. In the print media, space saved can be devoted to advertising. At the same time, many readers prefer brevity. The expectations of the target audience have to be satisfied.

In the mid-market newspapers and the broadsheets, of course, language tends to be much more expansive than in the tabloids.

MODES OF ADDRESS The ways in which newspapers seek to talk to their readers vary considerably. In the *tabloids*, the kind of language used tends to suggest commonsensical, forthright opinions, imbued with certainty and clarity. Unafraid to share their strongly held views, the writers have traditionally sought to achieve the relationship of 'the bloke in the pub' with their readers.

Following continual dips in circulation, however, some have moved more towards the tone of the *mid-market newspapers*. Here, the address is no less confident in expression, but rather more thorough in the detail and factual background given to stories. Sustained and serious arguments are made, and the effect is more of a campaigner who is keen to help you see things the 'right way'.

In the *broadsheets*, full and thoughtful consideration is extended to many of the topics covered. The topics themselves will be of rather more density, of course; however, it is the way in which they are addressed that marks them out as much as anything. The sensation is more one of sitting in on a series of lectures, where context and history (both recent and longer term) are as important as the immediate events.

SPEED Many readers skim newspapers. They only pause to read those stories that are directly interesting to them. Newspaper language has evolved to assist this process. Sentences are short. Headlines reduce the facts to just a few 'punchy' words. Key facts are carefully laid out in the opening sentence or two. In this manner readers can rapidly identify whether a given story will be of interest to them.

Location

Real estate agents say three factors set the price of a house: location, location and location. The print media operate on the same principle. The location of an article in a print media text is mainly determined by its importance and its genre.

The more interesting that readers will find a story, the closer it has to go to the front of the newspaper or magazine. The most exciting story or the most important story will appear on the front page, in the case of newspapers; or early on in the contents schedule, in the case of magazines.

READING NEWSPAPERS

How a newspaper is read

Headlines, news, then remainder	29%
Straight through front to back	28%
Front to back, then sections	12%
Sections, news, then remainder	8%
Look at all sections	87%

Editors place articles that are more interesting or important on pages one, three, five, seven and all the other right hand (odd-numbered) pages. This is because readers naturally look to the right hand side first, since the papers open towards the left. Similarly, a story above the fold of the paper has been placed there because the editors regard it as more important than those below the fold.

In all newspapers, and some magazines, there is a progression from hard news in the first few pages to comments and features towards the middle of the paper. This is followed by a further progression to classified advertisements, and then sports towards the back.

However, as newspapers in particular change in response to challenges from new media such as pay television and the Internet, comment is becoming more important. Some newspapers now put short argumentative commentaries by leading writers on the front page. Many feel little or no restraint in making their attitudes towards key topics crystal clear.

Page layout

The main elements of page layout are printed text, pictures and advertisements.

Each newspaper or magazine develops a page layout or format that is distinctively its own. Fonts, the size and nature of headlines and captions, placement and number of articles, the size and position of photographs – all combine to generate the 'house style'. All publications seek to apply a consistent style throughout – the page layout is like a brand image. Regular readers can recognise it and feel comfortable.

Figure 6.1
The location of a newspaper article will determine how many people see it.

Broadsheets, of course, have many more stories than do tabloids – which, in turn, favour larger-scale photographs, particularly on the front page. Similarly, the latter prefer short, punchy headlines, while the former tend to go for more serious topics. Middle-market newspapers such as *The Mail* fall somewhere between the two: they will often go for a single story on the front page, for instance, but it will usually be a serious one, and covered in some depth. This paper in particular has achieved a shrewd mix of formats. Sensationalist treatment of controversial stories and the forthright opinions of the tabloid on the one hand, together with the more expansive treatment of the generally more important topics of the broadsheets, on the other. This formula has proven to be a notable success for this publication in recent years.

Variations in layout

The design of a page will depend on its readership and the content of the publication. It can vary in the following ways.

ARRANGEMENT OF COLUMNS Some newspapers may put all stories in single columns. Often financial newspapers do this. Others may go for more sensationalism. They could spread the intro sentences of a main story across two columns.

FONTS The type of character selected is a way of giving a newspaper or magazine a personality. Fonts are a key means of establishing an identity that is different to that of competitors. They also suggest whether the newspaper is to be seen as serious or fun.

HEADLINE STYLE Some magazines and newspapers put headlines in block capitals to add urgency. Others use lower case, with only the first word and names capitalised. Some newspapers and magazines use a 'strapline' either above or below the main headline. This is a smaller headline that adds more detail.

SUBHEADINGS The use of subheadings is another distinguishing feature. A subheading is a means of visually breaking up a longer story, to make the text easier to digest. They can also be used for

picking out a particular feature of the following paragraph in the main body of the story.

USE OF GRAPHICS Graphics included above or below the masthead (title of the newspaper) can signal regular sections in the paper and add to the design possibilities. They are quite often used to promote special offers or competitions.

PHOTOGRAPHS The placement of photographs can also be a regular feature of page design. Page 3 in the *Sun* is probably the most renowned, but other papers also have detectable patterns in the nature and arrangement of the visual material used.

Story length and space

The length of a story indicates its importance, just as its location does. If the newspaper story is too long to fit its allotted space, editors cut paragraphs from the bottom. This practice has meant stories are written to tell all the important facts in the first few paragraphs.

The size of the 'news hole' is determined by the amount of space left after all the advertising has been included. Stories are cut to suit the overall news hole as well as their allotted order in it.

Photographs

Photographs make up a significant part of the overall package of newspapers. They have long been a key ingredient, offering useful and vivid illustration of particular stories. However, since their earliest usage they have also been subjected to a variety of methods of treatment and manipulation.

Many of these have been fairly innocent, in that they were developed to make the most of the features of a particular given photograph. Getting a photo to fit a predetermined physical space inevitably requires some means of changing its size or shape. (In the next section, however, some more dubious manipulations are examined.)

The following are some of the long-established methods of manipulating the photographic image.

SELECTION The first part of the process of treating photographs is in the choice of shot to be used. Most professional photographers take many

Figure 6.2
Hugh Grant, as William Thacker in **Notting Hill** *(UK, 1999), besieged by the press pack. In real life, Hugh Grant's celebrity and events in his private life have resulted in almost continual attention from the paparazzi.*

more than one shot of a subject. Differences can be substantial – a politician snoozing at a conference or, later, cheering a rousing speech.

CROPPING This involves trimming off parts of the picture that add little to the core subject or meaning. Sometimes, however, what is lost can change that meaning dramatically.

FRAMING This is the composition of the elements of the shot – what is included and what left out, how near or how far the subject, how things are positioned with relation to each other.

POINT OF VIEW Where a photograph of a subject is taken from will influence the way in which it is perceived. Perspective and background have major implications for the way in which we read an image.

LENSES Choice of lens can significantly alter the appearance of the relation of objects within a shot to each other (see pp. 148–9 on shots). Long lenses, of course, can pick out subjects without them being aware of it.

Today, it is often the photograph that comes first – sometimes, it may even *be* the story. The shot of a bloated Gary Glitter featured on p. 397 is *in itself* the only reason for including it. Celebrity-

hunting is a lucrative occupation for many freelance photographers. Catching famous people in unusual or embarrassing situations can pay big dividends.

Photojournalism

News photographers and photojournalists, playing by the old rules of engagement, find their pictures unpublished.

Even front-page pictures in the quality press are given over more and more to ironic portraits or photo-montages. Its news value usurped by television, its emotional power dulled, photographic reporting is in decline, as readers turn to the Hollywood profile or the shopping page.'

Liz Jobey, *The Guardian*
14 December 1996

▼ ▼ ▼

Photojournalism has been in the news itself for quite a long time. The antics of the *paparazzi*, intruding on people's privacy, have attracted much criticism. This very much came to head around the death of Diana, Princess of Wales (see p. 407).

However, it is not only the activities of the photographers that are stirring up controversy. There is considerable concern also about how the pictures that are taken are then *treated* when it comes to publication.

Figure 6.3
Children flee after a napalm attack on their village in June 1972, during the Vietnam War. This photograph was shown around the world and was widely credited with helping to turn the tide of opinion against the war.

A conference on the integrity of news photography, at New York University, identified two principle categories of news photograph, with distinct subgroups within each.

TAKING PHOTOGRAPHS

► *Photo reportage* where a photo is a spontaneous record of a naturally occurring event
► *Photo portraiture* where the subject is posed
► *Photo illustration* where people or things are used to illustrate more general points
► *Photo opportunity* where the subject dictates the conditions in which the photo is taken, in

an attempt to exert some control over the finished product

IMAGE MANIPULATION

► *Retouched photographs* in which cosmetic values have been enhanced, without significant alteration to the actual content
► *Composite photographs* in which the original content has been substantially altered
► *Computer-generated images* which need not involve a camera at all.

The impact of photographs is undisputed. The worldwide exposure of nine-year-old Kim Phuc burnt by a napalm attack, in Vietnam, is felt by many to have hastened the end of that war. The equally famous image of soldiers raising the flag at Iwo Jima, during World War II, was also felt by millions at that time to capture the heroism and suffering of victorious troops.

Where the first of these was an example of reportage, however, the second – despite appearances – was, in fact, posed and is actually an example of portraiture. The soldiers were asked to *re-enact* the original event, some time after it had occurred. The point would be made, in defence of this action, that it is not always possible to capture the original event at the time that it occurs. Wars are hazardous affairs and you cannot cover all the action all of the time. In any case, the event did actually take place, so there is no real deception involved.

Altering the original image, however, raises rather different concerns. At one level, this may be seen to be relatively harmless. In the cover shot of Yasmin Le Bon for *Harper's & Queen* (figure 6.4), only minor blemishes were improved. Rather more seriously, Soviet Russia was once notorious for 'rewriting history' – by removing from photographic records of official events the faces of those who later fell out of favour.

Where the ground becomes rather less solid, however, is when events are staged to convey a sense of some aspect of a dramatic story. In another famous example, a shot of a policeman carrying 'human remains' away from the notorious house where Fred West killed so many, the event was actually fabricated to give an impression of what was taking place. It is not that the things depicted did not occur – but this photograph was not the actual record of them it purported to be.

Figure 6.4
This cover shot of Yasmin Le Bon for Harper's & Queen was enhanced using digital manipulation. In all, some thirty minor blemishes were removed. (Source: The Independent)

Blemishes on forehead retouched

Wonky eyebrow hairs straightened

Bloodshot eye whitened out

Hints of bags under both eyes faded out

Pink blotch above top lip coloured over

Lips brightened

Stray hairs removed from face and neck

**Figures
6.5 & 6.6**
*The front pages
of* The Sun *and*
The Mirror,
9 March 2000.

FRONT-PAGE COMPARISON

ATTRIBUTE	THE SUN	THE MIRROR
Masthead/ title	Top left-hand corner – for prominence on newsstands One-half of page width	Left-hand justified Full page width
Typography	Italics Main script bold italic – suggests fun and urgency Sans serif lettering	Plain sans serif lettering, with black outline. Suggests straight, 'no nonsense' reporting
Headline	Single word – highly emotive language	Five words – ongoing story
By-line	Reveals shocking 'facts'	None for lead story
Banners	Occupies more space than main news story Use of innuendo	One for interior only Very small one for website
Choice/number of articles	Two: one playing on ongoing 'scare' story, the other on television celebrity *1/12 of page space*	One only: scandal with football players *1/24 of page space*
Pictures	Two: small one for news story; much larger one for Royals story inside	Two: tiny one for main news story; enormous one for celebrity story inside Note semi-nudity: the promise of sex inside is a tested selling device (even though it is not delivered in this case)
Advertisements	None	None

Once the notion is abandoned that the photograph is a true record of what takes place, there are all sorts of dangers as to what may get passed off as real in this form. This is a huge problem in terms of the subjects of photographs, and how they are represented. The effects of such changes may be highly damaging.

Sometimes the consequences of such actions can backfire, too. The Ford Motor Company once got into a lot of trouble for the retouching of a promotional photograph that air-brushed out some Black and Asian faces from a shot of its workforce.

With advances in computer manipulation of images, all sorts of possibilities now open up for complete fabrication. While many newspapers have 'fun' with this technology, the implications are really very serious. It is no longer possible to tell whether an image has been faked, or had even the vaguest connection with a real source. The photographic image cannot be trusted as a reliable record of the real world.

Newspaper front pages

The pages of the two popular tabloid newspapers shown on the previous page are both taken from the same day: Thursday, 9 March 2000. It is interesting to note the similarities and the differences. When there is a really huge story, such as the fuel depot blockades later on in the same year, then all the papers will cover it on their front pages. Generally, however, there is some variation.

Each has its own distinct house style, which it is keen to maintain and promote over its rivals'. Whether they are more alike or different from each other is debatable.

THE SUN In many ways, this is a 'classic' example of this newspaper's style and outlook. It condenses many of the core values and obsessive interests of the paper. On the one hand, it is irreverent, fun-loving, suggestive and highly indulgent of puns, especially those of a suggestive nature: there is the 'cheeky chappie' article concerning a Royal, with added-in sex angle (even though it does not really exist). On the other, the main 'news' story is a renewed attack on refugees. This newspaper is always ready to stir up antagonism towards foreigners of any kind and the flight of thousands of people from war-ravaged central Europe gave it

plenty of opportunities. Xenophobia is a forcefully promoted feature of the ideology of this paper. It finds little to celebrate in the achievements and contributions of people from other countries. Rather odd, given that it is owned by Rupert Murdoch, an Australian who renounced his own country of origin for financial reasons.

THE MIRROR Sex, of course, makes a up a very large part of the appeal of this front page – and always sells. The front cover picture of Kate Winslet is perhaps surprising only for *how little* it actually reveals – although more is promised (but not actually delivered) inside. Celebrities are a particular obsession of all the tabloids. The only thing they like more than idolising their fabulous lifestyles is tearing into them whenever they hit problems or crises.

The only story to be featured on this page concerns a nasty racial attack on a young Asian male. In some ways, the paper could be applauded for dealing with this vicious aspect of modern urban life. However, the involvement of football stars in the incident perhaps shows the true perspective on its interest in this particular story.

The values and ideologies of both these newspapers are readily identifiable from the materials they select for publication.

Issues of representation

The 'window on the world' that the media supposedly give us is not quite so transparent when studied closely. Far from being clear and transparent, the glass turns out to be highly tinted. Various values and beliefs are built into the pictures of events that they offer. This is most starkly apparent with newspapers.

To use the example of the refugee 'scandal' reported in the edition of the *Sun* shown on p. 395, the facts were not quite so clear-cut as the paper suggested. A more considered review, shortly afterwards, pointed out the many serious shortcomings in this coverage.

▼ ▼ ▼

Both the *Sun* and the *Times* presented their front page articles on the Gardiner report next to pictures of gypsy beggars and the *Sun*'s splash was unequivocal: 'Crooks, dole cheats and illegal immigrants

Figure 6.7
Front page of
The Guardian,
30 September
2000.

Figure 6.8
The front page of
the **Daily Mail,**
31 May 2000.

FRONT-PAGE COMPARISON

ATTRIBUTE	THE GUARDIAN	DAILY MAIL
Masthead/ title	Note unusual right-hand justification: distinctive style	Left-hand justified, across most of page Note use of royal crest
Typography	Interesting mixture of serif 'The' with much plainer, bold style for actual name Main script is very contemporary	Heavy Gothic script – suggestive of serious, 'weighty' publication
Headline	Serious story – though graphic, compressed language used	Focuses on emotive element of important story
By-line	Expands on key factual points	Offers some clarification of basic facts
Banner	Used to promote particular items inside – mainly based on personalities, whether the actual subjects or the writers covering them	Forthright opinion given by key writer on established celebrity Highly prejudicial language used
Choice/number of articles	Three on major political events, one on a sporting triumph *3/8 of page space*	Two: both apparently on serious topics, although the Gary Glitter item really only snoops on his privacy *1/8 of page space*
Pictures	Two: one small, head and shoulders shot shot of subject; the second, much larger one also depicts the article's subject, but is a much more dynamic shot, showing the action involved in the article	Three: interestingly, only two are of subjects of articles; the other is of a staff writer
Advertisements	One, quite prominent, across the full width of the paper	None

pocket £80 billion a year through the black economy'.

The fact that most of the report dealt largely with the activities of people born or long settled in Britain was irrelevant to the papers which had set their sights on fomenting prejudice in general against 'the asylum flood' (the *Mail*) and specifically against 'cadgers' (the *Times*).

Roy Greenslade,
The Guardian, 20 March 2000

▼ ▼ ▼

It is quite clear that newspapers have a particular set of concerns and views that they are keen to promote – some less subtly than others.

Another opportunity for foaming indignation on the part of the tabloids was the occasion of an anti-capitalist demonstration in London, on May Day 2000. The statue of Winston Churchill was notoriously defaced, principally by the addition of a green mohican haircut. The headline played on one of the wartime leader's most famous phrases and turned on the demonstrators with fury. 'Mindless thuggery' was how the march in general and this act in particular were portrayed.

However, the paper gave little coverage to the subsequent voluntary confession of the person who had done the deed. A former soldier, who had served in Bosnia and Croatia, he explained that he had wished to make a serious point.

▼ ▼ ▼

The May Day celebrations were in the spirit of free expression against capitalism. Churchill was an exponent of capitalism and of imperialism and anti-Semitism. A Tory reactionary, violently opposed to the emancipation of women … The reality was an often irrational, sometimes vainglorious leader whose impetuosity, egotism and bigotry on occasion cost many lives, unnecessarily, and caused much suffering that was needless and unjustified.

James Matthews, interviewed in
The Guardian, 8 May 2000

▼ ▼ ▼

The May Day protester was subsequently sent to jail. Whether or not one agrees with his point of view, or the tactics used, it is quite clear that the man is far from 'mindless'. He clearly had strongly held opinions and a serious message he wished to communicate. He was also quite capable of expressing them in detailed and considered language. As with the refugees, however, alternative views to simple jingoistic propaganda lie beyond the scope of the tabloid newspapers' agendas. Their chief aim is to present the world in simple black-and-white terms.

However, the stark reductions they offer also often conceal reactionary ideological viewpoints. Fervent opposition to all things European, for instance, is always presented as standing up for British culture and traditions. Even when EC directives may be of direct benefit to the United Kingdom and significantly improve its citizens' rights, the angle taken by most tabloids is that this is just another imposition from bureaucrats abroad. The Human Rights Convention, for example, adopted in 2000, was presented as an outrageous case of our own laws being overruled by foreign ones. In fact, it provides legal guarantees of rights for citizens of this country, in a manner that their own government has failed to do.

Many false stories are gleefully circulated about how Brussels issues endless nonsensical orders: the supposed attempt to banish bent bananas is a classic example of this. These stories have no basis in fact, but that does nothing to restrain the tabloid newspapers.

Curiously, there is virtually no resistance at all to the far greater cultural domination we are exposed to from the United States. Hollywood films, American music and American fast-food outlets have had a much greater impact on our lives than anything coming at us from Europe. Although equally 'foreign', these are allowed to be seen as beneficial.

▼ ▼ ▼ ▼ ▼ ▼

Newspapers and Magazines

activities

1. Look through a magazine or newspaper article and mark the emotive or highly symbolic words with a highlighter. Emotive or highly symbolic words are those that have strong associations with good or bad things. Try to establish the particular view of the story concerned that the article appears to be promoting.

2. Using a tabloid newspaper article, find examples of typical language that is either sensational or economical. Write these examples in another way, so that they suit a broadsheet newspaper. How would you have to change the nature of the words and the sentences used?

3. Survey the approach class members take to the print media. Devise questions designed to find out what they read in newspapers or magazines: which are their favourite sections, how long do they spend on each, which articles or headlines they remember, etc. Collate your results. Describe how you would design a newspaper or magazine to suit your classmates.

4. Re-read the six layout variables on p. 392. Compare two newspapers or two magazines by analysing them under each of these variables.

5. Investigate the graphic layout of a newspaper. Draw an outline map of the front page. Mark in the columns and boxes to represent photographs. Write the story headlines in the appropriate spaces and mark in the boundaries of each story. Draw boxes in the columns to indicate any advertising. Mark in any other graphics and the masthead (title) if a newspaper.

Now do the same thing for a page from another publication within the same medium, but aimed at a different market. How would the two have to differ?

The Medium of Newspapers

A great deal of the current shape of the newspaper and magazine output (the lifestyle variety, anyway) in Britain today can be traced back to a remarkable publication that first appeared in 1973. *The New Journalism*, edited by Tom Wolfe, was a collection of quite unprecedented variety and depth – and even more so of stylistic innovation.

Intensive social exploration, coupled with audacious experimentation in language and committed perspective, marked it out as unique in the history of journalism. Wolfe himself commented that he wanted to establish a 'journalism that would read like a novel'. For a time, it seemed possible that it might even supplant that particular form altogether.

▼ ▼ ▼

New Journalism's founding fathers were feature writers, at a time when that job was regarded as a mere 'motel' en route to a novel ... By 1973, largely thanks to the revitalising influence of the new wave, that marginalised past had become incredible. Writing for a Sunday magazine – a phenomenon that crossed the Atlantic in the mid-sixties – had become the most glamorous job in newspapers.

John Dugdale, *Media Guardian*,
16 November 1998

▼ ▼ ▼

Perhaps the most remarkable thing of all is the sheer range of publications over which it has cast its influence: from up-market glossies (*Harpers & Queen*), through the pop music press (*Rolling Stone* and *NME*), to the enduring successes of the so-called 'lad mags', or style magazines (*Loaded, The Face, More!*). Even further, newspapers themselves – and the broadsheets, especially, with their lifestyle supplements and specialist pull-outs – have succumbed to the attractions of this highly personalised approach. Sports, travel, even **motoring correspondents have all adopted its free-wheeling and committed tone.**

▼ ▼ ▼

Twenty-five years later, the special Sunday treat has been reinforced by the Saturday magazine, the style supplement, the daily feature tabloid, the host of

specialist sections and subsections, with feature writers advertised alongside columnists as the newspaper's stars. Like it or loathe it, today's journalistic power balance has been decisively shaped by the rolling revolution that began in the early sixties.

John Dugdale, *Media Guardian*,
16 November 1998

▼ ▼ ▼

Many have loathed it – including some of those who began it – in some of its derivations, at least. One of the original contributors, Hunter S. Thompson, later coined the term 'Gonzo journalism', to describe the incoherent ravings of less serious, or less capable, imitators.

Originally intended to bring a fresh new perspective, and an intensive exploration to pressing areas of social concern, it now seems to have deteriorated into a kind of pseudo-journalism. Self-centred and self-important, often the writer sets himself or herself up as the most interesting feature of any given topic.

One distinct variation of this genre was notably satirised by Chris Morris in the summer of 1999. The intention was to send up the confessional column. He wrote a spoof column for *The Observer*, under an assumed name, entitled 'Time To Go'. In it, he made out that he had decided on suicide and was gradually working his way through everybody he knew to say goodbye. It drew some venomously hostile criticism – not the first time Morris's humour has provoked such a response. However, as a journalist from *The Observer*'s sister paper was at pains to point out, people both inside and outside the industry too easily confuse the personal and the private:

▼ ▼ ▼

Media organisations sometimes get mistaken for purveyors of group therapy these days, but they are in fact simply selling private lives as commodities.

Decca Aitkenhead, *The Guardian*
28 June 1999

▼ ▼ ▼

A changing medium?

Are newspapers reaching the term of their natural life – about to become an endangered species in an electronic age?

The premature obituary of newspapers has been written for decades, but they have proven resilient survivors, refusing to lie down and die.

Despite being the first of the mass media, newspapers could scarcely be accused of being a medium of the past. They have been the quickest to experiment with digital transmission through the Internet. Many quality world newspapers are now available on the World Wide Web.

For many years now, supplements and specialised segments have been created to counteract the appeal of other media. In the past decade, *The Times* and the *Daily Mail* have doubled in size. Colour technology has been introduced across the board, and much cheaper computer technology adopted to enhance production.

In other words, newspapers have not lagged behind where modernisation is concerned.

Changing readerships

Newspapers have also refined their appeal to certain demographic groups (see pp. 336–8) and are engaging in much more audience research than they ever did in the past.

Advances in technology and changes in society have generated significant changes in both products, and the audiences they are aimed at. Some newspapers now identify their readership as the highly educated groups in society and leave the mass audience to television. A more highly educated readership demands more pages of background and more comment on the news, as well as greater depth in reporting. Providing comment on the news has become the major role of quality newspapers.

Forces reshaping the press

A number of technological and social factors are impacting on newspapers. They are forcing changes that seem more dramatic than those occurring in other media.

MEDIA CROWDING In a mature media market, new media can be added without necessarily wiping out audiences for the old media. Yet pay television and computer-based media have proved to be strong rivals for all of the traditional media.

THE INFORMATION SOCIETY Digital newspapers offer greater reader control of the information they receive. They also provide the possibility of an increased range of commercial and leisure

services. In an age of information overload, some people prefer to be able to be more selective.

DECLINING READERSHIP Many national daily newspapers seem to be suffering a slow, year-on-year decline in their circulation figures, especially among the tabloids. In the past decade, several well-known titles have ceased to appear.

COST INCREASES Another reason for the decline has been the increase in production costs and subsequent rises in the cover price. Newspapers are very price sensitive. People stop buying if they become too expensive. Price wars to increase circulation are increasingly common.

MORE CARS Changes in the habits of city commuters have also meant a decline in sales. Fewer people use public transport and so there are fewer people reading newspapers on the way to and from work.

The purposes of newspapers

From time to time, the press oversteps the mark in reporting matters that are felt by the subjects to be too intrusive into their personal or private affairs. Whenever this happens, long-running arguments surface once more about the need for laws to curb the powers of the press.

On the one hand, people look at countries such as France and point to the laws in place there to protect personal privacy. On the other, the press itself seeks to stress the invaluable role it plays in keeping a watchful eye over the powerful and making sure that they conduct themselves according to high moral and ethical standards. It is in this capacity that it refers to itself as a 'Fourth Estate' (the other three being the Church, the Monarchy and Parliament – all sources of power and influence in society).

Profit or service to the public?

The tobacco industry has been very much in the dock regarding the marketing and even manufacturing of its products in recent years. Shocking new accounts have emerged about how the contents of cigarettes have been concocted to induce addiction.

In general, we rely on our newspapers to keep us informed about the findings of medical research into matters as important as this. Yet American media analyst Mark Crispin Miller has revealed that damning medical evidence on the dangers of smoking was suppressed as far back as 1935. Tobacco companies, of course, were among the biggest advertisers in the mainstream press that colluded in this.

▼ ▼ ▼

It's the same old problem now, only it's infinitely worse. Reporters have to be careful not merely about offending some group of advertisers, they have to be aware of a whole range of corporations, including the one that owns the newspaper or network or television station they work for.

Mark Crispin Miller, Director of the Project on Media Ownership, New York University

The Guardian, 17 January 2000

▼ ▼ ▼

Media experts agree on one thing. While a newspaper is a business proposition, it is not like other businesses. Many people feel that the first duty of a newspaper should be to its public. Certainly, papers themselves have cultivated the image of watchdogs of the powerful in society, on the lookout for abuses and transgressions from high levels of public accountability. In this role, concern for profit should come second.

This is rather disingenuous view of the true nature and purposes of the press, however. Newspapers are in fact driven by the profit motive: they are, above all, businesses.

It is common to divide this duty to the public into five categories.

■ **A newspaper should provide truthful information**

Truth and accurate reporting of current events is one of the most important duties of the press. In a democratic country each citizen has a responsibility to take part in the making of decisions about national affairs. Voting for a particular political party is one of these decisions. This can only be effective if there is accurate information on current events.

■ **A newspaper should explain the news**

The mere reporting of news is often seen as not enough. People also want explanations as to what

Figure 6.9
One of the functions of a newspaper is to present the truth. By the time the reporter gives his or her opinion and by the time the editor has cut the story to fit into the space allocated, the truth may be looking very different!

it all means. As newspapers move towards a more highly educated readership and as television is such a serious competitor, many newspapers are giving more space to in-depth explanation of the news.

MOST-READ SECTIONS

	MEN	WOMEN
1	Page one	Page one
2	General news	General news
3	World news	World news
4	Sport	Inserted magazines
5	Television guide	Television guide
6	Inserted magazines	Entertainment
7	Comics	Comics
8	Business/finance	Sport
9	Entertainment	Business/finance
10	Classifieds	Classifieds

Figure 6.10
Men and women typically read the newspaper in a slightly different fashion. The breakdown of the paper into segments assists this.

■ **A newspaper should provide entertainment**

As newspapers are often read just to fill in spare moments, they should also be interesting and entertaining. Once again, strong competition comes from television. Slick television news packages have left newspapers with little choice but to follow suit. Humorous stories, stories about animals, exciting crime stories and so on are often simply to entertain. The modern trend towards pull-outs and weekend sections also fits the entertainment, or lifestyle, category.

■ **Newspapers should reflect diversity of public opinion**

In a modern democratic society, there will be a variety of political viewpoints and ideas. Wealth is distributed unevenly and the needs of one group are often quite different to the needs of another. To be truly fair, all groups should have the right of representation in the columns of newspapers. It may not be possible to reflect all opinions within any one publication; however, adequate coverage of the full spectrum of ideas should be possible across the medium as a whole. This is far from being the case at the moment.

■ **A newspaper should be able to give its opinion**

All newspapers give some of their column space over to opinion. Most people recognise this and many would claim not to be unduly influenced by it. However, for citizens to be able to make well-informed decisions they need an idea of the range of opinions on the issues facing them. This is particularly so when it comes to voting.

The ideal newspaper would be like this …

The following is a list of the elements of an ideal newspaper adapted from one prepared by media analysts Hirsch and Gordon.

▶ It should be reasonably independent from commercial pressure. Its main motive should not be just to make money.
▶ It should be truthful and accurate.
▶ It should provide fair and close coverage of major political parties, both in its news columns and its opinion sections.
▶ It should reflect the diversity of opinion available in the wider community.
▶ It should show the range of interests present in the community.
▶ It should be free of government manipulation and intervention, but should be subject to independent monitoring. Breaches of the Press Code should be punished formally and severely where necessary.

Readerships

Readers spend an average of forty minutes a day reading their favourite newspaper, while Sunday papers are read for rather longer. The most popular place for reading the morning newspaper is the home (70 per cent), followed by work (25 per cent); only 7 per cent read their paper in transport. The equivalent figures for Sunday papers are 96 per cent at home, 3.5 per cent at work and 0.5 per cent in transport.

The newspaper of the future

Will traditional newspapers soon be replaced by digital newspapers? In his book *Goodbye Gutenberg*, Anthony Smith argues that computerised news and information will revolutionise the newspaper industry. Videotext and teletext systems can present vast amount of information on such topics as stock exchange prices.

Internet newspapers are proving increasingly popular. Some papers are even experimenting with a system where consumers pay electronically for their subscription.

However, at the moment, newspapers enjoy a tremendous advantage over these systems. Newspapers are cheap, portable and permanent. They will be difficult to replace. Some believe that the answer for the press is to move towards a quality image aimed at the new generation of highly educated people.

National Newspaper Data for the month of: July 2001

Title	Overall Total Average Net Circulation	UNITED KINGDOM					REPUBLIC OF IRELAND					OTHER COUNTRIES
		Sub-Total Circulation	Full Rate Sales	Lesser Rate Sales	Pre-Paid Non-Postal Subscription Sales	Multiple Copy Sales	Sub-Total Circulation	Full Rate Sales	Lesser Rate Sales	Pre-Paid Non-Postal Subscription Sales	Multiple Copy Sales	
National Morning Popular												
The Mirror	2,222,151	2,066,466	1,831,267	183,229	-	51,970	86,746	86,746	-	-	-	68,939
Daily Record	597,418	567,465	551,268	5,072	-	11,125	1,969	1,969	-	-	-	27,984
Daily Star	627,532	599,570	536,430	62,907	-	233	-	-	-	-	-	27,962
The Star - Republic of Ireland	101,445	4,741	3,422	1,319	-	-	96,579	96,394	185	-	-	125
The Sun	3,516,681	3,306,554	2,926,635	378,883	-	2,836	107,822	107,822	-	-	-	102,305
National Morning Mid Market												
Daily Express	959,233	915,256	840,422	22,997	15	51,822	4,020	4,020	-	-	-	39,957
The Daily Mail	2,463,986	2,367,636	2,264,077	26,911	-	76,648	9,051	9,051	-	-	-	87,299
National Morning Quality												
The Daily Telegraph	1,009,369	970,162	544,051	77,924	296,833	51,354	3,996	3,996	-	-	-	35,201
Financial Times	461,888	162,681	138,465	4,154	801	19,261	5,260	4,540	3	-	717	293,947
The Guardian	397,411	351,442	331,343	3,843	-	16,256	3,952	3,864	88	-	-	42,017
The Independent	223,155	191,739	158,167	1,616	396	31,560	2,086	2,086	-	-	-	29,330
The Scotsman	85,021	84,992	74,112	699	133	10,048	-	-	-	-	-	29
The Times	701,142	646,450	451,004	52,689	93,561	49,196	5,172	5,172	-	-	-	49,520
National Morning Group												
The Mirror / Daily Record	2,819,569	2,633,931	2,382,535	188,301	-	63,095	88,715	88,715	-	-	-	96,923
Daily Star / The Star - Republic of Ireland	728,977	604,311	539,852	64,226	-	233	96,579	96,394	185	-	-	28,087
National Sunday Popular												
News of the World	4,051,360	3,785,970	1,810,117	1,973,021	-	2,832	158,014	158,014	-	-	-	107,376
Sunday Mail	701,523	671,316	653,310	4,638	-	13,368	3,074	3,074	-	-	-	27,133
Sunday Mirror	1,868,622	1,752,339	1,565,370	135,156	-	51,813	49,585	49,585	-	-	-	66,596
Sunday People	1,400,576	1,295,395	1,265,992	88	-	29,315	63,784	63,784	-	-	-	41,397
Sunday Sport	196,091	196,091	196,091	-	-	-	-	-	-	-	-	-
National Sunday Mid Market												
Sunday Express	888,148	843,187	808,742	2,969	15	31,461	5,687	5,687	-	-	-	39,274
The Mail on Sunday	2,407,481	2,305,467	2,147,793	75,670	-	82,004	20,468	20,468	-	-	-	81,546
National Sunday Quality												
Independent on Sunday	234,012	195,936	147,135	8,656	256	39,889	5,269	5,269	-	-	-	32,787
The Observer	460,825	412,344	370,099	1,787	724	39,734	10,471	10,465	6	-	-	38,010
Scotland on Sunday	87,463	87,368	83,477	583	-	3,308	-	-	-	-	-	85
Sunday Business	55,211	52,211	24,174	7,542	1,945	18,550	-	-	-	-	-	3,000
The Sunday Telegraph	787,109	754,784	227,980	199,885	290,712	36,227	4,274	4,274	-	-	-	26,051
The Sunday Times	1,316,206	1,155,142	948,380	85,385	91,879	29,596	90,796	90,774	22	-	-	70,268

Figure 6.11
National newspaper ABC Audited Circulation figures for the UK and the Republic of Ireland for July 2001 (Source: ABC)

activities

1. Newspapers may play down news items that would not be good for their profits. Make a list of possible news topics that a newspaper could play down in order to safeguard valuable advertising accounts.

2. The more newspapers are sold, the more profit is made. This can lead to varying degrees of hyping and sensationalism. Try to find examples of stories that have been exaggerated, in your opinion, simply to sell more papers.

3. Try to find examples of the same story in several different newspapers. Compare the story as it appears in, for example, a morning broadsheet, a tabloid and, if possible, an alternative newspaper. Use the checklist below as a guide for your comparison.
- How is the headline different?
- Do the story facts agree?
- Is one of the aspect of the story given more emphasis than another?
- Is there any difference in the language used?

- Is there any difference in the targeted audience?
- Is there any obvious bias?

Write a comparison of these different versions of 'truthful' reporting.

4. Make a list of the kind of people who never appear to be given a fair chance to put their views in print. Be careful to distinguish, however, between a teenager merely appearing in the news and teenagers being given a fair chance to say what they think about the issues that concern them.

5. Look at the cartoon at left (figure 6.12), then consider these questions.
- Is the press itself a watchdog or a lapdog (a tame pet)? In other words, whose interests do they look out for?
- What powerful groups would be capable of keeping the press under control?
- What influences could or should work against this?

Figure 6.12
Many critics feel that the press is not sufficiently regulated in Britain. The Press Complaints Commission (PCC) is made up of people from within the industry and has no legal powers.

major assignment

Written assignment

Choose one of the following tasks and write a 600-word response.

1. Analyse the front-page layout of a modern newspaper and the front page of a newspaper that is at least fifty years old (there are several collections of historic front pages available in book form). Compare the layout, the use of white space, advertising, photographs and typefaces. Evaluate the particular audience appeal of each front page. Conclude with your opinion about progress in the print media.

2. Evaluate the newspapers in your area against the criteria suggested by Hirsch and Gordon (see p. 403). Also consider the purposes of newspapers. How well are your selected newspapers fulfilling these criteria?

Print Media Readership

Of all the media, print is the one where establishing precise figures for the size of the audience presents the most difficulties. Analysts continue to discuss not only what makes up the actual number of people who read any given publication, but also even what exactly constitutes the act of reading itself.

Raymond Kent points out that some readers only glance casually through publications, while others spend hours carefully consuming every last word. Circulation figures have their limitations, too – as most print organisations will swiftly point out, many more people read newspapers and magazines than actually buy them.

Nevertheless, as with all other media enterprises, some calculation of audience size and type is crucial: for helping to set advertising rates, above all else.

In the publishing world, there are no state subsidies. A good deal of revenue comes from sales, but income from advertising is far greater.

National Readership Survey

Since 1992, the National Readership Survey (NRS) has been the principal means through which figures on readership levels have been calculated. Various methods have been used over the years. Computer-assisted personal interviewing (CAPI) was introduced as the NRS was set up. This continues to be the main method employed, although subsequently computer-assisted telephone interviewing (CATI) was also adopted.

Funded by a mixture of the industry, advertisers and the agencies, the NRS functions as an independent body, and provides quarterly reports. Drawing on a sample of people aged from fifteen years upwards, it seeks to establish readership levels and patterns across the whole of the UK.

The other body that monitors sales figures is the Audit Bureau of Circulation (ABC).

Patterns in sales

After a downward sales trend that has lasted thirty years, we cannot blind ourselves to what is happening. Fewer people are prepared to buy a paper every morning. They feel they can get their news – if they want it at all – from other sources.

Roy Greenslade,
The Guardian, G2, 17 January 2000

▼ ▼ ▼

National newspaper sales have been in steady decline for a long time. With the rise in alternative sources of news (television, radio and now the Internet), fewer people than ever are willing to buy a daily paper. The tabloids especially have seen significant falls: *The Sun* sold half a million copies fewer in 2000 than in 1994.

Broadsheets did slightly better, with some managing to increase sales. The reason for this is partly to do with their greater credibility in comparison to their red-top rivals: they attract a much more committed reader. At the same time, they have also adopted many of the concepts of the tabloids: greater use of popular news coverage, expanded sections on life-style and entertainment, extensive use of colour photography. Even with all this, only *The Financial Times* managed a significant increase – and the bulk of those were overseas.

Nevertheless, the scale of the tabloids should not be underestimated. On combined sales of more than ten million, their reach is reckoned to be nearer thirty million actual readers. The broadsheets manage sales of around 2.8 million, or some 8.5 million readers.

When the figures for the middle market papers are added in (some 3.3 million sales), it is clear that the vast bulk of the adult population are still exposed to a newspaper each day. It seems unlikely that they are in danger of disappearing, at least not in the near future!

Newspaper institutions

BACKGROUND The history of the press in Britain makes for a fascinating study. O'Sullivan details how independent publications began to appear from the early years of the eighteenth century onwards. Industrialisation in the later part of the century and rapid increases in the populations of cities led to appalling living conditions for many. This in turn fuelled considerable agitation for improvements –

some very radical pamphlets advocated revolutionary responses, especially after the French beheaded their monarch!

EARLY HISTORY Curran in particular has documented with considerable detail and interest how governments of the time first sought to suppress many of these publications by way of taxation. For many years, this policy failed miserably, as publishers simply refused to pay, and concealed their operations instead. Only in the middle of the nineteenth century did the authorities begin to succeed, when they actually *abolished* these taxes. From that point on, growing commercialisation forced most of the more radical presses out of business. More varied and higher-quality-finish publications became increasingly popular. The costs of production meant that single-perspective political publications could not compete.

Above all, advertising took hold in the newer papers and helped turn them into considerable businesses. At the same time, it exerted no little influence over the outlook that they maintained. Radicalism did not suit the purveyors of manufactured goods. A stable society was needed to encourage the people to buy things. From virtually the outset, capitalism recognised the importance and usefulness of the newspaper industry – and took steps to make sure it had control of it.

RECENT HISTORY The press in Britain underwent a significant period of development in the last part of the twentieth century: several factors contributed to this.

Without doubt, the greatest catalyst was the arrival of Rupert Murdoch. His relaunch of the *Sun* as a tabloid paper was probably the single most influential newspaper event of the century, both in terms of what it established as its own identity and in the impact it had on its rivals – not to speak of its effect on society.

Much later, his removal of operations to the new 'fortress' that was Wapping was to shake up the whole industry in yet other ways.

THE SUN ALSO RISES Since its rebirth in 1969, when Murdoch took over, the *Sun* has been keen to promote an image of itself as a lively, outspoken and populist publication. It often struck out at its targets in bold and hostile language, and has never been shy of venting its opinions on its receptive readers.

In those early days, it was much criticised for debasing standards of journalism – if not of society as a whole. Bare breasts on page three became a notorious rallying point, for both supporters and critics alike. At the same time, its irreverent attitude towards authority, particularly the royals, endeared it to many people of very different social and professional backgrounds.

In commercial terms, it turned an ailing concern into a 'soaraway' success. A circulation of fewer than one million was eventually to peak at well over four million. By 1978, it had overtaken its chief rival, *The Daily Mirror*, and was firmly established as the biggest-selling newspaper in the United Kingdom.

Other tabloids felt they had no choice but to copy its sex-saturated style. During the 1980s, obsession with television, celebrities, sport and, above all, the private lives of personalities in them came to dominate. This was the case not only on the inside and back pages, but increasingly on the front pages as well, where once the news had been firmly established. In effect, these items became the *new* news.

FLEET STREET DECLINES For a very long time, the publication of newspapers had come to be associated with the address in London where many of them had their presses: Fleet Street.

Early in 1986, however, Rupert Murdoch signalled the end of this historic association when he had all of his newspaper operations *secretly* transferred to a new headquarters. Surrounded by a steel fence topped off with razor wire, the new premises at Wapping had the appearance of a bunker that was designed to keep out hostile forces. There was good reason for this.

Thousands of employees were sacked and trades unions mounted large and angry pickets around the building. The protests were fierce and sustained. However, they proved inadequate in the face of the careful preparations made by Newscorp, Murdoch's company. Supported by the government, and protected by a heavy police presence, the new centre functioned well enough to cope immediately. This was thanks also, it must be said, to the willing support of the electricians' union – despite furious protests from fellow unions.

A simultaneous switch to new computer-based technology, to replace the old metal printing presses, soon led to significant increases in profitability. Before the year was up, the *Sun* alone was making more than a million pounds a year for the parent company, News International Ltd.

▼ ▼ ▼

It is almost impossible to underestimate the importance of the move to Wapping in the history of the Murdoch business. When he moved the papers to Wapping, the profits of his UK operation skyrocketed; and they rose at a time when he had serious financial problems. He had borrowed money all over the world to expand his business ... and he had to pay interest on that. The profits that he made every year as a result of moving to Wapping paid the interest on those loans. If he hadn't moved to Wapping, he would probably have gone bust.

Christopher Hird, author and film-maker

▼ ▼ ▼

On the other hand, it is also the case that the National Graphical Association (NGA), the old print unions, had an effective stranglehold over the way in which the industry was run. Costly manning levels and skill demarcations were preventing much-needed new investment. Only after this move was it possible to introduce the use of colour, for instance.

There are, however, tremendous social costs that still have to be weighed against the financial success of this industry. Many people lost their jobs; many more were arrested and sent to court simply for protesting about this. The full apparatus of the state was used to support this drastic action by one of the major employers in the newspaper industry.

THE PRESS COMPLAINTS COMMISSION The Press Complaints Commission (PCC) is the body responsible for dealing with apparent failures to keep to the code. It responds mainly to complaints from members of the public. It is made up largely of people from within the industry and has no legal powers. Moreover, it has long been criticised for being too lenient in its judgments, even within its limited capacities.

In reply, it insists it is much tougher now than previously. Also, it points out that the only alternative would be to introduce a stronger body to govern what can and cannot be printed in newspapers. A statutory body would have to be constituted by law and monitored by government. Political approval for free speech would be the outcome of this – a potentially very dangerous situation for democracy.

Many have questioned, however, the real importance of the topics that some newspapers have felt free to speak about. The private lives of celebrities and heart-tugging tales of individual suffering are not exactly fundamental to the survival of democracy.

THE NEW PRESS CODE The newspaper industry is regulated by a voluntary code that is intended to restrain it from the worst of its tendency towards excess.

This code was tightened considerably following the death of Diana, Princess of Wales. The *paparazzi* (freelance journalists and photographers who specialise in celebrity stories) who were chasing her car at the time of its fatal crash were felt by many to bear much of the blame for it. The resulting pressure to curb this element of the press led to many severe changes to the code. Even though the French judge investigating the crash later cleared the press altogether (the driver was found to be well over the alcohol limit), the changes have remained.

How rigorously the new code has been applied is another matter, however. The *Sun* notoriously broke it when it ran a big feature on 'SOPHIE TOPLESS', in May 1999. Only a few weeks before she was due to marry Prince Edward, holiday snaps of Sophie Rhys-Jones were splashed across several pages. Making matters much worse, it also later emerged that a glimpse of nipple in one of the main photos had been digitally grafted on, to 'enhance' the picture.

Critics from within television, particularly, point out that there are no effective punishments for breaking this code. Television companies can and do get fined – heavily, in some cases – by a separate regulatory body, if they break their own code. Newspapers, by contrast, only get told off, by a body of their peers.

There have been some very serious cases where newspapers have failed to abide by the requirements of the new code. In one case, at *The Mirror*, editor Piers Morgan was found to have profited from the share-purchasing tips his journalists were giving in their column. Suspected prior knowledge was a clear breach of the supposed stringency of the new code: yet all he received was a reprimand from the Press Complaints Commission.

Defenders of the system have suggested that the dishonour this brings is far more painful to people in this position than any mere monetary sanction. Others have different views on the enduring impact of such punishments.

Newspaper products

There is something of a paradox in the current provision of newspapers in the United Kingdom. Per head, we have one of the largest readerships of most countries in the Western world. The sheer number of *national* daily papers is virtually unrivalled. Yet parts of the industry are experiencing year-on-year declines in overall sales. Tabloids, especially, are steadily contracting.

Broadsheets, on the whole, are holding up in sales, if not expanding slightly. Few are economically viable, yet none seems to be ready to give up the ghost. Today, newspapers are mostly owned as part of a whole range of media and other interests, and are typically valued mostly for the influence that they bring once more.

Sales in most publications tend towards a steady decline. The *Daily Mail* and the *Financial Times* stand out against this trend: others fluctuate, but rarely sustain growth for more than a few months.

THE NATIONAL PRESS The market here has in some ways grown more diverse over the past ten years or so. There are three main types of daily newspaper: tabloid, broadsheet and middle-market publications. Until fairly recently, the only significant variation to this were the Sunday newspapers at the weekend. These have traditionally taken more of an overview of events. It is not so much what has happened just the day before that they report on, as how major developments have shaped up over the previous week, or even longer.

Today, many papers have also invested considerable money and effort in developing the style and contents of their Saturday publications, too. With some, it is no longer a question of difference of *kind*, but rather of title alone. The *Guardian* does not publish on Sundays; otherwise, its Saturday edition, with its ever-increasing pull-out sections and supplements, is more like its sister paper, *The Observer*, than it is the rest of the week's output. The same is true of other Saturday papers. The *Financial Times' Weekend* has been outstandingly successful in this respect.

On the other hand, the overall number of titles has declined also; even more significantly, the number of organisations that actually own those that remain has shrunk even further. Between 1947 and 1990, three leading media groups increased their ownership of newspapers by more than one-third, to a point where they owned some 60 per cent of *all* publications in this country, and *more than three-quarters* of the national papers.

In the early part of the twentieth century, the 'Press Barons' – wealthy magnates, often elevated into peerages – owned newspapers largely for social prestige. That, and for the moral and political influence ownership afforded them. As the century unfolded, the patterns of ownership, as well as the reasons for them, gradually shifted. The years following World War II saw the growth of a new breed of businessman-proprietor. Around the 1970s and 1980s, conglomerate ownership began to take over. Large multinational organisations, with diverse business interests around the world, bought up newspapers as part of their portfolio of interests. Their owners made no bones about using their possessions to further their wider business interests. Many of the old centre-Left papers had already been squeezed out of the market, by the steady withdrawal of advertising. Now, increasingly strident support for right-wing parties was taking over. On *The Observer*, *The Times* and *The Sun*, especially, proprietors made clear the views that they wished to see represented – and, in some notorious cases, the topics that they did not. Curran and Seaton have charted with careful detail the fates of those journalists who did not subscribe to the new agendas.

Electronic newspapers

The electronic newspaper has several advantages. It never arrives late, wet or in the shrubbery, points out Mike Gordon, managing editor of an on-line newspaper at the *Atlanta Journal-Constitution* in the United States.

The number of on-line newspapers available on the Internet nearly doubled every year during the 1990s. Experts predicted the total number would exceed 2000 when the increase finally stabilised. Most of these are supplements to the big traditional newspaper titles. But so far, no on-line newspaper has yet made any real money.

For the Internet surfer, the flood of electronic newspapers means he or she can get local news from anywhere in the world. A Londoner in Australia can get same-day news of home from *The Guardian* on-line. At the same time, a Sydney-sider in London can subscribe to the *Sydney Morning Herald* for the same reason. Both can connect to the *New York Times* to see what is happening in the 'Big Apple' – and then follow on by reading a Japanese electronic newspaper.

THE DEATH OF NEWSPRINT?

Every new medium is predicted to kill whatever existed before. When Caxton first cranked his printing press, I expect people thought that folk songs were finished. Television was predicted to destroy radio; radio has never been more popular. Television was predicted to eliminate cinemas; cinema has never had healthier attendances and advertising revenues.

Not long ago the experts were predicting that the Internet would sound the death knell for conventional media. It would begin to exterminate the printed word, they said.

Rubbish.

Rupert Howell, President of
the Independent Press Association,
The Guardian, 13 March 2000

▼ ▼ ▼

The economics of publishing may give electronic newspapers the push they need. It is estimated to be 400 times cheaper to distribute via the Internet than to print on paper – an enormously expensive commodity in itself. Start-up costs are much lower, too. Traditional printing presses cost millions of pounds. The computer servers used in running an electronic newspaper can be purchased for less than 1 per cent of the cost of a printing press. Unless they are forced to, however, people will not change medium until the product offered is significantly better.

Many electronic newspaper professionals feel that the magic number is ten – they have to be ten times better than the original product before

Figure 6.13
Even electronic newspaper industry professionals say that the traditional newspaper will be around for many years to come. Paper is a very useful technology.

people will consider changing. At the moment, they say, the product is not even half as good.

On-line newspapers are up against consumer laziness as well. Imagine a situation where you had to order your newspaper every day over the phone. Many people would find it too much trouble and would not subscribe. That is exactly the situation in which on-line newspapers are positioned.

Young professionals are the hope of the industry. Many of them have access to the Internet and e-mail at work. Reading the electronic morning paper at work may become a habit for them in the future.

Classified advertising is another weak spot for the traditional newspaper. The classifieds are the lifeblood of the newspaper, but a costly necessity for businesses. The prospect of reducing their advertising costs may encourage high-volume advertisers onto the Internet. Many real estate agents are already using the Internet to publicise their wares.

However, print is definitely the 'mother ship' for now. A survey of on-line newspaper editors conducted by journalist David Cracknell revealed them all to be enthusiastic about the survival of print. The electronic newspaper was seen as a being only a supplement – a different way of transmitting information. Newspaper owners and employees need to think of themselves as being in the information supply business. They cannot continue thinking they are just in the newspaper publishing business, advises Michael Hooker.

▼ ▼ ▼

Remington and Underwood saw themselves as being in the typewriter business. IBM saw itself as being in the word processing business. The rest is history.'

Mike Hooker, former President
of the University of Massachusetts

▼ ▼ ▼

All of these companies were powerful market leaders in their time, but they failed to move with new technology and were left behind by new arrivals keen to exploit the possibilities they saw in developing new products.

THE STORY SO FAR

Morgan Cartwright, On-line Manager for the *San Francisco Examiner*, says that most electronic newspapers have not yet succeeded in establishing themselves as popular enterprises. He cites the following reasons for their failure so far.

► **LACK OF CLEAR OBJECTIVES** Most simply repeat the 'wide-trawl' of traditional newspapers, but the Internet is actually about fine-targeting.

► **FAILURE TO MARKET** Publishers have not realised the need to *promote* these new products in a fiercely competitive area.

► **SALARIES** This is a problematic area. In other e-jobs, web staff command keen salaries. To recruit the right calibre of people, these have to be matched; yet, if they are, other staff on the papers are liable to complain.

► **INSUFFICIENT CAPITAL** In most cases, nowhere near enough is allocated to make the product attractive.

► **POOR MANAGEMENT** Not enough priority is given to what is needed to launch a significant new product.

THE PURPOSES OF ELECTRONIC NEWSPAPERS

The functions of an electronic newspaper are similar to those of a conventional print newspaper (see pp. 401–3).

Some say there is an additional function. We are experiencing an information explosion. It is beyond any individual to keep up with it. According to Chris Lapham, an on-line newspaper consultant, the most important function of an electronic newspaper may be to make sense of this avalanche of information. Defining what is news may be more important now than ever, Lapham says. Electronic newspapers have a duty to provide quality journalism and expert commentary.

THE FEATURES OF ELECTRONIC NEWSPAPERS

If you think you can dump the contents of today's edition on to the network and win subscribers, you're wrong. Paper is paper. A screen is something else. It isn't only that you *can* do different things on a screen. You *must*. Text on a screen is not newsprint, not a magazine, nor a book.

Melinda McAdams
Driving a Newspaper on the Data Highway

▼ ▼ ▼

Those organisations that have not recognised the special qualities of the new medium have been accused of dumping 'shovelware' into their on-line newspapers. Shovelware is defined as loads of text from the traditional print newspaper thrown on-line without changes.

Instead of being print on the screen, the new on-line journalism tells the story using the best techniques of the novel – and television, not to mention radio and also the data-bases of CD-ROM. Joseph Quittner, in an article for *Hotwired*, coined a term for it – 'way new journalism'.

▼ ▼ ▼

Like any on-line information product, a good translation of a newspaper to the Internet should use the power of computing. It should present information in a contextual (related using hypertext), searchable, and sortable manner.

As community resources the on-line additions should use the new media to build community, ask questions and host conversations of community members.

A depth of original 'made for on-line' content must be created and experimented with if we are ever going to learn how to story tell on-line.

Elizabeth Osder,
Content Development Editor
The *New York Times* Electronic
Media Company

▼ ▼ ▼

POSITIVE FEATURES

THE BOTTOMLESS NEWS HOLE Electronic newspapers have a *news hole* that is close to infinite. The news hole is a term for the total area left in a newspaper after the advertising space has been filled up. In the newsprint version subeditors ruthlessly cut stories to fit the allocated space that is available. A lot of information that will not fit in traditional newspapers can be included in the electronic versions. Stories with extended backgrounds can be included, along with accompanying maps and other graphics. The journalist can write to fully cover the story, rather than squeeze the facts into the space. Instead of being limited to a restricted coverage of the Budget, for example, some electronic newspapers have also included the whole Budget paper.

SEARCHES The opportunity for the reader to conduct searches of the electronic newspaper's database is one its most appealing features. A reader can enter keywords on any topic and search the newspaper right back to the first edition, if they want. All stories with the keywords in them will be listed in date order and the reader can access the desired story.

INDEXES These are another kind of searching mechanism available in some electronic newspapers. An index is useful for consumer information and access to the classifieds. For example, a reader can ask for all advertisements for a particular make of car to be indexed from the most expensive to the cheapest. Comparisons can be more easily made.

INTERACTIVITY Many people advocate electronic newspaper journalism as a way to reconnect with readers, says Wendell Cochran. Papers are experimenting with reader forums on selected subject areas. The community manages its own discussion without editorial control from the newspaper. Some see the electronic newspaper as a new kind of public space – like the Speakers' Corner in London's Hyde Park, with its traditions of people of all political persuasions sounding off about anything they choose. In the electronic newspapers, news presentations are often accompanied by opportunities for readers to join discussions.

The electronic newspaper can also be a source of people power. Some journalists are including details of how readers might take political action. For example, a story on Internet censorship may provide the e-mail addresses of government members, 'gopher' sites where legislation can be downloaded, access to relevant protest campaigns, news groups and so on.

THE 'DAILY ME' Interactivity can also mean readers can personalise their newspaper and select only the type of news they want to know about. David Cracknell suggests readers may want to access favourite topics, edit out boring news and even

Figure 6.14
The on-line newspaper requires a different approach to the presentation of information. Newspapers are experimenting in the hope of discovering the successful formula.

print up a 'Daily Me' on their home printer. Specific customers can get specific news.

MULTIMEDIA Multimedia frees up the printed page from its two-dimensional limits. Pictures are 'clickable' and a news photograph can become a short video with sound. Some companies are planning to develop television documentaries tied to stories in newspapers. This would be supplemented by more information also available in a multimedia format on-line.

NEGATIVE FEATURES

LIMITATIONS OF COMPUTER NETWORKS The Internet is agonisingly slow, even with a fast modem. Squinting to read a long newspaper story can be a frustrating experience. You also have to pay for the time that you are connected. The delays are expected to increase as electronic newspapers begin to make more use of multimedia. Waiting to download pictures and soundbites will be a disincentive for the busy professionals the papers are aiming at. The time taken to access different screens turns many people off the hypertext links (see p. 60) the electronic newspapers offer. In contrast, turning the page of a newspaper seems effortless – even on a windy station platform.

SCREEN LIMITATIONS The standard size screen does not allow a full page to be shown. The relative efficiency of paper is obvious – the eye can rove as it pleases. Screens are not portable. Even laptop computers are difficult to read in sunlight. Their screens are smaller than the standard screen size and so their disadvantages are magnified.

THE RELAXATION FACTOR Settling down with a newspaper can be a source of relaxation. Readers feel a sense of contentment that is lacking when they sit in front of a computer screen. Advertisers are concerned about this. Advertisements are not as effective if people have to search them out and click on them. If people are not relaxed, they will not be as receptive to the message of the advertisement.

AUDIENCE ISSUES

Whereas the Internet has proved the perfect harbinger of niche interests, serving individuals' peculiar tastes and diverse geographical demands, newspapers and national broadcasters are traditionally great generalists. They often seem ill-at-ease on the Internet: able to provide a breadth of information but unwilling to dig down to meet the diverse and specialist demands of their users.

Patrick Barkham, *Media Guardian*,
14 February 2000

▼ ▼ ▼

On-line newspapers have a problem when it comes to audience research. That also translates into a problem convincing advertisers that they can guarantee an audience. The great majority of online advertising is bound up in a very small number of large sites. Convincing advertisers of reach is the crux of the problem.

Traditional newspapers have always been good at delivering reliable demographics information to advertisers. Advertisers are willing to place millions of pounds worth of advertising in traditional newspapers because there is a long history of effective audience measurement.

There is no reliable way of telling how many people visit an on-line newspaper or what they do once they get there. According to Judy Black, who is working on demographic guidelines for on-line papers, the usual method of counting 'hits' is highly unreliable. Statistics on audience age and income are also unavailable for the electronic newspaper.

Web visitors are often reluctant to register by name or location. However, it is technically possible for websites to record details of each individual's identity. There is even an identifying signal called a 'cookie', which can be lodged in the visitor's hard drive and activated each time they return.

For commercial operators such as electronic newspapers, the use of these methods is not likely to be widely accepted. The privacy issues involved are still the subject of public debate.

CONTEXT

Originally all of the news media operated within the context of a one-to-many model of media communication. Information came from the top and was disseminated downwards to the general public. What the public actually thought about the news was of only minor interest.

Analysts of the Internet propose that it works in a different way on computer networks. News bubbles up from the bottom and winds its way upward from there, says Chris Lapham.

On-line newspapers have yet to wake up to the context of the Internet, according Jon Katz in *Wired* magazine. He says the real power in electronic newspapers is still held by a few editors in the editorial conference rooms. Readers have no more power than they do in a traditional paper.

According to Jack Lail of the New Information Technology Committee, there may be another contextual issue for electronic newspapers. Advertisers do not find them to be a strong drawcard. While traditional newspapers may get X per cent of their revenue dollars from advertisers and X per cent from subscribers, the reverse may be true for the electronic newspapers.

One thing that stays the same is the role of the journalist in the news organisation. The most expensive piece of capital equipment a newspaper has is its printing press. However, the most valuable asset is the team of journalists in the newsroom and the network of human contacts they have built up with the community.

It is the human touch that may be the key to success in the new environment. The insightful writer making sense of reality will be in high demand in the new media.

▼ ▼ ▼ ▼ ▼ ▼

1. Compare the size of the 'news hole' for the main story in a traditional newspaper and the main story in an electronic newspaper. Estimate the number of words in the traditional version and compare it with the on-line version.

Follow all of the hypertext links available in the on-line story and count the additional words found on these links. Have the on-line versions lived up to the analysts' predictions of infinite news holes?

2. Find an example of an electronic newspaper article or column that encourages readers to take action on a particular issue and provides them with the necessary information to do so.

3. Cut out a traditional newspaper story and convert it to an electronic article aimed at building citizens' action or 'people power'. Add various hypertext links to the bottom of the article to make it more interactive.

Discuss the likely effects on the political scene of this sort of reader action.

4. 'Way new journalism' is a term used by Joseph Quittner to describe the special features of electronic newspaper journalism. Select a traditional news story and plan a conversion to the new style. List the changes you would make.

Written assignment

Write a 600-word response to the following task.

Compare several electronic newspaper sites. Draw up criteria for evaluation before visiting each site. For example, you could compare the effectiveness of their search facilities, their interactivity, the extent of shovelware, the scope of news coverage and the size of the news hole, etc.

Production assignment

Select a front page from a recent edition of a newspaper. Redesign it as the opening screen of an electronic newspaper. Lay out the screen design on a sheet of paper the same dimensions as a computer screen. Mock up the masthead (title) and use colour as required. Hypertext links can be indicated through the use of colour, as in a computer screen.

Remember, a screen is not as big as a full newspaper page, so some information will have to be reduced to headings and links. The links can be to information somewhere else in the system. Describe where 'clickable' pictures and sound can be used for full effect on the page. Include a separate page explaining your decisions.

The Editorial

The editorial is the newspaper's official opinion or comment on the news. Sometimes it is called a *leader*, suggesting a discussion of the leading news of the day. It is not always written by the actual editor, but will be representative of the paper's general outlook. Good editorials will also give leadership in public affairs.

Types of editorial

Newspaper editorials can usually be divided into two categories: editorials that give opinions and editorials that explain.

► **EDITORIALS THAT GIVE OPINIONS** The main purpose for the writer in this common type of editorial is to persuade the reader to accept the newspaper's point of view. This is achieved by setting out the arguments that prove the opinion is correct and right. The language chosen is usually very persuasive, and can be very emotive, depending on the particular newspaper.

► **EDITORIALS THAT EXPLAIN** The writer's purpose in an interpretative editorial is to explain the news events to the reader without suggesting that one point of view is right. This is done by

diagnosing the news, explaining or predicting the news without giving arguments in support of an opinion. This editorial aims to inform rather than persuade. The language chosen is more neutral. Explanatory editorials are rare in modern newspapers.

The purposes of the editorial

The editorial fulfils several of the key functions of a newspaper. It leads opinion, it reflects opinion (although the range of opinion is limited) and it explains the news.

The editorial is the flagship of the newspaper's function in democracy. The opinion-leading role of the newspaper is seen as vital to the way it functions as the Fourth Estate of democracy (see p. 401).

The institutional context

The editorial or leader is not necessarily written by the editor. Most newspapers have their senior journalists write the editorials, although there is usually lengthy consultation with newspaper executives beforehand.

Topics for editorials will often be decided only on the day prior to publication. Generally, editorials deal with more weighty, ongoing topics and are not so much concerned with less important events or what has occurred that day only. Nevertheless, they do seek to highlight very current matters. Should a dramatic change take place around a chosen subject, an editorial could not afford to seem unaware of it.

The editor would normally have the final say on the selection of items to be covered in the editorial/s of the day.

Representation issues

There is surprisingly little variation in the general viewpoint of editorials. According to Noam Chomsky, all media enterprises 'serve the interests of state and corporate power'. Major newspapers may criticise particular policies of government, but on the whole they do not fundamentally challenge the institutions of state. Papers do not support widely different interest groups. Instead, they have mostly moved to a position on the conservative

side of the centre of the range of possible opinions. Even liberal left-inclined publications such as *The Guardian* generally support the current form of elective democracy.

Through out the 1980s and 1990s, most newspaper editorials accepted or actively supported the approach to national financial management known as 'economic rationalism'. Many argued forcefully for cuts to government spending, reductions in welfare and privatisation of state-owned industries. Most also supported the 'user pays' approach to higher education: the abolition of student grants and the introduction tuition fees. Editorial writers have not explained or supported alternatives to the economic rationalist model. This is despite a large segment of the community holding views opposed to the strictures imposed by economic rationalism.

In the past, British newspapers have rarely supported the election of Labour governments. In the early 1990s, the *Sun* famously claimed to have won the election for the Tory party, when it looked likely that their opponents were finally about to break their grip on government. Following this defeat, the Labour Party repositioned itself as a more conservative party in its policies, occupying the middle ground of politics. To make itself a winner, it felt it was necessary to drop much that distinguished it from its rival's outlook.

If the outlook of newspapers cannot easily be shifted, the orientation of political parties, it seems, can be.

The audience

Readership is the term normally used to describe the audience for newspapers. This is not the same thing as the number of copies they actually sell. Many more people read a newspaper than buy one. First of all, there is the natural recycling of newspapers around the members of a family or among friends, colleagues and so on. In addition, many producers also enter into bulk sales arrangements with particular outlets, such as hotels and other places with a large throughput of people.

The nature of readerships, of course, varies widely according to the kind of paper in question. Tabloids and broadsheets have quite different markets – although there is a very small amount of crossover, too.

Editors of broadsheets like to believe that the editorial is read by the well-educated reader with an interest in public affairs. The reading level of the editorial is often set a little higher than that of the front page news story. With tabloid papers, the editorial is largely used to deliver short, punchy messages – often reinforcing, if not creating, populist perceptions of very current events. Reading levels can vary considerably from paper to paper. Some tabloid newspapers even underline the main points in an effort to encourage people to read on.

Part I	The statement or news peg
Part II	The development of logical argument
Part III	The conclusion or kick

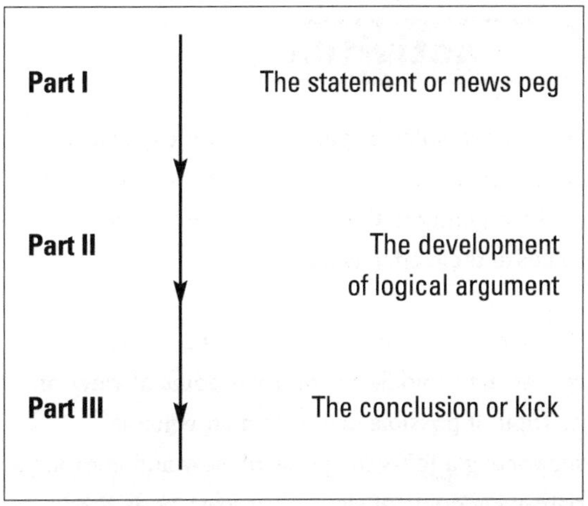

Figure 6.15
A diagram of the progress of an editorial or leader.

How to write an editorial

There is a story about a fiery editorial writer for *The Times* who was found slumped dead over his typewriter. There was a sheet of paper in the machine on which was typed one word: 'Notwithstanding …'. He was ever ready to begin an argument, even with death.

Like the editor of *The Times*, the editorial writer need only start at the beginning. However, a logical course needs to be followed to the end so that the readers are not left up in the air. The editorial is one of the most demanding and complex pieces of writing found in a newspaper.

Parts of an editorial

The editorial is most often written in three parts.

► the *statement of the subject* or the *news peg* on which the argument is hung. The subject is decided in an editorial conference. Normally it takes about one paragraph of fifty words to outline the subject.
► the *development of the argument* or the *expansion of the subject* takes up most of the editorial. The main points of the argument are given separate paragraphs. Paragraph length varies from about thirty words to around seventy words.
► the *kick* or the *conclusion* is where the writer drives home the point of his argument and delivers the kick. This sums up the editorial.

If a diagram were to be drawn showing the progress of the three-part editorial it would look similar to figure 6.15.

The title

The purpose of the title is the same as that of a news story headline. A good title will arouse interest and at the same time tell the reader what the editorial is about.

Layout of the editorial

Most newspapers use a vertical layout for their editorials. More rarely, a newspaper will lay out its editorials horizontally across the top of its page.

Newspapers often carry editorials on two, or even more topics. One is called the leader and the other/s the subleader.

▼ ▼ ▼ ▼ ▼ ▼ ▼

activities

1. Find examples of persuasive and explanatory editorials. In your own words, list the main points of the arguments the editorials make or examine. Evaluate their effectiveness.

2. Try to find an editorial that does not take a mainstream, middle-of-the-road point of view on its topic. If possible, try to find an editorial supporting a left-wing point of view and another a right-wing point of view; or at least ones that adopt opposing views on a given topic. Discuss the points of view raised and comment on the evidence used to support them.

3. Choose a topic and write a three-part editorial taking a strong point of view. Selectively present arguments and evidence to support the exposition. Conclude with a kick.

major assignment

Written assignment

Write a 600-word response to the task below.

Analyse a range of editorials, using the following headings as a guide.

▶ type of editorial
▶ structure – three-part or other?
▶ political opinion
▶ nature of language used (see p. 391 for Mode of Address).

Evaluate the persuasiveness of the editorials.

Production assignment

The arguments and facts for an editorial have been prepared. The notes are not in any special order. They must be rearranged and expanded. You may add some of your own ideas. You may like to leave out some from the notes.

Write them up into a powerful 400-word editorial persuading people that the slaughter on the roads must stop. Remember the three-part pattern:

▶ the statement of subject

▶ the expansion of the argument in a logical manner
▶ the kick.

▼ ▼ ▼

A major insurance company has made a detailed plea for more effective campaigns against the slaughter on British roads.

The car driver in Japan will often see in the distance a traffic officer sitting on his motor cycle by the side of the road. But as the driver gets closer, probably slowing down if he has been speeding, it becomes apparent that the officer – in most cases – is a carefully constructed model. The use of the model implies a determination to deter accidents by reminding drivers that care is needed.

The Parliamentary Road Safety Committee's latest report, *Staysafe*, makes a valuable contribution to road safety by presenting a persuasive case against the practice of collecting fines.

The committee found that police resources were concentrated on relatively safe stretches of road instead of at danger spots. There was too much interest in dramatic high-speed chases and a concentration of 'fining a small arbitrary percentage of the bulk of motorists who breach the road rules'.

The insurance company AAMI had more than humanitarian motives behind its hard-hitting and no doubt costly appeal for road safety sanity.

Payouts to accident victims and their families are rapidly growing in size and number, and the industry has justifiable commercial concerns.

According to research, a likely victim of a road smash incorporated these qualities: he's young, probably between 19 and 23, and he's just been to a party where he's consumed an amount of alcohol. It's late at night, probably midnight or beyond.

Without thinking twice about the consequences – and probably not once – he gets behind the wheel of his car, or onto his motorcycle, and heads off. With only minutes to live, and possibly with the lives of several other young people entirely in his hands, he perhaps drives through a country area.

Intent on impressing his peer group, he puts his foot down. Excited by alcohol and speed, and possibly the thrill of the chase if he's got a mate behind or in front, the driver ignores the rising speedometer needle.

The thought of something going wrong doesn't enter his alcohol-affected mind. But it does happen. He, or his passengers, perhaps his girlfriend, die horribly in the mangled wreckage. Worse still, they survive, brutally injured by flying torn metal, only to spend the rest of their lives a vegetable, or confined to a hospital bed or a wheelchair.

It's not a numbers game, it's a game of common

sense. Until we instil that sense into our young the carnage will continue unabated.

If the cost of general motor premiums also rose dramatically, the need for careful and thoughtful driving might become even more obvious.

It would be a shame if the community ignored the realities of road carnage until insurance companies revolted and driving a car became an expensive and exclusive privilege.

One fact is certain. Most people can drive a car, even youngsters barely into their teens. Not so many people can drive a car well. Most survive the next drive. But, a number don't.

The News Story

There is of course wide variation in the length and writing styles of stories as they are covered in three main types of newspaper in the United Kingdom – i.e. tabloid, middle-market and broadsheet.

However, the methodology of *how* stories are constructed remains essentially the same no matter what the publication in which they appear.

The structure of the news story

With most fictional stories, the pattern tends to be to build slowly towards a climax: the end is where all is revealed. With newspapers it is different: the most important facts – often even the outcome – are delivered first, at the top of the story. The reader's attention must be secured at the outset. Only once it has does the narrative move on to reveal more of the details.

The news story places all of the important information in the early part of the story and gradually tails off with less interesting information. This pattern of organisation is known as the *inverted pyramid*.

The intro

The introductory paragraph, or intro, as journalists call it, is found immediately below the headline.

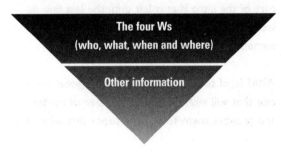

Since most headlines are written after the intro has already been finished, the intro could be called the most important party of the story.

The intro must 'sell' the story to the reader or else he or she will pass on to something more eye-catching. Most readers only scan the first few lines of a story before deciding whether or not it is interesting. The intro aims to attract by telling them what will interest them most.

Since the 1930s, the intro has answered four basic questions. They are 'Who?' 'What?' 'When?' and 'Where?'. Sometimes they may need to mention 'Why?' and 'How?'.

Journalists aim to write tightly and simply. All the important information has to be put across in as few words as possible. Most intros are only twenty-five words or less in length. Intros longer than this are in danger of crowding in too much for the reader to bother reading further.

Figure 6.16
The structure of a newspaper story is said to resemble an inverted pyramid. A huge breadth of information is at the top of the story. Just a few extra facts remain for those who read to the end.

WHO is a very important part of every intro. People are most of all interested in other people. Newspaper stories are about people. Tragedies, disasters, politics, good and bad fortunes and so on, are all about people.

Newspapers usually give people a label so that readers will know something about them and therefore relate to them right from the beginning of the story. This is the purpose of labels such as 'labourer' or 'youth'. It helps to place the person in the reader's mind. However, people who are well known to everybody will normally appear in the intro without a label. The Queen Mother would never be referred to as 'a woman' in a newspaper intro, for instance. Neither would Mel Gibson be labelled as 'an actor' or 'a man'.

WHEN is the factor that makes today's newspaper fascinating and last week's paper something to line the hamster's cage. The importance of the news declines as it gets older; however, it is also the part of the intro that is left until the last few words to mention – unless there is some immediacy that needs stressing.

WHAT is, of course, the news itself. A good story is one that will interest a great number of readers and provoke them to buy the paper. Just what this good story is in fact, is something that can perhaps never be answered.

WHERE determines the importance of the news in a similar way to the time factor. The further away the story occurred the less people will want to know about it. A disaster in some faraway part of the globe is, sadly, of less interest to most people than a minor accident in their own street. There used to be a saying on Fleet Street that explained the relative importance of numbers killed and injured according to how far away from England they were. 'One thousand Africans, or one hundred Italians, ten Frenchmen or one Englishman.'

Putting the news first

A shipwrecked solo yachtsman tells the newspapers that he lived on crabs, oysters and lizards for six days while stranded on an uninhabited part of the Northern Territory coastline. How would the newspapers report his diet? Crabs and oysters are served in restaurants. Lizards are not. A diet of lizards is sensational and not for the squeamish. The newspaper would head the list of foods with raw lizard.

▼ ▼ ▼

MAN LIVES ON LIZARDS FOR 6 DAYS

A BRISBANE man ate lizards, crabs and oysters for six days after his yacht ran aground last week on an uninhabited part of the Northern Territory coastline.

▼ ▼ ▼

The sensational news always comes first in a news sentence. The intro aims to communicate quickly and efficiently. The reader, most of all, wants to know what happened. This means that the 'what' in the intro must always come first, so that nothing comes in the way of the news.

An intro containing the details listed below could be written in several ways.

▼ ▼ ▼

Who	Mr Justice Booking
Where	in the Supreme Court
When	yesterday
What	said drug traffickers must expect to pay dearly for their crimes.

▼ ▼ ▼

Perhaps the quickest way would be to shift the position of 'said' and then add 'that' and join all the words up. The sentence would then read:

RUBES ® **By Leigh Rubin**

Figure 6.17
News reports focus on the most dramatic and startling aspect of the news and place it in the first few words of the lead sentence.

▼ ▼ ▼

Mr Justice Booking said in the Supreme Court yesterday that drug traffickers must expect to pay dearly for their crimes.

▼ ▼ ▼

This kind of sentence would be quite rare in a newspaper because the reader has to read all the way to the end of the sentence before he or she comes across anything newsworthy. Mr Justice Booking says things in the Supreme Court all the time. Few of these things would be worth

reporting. It is neither him that is newsworthy nor the Supreme Court, but the comment that in the future drug traffickers would be receiving heavy jail sentences. Therefore this piece of information must come first. Putting the news first would mean the sentence would read:

▼ ▼ ▼

Drug traffickers must expect to pay dearly for their crimes, Mr Justice Booking said in the Supreme Court yesterday.

▼ ▼ ▼

▼ ▼ ▼ ▼ ▼ ▼ ▼

activities

1. The following intro has been broken up into its factors. Identify each line as either 'who?' 'what?' 'when?' or 'where?'.

▶ A chief inspector of Police
▶ yesterday
▶ was charged with shoplifting
▶ in Birmingham

2. The following intro has also been broken up into its factors. Identify each line as either 'who?' 'what?' 'when?' or 'where?'.

▶ A man, 22
▶ on Thursday
▶ is in a satisfactory condition in hospital after being mauled by a crocodile
▶ in the McArthur River

3. Look at several intros from the newspaper and divide each of them into their elements. Label them 'who?' 'what?' 'when?' or 'where?'.

4. The following intros have been sequenced in the wrong way. The news does not come first. Change them around so that it does.

▶ Recovering in the Royal Free Hospital last night was a woman who spent four days cold and helpless in her bathtub.
▶ A boy unloading luggage from a bus roof touched a live overhead wire at a terminus in the western Indian state of Gujarat electrocuting nine passengers.
▶ Yesterday tribesmen in the south Indian state of Andhra Pradesh, as a religious sacrifice for the welfare of their village, killed a travelling salesman.
▶ A former prisoner said yesterday that jail is a 'junkies paradise' where drugs and money are freely available.
▶ The Hughes Aircraft Company in California is testing a clock that is accurate to within one second in 30 million years.

Grammar: using the active voice

Anything that happens can be written in either the active or the passive voice. This means that the focus of attention can be either the action or the person/object that the action happened to.

▼ ▼ ▼

The youth was punched by a skinhead.

▼ ▼ ▼

The sentence focuses attention on the youth who is passive or, in other words, not doing anything. In contrast, consider the following sentence.

▼ ▼ ▼

A skinhead punched a youth.

▼ ▼ ▼

Attention is focused on the skinhead, who is active and engaged in a most newsworthy activity. Generally, active voice sentences are more exciting than passive voice sentences and that is one of the main reasons they are used in newspapers.

One of the simplest ways to recognise the passive voice sentence is to look for the word 'by'. It appears in almost every passive voice sentence even if only by implication. If there is no 'by', it may be suggested. See if it can be added to the sentence. Look at the example below.

▼ ▼ ▼

The airbase was destroyed (… by enemy fighter aircraft).

▼ ▼ ▼

Sometimes passive voice sentences are preferable to active voice. Consider the most common use of passive voice in newspapers.

▼ ▼ ▼

Three people were run over by a train at Central Station, early today.

▼ ▼ ▼

This sentence is preferable to one in the active voice because the news comes first. Sometimes the active voice will be rejected in favour of the passive voice because it sounds odd or even at times ridiculous. Look at the following example of a sentence in the passive voice.

▼ ▼ ▼

A man was injured in a car accident.

▼ ▼ ▼

Although there is no 'by' in this sentence, it is there by implication or suggestion. To put this in active voice would make the sentence sound rather odd. 'A car accident injured a man' just does not sound right, even though it may be grammatically correct.

Sometimes a sentence may be written in passive voice so that the name of a famous person can go towards the front. Look at the example below.

▼ ▼ ▼

The President was hit by flying tomatoes.

▼ ▼ ▼

Except for these kinds of sentences, however, the active voice should be used at all times.

▼ ▼ ▼ ▼ ▼ ▼ ▼

activities

The intros below are written in the passive voice. Rewrite them in active voice to make them more exciting and suitable for newspapers to publish.

► Two wedding rings were stolen by thieves from a table piled with gifts moments before the ceremony was to take place in Bristol on Sunday.

► A hotel development is being fought by Kings Cross residents who claim it will destroy one of the last drug-free areas in the Cross.

► A can of cold WA beer was tasted by the lone British yachtsman James Hatfield yesterday off Fremantle.

► The body of a man found in the water off Cardiff Bay on Sunday has been identified by police.

The Structure of the News Story

Once the intro to a story has been written, there are several rules that must be applied to any following paragraphs.

► Each following paragraph should be about thirty words long. This is only slightly more than the intro paragraph. Readers only skim read the news stories. The thirty-word limit helps to present information in short doses and maintains interest longer.

► Each paragraph should be independent of the other paragraphs as far as possible. This means that the doses of information must be separate, so that some understanding of what happened can be reached if just a few paragraphs are read. Another reason for the independence rule is that a story may have to be cut to fit into the space allowed for it. If the paragraphs relied on each other to make sense of the story, then it would be impossible to cut.

Paragraph sequencing

The paragraphs in a newspaper story do not follow the natural order of events.

Suppose there had been a tragic aircraft crash at a major international airport. A novel or a film account of the disaster would focus on events leading up to the crash. We would be introduced to the characters. Background detail on their lives would be included. Then their journeys to the airport, and preparations for take-off. Perhaps an engine would catch fire. The pilot would become anxious and snap at the crew. The passengers would panic. Then the plane would hit the tarmac and burst into flames. Finally, the bodies of the dead and dying would litter the runway.

In contrast to this, a newspaper story would begin with the bodies on the tarmac. The headlines would shout: '200 Dead in Airport Horror'. The intro would give more details on the accident. The second paragraph may explain why it happened, while the third paragraph may mention the efforts of the pilot to control the panicking crew and passengers.

Newspaper stories are always set out with the most interesting information first. Often this results in the step-by-step order of events being disrupted for the sake of keeping the readers interested.

Story lay out follows one simple pattern: the most interesting news comes first. If people want to read more details they may find them out as the story goes on. For the skim readers, all the important information is at the top of the story. While not all the paragraphs in the story are thirty words in length, it is clear that some of them could be cut out without ruining the story. Each paragraph is independent.

The easy way to put a story in order

If the story is already in paragraph form, number each paragraph in the order that it will appear in the final draft. The most interesting paragraph will be number one.

If the story is only in its raw form of notes and unconnected items of information, then the most important item must be numbered 'one'. All information connected with this item can be numbered 'one A' or 'one B' and so on.

Some simple rules of sequencing

Once a few basic rules are followed when writing a newspaper story, then personal judgment can become the main consideration in paragraph sequencing.

Some rules of thumb are set out below.

► The most interesting news comes first.
► The names and ages of the people involved in the incident are usually given in the second paragraph. This is particularly true when they are not well known.
► Addresses and small personal details are almost never given. If for some reason they are, they are often included in the last paragraph. (Local papers are different in this respect, as readers will wish to know more of the smaller details.)

▼ ▼ ▼ ▼ ▼ ▼ ▼

activities

Imagine you are a tabloid journalist covering the police rounds. A police spokesman has given you the details of a freakish accident. You have made some notes and they are set out below. The notes need to be expanded and rephrased. Now write the story. Remember these points:

► The intro should be around twenty-five words long.
► Other paragraphs should be around thirty words long.
► Use the number system to plan the story. Give the most important point the number 1. Number all other points according to their importance and then organise the story. Some points will join together.
► Use active voice and past tense.
  ► The woman came from Newcastle.
  ► She was 32 years old.
  ► She was driving her estate car with her cat and dog as passengers.
  ► A workman was repairing power lines on top of a hoist lift on the back of a lorry.
  ► The woman's car clipped the lorry, which was parked on a bridge.
  ► The workman on the hoist held on, but his work-mate was thrown from the back of the lorry.
  ► The woman was uninjured.
  ► She got out and grabbed her pet cat.
  ► She made for the banks of the River Tyne and jumped in.
  ► She left her cat on the river bank.
  ► Two passing police constables dragged the woman out.
  ► Police spokesman said the woman had suffered severe shock.
  ► The workmen were not injured.
  ► The events happened yesterday afternoon.

major assignment

Production assignment – writing for newspapers

The three stories below are from the notebooks of foreign correspondents around the world. The stories need to be written up so that a national newspaper can print them. Headlines are needed as well.

Choose one of the stories and prepare it for publication after revising the guidelines below.

► The intro tells who, what, when and where in about twenty-five words.
► The news must come first.
► Use the active voice except in the circumstances outlined on p. 420.
► Do not let personal opinion, adjectives and adverbs change the news. Stick to the facts.
► Put the most sensational aspects of the story first and sequence the paragraphs accordingly.
► Write a headline that summarises the news and fits within a limited space.
► Keep all paragraphs to around thirty words in length.

STORY ONE

Syaifu Bachri walked backwards from Surabaya to Jakarta, Indonesia.

He strode triumphantly into Jakarta backwards, but staggered and fell over when he tried to walk forwards.

A small crowd welcomed Bachri, lining the street for about half a block.

Some of the crowd threw leaves and flowers onto the road ahead of Bachri.

Syaifu Bachri is a student at an Indonesian university.

'Most people I passed thought I was crazy,' he said.

Surabaya to Jakarta is a distance of 793 kilometres.

Mr Bachri arrived in Jakarta late yesterday.

He is 20 years old.

He wore out two pairs of track shoes on the trip.

The trip took twenty-eight days.

'Most nights I camped out beside the road. Before sleeping I would do a special programme of neck, back and leg exercises. Sometimes people would invite me home to stay at their place for the night,' he said.

Syaifu Bachri wore a knapsack across the front of his chest.

A pair of rear vision mirrors, attached to the knapsack, were used to watch for oncoming traffic.

STORY TWO

A fire hose ran out of control from the back of a fire engine in Liverpool.

The fire engine was rushing to a fire.

The hose whipped from one side of the street to the other.

About 60 metres of fire hose ran loose from the fire engine.

The hose smashed twelve shop windows as the fire engine sped down the street.

Firemen were rushing to a fire on derelict land in Toxteth.

Police believe the fire was lit by vandals.

The hose hit seven cars, breaking windows and windscreens and caving body panels.

Three people were injured in the process.

One bystander was hit by flying glass. He was taken to hospital.

A second was whipped across the legs.

He was standing beside his car, unlocking the door, when the hose lashed him.

A third person was cut in the chin when the hose broke through her car window.

A police motorcyclist behind the fire engine tried to alert the driver. He could not get past the lashing hose.

He finally managed to contact the driver on the radio, but he had to stop the motorcycle in order to do so.

When told of the mishap, the driver of the fire engine said, 'I had no idea. I'm very sorry.'

The mishap occurred yesterday.

STORY THREE

A baby was nearly thrown out with the laundry in a hospital in the United States.

The hospital was in Cadillac in the state of Michigan.

The baby was found after a full staff alert was declared and everybody searched the hospital for 90 minutes.

The baby's name was Hilary Harris and she was three weeks old.

A nurse had placed the baby on a pile of dirty bedsheets and turned away to do something else.

The baby's parents were unaware of the bungle until everything had been sorted out.

A hospital orderly had collected the bedsheets without noticing the baby.

He put the linen, with the baby in it, into a cart and wheeled it away.

Dirty linen is usually taken to the boiler room to be sterilised.

The linen was placed in a pile and the cleaner continued with other work.

The alarm was raised by the nurse when she returned to pick up the baby.

Boiler room staff found the baby.

The baby's parents were unavailable for comment, but the father's parents said the family was very shocked.

The family lives at 1427 North Lincoln Avenue, Cadillac.

The incident happened yesterday at 2 p.m.

Newspaper Representation Issues

Why is the news always bad?

Many people have asked why we only ever hear bad news. From time to time journalists themselves pose this question, and try to influence the selection of items for coverage. Usually, these efforts come to nothing. It seems most people *expect* the news to be negative. The reasons for this are complex. Media experts have some ideas on it.

Negative news appears more often than good news because it is easier to see. It can take seconds to kill a human being, but that same human being may have had years of nurturing and care that was not regarded as newsworthy. A house may take several months to build, yet it can be razed to the ground in seconds in an accidental fire. A negative event can easily occur between two issues of a newspaper and can therefore be easily slotted in to the front-page news story everyone is waiting for.

Negative news cannot be argued with. It is negative to everybody. For example, the building of a dam may be regarded by some conservationists as a serious problem, while developers may see it as a great benefit. However, the bursting of a dam wall and the subsequent flooding of a town would be seen by all as an undisputed terrible disaster.

The negative is more unexpected than the positive news item. Negative events are both more rare and less predictable than the more stable positive news.

Whose tragedy will make the headlines?

In the summer of 2000, the abduction of eight-year-old Sarah Payne was very closely covered by all the media. The efforts of hundreds of police and volunteers in the attempt to secure her safe return were a daily drama for the whole country. A few years prior to this, in a very similar story, a nine-year-old girl disappeared in Sydney, Australia. This, too, received extensive media attention. In the Sydney case, however, in the very same week a volcano erupted and poured clouds of lethal gas across the villages of the Cameroons, in Africa. Although 1500 people died in their sleep, this story was given very little coverage.

Some years before that, a gas leak at a Union Carbide factory, in India, had killed 2000 people. On this occasion, the event received widespread coverage, around the world. The factory had not heeded warnings and safety standards were not upheld. There remained a danger of similar accidents and, at the same time, the surrounding population demanded huge amounts of compensation.

What explains the difference in coverage between the three stories?

Geography is certainly one factor. The further away a story is, the less people are interested. But geography is not the only reason since India is even more distant (for us) than Africa.

News values (see pp. 13–14) clearly play a large part in all of this.

The bigger the audience response to a story, the more coverage it will receive. Possible emotional responses such as pity, sorrow or vengeance make for big stories. The Union Carbide disaster at Bhopal was therefore a 'better' story than the African volcano. Bhopal had a culprit – someone to blame. In the Cameroons, fate was the cause. The audience cannot blame nature. In Sydney, the disappearance of the little girl touched the public so much that thousands of volunteer mercy searchers turned out to help look for her. They had read of the parents' anguish in the newspapers and they wanted to help. An emotional response such as this from the public will keep a story on the front page for weeks.

How do you know if it is news?

A large national newspaper receives around one million words of news copy every day. The selection process is massive! Little more than 10 per cent of this avalanche ever appears in the paper.

Media analysts have prepared a shortlist of requirements they believe stories must have before they will be accepted into the newspapers (or television news). These requirements are:
- ▶ The news event must occur within a similar time frame as the newspaper. For example, a weekly newspaper may be able to focus better on long-term projects than a daily newspaper. This is why murders are common in daily

newspapers. They occur in a short space of time between each day's issue of the paper. Correspondingly, the building of a dam will not make a daily newspaper because the time frame is wrong. The start of construction or the official opening of the dam will make the paper, however. The timetable of the publication will determine the news on which it concentrates.

► The news event must fit in with what the majority of people in a society believe is important.

► The news event must be simple and easy to understand. Clear-cut issues are the best stories for newspapers. Anything too complex will often be rejected.

► There should be a conflict. The conflict can be between personalities, ideas or nations. A conflict with violence is even more newsworthy.

► News events must have a big impact on people. Journalists often ask themselves 'who will be affected by this story?' The story must be of some consequence to the audience. This is another way of saying there needs to be a legitimate public interest in the events.

► The news has to be familiar. Nothing too different or 'way out' will be included. In this sense all 'news' is actually a collection of 'olds'. It always consists of wars, murders, politics, earthquakes and so on. It is an endlessly repeated drama whose stories are familiar and very well understood.

Bias in newspapers

Accusations of newspaper bias are almost as old as the press itself. Bias is the favouring of one side or viewpoint over another. It is a lack of balance in the presentation of news and opinions. It may simply mean favouritism when it comes to a certain political party, or it may mean prejudiced treatment of certain groups in the community. Trade unions, women's groups, ethnic minorities, immigrants, refugees, unemployed youth and many other groups often accuse newspapers of bias.

The chief point to remember is that newspapers are not simply neutral organs for conveying objective information, but business products with very specific target markets. Their contents are designed to appeal to the tastes,

opinions and even prejudices of the consumers that they have in their sights. Media analysts say that bias can usually be seen to take the following forms: selectivity, sequencing, space or opinion.

SELECTIVITY

Newspapers can produce a biased report by selecting particular facts and opinions that agree with their own point of view. Other facts and opinions are left out. In this way the newspaper can say it is still printing 'the truth', but it is not printing the whole truth.

SEQUENCE

Giving some facts more importance than others can change the meaning of the truth. Placing the favoured facts at the top, near the headlines gives them greater impact. For example stories about strikes usually first tell readers how they will be affected. The reasons for the strike are often given last. This approach has led union leaders to claim that newspapers are biased against them.

▼ ▼ ▼

Paralysis of postal service set to spread

▼ ▼ ▼

Putting the effects of a strike in large headlines can introduce a certain amount of bias. Readers are led to believe that the reason for the strike is less important than the shock value of the effects. The use of the word 'paralysis' introduces an element of fear. 'Stoppage', for example, is less alarming.

SPACE

Newspapers may give more space to news and opinion that agree with their own opinions. Opposing news may be given less space.

OPINION

Editorials always support particular points of view and other opinions have little or no chance of being represented in the newspaper. For example, newspaper editorials very rarely support strikes or protest demonstrations.

Objective journalism, which is completely neutral and favours no point of view, is an impossibility. Like perfection, it can only be hoped for. It is important, however, that newspaper readers understand how bias can operate because often it is not obvious.

▼ ▼ ▼ ▼ ▼ ▼ ▼

activities

1. Decide in which daily newspapers the following stories would be most likely to appear. Give your reasons.

► The first trees are being felled along the route of the new four-lane bypass around the city of Nottingham, to allow easier access to the East Coast tourist resorts.

► A woman from the West Country has prepared a journal of each of the 728 lives she believes she has had in previous re-incarnations.

► Refugees in new dole cheat scandal.

► Banks set to adopt new software system to manage currency rate fluctuations.

2. Which of the following intros would be placed on the front page of a tabloid newspaper? Give reasons for your answer.

► Today the Prime Minister will set out plans for a new fiscal measuring system, based on a model devised by a group of financiers from Finland.

► An English rock band won the top award at the US National Rock Awards at the Hollywood Bowl Center last night.

► Panel beaters have priced themselves out of the market by ignoring public reaction to a 30 per cent increase in operating costs over the last two years, the Motor Trades Association said yesterday.

► Israeli archaeologists have dug up evidence of ancient dentistry work on a tooth more than 2000 years old.

3. Imagine you are a court reporter for a city newspaper and you have been sent to cover the day's events in the County Court. Choose the most likely story for the newspaper to publish and write an intro from the details given.

► A shoplifting case came first.
The accused was a mother of two children under five years old.
She was a claimant of state benefits.
She was accused of shoplifting goods to the value of £15.
She took them from a city supermarket.
The judge put her on a good behaviour bond for six months.

She lives in Tower Hamlets.

► The second case involved a drink-driving charge.
The accused was a young man aged twenty.
He had gone through a red light.
Breathalyser tests showed he was over the legal limit.
The judge gave him a fine of £400 and suspended him from driving for three months.
The man was a clerk in the public service.
He lives in the West End.

4. A newspaper can select the facts that suit its point of view. Other facts that do not support this view are left out.

Imagine that you are a reporter with two jobs. During the day, you work for a middle-market newspaper aimed at middle-aged conservative readers. This newspaper often features young people as 'drop-outs, dole scroungers and lazy layabouts'.

At night you 'moonlight' by writing stories for a newspaper aimed at younger readers. This paper tends to be sympathetic to the problems of today's young. It examines reasons for their actions.

You are asked to cover the story below for both newspapers. The details are as follows.

▼ ▼ ▼

The Centre for Youth studies has been studying youth unemployment in the city of Liverpool. A preliminary report has been released. Here are some of the findings. Divide them up to make two lists. The lists do not have to be of equal size.

► Youth unemployment in Liverpool is now about 40 per cent, with pockets of over 50 per cent.

► Thirty-six per cent of the unemployed youth had unemployed fathers. The unemployed young are more likely to come from wageless homes.

► A new shopping centre complex is being used as a hangout for unemployed youth.

► Eighty per cent of unemployed people visited the shopping complex at least once each year.

► Almost 100 per cent of female unemployed frequented the shopping complex.

► There are few other places for young people to go. There are no cinemas, no restaurants, no amusement arcades and no pool halls.

► Hundreds of young people parade for hours, not

buying, but displaying themselves inside the shopping complex. It is estimated that at least three or four hundred young people are inside the complex at any one time.

▶ Security guards are often forced to evict groups of young people from the shopping complex.

▶ Alcohol and drugs are often found on the groups of young people.

▼ ▼ ▼

From the report findings above, select the facts that you would use in a story for each of the two newspapers. Make a list of facts for each one. They will not necessarily be the same length.

5. A newspaper can push its point of view by putting some facts in a more important position than others. Many people only read the first few paragraphs of a story.

The following paragraphs are from a news story about a strike of railway technicians. Rearrange them to present the strike in a negative light, then rearrange them to feature the men's actions as understandable and reasonable. The intro remains the same for both stories.

▼ ▼ ▼

Major disruptions and delays plagued the suburban rail system in the city today.

Delays to train services are set to continue following the decision of technicians who fix signals and overhead wiring to continue their strike in support of five sacked workers.

In addition, thousands of peak-hour commuters on the Shoreditch and Bletchley lines today were late for work after the breakdown of an electric locomotive at Seven Hills.

Diesel trains were used on the Lime Grove line today, instead of electric trains during peak hour.

Commuters were delayed by the slower time of the diesels and also by altered schedules.

Signals technicians have been on strike for two weeks and refuse to fix any breakdowns in the signalling system.

Five technicians were dismissed last month.

A railway spokesperson said last night that the Railways

Department would not comment publicly on the sackings.

▼ ▼ ▼

6. A newspaper can be biased by only presenting those opinions that agree with its own viewpoint.

▶ Make a list of community groups that are 'invisible' to the newspapers. These groups almost never have a chance to show their viewpoint to the community.

▶ Select a well-publicised issue. Outline the range of views that could be held on that topic.

▶ Find an editorial and write down the issue and the standpoint that the newspaper has taken. Now write down any other possible viewpoints on that issue.

major assignment

Oral assignment

Brush up on the rules of debating, then prepare a formal debate on a media topic of your choice. Alternatively, select a topic from the following:

▶ You cannot believe a word you read in the newspapers.

▶ The government should set up a public-service newspaper corporation.

▶ Newspapers should be free to print whatever they want and be as biased as they want.

▶ It is not possible to prevent bias, nor should we try.

Production assignment

From the front pages of a newspaper, find a story with two possible viewpoints within it. Using selection, sequencing and space, create two biased 200-word stories from the original. Write a brief explanation of your methods and attach it to the original with the two biased stories.

The Feature Story

The features pages of newspapers are expanding as newspapers change in response to competition from other media. Radio delivers news faster than any other medium. It is difficult for the print media to compete with television's pictures. At the same time, magazines are increasingly giving over space to coverage of items that were once the exclusive domains of newspapers – and, indeed, even poaching some of their better staff.

It is equally difficult, however, for the other media to compete with the newspaper's ability to deliver breadth of coverage, news comment and in-depth analysis through feature articles.

Purposes of the feature article

Feature articles serve different purposes. Some are merely extended news stories. Others provide news analysis and interpretation. Another variety of feature article is the biography of a newsworthy person. These newspaper articles tell the story of a person's life. Often, the interview is used as the basis of this kind of feature.

Whatever the genre, the emphasis in all newspaper feature articles remains the news. The writer is said to 'hang' the story off the 'news peg'. The news peg is the newsworthy item that makes the story of immediate relevance to the public. It is the link back to the front page, or other pages carrying major stories. Newspaper feature articles fulfil several functions in addition to those carried out by other forms of journalism.

REPORTING ON EVENTS Just as the function of the news story is to tell what happened, a feature article may have the same aim. The difference between the two may simply be a matter of length. The feature has much more detail.

EXPLAINING EVENTS News reports do not analyse the news. The task of explaining what the news means belongs to the feature article writer.

EXPOSITION An exposition is an argument supported by evidence. Many feature articles are extended arguments in favour of a certain point of view. Their function is to extend public debate.

MULTI-EXPOSITION Sometimes a feature's purpose is to give an overview or summary of the range of viewpoints held on an issue of public debate.

Features of the newspaper feature article

Many elements of the feature article are shared with the newspaper news report. Other characteristics are held in common with the television and radio documentary. Different styles of feature article favour some elements over others.

The writing style of the feature article relies upon the same principles as the news story (see pp. 47–9). Verb tenses are often past tense or present perfect. The active voice is favoured over the passive voice. Economy and simplicity of wording are important.

The inverted pyramid structure of the traditional news story also applies to feature articles. This places most of the important information at the very beginning of the story (see p. 417). It is not necessary for the feature intro to contain the four Ws, however.

The structure has to be similar to the news story, as subeditors still cut paragraphs from the bottom if the article is too long. The only difference is that the subeditor begins the cut *above* the last, or last few, paragraphs. In this type of article, the end tends to draw to some kind of conclusion: there is more of a well-rounded shape to the whole.

Feature articles tend to use an extended headline structure. There is often a main headline and then a series of lower 'decks' or 'kickers'. The kicker adds further brief explanation to the main headline, or poses important questions.

▼ ▼ ▼

Aiming high

Listening to the young and helping them through troubled times are better options than tough crackdowns and new laws. That's the view of those who work with young people. Christine Jackman reports.

(Headline and kicker from *Courier-Mail*)

▼ ▼ ▼

The feature article headline is often extended to contain two parts: the main headline and the 'kicker'. The purpose of the kicker is to kick-start

the story by posing a question, stating an exposition, or summarising the content. Notice the reporter's by-line (name).

Like radio reporters, newspaper journalists include *eyewitness description*. This is to create pictures in the minds of the audience members. The description never strays far from the central news peg, however.

Interviews are an integral part of most feature articles. Interview quotes are interspersed throughout the article as supporting evidence for the exposition. Usually several people are interviewed and their comments can sometimes be placed in opposition.

The *exposition* is the central element of most feature articles. The exposition is what the article is saying. Even those articles that rely heavily on interviews contain some degree of indirect exposition. Since comment and opinion are clearly included in feature articles, there has to be an attribution. The writer of the article is named at the beginning in the by-line.

Writing a feature article

THE INTRO

Feature article intros aim to do two things: to attract attention, and to provide a focus or foretaste of the story to follow. This makes the feature intro quite different to the news story intro, which aims to give a summary of the story. In the news story, the intro must contain the 'four Ws' (see p. 417). The feature article intro is freed from that responsibility and its main role is to arouse reader interest and promise them a good story if they read on.

The feature intro is very similar in style to the magazine article intro (see pp. 440–1). Feature article intros tend to use what is known as 'suspended interest'. The reader is promised interesting information further into the story. Several different styles common in news features are listed below.

THE NEWS PEG INTRO
Some features begin in a similar style to a hard news story. The intros sound alike, but not all of the elements are present. Usually 'when' is deleted to give the article a longer shelf life.

THE TEASER
Beginning with a mystery is a sure-fire way to keep the audience reading on. In an article headlined 'The crying game', David Jones reported that: 'As the stadium rose to acclaim Steffi Graf as the World Sportswoman of the Year, her legendary composure vanished and she began to sob uncontrollably.' The intro is a teaser because we must read on to find out why she was crying.

DESCRIPTION OF AN INDIVIDUAL
A journalist can often attract interest in a story by focusing on a description of the behaviour of an individual. This 'close-up' of one person can then be broadened out to a 'long shot' showing the meaning of his or her actions. Some journalists refer to this technique as being 'filmic'.

PERSONAL NARRATIVE
In a news story the personal involvement of the reporter is frowned upon. The journalist is not supposed to say 'I' in a news story. In contrast, a feature writer can be a participant. This is even more acceptable if the person is himself or herself a public figure. For example, John Pilger often begins his articles with a story of something that happened to him, personally.

BEFORE AND AFTER
Before and after pictures always attract attention. A before and after intro uses the same technique. A typical intro might be about a rags-to-riches story. The interest comes from a desire to know how the transition was made.

For a range of other types of intros, refer to magazine articles, pp. 440–1.

THE BODY OF THE STORY
An intro of any style can open a feature article, but the content of the article has to get back to the news peg as soon as possible. Often this can be done in the second paragraph, so that the promise made by the intro is fulfilled as soon as possible.

When assembling the information for an article, the journalist arranges it in declining order of importance and interest. Journalism students are advised to modify the inverted pyramid for feature articles. In feature writing, they are told, the information is arranged according to its importance to the promise in the intro.

A practical way of doing this is to first put the information in categories and then number each

point according to its importance within its particular category. The categories of information can then become the central themes of the article. These are interlocked with joining words such as 'because' and 'however'. The themes are arranged in declining order of newsworthiness.

However, small climaxes or blockages to the train of events will keep the reader interested.

The traditional front-page news story does not interlock its paragraphs. For example, no paragraph begins, 'As a result ....' Words such as 'however' at the start of a paragraph can look strange if the subeditor has cut the previous paragraph.

In contrast, the feature article is rarely cut as ruthlessly as the news story. The journalist often has time to re-work the feature before it goes to print. Consequently, there is much more cohesion between paragraphs.

Feature writers use anecdotes or stories to keep their readers interested. These should be short and punchy. Their purpose is to support the exposition. They act as evidence. Consequently they are peppered throughout the story at crucial points in the argument.

Description is an important aspect of feature writing. Description comes from good observation. But the journalist should allow people to come to their own conclusions. Description avoids direct judgment, although of course there is a judgment made in the selection of the observations.

INTERVIEWS AND QUOTATIONS

Interviews are the basis of most journalism, whether it be the television documentary or the newspaper feature article.

Before an interview, a journalist spends a lot of time planning. Part of the research involves finding out *who* is the best person to interview in the first place. It may also be necessary to arrange comment from opposing points of view.

Journalists research the interview topics well beforehand. The background provides the basis for the questions. Most journalists have a list of prepared questions, but they are also quite willing to abandon them if they stumble upon a scoop comment.

Once the interview has been conducted, the quotations can be used to add life to the feature article. All quotations must fit the focus of the story. They must work as evidence to support the argument or the exposition.

Whenever direct quotations are used in a feature article, the writer loses control of the story and hands it over to the interview source. As a result, journalists never quote their sources at length. They often paraphrase most of the conversation and then quote the source at the 'punch line'. This is called 'foreshadowing' the quote.

THE CONCLUSION

The intro to a feature article does not contain all the main details of who, what when and where. The emphasis is more on the narrative qualities of the subject. As a result, there must be some kind of conclusion to a feature article.

The final section of a news feature is important in its own right. Subeditors know this and make any cuts above the conclusion.

The type of conclusion depends upon the subject matter of the article. Some common conclusions are:

▶ a final opinion or comment
▶ the logical outcome of an extended argument
▶ a question that re-orients the reader to investigate further
▶ a call for action.

For more information on the conclusion refer to the magazine article, p. 442.

▼ ▼ ▼ ▼ ▼ ▼ ▼

activities

1. Find examples of news feature articles that fulfil each of the purposes outlined on p. 428. Explain how each article corresponds to particular purposes and the way it fulfils them.

2. Identify the news peg in a feature article. If possible, try to match it with a news story dealing with the same issue.

3. Try rewriting the intros of feature articles in a different style. For example, you could turn a teaser into a news peg intro.

4. Categorise the intros and conclusions of a range of feature articles. Discuss the effectiveness of each and possible alternatives.

major assignment

Written assignment

Write a 600-word response to the following task. Analyse a newspaper feature article and conclude with an evaluation of its overall effectiveness. Your analysis should cover the following areas.

► the apparent purpose of the article
► the exposition (unless it is simply an expanded news story)
► an examination of the intro
► organisation of the main body of the article into themes
► structure (inverted pyramid?)
► use of interlocking paragraphs (cohesion)
► occurrences of comment and opinion from the journalist
► use of interviews
► an analysis of the conclusion.

Production assignment

Choose an area of concern with a current news peg. From the available information in a range of media forms, write a feature article of 600–800 words using the conventions of the genre.

You may also need to read the sections on news style (pp. 420–2). Give the article a headline and kicker, with your own by-line.

Magazines: The Medium

The explosion in the number of magazines regularly produced in the past ten years is simply staggering. Today, more than 8000 titles are available, on a wide range of interests and target markets. There has been an overall expansion in the sector of something like 25 per cent since 1990 alone.

Clearly, there are considerable attractions for both consumers and advertisers alike. According to the National Readership Survey (NRS) more than 80 per cent of adults read a consumer magazine. The market's buoyancy is in stark contrast to the general steady decline in the readership levels of many newspapers. The sector as a whole is now worth some £6.25 *billion*. Moreover, the medium is now the third largest, behind television and regional news-papers, in terms of earnings from advertising. A total of £1.9 billion was spent in magazines in 1999.

The fortunes of individual publications of course fluctuate widely. Some areas are seeing year-on-year decreases in readerships – many men's and women's magazines especially have recorded double-digit declines. Others appear to be booming irresistibly: computer magazines are up by 28 per cent over the past year, while Internet publications have seen an increase of 122 per cent. Overall activity in the sector, however, appears to be signalling a radical shift in the way people use print media.

▼ ▼ ▼

Magazines can offer something for everyone, and have earned the accolade 'medium of the decade' – consumers are spending 71% more on magazines than in 1990, copy sales have increased by 156m (13%) and the number of titles published has risen

by 39% to a staggering 8,000. The industry boasts a magazine for all interests – from fashion to fire-fighting, wallpaper to welding, and is dedicated to securing the title medium of the next decade.

Lucy Aitken,
Media Guardian, 17 May 1999

▼ ▼ ▼

There may be many reasons why this phenomenon is occurring. Certainly, the magazine offers a brighter, more durable publication, with much higher production values than newspapers. At the same time, as the traditional source of news, the daily newspaper is increasingly challenged by electronic means of news dissemination – the many new television channels, the Internet and now the WAP mobile phones.

Moreover, as people's lifestyles and work patterns evolve, so, too, do their leisure needs. Joke Hermes refers to the ease with which women's magazines can be picked up and put down, then picked up again later, as one of their strongest attractions. With the increasingly busy lives people lead, this observation may be taken to apply to magazines of many different kinds. Fragmentary reading is something that magazines cater for exceptionally well.

Niche markets

Magazines offer the opportunity for catering for particular interests. The magazine market is the most specialised of all media markets – this specialisation has increased dramatically in the past ten years. The rise of computer-based media, for instance, has created a huge market for technical magazines.

Even television has not so far been able to compete with the highly specialised niche markets that magazines can aim at. Traditionally, television has had to appeal to the great majority to succeed. The arrival of the multi-channel era – with the promise of numerous specialist channels – may well change all of this; however, for the moment, magazines remain a powerful marketing tool. Interestingly, the magazine format (where diversity of items are offered within the broad boundaries of a single programme) is one that television has adopted with some considerable success.

Magazines are able to reach minority audiences other media have to neglect, for two reasons. They are able to charge a substantial cover price that allows profit with a lower circulation. They are

also able to attract advertisers who wish to reach only a certain group in society – and charge premium rates for doing so. A computer magazine, for example, sells to enthusiasts or people wishing to buy a computer, or related products. Advertisers can reach this sought-after group if they place advertisements in that magazine. They could also reach them if they took out much more expensive television advertising; however, computer enthusiasts may only be a small portion of the television audience. The magazine is a far more cost-effective way of reaching a designated target market.

The purposes of magazines

The magazine is a medium of information and entertainment. Perhaps more than anything, it is a medium of advertising. In some publications, adverts make up as much as 60 per cent of the contents. They exist to *discover* social attitudes and sell products to the people who hold them. Glossy women's magazines, in particular, do not exist to *change* social attitudes.

Magazines exist to make money, of course. After all, they are businesses. To the advertiser, magazines offer a unique marketing environment. Readers read in a mentally active receptive sort of mood. If an advertisement strikes a responsive chord, it will be read in the same way as editorial matter is read. However, for most, the greater part of their income is from sales: 64 per cent in the case of consumer magazines. With business and professional titles, however, this drops to only 18 per cent (source PPA/Advertising Association 1999).

The magazine looks set to be with us for a long time. Primarily, this is because the medium is used for both information and relaxation. People can flick through magazines on the bus and the train. This is not possible with computer-based media.

▼ ▼ ▼

On the one hand women's magazines are valued because they fit in easily with everyday duties and obligations, whose execution they do not threaten because they are easy to put down. On the other hand, women's magazines need to provide a minimum of diversion and attractive information to make them interesting enough to pick up (though not so riveting they would be difficult to put down).

Joke Hermes

▼ ▼ ▼

Although it may sound an odd feature on which to base your appeal, the ease with which they can be put down is identified as a key factor in the success of magazines.

Types of magazines

Magazines can be classified according to their content and target audience. They can also be classified according to their frequency of publication. For example, some are weeklies, others monthlies and so on.

Magazines can be divided into three broad groups: consumer, business and now customer-orientated titles. This last, especially, has achieved a significant market position after only a short existence. Customer-orientated magazines are those publications that are produced by commercial traders of various kinds. Some outlets such as Sainsbury's produce a high-quality publication and charge for it. Others, such as ferry and airline companies, produce much slimmer volumes and distribute them free of charge.

Trade and business magazines exist for almost every occupation. Only a few are available for sale at the newsagents. Most are mailed out directly to subscribers.

Consumer magazines

This group contains a very broad range of publications, from generalised titles such as *Take a Break*, to more specific ones aiming at particular activities, such as *Today's Golfer*. They can be divided into the following main categories.

WOMEN'S MAGAZINES make up the largest sector of the market, as well as being the most varied. Almost any kind of topic can find a place in a women's magazine. Some specialise in fashion and luxury goods: designer décor and clothing, glamour and glitz. Others consist of varying mixtures of lifestyles, celebrities, personal and emotional matters, as well as broader concerns to do with food, home crafts and hobbies. Many men also read magazines of this kind.

MEN'S MAGAZINES are a relatively new phenomenon and are primarily aimed at men aged eighteen and over. The term used to refer to 'top-shelf', hard or soft-core pornographic publications, but the magazine market for men has seen phenomenal expansion over the past ten years – both in numbers of titles and in the range of topics covered.

The first of these were broadly re-creations of the women's magazine formulas, only with male-orientated topics – sportsmen, film stars, motoring and night life. During the 1990s, however, a new category of men's lifestyle magazine – the so-called 'lad mags' – shot to prominence in the market. They differ from women's magazines in having a much narrower range of subject matter: babes, booze and footie.

YOUTH MAGAZINES are aimed at the thirteen to twenty-one age group, although some youth culture magazines are aiming at an older audience, under thirty. Girls have a range of general titles aimed at them, concerned with fashions, music and celebrities. Boys tend to have only special interest ones, such as sport, or hobby-based.

HOUSE AND GARDEN MAGAZINES have been around for a long time, too. However, the success of television programmes on these topics has fuelled a considerable rise in sales.

MOTORING MAGAZINES are primarily aimed at men, although they have always been careful to ensure that plenty of women are included in their coverage.

RADIO AND TELEVISION MAGAZINES are among the top-selling titles on the shelves. They give programme guides and also offer feature articles about television stars and programmes.

HOBBY MAGAZINES specialise in a wide range of interests and hobbies. They provide information for enthusiasts of all ages.

COMPUTER MAGAZINES have experienced explosive growth since the mid-1990s.

GENERAL MAGAZINES deal with a range of topics without being tied to one particular interest group.

ORGANISATION AND INTEREST/LOBBY GROUP MAGAZINES are produced by groups such as conservationists, political parties, religious groups, service clubs, etc. Most are subscription only.

activities

1. Choose two magazines from the same category (such as *Autocar* and *Car* from the motoring category). Of the two, which one appeals to you the most? Examine the magazines under these headings to help you decide which you find the most appealing.

▶ cover
▶ advertising
▶ photography
▶ articles
▶ layout.

2. Survey your friends to find out their magazine reading habits. Use the list below to make a table and tick off the categories they read. Now ask them a few questions of the sort that might be of interest to advertisers. Sample questions are shown below.

▶ How much TV do you watch?
▶ How much do you spend on clothes each week?
▶ How much do you spend on entertainment each week?
▶ What is your (future?) occupation?

Now write a paragraph summarising your findings and drawing conclusions about what sort of people read particular magazines.

3. *The Reader's Digest* is a magazine of general interest. There should be something in it for everyone. Look through the contents of any issue and match up the articles with the intended audience. For example, some articles would probably appeal to older readers. Others appeal to younger audiences. Use the magazine categories as a guide to match some articles. Use your general knowledge about people for others.

4. Design an advertisement for a trade magazine aimed at advertising executives who are considering whether to advertise on television or in magazines. The theme of the advertisement is 'How to reach your television audience when they are not watching television'. The advertisement should point out the main disadvantages of television and the benefits of magazines.

5. Investigate the relative costs of advertisements in magazines and on television. Gather information from the companies and compare audience size and composition. Present your findings in the form of a report, as if to a board of directors, outlining the relative strengths of both media. Specify the one that you would recommend, with a summary of your reasons.

Magazine representation and audience issues

The magazine medium is dominated by carefully targeted appeals to narrow sections of the community. Critics have pointed to the equally narrow representations of people, events and ideas portrayed in magazines.

Women's magazines

All magazines have a formula that is used to create determine their identity, and hence market appeal. The effect of this is to create an image for the magazine that excludes certain representations while focusing on others.

The traditional formulas for women's magazines can be broken down into three basic types: all-age general (e.g. *Woman's Weekly*); over-eighteen glamour (e.g. *Elle*) and teenage (e.g. *J-17*).

GENERAL INTEREST WOMEN'S FORMULA Magazines that adopt the general interest woman's formula contain most or all of the following elements:

▶ *famous people* – the royal family, television personalities, politicians and their spouses, sporting celebrities and people in the news
▶ *fashion* – clothes to buy and (often) to make
▶ *babies and children* – child care and common problems
▶ *home improvement* – decorating ideas
▶ *food* – diets and recipes
▶ *exercise* – home fitness programmes

- *fiction* – short story romances or personal problem situations
- *travel* – usually within this country.

OVER-EIGHTEEN GLAMOUR FORMULA Magazines using this formula usually contain these elements:
- *relationships with men* – usually to be or not to be and how to
- *women and work* – careers, money, equal opportunity
- *fashion and style* – clothes to buy, rather than make
- *celebrities*
- *good looks and health*
- *travel* – usually overseas
- *fiction*
- *emotional problems.*

FORMULA FOR TEENAGE GIRLS' MAGAZINES Teenage magazines contain the following:
- *relationships with boyfriends*
- *fashion* – cult or fad fashions, in particular
- *celebrities and famous people* – from television and the music industry, in particular
- *pop news*
- *good looks and health*
- *emotional problem*
- *fiction* – romance and teenage problems.

CRITICISMS OF WOMEN'S MAGAZINES

There have been a number of criticisms of women's magazines and their effects. At the top of the list is the importance attached to good looks. In her classic study *Inside Women's Magazines*, Janice Winship identifies the feature of 'the gaze' that is used to shape all photographs of women. Essentially, every shot is composed to accentuate sexual allure and is arranged with an awareness of how men would respond. Even when the photograph is *for* women, it is designed to show how they should like to be seen *by* men.

Women come to see themselves as unworthy because they do not look as good as the models. The ongoing controversy about 'super-waif' models is now generally reckoned to be especially damaging to women's physical and mental wellbeing.

▼ ▼ ▼

There are lots of girls who are beautiful and spend lots of money on fashion, but they're not thin enough to be in *Vogue*.

Reading *Vogue* is like going to a movie. Don't believe any of it. Don't think any of it's really real. None of the models looks like this in real life. We make everyone look 1,000 times better. We're promoting the fantasy to sell the products. It's very easy when you work on it to see right through it for what it is; and it's a business. Those $40,000 dresses; you couldn't buy them anyway. Probably only two exist.

Plum Sykes, *Vogue* Executive,
The Independent, 8 July 2000

▼ ▼ ▼

Fashion articles make women anxious that they do not have the latest trendy gear. Few women ever seem to be able to catch up with the latest magazine trend before it is replaced. Those who cannot afford to keep up are seen within the magazine world as being inferior.

Celebrities are constantly pictured living fantasy lives ordinary women can only dream about. The magazines do not question the fairness, the honesty or the goodwill of the super-rich. Instead, they encourage the fantasy and promote envy. Advertising is so glamorous that it creates wants that are beyond the average person's income. It offers, says Winship, the illusion of the 'key to dreamland'.

Finally, most magazines are not socially progressive. Conservative viewpoints are the ones most often expressed. Serious questioning of society is not encouraged.

POSITIVE FEATURES OF WOMEN'S MAGAZINES

On the positive side, Winship also praises the ability of magazine publishers to put together a compilation of snippets that are both appealing and designed to fit in with women's multi-functional lives. Even before they entered the power jobs of the 1980s, she argues, women never had full control over their lives. Their time was scarcely ever their own: all they had was little bits of time snatched here and there from various other duties and obligations.

Moreover, these publications did put forward very strong messages that women's personal lives were worth bothering with.

Joke Hermes agrees with both of these points, and adds some others. Ease with which they can be picked up and put down comes first. This might sound like scant praise, but it is meant to point up the ingenuity of the format, and variety of the contents, which allow users to dip in as and when their leisure allows. As an aide to relaxation, they are without rival.

More importantly, perhaps, she also identifies a number of socially useful facets these magazines offer; chief among them being opportunities for 'connected knowing'. By this is meant that kind of knowledge that privileges intuition and experience over rational thought. 'Reading about other people's experiences ratifies your own … Stories related by others in the magazines may help give meaning to problems and experiences that could not be analysed before', Hermes says. This in turn helps reinforce the reader's grasp of how the world works, and how the self fits into it. It enhances the imaginative control the reader has over their life.

In addition to this, and not to be under-valued, are the tips and other practical knowledge that the publications offer. This can range from household and hobby orientations – knitting, baking, perhaps even DIY, and so on. But it can also extend to important medical topics, or emotional and psychological advice.

Men's magazines

The 1990s saw the dramatic rise to prominence of the new phenomenon of men's magazines – and in particular the so-called 'lad mags'. The main features of this last variant were the celebration of television, celebrities, football, alcoholic excess and babes of all kinds. Even the more up-market style magazines such as *GQ* felt they had to follow suit, as the up-front *Loaded* stormed the field in the circulation stakes At the end of the decade, *FHM* was outselling even the top woman's magazine, at more than 775,000 copies per month.

By the turn of the century, there was a growing feeling that things needed to change. The departure of James Brown from *GQ* was held to be a turning point in general orientation. A move towards a more serious and considered approach was forecast. 'I would rather put Kate Adie on the cover than Melanie Sykes,' said the editor of *Loaded*, Tim Southwell (*The Independent*, 18 January 2000).

Time will have told whether this was to be any more than a passing phase. As Nicolas Coleridge, Managing Director of British Condé Nast (publishers of *GQ*), put it: 'If you don't have babes you get punished at the news-stand.'

In the United Kingdom, sales at retail outlets do dominate the market: 89 per cent are distributed by this means, as opposed to only 11 per cent by subscriptions. In the United States, the emphasis is the other way around. The crucial role the front cover plays in this country is hard to overestimate.

Youth and style magazines

An audience somewhere between fifteen years old and the early thirties is the target for the magazines of youth culture. The magazines promote a sense of identity that allows the target groups to feel they stand out from the crowd.

Commentators see these magazines as being excessively consumerist. They have been said to offer 'the gaze of the yuppie consumer'.

Others see them as being too self-consciously generational – the only issue they ever deal with in depth is the issue of being young. They are always in danger of becoming magazines of peer pressure, critics say.

Audience issues

Naomi Wolf, in her book *The Beauty Myth*, says women's magazines offer the chance to connect with a worldwide women's culture of female solidarity.

While they acknowledge the pleasures of women's magazines, most analysts do not see them as completely harmless. In relation to eating disorders, it would be a mistake to ignore the power of magazine portrayal of women's dieting behaviour. The media discussion of eating disorders has come to influence the formation of femininity in Western societies. This is important because what audiences perceive as an objective viewpoint is actually based on a series of media myths and narratives.

▼ ▼ ▼ ▼ ▼ ▼

activities

1. Apply the women's magazine formulas to a sample of magazines from each category. How well does the formula describe the magazines' contents? What are some areas of interest to women you know that are not being addressed by the magazines? Evaluate the restrictiveness of the formulas.

2. Examine a range of magazines aimed at men, e.g. *Loaded*, *GQ* or *FHM*. Discuss the representation of men in the magazines and contrast it with the representation of women in magazines aimed at women. What kinds of images are promoted – of personality, outlook, lifestyle, social activity, etc?

3. Devise some questions and survey a group of your classmates to investigate their attitudes to, as well as the influence of the magazines they buy. Sample questions could include ones relating to reading pleasures, fantasies, use of advice, consumerism, fashion, role modelling, etc.

Analyse historical changes in the representation of gender in popular magazines aimed at men or women. Choose a period of time in which there has been significant change. Examples could include 1950 to the present for women, or 1980 to the present for men.

Evaluate the extent to which present-day depictions reflect social realities for either gender.

Production assignment

Imagine a magazine designed to appeal to a particular target group, such as youth, women aged twenty-five to thirty-nine, men aged eighteen to twenty-five, etc. You may also want to appeal to groups that the medium of magazines has traditionally ignored (such as people who are not consumerist).

Design a contents page for the magazine, listing articles that you think would constitute a formula the target group would find appealing. Also design a cover for the magazine. Part of the design of the cover and/or contents page should be a collage of images representing the target group as the magazine sees them.

Attach a brief written explanation of the magazine itself, the front cover and the proposed contents page.

major assignment

Written assignment

Write a 600-word response on the following topic.

Magazine Front Covers

The front cover of a magazine performs a crucial role in focusing all that the publication is about. A strong sense of both the contents and outlook must be conveyed literally in a single glance. This is increasingly true of many media products (e.g. programme trailers on television), as the markets become ever more crowded. Nowhere is this more evident than on the newsagents' shelves.

Hundreds of products fight for visual impact, many with little more than a couple of inches of display space. Design has responded to conditions at the point of sale, and features have been incorporated to maximise appeal.

Following is a selection of examples, some from the same sectors, so as to explore things that they have in common. However, publications in different areas have very distinctive formulae: of layout, pictures, lettering style, use of colour, etc. We cannot cover more than a few here, but it is worth trying to identify the particular features of different types of magazine.

COVER OF RED, JULY 2000

TITLE In this case the name is short, punchy and bold – like the colour itself (and by extension, the readers who buy it). The positioning in the top

Figure 6.18 *Cover of* **Red** *magazine, July 2000 edition.*

peg for all the goods the magazine is dedicated to promoting – including those for hair, lips and nails.

SELL-LINES These are arranged around the edges of the page, in a manner common to the genre. Although they are superimposed on the model, they do not actually obscure our vision of her. This is achieved by varying the colour of the different fonts. Red, black and white are used: were they all the same, the effect would be to blank out the image behind more. As it is, they are broken up visually, into separate segments. Differing font sizes and the use of upper and lower case add to this distinction, and also serve to draw our attention to the particular items on offer.

The chief function of the sell-lines is to offer little 'teasers' as to what is inside the magazine. Generally, there is always a title, which acts as a description, then a further comment that offers an intriguing or provocative elaboration.

COLOUR Apart from the red background to the title (which is also picked up in lettering), colour is minimal. Beige is the dominant colour of the clothes and is picked up in both hair and make-up. Tones used are pallid, to key in with clothing – all of which speak of elegance and fashion.

COVER OF WOMAN & HOME, AUGUST 2000

TITLE In this case, the title is spread right across the top of the magazine. The font used is a serif style (with elaborated ends to letters) and the effect is intended to be more elegant and decorative.

PHOTOGRAPH The model is again attractive and looks directly at us, with a warm, inviting smile. In this case, she is perhaps slightly younger and most definitely more 'natural' looking. There is evidence of make-up, but quite lightly applied. The hair looks simply swept back – but the credit to a hair stylist inside lets us know that the effect of dishevelled simplicity is in fact artfully arranged.

The pose is interesting: more often than not models are shot from the side, or slightly turning away. The head is then turned back towards the reader, with the effect that a special effort has been made to confront us. Intimacy and individual attention are increased by this gesture.

left-hand corner is designed to make it stand out in the overlapping stacks used on many newsagents' shelves, where space is limited.

The font used is distinctive, in the style of handwriting, where most others are print. This clearly seeks to mark it out as different and to establish a sense of individuality. At the same time, the style of the writing has an air of fun about it – a mood that is also conveyed by other features on the cover, from the model's smile to some of the articles highlighted.

PHOTOGRAPH In many ways, this is a traditional picture of a beautiful woman. The cover photo acts as a kind of mirror and offers the reader an image of how they would like to see themselves. Winship stressed the sexual nature of 'the gaze' – and the dual role it serves in both attracting interest from men and in offering a role model for women.

The gaze is outwards, directly at the reader. It invites an intimate individual contact: the connection it offers is warm and highly personal. Note also the gleaming Hollywood teeth and the carefully discreet make-up.

The one slightly odd feature is how the face is located in the upper right-hand corner of the page. In this case, it is to allow for the full range of the products on offer to be seen: earrings, jacket, blouse and trousers. The model is a living clothes

Clothing is much less in evidence – this is a high summer edition. Moreover, the target market denoted by the title is not the world of fashion and beauty, but rather of the domestic space, where one can relax and be one's self. Holidays are a key theme to this edition, too.

Strong key lighting has been used to give definition to the model's face, adding emphasis to the glow of her smile.

SELL-LINES A variety of items are used to arouse the reader's interest – from personal, to sexual, to cultural. The 'fabulous' competition is a stock device, working on the reader's desire not to exclude themselves from the chance of a dream win.

Sans serif (unadorned) lettering is used once more to outline the attractions, with variety of colour to avoid blocking out the all-important picture behind.

COLOUR The blurred-out background is difficult to pin down for certain, but the colours suggest a holiday setting, with blue water and abundant greenery.

The title is a rather dark gold, perhaps intended to suggest quality and value. Again, it is repeated in some of the other wording, especially the larger title at the bottom of the page. This offers some visual balance to the layout.

Cover photographs

The cover photograph is the key identifier for the whole publication. Both tone and outlook have to be established by the cover: it is a crucial factor in arousing audience interest.

Considerable attention has been paid to the nature of magazine cover photos. Marjorie Ferguson identified four types of facial expression in the cover photos of women's magazines:

▶ **SUPER-SMILER** Here, the view is of a full face shot, usually with a big smile. The head is often thrown back, and the hair appears windswept. The look is confident, assertive, and challenges the reader to match the subject in self-assurance. This look constitutes the hard sell.

Figure 6.19
Cover of Woman & Home, August 2000 edition

▶ **INVITATIONAL** In this case, the mouth tends to be shut, with only a suggestion of a smile, and the eyes are emphasised. The look is much more mysterious, with strong appeals to a sense of personal contact with the reader. The head is often tilted, or looking back over a half-turned shoulder, and the general appeal much more one of a soft sell.

▶ **CHOCOLATE BOX** This look features a slight parting of the lips, with only a glimpse of teeth, or even a mouth that is closed, but still with the all-important smile. The face is shot full-on or only slightly turned away; the general expression is non-specific. The emphasis in this case is on uniformity of feature and flawless beauty.

▶ **ROMANTIC OR SEXUAL** At one end of the spectrum, this is the overt 'come-on' look that promises sex and is largely directed at the single male. At the other, there is the more sensual, dreamy look of the self-absorbed icon of female beauty, which only hints at availability. Sometimes this is stretched to include shots of idealised couples, deeply attached to each other.

The Magazine Article

Most magazine articles are intended to entertain and inform. Some articles intend to entertain only. Magazine articles are based on fact in the same way as a news story. The entertainment value comes from the presentation of the facts. Interesting style and presentation are more important to the magazine article than they are for a front-page newspaper story.

Many articles work on the basis the need to engage interest is the first, and most important task. Selection of topic, liveliness of writing style and general provision of entertainment are the key priorities. Quantity and even quality of information are rather less pressing concerns.

Because of the long lead times of many magazines, news is the last thing they wish to get involved in. Stories and features that have ongoing interest are of much more importance to them.

Equally, liveliness and fun are crucial qualities that they wish to associate themselves with. Even though there may be serious topics being dealt with within the overall mix, the overriding identity they try to promote is one that will be positive and upbeat for their readers.

The subject matter

Almost anything can make a suitable subject for a magazine article. Certain kinds of articles have been tried and tested.

CELEBRITY FEATURES are common in women's magazines. A good personality profile does much more than just list a person's achievements. It should fill in the character and make the reader feel as if he or she is acquainted with the person. Quotes and descriptions combine to give the reader a picture of the subject. Extended interviews are a favoured way of doing this type of item.

ADVENTURE ARTICLES/TRAVEL WRITING describe exciting experiences in unusual, often exotic places for the benefit of readers who may never leave their armchairs.

HISTORICAL ARTICLES are often found in the general interest magazines such as *Reader's Digest*.

SEASONAL ARTICLES appear in many magazines around Christmas and New Year, especially. Spring and summer are also times when seasonal features often appear: items to do with gardens, holidays, new outfits and so on.

BACKGROUND AND EXPLANATORY ARTICLES are common in news magazines, but appear with frequency in most magazines. These articles examine almost any important topic.

LIFE SKILLS ARTICLES tell readers how to do something. Articles such as 'How to buy a house' and 'How to get a man and keep him' allow a magazine to educate, as well as to entertain, an audience.

Writing a magazine article

THE INTRODUCTION

The magazine article is not like a news story. It does not always place the most important facts first. The magazine article is similar to an essay. Its purpose is to convince, to instruct and, most importantly, to entertain.

The length of a magazine article varies from around 1000 words to a maximum of about 6000. Two thousand words is average.

▼ ▼ ▼

Openings for stories must grab the reader's attention. The first paragraph needs to be interesting. The headline is carefully chosen and so is the typeface. Subheadings are used to break up the type. A 'blurb' at the top, in heavier type, uses quotes from the story to attract the reader.

Pip Wilson, Editor, *Simply Living*

▼ ▼ ▼

The introductory paragraph, or lead as it is often called, is found immediately below the title of the story. The purpose of the intro or lead is to capture the attention of the readers and entice them to read further into the story. There are several well-known ways to do this. Some of them are shown below.

THE QUESTION INTRO poses a question of the reader. If he or she wants to find out the answer, he or she must read on.

THE ANECDOTE INTRO uses a short account of some interesting or humorous experience to get the reader interested. It may take two paragraphs to get to the humour.

THE QUOTE INTRO lets the subject of the article do the talking right from the beginning. It is often used in celebrity features.

THE ACTION/ADVENTURE INTRO begins with the high point of excitement. It starts as the bomb drops, the car runs off the road, the dam wall bursts or the aircraft engine is seen to be on fire.

THE DESCRIPTION INTRO can describe either places or people.

THE SUMMARY INTRO gives details about the subject in a brief lead. These details have to be interesting enough to make the reader want to continue.

THE SHOCK/HORROR INTRO uses sensational information to get the reader to read on.

THE BODY OF THE STORY

Like good comedians, magazine writers must know when to use their tricks. Some of these tricks, used for writing an article, are listed below. Some common questions are answered as well.

AM I ALLOWED IN? Traditionally, newspaper reporters are not permitted to write their articles in the first person – i.e. the word 'I' is not used. Magazine writers are given more freedom. They are encouraged to use 'I', especially in interviews. Even so, writers should remember that readers are not primarily interested in them, but instead in the actual subject of the article. Therefore the personality of the writer should intrude only when it helps the reader to understand the subject.

However, a feature of many magazines today – especially the newspaper supplements – is the promotion of the 'star' journalist as a personality. Their lives, opinions, thoughts and reflections are the real subject of their columns; the topics they deal with are very much secondary.

QUOTATIONS There are two kinds of quotation: single person speaking and dialogue (conversation) Both of these can be used to add life and personality to an article. However, a quote should only appear when necessary. Long-drawn-out and ordinary conversation should be converted to indirect speech. Quotes normally give a sense of getting to know a person. Readers expect a quote to reveal something important.

If people speak in a magazine article, the writer can tell *how* they spoke. 'Said' is not the only allowable word – some idea of the tone and manner of their speech can also be described. A news story reporter is not given this freedom.

PACE A magazine article should develop to give the reader only as much information in each paragraph as is needed. Too much, too soon kills the article and has the effect of boring the reader. A comedian spins the joke out. Similarly, a magazine writer does not go too fast. In the example below, the writer has moved too fast and lost the effect.

▼ ▼ ▼

Amanda had hardly got up to her evening jogging speed on the long, secluded beach when a man with a gun appeared in front of her. He fired point blank and Amanda fell to the water's edge – dead.

▼ ▼ ▼

The reader has barely had time to worry about Amanda jogging on a lonely beach in the evening before she is lying dead in the sea. The pace of an article should allow the reader to be drawn in.

HOW LONG SHOULD A PARAGRAPH BE? Unlike the thirty-word news story paragraph, the magazine paragraph can be of any length. A regular pattern is usually preferred, nevertheless. A magazine allows a paragraph to deal fully with its subject matter. However, it should not be so long as to discourage readers from reading it.

MOVING RIGHT ALONG … Paragraphs should flow so that the reader does not feel any sudden jolting changes of subject. The trick is to use a transition. A transition is a paragraph that connects para-graphs and takes the thoughts of the reader away from the old paragraph and into the new. Look at the paragraph below.

▼ ▼ ▼

Kings Cross again returned to normal as the police cleared onlookers. The incident was over and probably soon forgotten.'

▼ ▼ ▼

Suppose the writer wants to mention another incident that happened soon after. The reader has finished the paragraph above and thinks nothing more is going to happen.

▼ ▼ ▼

But violence flared again barely an hour later. Late night hooligans smashed a shop window.

▼ ▼ ▼

The transition has been made with one word – 'but'. The reader is drawn in yet again.

THE CONCLUSION

An article does not finish when the writer has run out of things to say. The conclusion can be an important part of the article. Readers of newspaper articles make their own conclusions by simply stopping reading and turning the page. A magazine reader, on the other hand is more likely to read to the end of the article. A conclusion should tie everything together and sum up the article. There are many ways to conclude – a few are listed below.

► an anecdote or story that explains the point of the article
► a return to some earlier statement that now means more than it did
► saving an explosive piece of information until the last paragraph
► an unexpected twist
► a 'call to action' or a recommendation.

▼ ▼ ▼ ▼ ▼ ▼ ▼

activities

1. Take an issue of one of the general interest women's magazines (such as *Prima* or *Essentials*). Count up the number of articles that fit into the category of personality study. Note whether the magazine places these toward the front or the back of the magazine (or otherwise). Comment on the use of the personality study in women's magazines in a brief paragraph.

2. Magazines aimed at a general audience, such as *Reader's Digest* often feature historical articles. Look at several issues of the magazine and list the subject of each historical article. Do you think there is a certain kind of subject that is featured often. Explain your answer in a paragraph that also lists the subject range.

3. List possible 'How to …' topics that might appear in a youth magazine.

4. Imagine you are a reporter for a general interest magazine. The editor wants a seasonal story that is fresh and different. The editor suggests 'Christmas on a turkey farm'. Suggest five more ideas of your own.

5. Search through the magazines that you regularly buy and find examples of the various kinds of intros. Cut out the intros and paste them into your workbook with the appropriate category written nearby.

6. Below are two treatments of the same topic. One uses 'I' and the other does not.

If you were the editor of a magazine, which one would you choose? Write a five-line memo to the author of the rejected approach explaining what was wrong with it.

▼ ▼ ▼

A. By Fred Germ
As we walked around the old convict ruins I felt a shudder as I heard the wind whistle through the roofless corridors and cells.

B. By Gertrude Hogg:
The wind howled through the unroofed corridors and cells, sending an involuntary shiver through anyone who chanced by.

▼ ▼ ▼

7. You are a magazine editor. One of your reporters covered a story, but you had to send someone else to do it after it was utterly ruined. All the excitement was taken out of it. Below is the acceptable style together with that of the unfortunate ex-employee of yours. Identify which is which and then send a note to each reporter to explain your decision.

▼ ▼ ▼

A. By Matilda Grubb

The phone rang. It was Terry. Could he come over? They were after him and he didn't think he had long to live.

'Okay,' I said, 'but what if they come here as well?'

B. By Jeremy Bean

Next Terry rang the reporter's home. He wanted to come over because they were after him. The reporter agreed but was worried about the consequences.

▼ ▼ ▼

8. Here is a short quotation and some information about the speaker. Combine the two into a smooth-flowing paragraph.

You can rearrange the sentences, reword them, reduce them or do whatever is necessary to achieve a good paragraph.

▼ ▼ ▼

'Somebody laced my drink and I woke up in the swimming pool drowning.'

John Martin is tall and athletic.

He is a strong swimmer.

He was lucky.

He struggled to the side of the pool.

He clung to the edge coughing.

He was safe.

major assignment

Production assignment

Write a magazine article on a topic of general interest. Use the conventions of the genre as outlined in this section. Research the topic, gather quotations or conduct interviews, collect anecdotes and combine the material into an article with a strong intro and conclusion.

Written assignment

Prepare a 600-word response to the following task.

Analyse a magazine article according to the features discussed on the previous pages. This might be referred to as a 'deconstruction' exercise – pulling apart something to reveal the means of construction. Following your analysis, evaluate the effectiveness of the article.

Magazine Display Advertisements

The advertisements are the best part of the magazine. Certainly, in terms of production values, the colourful, glamorous photographs of glossy magazine advertisements are the high point of technical representation. The world they promise is exciting, luxurious, soothing – whichever fits the nature of the product being promoted. Article and advertisement are certainly friendly rivals if not outright enemies. Each one competes for the reader's eye.

▼ ▼ ▼

Advertisements are carefully placed. A clash of colours is always to be avoided and so the different ads are presented to complement page presentation. Ads are not placed near clashing stories. A story on sheep kills is not placed next to an ad for wool, for example.

Pip Wilson,
Editor, *Simply Living*

▼ ▼ ▼

Features of display ads

Most magazine display advertisements are constructed to have three main parts: the headline, the picture and the written text.

THE HEADLINE

A good headline should say 'this message is for you, read on'. Veteran advertiser David Ogilvy says the reader must be 'flagged down' in the headline.

Selfishness is the secret of a good headline, advertisers say. The headline of an advertisement has to promise some benefit for the reader. A strong view from within the industry feels that this is best done by going to the essence of the product and showing the benefit to the consumer.

Although curiosity killed the cat, curiosity alone never sold anything. Advertisers aim to stop the reader in his tracks and they aim to arouse curiosity. But the advertisers must do much more

Figure 6.20

SAMPLE DISPLAY ADVERTISEMENT

This is a deceptively simple advertisement. Much of the motor industry relies on dynamic shots of their respective vehicles, often in exotic, open-road locations. This one relies on a verbal pun for its impact. At the back of the empty parking spaces are the familiar 'Reserved' signs.

Behind the car in the advertisement, however, the sign reads 'Outgoing'. The usual meaning of 'reserved' is played with, in order to label this particular model as different. The qualities are intended to transfer to the owner, of course. The colour used is simple metallic grey/green, suggesting a stylish, almost futuristic quality. The seats, however, are tinted dark red, conveying a hint of luxury, too.

than this – the product must be seen to be useful. The reader's self-interest is the key. Advertisers try to convince the reader the produce is something he or she needs.

The headline suggests it will be quick and easy for the reader to get his or her want. No advertiser mentions the hard-earned money that must be paid, or the dangers of debt.

There are five main categories of headline. Of course, there are countless combinations.

NEWS HEADLINES play upon the readers desire to keep up with the latest trends.

▼ ▼ ▼

MAYBELLINE LAUNCHES THE ULTIMATE MASCARA

▼ ▼ ▼

REWARD HEADLINES suggest the reader will benefit if the product is used.

▼ ▼ ▼

LONGER, STRONGER NAILS IN SEVEN DAYS

▼ ▼ ▼

CURIOSITY HEADLINES get the reader wondering what the advertisement is about. They are risky for advertisers, however, because people may not read on and may never get the message.

▼ ▼ ▼

IN THE SUMMER OF 426 AD, VILI VIKHELA, THE FINN TOOK HIS GIRL SIGHTSEEING, PROMISING TO BRING HER HOME BEFORE SUNSET. THREE MONTHS LATER, HER PARENTS GREW QUITE CONCERNED.

▼ ▼ ▼

This advertisement was for the Finnish airline,

Figure 6.21
The dynamics of an action photograph are combined with the fuller detail offered by text. The headline poses an intriguing inversion to the normally expected use of a mountain bike. Note how a very clear shot of the product is also included.

Finnair. It goes on to make the point that the sun never sets in Finland in summer, and suggests a visit to experience this remarkable phenomenon.

SELECT GROUP HEADLINES aim at particular audiences such as older people, overweight people and so on.

▼ ▼ ▼

MUSIC LOVERS. TIVOLI HI-FI ARE THE SPECIALISTS

▼ ▼ ▼

COMMAND HEADLINES order the reader to buy the product.

▼ ▼ ▼

BUY NOW AND SAVE

▼ ▼ ▼

THE PICTURE

The picture is the best means available to attract attention. Readers often flip through newspapers and advertisers need a strong picture to arrest the reader's attention and make them stop flipping. A picture can also be used to give the message quickly to those who do not bother reading. Some advertisers hope that the eye registers pictures even though the conscious mind is unaware of it.

The picture enables advertisers to achieve the following:

▶ build an image and a personality for the product
▶ show the product in use, and how it works
▶ show the users, show the kind of people and their lifestyle
▶ exaggerate the benefits of using the product.

Advertisers want the picture to convey a certain mood as well. They hope this mood will suit the desires of the intended audience. A common mood created is a feeling of wealth, status and exclusive quality.

THE PERSUASIVE POWER OF COLOUR It may be surprising to find out that advertisers use colour to produce certain feelings in the audience. The colour is not just chosen because it 'looks nice'.

▶ *Blue* can show the law or authority, the sea, coolness, the sky and traditional masculinity.
▶ *Pink* expresses tenderness, sweetness and traditional femininity.

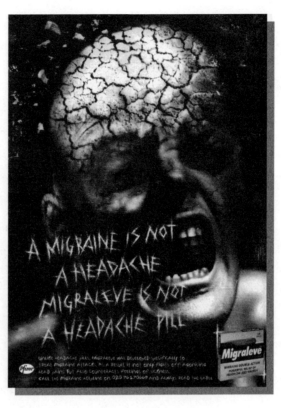

Figure 6.22
In this advertisement, the picture seeks to generate a visual sense of the grating headache that the product offers to cure.

▶ *Green* shows the country, the earth, naturalness and fertility. It also calms the nerves and is used for restful products.
▶ *Red* shows warmth and fires. It is a strong colour. It can also stand for passion and excitement. It can mean danger.
▶ *White* represents purity and hygiene. It can mean virginity. It also suggests hospitals, doctors and nurses.
▶ *Purple* stands for royalty and luxury.
▶ *Yellow* shows cheerfulness, sunlight and heat. Yellow is a common colour for packages because it makes them seem bigger.

PICTURES RICH IN MEANING The pictures created by advertisers speak just as loudly as their words. They often contain 'signifiers' that are more powerful than words. These signifiers work like signals in that they have special meanings (significances) for the audience. In the Barnardo's advertisement (see figure 6.24, p. 446), the inclusion of a baby is intended to signify the original innocence of the person who later becomes a victim.

THE TEXT

The written text is usually the least read part of the advertisement – even though it is the most detailed. The rules of newspaper layout are often

Figure 6.23
One of a series of highly controversial advertisement for the charity Barnardo's which worked by mixing shocking images of failing adult scenarios with the innocence of early childhood.

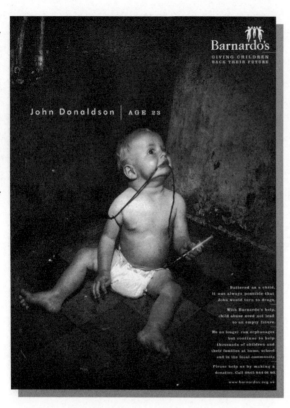

applied to advertising material as well. People expect the text to be set out in columns and to begin with the most interesting material. Sentences are kept short and words are not usually very complex.

The text of an advertisement should concentrate on the self-interest of the reader. The

word 'you' will appear to the total exclusion of any other pronoun. The key advertisers use to cash in on the consumer's selfishness is to let the person feel what it is like to *be there*. The text aims to let the reader experience what it is like to use the product. Car salesmen used to say that if the customer gets behind the wheel, then he or she is sold on it. The text encourages the reader to 'get behind the wheel'.

Some advertising is similar to poetry. R. B. Heath, in his book *The Persuaders*, has compared an advertisement to a poem. Consider the following extract from a perfume advertisement:

▼ ▼ ▼

... it is warm, rich and narcotic with a come-on sexiness. It is redolent of burgundy, roast chestnuts, summer night smells and approaching bedtime.

▼ ▼ ▼

Heath believes the ad writer is poeticising the product. This means it is the image that is sold rather than the actual product itself.

JOURNALISTIC PERSUASION Short sentences and frequent commands make up the style of ad called journalistic. This form of writing has more orders and commands in it than any other type of language. Its only close relative is the language of public notices and government forms. Common commands might include: 'Get Brand X', or 'Ask for Y'.

Questions are constantly asked of the reader. These are the reverse of the commands. A question forces the reader to think of an answer and gets him or her involved. Common questions could include: 'Choosing a new car?' and 'Remember when ...?'

Advertisements consist of two parts: the core message about the product (its use or function) and the decorative poetic imagery.

Language

Both traditional and functional grammar can provide a means of understanding the language of magazine advertising.

FUNCTIONAL GRAMMAR

In functional grammar sentences can be divided into *participants* (who or what), *processes* (verbs) or *circumstances* (where, when, why or how).

The main participant in the display advertisement is 'you'. The other main participant is the product being sold. Processes are usually action

Figure 6.24
Here, the wit is almost entirely visual. The picture is carefully designed to resemble the scene of a crime: yellow banners to isolate the area, faces and registration digitally obscured, as in television crime reports. In this case, the 'crime' is the use to which the product is being put. Promoted as a rugged off-road vehicle, shopping is clearly a sad alternative for this expensive machine.

processes such as 'buy' and 'save'. Circumstances in magazine advertising are often related to time (when). Words and phrases such as 'now' and 'only while stocks last' are circumstances of time.

Advertisers use a variety of sentence structures (moods) to get their messages across. Declarative sentences make statements about the product. Interrogative sentences ask questions of the reader. Advertisers are also fond of imperative sentences such as 'Act now!'

The first chunk of meaning in a sentence is called the *theme*. Advertisers are careful to choose the theme so it will attract the reader's attention. Sometimes 'you' will be the theme. Often, the product will be in theme position – up at the front of the sentence.

The modality of a sentence refers to the degree of certainty or obligation. Advertisers are very definite about the benefits of their products. They make this clear in sentences with strong modalities, such as 'Simply the best!'.

TRADITIONAL GRAMMAR

VERBS Advertisers prefer the present tense. This is because it is more spectacular than past tense. Verbs are stronger than adverbs. Advertisers try to choose descriptive verbs, rather than use less exciting verbs with colourful adverbs. Compare 'she cleans the house quickly' with 'she breezes through the cleaning'. However, the simple verb 'get' remains the most often used verb in advertising.

In functional grammar, verbs are referred to as processes. Advertisers usually choose action processes such as 'buy' and 'save'. Sometimes relational processes are used to describe the product. These are processes such as 'is' and 'has'.

ADJECTIVES Advertisements are rich in adjectives. The most frequent to appear is 'new', followed by 'good/better/best'. So anxious are they to describe their products that advertisers pile adjective after adjective in patterns called *compounds*. Adjectival compounds are groups of words that describe a noun. Compounds are usually hyphenated. Examples include: 'top-quality bread', 'farm-fresh eggs' and 'crispy-light flakes'.

NOUNS Aside from the use of nouns to name products, advertising language sometimes uses

noun compounds. These are combinations of nouns set out in a similar way to adjectival compounds. Examples include: 'gives a girl sex-appeal', and 'long-lasting flavour freshness'.

FLOATING COMPARISONS Advertisers never say bigger than anything in particular. They never say better or stronger than anything in particular. Advertising comparisons are not tied down to anything and so they are said to be 'floating'.

At least one reason for the use of floating comparisons is that nothing has to be proved. 'Bigger' sounds good, but is meaningless.

EXPLODED SENTENCE STRUCTURE Sentence structure in advertising follows the same basic rule as all advertising. Emphasise, stress and get attention at any cost. This leads to sentences without verbs or even without subjects. Parts of sentences have been shaken loose from the main structure and left standing on their own. 'New, Improved!' and '20% Off!' would be examples of this.

EMOTIVE WORDS Call someone stubborn, crafty and miserly and they may cancel your friendship. Instead call them firm, shrewd and economical and they might thank you for the compliment. The nature of the person is the same – the opinion of the speaker is the only change.

Emotive words are words that provoke an emotional reaction – usually approval or disapproval. Advertisers use emotive words to create positive, approving images of their products. They are used to create desirable personalities for often quite ordinary items of merchandise. The choice of word is all-important.

NEOLOGISMS 'Schweppervescence' is a neologism made up of the brand name Schweppes and the word 'effervescence', which means fizzy or bubbling. Neologisms of this kind are new words invented especially for an advertising purpose. Usually, it is a combination of two more common words.

Neologisms are also used elsewhere, for instance in science and technology. Technological neologisms include microwave, polystyrene and byte. These have now become accepted as part of the language.

Advertising neologisms have short lives and never really become accepted as real words.

activities

1. Write your own display advertisement headlines. Write one for each category and also write a couple of combination headlines.

2. Collect some advertisements with obvious signifiers. Suggest alternative signifiers that would destroy the images the advertisers are trying to create. For example: a luxury car at the steps of a mansion (effective); a luxury car outside a corrugated iron shed (destructive to the image).

3. Write a fifty-word text for a magazine advertisement selling a holiday or travel destination. Let the readers experience 'being there'.

4. Write 100 words of poetic advertising text. Choose any product you like.

5. Make a list of products you would like to advertise. Think up some adjectival compounds to describe the products.

6. Collect some magazine advertisements and look for floating comparisons. Make a list of them. Then write your own short text of around fifty words that has at least three floating comparisons.

major assignment

Magazine production

Design a magazine advertisement. Give it a headline that promotes self-interest. Describe or draw an eye-catching picture with a signifier. Write about 100 words of text. Make sure the text has:

► 'you' appearing regularly
► persuasive language
► emotive words
► advertisement-style punctuation
► floating comparisons.

glossary

Numbers in **bold** indicate where there is a longer description(s) of a term in the preceding text

AESTHETICS literally, the appreciation of beauty. In study of the media, the focus tends towards the formal qualities of a product – how it is organised and constructed

AGENDA a set of values or goals that governs how media practitioners proceed in their work. Agendas may be openly stated, or subconsciously adopted

ANCHORAGE the process of pinning down meaning. Many media products can be interpreted in different ways – photographs especially. Material of this kind will often use a written caption to indicate the correct way to read the visual image

AUTEUR a term that proposed the director of the film as similar to the author of a novel – i.e. the main or even sole creative force. Derived from highly influential French film criticism journal *Cahiers du Cinema*

BANNER ADS are the most common form of advertising on computer-based media. They are typically at the top of each page on the screen, and are normally long, narrow graphics

BINARY OPPOSITIONS are concepts or forces that are set against each other, such as good versus evil or nature vs culture. Claude Lévi-Strauss first identified them in literature, and other media products

BROADBAND is a reference to the carrying capacity of cable delivery systems – in other words, the number of television channels they can supply

BROADSHEET sometimes referred to as the 'quality press'; essentially, the larger format newspapers

CENSORSHIP the act of prohibiting an item from print or broadcast media **(21)**

CGI computer-generated imagery, principally. Much used by film post-production companies for digital special effects

CLOSED NARRATIVE a story where the principal threads of the plot are neatly resolved

CODES are systems of signs, put together to create meaning. They are a product of the social and cultural contexts of media production. Study of their meanings is known as *semiotics* **(47, 203–4)**

COMMUTATION TEST current meanings of signs and symbols can be tested by swapping one symbol for another – e.g. items of dark and light clothing on traditional screen villains and heroes **(49)**

CONGLOMERATES very large commercial organisations with diverse business interests, often operating in an international arena **(11)**

CONNOTATION a term in semiotics that refers to associated, or more abstract, meanings that a particular sign brings to mind **(47)**

CONSTITUENCY the audience or client-base that a media product, or outlet, aims to attract

CONTEXT refers to all of the natural, cultural and social aspects of an environment that help shape the final meaning of a text **(51)**

CONTINUITY EDITING a collection of cinematic conventions developed by Hollywood that has dominated mainstream film production **(154)**

CONVERGENCE The blurring of the boundaries , or bringing together of different telecommunications media such as telephone systems, television, radio and newspapers **(65, 120–242)**

COOKIES are small pieces of computer code that are placed on your hard drive by web sites and advertisers. They are usually used to track a visitor's progress through a web site allowing the operator to evaluate which pages are the most popular **(89)**

COPY written material supplied by a journalist, or to accompany an advertisement

CRITICAL LITERACY is being able to 'read' media texts. understand how they work and the institutional and cultural contexts in which they are produced **(54)**

CROPPING the process of trimming a photograph to concentrate on particular features of the captured image

CULTIVATION STUDIES aim to pinpoint the variable of media consumption in among the complexities of everything else people do. Typical studies would compare the attitudes of heavy television viewers with the attitudes of infrequent viewers **(31, 179)**

CUTAWAY a change of shot to another subject to conceal a noticeable mismatch of images in a scene that is being edited

DECODE to use signs and symbols to make sense of a media artefact **(49)**

DECONSTRUCT to attempt to make sense of a media product by breaking it down into its signifying components (see **CODES**)

DEEP FOCUS is a stylistic choice that allows for the fore, middle and background to be in focus at the same time

DEFAMATION a legal term referring to deliberate and unjustified damage to a person's reputation. It consists of two distinct elements: slander for the spoken word, and libel for the written word **(21)**

DENOTATION is the functioning of a sign at its most literal level – e.g. the road sign picture of a car going over the edge of a harbour (see also **CONNOTATION**) **(47)**

DEREGULATION literally, the lifting of constraints, rules or limitations on the way organisations function **(244)**

DIEGETIC refers to the 'world' of film, television and radio products – i.e. the people, places and events that occur within the narrative. It applies mainly to sounds that arise naturally from this environment. (Non-diegetic sound is that which is superimposed, such as music)

DIGITAL currently the most advanced, accurate and versatile form for storing and transmitting a wide range of information, from musical and video recordings, to television and radio broadcasts. Reduction of an original to a series of electronically recorded numbers allows for near-perfect reproduction

DISCOURSE ANALYSIS is concerned with the study of modes of communication. All human communication, it suggests, is composed of complex structural processes. If these can be scrutinised carefully, then the underlying assumptions can be traced, and the processes of ideological transmission laid bare. In this discipline, there is a particular fascination with social control and the persuasive potential of dominant interest groups

DIVERSIFICATION is the process of enlarging a company by taking over or merging with other companies. Sometimes these other companies can be in similar, or related areas of business; sometimes they are not. Unpredictable trends in consumer tastes are guarded against, by spreading activity over a wider area of production **(12)**

DOCUDRAMA is a re-enactment of events as they are supposed to have actually happened. Fidelity to the facts is intended to be the foundation on which the drama is built **(207, 277)**

DOCUSOAPS are a self-professed form of documentary that claim to follow the lives of real people. They are distinguished from the more traditional ones by their exclusion of complex filming procedures and low production costs **(277)**

DOMINANT READINGS refer to the way in which the majority of people are believed to respond to a particular media text

DUOPOLY a state of affairs where only two organisations are competing to provide a product **(11)**

DVD (DIGITAL VERSATILE DISC) is the latest format for recording of sound and images in digital form. Greater clarity, and compression allow for more extensive materials to be included, particularly in film recordings

EDIT is the act of preparing a text for publication, transmission or screening. It is often seen as the process of cutting something down, where in fact it is more accurate to see it as the process of shaping, or even of building up **(154)**

EFFECTS effects studies have tried to find out whether the media change people's behaviour. Studies of film or television violence and political influence have been the main focus of effects research **(30, 179)**

E-MAIL allows users to send and almost instantaneously receive messages from any other user in the world. An e-mail message may also include 'attached' files such as pictures and documents. Each user on the Internet has a unique e-mail address. It is made up of a 'username', the name and type of the Internet Service Provider (ISP) and the country code **(74)**

ENCODE the process of making codes **(49)**

EQUILIBRIUM is a state of affairs that exists at the beginning of a narrative, which is then disrupted as the story unfolds

ETHNOGRAPHIC STUDIES has investigated the ways audiences make meanings from media texts. media researchers observed and interviewed media fans **(180)**

GATEKEEPERS are key personnel within media organisations with some kind of operational control over what passes through the particular institution **(18)**

GENRE is a means of classifying products according to the elements they have in common – most notably narrative form, setting, characters, subjects and themes **(41, 191)**

GLOBALISATION is the process of any organisation extending its operations across a number of different countries **(55, 242)**

HEGEMONY the concept developed by political theorist Antonio Gramsci to describe how governments solicit the consent of their peoples to be governed. This is done largely by persuading them that their best interests are served by the social organisation that exists at the time **(11)**

HIGH-CONCEPT film one that has a single, crystal-clear defining idea at its core **(169)**

HORIZONTAL INTEGRATION is when companies expand sideways. An example might be a broadcasting company such as the BBC selling toys

HOTSPOT a link to another piece of information, website page or multimedia element such as a video clip **(60)**

HOUSE STYLE is the combination of contents and the ways in which they are presented that typically apply in any given publication

HTML (HYPERTEXT MARK-UP LANGUAGE) the computer language that web pages are programmed in

HTTP: stands for hypertext transfer protocol. Each Internet site has its own unique address. Each address starts with http://. This instructs the user's 'browser' how to negotiate the transfer of information from the 'server' computer on which it is stored to the user's machine **(73)**

HYBRID TEXTS mix and match a range of genres. They draw on formats that have proven popularity. At the same time, they also prevent those formulas from becoming stale.

HYPERTEXT the system of navigation in the Internet and multimedia is called 'hypertext' and each link, whether it is a word, an icon or a picture, is known as a hypertext link **(60, 73)**

HYPERTEXT LINKS are in two forms: either highlighted or underlined words or sentences describing something, somebody or a subject title, or as images or icons, called *hotspots* **(60, 73)**

HYPODERMIC NEEDLE is a term used to describe one model for media effects. The supposition is that a media text directly 'injects' a message into its audience, who have no power to resist it **(30)**

ICONS are signs that resemble the object they refer to. Photographs are good examples of this; so are road signs of cars and motorbikes **(47)**

IDEOLOGY is an organised system of beliefs and values that inform the basis on which a particular society operates **(39)**

INFORMATION RICH/INFORMATION POOR refers to populations who either do or do not have access to computer-based equipment – particularly that which offers access to the Internet **(66)**

INFORMATION SUPERHIGHWAY a massive 'datasphere' containing an unlimited amount of information in the form of text, images and sound **(64)**

INTERACTIVE MODES OF COMMUNICATION are those where audiences are offered some means to respond to a source, and to have some impact on it

INTERFACE an interface allows a user to manipulate a complex technological system (such as a computer) to achieve their desired outcome **(61)**

INTERTEXTUALITY the use of references to existing media texts. Audience pleasure comes partly from spotting sources, then from how the reference is worked in

ISP (INTERNET SERVICE PROVIDER) the individual domestic computer does not connect directly to the Internet, the ISP provides that service

JUMP CUT an edit where roughly the same scene/shot is being filmed, but a section has been removed, causing the image to 'jump'. Using a cutaway shot can conceal this

JUXTAPOSITION the placing together of two opposing images or forces. The impact of both combine to produce new insights or observations

MAINSTREAM a term signalling the dominant forms and values in any given society

MASS MEDIA modes of communication that are able to address large numbers of people. In the past, this has largely been a 'one-to-many' form of communication. With the Internet, a 'many-to-many' mode becomes possible **(2)**

MASTER SHOT the filming of a single scene, usually in a continuous long shot (sometimes by multiple cameras), parts of which are later shot in medium and close-up and edited together **(154)**

MEDIA INSTITUTIONS refers to the organisations that are responsible for producing media artefacts. Structures, beliefs and practices are the main areas of study

MEDIA MANIPULATION consists of deliberate attempts to induce certain beliefs, or modes of behaviour in audiences. Advertising is the most apparent form; more subtle persuasions come from many other kinds of output

MEDIATION the process of relaying something via a media outlet and the necessary changes that are made in doing so

MISE-EN-SCENE French for 'putting-in-the-scene' – it refers to everything that can be perceived within any single shot, or extended sequence of shots within one scene, including sets, props, costume, lighting, actors and so on **(150)**

MODE OF ADDRESS concerns the language that media organisations use to communicate with their audiences. Both the kinds of words they select, and the manner, or tone in which they speak: tabloid newspapers adopt a deliberately informal tone **(28)**

MONOPOLY where a single organisation has sole control of supply of any kind of product **(11)**

MONTAGE is the placing together of separate images to create suggested narratives from the clashing images **(155)**

MORPH to change from one state into another – particularly used in film special effects (see CGI)

MULTIMEDIA the blending of sound, text and visual images to create computer-based products **(114)**

NARRATIVE at its simplest, a sequence of events building to coherent story

NARROWCAST targeting very specific audiences for television and radio programmes

NEGOTIATED READINGS are made when mental negotiations are needed to overcome some incompatibility or disagreement with the overt messages of a text **(27)**

NEWS AGENCIES organisations dedicated to gathering news items and developing them into stories, but not involved in actually producing them in print. They sell them on to news producers instead

NEWS VALUES criteria that determine the selection, treatment and presentation of news items **(13)**

OLIGOPOLY where a small number of companies dominate the supply of particular products or services **(11)**

180-DEGREE RULE an imaginary line drawn between two or more actors to keep the camera on one side of the action so that the audience's perspective is consistent, even if several viewpoints are edited together. If the camera 'crosses the line', the audience might feel disorientated by the change of perspective **(154)**

OPEN NARRATIVE is one where not all the threads of the story are neatly tied up at the end. Some elements are left unresolved, to allow audiences to imagine likely outcomes

OPPOSITIONAL OR RESISTANT READINGS are made when people find their own life experiences are at odds with the views in the text **(27)**

OUTLINE in film terms, a very brief summary of a proposal, giving suggestions of setting, genre, main characters and action

PAPARAZZI freelance photographers who specialise in celebrity-snapping

POLYSEMY refers to the capacity of all signs to have more than one meaning **(47)**

POSTMODERN a concept that derives from very complex theories about art and ideology. Postmodern theory and practice emphasises 'borrowing' from previous works, mixtures between all different kinds of high or 'low' art forms. It rejects the idea of 'universal' characteristics and originality in culture

PREFERRED OR DOMINANT READINGS are the readings that are closest to those intended by the producers of a text **(27)**

PRESS CODE a set of guidelines intended to govern the behaviour of journalists, and the organisations they work for, in the stories that are gathered, how they are gathered, and also presented in publication **(19)**

PRIVATISATION the transfer of publicly owned companies into private commercial ownership

PROFESSIONAL VALUES guidelines, usually unwritten, about the proper ways to conduct business within a particular organisation

glossary

PROGRAMME FORMATS the outline structure and key ingredients of any individual programme. There is a quite large trade in successful formats around the world today, with some adaptation for language and cultural differences (e.g. *Big Brother*)

PROPAGANDA material that is produced in order to persuade an audience of a particular point of view or belief

PUBLIC SERVICE BROADCASTING (PSB) is dedicated to providing essential services and information, as well as some entertainment and is funded by the public, in the United Kingdom by the licence fee. **(243)**

READINGS the ways in which particular texts are understood

REALISM a form of presentation across various media which attempts to portray 'real life'. It is often contrasted (and mixed with, e.g. soap opera) spectacular or melodramatic modes of narrative **(168, 295)**

RECEPTION STUDIES have tried to study how people use and interpret the media **(31, 180)**

REPORTAGE coverage of actual events in which the style of writing is intended to convey something of the raw experience

REPRESENTATION is a depiction, a likeness or a constructed image, of something in real life **(35)**

RUSHES original, unedited footage

SEARCH ENGINE the main way information is found on the World Wide Web. The organisations that operate search engines use super-computers to scan Internet sites across the globe for keywords and phrases which they store on massive databases **(74)**

SEMIOTICS the study of signs and symbols

SERIF a form of lettering in print products that has a slightly more ornate style (as opposed to the plainer sans serif)

SHOT the smallest unit in the visual language of photography, television and film **(148)**

SIGNIFIED is an object or concept which is referred to by a sign

SIGNIFIER is the sign which refers to an object or concept

SIGNS components of communication referring to things other than themselves **(46)**

SOUNDBITE a very short statement, usually from a politician or other public figure. It is constructed to suit the pressures on time and space in the media industries, and is necessarily reductive of the subject under discussion

SPIN DOCTOR an employee of a political party who wields considerable control over the way in which information about government activity is released **(17)**

STEADICAM a type of camera that is mounted on the body of its operator, and allows for a very fluid and stable image to be recorded, even when following rapid movement

STEREOTYPE is a 'typical' or mass-produced image, repeated so many times it seems to have established a pattern. It is a simplified and judgmental type of representation. Repetition establishes stereotypes and over time allows them to appear 'natural' **(38. 314, 332)**

SYMBOLS are signs that do not resemble the thing they refer to – e.g. a turtledove as a symbol for love **(47)**

SYNERGY is the process whereby two or more products are used to promote each other: a hit film makes associated products desirable; then, in turn, the array of merchandise available helps to keep the film itself in the public eye **(12)**

TELEVISION RATINGS are calculated from a random sampling of the population, drawn from monitoring devices installed on volunteers' television sets, and from questionnaires. The figures gathered by this means are highly important; in the commercial sector for setting advertising rates, and in the public sector for justifying continuation of the licence fee

TEXT is a term that can include any sequence of communication, such as an article, a video clip, a radio broadcast or an internet home page. It is a unit of meaning that is complete in some way **(54)**

TREATMENT is the broad plan of a film proposal (see **OUTLINE**) describing each scene in a paragraph or two

URL any Internet page should have contact information on it. This can include its URL (uniform resource locater) address, the identity of its creator, and their e-mail address so that people who require more information or who wish to contribute information can contact them.

USES AND GRATIFICATIONS a theory of media consumption which argued that audiences used the media to satisfy certain basic psychological needs **(31)**

VERTICAL INTEGRATION is when industrial expansion 'up' or 'down' the production process occurs. A television manufacturer may buy a film production company, and then even broadcasting outlets which are at different stages up or down the production chain

VOX POP interviews conducted with 'ordinary' people, often in the street, and in number rather than depth **(279)**

list of contacts

Much of the following information is drawn from the British Film Institute's website, www.bfi.org.uk, which includes more information of relevance to media and films studies teachers and students

The Education Projects section of the BFI (www.bfi.org.uk/education/projects) provides services to teachers and learners which include courses and conferences for teachers and students, in-service training, events linked to screenings and seasons, classroom resources, research and policy development.

BFI Publishing (www.bfi.org.uk/books) publishes a wide range of books for students,

teachers and general readers in the area of film and media studies.

More information on the BFI is available at www.bfi.org.uk or at the:

British Film Institute
21 Stephen Street
London WIT ILN
(020) 7255 1444

The BFI exists to promote greater understanding and appreciation of, and access to, film and moving image culture in the United Kingdom.

Examination boards
ADVANCED LEVEL MEDIA STUDIES
OCR (Oxford Cambridge RSA)
Subject Officer (Media Studies)
Mill Wharf
Mill Street
Birmingham B6 4BU
Tel: 01223 552933
Fax: 01223 553030
Website: www.ocr.org.uk

Welsh Joint Education Committee
Subject Officer (Media Studies)
245 Western Avenue
Cardiff CF5 2YX
Tel: 02920 265038
Fax: 02920 575994
Website: www.wjec.co.uk

Assessment and Qualifications Alliance
(AQA)
Subject Officer (Media Studies)
Devas Street
Manchester M15 6EX
Tel: 0161 9531180
Fax: 0161 9537576
Website: www.aqa.org.uk

BTEC
Edexcel Foundation
Product Manager
Media GNVQ & National Diploma
Stewart House
32 Russell Square

London WCI 5DN
Tel: 0870 240 9800 (x4117)
Fax: 020 7758 6960
Website: www.edexcel.org.uk

CITY & GUILDS
Customer Services Enquiries Unit
Tel: 020 7294 2468
Website: www.city-and-guilds.co.uk

A-LEVEL FILM STUDIES
Welsh Joint Education Committee
Subject Officer (Film Studies)
245 Western Avenue
Cardiff CF5 2YX
Tel: 02920 265038
Fax: 02920 575994
Website: www.wjec.co.uk

GCSE MEDIA STUDIES
AQA (formerly SEG)
Francine Kobel
Stag Hill House
Guildford
Surrey GU2 7XJ
Tel: 01483 477763
Fax: 01483 300152
Website: www.aqa.org.uk

Welsh Joint Education Committee
Subject Officer (Media Studies)
245 Western Avenue
Cardiff CF5 2YX
Tel: 02920 265038

Fax: 02920 575994
Website: www.wjec.co.uk

OCR (Oxford Cambridge RSA)
Subject Officer
Mill Wharf
Mill Street
Birmingham B6 4BU
Tel: 01223 552933
Fax: 01223 553030
Website: www.ocr.org.uk

Qualifications & Curriculum Authority
Principal Subject Officer –
Qualifications Framework/AVCE Media
83 Piccadilly
London W1J 8QA
Tel: 020 7509 5555 (x5622)
Fax: 020 7509 6666
Website: www.qca.org.uk

Local contacts
Cinema/venue-based education contacts

List of local teachers' groups

Details of regional film officers
(who now have a responsibility for education with their remit), regional arts boards and development agencies and contact names

All the above can be found at the Contact Sheet on the BFI's website

National organisations

Advertising Standards Authority (ASA)
2 Torrington Place
London WC IE 7HW
Tel: 0207 580 5555
Website: www.asa.org.uk

British Broadcasting Corporation (BBC)
Television Centre
Wood Lane
London WI2 7PJ
Tel : 0208 743 8000
Website: www.BBC.co.uk

British Board of Film Classification (BBFC)
3 Soho Square
London WIV 6HD
Tel: 0207 439 7961
Website: www.bbfc.co.uk

British Universities Film & Video Council (BUFVC)
77 Wells Street
London WIT 3QS
Tel: 020 73931500
Fax: 020 73931555
Website: www.bufvc.ac.uk

Broadcasting Standards Commission
7 The Sanctuary
London SWI P 3JS
Tel: 0207 233 0544
Website: www.bsc.org.uk

The English and Media Centre
18 Compton Terrace
London NI 2UN
Tel: 020 7359 8080
Fax: 020 73540133
Website: www.englishandmedia.co.uk

Film Council
10 Little Portland Street
London WIW 7SG
Tel: 020 7861 7861
Fax: 020 7861 7862
Website: www.filmcouncil.org.uk

Film Education
Alhambra House
27–31 Charing Cross Road
London WC2H 0AU
Tel: 020 79762291
Fax: 020 78395052
Website: www.filmeducation.org

Institute of Practitioners in Advertising (I PA)
44 Belgrave Square
London SWI 8QS
Tel: 0207 235 7020
Website: www.ipa.co.uk

Independent Television Commission (ITC)
33 Foley Street
London WIP 7BL
Tel: 0207 255 3000
Website: www.itc.org.uk

National Museum of Photography, Film & Television
Pictureville
Bradford BDI INQ
Tel: 01274 203310
Fax: 01274 772325
Website: www.nmpft.org.uk

Press Complaints Commission
I Salisbury Square
London EC4Y 8AE
Tel: 0207 353 1248
Website: www.pcc.org.uk

The Radio Academy
5 Market Place
London WIN 7AH
Tel: 0207 255 2029
Website: www.radioacademy.org

Radio Authority
Holbrooke House, Great Queen Street
London WC2B 5DG
Tel: 0207 430 2724
Website: www.radioauthority.gov.uk

NORTHERN IRELAND

Northern Ireland Film Commission (NIFC)
21 Ormeau Avenue
Belfast BT2 8HD
Tel: 02890 232444
Fax: 02890 239918
Website: www.nifc.co.uk

Northern Ireland Media Education Association (NIMEA)
David McCartney
c/o Belvoir Park Primary School
Belvoir Drive
Belfast BT8 7DL
Website:
www.mediaed.org.uk/links/nimea
Tel: 02890 491810
Fax: 02890 492356

SCOTLAND

Scottish Screen
Media Education Officer
249 West George Street
Glasgow
G2 4QE
Tel: 0141 3021700
Fax: 0141 3021711
Website: www:scottishscreen.com

The Association for Media Education in Scotland (AMES)
24 Burnett Place
Aberdeen AB24 4QD
Tel: 01224 481976
Website: www.ames.org.uk

WALES

Sgrin, Media Agency for Wales
The Bank 10 Mount Stuart Square
Cardiff Bay
Cardiff CF10 5EE
Tel: 02920 333300
Fax: 02920 333320
Website: www.sgrin.co.uk

Media Education Wales
University of Wales Institute Cardiff
Cyncoed Road
Cardiff CF23 6XD
Tel: 02920 689101
Fax: 02920 416076
Website:
www.mairtom.demon.co.uk/mediaed

bibliography

CHAPTER 1 – KEY CONCEPTS

Blumler, J. G., *Television and the Public Interest: Vulnerable Values in West European Broadcasting* (London: Sage Publications, 1992).

British Film Institute, *The Companies You Keep* (London: BFI Education, 1982), p. 1.

Brenton H. and Hare D., *Pravda* (London/New York: Methuen, 1986).

Burton, G., *More than Meets the Eye* (London: Edward Arnold, 1990), p. 48.

Chomsky, N., *Necessary Illusions: Thought Control in a Democratic Society* (London: Pluto, 1989).

Chomsky, N. in Mark Achbar (ed.), *Manufacturing Consent: Noam Chomsky and the Media* (Montreal/New York: Black Rose Books, 1994).

Cumberbatch G., *Psychology Review*, Vol. 3 No. 4, April 1997.

Fairclough, N., *Language and Power* (Harlow: Longman, 1989).

Fiske, J., *Introduction to Communication Studies* (London: Methuen, 1982).

Henningham, J., 'How Political Correctness Shapes the Media', *The Independent Monthly*, February 1996, p 16.

Hermes, J., *Reading Women's Magazines: An Analysis of Everyday Media Use* (Cambridge: Polity Press, 1995).

Lewis, J., *The Ideological Octopus* (London: Routledge, 1991), pp. 58–67.

McMahon, B. and Quin, R., *Real Images: Film and Television* (Melbourne: Macmillan, 1986).

McQuail, D., *Mass Communication Theory* (London: Sage Publications, 1989), p. 51.

Moon, B., *Literary Terms: A Practical Glossary* (Scarborough, WA: Chalkface Press, 1993).

O'Sullivan, T., Dutton, B., and Raynor, P., *Studying the Media: An Introduction* (London: Edward Arnold, 1994), p188.

Pilger, J., *Hidden Agendas* (London: Vintage, 1988).

Windschuttle, K., *The Media: A New Analysis of the Press, Television, Radio and Advertising in Australia* (Ringwood: Penguin, 1985), p. 414.

Wittgenstein, L. in Inglis, F., *Media Theory: An Introduction* (Oxford: Basil Blackwell, 1990).

CHAPTER 2 – COMPUTER-BASED MEDIA

Bok, S., *Mayhem: Violence as Public Entertainment*, (Reading, MA : Perseus Books, 1999).

Branwyn, G., Frauenfelder M. and Sugarman P., *Beyond Cyberpunk: A Do-It-Yourself Guide to the Future* (HyperCard Stack) (Louisa, VA: The Computer Lab, 2001). An 18-page comic book drawn by Mark Frauenfelder is also available from The Computer Lab.

Feldman, T., *Multimedia in the 1990's* (British National Bibliography Research Fund, 1998).

Gibson, W., *AGRIPPA (A Book of The Dead)*; etchings by Dennis Ashbaugh (Kevin Begos Publishing, 1992). Entire text (in non-interactive format) can be found at: www-personal.umd.umich.edu/~nhughes/cyber/gibson/agrippa.html.

Gilder G., *Life after Television* (New York: W.W. Norton, 2001).

Landow G. P., *Hypertext: The Convergence of Contemporary Critical Theory and Technology* (Baltimore, MA: Johns Hopkins University Press, 1992).

Lynch P., *Yale University Web Style Manual*, http://info.med.yale.edu/caim/manual/sites/site_struct ure.html.

Mallory, J., *Its Name Was Penelope* (Watertown MA: Eastgate Systems, 2001), www.eastgate.com/catalog/Penelope.html.

Samsel J. and Wimberly D., *Writing for Interactive Media: The Complete Guide* (New York: Allworth Press, 1998).

Slade, A., *Information Technology, Issues and Implications* (Collingwood: VCTA Publishing, 2000).

Wark, McKenzie, 'The Multimedia Thing', *Metro Magazine*, No. 103, *Metro Magazine* is run by Australian Teachers of Media (ATOM). www/cinemedia.net/ATOM

CHAPTER 3 – FILM

Altman, R., *Film/Genre* (London: BFI, 1999).

Andrew, D., *Concepts in Film Theory* (New York: Oxford University Press, 1984).

Ang, I., *Living Room Wars: Rethinking Audiences for a Postmodern World* (London: Routledge, 1996).

Arroyo, J. (ed.), *Action/Spectacle Cinema: A Sight & Sound Reader* (London: BFI, 2000).

Bone, J., and Johnson, R., *Understanding the Film* (Lincolnwood, IL: National Textbook company, 1991).

Bluestone, G., *Novels into Film* (Baltimore, MA: Johns Hopkins University Press, 1957).

Bordwell, D. and Thompson, K., *Film Art: An Introduction* (New York: McGraw-Hill, 1979).

Chatman, S., 'What novels can do that films can't (and vice versa)' in Mast, G., *Film Theory and Criticism* (New York: Oxford Press, 1992).

Cohen, K., *Film and Fiction: The Dynamics of Exchange* (New Haven: Yale University Press, 1979).

Cook, P. and M. Bernink (eds), *The Cinema Book 2nd Edition* (London: BFI, 1999).

Dyja, E. (ed.), *BFI Film and Television Handbook 2001* (London: BFI, 2000).

Ellis, J., *Visible Fictions* (London: Routledge, 1992).

Grindon, L., *Shadows on the Past* (Philadelphia: Temple University Press, 1994).

Herlihy, D., 'Am I a Camera?', *The American Historical Review*, Vol. 93, December 1988.

bibliography

Hill, J., 'Cinema' in Stokes, J. and Reading, A. (eds), *The Media in Britain* (London: Macmillan, 1999).

Jinks, W., *The Celluloid Literature* (Beverley Hills, CA: Glencoe Press, 1971).

Kent, R., *Measuring Media Audiences* (London: Routledge, 1994).

Keuhl, J., 'Truth Claims' in Rosenthal, A., (ed.), *New Challenges for the Documentary* (Berkeley: University of California Press, 1988).

Martin, A., 'Teacher I Need You' in *Metro*, No. 84, Summer, 1990-91, p. 13.

McDougal, S., *Made into Movies: From Literature to Film* (New York: Holt Reinhart and Winston, 1985).

McFarlane, B., *Words and Images: From Page to Screen* (Richmond, PA: Heinemann, 1983).

McMahon, B., and Quin, R., *Real Images* (Melbourne, Macmillan, 1986).

Monaco, J., *How to Read a Film* (Oxford: Oxford University Press, 1981).

Norman, B., *Talking Pictures* (London: BBC/Hodder & Stoughton, 1987).

O' Sullivan, T., Dutton, B., and Rayner, P., *Studying the Media* (London: Andrew Arnold, 1994).

Ranciere, J., 'Histoires d'ecole', *Cahiers du Cinema*, No. 431, May 1990.

Reisz, K., and Millar, G., *The Technique of Film Editing* (New York: Hastings House, 1975).

Rosenstone, R.A., 'History in Images/History in Words: Reflections on the Possibility of Really Putting History onto Film', *The American Historical Review*, Vol. 93, December 1988.

Sussex, E., 'Getting it Right' in Rosenthal, *New Challenges for the Documentary*, 1988.

Thompson, F., 'Blurbmeisters', *American Film*, September/October, 1991.

Thomsen, S. R., 'A Worm in the Apple: Hollywood's Influence on the Public's Perception of Teachers'. Paper presented at the Joint Meeting of the Southern States Communication Association and the Central States Communication Association, Lexington, Kentucky, April, 14–18, 1993 (ERIC document).

Todd, P., 'The British Film Industry in the 1990's' in Murphy, R. (ed.), *British Cinema of the 90s* (London: BFI, 2000).

Udwin, L. *Black Filmmaker*, Vol. 3 No. 9, 1999.

Willis, E. and D'Arienzo, C., *Writing Scripts for Television, Radio and Film* (New York: Holt, Rinehart and Winston, 1981)

Wurtzel, A., *Television Production* (New York: McGraw-Hill, 1983).

CHAPTER 4 – TELEVISION

Abt, V. and Mustazza, L., *Coming after Oprah: Cultural Fallout in the Age of the TV Talk Show* (Bowling Green, IL: Bowling Green State University Popular Press, 1997.)

Adams, P., 'From the global village to the tribal ghetto', *The Weekend Australian*, April 22–23 1995, p. 27.

Anderson, R., *Consumer Culture and TV Programming* (Colorado: Westview Press, 1995).

Baehr, H. and Dyer, G., (eds), *Boxed In: Women and Television* (Pandora Press, London, 1987).

Cashmore, E., *And There Was Television*, Routledge, London, 1994

Chomsky, N. quoted in Boyd, J., and MacLennan, G., 'From Consent to Dissent: Chomsky and the Media Teacher', *Metro*, No. 93, Autumn, 1993, p. 15.

Corner, J., *Television Form and Public Address* (London: Edward Arnold, 1995), p. 77.

Day-Lewis, S., *Talk of Drama* (Luton: University of Luton Press, 1998).

Frisby, C. and Weigold, M. F., 'Gratifications of Talk: Esteem and Affect related consequences of viewing television talk shows' at: http://web.missouri.edu/~advcf/tv_talk_shows.html

Gamson, J., 'Freak Talk on TV', *The American Prospect Online*, No. 23, Fall 1995, www.prospect.org/archives/23/23gams.html.

Gamson, J., *Freaks Talkback: Tabloid Talk Shows and Sexual Nonconformity* (Chicago, IL: University of Chicago Press, 1998).

Gerbner, G., *Adbuster*, Winter 1989–90, quoted in *Media Asia* (Singapore) Vol. 18 No. 2, 1991.

Glasgow University Media Group, *Really Bad News* (London: Writers and Readers Co-operative, 1982).

Greer, G., 'Dinkum? No, Bunkum!', *Radio Times* (UK), March 11–17, 1989.

Heath, R., 'Tuning into Talk', *American Demographics*, February 1998.

Heaton, J. and Wilson, N., *Tuning in Trouble: Talk TV's Destructive Impact on Mental Health* (San Francisco: Jossey-Bass Publishers, 1995).

Kent, R. *Measuring Media Audiences* (London: Routledge, 1994).

Kilborn, R., *Television Soaps* (London: B.T. Batsford, 1992), p. 40.

Kurtz, H., *Hot Air: How the Talk Show Culture Has Changed America* (New York: HarperCollins (Basic Books), 1997).

Leone, R., 'What's Trust Got to Do With it?', *The American Prospect Online*, No. 17, Spring 1994, www.prospect.org/archives/17/17leon.html.

Mayeux, P., *Writing for the Electronic Media* (Madison, WI: Brown and Benchmark, 1994), pp. 211–12.

Modelski, T., *Loving with a Vengeance: Mass-produced Fantasies for Women* (London: Methuen, 1982).

Morton, S., 'Dusenberry: Eyes Have It', *B&T*, 3 May 1996, p. 18.

O'Rourke, D., from a lecture reprinted in *Metro*, No. 92, Summer, 1993, p. 40.

Pryluck, C., 'Ultimately we are all outsiders' in Rosenthal, *New Challenges for the Documentary*, 1988, p. 263.

Putnam R., Dillon Professor of International Affairs, Harvard, quoted from *The Courier-Mail*, 11 September, 1995, p 13. Original article from *The Daily Mail* (UK).

Rabiger, M., *Directing the Documentary* (Boston, MA: Focal Press, 1987), p. 4.

Rosen, R., 'The Search for Yesterday' in Gitlin, T., (ed.), *Watching Television* (New York: Pantheon Books, 1986), p. 46.

Rosenthal, A. (ed.), *New Challenges for the Documentary* (Berkeley: University of California Press, 1988).

Scannel, P., 'For a Phenomenology of Radio and Television', *Journal of Communication*, Vol. 45 No. 3, Summer, 1995.

Shattuc, J., *The Talking Cure: TV Talk Shows and Women* (New York: Routledge, 1997).

Willis, E., and D'Arienzo, C., *Writing Scripts for Televsion and Film* (New York: Holt, Rinehart and Winston, 1981), p. 70.

Winston, B., *Claiming the Real: The Documentary Film Revisited* (London: BFI, 1995), p. 11.

Winston, B., 'Documentary, I Think We Are in Trouble' in Rosenthal, *New Challenges for the Documentary*, 1988, p. 31.

Wood, P., 'Television as Dream' in Adler, R. (ed.), *Television as a Cultural Force* (New York: Praeger, 1981).

CHAPTER 5 – RADIO

Barnard, S., *Studying Radio* (London: Edward Arnold, 2000).

Crisell, A., *Understanding Radio* (London: Methuen, 1986).

Hind, J. and Mosco, S., *Rebel Radio* (London: Pluto Press, 1985).

Kent, R., *Measuring Media Audiences* (London: Routledge, 1994).

McLeish, R., *The Techniques of Radio Production* (London: Focal Press, 1978).

Wilby, P. and Conroy, A., *The Radio Handbook* (London: Routledge, 1994).

CHAPTER 6 – NEWSPAPERS AND MAGAZINES

Barrel, J. and Braithwaite, B., *The Business of Women's Magazines* (London: Associated Business Press, 1998).

Braithwaite, B., *Women's Magazines: The First 300 Years* (London: Peter Owen, 1995).

Chomsky, N. in Mark Achbar (ed.), *Manufacturing Consent: Noam Chomsky and the Media* (Montreal/New York: Black Rose Books, 1994).

Cochran, W., 'Searching for the Right Mixture', *The Quill*, May 1995.

Cracknell, D., 'The pros and cons', *News of the World Wide Web*, http:///www.warwick.ac.uk/guest/cracknel/proscon.html

Curran, J. and Seaton, J., *Power without Responsibility: The Press and Broadcasting in Britain* (5th edition) (London: Routledge, 1997).

Glasgow University Media Group, *Bad News and More Bad News* (London: Routledge, 1980).

Hermes, J., *Reading Women's Magazines: An Analysis of Everyday Media Use* (Cambridge: Polity Press, 1995).

Hodgson, F. W., *Modern Newspaper Editing and Production* (London: Heineman, 1987).

Keeble, R., *The Newspaper Handbook* (London: Routledge, 1994).

Kent, R., *Measuring Media Audiences* (London: Routledge, 1994).

Lapham, C., 'The Evolution of the Newspaper of the Future', *Computer Mediated Communications* magazine, http://sunsite.inc.edu/cmc/mag/1995/jul/lapham.html.

McAdams, M., 'Driving a newspaper on the data highway', http://www.well.com/user/mmcadams/online.newspapers.html#footnotes.

McCracken, E., *Decoding Women's Magazines* (London: Macmillan, 1993).

O' Sullivan, T., Dutton, B. and Rayner, P., *Studying the Media* (London: Andrew Arnold, 1994).

Quittner, J., quoted in Cracknell, D., 'The role of the journalist', *News of the World Wide Web*, http:///www.warwick.ac.uk/guest/cracknel/jrnrole.html.

Winship, J., *Inside Women's Magazines* (London: Routledge, 1987).

Wolf, N., *The Beauty Myth* (New York: Anchor Books, 1992).

Wolfe, T. (ed.), *The New Journalism* (New York: Harper and Row, 1973).

list of figures

Whilst considerable effort has been made to identify and contact the copyright holders and originators of figures, this has not been possible in all cases. We apologise for any apparent negligence. Any ommisions or corrections brought to our attention will be remedied in any future editions.

KEY CONCEPTS

1.1 – Frazzled Cat Productions; 1.3 – Carlton Television; 1.4 – *Australian Financial Review*/Tony Edwards; 1.5 – Pearson Television; 1.6 – Frazzled Cat Productions; 1.8 – Guardian Newspapers Ltd; 1.9 & 1.10 – Frazzled Cat Productions; 1.11 – © Stuart Krygsman, 2001; 1.12 – Children's Film Foundation/The Moviestore Collection; 1.13 – Columbia Pictures/The Moviestore Collection; 1.14 – Frazzled Cat Productions; 1.15 – ITV/United Film and Television/Meridian; 1.16 – Thames/Pearson Television; 1.18 – © DaimlerChrysler Aktiengesellschaft, 2001; 1.20 – Ivan Reitman Productions/ Northern Lights Entertainment/Universal Pictures; 1.21 – 20th Century-Fox/Redwave Films/Pictorial Press; 1.24 – 20th Century-Fox/Pictorial Press

COMPUTER-BASED MEDIA

2.3 – Sony Corporation/www.sony.com; 2.6 – William Shakespeare's Romeo and Juliet ™© 1996, Twentieth Century Fox Film Corporation. All rights reserved/ www.foxinteractive.com; 2.7 – © The Corner Spyshop; 2.8 – © www.thismodernworld.com; 2.11 – Jacaranda Wiley Ltd; 2.12 – Tesco PLC/www.tesco.co.uk; 2.13 – http://misato.iserver.net; 2.14 – www.altavista.com; 2.16 – © Times Newspapers Ltd, 2001/www.thetimes.co.uk; 2.17 – © CNN Corp./www.cnn.com; 2.19 – © Time Warner Inc./www.time.com; 2.20 – © www.netnanny.com/ © www.surfcontrol.com/ © www.cybersitter.com; 2.21 – © www.travelscape.com/http://travel.discovery.com/www.village.co.uk; 2.23 – screen shot reprinted by permission from Microsoft Corporation; 2.24 – Adamate Design; 2.25 – Sony Corporation/www.sony.com; 2.26 – Vauxhall Motors Ltd/www.vauxhall.co.uk; 2.27 – www.smartlinks.com/www.oracle.com/ www.backup.com/oncology.com; 2.28 – © Charles Deemer/cdeemer@teleport.com; 2.29 – © Eidos Interactive Ltd/www.edios.co.uk/Universal Pictures; 2.31 & 2.32 – © Sierra Studios/www.sierrastudios.com; 2.33 – © id Software Inc./www.idsoftware.com; 2.34 – © Eidos Interactive Ltd/www.edios.co.uk; 2.35 – © Epic Games/www.epicgames.com; 2.36 – © Sega Corp./www.sega.com/www.heat.net; 2.37 – © Blaze International Limited; 2.38 – Veam Software

FILM

3.1 – Jacaranda Wiley; 3.2 – Magnum Photos/Cornell Capa; 3.3 – Columbia Pictures/The Moviestore Collection; 3.4 – Paramount; 3.7 – Twentieth Century Fox Film Corporation; 3.9 – details in text; 3.12 – © Universal Pictures; 3.13 – © Film Four Ltd/Miramax; 3.14 – Carolco Pictures; 3.16 – Steven Moore/*Australian*; 3.17 – New Regency Films/Warner Bros/Alcor Films; 3.19 Screen Finance/X25 Partnership/BFI/British Council; 3.20 – Twentieth Century Fox Film Corporation/Paramount Pictures/Lightstorm Entertainment; 3.22 – Warner Bros; 3.23 – Universal Pictures/DreamWorks; 3.24 – Universal Pictures; 3.25 – © New Line Cinema; 3.27 – Camelot/Ixtlan Productions/Canal+/Warner Bros; 3.28 – Columbia Pictures; 3.29 – Hell's Kitchen Films/Universal Pictures; 3.30 – 40 Acres and a Mule/Marvin Worth/Largo Entertainment; 3.31 – Paramount Pictures Corporation; 3.32 – Talisman/Scottish Film Production Fund/United Artists; 3.33 – Channel Four/Figment Films/Noel Gay Motion Picture Company Ltd/Universal; 3.34 – Merchant Ivory Productions Ltd; 3.35 – United Artists/First Look Pictures/Mayfair Entertainment; 3.36 – Merchant Ivory Productions Ltd; 3.37 – Woodfall Film/Kestrel Films; 3.38 – Touchstone Pictures

TELEVISION

4.4 – www.laplanteproductions.com; 4.5 – courtesy of Sean Leahy/Jacaranda Wiley; 4.6 – courtesy of Patrick Cook; 4.7 – ITC/www.itc.org.uk; 4.8 – Paul Lennon/Jacaranda Wiley; 4.9 – Frazzled Cat Productions; 4.12 – Frazzled Cat Productions; 4.13 – courtesy of BBC; 4.14 – Colin Wheeler from *Really Bad News* (Glasgow Media Group); 4.15 – reproduced courtesy of Film Australia; 4.16 – Paul Lennon/Jacaranda Wiley; 4.17 – Anthony Thomas/WGBH/Pictorial Press; 4.18 – Channel 4; 4.21 – Granada; 4.23 – BBC; 4.24 & 4.25 – Pearson Television; 4.26 – Frazzled Cat Productions; 4.27 – Channel 4/Pearson Television; 4.28 – Patrick Cook; 4.29 – BBC/Terry Gilliam; 4.30 – Pearson Television; 4.31 – Twentieth Century Fox Television, 1992; 4.32 – Pearson Television; 4.33 – BBC; 4.34 – Lynda La Plante/Granada; 4.35 – Pearson Television; 4.36 & 4.37 – © Thames TV (Pearson Television); 4.38 – Frazzled Cat Productions; 4.39 – Jenny Coopes/*Sydney Morning Herald*; 4.40 – Loctite; 4.41 –Volkswagen UK; 4.42 – Roadshow Interactive; 4.44 – Ad News;Yaffa Publishing

RADIO

5.2 & 5.3 – Frazzled Cat Productions; 5.6 – Twentieth Century Fox Film Corporation, all rights reserved/; 5.7 & 5.8 – Frazzled Cat Productions; 5.9 – Paul Lennon/Jacaranda Wiley; 5.10 – BBC/Pictorial Press; 5.11 – Jeff Busby; 5.13 –Tony Edwards; 5.14 – Frazzled Cat Productions

THE PRINT MEDIA

6.2 – Working Title/Polygram/The Moviestore Collection; 6.3 – Nick Ut; 6.4 – © The National Magazine Company/Independent Newspapers; 6.5 – News International; 6.6 – The Mirror Group; 6.7 – Guardian Newspapers; 6.8 – The Daily Mail; 6.9 – Frazzled Cat Productions; 6.11 – ABC; 6.12 & 6.13 – Frazzled Cat Productions; 6.14 – Guardian Newspapers; 6.17 – © Creators Syndicate Inc.; 6.18 – © EMAP Elan; 6.19 – © IPC; 6.20 – © Peugeot; 6.21 – © Scott USA/www.scottusa.com; 6.22 – © Pfizer Inc.; 6.23 – Barnardo's/www.barnados.org.uk; 6.24 – © Toyota/www.toyota.co.uk

index

t= table (or other text insert).
Italic text = illustrations where
    picture or caption contains
    matter not in the text.
Bold text = glossary term
Bold caps = key terms used
    thoughout the book

Absolutely Fabulous 304
accents (of broadcasters) 28, 45, 352
action/spectacle films 166, 196–200
adaptations 195, 217–23, 379
The Addams Family 304
ADVERTISING
    characteristics of adverts 326–31,
        386–7
    in cinema 172–5, 183–4
    of computer games 120, 132, 133–4
    as driving force of media 26, 29,
        85, 321
    on the internet 66, 88–9, 90–1, 98,
        102, 104–7, 409, 412
    in magazines 432, 435, 443–7
    in newspapers 401, 409, 412
    on radio 285, 363, 384–7
    stereotypes, use of 193, 195, 332–4
    targeting of audience 29, 67, 90,
        105–7, 173, 235, 238, 327, 336–9,
        385
    on television 287, 321–41
    types of advert 323–5
aesthetics **449**
agenda **449**
Alien 42, 162, 192
All the President's Men 17
Allen, Keith 361
Altman, Robert 162
Amin, Idi, President 370
anchorage **449**
animation, in multimedia 107, 110–11
Apocalypse Now 161, 223
The Archers 294
Atkinson, Rowan 304
The Atomic Train 13
Attenborough, Richard 208
attention spans/levels 138, 166–7,
    285, 357–8, 370
AUDIENCE(S)
    active involvement 2, 5–6, 8, 25–6,
        114–16
    age 77, 136, 141, 177, 182, 247,
        337, 346, 358, 367–8, 371, 384
    attitudes 26–7, 31, 235, 237, 251,
        285, 297, 357–8, 359
    cinema 182, 183–4, 187–8
    composition 77–8, 81, 237, 285,
        297, 336–8, 342, 347, 358

effects on 25, 30–1, 32–3, 78, 136,
    138–40, 141, 178–80, 297, 317
expectations 35, 42–3, 192
and radio 355–6, 357–9, 367–8,
    369–70, 371
ratings 239–40, 274, 358–9, 364,
    367–8
research 29–32, 179–81, 183–4,
    238–41, 338–9, 412
responses 25, 26–7, 31–2, 301, 339
and soap opera 32, 285–6, 297–8
and talk shows 342, 345–7
targeting of 26, 28, 29, 99, 132, 177
    (*see also* advertising)
auteur **449**
authorship, multiple 16, 221
Ayckbourn, Alan 378

Baer, Ralph 143
Baird, John Logie 245
Baker, Danny 364
Ball, Zoe 353, 362
The Ballad of Little Jo 194–5
banner ads **449**
Barbie 132
Barr, Roseanne 11
Barry, John 160
Barthes, Roland 44, 46
Basic Instinct 177
Batman (and sequels) 12, 170, 227
The Battle for Chile 276
Battleship Potemkin 156, 166, 209
Beaverbrook, Lord 9
Beckett, Samuel 378
Berlusconi, Silvio 10
Bert, Albert 187
Bethell, Andrew 277
Betrayal (documentary, 1982) 272
Bewitched 304
The Big Breakfast 251
Big Brother 235, 276
The Bill 44, 288, 294, 309, 314, 316
Billy Elliot 225
binary oppositions **449**
The Birds 152
Bjelke-Petersen, Sir Joh 273
Black, Conrad 9
Blackadder series 304, 306
The Blackboard Jungle 225–6, 227,
    229–30, 231
Blade Runner 196
Blair, Tony, PM 9–10, 297
The Blair Witch Project 172
Blazing Saddles 195
Bond (James) films 192, 196
Bonnie and Clyde 152
Bram Stoker's Dracula 196

Brand, Jo 300
Branson, Richard 363
Brass Eye 273
Braveheart 188, 200, 210–11
The Breakfast Club 225
Brenton, Howard 15
The Bridges of Madison County 194
British Broadcasting Corporation
    (BBC)
    history and traditions 9, 26, 45,
        245–6, 360
    present activities 190, 246, 361–3
    structure/governance 9, 15, 20, 84,
        243
British Film Institute (BFI) 184,
    188–9, 270–1
broadband **449**
broadsheet **449**
Brookside 288, 294, 296, 298
A Bug's Life 119, 191
Bulger, Jamie 25, 32, 181
Buñuel, Luis 169
Burton, Tim 160
Bush, George (sr.), President 210
Butch Cassidy and the Sundance Kid
    195

The Cabinet of Dr Caligari 201
camera techniques *see*
    cinematography
Campbell, Neve 204–5
Campion, Jane 219–20
Cane Toads: an Unnatural History 272
Cannibal Tours 276
Capra, Frank 178
Carmageddon 140
Casablanca 150
Castaway 2000 276
casting 27–8, 160, 173, 192, 292
Casualty 294
Catch-22 217
The Catcher in the Rye 221–2
'catharsis' 141, 179
Cathy Come Home 273
censorship
    computer games 140–1
    film/TV 21–3
    internet 4, 94–7, 118
CGI **449**
Chandler, Raymond 309
Channel Four 190, 247–8
CHARACTERISATION
    computer games 125, 126–7, 130,
        132–4
    crime dramas 309, 310–11, 314–15
    docudramas 207–8
    horror films 201–2, 204–5

index

Characterisation *Cont.*
  and narrative 217, 218
  school films 226, 227–8, 230
  soap operas 287–8, 290–2
  Westerns 51, 52–3, 192–3
The Charge of the Light Brigade (film, 1968) 217
Charlie's Angels 196
chat shows *see* talk shows
Un Chien Andalou 169
Child of the Death Camps 272
children
  and computer games 136, 138–41
  and the internet 78, 96
  and screen violence 179, 181
Chomsky, Noam 11, 26, 39, 85, 414
Churchill, Sir Winston, PM 398
cinéma-vérité 169, 276
cinemas, multiplex 166, 182, 183, 188
cinematography 148–53, 198–200
  camera angle/movement 152–3, 220
  focus 151–2, 200
  lighting 151, 220
  shot construction 149–50, 150, 200
  shot sizes and types 148–9, 153, 198, 199, 287
  shot-to-shot transition 155–6, 157, 158t, 198
Citizen Kane 151
City Slickers 195
Clayton, Jack 222
Cleese, John 324
Clinton, Bill, President 3
A Clockwork Orange 161, 176–7
closed narrative **449**
codes 44, 47–8
  in audiovisual media 48–9, 48t, 192, 220
  on the internet 75, 94
Collins, Wilkie, *The Moonstone* 308
Collision Course 214
Coltrane, Robbie 315
comedy 299–307
  categories 299–300, 375
  conventions 300–2
  radio 374–7
  see also situation comedy
communication(s)
  growth in 3, 240–1, 242
  internet 3, 60, 69, 70, 74–7, 85–6
computers *see* games; internet
The Connection 270
Conrad, Joseph, *Heart of Darkness* 223
constituency **449**
convergence (technological) 4–5, 60, 65, 120, 240, 242
cookies 88–9, 105, 412
Coppola, Francis Ford 186, 223
The Cops 310, 314
copy **449**
'copycat' crime 25, 32–3, 176, 178, 181

copyright (and the internet) 66–7, 75, 91–3, 118
The Corn Is Green 229
Coronation Street 297
Costner, Kevin 207
Cracker 309, 310, 315
Craven, Wes 202
crime drama (TV) 308–20
Crimewatch UK 317
critics 170–2
Cronenberg, David 177–8
cropping **449**
Crouching Tiger, Hidden Dragon 196
Crowe, Russell 197, 198
Cruise, Tom 193
Cudlipp, Hugh 9
Cuerpo E Alma 297
cultural imperialism *see* United States
culture
  as context for drama 43–4, 52–3, 205
  national/regional 43, 55–6, 242
Curtis, Jamie Lee 205
cutaway **449**

Dad's Army 300
Dahl, John 201
Dalí, Salvador 169
Dallas 286–7
Dances With Wolves 52–3, 194
Dangerous Minds 230
Dante Alighieri, *Inferno* 202
Davis, Bette 302
Dazed and Confused 225
De Niro, Robert 186
de Sica, Vittorio 169
Dead Poets' Society 226–7, 230, 231
Death of a Princess 275
Death Race 2000 140
deep focus **449**
defamation, laws of 21, 87
Despatches 270
diagetic **449–50**
Diana, Princess of Wales 15, 18, 393, 407
Dickens, Charles 285
Die Hard (and sequels) 172, 193
digital **450**
The Dinner Party 276
Dirty Harry (and sequels) 194
disc jockeys 353, 358, 362, 367
discourse analysis **450**
Dixon of Dock Green 308
'docudrama' 207–11, 213–15, 277
  vs. traditional documentary 211
  vs. written history 214–16
documentaries 270–83
  characteristics 271, 279–80, 281–3, 372–3
  and controversy 273, 274–5, 372
  criticisms of 273, 275–6
  notable examples 211–12
  radio 372–3
  subject matter 273, 274–5, 279, 372

  types 211, 276–7, 372
  vs. current affairs 273
'docusoaps' 244, 277
dominant readings **450**
Donahue, Phil 342, 344
Doom 126, 140
Doyle, Sir Arthur Conan, *Sherlock Holmes* stories 200, 308
Dracula (1931) 203–4t
Dragnet 308, 309
dreams (and TV) 235–6
'dumbing down' 85, 251
DVD 3, 61, 187, 218, 220
  'special editions' 163, 196–7, 200, **450**

e-mail 74–5
East Is East 174, 175
East Timor 5, 21
EastEnders 285, 286, 288, 289, 291, 293–4, 296, 298
Eastwood, Clint 51, 52, 193–4
eating disorders 436
Eclair, Jenny 300
economics
  and advertising 29, 287, 322, 323, 338, 384–5
  of film/TV production 8–9, 12, 84, 196, 223
  project funding 42, 188, 190
  of publishing 8, 29, 409, 412, 432
education (and TV) 8, 243
Edward, Prince 18, 407
Eisenstein, Sergei 116, 155, 156, 166, 169, 209, 210
The Election 231
The Electric Horseman 193
Elfman, Danny 160
Elizabeth (film, 1998) 174
Elton, Ben 33, 300
Emmerdale 294
environment(s)
  computer games 122, 123, 124, 127–8
  crime drama 319–20
  film 169, 209, *218* (see also landscape)
  soap opera 293–4
equilibrium **450**
Eraserhead 169
Erin Brockovich 208
E.T. 120
ethos *see* moral values
European Convention on Human Rights 398
Evans, Chris 353, 362, 363
Evans, Nicolas 195
expressionism, in German cinema 169, 201

The Fall and Rise of Reginald Perrin 300
family life *36*
  in sitcoms 25–6, 305, 306
  in soap operas 294, 295

Fangface 181
Fawlty Towers 305
Figgis, Mike 187
Fight Club 197
file transfer protocol (FTP) 75
Film Council (UK) 189–90
film(s)
  editing 154–8, 199–200
  genre(s) 191–205, 225–6 (*see also*
    separate entries, e.g. Westerns)
  high-concept 169–70, 196
  history 166, 186–8
  influence on computer games 123,
    127
  influence on narrative fiction 217
  narrative structures 167–9, 217–19
  photographic techniques *see*
    cinematography
  promotion 172–5
  screenplays,
    preparation/presentation 162–5
  soundtrack *see* music; sound
  special effects 187, 191, 200, 220
  stars (persona/use of) 173, 174,
    192, 198, *213*
  US *vs.* UK industries 182–3, 188
  viewing, experience of 167, 168
  violent content 176–82
Final Fantasy series 122, 123
finance *see* economics
A Fistful of Dollars (and sequels) 193
'fly-on-the-wall' TV 276
football 14, 35–7
Ford, Henry 16
Ford, John 52, 148, 193
Foucault, Michel 241
Four Weddings and a Funeral 175, 182,
  188
Freud, Sigmund 235
Friday the 13th series 202
Friends 321
The Full Monty 9, 51–2, 53, 169, 182,
  183, 188

games, computer/video 119–45
  addiction 136, 139
  and computer design 120
  defining characteristics 119–20,
    130–1
  'girl games' 132–3, 137
  history 121, 141–3, 142t
  multiplayer 123–4
  narrative structure 124–9
  player characteristics/responses
    136–41
  role of technology 120, 128–30
  types 121–3
Gandhi 208
Gangsters 308–9
Garnett, Tony 311
Garrison, Jim 208
Gates, Bill 66, 118
GENDER, issues of
  in adverts 332–3, 336–7

Gender *Cont.*
  in characterisation 27, 35
  in comedy *49,* 300
  and computer games 132–4,
    136–7, 137t
  in crime drama 310
  in horror films 200, 204–5
    and the internet 77, 81–2
and language 45
  in newspaper/magazine readers
    402t, 434–6
  in school films 230
  in soap operas 286, 287, 296
  TV presenters 250
  in Westerns 194–5
GENRE(S)
  comic 299–300
  computer games 119–20, 121–4
  conventions of 192–3, 202–5,
    208–9
  cultural background to 43–4
  film 6, 41–4, 191–205, 225–6
  hybridity 42, 44, 104, 192, 196
  listed/defined 41, 104, 119–20,
    191–2, 196, 200, 207, 321, 342,
    433
  use in advertising 173
geography *see* landscape
Gerrard, Lisa 198
Gibson, William 66, 69, 114
Gladiator 196, 197–200
globalisation 55–6, 83, 85–6
  effect on TV 240, 242, *243,* 334
Godard, Jean-Luc 29
The Godfather (and sequels) 196
Goldberg, Whoopi 27
good *vs.* evil *see* moral values
Good Will Hunting 230
Goodbye Mr Chips 225–6, 227, 231
Goodness Gracious Me! 375
The Goon Show 374, 376–7
Grand Theft Auto 118, 141
graphics
  in computer games 120, 122,
    128–9
  on websites 101–2, 112
The Great Train Robbery (1903) 192
Grierson, John 211, 270, 271, 272
Grisham, John 180, 181
The Guiding Light 285

'hackers' 77, 86
Haley, Bill 226
Half Life (computer game) 125,
  126–7, 130
Half Life (documentary) 282
Halloween (and sequels) 153, 202, 205
Hammett, Dashiell 217, 309
Hanks, Tom 177
Hannibal 201–2
Hardy, Thomas 195
Hare, David 15
Hearst, W.R. 390
Heathers 225

Heaven's Gate 9
Heller, Joseph, *Catch-22* 217
Henry VIII, King 208
Hercules 12
Herrmann, Bernard 159, 161
High Noon 195, 226
High Plains Drifter 193
Hill Street Blues 309
Hillsborough disaster 14, 277
The Hitch-Hiker's Guide to the Galaxy
  375, 376
Hitchcock, Alfred 155, 159, 161, 218,
  221
Home Alone 172
home video *see* video, amateur
horizontal integration **450**
Horner, James 160
horror films 200–5
  conventions 202–5, 203–4t
The Horse Whisperer 195
The House 277
house style **450**
Howards End 222
HTML **450**
Hunter, Holly 219
Hussein, Saddam 39
hybrid texts **450**
hypertext 60–1, 73, 102, 411
  and narrrative 114–16

I Dream of Jeannie 304
I Know What You Did Last Summer 202
ideology/ies 45–6, 205
  and media presentation 39, 46,
    203–4, 241, 398
If... 231
images
  in advertising 173–4, 445
  cultural significance 46–8
  falsification 18, 81, 394–6, 407
  in film 220–1
  on magazine covers 438–9
  vs. words 46
imagination, role of 355, 375–6, 380
In the Name of the Father 210
Independence Day 37
Independent Television Commission
  15, 20, 244, 245
industrial action, news coverage of
  11, 39, 246, 268, 425
information
  access to 3–4, 5t, 65, 66–7, 81, 91
  monitoring of 88–90, 94
  organisation 73, 112–13
  ownership 66, 92–3, 118
  reliability 79–81
  storage 60–1, 67, 71
  'superhighway' 64, 67
The Innocents 222
Inspector Morse 309
interactive drama/movies 114–16,
  123
interactive modes of communication
  451

index

interface 61–2, 62, 63t, 122, 129
internet 69–108
  commerce 72, 81, 85, 88–9, 90
  communication systems 74–7
  control of 84–6
  and criminal activity 67, 78, 81, 82,
    86, 90, 91–2, 95–6
  decentralisation 20, 70, 84–5, 94
  development 4, 69–70
  drama 286
  games 123–4
  links 73, 92–3, 101
  newspapers 403, 408–12
  regulation (problems of) 84–5, 94,
    117–18
  reviews 170–1
  searching 71, 74, 411
  service providers (ISPs) 70, 95
  size and scope 2–3, 65, 69, 71, 72,
    74
  social role 71, 72
  vs. traditional media 3, 70–1,
    408–12
  see also e-mail; websites; World
    Wide Web
intertextuality **451**
'inverted pyramid' structure 102–3,
  256, 417, 428, 429–30
Ishiguro, Kazuo 220
ISP **451**

James, Henry 222
Japan, role in games industry 141–3
Jarman, Derek, *Blue* 169
Jaws 162, *173*
JFK (film) *207*, 208, 210, 277
The Joy Luck Club 218
jump cut **451**
Junior 49, 196
Jurassic Park 12
juxtapostion **451**

Keeping Up Appearances 302, 305
Kennedy, John F., President 37, 207,
  210
Kes 225
Khouri, Callie 162
King, Rodney, beating of 5–6
King, Stephen 202
King's Quest 122–3
Krusenstjera, Frederik von 272
Krushchev, Nikita, President 213–14
Kubrick, Stanley 161, 176–7

La Plante, Lynda 310
Land and Freedom 209
landscape, use of in film 51–3, 148,
  219–20
Lang, Fritz 169, 201
**LANGUAGE (OF MEDIA) 6, 28,
  46**
  adverts 327–8, 445–7
  comedy 302
  and ideology 45

newspapers/magazines 390–1,
  418–20, 428, 430, 441
  reviews 171
  TV news 259–61, 268
Last Action Hero 8–9
The Last of the Mohicans 194
Laurel and Hardy 302
Lawrence, Stephen, murder of 270
Lawrence of Arabia 148
Le Bon, Yasmin 394
Leacock, Stephen 302
Lean, David 148
Lean on Me 226, 227, 230
Lee, Spike 213
Leigh, Mike 221
Leland, David 225
Leonardo da Vinci 168
Leone, Sergio 193
Lewis, Martyn 14
Lineker, Gary 324
The Lion King 27
Little Big Man 194
Liverpool One 314
Loach, Ken 209, 225, 273
Loch Ness (film) 173
Lock, Stock and Two Smoking Barrels
  174
Lucas, George 66
Lukwiya, Rev. 370
Lumière brothers 155, 166, 167
Lynch, David 42, 166, 169

Made in Britain 225, 231
magazines
  articles 439–42
  circulation 431–2
  covers 437–9
  men's 433, 436
  range of titles 431
  social/political viewpoint 432, 435
  types of 433, 436
  women's 433, 434–6, 437–9
The Magnificent Ambersons 151
mainstream **451**
Malcolm X 213
A Man Called Horse 194
The Man from Snowy River 217
Mann, Anthony 193
Marconi, Guglielmo 360–1
marketing see advertising
Marx, Karl 10
Mary Shelley's Frankenstein 218–19
M*A*S*H 304, *305*
The Matrix 187, 191
Matthews, James 398
Maupassant, Guy de, *Boule de Suif* 195
Maxwell, Robert 8, 408
McCabe and Mrs Miller 195
McCarthy, Cormac, *All the Pretty
  Horses* 195
McCarthy, Joseph, Senator 177
McGovern, Jimmy 277
McKenzie, Kelvin 364
McLuhan, Marshall 242, 355

MEDIA (INSTITUTIONS)
  characteristics 5t, 8
  conglomerates 3, 11–13, 18, 85,
    242, 246, 408
  contextual factors 51–4
  growth/diversity of 2, 51, 64
  influence on public affairs 9–10, 11,
    31, 273 (see also politics)
  manipulation **451**
  ownership 8, 9–10, 39, 408
  relative popularity 4t, 136, 139
  'mediation,' process of see
    representation
mediation **451**
Mel and Sue 375
melodrama, influence on modern
  media 49, 285, 290–1, 308, 342–3
Men Behaving Badly 304
Men in Black 163
merchandising 12, 170, 196–7
Merchant-Ivory films 188, *222*
Metal Gear Solid 122, 130
Meyrink, Gustav, *The Golem* 200
Michael Collins 210
Midnight Cowboy 193
Minghella, Anthony, *Cigarettes and
  Chocolate* 378
minority interests
  catered for 65, 83, 239–40, 242,
    247–8, 347, 432
  neglect of 2, 55
mise-en-scène 150, 199, 201, 202,
  215–16, 219, 271
Mission Impossible 1/2 166, 193, 197
montage 155, 166
Monty Python's Flying Circus 300, 302,
  374
Moonlight State 273
Moore, Michael 212, 272
moral values 43
  of film genres 51, 193, 227
  of TV dramas 285, 308
Morgan, Piers 407–8
morph **451**
Morricone, Ennio 160, 193
Morris, Chris 273, 400
Morris, Errol 212, 270
Mortal Kombat 122, 138, 140
Morton, John 272
Mr Bean 304
Mr Holland's Opus 226
Much Ado About Nothing (film, 1993) 153
multimedia 60–1, 102–3, 109–18
  elements of 109–12
  and narrative 114–16
  and news coverage 410, 411–12
The Munsters 304
Murdoch, Rupert 9–10, 11, 20, 29,
  186, 242, 245, 248, 396, 406–7
Murnau, F.W. 169, 201
music
  in advertisements 322, 331, 387
  in films 159–60, 161, 193, 197, 198,
    199–200, 215, 226

internet piracy 91–2
on radio 353, 362, 363, 365–8, 381
The Music Quiz 375
Myst 122, 124

NARRATIVE(S)
comedy 306–7, 377
computer games 124–9
documentaries 281–3, 282t
film 166, 167–9, 217–19
multimedia 114–16
perspectives 217, 221–2
prose fiction 217–19
soap operas 287–9
narrowcast **451**
Native Americans, portrayals of 27–8, 35, 52–3, 193, 194
Natural Born Killers 180, 181
'negativity' (of news coverage) 14, 424
Neighbours 288, *294*, 296
Neighbours From Hell 244
Neill, Sam 220
'New Journalism' 399–400
news coverage (TV) 250–69
(alleged) bias 10, 11, 22t, 23, 246, 267–8
language 259–61, 268
leads 256–8, 263
presenters 250, 253, *257*
scripts 262–3, 264t, 265t
selection of material 13–14, 16–17, 256, 267–8
speed 2, 3
structure 256–8, 264, 266, 268
subject matter 252–3
news agencies **451**
The News Quiz 375
Newsnight 270
newspapers
broadsheet *vs.* tabloid 18, 390–1, 392, 397t, 405, 414–15
circulation 401, 405, 408
editorials 413–15, 425
electronic 403, 408–12
as 'endangered species' 400–1, 403, 405, 409
features 428–30
history 2, 341, 405–7
news presentation 256, 395t, 397t, 417–19, 421–2
page layout 391–2, 395t, 397t
photographs, use of 392–6, 395t
readership 391, 402t, 403, 405, 412, 414–15
selection of material 267, 390, 424–5
sensationalism 18, 341, 392, 395t, 396, 398, 406, 424, 425
space limitations 55, 392, 410–11, 425
Nixon, Richard, President 17
No Harvest for the Reaper 273
Nosferatu (1922) 200, 201
Not the Nine O'Clock News 11, 375

Notting Hill 169
novels *see* adaptations
nuclear industry, TV coverage of 13, 15–16
Nyman, Michael 160
NYPD Blue 311, 316

Oligiati, Christopher 272
Once Upon a Time in America 193
Once Upon a Time in the West 193, 195
Only Fools and Horses 300, 305
open narratives **451**
O'Rourke, Dennis 276, 282
Orwell, George, *1984* 39
outline **451**
ownership, issues of *see* copyright; information; media

Pabst, G.W. 201
Pac Man 121, 134, 138
Pacino, Al 186, 192
Pakula, Alan J. 177
Pale Rider 193
Panorama 32
paparazzi 15, 18, 393–5, **451**
Parker, Dorothy 302
Parkinson, Michael 362
parodies 377
advertisements 321
documentary 272–3
film 195, 196
Patten, Chris 9
Payne, Sarah 424
Peirce, Charles 46
People Like Us 272–3
Pfeiffer, Michelle 230
Pharaoh 123
photographs/photography *see* cinematography; images
photojournalism *see* newspapers: photographs, use of; *paparazzi*
The Piano 160, 162, 219–20
Pilger, John 20, 21
Pinter, Harold 378
pirate radio 360–1
'pitches' 42, 162
Platoon 199–200
The Player 162
Pocahontas 35
Pokèmon 120
Poliakoff, Stephen, *City Sugar* 28
police, TV coverage of 5–6, 11, 17
see also crime drama
'political correctness' 45
politics
and comedy 300, 304
of individual journalists 16, 17–18, 408
of media organisations 9–11, 16, 18, 39, 245–6, 408, 414
Pong 138, 143
pornography, internet 78, 82–3, 95–6
Porridge 304
Posse 194

postmodern **451**
Press Code/Press Complaints Commission (PCC) 14–15, 18, 19t, 20, 407–8
The Prime of Miss Jean Brodie 226
Prime Suspect 309
Principal 226
Prisoner: Cell Block H 27
privacy
and the internet 75, 83, 87–90
and print media 401
privatisation **451**
professional values **451**
programme formats **452**
propaganda 4, 7, 11, 29, 39, 83
Psycho 152, 161
Public Service Broadcasting (PSB) **452**
Puttnam, David 178

Quake 122, 125, 126, 127, 130, 140
The Quick and the Dead 195, 196

RACE, issues of
in advertising 175, 333–4, 396
in computer games 134
internet sites 81, 96
in print media 396, 398
in soap operas 295, 296
in Westerns 27–8, 52–3, 193, 194
radio
characteristics of medium 355–6, 369–70, 379
drama 378–82
history 245, 360–1
and the internet 3
local 363
news coverage 369–71
presenters 28, 54, 356
regulation of 20, 364
scripts 353–5, 370, 380–1
serials 285
stations 356, 361–4
vs. television 355–6, 369, 370
Raiders of the Lost Ark 193
Raimi, Sam 195
readings **452**
Reagan, Ronald, President 192–3
realism 168–9
of news coverage 37, 234–5
in soap operas 285, 295–6
Red River 195
Red Rock West 201
Redford, Robert 193
Redmond, Phil 298
Reds 214
Reith, Lord 245–6
The Remains of the Day 220
reportage **452**
REPRESENTATION, issues of
in multimedia 117–18
in newspapers 396–8, 414
in TV news 6–7, 35–8, 39–40, 54, 234, 267–8
Restoration 223

index

reviews, film 170–2
Rhys-Jones, Sophie 18, 407
Richard III (film, 1996) *221*
Ride with the Devil 195
Riefenstahl, Leni 166
Rimes, Leanne 195
Rising Damp 305
Rob Roy 52, 215
Robin Hood: Prince of Thieves 215
Rockett's New School 132
Roger and Me 212, 272
A Room with a View 219
Rope 155
Roseanne 305
Rossellini, Roberto 169
Roth, Tim 225
Rowland, Tiny 12–13, 22
The Royle Family 25, 305
rushes **452**
Ryan, Meg 192
Ryan, Michael 32

Salinger, J.D. 221–2
Salvador 209
satellite/cable TV 235, 242, 248–9
   deregulation 26, 249
   multimedia capabilities 4–5, 240, 249
satire 11, 259, 272, 299, 400
   see also parodies
Saussure, Ferdinand de 46
Savalas, Telly 213–14
Saving Private Ryan 188, 196, 200, 214
Scary Movie 202
school, films about 225–31
Schwarzenegger, Arnold 9, 173
Scorsese, Martin 186
Scott, Ridley 160, 197, 198, 199–200
Scream series 202, 203–4t, 204–5
selection (of material presented) 2, 54, 211
   see also news coverage
semiotics 46, **452**
serif **452**
settings *see* environment
Se7en 201, 202
Seven Up (documentary series) 275
sex (as subject matter) 35, 53–4, 177, 182, 223
   of comedy 300, 302
   and newspaper sales 10, 396, 406
sexism *see* gender, issues of
Shadow of the Vampire (2001) 200
Shadowlands 52
Shakespeare, William 285
   Julius Caesar 199
Sheen, Martin 161
Shelley, Mary, *Frankenstein* 200
The Shining 153
shooting/shots *see* cinematography
signified **452**
signifier **452**
signs *see* images
The Silence of the Lambs 181, 200–2, 310

Simpson, John 22t, 23
The Simpsons 243, 305
Singin' in the Rain 159
situation comedy 300, 304–7, 375
   formulae 304–5
Skinner, Frank 300
Smith, Joan 15–16
Smith, Julia 285
soap operas 32, 43, 55, 56, 285–98
   and crime drama 44, 309
   on the internet 286
   longevity 285, 286t
   subject matter 37, 54, 286, 287–9
   social context 53–4, 201, 210–11, 222–3, 228, 295, 296, 304, 316
Soldier of Fortune 134
Sonic the Hedgehog 121, 133
sound
   in computer games 129–30
   in documentaries 281–2
   in films 158–61, 187, 197, 198, 199, 200, 222
   on radio 352–3, 370, 373, 377, 379–80, 381, *383*
soundbite **452**
Space Invaders 121, 134
Spielberg, Steven 159–60, 214
'spin doctors' 17
sport, coverage of 156, 362, 363–4
Springer, Jerry 341, 343
Stagecoach 195
Stand and Deliver 226, 227, 230–1
state control (of media) 5t, 18–20, 21
   ISPs 4, 96–7
   radio/TV 21–3, 39, 83, 241
Steadicam **452**
Steptoe and Son 300
stereotypes 38–9
   in comedy 38, 300–1, 376–7
   in computer games 127, 132–4
   and talk shows 344–5
   see also advertising
Stevenson, Robert Louis, *Dr Jekyll and Mr Hyde* 200
Stewart, James 193
Stoker, Bram, *Dracula* 200
Stone, Oliver 177, 181, 208, 209, 210, 277
Stoppard, Tom 378
Streep, Meryl 194
Strike (USSR, 1924) 210
Summer School 229
Super Mario Brothers 120, 121
surveillance 65–6, 88–9
   governmental 89–90
Svankmajer, Jan, *Alice* 169
The Sweeney 309

Taggart 315, 317
talk shows 341–6
   criticisms of 341, 347–8
   social role 346–7
Tan, Amy 218
Tarkovsky, Andre 166

Teachers 230
technology
   advances in 64, 128–9, 187, 240
   speed of advance 66, 120
   'worship' of 64
Teletubbies 12
television
   channels, proliferation of 235, 240, 242
   genres 285–320 (*see also* specific entries, e.g. soap opera)
   and the internet 3, 4–5, 83, 250
   as 'necessity' 2, 234
   networks 245–50 (*see also* BBC; Channel Four; ITC)
   profit/ratings *vs.* quality 239–40, 243–4, 277
   programming policy 239–40, 277
   public service *vs.* commercial 242–5, 267
   ratings **452**
   regulation of 15, 20, 241, 243, 244–5
   role in society 234–7, 251
   see also news coverage (TV)
Terminator 2 126, 173, *191*, 197
texts 54, **452**
Thackeray, W.M. 223
Thatcher, Margaret 39
Thelma and Louise 162, 195
The Thin Blue Line (documentary, USA 1988) 212, 270
Third World
   technology 66–7, 83
   TV 273
Thomas, Dylan, *Under Milk Wood* 378–9
Thompson, Lord, of Fleet 8
'three-act' structure 114, 125, 226, 288
time
   in film narrative 157–8, 166, 167–8
   as medium of radio 352
   and TV scheduling 55, 235, 268, 321–2
Timecode 2000 187
Titanic 8, 169, 186–7, 191, 196
Tomb Raider 120, 122, 126, 127, 132
Tonight with Trevor McDonald 270
Took, Barry 304
A Touch of Frost 309, 315
Toy Story 1/2 187, 191, 195
Toynbee, Polly 18
Trainspotting 218
Tremain, Rose 223
truth
   in advertising 321, 334–5
   in docudrama/documentary 37, 213–15, 274
   in news coverage 17, 37, 401, 425
   see also news coverage; representation
The Turn of the Screw 222
Twain, Shania 195

Twin Peaks 42, 169
Twins 162
The Two Ronnies 302
2001: A Space Odyssey 157, 161

Ulysses (film, 1954) 217
Unforgiven 51, 194
United Kingdom, film industry 182–3, 187–90, 189t
United States
    domination of media culture 55, 83, 117–18, 133–4,
        182–3, 186, 193, 240, *243,* 398
    film industry 182–3, 186–7
Unreal 132
URL **452**

van Outen, Denise 324
Vanessa 341
Vanity Fair 223
vertical integration **452**
video, amateur 13, 65
    as anti-establishment force 5–6
villians (TV drama) 290–1, 314, 315
VIOLENCE
    in ancient world 177, 178
    in cartoons 30, 316
    in computer games 134, 136–7, 139–40
    in films/TV drama 176–82, 316–17
    media-inspired 25, 30–1, 32–3, 78, 95–6, 136, 139–40,
        176, 178–82
    news coverage of 5–6, 11, 35–7
Violence in America 274
Visconti, Luciano 169
Voigt, Jon 193

Wadhams, Steve 370
Walkabout 52
Wang, Wayne 218
war
    and comedy 304, *305,* 306
    and computer games 140
    documentaries 271–2
    internet sites/discussions 3, 4, 83
    journalism 394
    TV/radio coverage 2, 22–3, 356

The War Game 21–2
Wayne, John 193, 194, 195
websites 71, 98–103, 110–13, 240
    addresses 73–4
    content 97, 98, 100, 103
    design 98–101, 102–3
    film-related 172, 184
        regulation of 97
Welles, Orson 151, 221
West, Fred 87, 394
Westerns 43, 192–5, 227
    ethos 51, 52–3, 192–3
    influence on popular culture 193, 195
Whaley, Jim 172
What's My Line? 375
When the Dog Bites 280
Wiene, Robert 169
Wild at Heart 166, 169
Wild Wild West 195
Wilde, Oscar, *The Picture of Dorian Grey* 200
Wilkomirski, Binjamin 272
Williams, John 159–60
Williams, Robin 231
Willis, Bruce 193
Winfrey, Oprah 342, 343, 344
Winslet, Kate 396
Winterbottom, Michael 195
Wolfe, Tom 399
Woodhead, Leslie 214
Woodward, John 189
World Wide Web 72, 73, 92–3
Wright, Steve 362

Young, Kirsty 250
Young Guns 1/2 195
The Young Ones 302, 306

Z Cars 308, 314
Zimmer, Hans 160, 197, 198